19th Century European Art

in the Collection of the **Museum of Fine Arts, Budapest**

Budapest, 2025

Editor, author of introductions:
Ferenc TÓTH

Project coordination:
Anna Zsófia KOVÁCS

Contributors:
Csenge Júlia BÉRES
Dávid FEHÉR
Judit GESKÓ
Bianka IZSÁK-BODA
Luca KESERÜ
Adriána LANTOS
Dóra LOVASS
Rebeka MRÁZIK
Dominika SODICS
Anett SOMODI

Budapest, 2025

19th Century European Art

in the Collection of the Museum of Fine Arts, Budapest

Contents

The Shaping of the Nineteenth-Century International Art Collection

International works of art from the nineteenth, twentieth, and twenty-first centuries are kept together in the Budapest Museum of Fine Arts in what is now known as the Department of International Art after 1800. The department has a collection of almost 1,000 nineteenth-century artworks, including 578 paintings, 160 sculptures, and 230 medals and plaquettes. Rich in terms of both size and quality, the collection has never before been presented to the public in its full diversity. All earlier exhibitions have shown a drastically filtered selection – due either to space constraints or pressure to reflect prevailing tastes. The present publication can be considered a pioneering work: our aim was to provide as varied and extensive an overview of the collection as possible, taking into account how preferences and value judgements change over time.

With the establishment of the Museum of Fine Arts in 1896, the entire collection of works from after 1800 held in the Picture Gallery of the Hungarian National Museum – including both Hungarian and foreign paintings and sculptures – was transferred to the new institution. When the museum opened to the public in 1906, one of its most important units – the Gallery of Modern Art – comprised these holdings, together with later acquisitions. The prehistory of the present-day Department of International Art after 1800 thus begins not in 1906, but with the founding in 1808 of the National Museum, the first Hungarian public collection with a broad collecting scope.[1]

When the collecting activities of state art institutions were reorganised in the 1870s, in line with the new approaches to museology, artworks dating from after 1800 began to be referred to as "modern", to distinguish them from other art historical periods. As twentieth-century avant-garde movements gained ground, the term was later restricted mainly to the avant-garde era. With the emergence of new perspectives on nineteenth-century art, it has been suggested on numerous occasions in recent decades that the new approach to painting originated either from the birth of the Biedermeier, or from the birth of romanticism, or even from various periods in the eighteenth century.[2] Based on historical collecting traditions, in our museum, we draw the chronological divide after which the collection in question begins at around 1800, and we still refer to it with the overall term "modern".

1   On the acquisition of modern foreign works of art that were transferred to the Museum of Fine Arts when the institution opened, see Tóth 2012.

2   Crucially important essays on the origins of the artistic approach leading to the reformation of art in the twentieth century: Rosenblum and Janson 1984; Hofmann 1987; Craske 1997.

**The development of the National Museum's Picture Gallery
during its operation as a public trust**

With its legal establishment, the National Museum housed a variety of historical and cultural relics, including various types of images.[3] Initially, national themes were central in the acquisition of artworks. The underdevelopment of artistic life in Hungary meant that the majority of institutional and private commissions – and orders for more substantial, representative works in particular – were given to Austrian artists. Several such works were donated to the museum, although the majority were transferred to the Hungarian Historical Gallery when it was established in 1884. In terms of today's international holdings, the earliest acquisitions, and those that can be considered the most significant during these early years, were initiated by the museum's patron, Archduke Joseph of Austria, Palatine of Hungary. In 1821, with the emperor's blessing, the National Assembly commissioned the Viennese court painter Peter Krafft to produce monumental depictions of two historic events.[4]

The 1832–1836 National Assembly marked a turning point in the evolution of the National Museum's collection of art. In the final year of the assembly, the deputies approved the purchase of the art collection of Miklós Jankovich, and also accepted a valuable donation of paintings from János László Pyrker, archbishop of Eger. Following earlier, sporadic acquisitions, the museum's art gallery was established with what amounted to almost 250 paintings. Of a European standard and pertaining to universal art history, the collection also included recent artworks. Pyrker's donation included several modern works, the most prominent being eight oil paintings by Josef Danhauser. All the works donated by the archbishop were on public display in the new museum building, designed by Mihály Pollack, which opened on 19 March 1846.[5]

Ágoston Kubinyi, who was appointed to the position of museum director on 8 April 1843, strove from the outset to support Hungarian art and ensure its representation within the museum's collection. However, this meant that, before the 1867 Compromise, foreign paintings were acquired merely by way of occasional donations. All the museum's departments (with the exception of the Library) opened to the public on 24 January 1848: the Department of Coins and Antiquities on the first floor, and the Picture Gallery on the second. An examination of the provenance of the modern international works currently held by the Museum of Fine Arts reveals that, apart from the above-mentioned painting by Krafft and a few from the Pyrker collection, only Friedrich von Amerling's portrait *Writing Scholar* and Franz Eybl's *Slovak Boy Selling Onions* originate from the then collection of the National Museum's Picture Gallery.[6] The Collection of Antiquities – as the department responsible for all works of sculpture – likewise owned a few of the works that are now part of the Museum of Fine Arts' collection. The neoclassical sculptures *Metabus and His Daughter* by Francesco Massimiliano Laboureur, and Adamo Tadolini's *Venus and Amor*, were donated to

---

3   On the early days of the National Museum and on the development of its collections, see Tóth 2017.

4   The painting *Emperor Francis II being Crowned King of Hungary in Buda* was finished in 1823, and *Miklós Zrínyi's Sortie from Szigetvár* was completed in December 1824. The former painting later ended up in the Hungarian Historical Gallery.

5   Mátray 1846.

6   Since both the acquisition register and the inventories of the collections are missing, the starting point for research on Picture Gallery acquisitions are the inventories compiled by János Peregriny at the time of the establishment of the Museum of Fine Arts. Peregriny 1909.

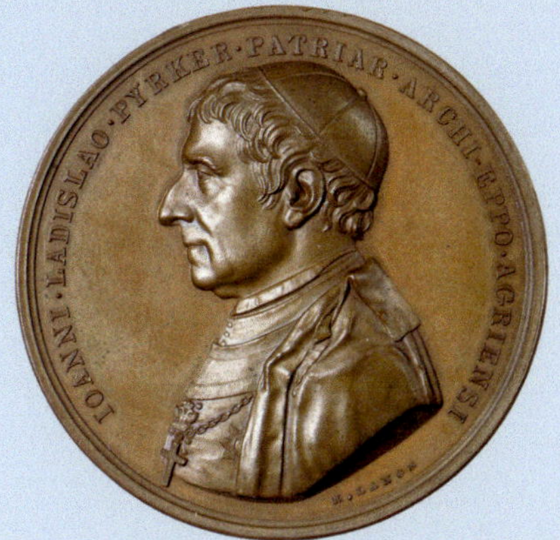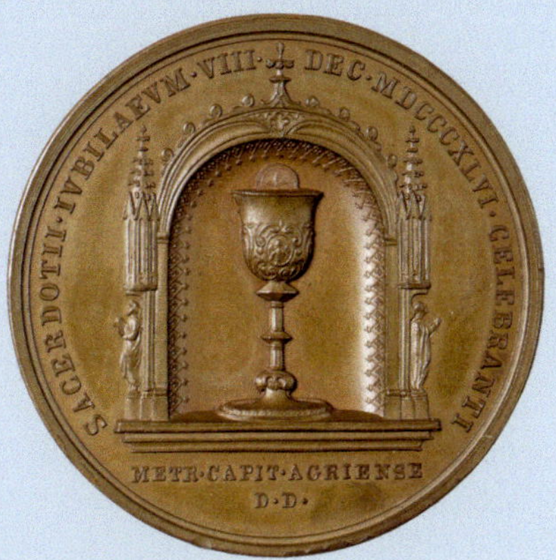

Konrad Lange, *János László Pyrker
commemorative medal*, 1846

the museum by Prince Pál Esterházy in 1847, and in the same year Raffaele Monti's bust of Emperor Ferdinand V (King Ferdinand I of Hungary) was given to the museum by the Royal Curia. At the same time, many works purchased by their former owners from exhibitions of the Pest Art Society later came to be owned by the National Museum, and subsequently by the Museum of Fine Arts.[7]

Amidst the straitened financial circumstances of the period of open absolutism that followed the Hungarian Revolution of 1848, works by foreign artists could still only be acquired in the form of private donations. In 1864, the museum's collection was enriched with the bequest of Countess Mária Eltz, which included modern works, several of which were destroyed in the Second World War.[8] The marble bust of Károly Markó by Hans Gasser, which was shown at the Pest Art Society exhibition in 1855, was purchased by Emperor Franz Joseph and then donated to the museum in 1864. Two years later, plaster reliefs by Bertel Thorvaldsen, which, to this day, are extraordinarily valuable examples of nineteenth-century sculpture, were given to the museum by the composer and violinist Ede Reményi.

Works purchased for the National Museum from the state budget

The most important consequence of the 1867 Austro–Hungarian Compromise for Hungarian museums was that public collections were placed under state management. Direct ministerial oversight and regular funding from the state budget meant a substantial increase in support, which allowed museums to begin systematically building their collections in earnest.

7   Gabriella Szvoboda Dománszky has identified several works from the exhibitions of the Pest Art Society that later ended up in the public collection via various channels. Szvoboda Dománszky 2007.

8   Jeszenszky 1952.

Following Ágoston Kubinyi's retirement, the minister for religion and public education, József Eötvös, appointed Ferenc Pulszky as the new director of the National Museum on 4 March 1869. In terms of Pulszky's approach to developing the museum and shaping its profile, the presentation of universal cultural progress was just as important as the conservation of national heritage.[9] The beginning of his tenure as director of the museum coincided with the transfer of the Esterházy collection to Pest and its subsequent purchase by the state. With the establishment, in 1871, of the National Picture Gallery dedicated to the management of this collection, the role of the National Museum's collections and the collecting scope of the two institutions had to be rethought. The tasks of the National Picture Gallery included the presentation of universal (and Hungarian) art history and the collecting of "old" paintings and prints, while the National Museum's Picture Gallery covered contemporary and recent paintings and sculpture – that is, works dating from after 1800. The paintings were regrouped accordingly, and modern sculptures were reclassified from the National Museum's Collection of Antiquities to its Picture Gallery.[10] The outlines of the two main units of collection in the future Museum of Fine Arts, the Old Picture Gallery and the Gallery of Modern Art, began to take shape. The Esterházy collection also contained a few more recent foreign paintings. Among the works acquired by the museum in this way, Ferdinand Georg Waldmüller's well-known genre painting *Man with a Peep Box* stands out in particular.

Private donations continued to play an important role in the National Museum's acquisitions. In 1871, the bequest of Mihály Erny resulted in the addition of almost fifty nineteenth-century foreign, mainly Austrian Biedermeier paintings to the museum's collection, laying the foundations for one of the Museum of Fine Arts' significant collection units. In terms of later acquisitions, the bequest of Baron Albert Wodianer the Elder, made in 1892, deserves particular mention. (The bequest included eleven German and Austrian landscapes and genre scenes, although six are listed among works that were lost in the Second World War.)

Besides private donations, the international exhibitions organised by the Hungarian National Society of Fine Arts, founded in 1861, became an increasingly important source of acquisitions.[11] In the early years, most of the works purchased were landscapes and genre paintings – popular genres among the most successful Central European artists of the day – from Vienna, Munich, and Düsseldorf. Beginning in the 1880s, the Society of Fine Arts strove to expand its institutional connections, and this too left its mark on museum acquisitions: besides Dutch and Belgian artists, representing the spread of *plein air* painting on the Continent, works by increasingly popular artists from Italy and Scandinavia were also acquired.

In the three decades following the 1867 Compromise, sculptures were purchased on only two occasions: the state bought a study for a woman's head by the Belgian artist Paul de Vigne in 1890 and Franz von Stuck's *Athlete* in 1893 from exhibitions of the Society of Fine Arts. Only three, relatively insignificant donations were made during this period.

The first acquisitions by the Museum of Fine Arts

By the 1890s, the public collections had outgrown their allotted space, making radical reorganisation inevitable: this meant merging the state-owned art galleries and

9 Pulszky 1875, 242–257.

10 Tóth 2017, 180, 198–202.

11 The Hungarian National Society of Fine Arts began to organise international exhibitions only from 1871. For a list of state purchases made at these exhibitions, see Szmrecsányi 1911.

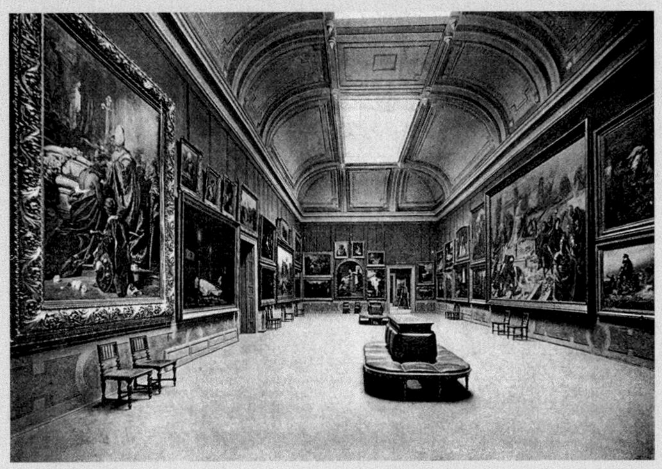

The major picture hall of the National Museum,
ca. 1880

creating an independent museum of art history in a purposely constructed building. Thus, the core of the Museum of Fine Arts, which was established by Article 1 of Act VIII of 1896, comprised the National Picture Gallery and the fine art holdings of the National Museum. Károly Pulszky (the son of Ferenc Pulszky), who elaborated the concept for the new museum, developed a collection of old paintings of international standing, using the financial resources earmarked for collection development. Following the establishment of the Museum of Fine Arts, the most important tasks were to structure the new institution and fill the biggest gaps in terms of its holdings. For this task, the minister of culture, Gyula Wlassics, appointed Ernő Kammerer[12] as head of the National Picture Gallery on 22 May 1896; Gábor Térey, lecturer at the University of Freiburg, also soon joined the museum's staff. In the following years, Térey was given an increasingly important role in terms of organisation and purchases.

In the following period, the state prioritised support to Hungarian art from funding earmarked for the development of the museum's collections. At the same time, using a separate sum set aside for the 1896 Millenial Exhibition of the Hungarian state, works by Vlaho Bukovać, Celestin Medović, and Robert Frangeš-Mihanović, the most prestigious Croatian artists of the day, were purchased from the Croatian pavilion. The National Museum's Picture Gallery was also able to use its own annual budget to purchase foreign works. In 1896, it bought the imposing painting *The Kiss of the Sphinx* by Franz von Stuck from an exhibition at the Budapest Kunsthalle, its most important acquisition in the years before the turn of the century.

In 1899, the ministry of culture opened up the possibility of making purchases on the international art market. One of the objectives for the following years was to elevate modern (foreign and Hungarian) art to the same level as the museum's prestigious historical

12   The rapidly deteriorating health of Károly Pulszky, who had earlier been put in charge of organising the establishment of the Museum of Fine Arts and shaping its collections, as well as the criminal proceedings launched against him because of earlier incidents in which he had overstepped his authority and mismanaged funds, made him unsuitable to fulfil these tasks. On this, see Tóth 2007.

holdings, among the most renowned in Central Europe; a significant sum was made available for this by the redistribution of budget resources.[13] In the following years, the museum acquired new works by eminent artists. At the turn of the century, it was not only the large-scale annual exhibitions of the Society of Fine Arts that provided an opportunity for selection when it came to the dynamically increasing state acquisitions. The museum also made regular purchases from the international exhibitions of the National Salon that were launched in 1901, while direct acquisitions from outside Hungary also gained momentum. Museum experts negotiated with foreign owners and closely followed international auctions. One of Gábor Térey's greatest achievements was his purchase of five sculptures for the Museum of Fine Arts personally from Auguste Rodin. When the artist István Delhaes drew up his will in 1893, he left his art collection to the Hungarian state. On his death in 1901, the extremely valuable pieces acquired by the public collection included twelve modern paintings, mainly the work of German and Austrian masters.

At the proposal of Ernő Kammerer, Emperor Franz Joseph, during a visit made on 1 December 1906, granted permission for two galleries showing "old" and "modern" paintings to be opened to the public on the first floor of the new building of the Museum of Fine Arts. When the Museum of Fine Arts began operation, there were no specialist departments for the management of individual collection units, in today's sense of the word. (The names Old Picture Gallery and Gallery of Modern Art merely referred to the structure according to which the holdings were displayed.) Besides his administrative management tasks, Ernő Kammerer was responsible for the collection of plaster casts of famous sculptures and the presentation of Hungarian art, while Gábor Térey was responsible for the management and acquisition of old and modern foreign art, as well as the collection of graphic art.

Following the inauguration of the Museum of Fine Arts' new building, the purchasing of modern works of art continued. By the time the museum opened, the winter international exhibition at the Budapest Kunsthalle was already under way, from which a large number of Scandinavian works, which were hugely successful throughout Europe at the time, were acquired for the collection. The National Salon also joined the European travelling exhibition that was initiated in 1907 with the aim of familiarising the public with modern French painting. Of the works represented here, the museum successfully negotiated for the purchase of paintings by Eugène Boudin, Charles-François Daubigny, Paul Gauguin, Camille Pissarro, and Alfred Sisley. The sculpture collection also underwent dynamic development. The state purchased eight bronzes and one marble sculpture from the exhibition of works by Constantin Meunier that took place in the Kunsthalle in 1907. In the following year, it acquired a monumental marble sculpture by Égide Rombaux, while four bronze portraits by Jules Lagae were added to its holdings of Belgian sculpture in 1909.

Acquisitions of modern French works continued in 1912 with the purchase of Claude Monet's *Plum Trees in Blossom* and Jean-François Millet's pastel *The View of the Puy de Dôme*. In 1913, Gauguin's *The Black Pigs* and Henri de Toulouse-Lautrec's *These Ladies in the Dining Room* were acquired for the collection from the Ernst Museum's exhibition *Great French Masters of the Nineteenth Century*.

In the early 1910s, two famous private collections were bequeathed to the museum, resulting in the sudden expansion of the museum's modern international holdings. In 1907, Count János Pálffy drew up a will stating that the collection of artworks in his mansions

13   On the changes in the direction of acquisitions, and on the new financial conditions for purchases, see Tóth 2012, 77–78, 104–107.

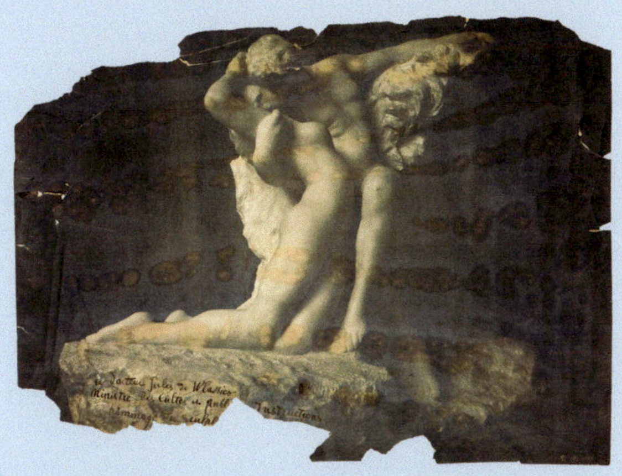

The photo of Auguste Rodin's *Eternal Springtime*,
dedicated by the artist for Gyula Wlassics

and palaces was to be left to the Museum of Fine Arts. On his death in 1912, the museum acquired 121 old and forty-five modern foreign artworks, including further valuable nineteenth-century French paintings. However, the majority of the collection comprised German, Belgian, and Dutch landscapes and genre scenes, which formed another distinct unit within the museum's modern art holdings. The museum acquired 136 modern foreign paintings and eight sculptures through the 1912 will of Count Dénes Andrássy. The bequest included several outstanding works from the end of the previous century, one of the most striking being *Spring Evening* by the leading symbolist Arnold Böcklin. Unfortunately, fifty-five paintings, a substantial proportion of Dénes Andrássy's bequest, were lost in the Second World War. The museum building had not been designed to accommodate such providential and unexpected expansion (or the similarly dramatic expansion of its Hungarian holdings and the establishment of its collection of antiquities), thus the museum had to contend with a significant shortage of space in the decades that followed.

Between the two World Wars

When Ernő Kammerer was obliged to step down as director of the museum due to ill health, the emperor appointed Elek Petrovics, previously head of the Law Drafting Department at the Ministry of the Interior, as director of the Museum of Fine Arts on 21 March 1914. Gábor Térey, as head of department, was subsequently responsible only for the Old Picture Gallery, while the modern Hungarian and foreign holdings were managed directly by Petrovics.

When Petrovics took over as head of the museum, it already owned a substantial collection of nineteenth-century international art, offering a wide geographical overview of the various trends on the Continent. In the years that followed the opening of the building, works by French impressionists and representatives of the younger generation also began to appear among the museum's acquisitions. When determining the focus of further acquisitions, Petrovics was obliged to consider the narrowed opportunities resulting from the war, market recession – experienced mainly at international level – and the Hungarian currency's reduced purchasing power. Compared to the museum's initial period, when the goal of acquisitions was to represent the greatest possible variety of trends in contemporary art,

Petrovics significantly restricted the scope of collecting. He prioritised acquisitions of Hungarian art, while in terms of modern European art he considered the acquisition of only the most influential artists to be worthwhile, and especially those who had reinvigorated French painting in the preceding century.[14]

The budget that had earlier been available to the museum for its independent use – even despite the wartime circumstances – ensured satisfactory opportunities for Petrovics in the initial years. Relying on the excellent taste and active cooperation of Simon Meller, Petrovics managed to purchase two landscapes by Jean-Baptiste-Camille Corot in this period, as well as works by Eugène Delacroix, Édouard Manet, Claude Monet, and Aristide Maillol.[15] A few years later, however, having emerged from the war on the losing side, the country faced financial hardships. It was then that Petrovics's talents and his extraordinary capacity for networking came to the fore. By virtue of his role at the ministry, he cultivated direct, personal connections with Hungarian art collectors, which enabled him to obtain the works he required.[16] The collection of modern French holdings expanded with donations of works by Théodore Chassériau, Gustave Courbet, Paul Cezanne, Camille Pissarro, Pierre Puvis de Chavannes, Maurice Denis, Pierre Bonnard, and Aristide Maillol, and with the financial support of private individuals wealthy enough to contribute to the arts, as well as enterprises and banks. During Petrovics's tenure, eighteen extremely valuable modern French works were acquired by the museum, raising the standard of the collection to an international level. At the same time, he did not entirely neglect nineteenth-century art from other countries. On his initiative the collection acquired – by means of donations or purchases – works by outstanding masters of realism, primarily from Austria (Ferdinand Georg Waldmüller, August von Pettenkofen, Carl Rahl) and Germany (Adolph Menzel, Adolf von Hildebrand), while compositions by Ivan Meštrović and George Minne were another significant addition. Bearing in mind the relatively more modest acquisitions of works of sculpture, it was considered a great achievement when the first permanent exhibition of the museum's collection of modern sculpture opened in the Baroque Hall in 1926, organised by Elek Petrovics and Zoltán Oroszlán.[17]

Amidst the economic hardships and the difficult political situation that persisted throughout Petrovics's tenure as director – yet still following his own tastes – he was obliged to be selective, concentrating his foreign collecting on what could by then be considered a historical period. In so doing, however, he neglected to present the international art of his own day, leaving gaps in the collection that were subsequently impossible to fill.

In 1935, the ministry of culture forced Elek Petrovics to retire, on the grounds that the sixty-two-year-old had already been seriously ill for six months. Dezső Csánky was appointed in his place. Csánky – like his predecessor – was directly responsible for the management of the modern Hungarian and international collection. During his tenure, the development of the collections suffered a considerable decline, which is particularly noticeable with respect to modern foreign art.

The final phase of the Second World War was a dramatic ordeal for every one of the museum's collections. On 8 November 1944, the most valuable paintings were transported to the Archabbey of Pannonhalma, and from there to Szentgotthárd; as the fighting intensified, they were then taken by train to Germany. The collection of sculptures remained

14   Petrovics 1918.

15   Geskó and Molnos 2003, 15–16, 19–20.

16   Petrovics 1921.

17   Petrovics 1926.

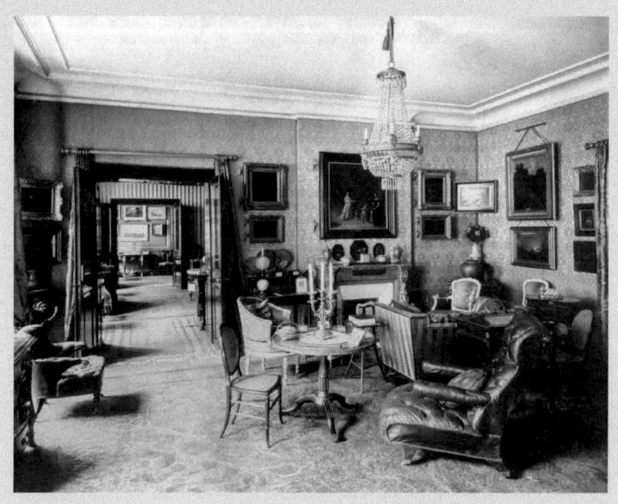

The lesser salon of Count János Pálffy's
Bratislava palace, 1910

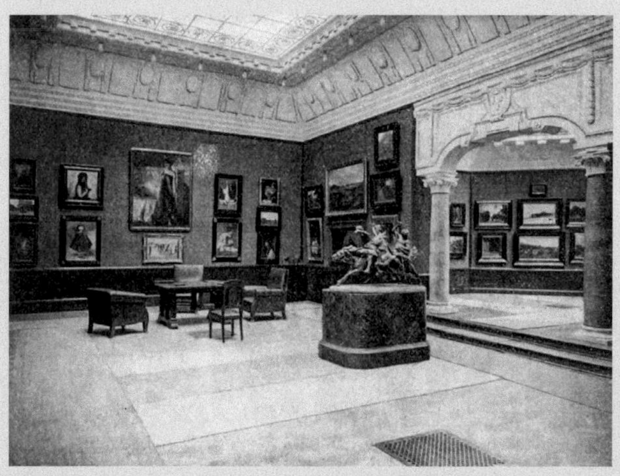

A room in Count Dénes Andrássy's gallery
in Krásna Hôrka

in the museum building throughout, packed into crates. These precarious conditions led to substantial losses among the museum's modern holdings. The most painful loss was Max Klinger's plaster bust of Franz Liszt, although our overall picture of nineteenth-century art is also poorer for the absence of Jean-Baptiste Isabey's *Portrait of a Man*, Ferdinand Waldmüller's *Grey-Haired Man*, Eduard Grützner's *The Miniaturist*, Max Liebermann's *Memorial Service in Kösen*, Henri Le Sidaner's *Woman and Child in the Garden*, Carl Moll's *Spring Trees*, and Antoine-Louis Barye's bronze sculpture *Horse*.

In the period between the two World Wars, the museum placed a substantial number of artworks with ministries and with the Directorate of Public Foundations, partly to decorate their own offices, and partly – in the case of the Ministry of Foreign Affairs – to decorate consulates abroad. A good number of these works were never returned and are currently

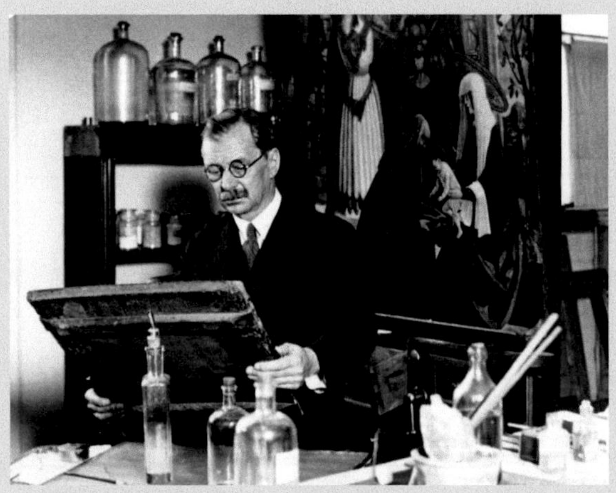

Elek Petrovics in the restoration workshop
of the Museum of Fine Arts

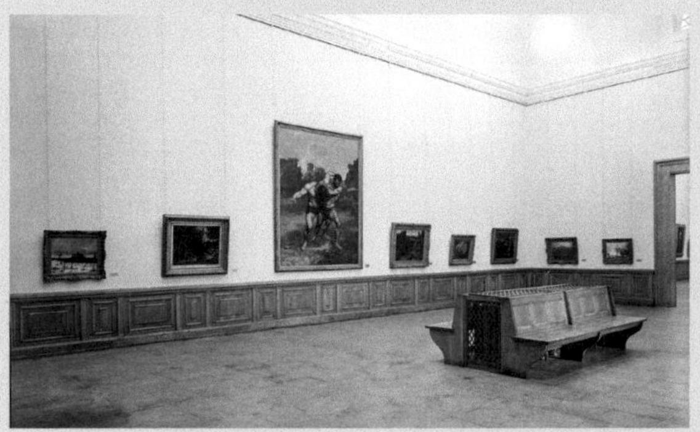

Permanent exhibition of the Gallery of Modern Art on the 1st floor
of the Museum of Fine Arts in the 1960s

listed as missing. In 2019, museum staff working in the Department of International Art after 1800 began to investigate the fate of these works, as a result of which twenty-one of them have been tracked down to date in various government bodies, including pieces that add nuance to the overall picture of the museum's exhibitions, such as Jacques-Émile Blanche's *Woman Reading*, Pio Joris's *The Via Flaminia in Rome*, Adolf Lier's *The Mill*, Willem Maris's *Grazing Cows*, or Carl O'Lynch of Town's *The Blue Lake*.

Recent decades

In the years following the Second World War, the museum's institutional structure underwent significant changes.[18] In 1952, István Genthon took over as head of the Gallery of Modern Art, which comprised the combined collections of international and Hungarian paintings dating from after 1800. Following the establishment of the Hungarian National Gallery, the Gallery of Modern Art, now with the name the Gallery of International

18   For a summary, see Tóth 2010.

16

Modern Art (later the Department of Modern Art), also took over guardianship of foreign paintings and sculptures from the period.

Thanks to the restructuring of Hungary's public collections, the museum acquired further important works in the years following the war. The Museum of Applied Arts, which had previously managed collections of small bronzes and medals, handed over these holdings in 1950; then, with the closure of the Municipal Picture Gallery in 1953, its entire collection of art was transferred to the Museum of Fine Arts. These changes resulted in the acquisition of three sculptures by Albert-Ernest Carrier-Belleuse from the Museum of Applied Arts, and 142 foreign medals from the Municipal Picture Gallery. The collection of modern medals and plaquettes, which includes works by the most outstanding artists of the nineteenth century, and especially the turn of the century, is today one of the lesser-known but valuable units within the Museum of Fine Arts.[19]

The funds available to the museum did not allow for the expansion of its modern international holdings to the same extent as in the first decades of the century. However, it remains the case that the most valuable items have been acquired for the collection by means of purchases. The first years after the war saw the purchase of several important French works (Pierre-Auguste Renoir's *Portrait of a Young Girl*, Claude Monet's *Three Fishing Boats*, Eugène Fromentin's *Reed Cutters on the Nile*, as well as the donation of Gustave Courbet's *Cedar Tree at Hauteville* by the wife of Count Gyula Andrássy), although the critical political situation occasionally prompted owners to part with their valuables. Later, the collection of sculptures also acquired some outstanding items, with the purchase of Jules Bastien-Lepage's *Shepherd Girl*, Égide Rombaux's *Cakewalk*, George Minne's *Bust of a Woman*, and three bronzes by Constantin Meunier.

Following István Genthon's retirement, Éva Kovács took over as head of department in January 1969, and was succeeded a year later by Dénes Pataky. In 1970, Krisztina Passuth joined the staff of the Department of Modern Art and was head of department between 1975 and 1977. Starting from this period, the focus was on developing the collection of foreign contemporary art, which had received minimal attention since the second half of the 1910s. The heads of department who succeeded Passuth (Brigitta Cifka, 1977–1995; Ferenc Tóth, 1995–2000; Péter Ujvári 2000–2005; Judit Geskó 2005–2018; and Anna Zsófia Kovács, 2018–) shared the goals that she had defined, however they no longer confined themselves to the activities of foreign-based Hungarians. At the same time, acquisitions of exemplary nineteenth-century and early twentieth-century artworks were extremely limited – largely due to their unaffordability. Passuth's most significant acquisition was the Delacroix painting *An Arab Camp*, although there were also later opportunities for important purchases, despite the financial constraints: Carl Moll's *Winter Courtyard* (1983), Ludwig von Herterich's *Nocturne* (1984), Pascal Dagnan-Bouveret's *Landscape with Trees* (1986), Friedrich von Amerling's *Moses and the Brass Serpent* (1991). In the past few years – in addition to contemporary works – the Department emphasized the development of this segment of the collection. After acquiring Pierre-Auguste Renoir's Reclining Act and a woman's portrait attributed to Johann Friedrich August Tischbein (both in 2019), in 2024 the collection was enriched by two exceptional purchases, two portraits: *The Odalisque* by Anne-Louis Girodet de Roucy-Trioson and *Young Girl at the Mirror. The Allegory of Vanity* by Anton Romako.

19   Including works by Bertel Thorvaldsen, Jean-Baptiste Carpeaux, Jules-Clément Chaplain, Jules Lagae, Oscar Roty, Alexandre-Louis-Marie Charpentier, Adolf von Hildebrand, Hans Stoltenberg-Lerche, Robert Frangeš Mihanović.

Collection Focal Points Recontextualised

The Museum of Fine Arts' nineteenth-century international collection took shape over a period of around a hundred years, from the substantial donation made by János László Pyrker
(in 1836) to the retirement of Elek Petrovics as director of the museum (in 1935). From
Pyrker's donation right up until the emergence of new acquisition sources – following the legal establishment of the Museum of Fine Arts – exhibitions organised by the Pest Art Society,
and subsequently by the Hungarian National Society of Fine Arts, represented almost the
only opportunity for (state and private) acquisitions.

Founded in 1839, the Pest Art Society established close relationships mainly with
the *Kunstvereine* operating in German and Austrian cities. On the one hand, this meant that
it was part of a network submitting foreign works to exhibitions organised by partner institutions, while on the other hand it strongly demarcated the Hungarian public's opportunities
to gain direct insight into regional trends. Many of the foreign works shown at exhibitions of
the Pest Art Society that ended up in private ownership are today part of the Museum of Fine
Arts' collection – acquired either via the National Museum, or later by a more direct route.
It is to acquisitions such as these that the museum owes its rich and high-quality selection of
Biedermeier paintings.

The Hungarian National Society of Fine Arts was established in 1861 by a broad
circle of Hungarian artists, along with other players in the artistic life of the country, in order
to represent their interests more effectively. The Hungarian art scene was not yet divided
by the kind of fierce conflicts that would later emerge. The Society represented the tastes
of an artistic community that could still be considered homogeneous – tastes that were not
essentially questioned by the public or art critics. In the twenty-five years that followed the
1867 Compromise, the works acquired by the Picture Gallery of the National Museum thus
reflected the shared artistic tastes of the period.

In terms of the international material shown in the period before the turn of the
century, exhibition organisers and mediators strove to attract successful figures from the artistic centres of Europe to take part in exhibitions in Pest. During the Society's first decades,
exhibitions were dominated by representatives of landscape and genre painting from Munich,
Düsseldorf, and Vienna, who were also under the patronage of the Society's partner institutions in Central Europe. Alongside them, however, outstanding representatives of Hungarian
and international historical painting were long guaranteed a place. By the last two decades
of the century – besides the leading role played by Paris – artists from countries hitherto far
less in the spotlight gradually won respect and acclaim in the salons and galleries of Europe.
The impact of this was soon apparent in terms of the international works shown at Society

exhibitions, as well as in state acquisitions: works classified as belonging to realism or naturalism were submitted to exhibitions (and subsequently remained in the country) from almost every corner of Europe – from Austria to England, and from Spain to Norway.

Following the legal establishment of the Museum of Fine Arts, the minister of religion and public education Gyula Wlassics, played an active role in managing the construction of the museum and was keen to take part in acquisitions, or rather to determine their direction. The team of experts involved in the preparatory work for the new museum included Ernő Kammerer, who was responsible for administrative management tasks, and Gábor Térey, who essentially became the museum's academic director. The upturn in purchases of modern artworks after 1900, and the impressive results achieved in terms of collection development, can be associated with his tenure.

By the time the Museum of Fine Arts began its operations and opened its doors in 1906, it owned an extremely rich and surprisingly high-quality contemporary collection. The substantial number of new acquisitions included an impressive proportion of works belonging to the aesthetic world of naturalism, symbolism, and Art Nouveau. When evaluating bulk acquisitions, the question arises as to how far the individual tastes and stylistic preferences of decision makers influenced the selection of works. Wlassics's liberal cultural nationalism and Térey's predilection for fifteenth- and sixteenth-century German art cannot explain the purchasing of works by prominent artists of the end of the century. Personal taste was thus not the deciding factor in the initial development of the museum's modern foreign collection. In summary, the collection taking shape at that time can be said to represent not personal preferences but the tastes of the intelligentsia, and the decisions that were made are a reflection of contemporary tastes.

Those in charge of the newly founded Museum of Fine Arts set themselves the goal of establishing a contemporary collection of European relevance. But in this case, why did the museum's early acquisitions not include the great French masters, who have been regarded since the early twentieth century as the most outstanding artists of the modern reform movement? Why did several decades pass before the management of the country's foremost artistic institution took notice of them? In short, how may we evaluate a collection that had been assembled by the time of the inauguration of the museum, and later expanded, with a special emphasis on late-nineteenth-century art? When assessing the composition and quality of the modern foreign collection, we must be guided by the changes that have taken place – over the past four or five decades – in the international literature on the art of this period.

Until the twentieth century, the public in continental Europe – with the exception of Brussels – had very little first-hand experience of the innovative approach of the impressionist painters.[1] They were acquainted with French trends largely by hearsay, and what did filter through to them was vehemently rejected. Exhibitions of work by impressionist painters, organised by art dealers and private galleries – and targeted at potential clients: the new generation of art dealers and well-to-do art collectors – attracted a relatively limited audience even in Paris until the last years of the nineteenth century.[2] The activities of the next, radi-

1   On the spread of impressionist works in Europe, see Jensen 1994; *Atlanta–Seattle–Denver* 1999.

2   According to the Swiss art historian Oskar Bätschmann, at the first three exhibitions of the impressionist group, the paintings were arranged to evoke a studio or an apartment, thus, from a marketing point of view, the exhibitions deliberately targeted a selected clientele. Bätschmann 1997, 144–145.

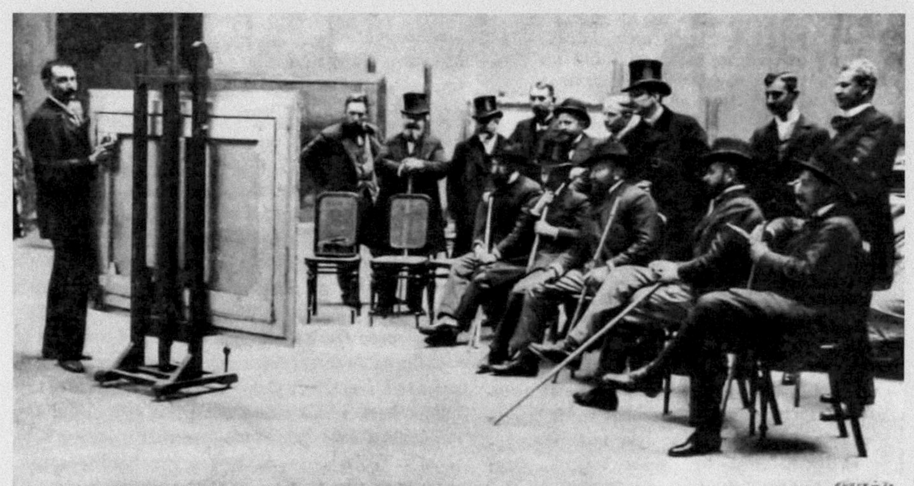

The jury of the Budapest Kunsthalle's
1900–1901 winter exhibition

cally innovative generation, which would later achieve cult status, similarly became known throughout Europe only from the first decade of the next century. Impressionist painters gained international acclaim following the World Exposition in Paris in 1900. Outside France, their work was first acquired by public collections in Germany, thanks to the efforts of Hugo von Tschudi, director of the Nationalgalerie in Berlin at the turn of the century. The purchases made by the Budapest Museum of Fine Arts in 1907 placed it second only to Berlin in terms of the collecting of impressionist works – ahead of other European countries. As a result of his remarkable efforts, Elek Petrovics was able to elevate this unit of the museum's collection to a level of internationally renowned excellence, several decades after the first wave of reform in France.

The predominant the predominant theory in twentieth century aesthetics was that of development from impressionism, via post-impressionism, to cubism and the avant-garde, which, at the same time, marked the evolutionary path of European modernism.[3] Thus, all forms of painting that were connected in any way with academism or the realm of romantic imagination remained for a long time outside this artistic progress. However, recent representative exhibitions have indicated a change in this respect. Research carried out by curators and aesthetes has turned towards geographical regions that attracted little interest earlier, while previously neglected artists are now being elevated among the ranks of artistic pioneers. Just as the orientation of art history has changed in recent decades, and exhibitions have presented the nineteenth century in a new light, so developments in the art of that period, especially during its last decades, have been re-evaluated.[4] The most important lesson concerns the untenability of a model in which the progressive art of the period "radiated"

3   The art critic Julius Meier-Graefe, who was born in the Banat region of Austria–Hungary, established the theory behind the international popularity of impressionism. Meier-Graefe 1904.

4   Among others: Schorske 1979; *Washington – New York – Minnesota* 1982–1983; Rosenblum and Janson 1984; Makela 1990; *London – New York* 2000; Jensen 2007; *Amsterdam–Helsinki* 2010–2011.

from a single prominent European centre (Paris) towards the peripheries. There were several such centres in continental Europe in the 1890s, each one with its own circle of influence.

Art reformers everywhere had to adjust to local conditions and traditions when fighting for their own "secession" and waging their own war of independence.[5] In the late nineteenth century, demands for institutional and educational reform were emerging almost simultaneously in the art centres of Europe, along with initiatives for the elimination of academic expectations that restricted artistic expression. Paris was appealing primarily because of its cultural vibrancy and modern lifestyle, its innovative forms of art education and trade, its progressive art criticism, its freely established art colonies, its public debates, and its occasionally enigmatic private salons.

With the demolition of the academic bastions of painting, the progress of the liberation of forms and the emergence of dynamic visual expression cannot be described as a linear development of consecutive tendencies that built on one another. Changes took place via several paths in parallel, in Paris as well as in Central Europe, Britain, the Low countries, and Scandinavia. Within this diversity, it is still possible to discern the outlines of two universal languages of form, countless variants of which emerged throughout the continent, which can be summarised under the collective terms "naturalism" and "symbolism". One shared feature of late-nineteenth-century European art centres was that both these – only apparently contradictory – stylistic trends found a place in the struggle of local progress against the powers of conservativism: naturalism, with its lighter colours and its insistence on the truth of observation as opposed to official precepts; and symbolism, which subordinated the reality of nature in the service of expression.

The composition of the nineteenth-century art collection in the Budapest Museum of Fine Arts reflects the changing perspectives of successive eras of art lovers, as well as the relationship between the cultural elite and the arts. The present publication aims to reconstruct these changes. For this reason, alongside artists who are highly acclaimed even now that a century has passed, it also includes artists whose work achieved success at exhibitions in their day but who have since been forgotten, and in many cases rediscovered – or who are still perhaps awaiting rediscovery. When it comes to changing tastes, the present publication that introduces the diversity of the collection will be followed by the second chronological unit in the Department of International Art after 1800 – a similarly comprehensive volume examining works from the twentieth century and the first decades of the twenty-first century.

5   In England, the beginnings of the reform movement can be traced back to the founding of the Pre-Raphaelite Brotherhood in 1848, which, with the Arts and Crafts movement, later became extremely popular throughout Europe. In Scandinavia, the new wave of painting began in the mid-1870s with the Skagensmalerne school of painting, founded in Skagen, Denmark. The group of artists known as Les XX was founded in Brussels in 1883, its international exhibitions making it influential throughout Europe; from 1893, it operated under the name La Libre Esthétique. In the German-language territory, groups established under the name "Secession" broke away from the official frameworks of exhibitions and patronage in Munich in 1892, Vienna in 1897, and Berlin in 1898. In Hungary, the two key dates are the founding of the artists' colony in Nagybánya (now Baia Mare, Romania) in 1896 and of the Gödöllő artists' colony in 1901.

List of Illustrations

Chronology

1808

→ The Hungarian Parliament passes a law providing for the establishment of the first national public collection, the Hungarian National Museum, that will also include works of art.

1824

→ The painting *Miklós Zrínyi's Sortie from Szigetvár*, commissioned from Peter Krafft, is acquired by the Hungarian National Museum; it is the earliest acquisition among the nineteenth-century international artworks now owned by the Museum of Fine Arts.

1844

→ **20 July** The collections of the National Museum are enriched by the donation of the art collection of János László Pyrker, Archbishop of Eger. The gift includes thirteen modern paintings from outside Hungary.

1846

→ **19 March** The first display of modern paintings from outside of Hungary in the new building of the National Museum on the occasion of the opening of the Pyrker Gallery.

1847

→ The first works of sculpture from outside Hungary (Laboureur, Tadolini, and Monti), in what will later be the modern collection of the Museum of Fine Arts, are acquired by the Collection of Antiquities of the National Museum, donated by Prince Pál Esterházy and the Royal Curia.

→ **20 October** Following the appointment of Bálint Kiss, the Picture Gallery of the National Museum becomes an independent department.

1848

→ **24 January** Opening of the permanent exhibitions of the National Museum, featuring the museum's nineteenth-century international holdings, including paintings held in the Picture Gallery and sculptures from the Collection of Antiquities.

1864

→ Bequest of Countess Mária Eltz, containing six contemporary genre paintings by artists of different nationalities.

1871

→ An annual sum of 5,000 florins is earmarked from the state budget for the Picture Gallery of the National Museum for the purchase of international works from exhibitions of the Hungarian National Society of Fine Arts.

→ With the purchase of the Esterházy collection, nine modern paintings from outside Hungary join the public collection (e.g., Waldmüller: *Man with a Peep Box*). With the establishment of the National Picture Gallery, and the later reorganisation of the holdings of the two galleries, the National Picture Gallery assumes guardianship of the old fine arts holdings, and the National Museum's Picture Gallery becomes the guardian of the modern fine arts holdings.

→ The National Museum acquires the bequest of Mihály Erny, a large portion of which are Austrian Biedermeier paintings. The bequest contains a total of forty-nine nineteenth-century paintings from outside Hungary.

1892

→ The bequest of Baron Albert Wodianer the Elder to the National Museum includes eleven nineteenth-century German and Austrian paintings.

1895

→ Gyula Wlassics, minister for religion and public education, puts a hold on foreign purchases by the new Museum of Fine Arts until the institution's organisational structure and unregulated financial situation have been clarified.

1896

→ With the passing of Act VIII of 1896, the setting up of the Museum of Fine Arts and the development of its collections become the responsibility of the National Picture Gallery.

→ **1 November** Appointment of Dr Gábor Térey, who is responsible for managing and developing Museum of Fine Arts' international holdings.

1896–1906

→ The museum acquires 120 modern international artworks, most of them contemporary.

1900

→ A sum of 180,000 kronen is set aside in the state budget for the expansion of the collection of paintings; of this, 40,000 kronen are earmarked for modern international works. The sum is available annually until 1918.

→ Gábor Térey visits the studio of Auguste Rodin, following which the museum acquires five Rodin sculptures.

1901

→ In the will of István Delhaes, dated 1893, twelve modern international paintings from his collection, mainly from Germany and Austria, are bequeathed to the future Museum of Fine Arts.

1906

→ **6 December** The permanent exhibitions of the Old Picture Gallery and Gallery of Modern Art open on the first floor in the new building of the Museum of Fine Arts.

1907–1913

→ The modern international collection acquires 273 works, 150 of which date from the turn of the century or after.

1907

→ Purchase of eleven Scandinavian paintings from the 1906/1907 winter exhibition at the Budapest Kunsthalle (including works by Johansen, Gallen-Kallela, Halonen, Stenersen, and Tuxen).

→ The state purchases five paintings, by Boudin, Daubigny, Gauguin, Pissarro, and Sisley, from the exhibition series of modern French paintings at the Hungarian National Salon.

→ The state purchases eight bronze statues and one marble sculpture from the exhibition of Constantin Meunier's works at the Budapest Kunsthalle.

1912

→ The Museum of Fine Arts acquires forty-five modern international artworks through the 1907 will of Count János Pálffy.

1913

→ The bequest of Count Dénes Andrássy to the Museum of Fine Arts contains 136 modern international paintings and eight sculptures.

1914

→ **21 March** Elek Petrovics is appointed director of the Museum of Fine Arts; he is directly responsible for the collections of both Hungarian paintings and modern international paintings.

1914–1934

→ On the initiative of Elek Petrovics, eighteen outstanding modern French works of art are acquired by the museum.

1926 → The first permanent exhibition of modern sculpture opens in the Baroque Hall of the Museum of Fine Arts.

1950 → The Museum of Applied Arts transfers the fine arts holdings in its collection – small bronzes and medals – to the Museum of Fine Arts.

1952 → The newly published inventory of artworks that were lost during World War II includes around 120 paintings and thirteen sculptures from the museum's modern international holdings.

1953 → Several modern international artworks from among the fine arts holdings of the abolished Municipal Gallery are transferred to the Museum of Fine Arts, including, among other things, 142 medals and plaquettes.

1957 → In parallel with the establishment of the Hungarian National Gallery, the Gallery of International Modern Art (later the Department of Modern Art, then the Department of International Art after 1800) is created in its present-day form to manage international paintings and sculptures dating from after 1800

since 2019 → From among the holdings of the Department of International Art after 1800 previously recorded as missing, twenty-one modern international paintings have successfully been traced and reclaimed from ministries and governmental institutions.

Catalogue

CSJB: Csenge Júlia Béres
DF: Dávid Fehér
JG: Judit Geskó
BIB: Bianka Izsák-Boda
AZSK: Anna Zsófia Kovács
LK: Luca Keserü
AL: Adriána Lantos
DL: Dóra Lovass
RM: Rebeka Mrázik
DS: Dominika Sodics
AS: Anett Somodi
FT: Ferenc Tóth

———————

cat. no.: catalogue number
Inv. no.: Inventory number
HNSFA: Hungarian National Society of Fine Arts

I

Order and Ideal

The period covered by the present publication is the nineteenth century, the age of the bourgeoisie. The beginnings of this era can, however, be traced back to the mid-eighteenth century, when the Industrial Revolution and early advances in manufacturing and transportation began to frame the bourgeois perspective that was consolidated during the nineteenth century. The changes then taking place in social, economic, and cultural life in every country of Europe were as significant as those in the early twentieth century. The two Enlightenment catchwords with the biggest impact on the worldview of this period were reason and liberty: the new order instituted by rationality and the systematisation of existing knowledge; and human and intellectual freedom, natural *joie de vivre*, and the elimination of barriers to desire. Corresponding to this polarity, the art of the period that lasted until around the mid-nineteenth century is far from uniform: in art historical tradition, the labels "neoclassicism" and "romanticism" have been applied to its two extremes, although it would be far more appropriate to talk of the synergy, combination, and varying emphases of complex forces. The first section of this volume introduces selected works, which, in terms of their formal elements and aesthetic orientation – or ethos – bear the hallmark of the first of the polarities mentioned above.

The Enlightenment accorded a special role to art: rather than eliciting and intensifying religious feelings, it was seen as being morally improving and revealing the power of reason. The role of art as edification found expression not in its earlier ecclesiastical function but in the representation of the certainty afforded by reason and order. These basic principles, formulated by the German art historian Johann Joachim Winckelmann, also engendered a sensitivity towards history. The paradigm for the framing of universally applicable laws of art was provided by antiquity; in their choice of subjects, the artists of the time drew primarily from this source, and occasionally from the Old and New Testaments.

This artistic aesthetic was not homogeneous, nor did not emerge simultaneously in every country of Europe. As a stylistic category, "neoclassicism" is a collective term applied to artistic tendencies that emerged either in parallel or after a certain delay. The selected works in this category have been grouped together based on their aesthetic kinship and their shared artistic goals and principles. Besides content-related aspects, such as the rule of order, morality, and reason, there are other recurring features that might also merit definition as a stylistic category – clear, pure lines, symmetry, and the symbolism of precisely distributed proportions, suggestive of organisation.

This collection starts with the year 1800, shortly before the establishment of the first national public collection in Hungary. However, the institutional collecting of artwork from the first decades of the nineteenth century was not carried out systematically until far later, giving rise to significant omissions and the inclusion of somewhat arbitrary examples. Besides the leading artists of the period, such as Heinrich Füger, Bertel Thorvaldsen, Pietro Tenerani, and Johann Baptist Lampi, among others – as the students of distinguished masters or those who continued their work – are worthy representatives of the distinctive aesthetic of these decades.

Johann Claudius HERR

(Vienna, 1775 – Vienna, after 1838)

After Andries Cornelius Lens (Antwerp, 1739 – Brussels, 1822)

Zeus and Hera on Mount Ida, 1821 | Viennese porcelain, 30 × 40 cm

Purchase, 1992 | Inv. no. 92.7.B

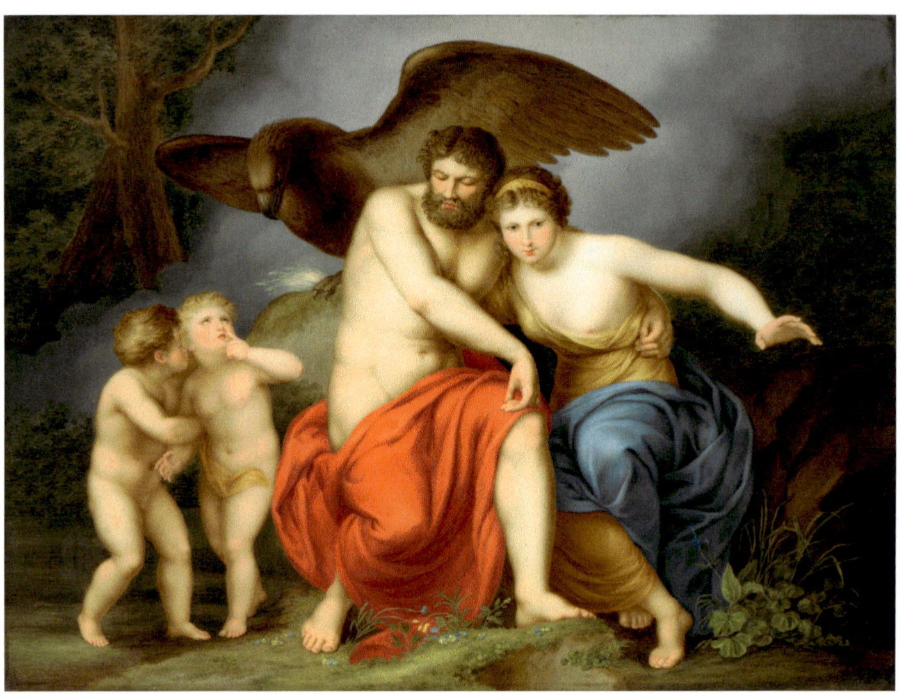

Founded in 1718, the Vienna Porcelain Manufactory began operation as the second in Europe, just a few years after the Meissen manufactory. Besides the mass production of household tableware, the factory also made genuine curios such as this, executed with exquisite artistry and intended as decorative items for aristocratic palaces – individual miniature replicas of the most famous works in the Belvedere in Vienna, painted on porcelain. Such pieces demanded enormous technical skill, and one of the greatest talents in this field was Johann Claudius Herr. Born into a family of porcelain painters, he was already working in the manufactory at ten years of age; by the age of twenty-five, he was considered the most brilliant of figurative painters, whose works were even presented as gifts by Emperor Francis I.

The original work, representing the classical ideal of beauty, was painted in 1775 by the Flemish artist Andries Cornelis Lens. Herr recreated the work in luminous colours, the unique texture of the porcelain emphasising the sculptural beauty of the nude figures. According to Chapter 14 of Homer's *Iliad*, Hera seduces Zeus, then lulls him to sleep with the help of Hypnos, the god of sleep. While her husband slumbers, she helps the Greeks to victory over the Trojan forces. – AL

T. V. 1993, 89 | *Budapest* 2022b, 7

Heinrich Friedrich FÜGER

(Heilbronn, 1751 – Vienna, 1818)

Jupiter Enthroned, after 1810 | Oil on canvas, 103 × 79 cm
Donated by art historian Charles de Tolnay, 1938 | Inv. no. 418.B

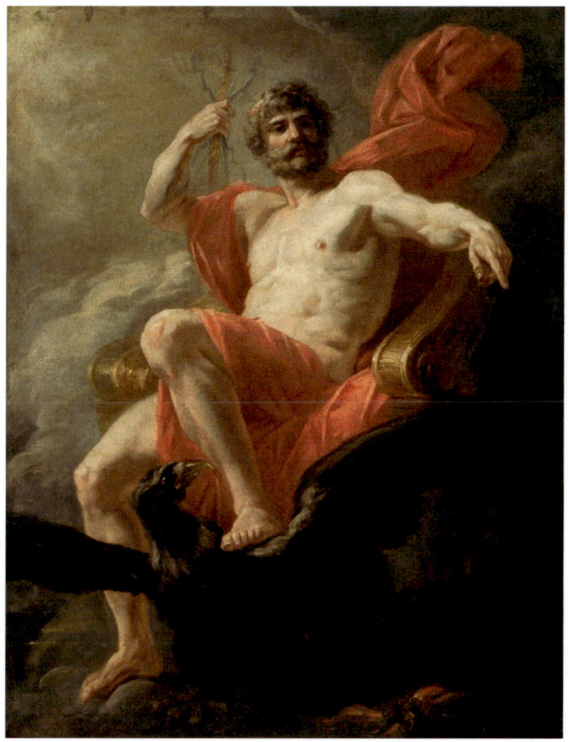

German-born artist Heinrich Friedrich Füger moved to Vienna in 1774, and two years later he was awarded a scholarship to Rome by the imperial court. Although familiar with the neo-classicist ideal from his studies in Leipzig, his time in Italy proved decisive in terms of his painting. On his return home, he was appointed to the Vienna Academy, becoming its director in 1795. This influential position meant that his artistic ideals determined the teaching ethos at the academy for decades.

Initially successful as a portraitist, in the late 1790s Füger was mainly producing large-scale historical paintings, although around 1810 he showed a marked preference for mythological scenes featuring one or two figures. In this example, Jupiter is depicted with thunderbolts in his hand and his emblem, an eagle, at his feet. Features of the artist's later style can be observed in the plasticity of the figure and the vivid red of the drapery. The looser brushwork employed in the background accentuates the precise elaboration of the nude figure. The rendering of the clouds and the diagonal composition lend this painting greater dynamism than is found in Füger's other depictions of mythological subjects. – DS

Szombathely 2001, cat. no. 1.33 | Keil 2009, 387, cat. no. 570

Gaspare LANDI

(Piacenza, 1756 – Piacenza, 1830)

Alcibiades Spies on a Beautiful Greek Girl in Her Bed, 1805–1806 | Oil on canvas, 147 × 197 cm
Purchase, Esterházy Collection, 1871 | Inv. no. 2.B

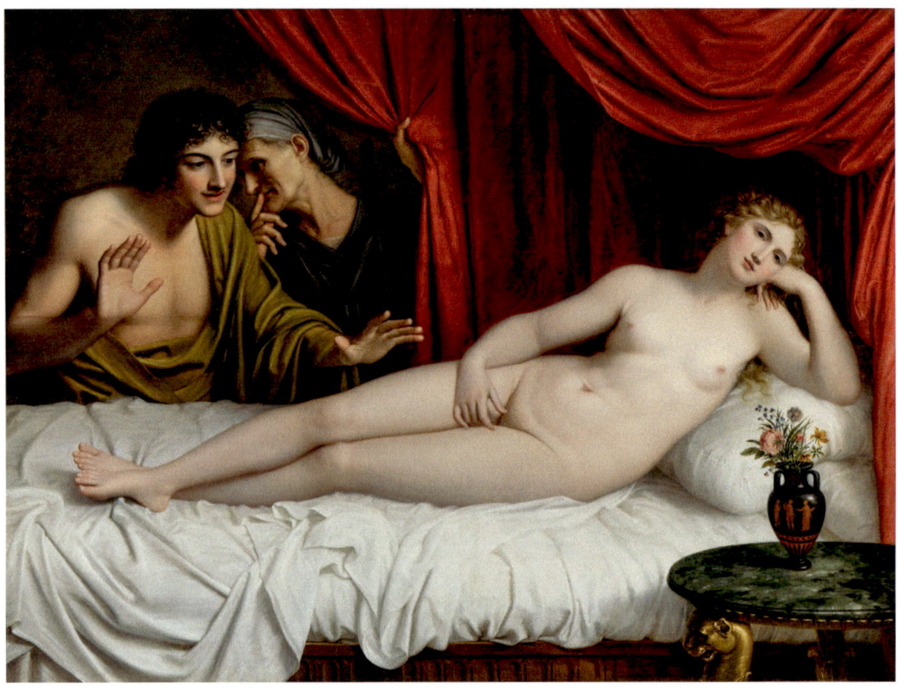

In 1817, the year in which Prince Nikolaus II Esterházy purchased this painting in Rome, Gaspare Landi, one of the city's most outstanding colourists, was elected president of the Accademia di San Luca in recognition of his services. This painting, which Landi kept in his studio for almost ten years, perfectly encapsulates his qualities as an artist. In it, he brilliantly renders the contrast not only between the figures but also between the different textures – from the cool marble and gilt and carved details to the crumpled linen sheet and the heavy velvet folds of the curtains. Landi's concern in this painting, which is reminiscent of the depictions of Venus by Titian and Giorgione, was to give expression not only to ideal beauty but also to differences in gender and age, while at the same time he drew inspiration from Antonio Canova's hugely influential reclining female nude, modelled on Paolina Borghese between 1804 and 1808. Standing behind the young daydreamer are an elderly procuress and a well-built young man with a lascivious eye, identified in contemporary descriptions as Alcibiades. The handsome Greek general, who lived in the fifth century BC, was famous not only for his brilliant intellect but also for the weak morals that proved his undoing, making him a popular subject of works produced in Rome at the turn of the seventeenth and eighteenth centuries. – AL

Cifka 1996b, 111–114 | Grandesso 2008, 22–23

Natale SCHIAVONI

(Chioggia, 1777 – Venice, 1858)

Venus with Doves, ca. 1844 | Oil on canvas, 122 × 155.5 cm
Bequest of Countess Miklós Dessewffy, 1939 | Inv. no. 424.B

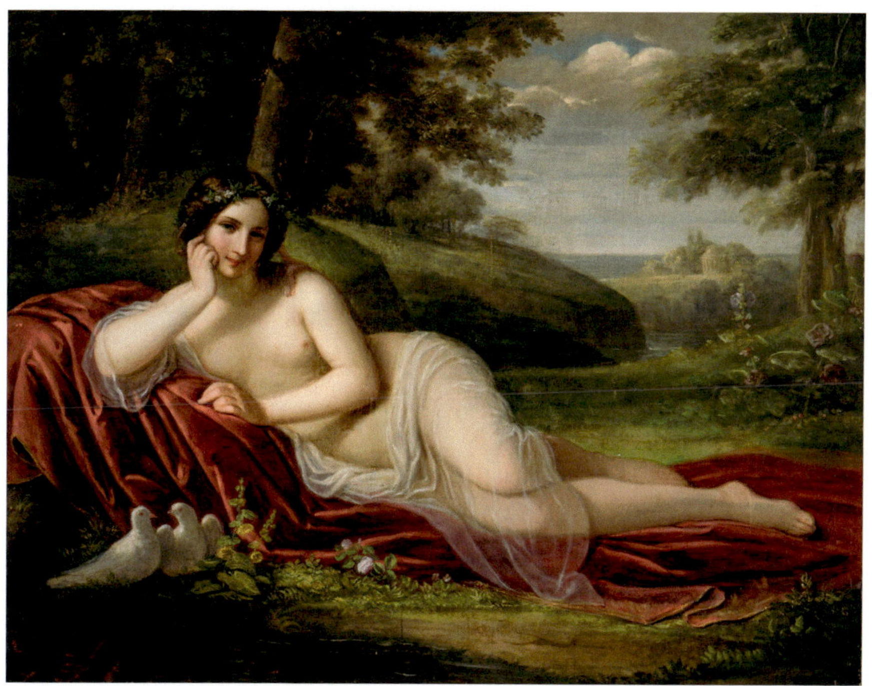

Portraits and depictions of idealised feminine beauty by Natale Schiavoni, the most successful neoclassical painter in Venice, enjoyed huge popularity in Vienna, where the artist worked
for six years as court portraitist of the Austrian emperor Francis I. With his fluid forms and
luminous colours, Schiavoni was, in the eyes of his admirers, the talented heir to the centuries-old Venetian painting tradition.

Following the first exhibition of the Pest Art Society in 1840, Schiavoni was an immediate favourite with audiences. He featured regularly in exhibitions of Hungary's first art
society, with a succession of paintings of sweetly charming girls, posing shyly or smiling co-
quettishly. His sensual paintings of Venus, the Roman goddess of love, were also extremely
popular at this time. The Budapest painting is a copy made by Schiavoni himself; the original
painting, produced in 1844, can now be found in Brescia.

Despite references to antiquity, and Venus's traditional attributes – cooing doves
and roses – the reclining woman on the island of Cyprus is in fact an idealised, fashionably
coiffured Biedermeier beauty, leaning seductively on her elbow, her allure intensified by her
nakedness, scarcely concealed beneath the veil. – CSJB

Sernagiotto 1881, 493–495, 580 | Szvoboda Dománszky 2016, 17, 182, cat. no. 9

Francesco Massimiliano LABOUREUR

(Rome, 1767 – Rome, 1831)

Metabus and His Daughter, 1820 | Marble, 159 × 88 × 93 cm
Donated by Prince Pál Esterházy, 1847 | Inv. no. 3658.U

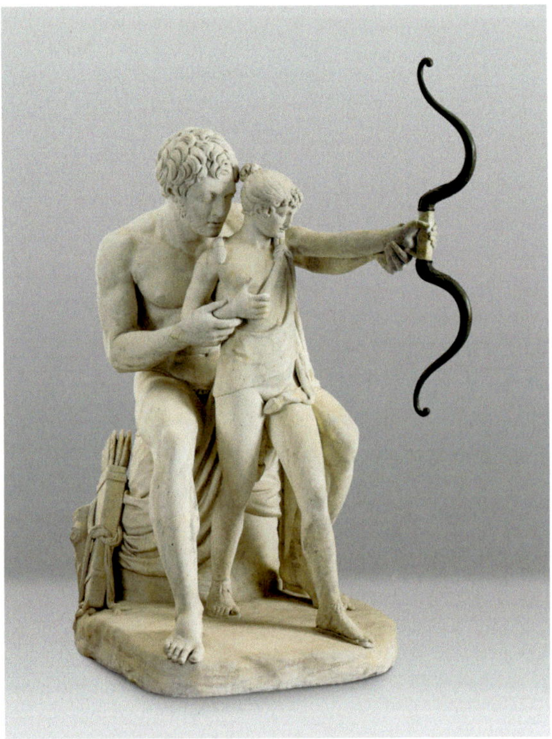

During his travels in Italy, Nikolaus II Esterházy was fond of commissioning artworks from the most famous artists of the day. This is exactly how this exquisite, neoclassical sculpture came about. Laboureur, who had been taught by his Belgian father, owed his reputation to the monumental statue of Napoleon, dressed as a Roman consul, which stood in Ajaccio. When Prince Nikolaus II Esterházy made the sculptor's acquaintance, he was teaching at the San Luca Art Academy in Rome, shortly afterwards becoming its president.

The subject of the composition is a rarely depicted scene from Virgil's *Aeneid*. The Volsci, no longer willing to bear the tyranny of their king, Metabus, banished him. As he fled, he took with him his infant daughter Camilla. On reaching the river Amasenus, then in full flood, Metabus feared that he would not get across without the waters snatching her from his arms, so, entrusting the baby girl to the goddess Diana, he bound her tightly to his spear, which he threw to the opposite bank. Following their escape, father and daughter lived in the wilderness. Laboureur's sculpture shows the king teaching the little girl to use a bow and arrow. – AL

Horváth 1924, 287 | Körner 2013, 284

Adamo TADOLINI

(Bologna, 1788 – Rome, 1868)

Venus and Amor, 1818–1824 | Marble, 102 × 152 × 73 cm
Donated by Prince Pál Esterházy, 1847 | Inv. no. 3665.U

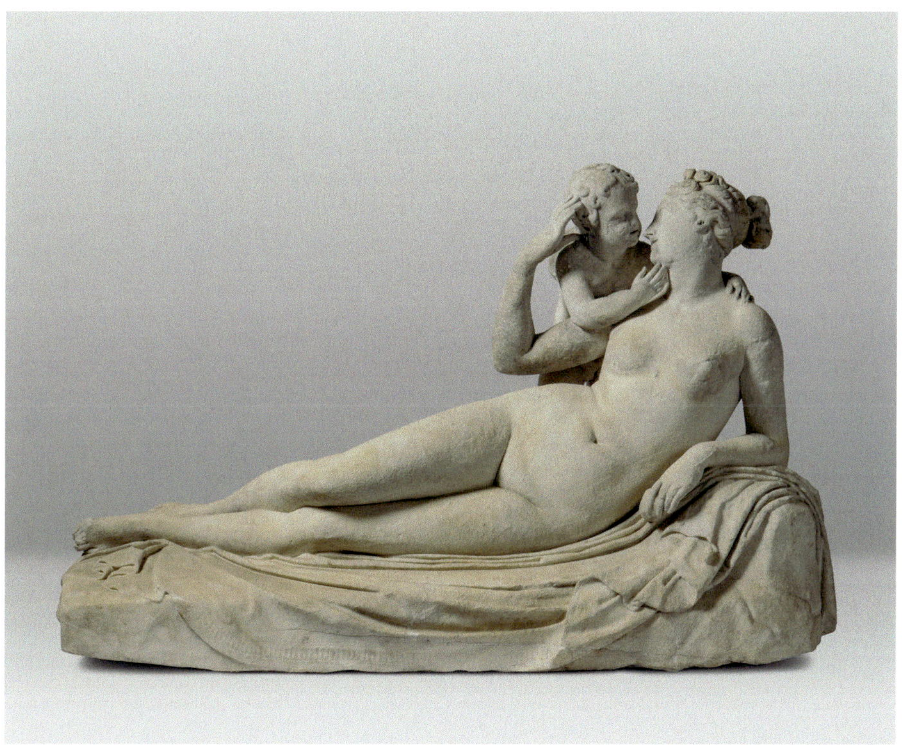

Like his teacher, the distinguished neoclassical sculptor Antonio Canova, Tadolini strove to express in his sculptures the antique ideal of beauty. His talents quickly set him apart from his contemporaries: at just twenty-two years of age, he was a member of the San Luca Art Academy in Rome, besides being a professor of anatomy. It is no accident that while in Rome between 1817 and 1819, the keen art collector Nikolaus II Esterházy visited not only Canova and Thorvaldsen, but also the studio of Tadolini. It was there that he caught a glimpse of Tadolini's statue of Venus, whose Titianesque beauty also evoked Canova's semi-nude sculpture *Paolina Borghese Bonaparte as Venus Victorious* (1804–1808, Galleria Borghese). We know from Tadolini's memoirs that the prince took such a liking to the sculpture that he wished to purchase it immediately from the artist, who had originally produced it at the request of his patron, Prince Hercolani. The prince was unwilling to part with the work, although at his suggestion Tadolini produced a replica of it, also from high-quality Carrara marble but for a far higher price than the original. The work eventually entered the collection of Nikolaus II Esterházy in Vienna in 1824. – AL

Ricordi autobiografici 1900, 101, 105, 251 | Körner 2013, 284–285

Bertel THORVALDSEN

(Copenhagen, 1770 – Copenhagen, 1844)

Tobias, 1840–1844 | Plaster, 105 × 204 × 13 cm
Donated by Ede Reményi, 1866 | Inv. no. 3678.U

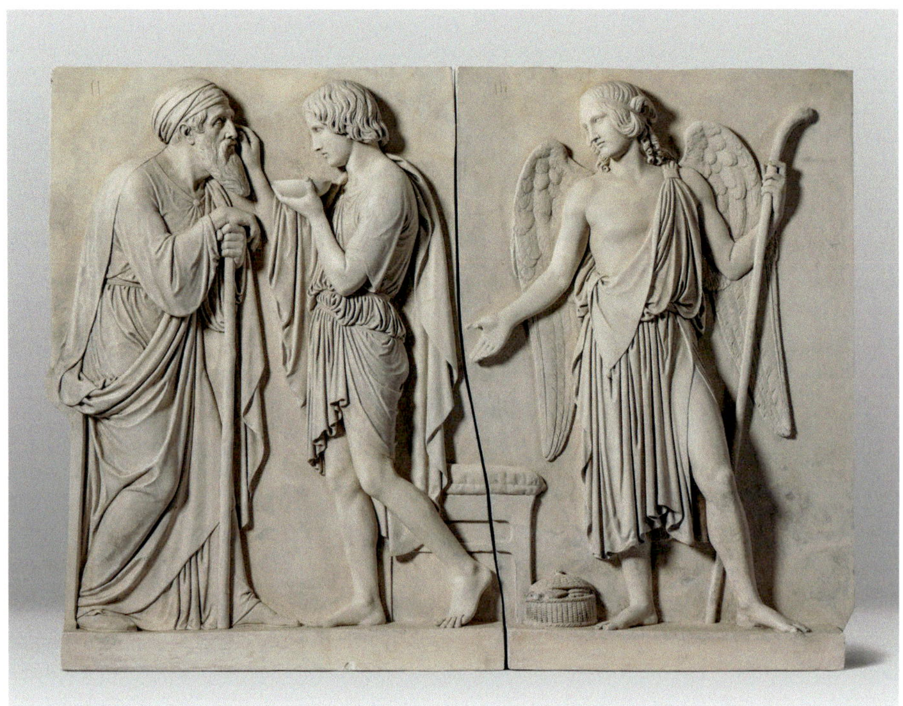

Danish artist Bertel Thorvaldsen was one of the leading figures in neoclassical sculpture. He spent a significant part of his life in Rome, where, like his great rival Antonio Canova, he ran a well-staffed workshop. Besides countless portraits of aristocrats, artists, and writers of the period, Thorvaldsen chiefly produced works inspired by mythology, although occasionally he also turned to biblical themes.

This relief alludes to the Old Testament book of Tobit, in which, with the help of the Archangel Raphael, the young Israelite Tobias cures his father Tobit's blindness. The composition was produced for the marble tomb of the famous Italian eye surgeon Andrea Vaccà Berlinghieri in the Campo Santo next to the Cathedral of Pisa. Unlike the other known version of the plaster sculpture (in the Thorvaldsens Museum, Copenhagen), the Budapest version has survived incomplete: the first, left-hand section of the three-part cast – featuring Tobias's elderly mother and a dog – was probably destroyed during the Second World War. The work was given to the Hungarian National Museum by the world-famous violinist and composer Ede Reményi; this, and six other Thorvaldsen plaster sculptures acquired by Reményi, were delivered to Budapest with the help of Franz Liszt. – AZSK

Soós 1963 | *Rome* 1989–1990, 16–18

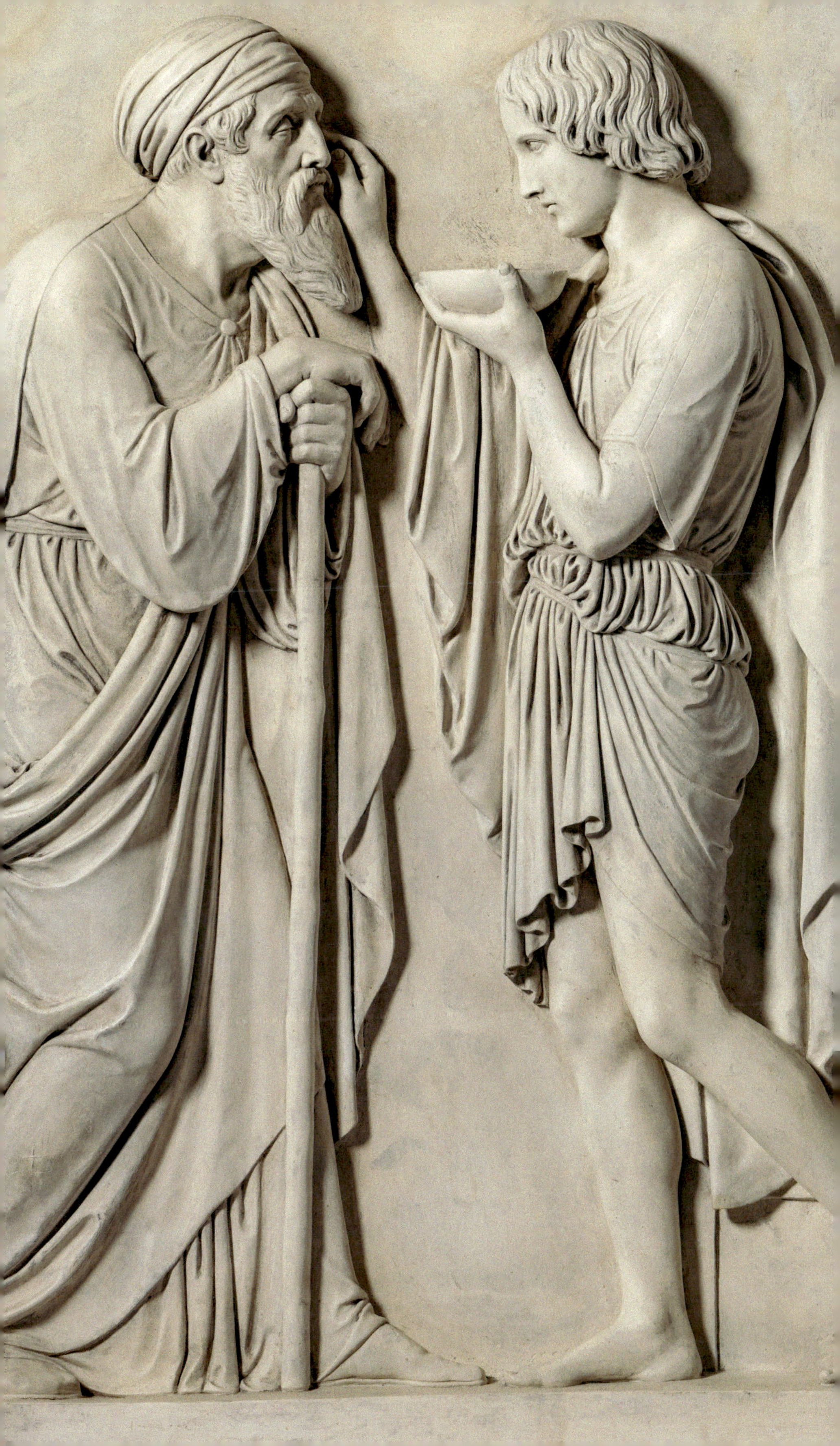

Filippo AGRICOLA

(Rome, 1795 – Rome, 1857)

The Virgin Mary with Jesus and St John the Baptist, 1819 | Oil on wood, 76.5 × 77.5 cm (tondo)
Transfer, 1951 | Inv. no. 468.B

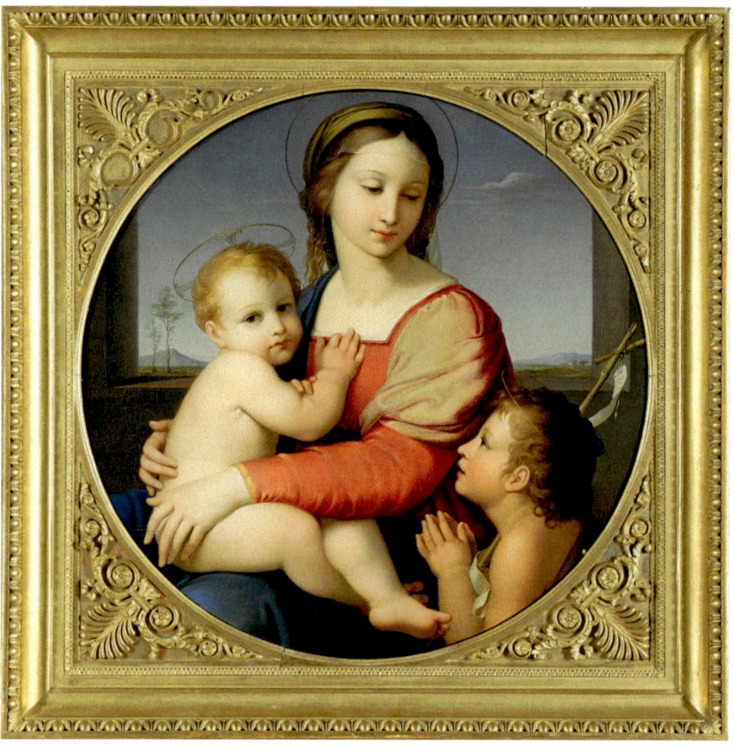

Regarded by some as "the Raphael of the nineteenth century" – owing to one of his most important paintings, the portrait of Constance Monti Perticari – Filippo Agricola was barely seventeen when he caught the attention of Antonio Canova, who gave him a three-year scholarship. Highly successful at a young age, Agricola saw Raphael as the embodiment of artistic perfection: not only did he copy Raphael's works, but he also drew his primary inspiration from them. This intimate, neoclassical work, commissioned by Prince Nikolaus II Esterházy, is distinguished by its polished execution and elegant, exquisite brushwork. Despite its decorativeness, it lacks – as do the artist's other works – the vigour and vitality of the output of his great Renaissance role model, as pointed out by Stendhal in his 1828 book on his experiences in Rome.

Greatly admired by contemporaries, the painting was given by Prince Esterházy to István Széchenyi, the "greatest Hungarian", just a few years after his arrival in Vienna. Széchenyi's son then donated the charming painting to the Hungarian Academy of Sciences, from where it was transfered to the Museum of Fine Arts in the mid-twentieth century. – AL

Nuova Enciclopedia Popolare Italiana 1857–1864, 9–10 | Crielesi 2019, 119–140

Friedrich von AMERLING

(Vienna, 1803 – Vienna, 1887)

Moses and the Bronze Serpent, 1829 | Oil on canvas, 178 × 236 cm
Exchange, 1991 | Inv. no. 91.2.B

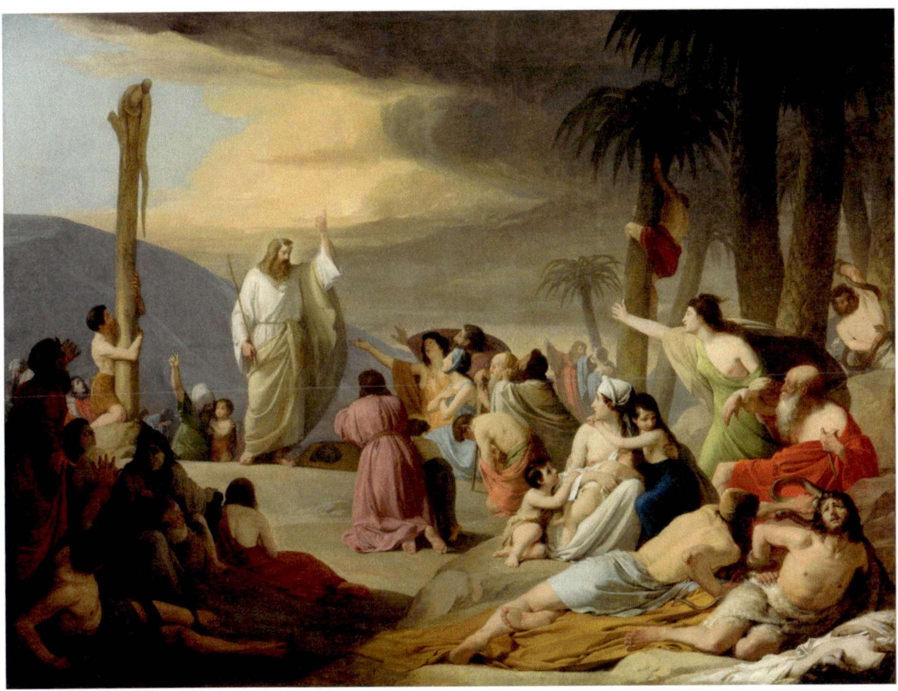

Friedrich von Amerling, the most sought-after portraitist in Biedermeier Vienna, studied art in Vienna and Prague. In 1829, he entered a competition for the Grand Court (or Imperial) Prize, offered by the Vienna Academy for a painting on the theme of "Moses and the Bronze Serpent". Amerling's was judged the best of the six submitted works: the jury particularly commended its accomplished composition, the arrangement of the figures, and the brilliantly executed play of light and shadow. However, the prize was not awarded to Amerling, as the disparity between the finished work and his preparatory sketch represented a breach of the competition criteria. The Old Testament story illustrated in the painting can be found in the Book of Numbers, which describes the Jewish people's rebellion in the wilderness and their punishment by God. The men in the foreground, writhing in agony, are being tormented by poisonous serpents, while the figure of Moses stands tall against the pale background. Moses has made a bronze snake, and those who repent of their sins are forgiven if they look at it. In Christian symbolism, the scene prefigures the crucifixion of Christ. – DL

Cifka 1996a, 61–68 | *Vienna* 2003, 210–211

Johann Baptist LAMPI the Younger

(Trient [Trento], 1775 – Vienna, 1837)

The Duke of Reichstadt, ca. 1830 | Oil on canvas, 99 × 76 cm
Bequest of Mrs István Hirsch, née Anna Krafft, 1910 | Inv. no. 485.B

The Austrian portraitist Johann Baptist Lampi was the son of the painter Johann Baptist Lampi, known as "the Elder". He moved to the imperial capital with his father in 1783, where, from 1786, he studied at the Academy of Fine Arts under Heinrich Füger and Hubert Maurer. He left the academy in 1794 to continue his training in his father's studio. From 1796, he worked at the court of Catherine the Great in Saint Petersburg, where he was appointed an honorary member of the city's academy of art. After returning to Vienna, he became the sought-after portraitist of the Habsburg Empire and received numerous court commissions. In 1813, he was made a professor and became a member of the board of the Academy of Art. He took over his father's studio in 1822. He was primarily a portrait painter, although he also produced genre paintings and religious works.

The Duke of Reichstadt was the first, legitimate son of Napoleon I of France and his wife, Archduchess Marie Louise of the House of Habsburg-Lorraine. Following the defeat of Napoleon, he was brought up at the Viennese court where, according to contemporary accounts, he blossomed into a charming young man. Although he was the longed-for, designated successor of the French emperor, his bloodline and his personality aroused misgivings in the minds of contemporary political figures. He died at a tragically young age without ever holding high political office. In this portrait, he wears the Grand Cross breast star of the Hungarian Order of Saint Stephen; in the background is a cloudy sky and a pillar symbolising his nobility. Known as the "Eaglet", he died of tuberculosis in Schönbrunn in the summer of 1832, at the age of twenty-one. – DL

Trento 2001, 109

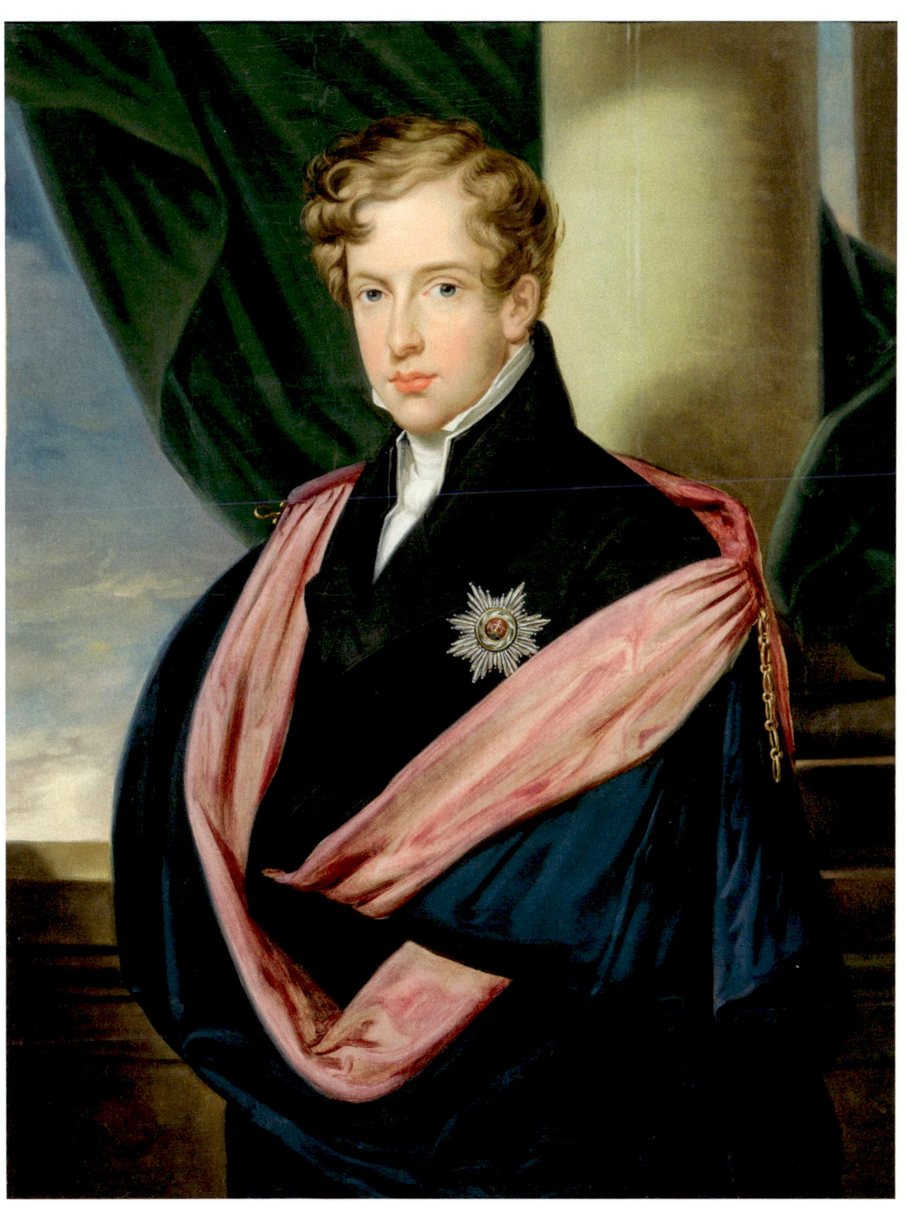

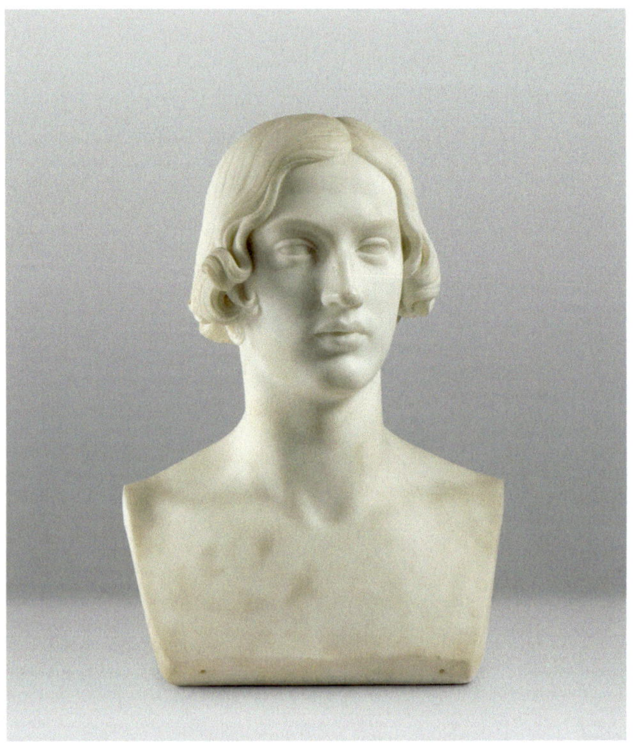

Tenerani grew up not far from the Carrara marble quarries, and having mastered the rudiments of sculpture from his uncle, he distinguished himself from his contemporaries at an early age. Having won several sculpture competitions, he moved to Rome on a scholarship at merely seventeen, and began working in the studio of the Danish sculptor Bertel Thorvaldsen. The excellence of his work quickly brought him acclaim not only in Rome but throughout Europe: his clients included members of the nobility as well as kings and emperors.

Tenerani's numerous busts – which offer a remarkable panorama of the aristocracy of his day – capture the personality of his models with exceptional sensitivity, conveying a sense of distinction without any idealisation. A representative of purism – an artistic tendency inspired by the purity of form of the early renaissance – he typically depicted his subjects dressed in garments from antiquity, or in the case of male figures, with a bare chest. Here, he almost imperceptibly disrupts the rigid symmetry typical of many of his sculptures: by turning the head slightly to the left, the gaze of this unknown young man becomes alive and contemplative. – AL

Soós 1964a, 107–108 | Grandesso 2003

Marco CASAGRANDE

(Campea, 1804 – Cison di Valmarino, 1880)

Bust of Mihály Siskovics, Engineer of the Archdiocese of Eger, 1835
Plaster, 77 × 52 × 32 cm | Purchase, 1960 | Inv. no. 60.1.U

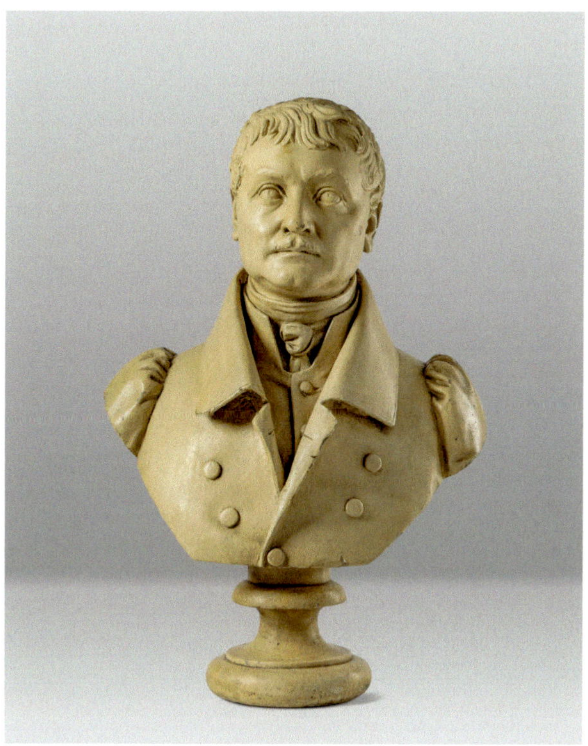

Marco Casagrande studied sculpture at the Academy of Fine Arts in Venice under Luigi Zan-
domeneghi. He worked in the Veneto region but was invited to Hungary in 1833 by János
László Pyrker, Archbishop of Eger, with whom he was acquainted as the Patriarch of Venice.
Casagrande's commission to produce ornamental sculptures for the Basilica of Eger marked
a turning point in his life, as its success led to further large-scale commissions from the church
and the aristocracy. While in Eger, he stayed with Mihály Siskovics, the archepiscopal engineer.
Casagrande produced a plaster bust of his host, which he coated in yellow oil paint. It was
preserved by the engineer's family who sold it to the Museum of Fine Arts. Casagrande's
secular commissions and portraits – free of the iconographic and conceptual expectations of
his ecclesiastical works – are more relaxed in execution, allowing greater scope for the force
of the subject's personality.

     Casagrande played a key role in advancing Hungarian sculpture. For his ornamental
works, he employed several assistants, thus – in the absence of a teaching institute – his workshop became an important setting for practical training in sculpture. – FT

Pálinkás 1942, 743 | Soós 1964a, 107

II

Picturesque Views,
Everyday Passions

———

Andreas ACHENBACH	Louis GALLAIT
Victor ADAM	Anne-Louis GIRODET DE ROUCY-TRIOSON
Leonardo ALENZA Y NIETO	François Marius GRANET
Antoine-Louis BARYE	John Frederick HERRING
Luigi BISI	Leopold KUPELWIESER
Giuseppe CANELLA	Joseph-Fortuné Séraphin LAYRAUD
Consalvo CARELLI	Sir Joseph Noel PATON
Jean-Baptiste CARPEAUX	Johann Mathias RANFTL
Franz Ludwig CATEL	Ludwig Michael von SCHWANTHALER
Théodore CHASSÉRIAU	Bernhard STANGE
Vincenzo CHILONE	Eduard Jakob von STEINLE
Jean-Baptiste Auguste CLÉSINGER	Joseph Édouard STEVENS
Jean-Baptiste Camille COROT	Johann Friedrich August TISCHBEIN
Alfred DE DREUX	Wouterus VERSCHUUR
Eugène DELACROIX	Petter Gabriel WICKENBERG
Gustave DORÉ	John WILSON
Félicie de FAUVEAU	→

The introduction to the first section referred to the grouping of tendencies that are similar in ethos but differ in terms of execution, and this observation is even more pertinent in relation to our second theme. The term "romanticism", as applied to the parallel yet apparently contrasting aesthetic trend of the period, denotes the artistic expression of emotional states rather than a stylistic category. The works included here are differentiated from those introduced on the preceding pages by their distinctive sensibility.

The essential feature of strictly regulated academic training was not only that it produced painters and sculptors endowed with genuine professional skills, but also that it guaranteed status and artistic identity. It was precisely this, however, that ultimately turned it into a source of conflict: it became an obstacle to any expression of individuality. By the end of the eighteenth century, emotional freedom was being championed in the arts in place of the rules dictated by reason. Liberation from the prescriptive approach of academicism, and a rhetoric that accommodated the expression of the passions, culminated in the 1820s in France, in the work of Eugène Delacroix in particular, although its influence would be felt throughout Europe for decades.

The historical roots of what we call romanticism – in contrast to the idealisation of antiquity – go back to the Middle Ages and Gothic art, and to the sensory expression of rapture and ecstasy. The goal of the group of German painters called Nazarenes as well as the British Pre-Raphaelites was to restore the pure, spiritual values of art before Raphael. Several of the works in the present selection can be associated with these tendencies: works by Franz Ludwig Catel, Leopold Kupelwieser, and Eduard von Steinle with the former; and Joseph Noel Paton with the latter. Other artists were drawn rather towards the unfamiliar and exotic. Artists were ready to face adventures, long journeys, and danger in the interests of discovering unknown worlds. They were fascinated by landscapes, people, events of all kinds; their inspiration might come from mythology, religious sentiment, the customs or clothing of unfamiliar peoples, everyday passions, or a stormy coastline.

The depiction of animals was a typical theme in this period, whether in connection with mythology (Antoine-Louis Barye) or associated with hunting scenes or exotic settings. Other, traditional themes were imbued with new significance, and above all new emotions. Human faces mirror internal states of mind and reflect the emotions (Johann Heinrich Wilhelm Tischbein, Anne-Louis Girodet de Roucy-Trioson, Jean-Baptiste Carpeaux). The cult of nature was ignited in followers of Jean-Jacques Rousseau, ultimately leading to a revival in landscape painting. The painter, standing in awe before the landscape, broke with the formulas inherited from the seventeenth century: artists now observed nature with wonder and captured its grandeur, power, and majesty. Painters of various nationalities were inspired to record the sublimity of the landscape during their tours of Italy. The lasting impact of Camille Corot's experiences in Rome between 1825 and 1828 deserves particular mention. During their later excursions in the Barbizon region, Corot and his friends recorded their observations and impressions of the landscape not only in sketches but directly in oils, giving rise to a Europe-wide fashion for *plein air* painting.

Johann Friedrich August TISCHBEIN (attributed)

(Maastricht, 1750 – Heidelberg, 1812)

Portrait of Caroline Tischbein, ca. 1804 | Oil on canvas, 54.5 × 43 cm (oval)
Purchase, 2019 | Inv. no. 2019.2.B

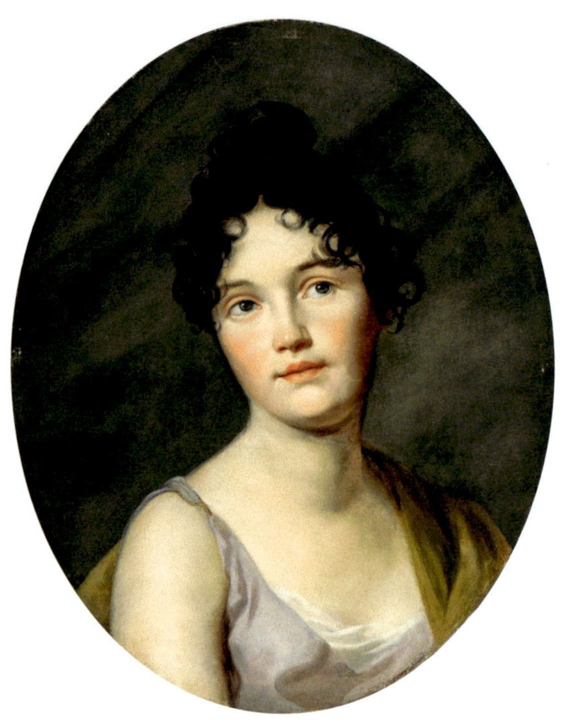

Johann Friedrich August was the foremost artist of the second generation of the influential Tischbein family of painters, who came originally from the northern part of the German province of Hessen. Initially court painter to the prince of Waldeck and Pyrmont, Tischbein spent time in Paris, Rome, and Naples as a young man, before devoting himself to portraiture following a lengthy stay in the Netherlands. In 1800, he was appointed director of the Academy of Art in Leipzig, later becoming known as "Leipziger Tischbein". By the turn of the eighteenth and nineteenth centuries, he was particularly popular for his portraits: inspired by French and English examples, he was among the first to combine the purity of neoclassical painting with the sensitivity and psychological insight of romanticism. As in this medallion, he often painted members of his own family. This charming young lady, her eyes gazing dreamily upwards, is his oldest child Caroline, who continued the family tradition as a graphic artist. She appears in an almost identical pose and attire in Tischbein's signed painting of his two daughters, now in the Academy of Fine Arts in Vienna, in which the girls are portrayed as the Muses of painting and music. – AL

Stoll 1923 | Osten-Sacken 2023, 78–83

Franz Ludwig CATEL

(Berlin, 1778 – Rome, 1856)

Portrait of a Man, first half of the 19th century | Oil on canvas, 36 × 27 cm

Purchase, 1977 | Inv. no. 77.2.B

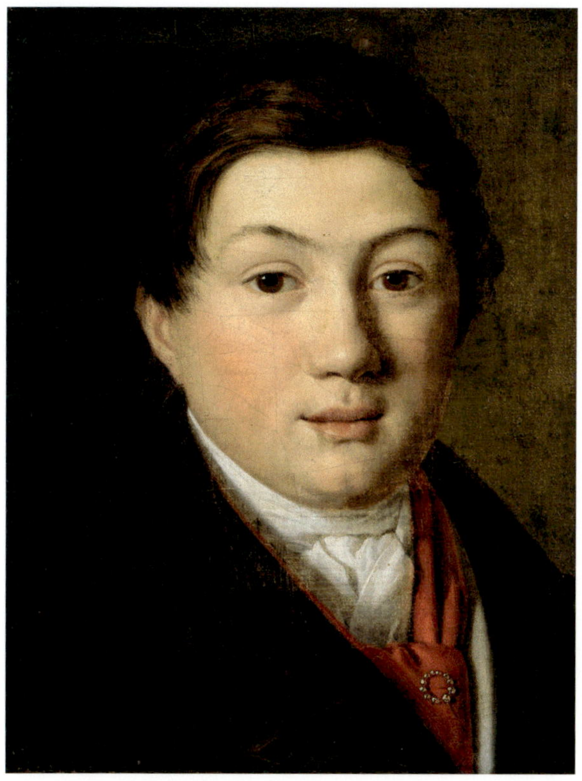

Franz Ludwig Catel was born in Berlin to French Calvinist parents. He began his studies in 1797 at the Academy of Arts in Berlin, but from the following year attended the École des Beaux-Arts in Paris. His first commission came from Johann Wolfgang von Goethe, who asked him to illustrate the poem *Hermann und Dorothea*, which was published in 1799. Catel moved to Rome in 1811 and spent the remainder of his life largely in Italy. His membership of the group of German artists in Rome known as the Nazarenes gave impetus to his artistic development. However, he was more interested than the other Nazarenes in genre and landscape painting, in which he achieved extraordinary success, becoming a leading figure in the city's artistic community. As a favourite painter among the German elite in Rome, he received numerous commissions for portraits. The young man, whose open gaze and soft features are captured in this small painting owned by the Museum of Fine Arts, may well have been one such visitor to Rome. The harmonious but vibrant colours and polished technique attest to the artist's training in France and follow the style of early romanticism. – FT

Hamburg 2015

Anne-Louis GIRODET DE ROUCY-TRIOSON

(Montargis, 1767 – Paris, 1824)

The Odalisque, ca. 1820 | Oil on canvas, 40.3 × 32.7 cm
Purchase, 2024 | Inv. no. 2024.12.1.B

Anne-Louis Girodet was one of the most successful pupils of Jacques-Louis David, the leading figure in the French neoclassical school. Although he mastered to perfection David's fine, polished painting technique, Girodet's approach differed entirely from the strictness of his master's style, transcending the traditional antithesis between neoclassicism and romanticism. His entire career was characterised by originality and an inclination towards the bizarre and exotic.

Although he favoured orientalist themes, he never travelled to the East – the models for his lofty scenes and characterful male portraits were found in Paris, among the Egyptian Mamelukes of Napoleon's Imperial Guard. After 1820, he painted numerous portraits of beautiful women in turbans. However, since he never had an opportunity to meet oriental women, Girodet used a European model, whose features are recognisable in several works. This same charming face appears in *The Odalisque*, the round chin and long, straight nose reflecting the classical ideal of beauty. The woman's downcast eyes suggest that this is a head study rather than a portrait. The odalisque's shoulders are draped in an Indian shawl, and she wears a striped silk turban on her head. This wealth of colours and patterns throws into relief the subtle shades of her skin and the pink flush that animates her pale face. Reminiscent of the Sybils of Domenichino and the Madonna paintings of Guido Reni, the odalisque also has an affinity to the turbaned figures of Jean-Auguste-Dominique Ingres. Although he did not exhibit the painting, Girodet must have been satisfied with it, as it was reproduced as a lithograph and as an engraving. Until recently, this work was known only in its printed form. – AZSK

Paris 2005, 394–397 | Montargis 2010

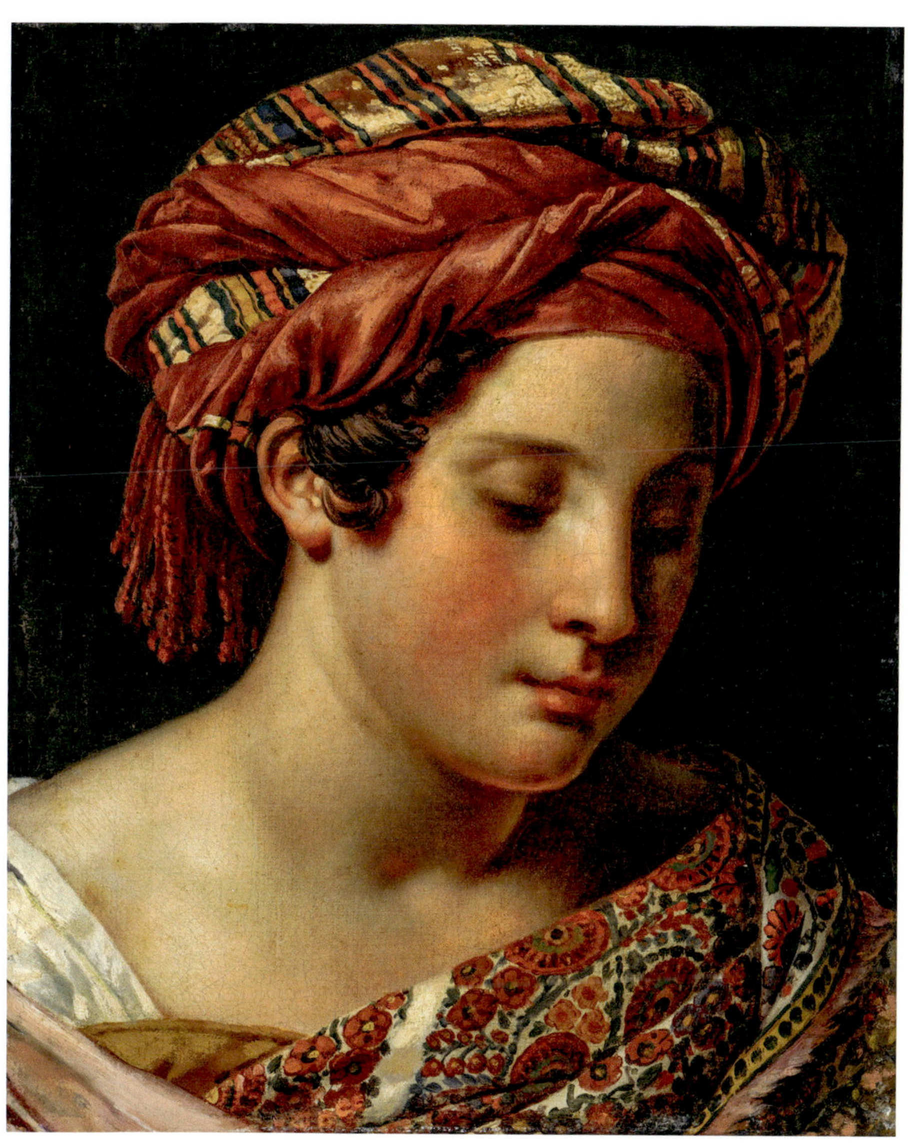

François-Marius GRANET

(Aix-en-Provence, 1775 – Malvalat, 1849)

Capuchin Monks at Prayer, ca. 1815–1830 | Oil on canvas, 47 × 36.5 cm
Donated by Archbishop János László Pyrker, 1836 | Inv. no. 94.B

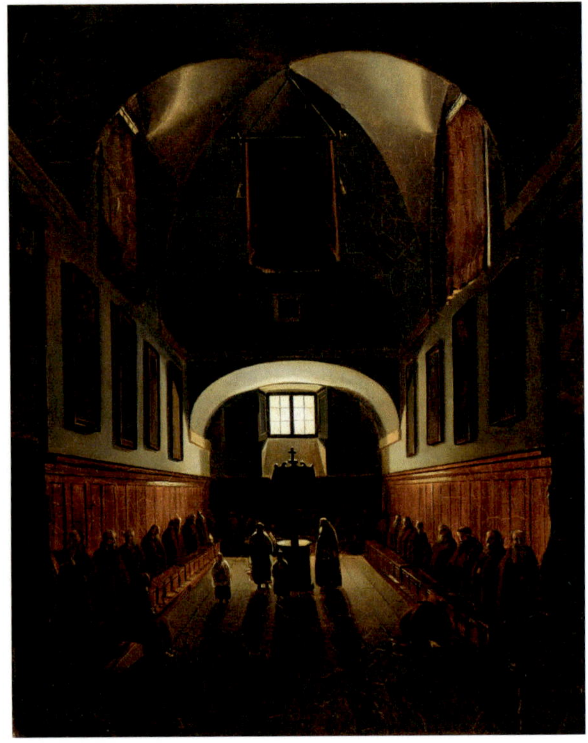

Born in Provence, François-Marius Granet was a student of Jacques-Louis David in Paris before settling in Rome in 1802, where he lived for over two decades, painting evocative interiors and sun-drenched landscapes. His works display both the precise, strict compositional principles of neoclassicism and the evocative approach to nature of Romanticism.

The interior of the Chiesa dell'Immacolata Concezione on the Piazza Barberini in Rome, belonging to the monastery of the Capuchin order, was one of Granet's most popular subjects. This hugely successful painting was executed in more than a dozen variations: the original version was inspired by Napoleon's occupation of Rome between 1808 and 1814, when the Mass and church services were banned. Granet found his favourite church empty, and the profoundly religious painter turned to his canvas to protest the restrictions. In the Budapest version, too, he accurately renders the perspective of the building and the details of the interior ornamentation, while sensitively depicting the effects of light and shadow that intensify the enigmatic, intimate atmosphere of the space and the deep piety of the praying monks. – AZSK

Aix-en-Provence 2008, 195–205

Luigi BISI

(Milan, 1814 – Milan, 1886)

Detail of the Basilica of Sant'Ambrogio in Milan, 1839 | Oil on canvas, 49 × 69 cm
Bequest of Mihály Erny, 1871 | Inv. no. 92.B

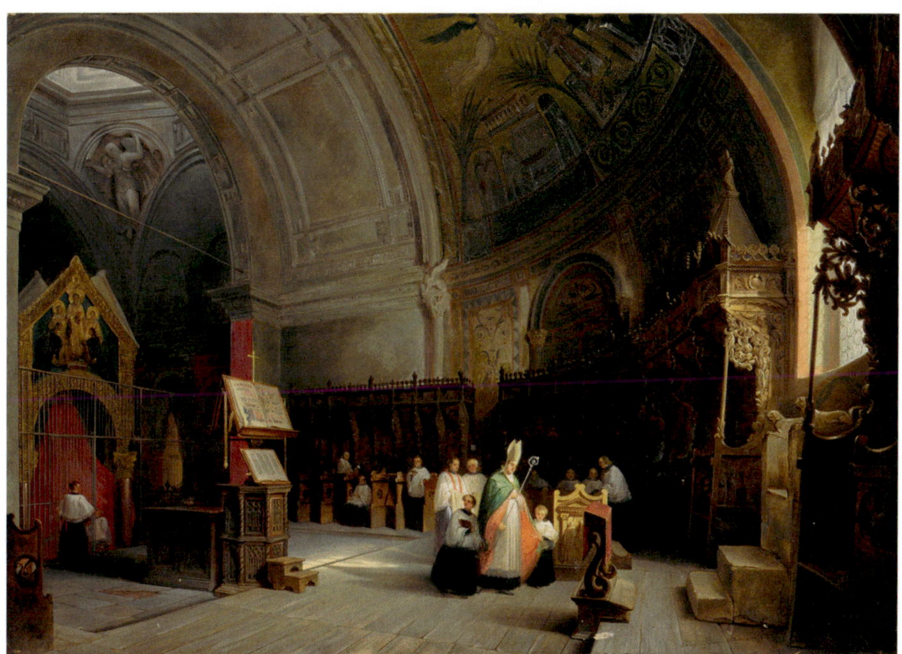

Luigi Bisi was born in Milan into a successful family of artists. A painter and architect, he became a member, and later professor, of the Brera Academy, where he taught the methods of perspective. He was elected president of the academy in 1879. His painting was permeated by his interest in architecture: he produced numerous vedute of Italian cities and famous buildings, although it was church interiors that eventually became his favourite subject. He focused primarily on the churches of his native city: by his own reckoning, he painted Milan Cathedral on almost ninety occasions.

In this image of the chancel in the Basilica Sant'Ambrogio, the second most important church in Milan, preparations are underway for Mass, although Bisi is more interested in the architectural details and eclectic ornamentation. Besides the Byzantine mosaics in the apse, he includes an accurate depiction of the later baroque alterations. Interestingly, the painting shows the interior in a condition that no longer exists. Originally founded in the fourth century, the building was renovated after 1857 – under the supervision of Bisi, among others – with the goal of restoring its early Christian and Romanesque character. As a result, by the late nineteenth century the basilica had regained the simplicity of its medieval appearance. – AZSK

Ottino della Chiesa 1968 | Castelnuovo ed. 1990, 701

Leopold KUPELWIESER

(Piesting, 1796 – Vienna, 1862)

The Assumption of the Virgin Mary, 1852 | Oil on canvas, 53.5 × 30 cm
Bequest of Béla Tárkányi, 1886 | Inv. no. 156.B

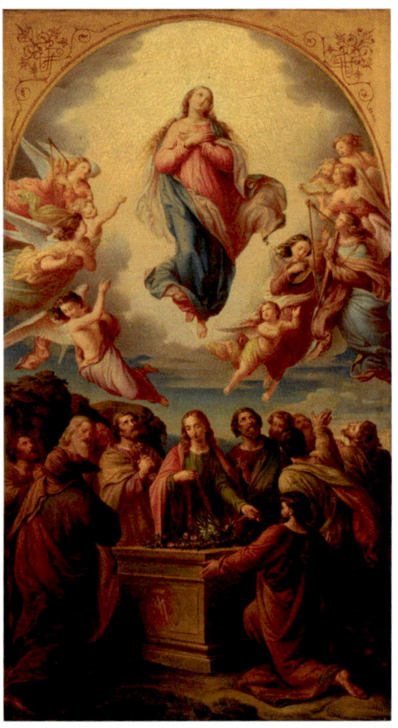

Leopold Kupelwieser's talents were recognised early: he was given a place at the Academy of Fine Arts in Vienna at just twelve years of age. He lived in Rome between 1823 and 1825, where he came under the influence of the Nazarene movement. After settling in Vienna, he made a name for himself as an illustrator, a painter of shopfronts, and a portraitist. He later turned to religious frescos and altarpieces, earning a reputation as an ecclesiastical painter. He decorated countless churches in Vienna, produced several paintings for Pécs Cathedral, and painted the main altarpieces in Kalocsa Cathedral and the Józsefváros parish church in Budapest. In 1837, he became a professor at the academy, and in 1850 was awarded the Knight's Cross of the Order of Franz Joseph.

This relatively small painting of the Assumption of Mary may have been produced as a proposal for a commission; it was eventually painted full size as the main altarpiece of the Convent Church of Our Lady in Pécs. The impact of renaissance painting, chiefly that of Raphael, is discernible in the composition. The painting was purchased in Rome by Béla Tárkányi, canon of Eger, who then bequeathed it to the picture gallery of the Hungarian National Museum in 1886. – AS

Fővárosi Lapok 1878 | Peregriny 1909/1, 305

Eduard Jakob von STEINLE

(Vienna, 1810 – Frankfurt am Main, 1886)

Mary Adoring the Sleeping Jesus, 1847 | Oil on canvas, 47 × 54.7 cm
Bequest of Béla Tárkányi, 1886 | Inv. no. 168.B

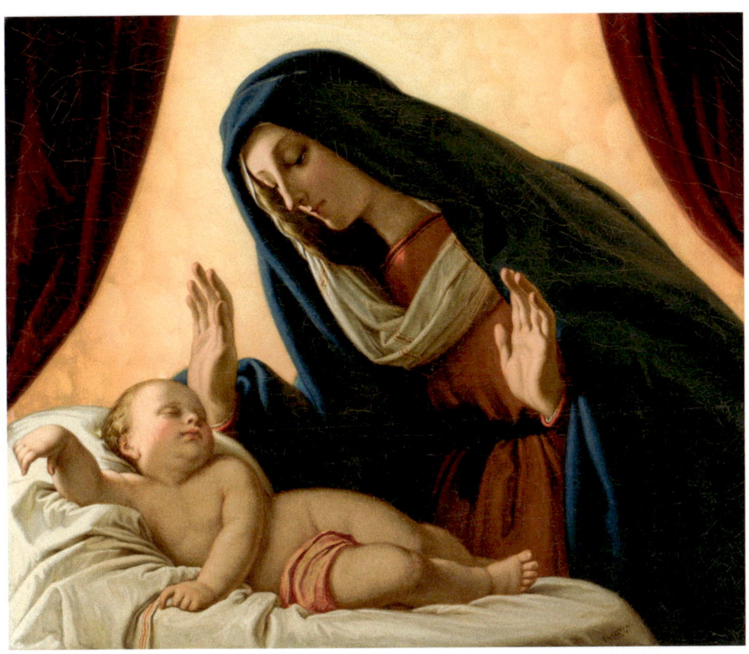

Eduard von Steinle, who was born in Vienna but worked for much of his life in Rome and Frankfurt, was one of the most important church painters of his day. He studied at the Academy of Fine Arts in Vienna under Leopold Kupelwieser. From 1828, he pursued his studies in Rome, where he joined the German Nazarene movement that gathered around the painters Johann Friedrich Overbeck, Philipp Veit, and Peter Cornelius.

The Nazarenes rejected academicism and neo-classicism, turning rather to the example of Dürer and the formal purity and religious devotion of Quattrocento Florence. Their ambition was to bring about an artistic renewal according to the romantic and pietist views of the period, in the spirit of pre-Reformation Christianity, and to establish a new kind of religious and patriotic art. Steinle received numerous commissions for decorative work and painted frescos in the chancel of Cologne Cathedral and the Church of Saint Giles in Münster, among others. He also undertook important teaching work in the Städelschule in Frankfurt.

The Budapest painting shows the Mother of God gazing in wonder at the beauty of the sleeping Jesus, as she leans her gentle face over the slumbering infant. The meaning behind the position of her hands is deliberately ambiguous: it might be interpreted as a gesture of spontaneous surprise or as a blessing. The faint outlines of angel heads can be discerned in the golden background bordered by red drapes. – DL

Wurzbach 1879 | Mainz 2012

(Dunfermline, 1821 – Edinburgh, 1901)

The Virgin with the Sleeping Child and Saint John the Baptist, 1844 | Oil on canvas, 76 × 61 cm

Purchase, 2002 | Inv. no. 2003.2.B

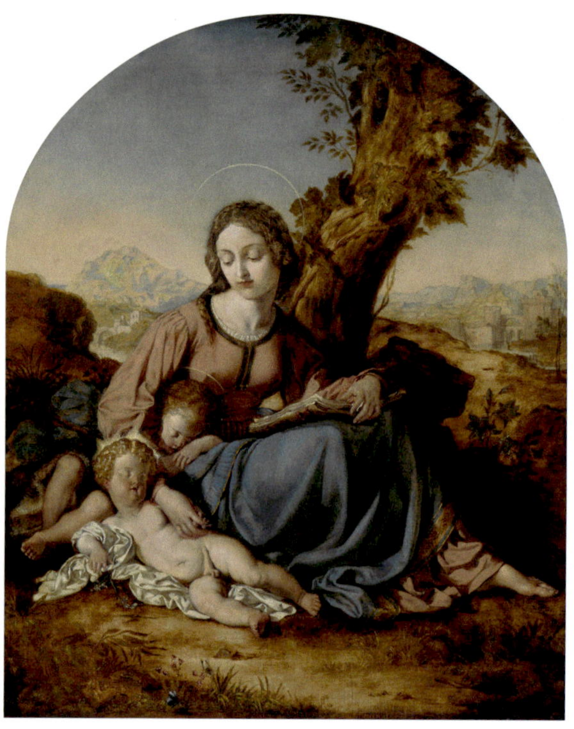

Sir Joseph Noel Paton's mother and father both worked as damask designers and weavers in Dunfermline. After studying in his native city, the Scottish painter, illustrator, art collector, sculptor, and poet briefly attended the Royal Academy in London in 1843, where he was taught by George Jones. While studying in London, he made the acquaintance of John Everett Millais, who invited him to join the Pre-Raphaelite Brotherhood. Paton did not like London and declined the invitation, although he remained associated with the group. The art critic John Ruskin, theoretician of the Pre-Raphaelite Brotherhood, referred to him as the "genius of Edinburgh". He received numerous commissions from Queen Victoria, and was given a knighthood for his services.

Paton's contemporaries called him the "fairy painter", owing to his familiarity with Scottish folklore and Shakespeare's *A Midsummer Night's Dream*. He often painted biblical scenes and religious subjects, looking to Renaissance Florence, to Raphael and Leonardo's Madonnas as his models. In the Budapest painting, the landscape elements and the tree in the background, painted with highly detailed realism, lend an unusual, romantic atmosphere to the classical composition. – DL

Story 1895 | Cifka 2003

Louis GALLAIT

(Tournai, 1810 – Brussels, 1887)

Travelling Players, 1864 | Oil on wood, 75.5 × 60.5 cm
Bequest of Count János Pálffy, 1912 | Inv. no. 254.B

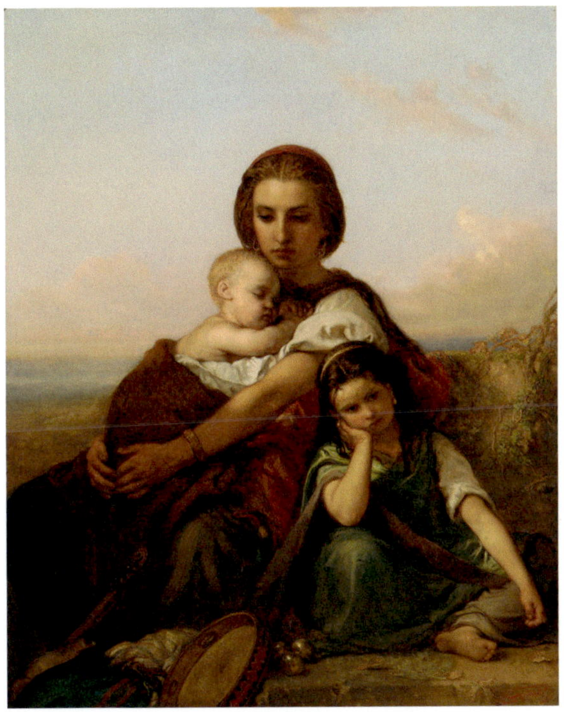

Louis Gallait studied in Tournai and Antwerp before moving to Paris, where he lived from 1834 to 1841. There, the romantic historical painting of Ary Scheffer and Paul Delaroche profoundly influenced his artistic development. His large-scale, realist depictions of dramatic events from the nation's past were not only popular in Belgium, a country that gained its independence in 1830, but also earned acclaim throughout Europe. Works exhibited by Gallait in Germany also had an indirect influence on Hungarian historical painters, including Bertalan Székely, via the teaching of Karl von Piloty at the Munich Academy.

This painting, illustrating the hardships of life as a travelling player, is one of Gallait's smaller, intimate genre paintings and evokes the Madonnas of Raphael. The woman, seated at the centre of the pyramidal composition, creates an intimate unity with the child asleep in her arms and the little girl wearily resting her head in her hand. The musical instruments, juggling balls and costumes at their feet are the tools of a trade that was both celebrated and scorned. The subtle, warm light of the setting sun emphasises the group's exotic, melancholy beauty. Gallait painted several variations of the scene. – AZSK

Térey 1913, 53 | *Tournai* 1987, 256–258

Félicie de FAUVEAU

(Livorno, 1801 – Florence, 1886)

Water Sprite, 1851 | Stone, 75 × 50 × 50 cm
Transfer, 1953 | Inv. no. 2024.1.1.U

Born into a French aristocratic family, Félicie de Fauveau was an eccentric personality and an unconventional artist. A self-taught sculptor, her artistic approach was close to the historical paintings of Ary Scheffer and Paul Delaroche: she was a representative of the so-called troubadour style, which took its inspiration from the medieval and renaissance periods, and her romantic, historicist works even inspired the novelist Alexandre Dumas. She attracted notice for her masculine appearance, although she was also conspicuous for her profound religiosity and radical political views. In 1831, she took part in the Bourbon uprising against Louis Philippe, and following its defeat she was forced into exile. She settled in Florence, where she received commissions from the Russian tsar and from members of the European nobility, including the Hungarian count Edmund Zichy. Although Fauveau's name disappeared into oblivion in the late nineteenth century, interest in her unique art has recently revived among researchers and museum curators.

The Budapest sculpture was made in Florence, as evidenced by the inscription "Florentiae" on its base. The work exemplifies Fauveau's characteristic decorative approach. The figure, whose wavy hair is adorned with water lily leaves, is probably a water sprite. Her dress, as well as her wings, reminiscent of butterfly wings or fish fins, are decorated with gold details. The figure forms a dynamic, upward-curving spiral, and the gown that clings to her body brings to mind underwater ripples. Her hand, raised to her ear, suggests that she is trying to make out voices penetrating from the surface of the water. The work is very similar to a marble sculpture that Fauveau produced twenty years later, which likewise depicts a mythical water nymph, Undine, who longs for a human soul. – AZSK

Mascalchi 2012 | *Les Lucs-sur-Boulogne – Paris* 2013

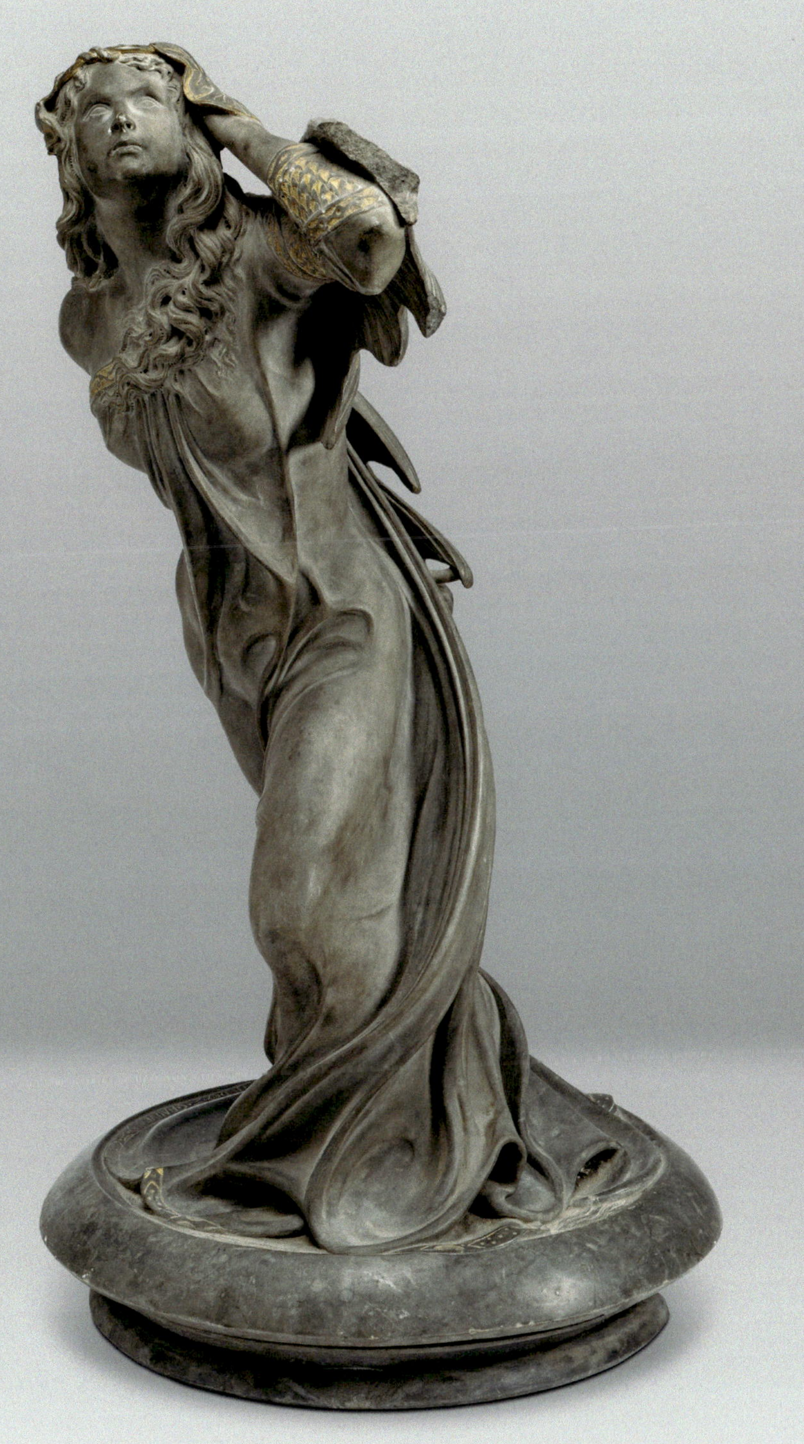

Antoine-Louis BARYE

(Paris, 1796 – Paris, 1875)

Theseus Defeating the Centaur Bienor, model: 1849; cast: 1875–1918
Bronze, 76 × 67 × 30 cm | Purchase, 1974 | Inv. no. 74.1.U

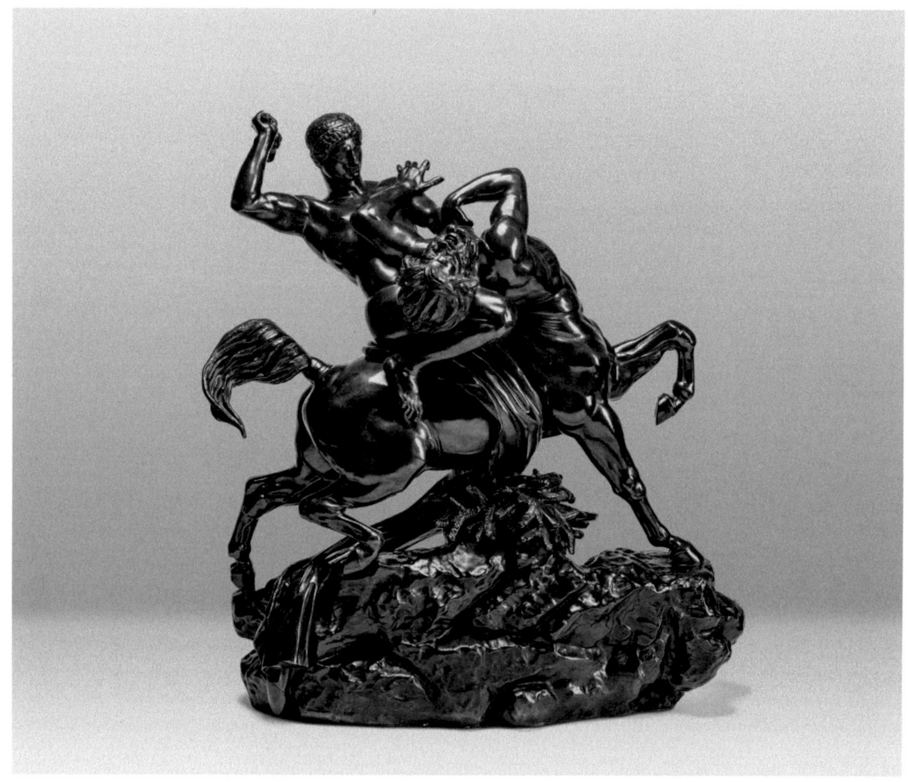

Antoine Barye was an outstanding exponent of French romantic sculpture, whose work was largely inspired by the exotic, alien world of animals. He and his close friend Eugène Delacroix regularly visited the Paris Zoological Garden to study the behaviour and anatomy of the different species. His compositions often depict fighting animals, accentuating, in these occasionally brutal encounters, their savage beauty and unbridled strength.

This representation of Theseus, which was shown at the 1850 Paris Salon, is a romantic interpretation of a Greek myth: when drunken centaurs ran riot at a wedding feast and assaulted the women, Theseus intervened, killing Bienor as he attempted to carry off the bride. Barye presents the classical story with characteristic charge and vitality. The composition is based on powerful diagonals: the muscular bodies of demigod and centaur – a hybrid creature with the lower body of a horse and the chest and head of a man – are forged into a dynamic yet balanced whole as they strain against each other. The hero's defeat of the centaur symbolises victory over the bestial instincts latent within the human psyche. – AZSK

Poletti and Richarme 2000, 109–110 | Illyés 2001, 14–16

John Frederick HERRING

(Surrey, 1795 – Meopham, 1865)

Fox Hunting, 1831 | Oil on canvas, 86 × 103 cm
Purchase, 1969 | Inv. no. 570.B

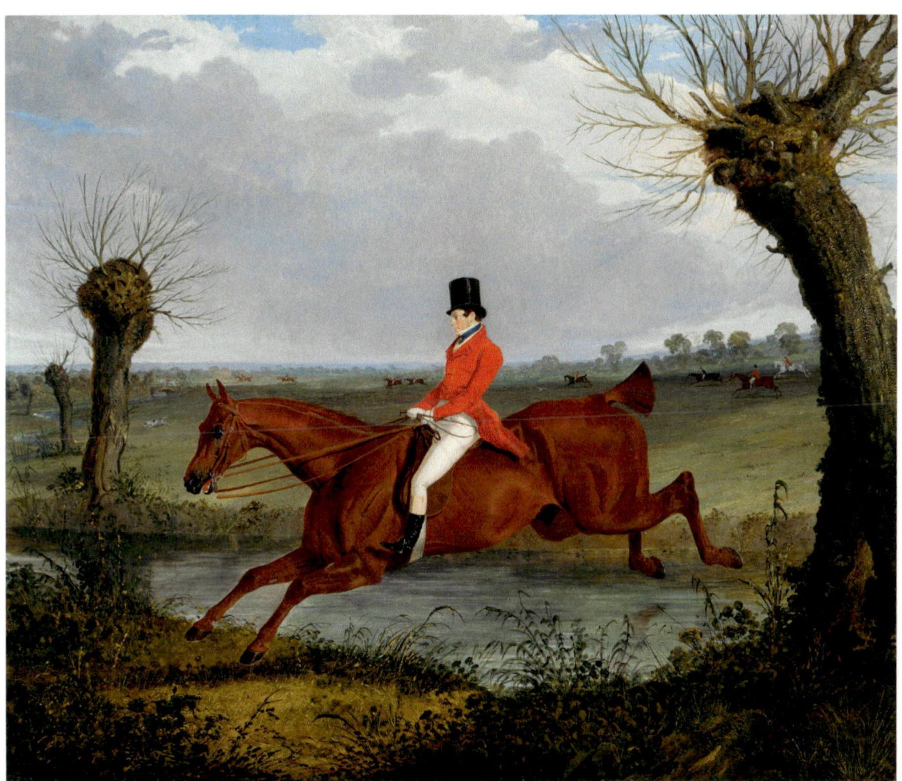

From the eighteenth century, foxes were hunted in England not only for their fur, or as a means of culling, but also by way of recreation. By the nineteenth century, fox hunting was no longer the preserve of the nobility: increasingly enjoyed by the middle classes, it soon became the – rather expensive – English national sport. In parallel, paintings of foxhunts grew in popularity.

This was a world with which Herring was familiar: previously employed as a professional coachman (a respectable position at that time), he then painted inn signs and equestrian portraits. In the 1830s, he became a full-time artist and was regularly commissioned by members of the English gentry to paint hunting scenes and portraits of racehorses. He even attracted the attention of Queen Victoria, who became his patron. Reproductions of his paintings reached a wide audience and thus may well have influenced the work of Édouard Manet and Edgar Degas. – BIB

Gaunt 1964, 89–98 | *London–Leicester–Liverpool* 1974–1975, 18–19, 104

Victor ADAM

(Paris, 1801 – Viroflay, 1866)

Military Field Forge, 1835 | Oil on canvas, 46 × 55.5 cm

Transfer, 1951 | Inv. no. 475.B

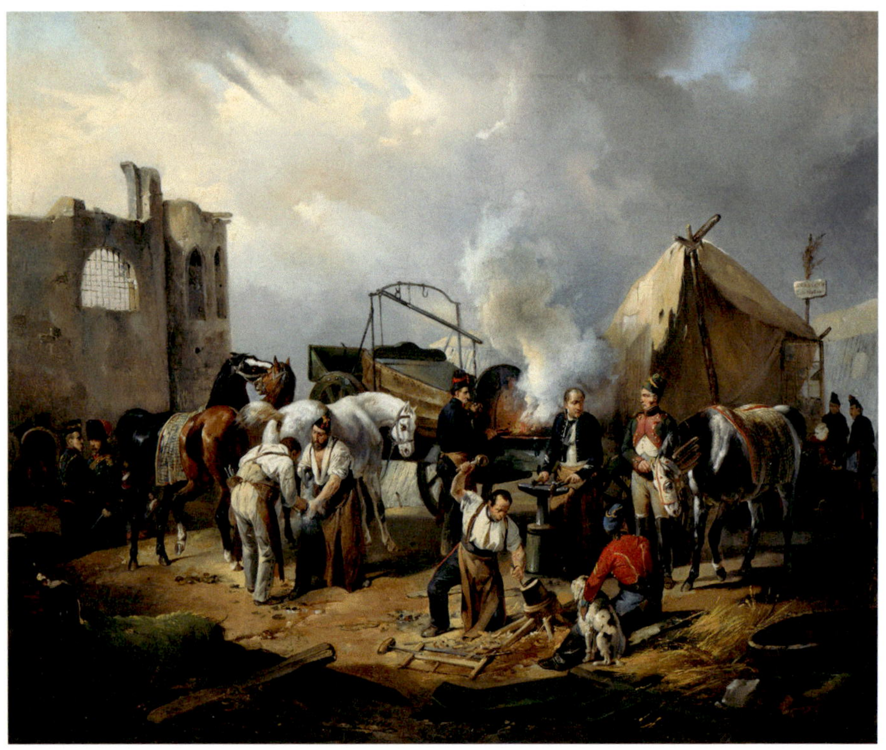

Victor Adam's talents were recognised early: he was admitted to the École des Beaux-Arts at just thirteen years of age. His career got off to a promising start when, after 1819, he was commissioned to produce several paintings of the Napoleonic Wars for the historical museum at the Palace of Versailles. Besides these, he favoured smaller-scale genre scenes of horsemen and soldiers. Lithography played an increasingly important role in his artistic output and eventually he specialised in illustrations and albums. A fast and prolific artist, he produced around seven or eight thousand prints.

    This painting of a forge in a military camp captures a less heroic moment in army life, as the soldiers garrisoned beside a ruined church maintain their equipment and tend to their horses. In his customary style, Adam has painted the animals and the minutiae of everyday life with both immediacy and accuracy. The kneeling figure in the foreground mends a wheel, the farrier shoes a horse, while behind him, the glowing embers are fanned by bellows mounted on a cart. In the tent in the background – according to the sign on the pole – meals are served by the camp cook, Françoise. – AZSK

Béraldi 1885, 15–22 | *Benezit 2006*, 95

Alfred DE DREUX

(Paris, 1810 – Paris, 1860)

Resting Horses, ca. 1848–1850 | Oil on canvas, 32.8 × 46 cm
Purchased from the HNSFA's 1877–1878 winter exhibition | Inv. no. 68.B

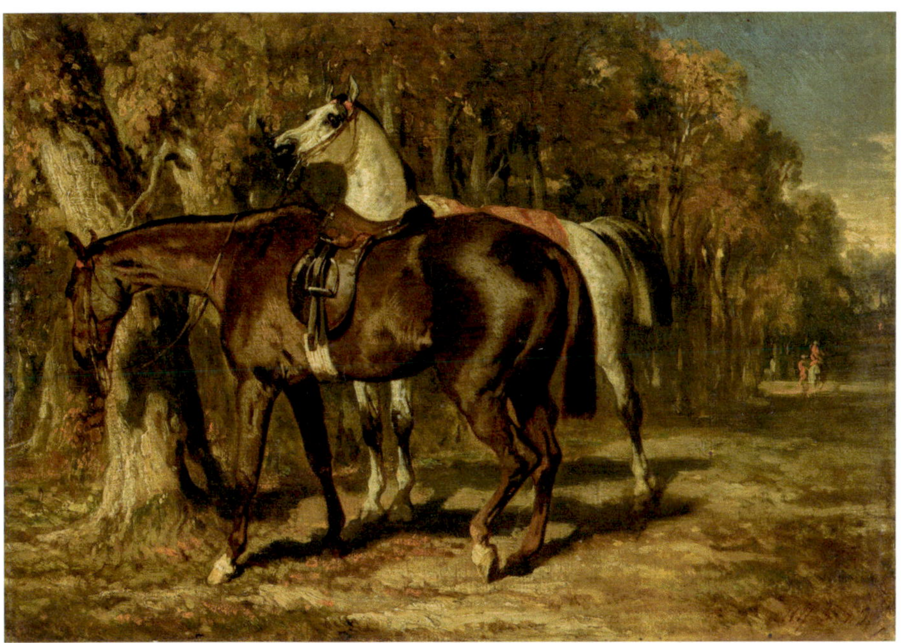

Acclaimed as both an animal painter and a portraitist, Alfred de Dreux was profoundly influenced by Théodore Géricault. Although still only a child when he met his role model – during his short life Géricault was a close friend of De Dreux's uncle, the painter Pierre-Joseph Dedreux-Dorcy – his love of horses and interest in animal painting can be traced back to the romantic artist. He ultimately became the favourite painter of Paris's exclusive equestrian society, receiving numerous commissions from the court of Louis Philippe and Napoleon III. Besides paintings of fashionable equestriennes and sporting aristocrats, he produced portraits of horses, in which the animals are depicted in the same meticulous detail and with the same empathy as his human models.

In this small-scale, brown-toned picture, two horses stand tethered to a tree. Not even the two tiny figures, heading into the background, distract the viewer's attention from the animals, who rest by an autumnal wood. The anatomical details, the pose of the noble animals' heads and bodies, and their lustrous coats are rendered with De Dreux's customary sensitivity. – AZSK

Paris 1997, 163 | Renauld 2008, cat. no. MCR 287

Eugène DELACROIX

(Charenton-Saint-Maurice, 1798 – Paris, 1863)

An Arab Saddling his Horse, 1857 | Oil on canvas, 50 × 61.5 cm
Purchased from the Galerie Bernheim-Jeune (Paris), 1915
Inv. no. 385.B

An Arab Camp at Night, 1863 | Oil on canvas, 55 × 65 cm
Purchase, 1972 | Inv. no. 72.7.B

His fervent, dynamic compositions, a sensual, intensive use of colour, and masterful brushwork ensured Eugène Delacroix's position as the leading figure in French romanticism. Although these two Budapest works date from the final phase of his career, the artist drew on memories from almost thirty years earlier for his oriental theme: his months spent travelling in Morocco in 1832 served as a source of inspiration for decades.

An Arab Saddling His Horse, painted in 1857, is dominated by vibrant, powerful tones. The painter renders the exotic everyday scene and the Arab's brightly coloured clothing with both exactitude and passion. Delacroix observed the unfettered animal world with the same attention to detail, brilliantly capturing the spontaneous movement of the unsettled horse as it turns towards the yapping white dog.

Completed in April 1863, *An Arab Camp at Night* is one of Delacroix's last paintings. Here too, the painter was working from memory: while in Morocco, he had crossed the desert as part of a large caravan, and this painting recalls his impressions of the nights he spent there. The Arab men in the camp gather around the fire in the darkness of the desert night for a time of rest and free-flowing conversation. The composition relies on the powerful effects of light and shadow, the contrast between the cold moonlight filtering softly through the clouds and the burning flames. – AZSK

Johnson 1986, cat. no. 404 and cat. no. 418 | *Paris* 1994–1995, cat. no. 97
Paris – New York 2018–2019, cat. no. 175

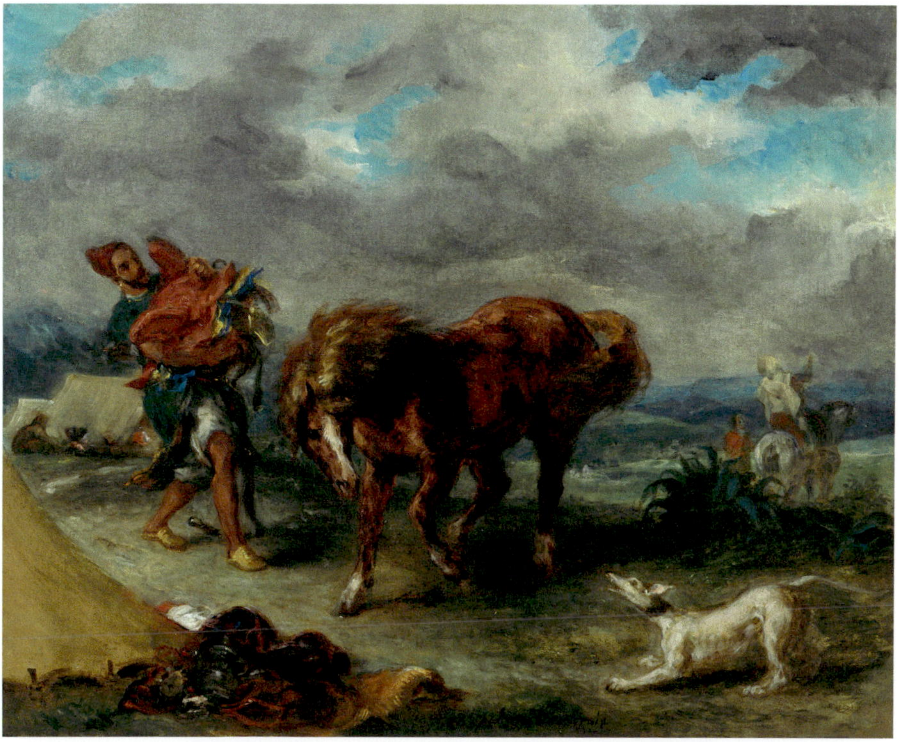

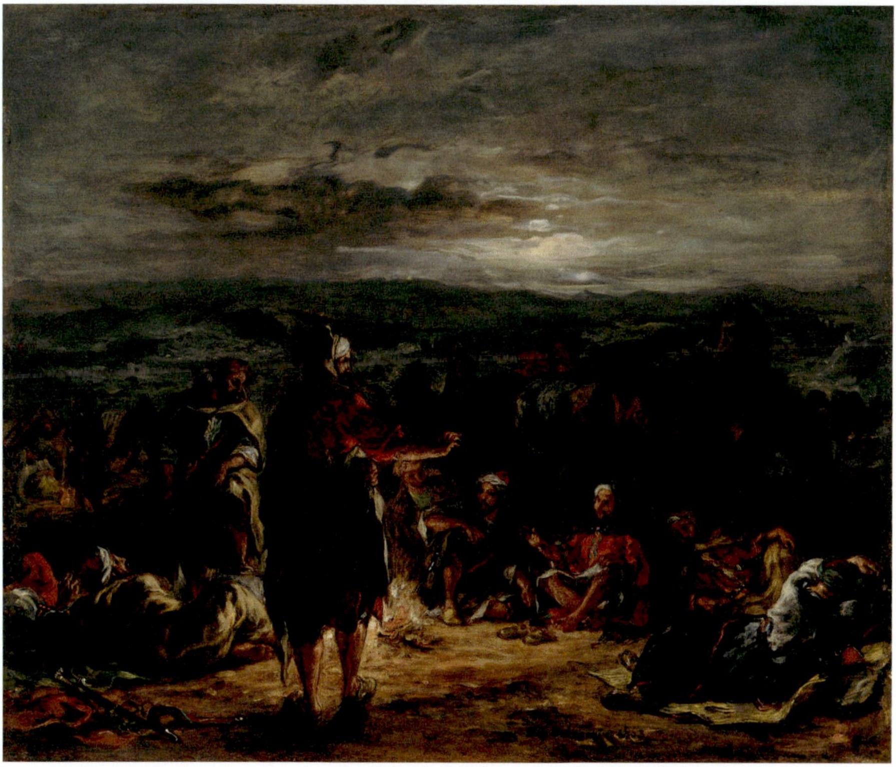

Théodore CHASSÉRIAU

(El Limón, 1819 – Paris, 1856)

Petra Camara, 1852 | Oil on wood, 32.2 × 23.4 cm
Donated by Ferenc Hatvany, 1916 | Inv. no. 365.B

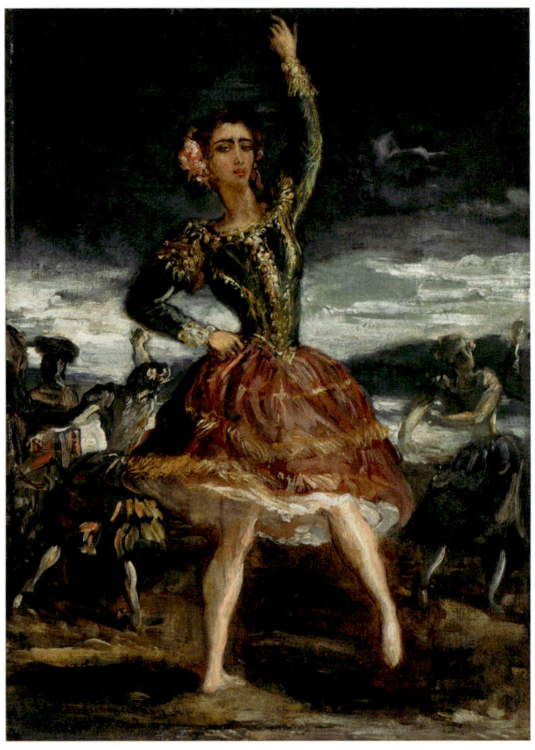

Théodore Chassériau was one of the leading figures of the French Romantic school. While both the rich painterly quality of Eugène Delacroix and the classic elegance of Jean-Auguste Dominique Ingres are discernible in his work, Chassériau represented a unique vision in a career cut short by his early death. Orientalism played a major role in his work, and his Spanish subjects, too, are imbued with the rich colours and exotic appeal of the East. This small painting shows the Spanish dancer Petra Camara, who performed in Paris in 1851. Chassériau made several sketches of the impassioned performance. The model turns towards us, her dark eyes set off by her black hair adorned with roses. The dancer's embroidered dress and the energetic, unfamiliar dance step have been painted with vigour. The glimpses of the other dancers and the cloudy sky in the background enhance the dynamism of the scene; the painting calls to mind the bold brushwork of Francisco de Goya and the palette of Delacroix. The work was owned by the poet, writer, and art critic Théophile Gautier, a defining figure of the French Romantic generation. A great admirer of Petra Camara, Gautier celebrated the dancer's beauty in several writings. – AZSK

Sandoz 1974, cat. no. 179 | Illyés 2001, 24–26

Jean-Baptiste Auguste CLÉSINGER

(Besançon, 1814 – Paris, 1883)

The Death of Lucretia, model: 1865; cast: 1868 | Bronze, 78 × 107 × 40 cm

Transfer, 1951 | Inv. no. 56.9.U

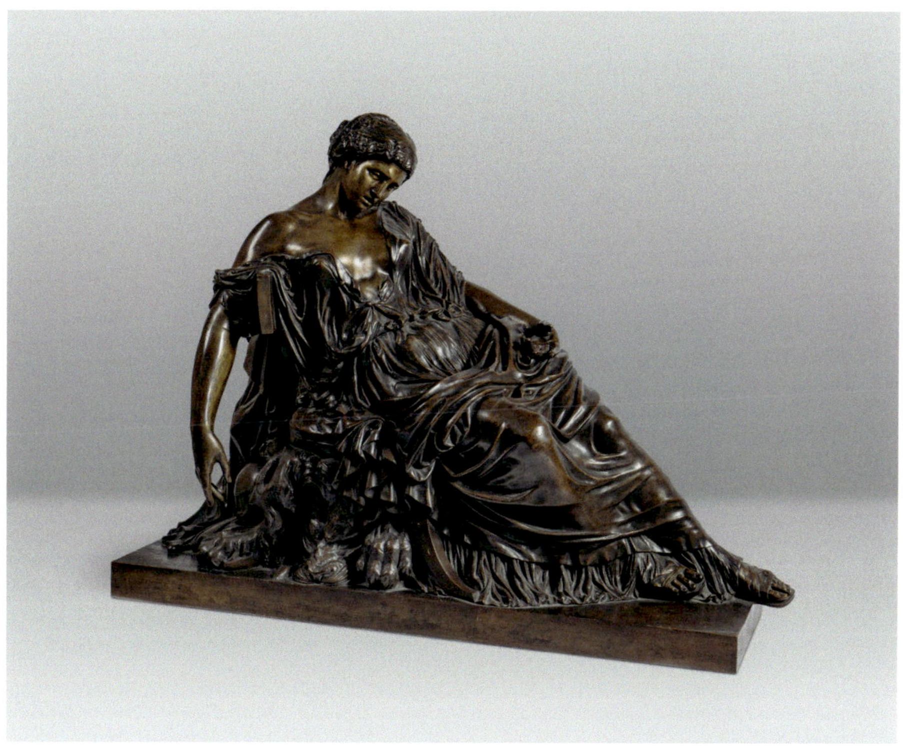

Auguste Clésinger was one of the most prominent French romantic sculptors. Although the bold sensuality of his most famous work – *Woman Bitten by a Serpent*, shown at the 1847 Paris Salon – provoked controversy with its realistic depiction of the female body, he was also inspired by more restrained classical subjects, as in the case of this representation of the dying Lucretia. A Roman noblewoman famed for her beauty and virtue, Lucretia committed suicide after being raped, plunging a dagger into her heart in the presence of her husband and son. The significance of this dramatic event went beyond personal tragedy: it aroused widespread indignation, and, because of its political implications, contributed to the abolition of the Kingdom of Rome and the establishment of the Republic. Clésinger's sculpture depicts Lucretia in her dying moments: the dagger has just fallen from her hand and her body lies limp. The paler, more yellow patina used for her skin draws attention to the pain in her face and the wound to her chest, while the fluidity of the rippling fabric intensifies the drama of the moment. Several copies of the sculpture are known – versions of it were produced in bronze, terracotta, and marble. – AZSK

Illyés 2001, 35–37 | *Ornans* 2011, 137-138

Jean-Baptiste CARPEAUX

(Valenciennes, 1827 – Courbevoie, 1875)

Laughing Girl with Roses, model: 1872; cast: 1873 | Terracotta, 54.5 × 30 × 25 cm

Donated by Sándor Apponyi, 1934 | Inv. no. 6811.U

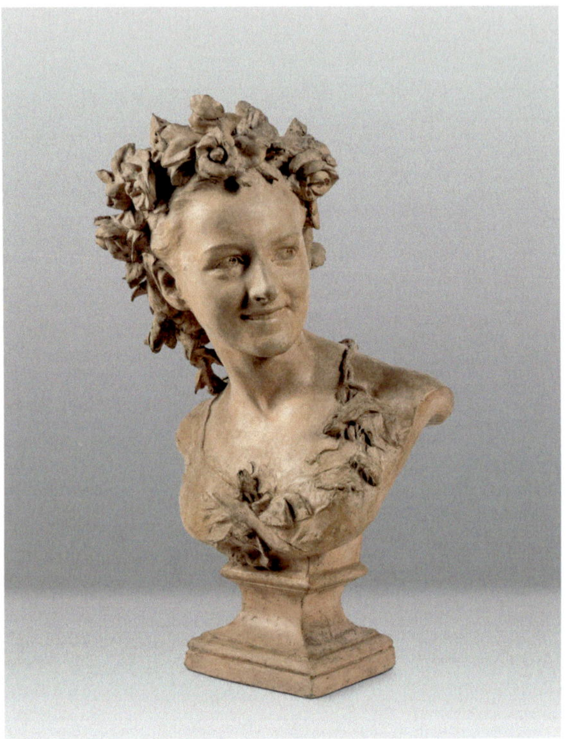

Jean-Baptiste Carpeaux was an idiosyncratic figure in nineteenth-century French sculpture. Although he studied under François Rude at the École des Beaux-Arts and was awarded the Prix de Rome, he was unable to reconcile himself to the constraints of the academy. In great demand during the Second French Empire, his success was marred by scandal: the unrestrained sensuality of his sculpted allegory of Dance on the façade of the Paris Opera aroused huge indignation.

Following the Franco-Prussian War, he established his own studio, giving him personal oversight of the production and sale of his works. Among his most popular pieces were his decorative female busts, such as *Laughing Girl with Roses*, also known as *Spring*. The sense of movement suggested by the tilt of her head, and the glimpse of her teeth as she smiles, reflect the dynamism, the directness that were a hallmark of his work. The bust is a likeness of Anna Foucart, daughter of one of the sculptor's close friends. Although he modelled her features in 1860, the girl's joyful expression can also be found in later works. There are several known copies of the bust in plaster, marble, and terracotta. – AZSK

Illyés 2001, 74–77 | Czére ed. 2006, 133–134

Gustave DORÉ

(Strasbourg, 1832 – Paris, 1883)

Young Woman with White Shawl, ca. 1870 | Oil on canvas, 128 × 95 cm

Donation, 1976 | Inv. no. 77.3.B

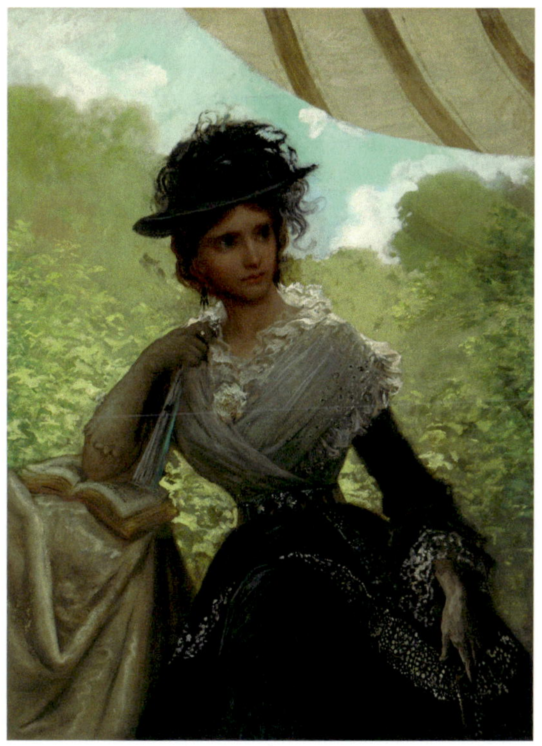

Known primarily for his illustrations of literary works and the Bible, Gustave Doré always remained open to other artistic genres and techniques. Extremely successful and prolific, he also developed his talents in the fields of painting, sculpture, and even furniture design. Wishing to establish himself as a painter, he exhibited monumental religious compositions at the Paris Salon, but also executed more intimate genre scenes and portraits, such as the one held in Budapest.

The work shows a beautiful, fashionable young woman sitting in a garden. Her slender, elegant figure is accentuated by the white shawl wrapped around her bust and by the belt encircling her waist. The wide, black skirt, adorned with white lace, the feathered hat and the fine white gloves beautifully complement her garment. As if something had caught her attention while reading, she is looking in the distance, away from the viewer. Protected from the harsh summer light by a striped sunshade, she appears in the shadow against the fresh green backdrop. The strong contrast between the woman and her environment, however, suggest that the model was probably painted in the artist's studio, not in the open. – AZSK

Illyés 2001, 78-80 | *Tokyo* 2019, cat. no. 76

Ludwig Michael von SCHWANTHALER

(Munich, 1802 – Munich, 1848)

Franz Liszt, 1843 | Bronze relief, 39 × 39 cm
Donated by Vilmos Kurz, 1939 | Inv. no. 7659.U

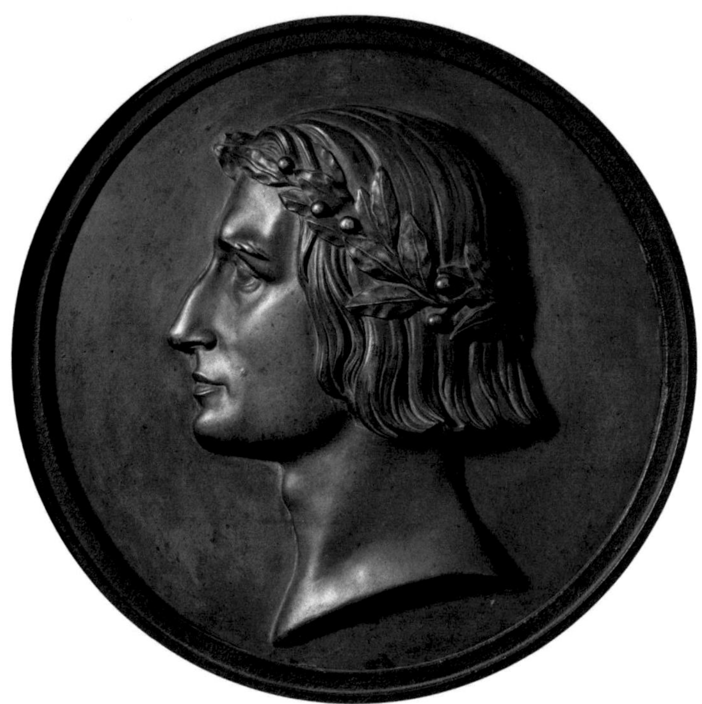

Ludwig von Schwanthaler – who was born into a family of German sculptors going back seven generations – was the most distinguished figure in German romantic and historical sculpture. When Liszt visited him in his Munich studio in October 1843, Schwanthaler was working on his most important piece, a monumental allegorical female figure representing Bavaria, commissioned by Ludwig I of Bavaria. In a cordial letter, the composer referred to the sculptor as a friend who found time in his hectic schedule to work on a portrait of him. In that same year, Schwanthaler even produced a second version of the relief that appears on the medallion, this time with a laurel wreath, several copies of which he sent to Liszt. In 1848, the composer was appointed official court kapellmeister in Weimar and moved to the mansion that became known as the Altenburg, where he lived with Princess Carolyne zu Sayn-Wittgenstein. The so-called green room in the mansion, which became an important centre of Weimar cultural life, was decorated with Liszt's awards and honours, among which a copy of the medallion was given pride of place. – AL

Kapp 1911, 38 | Kovács 1988, 331–332

Joseph-Fortuné Séraphin LAYRAUD

(La Roche-sur-le-Buis, 1834 – Valenciennes, 1912)

Portrait of Franz Liszt, 1869 | Oil on canvas, 62.5 × 35 cm
Purchased from Jules Pillion (Valenciennes), 1911 | Inv. no. 4060.B

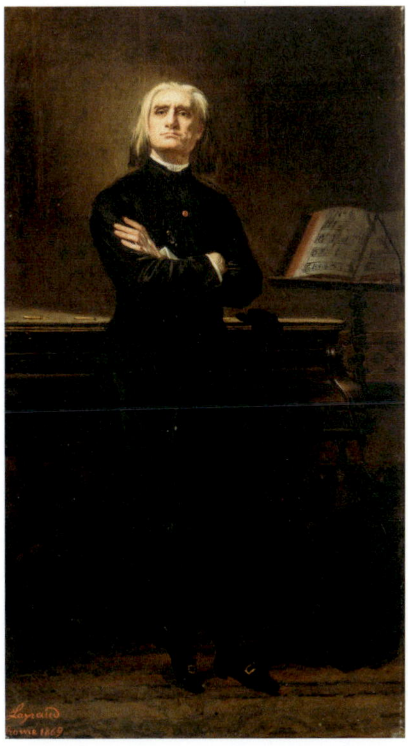

Fortuné Layraud initially worked as a shepherd and only began painting at the age of twenty. In 1856, he gained admission to the École des Beaux-Arts in Paris, and in 1863 was awarded the Prix de Rome. During his long, eclectic career, he worked in many different styles, producing historical scenes, modern genre pieces, landscapes, and portraits.

This portrait of Franz Liszt was painted in Rome in 1869, at the end of Layraud's time in Italy. It was inspired by their first encounter, when, following an impassioned performance, the composer refused the audience's pleas for an encore, closed the lid of the piano, and crossed his arms, indicating that the concert was over. Layraud was so taken with Liszt's demeanour that he produced this somewhat defiant portrait, which displeased some critics. The full-length portrait, painted in Layraud's studio with Liszt's collaboration, shows the composer dressed in the long black cassock of a priest, the red ribbon of the French Legion of Honour pinned to his chest. A life-sized version of the portrait – for which the Budapest painting may have been a first draft – was shown at the Paris Salon in 1870 and is now in the Valenciennes Museum. – AZSK

Eckhart 1986, cat. no. 172 | *Valence* 1993, 28

Leonardo ALENZA Y NIETO

(Madrid, 1807 – Madrid, 1845)

The Last Parting, ca. 1837–1839 | Oil on canvas, 34.8 × 25.5 cm
Donated by the art critic Robert Langton Douglas (London), 1908 | Inv. no. 214.B

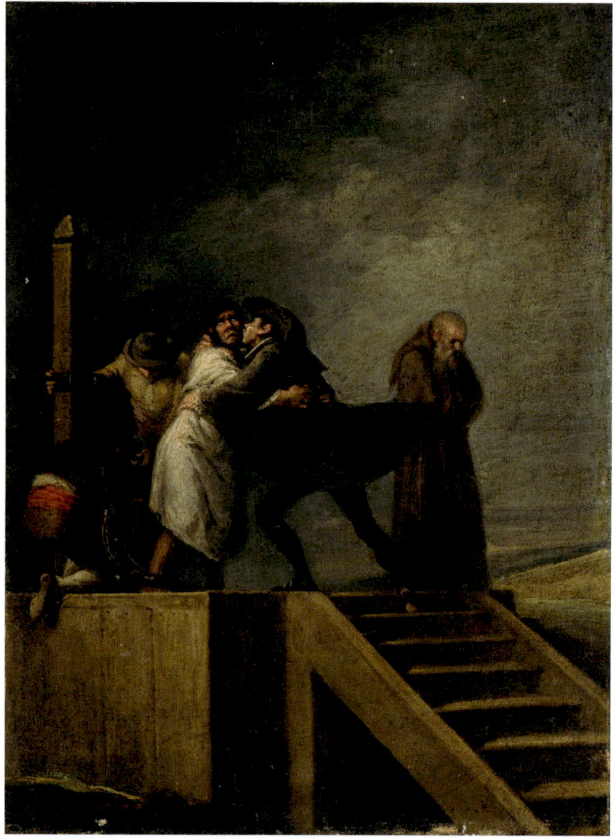

Regarded as one of the most talented followers of Francisco de Goya, Leonardo Alenza y Nieto was a consummate Romantic who produced primarily genre scenes during his poignantly short life. In his predominantly small-scale works, executed in dark tones with rapid, loose brushwork, he tended to present popular Romantic themes in an ironic or comical way. Images depicting various manners of death, conveying covert social criticism, form a distinct thematic unit within his oeuvre: his *Satire on Romantic Suicide* and *Satire on the Romantic Lover's Suicide* (both ca. 1839, Museo Nacional de Romanticismo, Madrid) resemble *The Last Parting* in terms of style and dimensions. Here, the viewer is presented with the final moments before an execution: the executioners are adjusting the ligature, or *garrote vil*, the most common device for asphyxiation at the time, while the condemned prisoner, raising his eyes to heaven, bids a reluctant farewell to a man indubitably overcome with emotion. – AL

Térey 1916, 336 | Nyerges 2008, cat. no. 95

Joseph Édouard STEVENS

(Brussels, 1816 – Brussels, 1892)

Animal Idyll, 1852 | Oil on wood, 42.5 × 51 cm
Bequest of Count János Pálffy, 1912 | Inv. no. 229.B

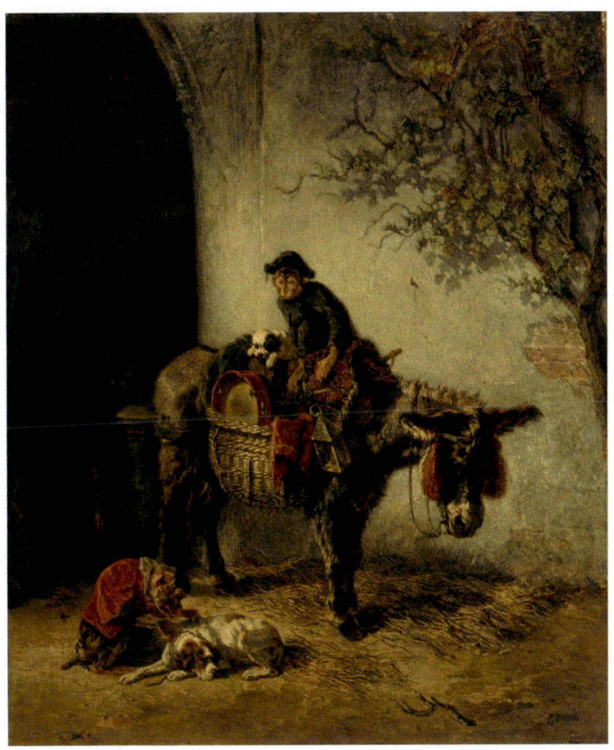

The Belgian animal painter and engraver Joseph Édouard Stevens, like his older brother Alfred, turned to painting with the encouragement of his art-loving father. Originally self-taught, he went on to study in Brussels under the animal painters Louis Robbe and Eugène Verboeckhoven. He later studied and lived in Paris and showed his work throughout Europe. He was one of the founders of the Société Libre des Beaux-Arts in Brussels.

His contemporaries saw him as a successful, prosperous artist, whose sympathetic depictions of dogs, cats, birds, donkeys, horses, and circus monkeys they particularly admired. In Paris, he made the acquaintance of Charles Baudelaire, whose prose poem *Good Dogs* is dedicated to Stevens. Influenced by the Barbizon School, his art developed from romantic sentimentality to keen-eyed realism, and he became one of the precursors of Belgian realist painting. His principal subject was the sensitive depiction of snarling dogs, urban strays, and abandoned animals. His goal of arousing sympathy for the animals in his paintings can be seen in parallel with a desire to overcome indifference towards the city's impoverished workers, beggars, and itinerant players. – DL

Térey 1913, 66 | Fierens 1931

Vincenzo CHILONE

(Venice, 1758 – Venice, 1839)

Saint Mark's Square, Venice, 1820s | Oil on canvas, 46 × 63.5 cm
Donated by Archbishop János László Pyrker, 1836 | Inv. no. 90.B

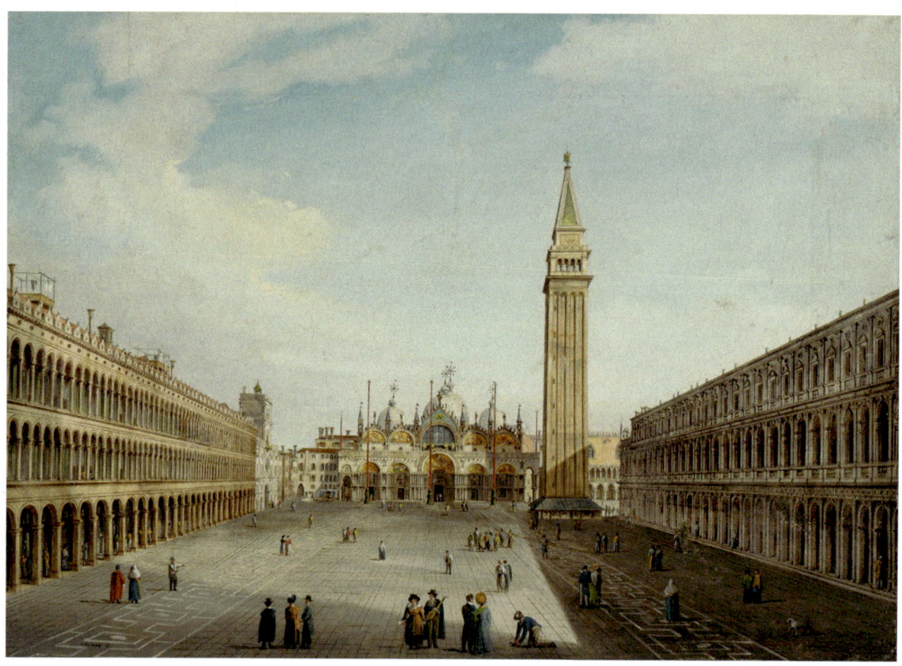

Vincenzo Chilone was born into a family of poor Venetian artisans and began his career as a maker of silk stockings and a wood carver before training in the studio of the vedutista Francesco Battaglioli. He also had to rely on designing stage sets and painting scenery and frescos to earn a living.

Chilone followed in the footsteps of the great eighteenth-century Venetian landscape painters and vedutisti, especially Canaletto, and was regarded as one of the great master's most devoted followers. Based on the English example, the Europe-wide fashion for the Grand Tour created a huge demand for vedute, or perspective views of Venice, which ensured a livelihood for Chilone. The high technical standard of his work and the wealth of topographical detail were recognised even by his contemporaries, and his paintings were often sold as Canalettos.

Chilone made several paintings of this iconic view of Saint Mark's Square looking towards the basilica. Executed with the precision of an engineer, using one-point perspective, the view is structured in such a way that the eye is led towards the entrance of the basilica. Framed by exquisite, jewel-like buildings that gleam in the crystal-clear light, the square is animated with a staffage of strolling figures admiring the view, as traditional for this genre. – DL

Mátray 1846, 36 | Peregriny 1909/1, 14

Giuseppe CANELLA

(Verona, 1788 – Florence, 1847)

Landscape in Cloudy Morning Light, 1836 | Oil on canvas, 53.3 × 74.5 cm
Bequest of Mihály Erny, 1871 | Inv. no. 178.B

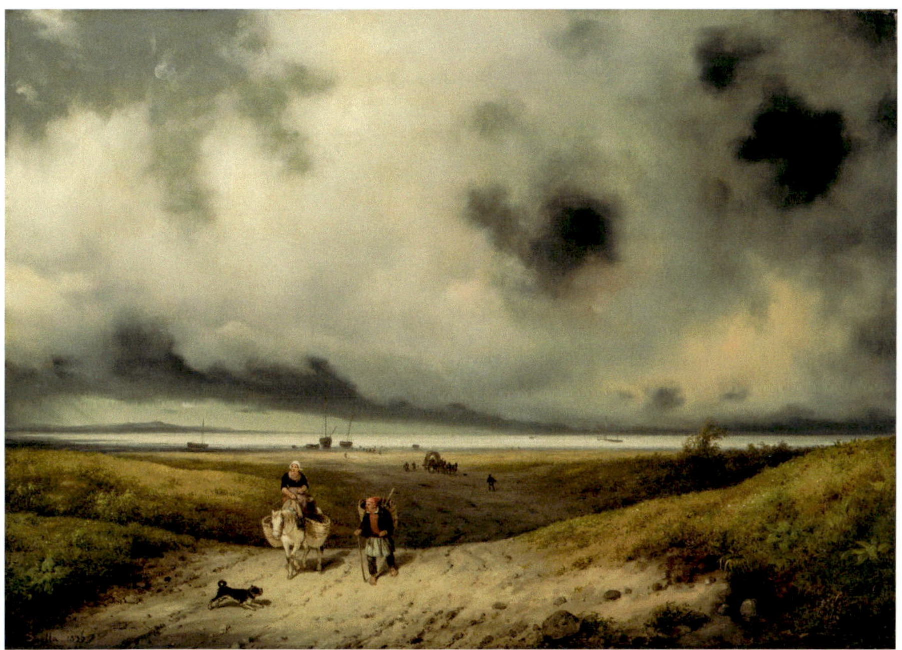

Giuseppe Canella was one of the pioneers of "dal vero", or realistic landscape painting in early nineteenth-century Italy. He began his career in Verona as a painter of stage sets and architectural ornamentation, working alongside his father, an architect and stage designer, although he soon devoted himself to working on canvas, painting vedute and landscapes. Unlike a significant number of his contemporaries, he painted his urban and natural vistas outdoors, rather than in the studio.

Not only did he live and work in several of Italy's most important cities – Milan, Venice, Rome, and Naples – but he also travelled throughout Europe: he lived in Spain (Madrid, Barcelona, Valencia, and Alicante) and France (Paris and Fontainebleau), travelled extensively in Normandy and the Netherlands, and also visited Vienna, Pest, Prague, Dresden, and Berlin.

In this view of the Dutch coast, Canella emphasises the complex visualisation of the landscape and the changing light and atmospheric conditions. The dog, unsettled by the impending storm, the pacing mule and the woman on its back, as well as the man trudging beside her with a basket on his back, indicate the scale of the landscape. The low horizon and plain, parched countryside accentuate the ominous clouds that cast unusual, permanently shifting shadows across the landscape. – AL

Brescia 1994 | Brescia 2008

Jean-Baptiste Camille COROT

(Paris, 1796 – Paris, 1875)

Souvenir of Italy, 1826–1827 | Oil on canvas, 36.3 × 28.3 cm
Purchased from Galerie Heinemann (Munich), 1916 | Inv. no. 364.B

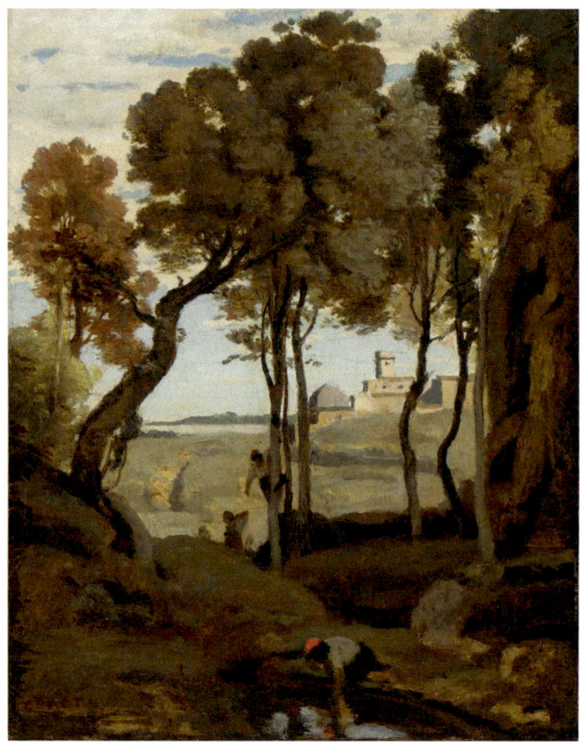

Camille Corot was one of the foremost figures in the renewal of French landscape painting.
He further developed the techniques of his forerunners, Pierre-Henri de Valenciennes and
Achille-Etna Michallon, whose classical, historical landscapes were based on sketches executed outdoors; his approach to nature and his light palette laid the foundations for the *plein
air* method espoused by the Barbizon school and later the impressionists.

This small work, also known as *The Nest Robbers*, is linked to Corot's first visit to
Italy, from 1825 to 1828, and may depict the area near Castel Gandolfo. Although it has the
freshness and spontaneity of Corot's early works, as if painted in situ, it was probably executed later, from his sketches of the Roman Campagna. The harmony of greens, ochres, and
browns predominates, while the distant, sunlit landscape is bathed in golden light. The dab of
bright red, the hat of the figure leaning over the water, is a recurring motif in Corot's paintings,
a counterpoint that animates the whole scene. Late in life, Corot reworked the composition
and the motif of the nest robbers, but this time his far-off memories of Italy were rendered in
the silvery tones of his late style. – AZSK

Kovács 1957, 85–87 | Illyés 2001, 11–13

Consalvo CARELLI

(Naples, 1818 – Naples, 1900)

Landscape near Naples, 1839 | Oil on canvas, 128 × 184 cm
Purchase, 2014 | Inv. no. 2014.2.B

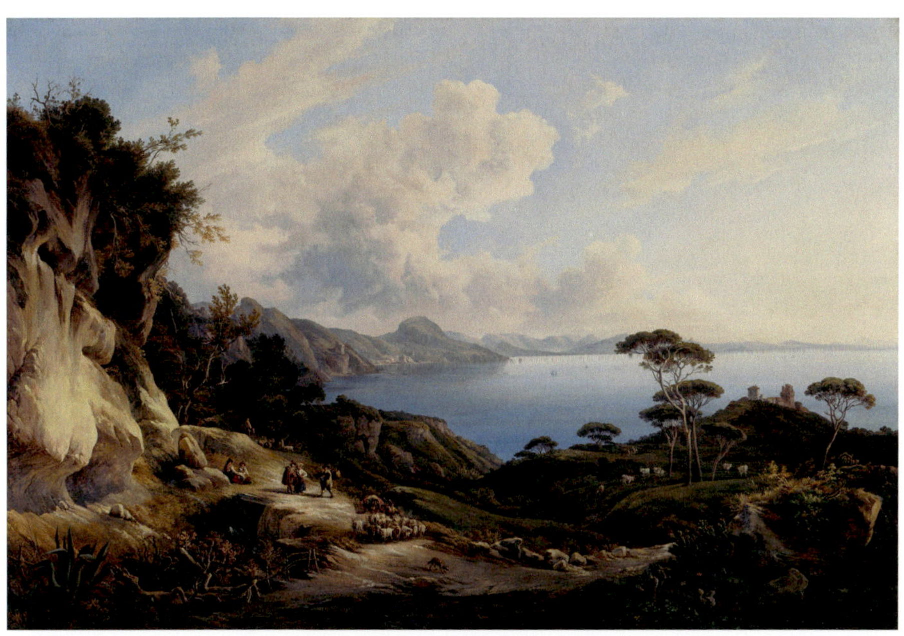

In 1820s and 1830s Italy, landscape painting was a minor genre that, for artists longing to escape the shackles of academic painting, offered relative creative freedom and the opportunity
to align themselves with the more modern artistic aspirations associated with the names of
J. M. W. Turner, Camille Corot, and Richard Parkes Bonington. Consalvo Carelli drew inspiration from the direct observation of nature. Like other members of his family – his father and
two brothers, who were also painters – he was a member of the so-called Posillipo school:
rather than ideal landscapes, he chose as his subjects the surrounding countryside, the Bay
of Naples. His lyrical, emotive landscapes, with their brilliant colours and light effects, featuring figures in typical local costume going about their everyday lives, not only contributed to
a greater appreciation of local values but also strengthened the desire for Italian national unity.

In a letter to a friend, Carelli spoke of how art must firstly touch the heart: beauty
that is beyond words is revealed to the soul, not the intellect. This picturesque view of the Bay
of Naples, with its varied terrain and vegetation, is an embodiment of that idea. – AL

Castelnuovo ed. 1990, 740 | AKL 1997, 375–376

John WILSON

(Ayr, 1774 – Folkestone, 1855)

Shipwreck, 1830s–1840s | Oil on canvas, 90.5 × 128.5 cm
Donated by Frigyes Glück, 1905 | Inv. no. 190.B

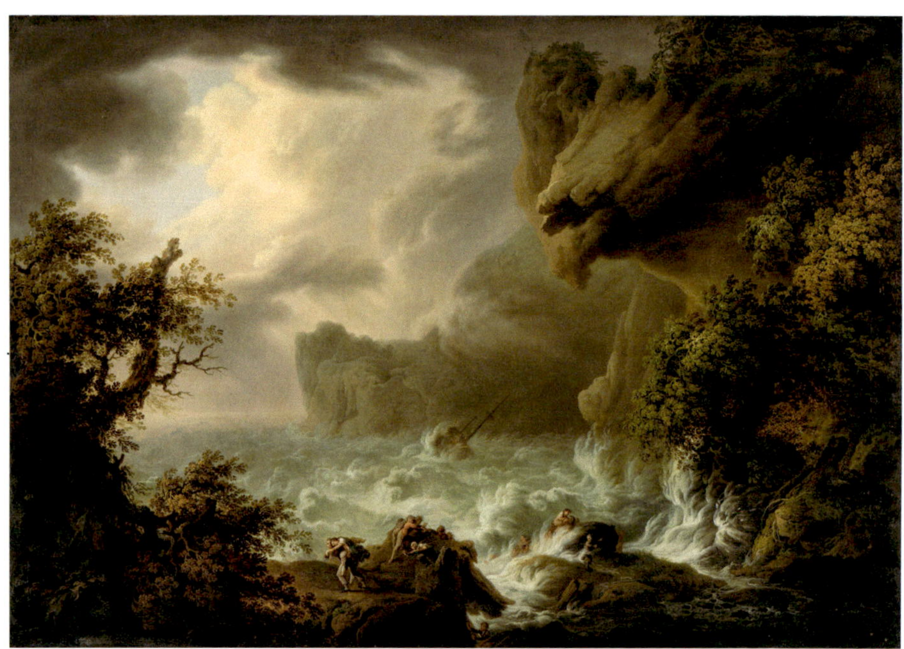

Marine art is an integral and fascinating aspect of British culture, and British maritime painters generally had a close and immediate connection with their preferred subject matter. John Wilson was the son of a Scottish captain in the merchant navy. In 1798, Wilson moved to London, where for many years, at least until 1827, he worked as a scenic painter. During this period, he began to make oil paintings, chiefly on a maritime theme. From 1807 until his death, Wilson regularly featured in the exhibitions of the Royal Academy of Arts; in 1823, he founded the Royal Society of British Artists, becoming its president in 1827.

This painting depicts a shipwreck, one of the most important sub-genres in British maritime painting and one of the most popular themes in romanticism. Contemporary audiences were fascinated by the dangers and challenges of seafaring, and their curiosity brought them flooding to exhibitions, where they could see hair-raising paintings of storms at sea and wrecked ships. Wilson's work focuses on the destructive power of nature, depicting the moment when the storm strikes the ship and its imperilled sailors with elemental force. – RM

Peregriny 1914–1915/1, 412 | Tóth 2012, 174

Johann Matthias RANFTL

(Vienna, 1805 – Vienna, 1854)

The 1838 Flood in Pest, 1839 | Oil on wood, 100 × 136 cm
Acquired from the Imperial Collection, Vienna, 1934
Inv. no. 405.B

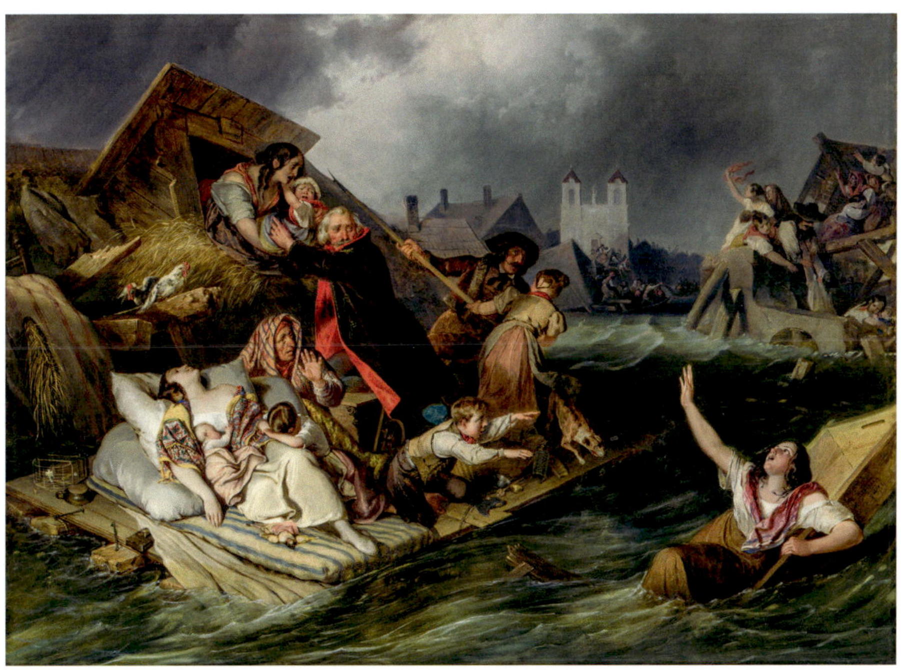

Numerous contemporary artists produced depictions of the 1838 flood in Pest, which claimed
a great many lives and caused substantial material damage. Johann Matthias Ranftl of Vienna
– in collaboration with Karl Klotto   produced a series of ten drawings of the incident, which
were then reproduced as lithographs. One of these drawings probably served as the inspiration for Ranftl's 1839 painting. The towers of what is presumably the Józsefváros church can
be seen in the background, suggesting that the artist has placed the scene in the part of the
city worst affected by the flood. The raft, set diagonally across the pictorial space, and the
gestures of the figures arranged in a triangular composition, suggest the influence not only
of Peter Fendi's depiction of the 1830 flood in Vienna (1830, Vienna, Wien Museum) but also,
perhaps, of the period's most iconic painting of a catastrophic event – Théodore Géricault's
The Raft of the Medusa (1819, Paris, Musée du Louvre). Like its antecedents, Ranftl's painting
is both the documentation of a contemporary event and, at the same time, a historical work
that exploits the visual tropes of academic painting. – DS

Feuchtmüller 1983, 414 | Basics 2018, 336

Petter Gabriel WICKENBERG

(Malmö, 1812 – Pau, 1846)

Fishing in Winter, 1839 | Oil on canvas, 83 × 118 cm
Purchase, 2024 | Inv. no. 2024.5.1.B

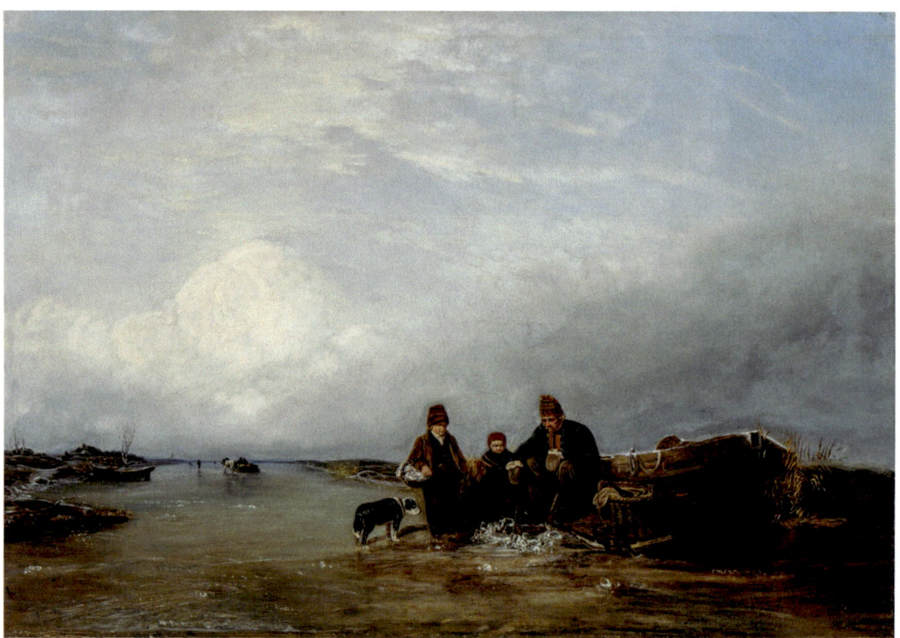

Also known as Per or Pehr, Petter Wickenberg studied at the Royal Academy in Stockholm and initially made a name for himself in his native country with his mythological and historical paintings. In 1837, he travelled on a scholarship first to Berlin and then to Paris, where he lived until 1842. While abroad, his style underwent a radical change, influenced by contemporary trends and the seventeenth-century Dutch masters Adriaen von Ostade and David Teniers the Younger; the realist genre scenes and northern winter landscapes he exhibited at the Salon attracted the interest of critics and collectors. He was one of the first Swedish artists to achieve real success in France: in 1841, Louis Philippe purchased one of his works (now in the Musée du Louvre, Paris), and shortly before his early death he was awarded the Legion of Honour.

    The painting *Fishing in Winter* is typical of his oeuvre, inspired by the severe winters of his native country. In the foreground, the elderly man and two children have broken the ice to get food for the day. They are surrounded by a bleak, wintry landscape, with a cloudy sky above them. Wickenberg painted this subject on numerous occasions, with different figures and backgrounds. One version of the popular theme was shown at the 1839 Paris Salon. – AZSK

Kruse 1901, 53 | *Stockholm* 1976

Wouterus VERSCHUUR

(Amsterdam, 1812 – Vorden, 1874)

The Ferry, 1847 | Oil on canvas, 88 × 113 cm
Bequest of Count János Pálffy, 1912 | Inv. no. 228.B

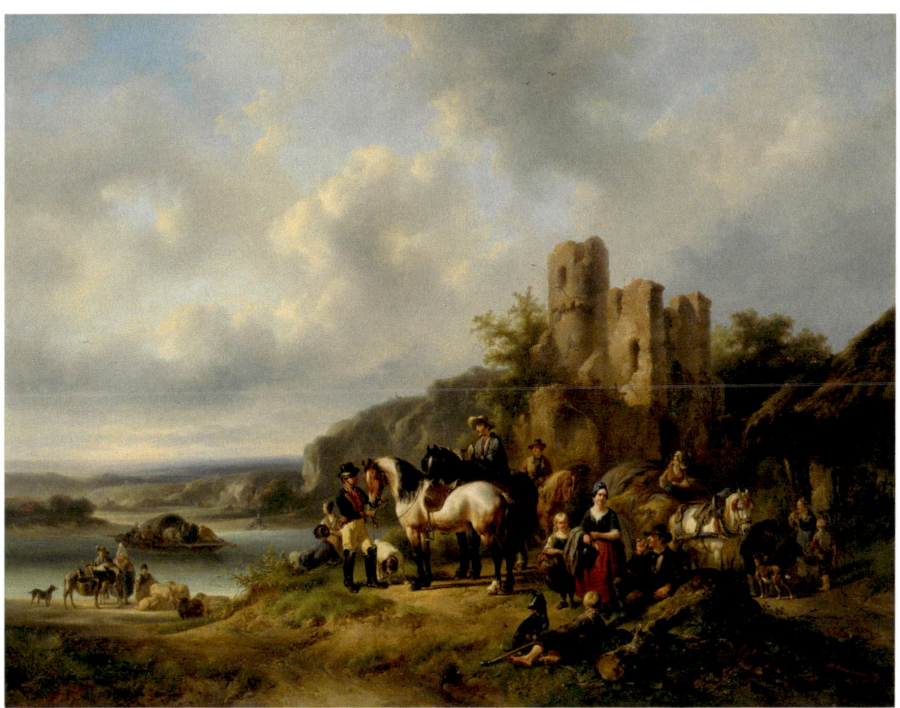

The painter Wouterus Verschuur carried on the traditions of seventeenth-century Dutch paint-ing. He specialized in painting horses and is regarded as the most important artist of his day in this field. Anton Mauve, an animal painter belonging to the Hague School, was a famous pu-pil of his. Verschuur's horses are painted skilfully, with anatomical exactitude. His horses tend to be large, baroque animals, and his rural settings also betray the influence of the northern Baroque masters, especially Philips Wouwerman and Peter Paul Rubens. Verschuur belonged to the last generation of the Romantic school, and his work bears the late marks of this period. He achieved significant recognition even during his lifetime, and his works were purchased by many foreign collectors, including Napoleon III.

The Museum of Fine Arts owns four Verschuur paintings, all of them scenes featur-ing horses. The large-scale work *The Ferry* shows a group of people presumably waiting to cross the Rhine. The majestic, ruined castle in the background, a typical feature of romantic paintings, provides a contrast to the peasants in the foreground, who are going about their everyday activities in this idyllic setting. – BIB

Matits and Sillevis 1992 | *Budapest* 1995–1996, 66

Andreas ACHENBACH

(Kassel, 1815 – Düsseldorf, 1910)

Waterfall, 1842 | Oil on canvas, 97 × 131 cm
Bequest of Baron Albert Wodianer the Elder, 1892 | Inv. no. 18.B

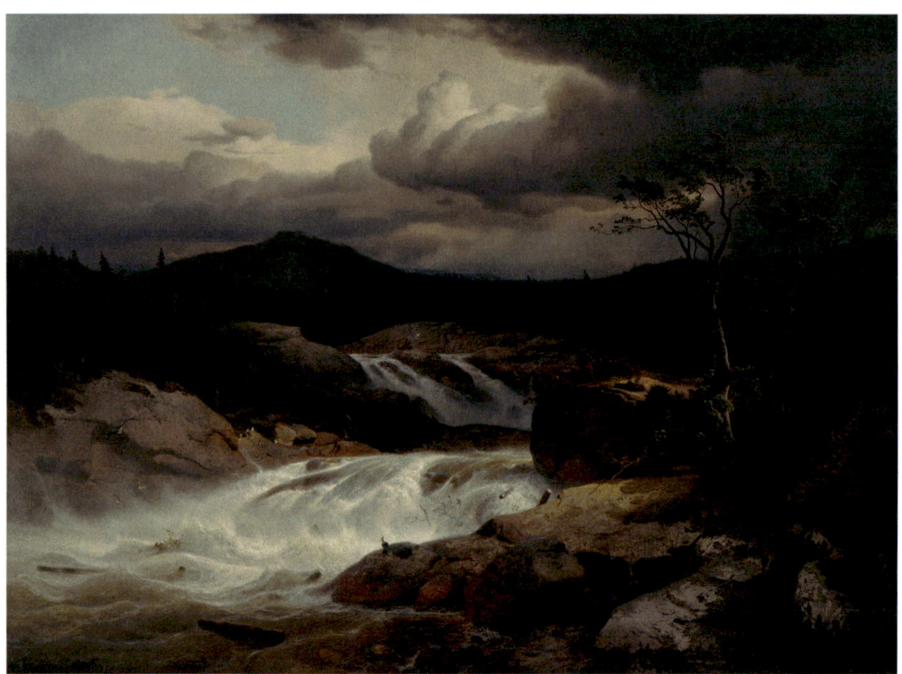

A member of the second generation of the Düsseldorf school of landscape painting, Andreas Achenbach studied in Saint Petersburg early in his career and was later influential among Russian landscape artists eager to train in Düsseldorf. His pupils included his younger brother, Oswald, who was likewise a landscape painter. Although he was highly respected in the nineteenth century, his paintings had disappeared from the walls of German museums by the end of the century and were only rediscovered in the late 1990s. He was chiefly inspired by his travels in Scandinavia and Italy: his favourite subjects were the bleak northern countryside and the Norwegian fjords, lending him a reputation as one of the first artists to discover the northernmost regions of Europe. He worked with intense whites and thick, rough streaks of paint, and his predilection for dramatic expanses of roaring water made him influential among German maritime artists.

 Waterfall is an early work, in which – true to the spirit of romanticism – the landscape is depicted theatrically. As forces of nature far superior to any human power, the combination of lofty mountains, gathering storm clouds, and cascading water evokes a sense of the sublime – a concept that emerged in eighteenth-century aesthetics. – BIB

Wappenschmidt 1998, 57–63 | Ziegler 2001, 179–184

Bernhard STANGE

(Dresden, 1807 – Sindelsdorf, 1880)

Night (The Last Gondolier), 1864 | Oil on canvas, 151 × 214 cm
Bequest of Count János Pálffy, 1912 | Inv. no. 235.B

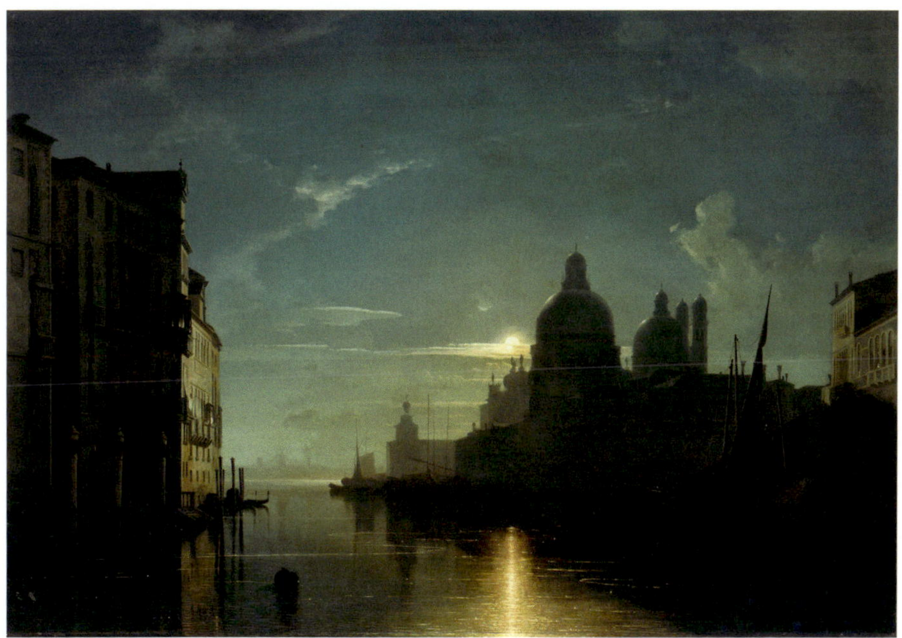

Having studied law in Leipzig, the German romantic landscape artist Bernhard Stange turned
to painting, influenced by the work of Caspar David Friedrich and Carl Rottman. Initially self-
taught, he subsequently studied in Munich. He was a friend of Carl Spitzweg and Friedrich
Voltz. He first achieved success with his atmospheric alpine landscapes. In 1849, he visited
Northern Italy and Venice, where he was captivated by the sight of the buildings emerging from
the water and the ephemeral, magical play of light. He immersed himself in the centuries-old
Venetian vedute tradition associated with Canaletto and Bellotto, but rather than perspective
and topographical accuracy, he was more intent on capturing the atmospheric effects of light.

    Night may have belonged to a four-part series, named for the times of the day, and
it was purchased, together with the companion piece *Evening (The Doge's Funeral)*, by the fa-
mously discerning art collector Count János Pálffy. The Budapest painting shows the Canale
Grande in Venice by night: the surface of the water, shimmering in the moonlight, is framed on
the right by the church of Santa Maria della Salute, veiled in shadow, and on the left by a row
of gothic buildings. – DL

Térey 1913, 65 | Szvoboda Dománszky 2015, 32–33

III

Images of the Bourgeois Milieu

———

The rise of the middle classes in the 1830s and 1840s opened up a new market for the arts. The bourgeoisie who took the place of the old aristocracy desired a more intimate world; with the end of the Napoleonic Wars came a yearning for a life free of politics and a focus on the comforts of domesticity. Bourgeois citizens who took pride in their social status and increasing financial ease, and the style of art and interior design that became fashionable in Central Europe, were given the slightly satirical label "Biedermeier" (from *bieder*, meaning "respectable", and the commonplace German surname Meier), evoking the worldview of the upright, honest, compliant middle class. This aspirational social group strove to fashion its environment according to its own tastes. A growing emphasis on family life brought with it the golden age of furniture design and interior decoration.

As an expression of bourgeois consciousness, homes were adorned with portraits of the occupants and with scenes and objects that conveyed a sense of peace and harmony. As idealism and grandeur lost prominence, the focus turned to the objective portrayal of the material world, to restraint and intimacy. The subject matter of paintings reinforced a sense of security, decency, and even-tempered restraint, with the avoidance of political and social issues. Portraits that captured the personality of the sitter as well as the clothing and hair-styles fashionable at the time were a popular genre. Everyday scenes and daily events were represented through the meticulous depiction of every last detail of the surrounding milieu. Serenely empathetic depictions of the poor formed a distinct branch of genre painting. The mood of landscape paintings conveyed a sense of purity and pleasantness: rather than the remote grandeur of the Alps, artists depicted congenial locations accessible to city dwellers.

As the region's political and cultural centre, Vienna was the undisputed artistic capital of Central Europe. With artistic life still only emerging in the other regions of the Habsburg Empire, the fashionable painters of the imperial city enjoyed huge popularity. As a result, their works were acquired in huge numbers for private and public collections in Hungary. Formed from the merging of existing fine art collections, the Museum of Fine Arts already owned a notable collection of outstanding Austrian Biedermeier paintings at the time of its opening. Supplemented by new acquisitions in later decades, these holdings form one of the most important units in the museum's modern collection, impressive even by international standards and highly popular among visitors.

The strong reservations expressed about Biedermeier taste in the second half of the nineteenth century, as being that of the petty bourgeoisie, were reinforced during the twentieth century. However, by stressing the formal simplicity and functionality of the Biedermeier, exhibitions organised from the 1980s presented this period as the pioneer of a new style of interior decoration, the forerunner of the applied arts revolution at the turn of the century, and, in relation to the fine arts, an important stage in the development of modern painting.

Johann Nepomuk ENDER

(Vienna, 1793 – Vienna, 1854)

Portrait of a Young Woman, 1837 | Oil on canvas, 114 × 87 cm
Purchase, 1963 | Inv. no. 541.B

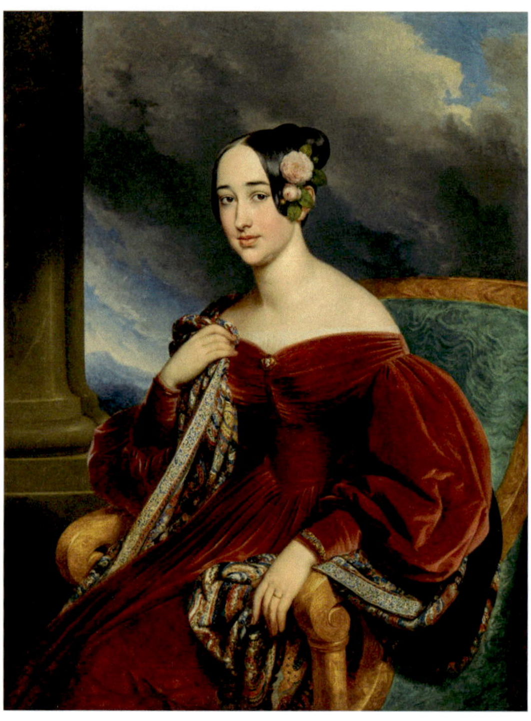

The acclaimed Austrian Biedermeier portraitist Johann Nepomuk Ender grew up on the out-skirts of Vienna, the child of a poor merchant family of Silesian origin. He and his twin brother Thomas attended the Academy of Fine Arts in Vienna, although while Thomas was drawn to landscape painting, Johann preferred classical mythology and historical themes. He was chiefly influenced by the French artist Jean-Baptiste Isabey, Napoleon's favourite miniaturist, who travelled to the imperial capital in 1814 to paint portraits of the distinguished visitors par-ticipating in the Congress of Vienna. Thanks to the connections he cultivated with the nobility of the Habsburg Empire, he made the acquaintance of Count Ferenc Széchényi and his family, and produced a full-length representative portrait of the count in 1823. In 1831, he was asked by Count István Széchenyi to paint *From Darkness, Light*, an allegorical work now familiar as the crest of the Hungarian Academy of Sciences.

The present painting is a typical example of a refined, elegant, slightly aloof portrait of a Biedermeier woman, in which emphasis is given to the model's graceful hands, gentle charm, and characteristic cashmere shawl, which the artist uses to counterpoint the discreet elegance of her red velvet dress. – DL

Gonda 2001, 11–27 | *Vienna* 2016

Ferdinand Georg WALDMÜLLER

(Vienna, 1793 – Helmstreitmühle in der Hinterbrühl, 1865)

Portrait of Mrs Imre Szentgyörgyi, 1844
Oil on canvas, 70.9 × 58.2 cm
Purchased from Albert Szentgyörgyi, 1917
Inv. no. 375.B

Portrait of Court Councillor Imre Szentgyörgyi,
1846 | Oil on canvas, 71.5 × 59.3 cm
Purchased from Albert Szentgyörgyi, 1917
Inv. no. 374.B

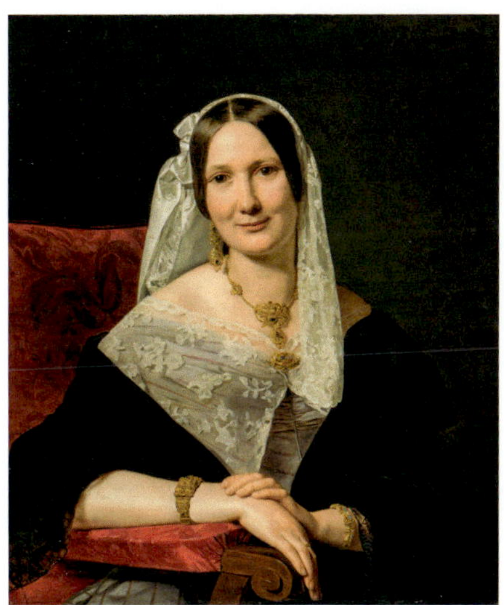
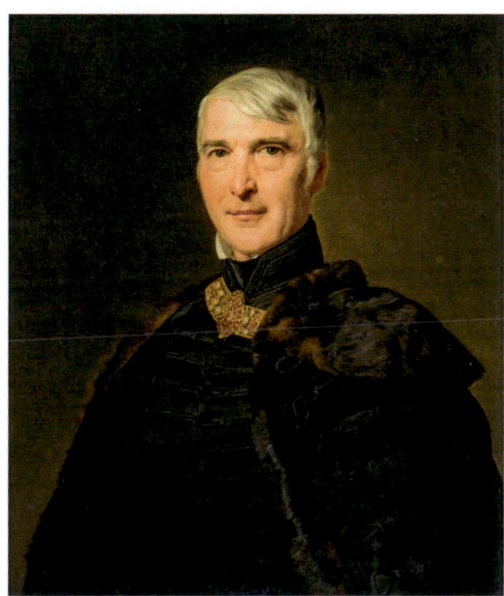

The portraits of Imre Szentgyörgyi and his wife, Borbála Kirchlechner, were painted by Ferdinand Georg Waldmüller, one of the most popular portraitists in Vienna in the Biedermeier period. The couple were married in 1825. Szentgyörgyi, who was born into a Transylvanian gentry family, was a qualified lawyer and a councillor in the Viennese Court Chancellery. He was tried for his role in the events of the 1848–49 War of Independence and subsequently discharged from his post.

In contrast to the academic approach, which relied on copying old works of art, Waldmüller favoured the direct observation of nature; he recalled how he came to this realisation precisely in the context of a commission for a portrait. At the same time, the kind of idealisation typical of Biedermeier portraiture remains perceptible in his work: in the case of the Szentgyörgyi portraits, it is apparent in the thin layering of the paint, the handling of light, and the subtle facial expressions that alleviate the formality of the paintings.

The museum purchased the portraits from the couple's son, Albert Szentgyörgyi, great-uncle of the Nobel Prize–winning scientist, in 1917. – DS

Cifka 1980, 87 | Feuchtmüller 1996, cat. no. 723–724

Anton EINSLE

(Vienna, 1801 – Vienna, 1871)

Woman in a Red Dress, 1838 | Oil on canvas, 80 × 63 cm
Purchase, 1966 | Inv. no. 558.B

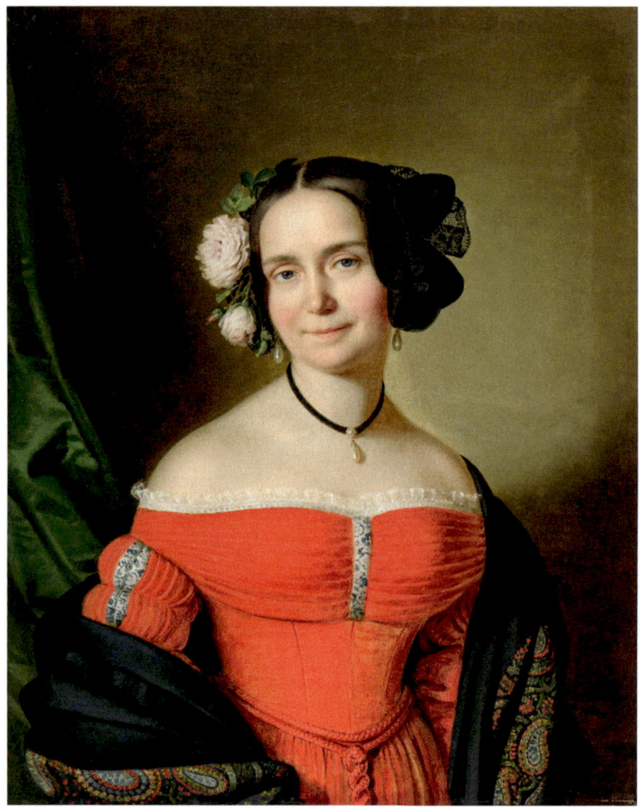

Anton Einsle painted more than thirty portraits of Franz Joseph during the first two years of the emperor's reign and even had his own studio in the Hofburg. In 1832, he moved to Pest-Buda, where he soon became a protégé of Palatine Joseph of Hungary and his family's favourite portraitist. The success of his portraits of the emperor and palatine brought further commissions from secular and church dignitaries. In 1838, he was appointed official court painter. On his return to Vienna, he was elected as a full member of the Academy of Fine Arts in 1843. He enjoyed fame and success throughout his life.

The elegant woman in this portrait of an unknown model wears clothing typical of the 1830s: an off-the-shoulder red dress, cinched at the waist and gathered at the bust, pearl drop jewellery, and an elaborate hairstyle with a central parting. The fashionable dress, expensive accessories, and olive-green background emphasise the model's face and gaze, which, directed towards the viewer, is extraordinarily suggestive despite its idealised modesty. – DL

Vienna 1993

Friedrich von AMERLING

(Vienna, 1803 – Vienna, 1887)

Reading Woman, 1834 | Oil on canvas, 63.5 cm × 52 cm
Purchased from Mrs István Konja, 1903 | Inv. no. 59.B

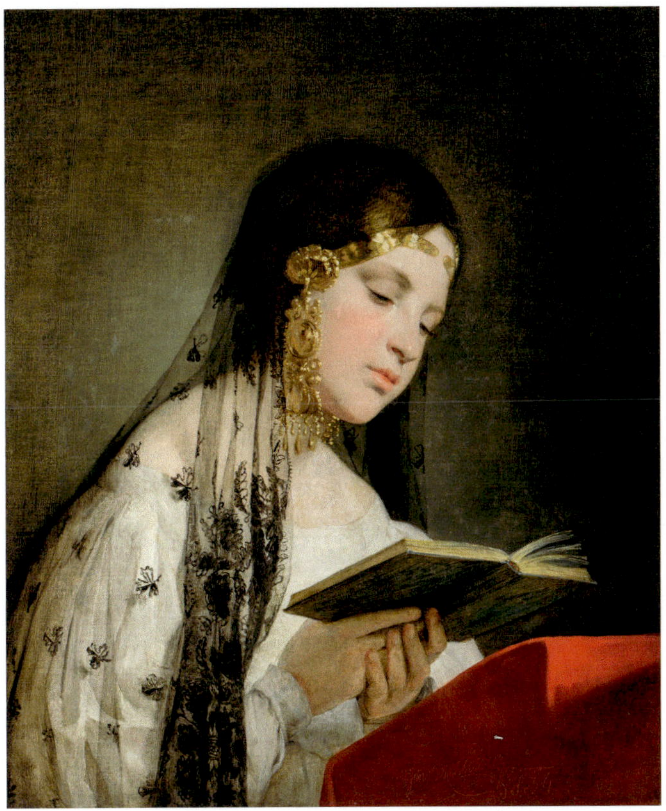

The most significant period in Friedrich von Amerling's successful career as a portraitist in Vienna was the 1830s, when he integrated skills acquired from the English portrait painter Thomas Lawrence with his own artistic experience. The subtle play of light and shadow typical of his work, the rendering of different surfaces and materials, and his brilliant handling of colour are particularly apparent in his portraits of young girls and elegant women. Neither a portrait nor a genre painting, *Reading Woman* is in fact a kind of transition between the two, a so-called *Rollenportrait* (role portrait). It captures a candid moment, a fleeting mood. The viewer can do no more than contemplate the private world of the girl immersed in her book; the composition prevents the model from seeking to meet the viewer's eye. The painter has masterfully arranged the various accessories – the sitter's black veil, gold jewellery, and white blouse – to frame her delicate, porcelain face. The viewer's space and that of the model are separated by a lectern covered with a red cloth, further emphasising the girl's remote, angelic beauty. – DL

Cifka 1996a, 61–68 | *Vienna* 2003, 214–215

Franz EYBL

(Vienna, 1808 – Vienna, 1880)

Self-portrait, ca. 1840 | Oil on canvas, 79 × 63.2 cm
Bequest of István Delhaes, 1902 | Inv. no. 35.B

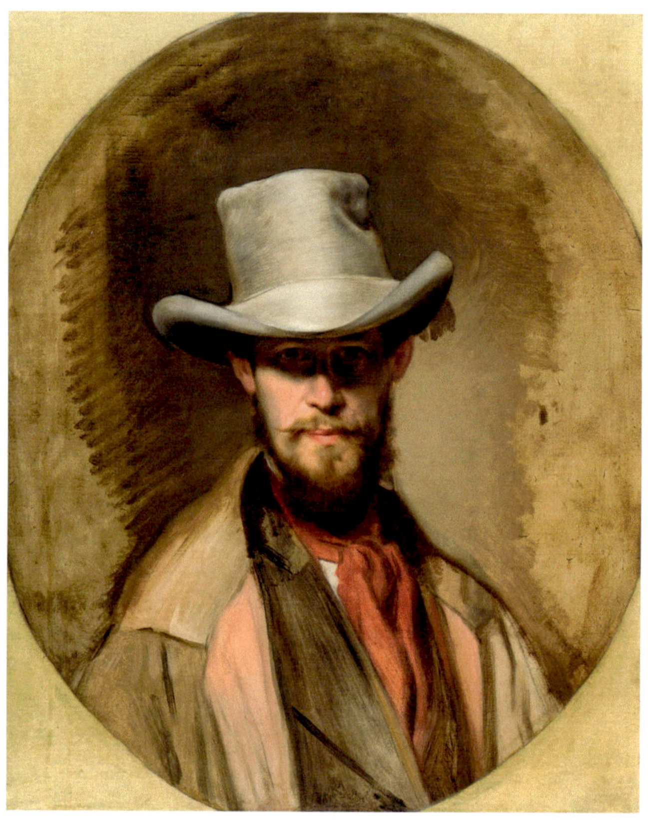

Franz Eybl was a student of Johann Baptist Lampi and Peter Krafft at the Academy of Fine Arts in Vienna, but was later one of a group of artists who helped steer rigid neoclassicism in a new direction. There was huge contemporary demand for Eybl's bourgeois genre paintings and portraits. His portraiture was greatly influenced by the Dutch master Rembrandt van Rijn, as can be seen in the self-portrait by Eybl preserved in the Museum of Fine Arts, and most obviously in the dramatic use of shadow that was alien to the Biedermeier style.

The face of the fashionably attired young man is lit from above, with the result that the brim of his grey hat casts a shadow over his eyes. While the head has been executed in meticulous detail, the body and clothing are sketchy, and the shadow in the background is no more than hatching. The work was painted in around 1840 and may have been a preliminary study for a smaller self-portrait using a different colour palette – presumably the painting now kept in the in the Belvedere in Vienna. – BIB

Kastel 1983, 130 | *Turin 2004–2005a*, 132

Franz EYBL

(Vienna, 1806 – Vienna, 1880)

Slovak Boy Selling Onions, 1835 | Oil on paperboard, 25 × 30.3 cm
Donated by János Müller, 1844 | Inv. no. 155.B

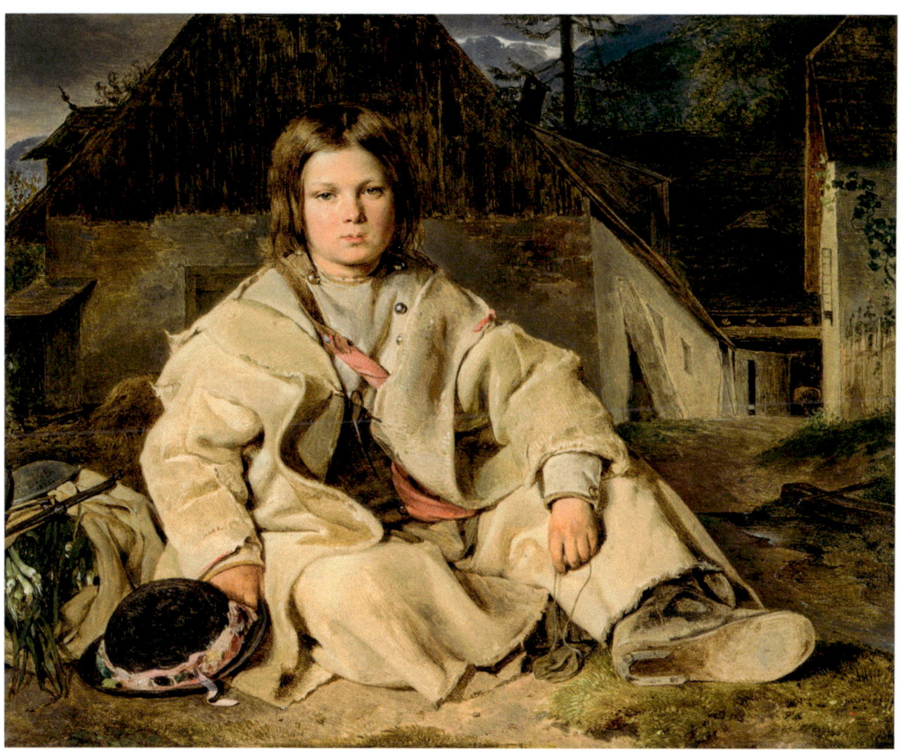

Alongside idealisations of rural life, depictions of the hardships suffered by the peasantry enjoyed huge popularity in the nineteenth century, leading to a demand for genre paintings. Such paintings often contained some kind of moral message.

This is certainly the case with Franz Eybl's *Slovak Boy Selling Onions*, a work that conveys an almost palpable sense of compassion for the marginalised peasant boy in his ragged clothes. The young boy stares straight out from the painting, while the light directed onto him makes him into a monumental figure. The artist has endeavoured to depict the boy's clothing as accurately as possible – like other painters of the period he was fascinated by peasant dress. The rough linen garments, typically worn by poorer peasants, lend even greater emphasis to the boy's poverty.

As a renowned lithographer and portraitist, Eybl often visited the Hungarian territories of the Habsburg Empire and presumably also drew inspiration for his genre paintings from his travels. This may well have been the case here, as Slovaks formed a substantial minority population in the then Hungarian territories. – BIB

Allgemeines Lexikon 1915, 127 | Szvoboda Dománszky 2015, 23

Josef DANHAUSER

(Vienna, 1805 – Vienna, 1845)

Slumbering, 1831 | Oil on canvas, 68.5 × 51 cm
Donated by Archbishop János László Pyrker, 1836
Inv. no. 171.B

Josef Danhauser studied at the Academy of Fine Arts in Vienna, where he was taught by Johann Peter Krafft and Johann Baptist Lampi the Younger. His father, the founder and owner of the famous Danhauser furniture manufactory in Vienna, was a good friend of János László Pyrker, archbishop of Eger and patriarch of Venice, whose friendship was decisive in the development of Danhauser's career as an artist. In 1828, he travelled to Eger at the invitation of Pyrker, where he worked on altarpieces and historicist works, among other things.

This painting occupies a special place in Viennese Biedermeier painting, as its iconography offers a unique commentary on the ideal and bourgeois idyll of the Habsburg Empire. The balanced, symmetrical composition shows an elderly couple enjoying a well-deserved afternoon nap in the company of their pets. The man holds a tobacco pouch and pipe, while the woman has nodded off over her book. A dog stretches at their feet with a cat asleep on its back, while a canary dozes in a cage on the windowsill. The interior, painted in warm, brown shades, contrasts strongly with the landscape outside the window, which Danhauser has depicted with meticulous realism. The tower in the background is that of the Serbian Orthodox church in Eger. The window is positioned in parallel to the picture plane, and the painter has used the panes to direct the light pouring through it onto the scene, creating an intense play of light and shadow. The subtle humour here anticipates Danhauser's later attitude as a genre painter, who illustrated contemporary social phenomena through a combination of moral content and humour. – DL

Cifka 1990–1991, 27 | Grabner 2011, 41

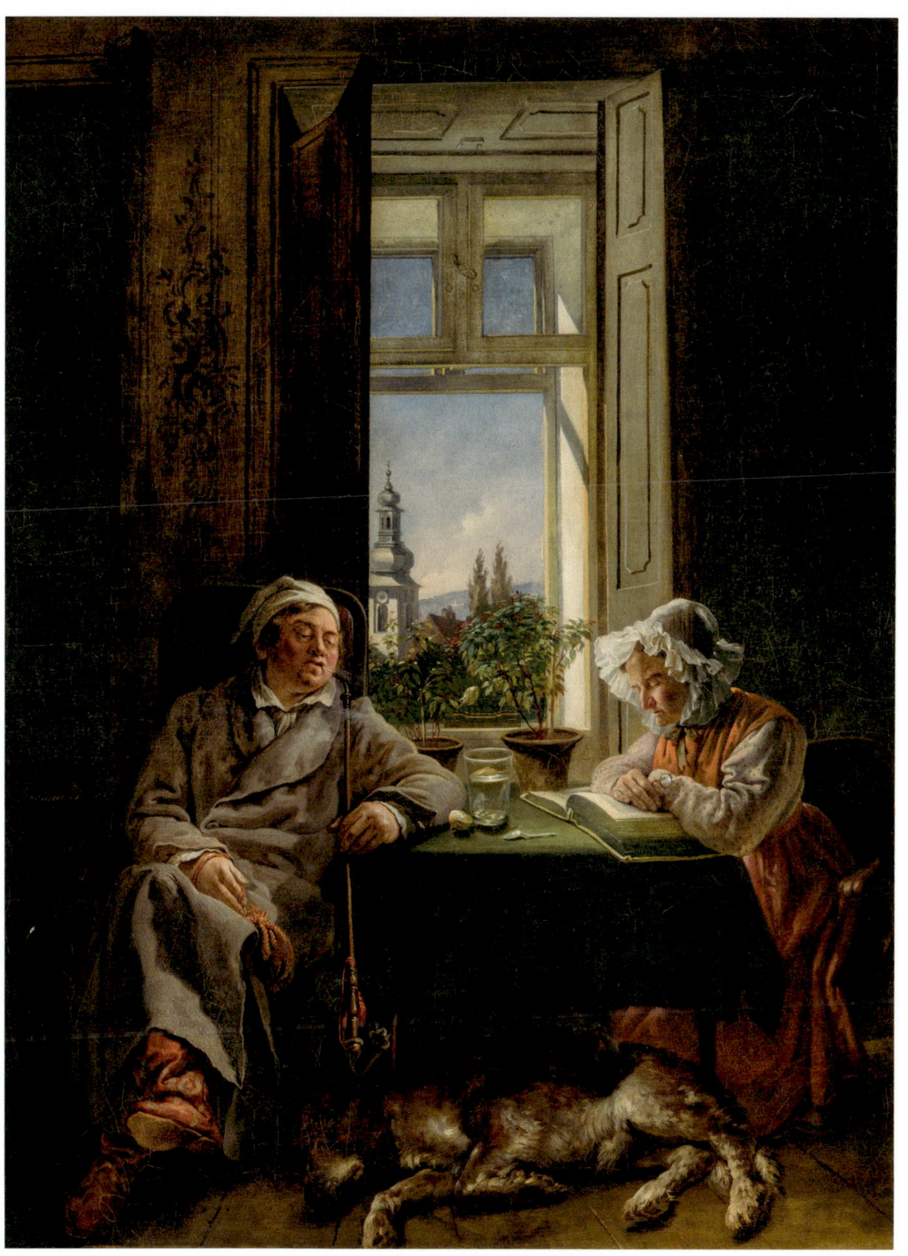

Johann Nepomuk ENDER

(Vienna, 1793 – Vienna, 1854)

Fishing Boy, 1825 | Oil on canvas, 145 × 113.5 cm
Transfer, 1949 | Inv. no. 442.B

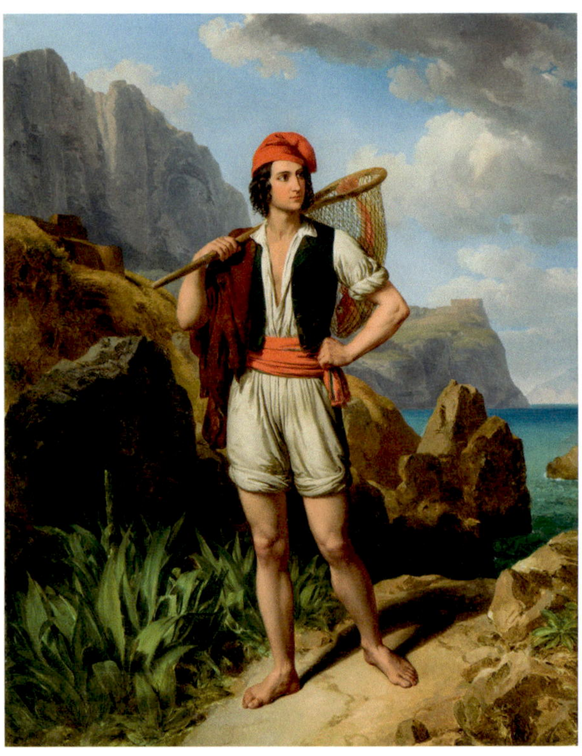

When István Széchenyi set off from Greece in 1818 on a tour of several months, crossing Italy and ending in Malta, the painter Johann Nepomuk Ender was part of the small entourage that accompanied him. Thanks to his portraits of the Széchenyi family, Ender had by then been a close friend of Széchenyi for a couple of years. It was the Austrian painter's task to capture for the count notable sights on the journey, although he also filled his own sketchbook with drawings, collecting subjects and ideas for later use. Travelling by boat gave him an opportunity to study water-related occupations, people's clothing, their facial types, and the details of their employment.

Not long afterwards, Ender and his brother Thomas spent several years in Italy, thanks to a scholarship awarded by Chancellor Metternich. It was then that he painted the *Fishing Boy*, a condensation of his impressions of Italy inspired by the cheerful, more direct approach of Italian genre painting. The figure of the fisherman in the painting is depicted as a hero of antiquity, his fishing net resting on his shoulder like an attribute. In the background are the rocks and coastline of the island of Capri. – BIB

Gonda 2001, 15–19

Johann Nepomuk ENDER

(Vienna, 1793 – Vienna, 1854)

Genre Scene, 1841 | Oil on canvas, 73 × 57.5 cm
Bequest of Mihály Erny, 1871 | Inv. no. 153.B

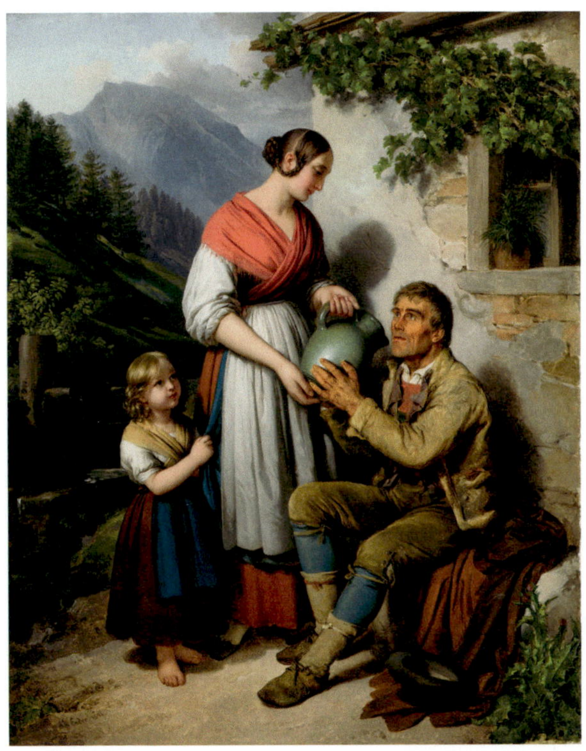

Johann Nepomuk Ender was accepted to the Academy of Fine Arts in Vienna at the age of thirteen. Success came quickly: by the end of his time at the Academy, he lacked neither commissions nor acclaim. He was a sought-after portraitist in both Austrian and Hungarian aristocratic circles. His precise drawing and relief-like figures bear witness to his thorough mastery of the elements of classicist style.

From the 1840s, due to strong competition, he began to experiment with religious themes and genre scenes alongside his portraits. Italian pilgrims and beggars resting at a well were frequent subjects among his genre scenes. In this early genre painting, a woman offers a beggar a drink from a jug of water. The clothes worn by the woman and her child, the mountains in the background, and the water flowing from the well are characteristic, recurrent elements in Ender's Italianate genre scenes. – BIB

Genthon 1956, 211 | Gonda 2001, 11–27

Eduard RITTER

(Vienna, 1808 – Vienna, 1853)

At the Well, 1839 | Oil on canvas, 48.3 × 36.3 cm
Bequest of Mihály Erny, 1871 | Inv. no. 169.B

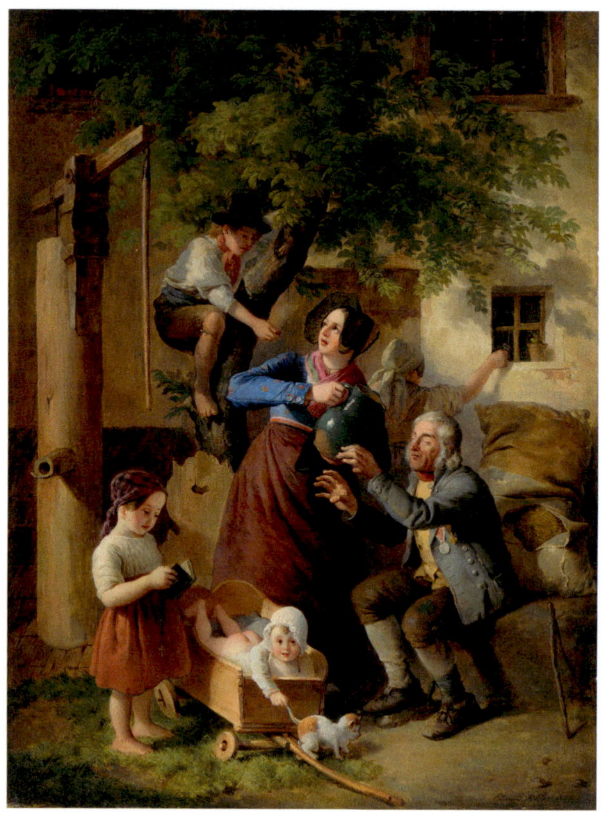

Eduard Ritter attended the Academy of Fine Arts in Vienna between 1829 and 1834. The works that he showed at the academy's annual exhibitions from 1830 bear witness to the important influence of seventeenth-century Dutch painting, rather than the direct observation or study of nature. Ritter was considered highly successful in his own day, less as a reformer than as a pioneer in the popularisation of genre painting.

Ritter tended to paint anecdotic or narrative peasant and rural scenes, such as this theatrical genre painting, which is not without an element of humour. The characters in the scene taking place around the well are familiar types: in the centre stands a pretty young woman, who keeps one eye on her mischievous young children while pouring water for the helpless, blind veteran. The playful mood of the work is conveyed by details such as the bare-bottomed baby lying on its front in the little wooden cart, pulling the kitten's tail, and the old man groping clumsily for the water jug. – RM

Peregriny 1909/1, 313–314 | Tóth 2012, 149

Felice **SCHIAVONI**

(Trieste, 1803 – Venice, 1881)

The Tea Maid, mid-19th century | Oil on paperboard, 44.4 × 36.5 cm
Bequest of Baron Albert Wodianer the Elder, 1892 | Inv. no. 14.B

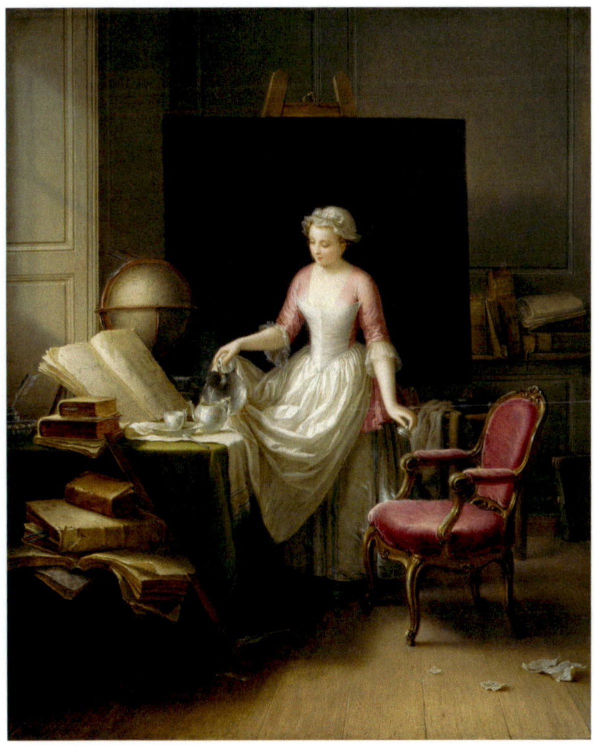

Felice Schiavoni first studied under his father, the famous painter Natale Schiavoni. He moved to Venice in 1821, where he produced altarpieces and depictions of the Virgin Mary and the saints in a style reminiscent of sixteenth-century Italian painting, especially Raphael. In 1840, he was invited to Russia, where he lived until 1847, producing several acclaimed paintings of the tsar's family.

The genre scenes that he painted in the mid-century revealed a new side to his drawing skills and shaping talent. The posture of the maid making tea in a scholar's study is more graceful and informal than was required in the case of representative portraits commissioned by the well-to-do. The piles of books and academic instruments tell us something about the room's absent owner. The apparently disordered spatial arrangement and the play of light and shadow here take the place of the closed composition employed in his earlier works. In similar genre scenes by Schiavoni, even those evoking the coquetry of rococo style, one can already sense the influence of the period's new artistic trends – romanticism and the Biedermeier style that was gaining popularity, especially in Central Europe. – FT

Gunma–Sapporo–Tokyo 1981, cat. no. 37 | *Tokyo* 2019, cat. no. 66

Ferdinand Georg WALDMÜLLER

(Vienna, 1793 – Helmstreitmühle in der Hinterbrühl, 1865)

Man with a Peep Box, 1847 | Oil on wood, 76 × 92.5 cm
Purchase, Esterházy Collection, 1871 | Inv. no. 3.B

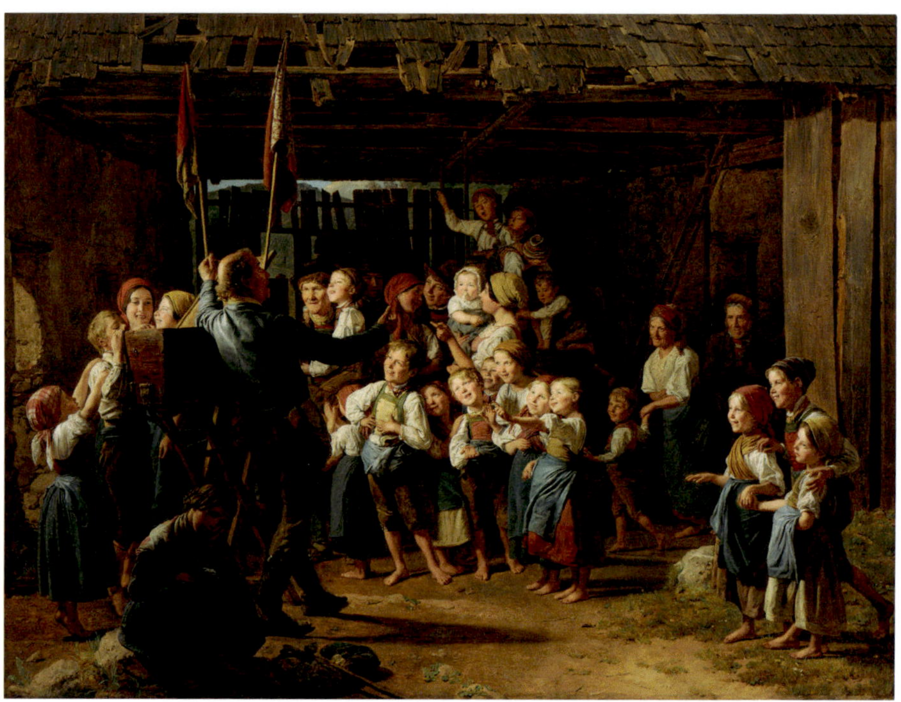

From the 1840s, Ferdinand Georg Waldmüller devoted himself intensively to genre painting. Typically depicting the lives of the peasants in the countryside around Vienna, his genre pictures were soon as popular with the public as his portraiture.

In this scene, a travelling performer is projecting pictures for an enthralled village audience. The spectacle itself is not shown in the painting: as the original title of the work (*Kinderlust*, or *Childhood Joy*) suggests, Waldmüller wanted the emphasis to remain on the children's reactions. Shown standing almost in one plane in the narrow pictorial field, the audience is divided into groups that might be interpreted as a series of small genre paintings, woven together by the carefully calculated angles of the arms and heads, the direction of the gazes, and the representation of the contrast between light and shadow. This last aspect was particularly important to Waldmüller: in his polemical essays submitted to the Vienna Academy in 1846–1847, he defined the correct rendering of the contrast between light and shadow as the foundation of painting. Even before it was shown for the first time at the 1848 exhibition at the Vienna Academy, the painting was acquired from the artist for the Esterházy Collection, where Waldmüller had spent some time working as a conservator. – DS

Cifka 1980, 84–85 | Feuchtmüller 1996, 169, cat. no. 777

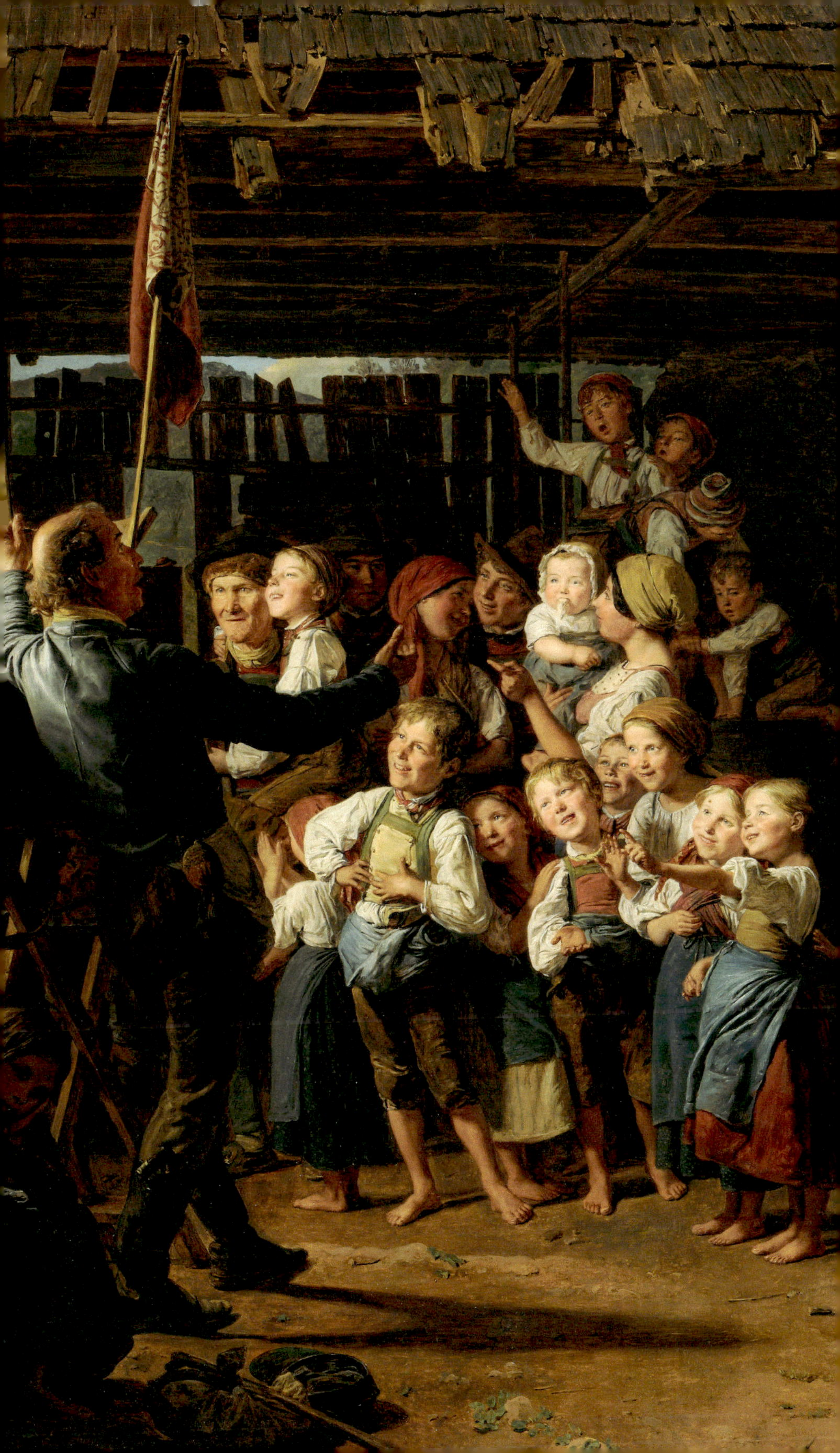

Johann Baptist REITER

(Urfahr bei Linz, 1813 – Vienna, 1890)

The Little Jewellery Dealer, 1850 | Oil on canvas, 50.6 × 50.6 cm
Bequest of Mihály Erny, 1871 | Inv. no. 186.B

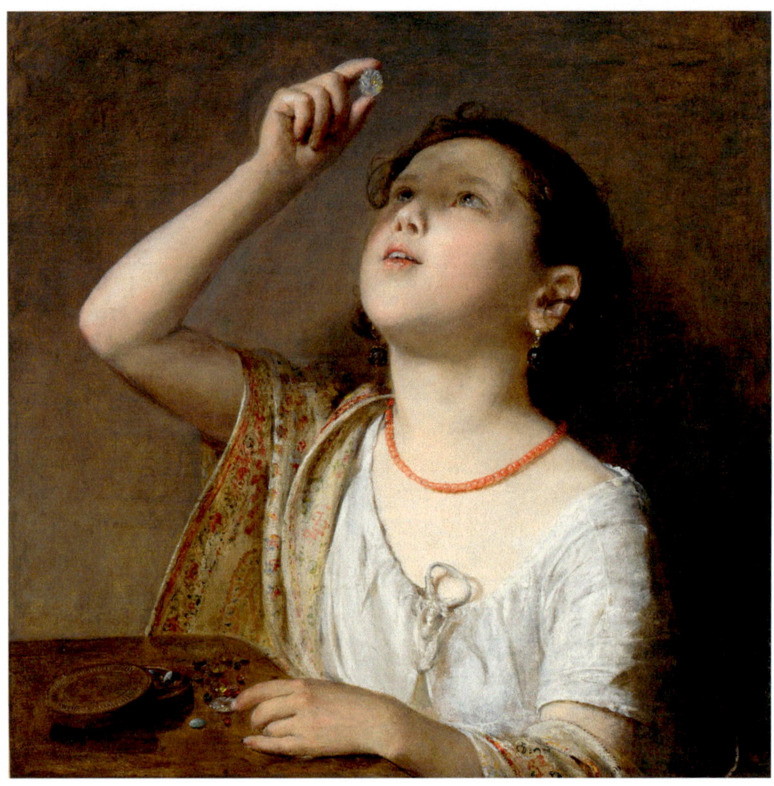

Reiter studied at the Academy of Fine Arts in Vienna, where he was taught by Leopold Kupelwieser and Thomas Ender. His talent was recognised early and he achieved success at a young age, his portraits and genre paintings ensuring his place as the definitive painter of the Viennese Biedermeier. He was known for his surprisingly innovative approaches to composition and for the novelty of his subjects. The portraits that he painted around 1850 occupy a prominent place within his oeuvre.

His portraits of children are among his most eye-catching works, and *The Little Jewellery Dealer* is one of Reiter's most charming. The little girl, shown in three-quarter profile, has apparently just found the family treasure box and is gazing enthralled at a glittering precious stone. The light shining from the gemstone and from the little girl's lips and eyes contrasts sharply with the dark shades and brown tones. The pale pinks of her lips, her coral necklace, and the pattern on her shawl add fresh dashes of colour. The painting is also remarkable for its unusual square format and close-up perspective. – AS

Linz–Grafenegg 1990, cat. nos. 55, 61 | *Linz* 2013, cat. no. 212

Johann Baptist REITER

(Urfahr bei Linz, 1813 – Vienna, 1890)

Worker, 1848 | Oil on canvas, 39.5 × 29 cm
Bequest of Mihály Erny, 1871
Inv. no. 173.B

Woman Worker, 1848 | Oil on canvas, 39.5 × 28.5 cm
Bequest of Mihály Erny, 1871
Inv. no. 172.B

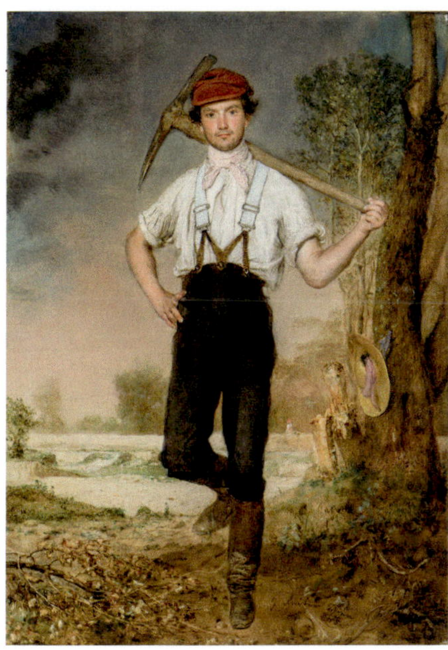 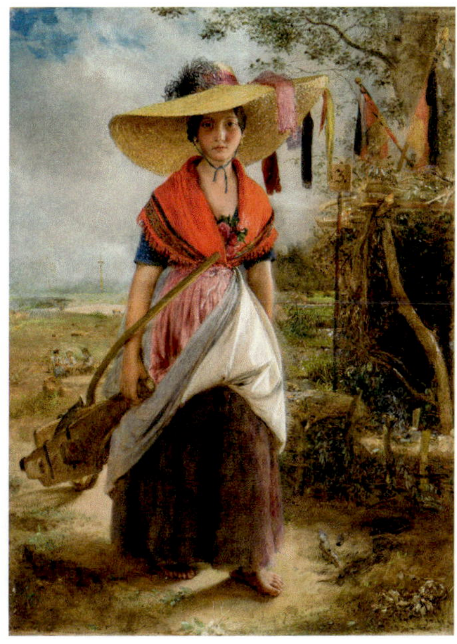

This charming pair of portraits, apparently depicting ordinary agricultural workers, is hard to categorise and can be interpreted in several ways. They can be seen as a transition between idealised self-portrait and genre piece, while at the same time they encapsulate Reiter's personal and political beliefs. The son of a Linz carpenter, Reiter sympathised with the ideals of the 1848 Vienna Uprising. Political and economic tensions in Austria's multiethnic empire had culminated in the resignation of Chancellor of State Metternich and initial concessions on the part of Emperor Ferdinand I, and many artists and intellectuals took part in the resulting armed clashes alongside members of the working class.

The two figures, shown in the prime of their youth against an idyllic backdrop featuring symbols of the revolution, are in fact the painter and his first wife, Maria Anna Hofstötter. The barricades and trenches discernible in the background, the straw bonnet and so-called barricade hat, as well as the yellow, red, and black flags and May Pole, are allusions to the events of May 1848 and the riots that devastated Vienna in the second wave of the revolution. – DL

Vienna 1993, cat. nos. 86–87 | *Linz* 2013, 112

Franz STEINFELD

(Vienna, 1787 – Písek, 1868)

Lakeside Landscape, 1830s | Oil on canvas, 25 × 34 cm

Purchase, 1990 | Inv. no. 90.2.B

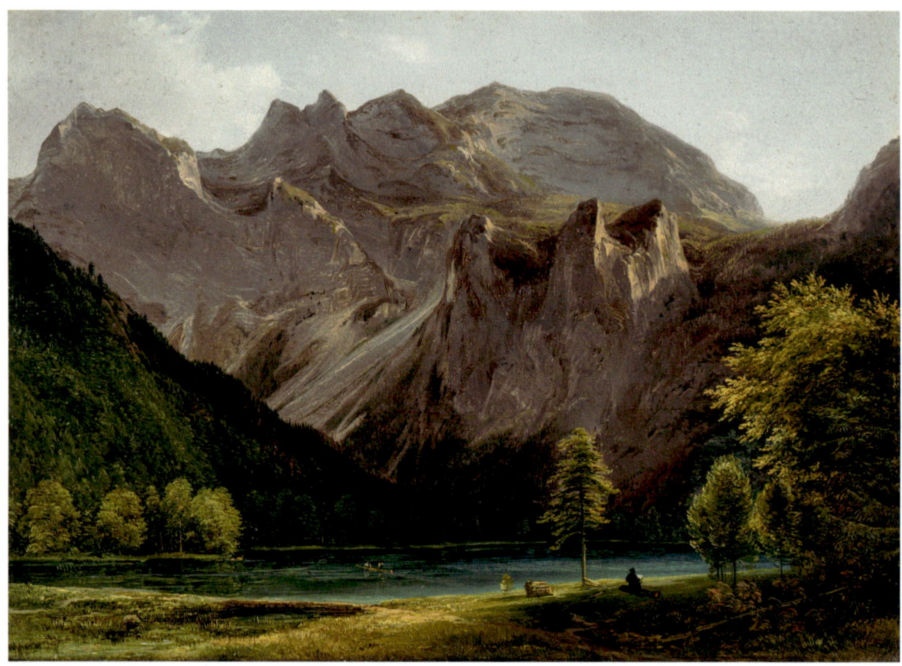

Franz Steinfeld was one of the Monarchy's most famous and most sought-after landscape painters in his day: he was compared in the contemporary press to Ferdinand Georg Wald-müller and Friedrich Gauerman. He was among the first to paint in the *plein air* style, in which the faithful depiction of nature was considered paramount. He spent the summer months in the Alps and was particularly fond of the Salzkammergut region and its centre, the spa town of Bad Ischl that also served as an imperial residence. Rather than continuing the tradition of baroque or romantic landscape painting, Steinfeld sought his own path, through the accurate observation of natural phenomena, and by doing so created the prototype of Austrian Bieder-meier landscape painting. In this exquisite, meticulously executed work, measuring scarcely the size of two palms, it is probably the Hohen Spielberg mountains that block the horizon, with the valley and a crystal-clear alpine lake in the foreground. The artist himself can be seen, painting by the lakeside, his back to the viewer. – DL

Graz 2023

Friedrich GAUERMANN

(Miesenbach, 1807 – Vienna, 1862)

Cows before the Stable, ca. 1830 | Oil on wood, 37 × 45 cm
Transfer, 1950 | Inv. no. 450.B

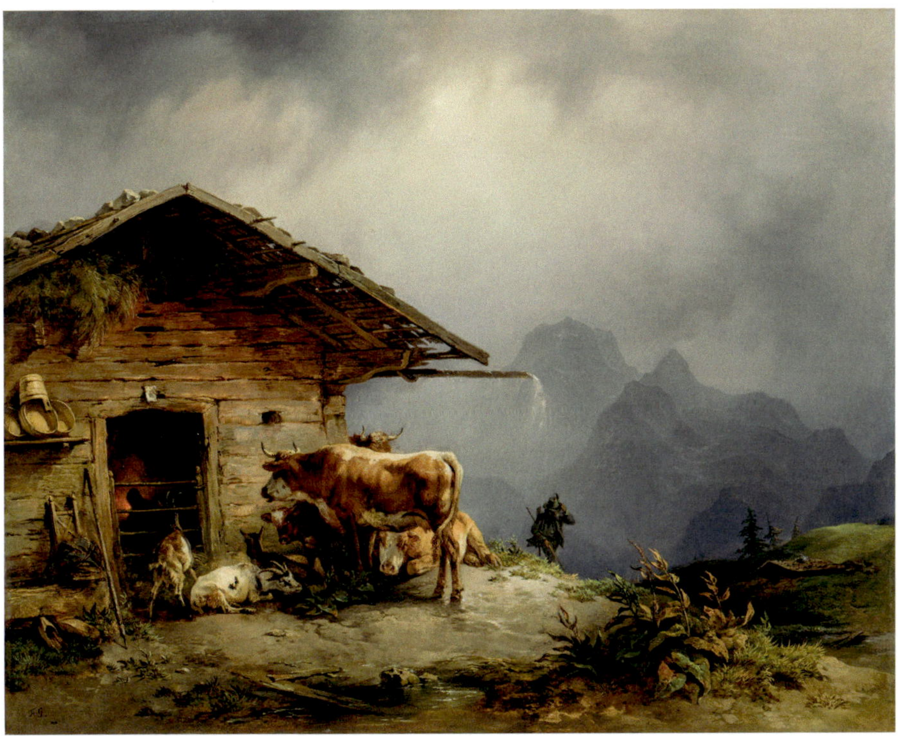

Friedrich Gauermann was given his first lessons in painting by his father, a landscape painter, before studying at the Academy of Art in Vienna from 1824 to 1827. The principal source for his artistic development comprised seventeenth-century Dutch landscapes and paintings of animals fighting. His parents spent each summer on their farm in Miesenbach, and it was during his excursions and travels that he discovered the grandeur of the alpine mountains and pastures. Back in his studio, he produced finished compositions from the nature studies and sketches made in these awe-inspiring locations. Despite the similarities among paintings featuring his almost trademark cows, farm animals, hardworking peasants, and alpine huts, they are not monotonous but always preserve something of the freshness of the original impression. Gauermann integrated animals and human figures into his landscapes with remarkable sensitivity, creating a kind of crossover between genre paintings and landscapes. Like his baroque forerunners, he preferred a dramatic atmosphere over cloudless sunshine. He was highly skilled at rendering a suddenly darkening sky, or sunshine gleaming between the clouds after a storm. – DL

Vienna 1962 | Feuchtmüller 1987

Joseph ALTENKOPF

(Vienna, 1818 – ?, after 1868)

Pottendorf Castle, 1855 | Oil on canvas, 76 × 105 cm
Purchase, Esterházy Collection, 1871 | Inv. no. 4.B

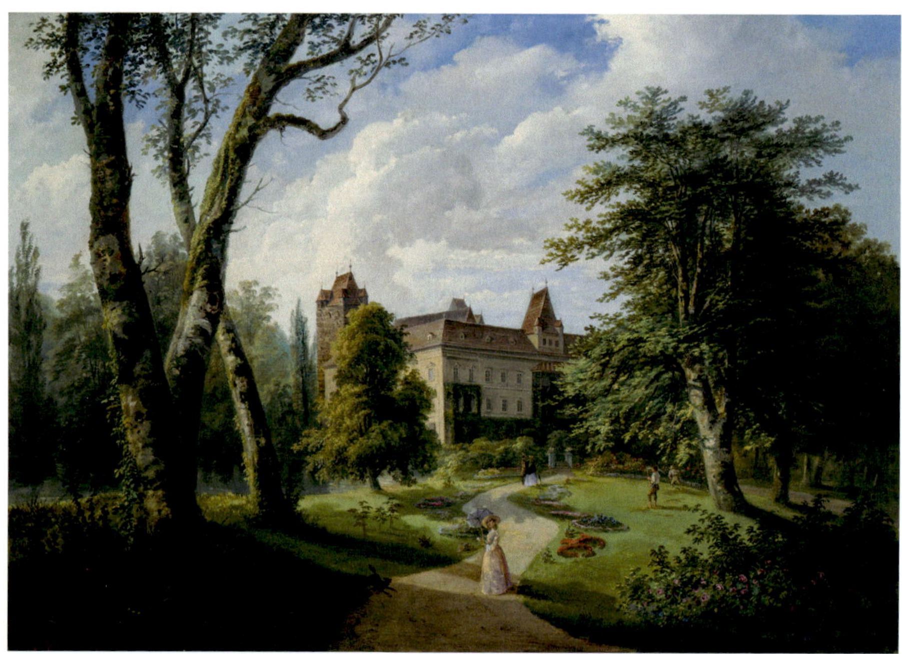

Joseph Altenkopf achieved popularity among Viennese art lovers as a painter of genre scenes and landscapes. The high point of his career came in 1855, when Pál Antal Esterházy entrusted to him the management of his picture gallery and print collection. However, his employment proved short-lived: he was arrested after just eighteen months, then sentenced to imprisonment for appropriating the artworks in his care and selling forty paintings and numerous highly valuable prints.

While in the prince's employment, Altenkopf produced several paintings for him, including this view of Pottendorf Castle, where Pál Antal lived with his family after serving as ambassador in London. The focus here is on the romantic English landscape garden in the foreground. Circled by the river Fischa, Pottendorf Castle was once owned by the ill-fated Count Ferenc Nádasdy: it was from here that the lord chief justice was taken in 1670, before being executed for his part in the Wesselényi Conspiracy against Emperor Leopold I. Some 130 years later, the castle, which had been reconstructed during the eighteenth century, was purchased by Pál Antal's father, Nikolaus II Esterházy, to house his scattered art collection. Pottendorf was home to the picture gallery for just five years: the paintings were moved in 1810 to Laxenburg, and in 1814 to Vienna, to protect them from the Napoleonic troops. – AL

Meller 1915, 251 | *Eisenstadt* 1995, 413, cat. no. XXIV/4.41

Hermann GRAF

(Frankfurt am Main, 1873 – Frankfurt am Main, 1940)

Biedermeier Room, 1906 | Oil on canvas, 60 × 55 cm
Bequest of Count Dénes Andrássy, 1913 | Inv. no. 270.B

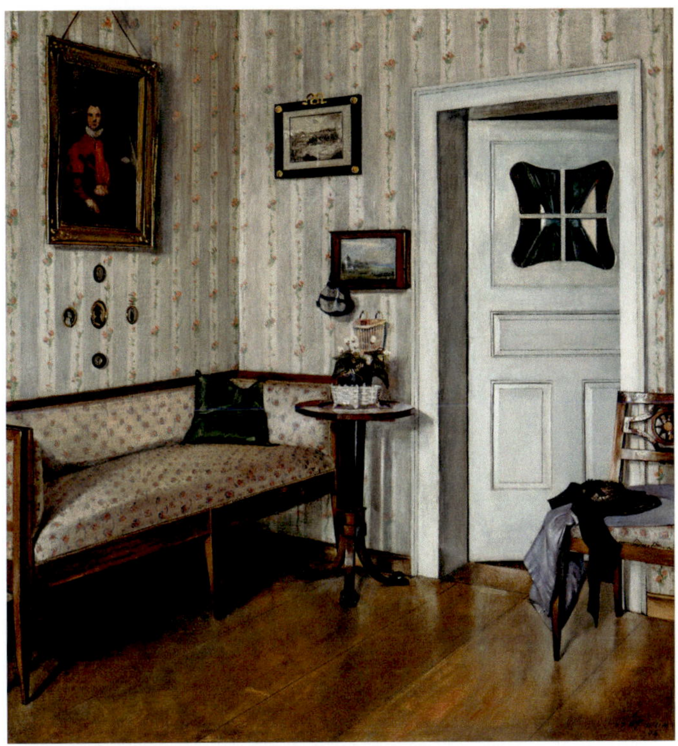

Hermann Graf is a little-known artist of late German realism. Although a member of the Munich Kunstverein, his career lasted for only a few years: his work was shown regularly only after 1904, while his last dated work was painted in 1908. He produced mainly portraits, still lifes, and interiors. His style is reminiscent of Jan Vermeer's: he captured motionlessness on canvas and often depicted figures absorbed in solitary tasks. Like the Dutch master, he too was fascinated by the glint of light on objects and by interiors luminous with sunlight.

The painting *Biedermeier Room,* of which there are a few versions, allows us a glimpse into a bourgeois interior. All versions show the same corner of the room but differ in terms of the furniture and whether the door is open or closed. In the Budapest painting, fine particles of dust glisten in the light reflected from the glass in the door. The small family portraits on the wall lend the painting the sense of intimacy and privacy that was typical of the Biedermeier period. The date of the painting, 1906, is a clear indication of the prevailing presence of Biedermeier tastes in the style of interior design and furniture. – BIB

Hanfstaengl 1895, 213, 220 | *Allgemeines Lexikon* 1921, 483

IV

The Real World

———

Rudolf von ALT

Friedrich von AMERLING

Louis-Ernest BARRIAS

Charles-Édouard BOUTIBONNE

Albert-Ernest CARRIER-BELLEUSE

Jean-Baptiste Camille COROT

Gustave COURBET

Thomas COUTURE

Giacomo FAVRETTO

Eduard FRANKFORT

Eugène FROMENTIN

Hans GASSER

Victor Julien GIRAUD

Cyprien GODEBSKI

Jozef ISRAËLS

Friedrich August von KAULBACH

Wilhelm LEIBL

Franz von LENBACH

Guillaume François-Gabriel LÉPAULLE

Wilhelm LINDENSCHMIT

Édouard MANET

Adolph MENZEL

Albert NEUHUYS

August von PETTENKOFEN

Carl RAHL

Théodule RIBOT

Mathias SCHMID

Alfred STEVENS

Eugène VERBOECKHOVEN

Kaspar Clemens von ZUMBUSCH

In the mid-nineteenth century, the quality and dynamics of life changed dramatically. Thanks to industrialisation, a significant proportion of the population were by then living in cities. Painters of the new lifestyle perceived the changed reality and human fate in the context of urban existence. Technological advances significantly affected the rhythm of daily life and the way in which people navigated the world. The invention that had the biggest impact on the fine arts was photography. Seen at the time as a way of reproducing almost any scene or detail with perfect objectivity, it gradually became accessible to the wider public, too. This new perspective on how things were perceived and recorded affected the way people saw the world: the contemplation of what had previously been outside common perception or considered insignificant, spontaneous spatial correlations among visual elements, instantaneity and chance represented a challenge for art. The success of a depiction was now measured in terms of its realism.

Art historians use the term realism in an extremely broad sense. It is occasionally even applied to medieval and Gothic art, to refer to depictions that emphasise the human quality of the protagonists in religious scenes; or to characterise the illusionism of early Dutch painting. In a narrower sense, realism in the mid-nineteenth century – as a response to both idealisation and excessive sentimentality – refers to a pan-European shift in attitude, the immediate, lifelike depiction of everyday existence, devoid of any ideational element. The first paintings by Gustave Courbet generated the most far-reaching impact. Many of the artists of this period chose to portray social themes, and for Courbet the objective portrayal of people and situations entailed the acknowledgement of imperfection and the visualisation of ugliness and indecency. The radical approach of his art initially provoked scandal, although it would later be highly influential in liberating the artistic outlook of the next generation.

Social sensitivity and the rendering of directly perceived reality emerged in parallel almost everywhere on the continent. The desire to communicate personal experience prompted artists to observe human features in meticulous detail, while the visualisation of unfamiliar areas of life led to a quest for new subject mattor. Artists began to be interested in agricultural and industrial labour, rural and urban poverty, the everyday environment, or even in the often grotesque representation of awkward episodes from the past. While in France the changes that occurred in the middle of the century provoked an explosive reaction to neoclassicism and romanticism, elsewhere the same process required a shorter or longer period of transition. In Belgium, it took the form of scarcely perceptible changes to romantic landscape and genre painting, and in the Netherlands, likewise, it involved the revival of rich, local traditions dating back to the seventeenth century. In Central Europe, the careers of Biedermeier artists belonging to the previous generation – Ferdinand Georg Waldmüller and Friedrich von Amerling – carried over directly into the following period.

Guillaume François-Gabriel LÉPAULLE

(Versailles, 1804 – Aÿ, 1886)

Portrait of General Eugène Cavaignac, 1848 | Oil on canvas, 130 × 97 cm
Bequest of Count János Pálffy, 1912 | Inv. no. 246.B

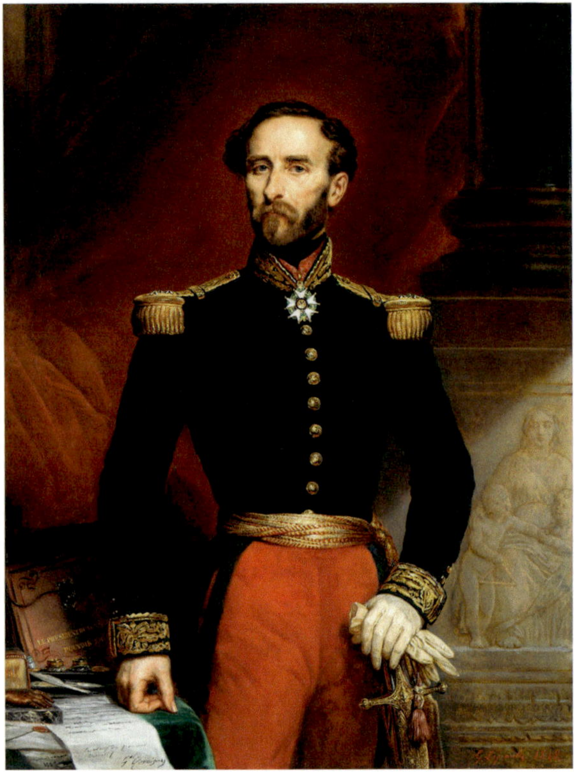

Guillaume Lépaulle studied at the École des Beaux-Arts in Paris, and his oeuvre comprises genre paintings and portraits. One of his most famous subjects was Eugène Cavaignac, who enjoyed a remarkable military and political career: in 1848, he became Governor of Algeria, and later that year, on his return to France, he played an important role in the suppression of the workers' revolts as minister and head of executive power in France. However, at the presidential elections following the Revolution he lost to Louis-Napoléon Bonaparte, later Napoleon III.

Lépaulle's portrait of Cavaignac, as a statesman posing confidently in his uniform, was painted amidst these complex political circumstances. The subject's unwavering gaze is fixed on the viewer; beside him on the table are the symbols of his authority, while in the background a relief carving of the allegory of the Republic can be seen. The painting was shown at the 1849 Paris Salon, together with two other portraits of Cavaignac. Something of a competition arose between the personal, intimate work by Horace Vernet, Jean-Adolphe Lafosse's portrait, which was considered less successful, and this official portrait by Lépaulle.

– AZSK

Lauzac 1859–1861, 517 | Illyés 2001, 17–19

Friedrich von AMERLING

(Vienna, 1803 – Vienna, 1887)

Berta Gyertyánffy, Countess Nákó, 1855 | Oil on canvas, 128 × 107 cm
Purchase, 1969 | Inv. no. 572.B

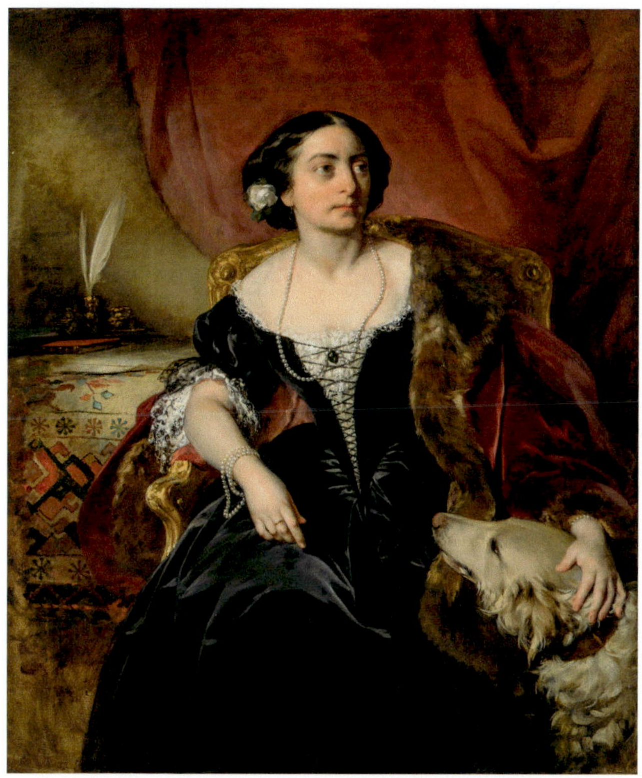

Having been commissioned to paint the portrait of Emperor Francis I in 1832, Friedrich von Amerling spent the next two decades as Vienna's most fashionable portraitist, working for the most distinguished clientele. Although his prestige doolined somewhat in the 1850s, his portrait of Berta Gyertyánffy, wife of Count Kálmán Nákó, has a quality that sets it apart from other paintings of illustrious aristocratic ladies and the wives of magnates. With a strong, independent personality unusual for the period, the wife of Count Kálmán Nákó of the Banat was not content to fill her days with the kind of activities typical of wealthy aristocratic women. She was admired for her talents as both a musician and a fine artist: she was taught painting by Amerling, among others, while her virtuoso piano playing was commended by Richard Wagner and Franz Liszt, who made her acquaintance at the Nákó residence in Vienna. Typical of an Amerling portrait, the sitter gazes into the distance, lost in her thoughts, with one hand resting on her dog's head. The naturalness of the pose, the model's charismatic charm, and, last but not least, the richness of textures, make this one of Amerling's most attractive portraits. – DL

Probszt 1927, 144 | Cifka 1996a, 61–68

Hans GASSER

(Eisentratten, 1817 – Pest, 1868)

Bust of Károly Markó, ca. 1855 | Marble, 58 × 37 × 30 cm
Donated by Emperor Franz Joseph, 1864 | Inv. no. 56.23.U

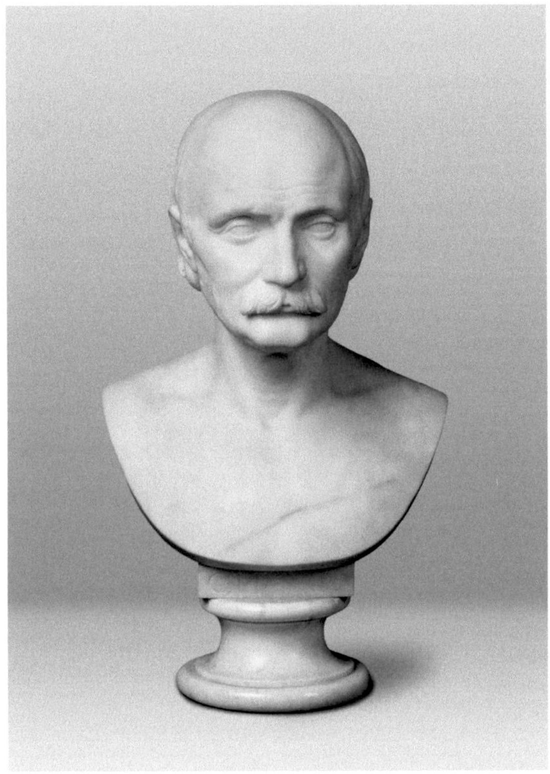

Hans Gasser began his career as a wood engraver but achieved fame as a sculptor in the 1840s, when his work became increasingly fashionable in Vienna, Pest, and Munich. Between 1850 and 1851, he worked as a professor at the Academy of Fine Arts in Vienna. Besides public sculptures, he produced busts of many of the important artists (Carl Rahl) and prominent Hungarian personalities (Count István Széchenyi, the poet Sándor Petőfi) of his day. This portrait of Károly Markó the Elder, founder of Hungarian landscape painting, was modelled during the ageing master's last visit to Vienna in 1853. Gasser has portrayed the revered and celebrated painter in keeping with the traditions of neoclassicist sculpture, while emphasising his subject's distinctive features without idealisation. Gasser showed the marble sculpture in Pest in 1855, but it was only later, in 1864, four years after Markó's death, that it was purchased by Emperor Franz Joseph, who donated it to the Hungarian National Museum. The bust was displayed in the so-called Markó Hall up until the early 1870s, before becoming part of the collection of the newly established Museum of Fine Arts. – AS

Budapest 1995, 26–27 | *Budapest* 2011, 37, 219, cat. no. 219

August von PETTENKOFEN

(Vienna, 1822 – Vienna, 1889)

Portrait of József Borsos, ca. 1850 | Oil on canvas, 91 × 72 cm
Purchased from the auction house C. J. Wawra (Vienna), 1901 | Inv. no. 128.B

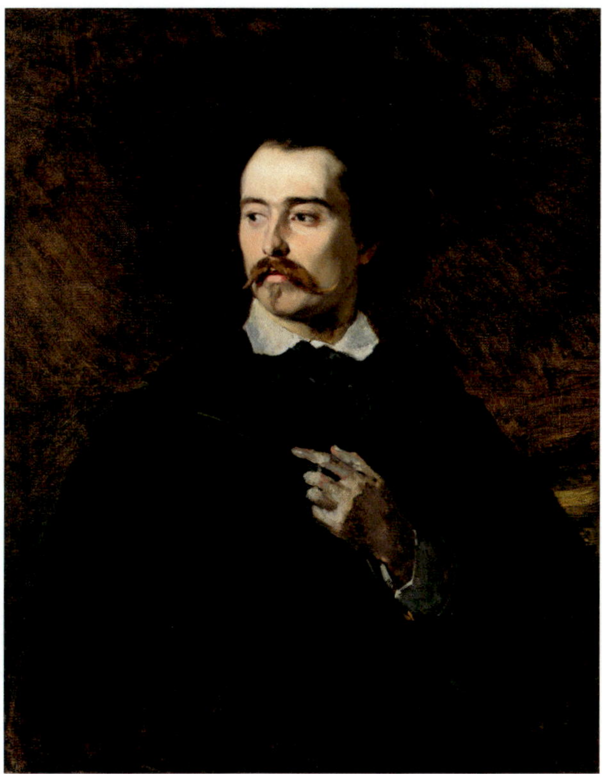

The friendship between August von Pettenkofen and the Hungarian painter, József Borsos, dated from their days as students at the Academy of Fine Arts in Vienna. The two men even rented a studio together in Vienna between 1845 and 1848. According to Árpád Weixlgärtner, a personal acquaintance of Pettenkofen and the author of an early monograph on the artist, Borsos's style had a profound influence on the Austrian artist.

The precise year in which Pettenkofen produced this life-sized half-portrait of József Borsos is not known, as Pettenkofen rarely dated his works. The length of Borsos's hair, however, suggests that he was fairly young when the portrait was painted. The greyish-brown tone of the painting was typical of the period between 1847 and 1853, before Pettenkofen's association with the Barbizon School, while another well-known portrait of Borsos might also provide a clue to the dating of the work: in the 1861 lithography by József Marastoni, the Hungarian painter is already portrayed with short hair. – BIB

Weixlgärtner 1916, 140, 374 | *Budapest 2009*, 9, 13

Carl RAHL

(Vienna, 1812 – Vienna, 1865)

Portrait of Countess Miklós Zichy, 1856
Oil on canvas, 63.5 × 50 cm
Bequest of Countess Leona Zichy, 1914
Inv. no. 361.B

Portrait of Count Miklós Zichy III, 1856
Oil on canvas, 63 × 50 cm
Bequest of Countess Leona Zichy, 1914
Inv. no. 360.B

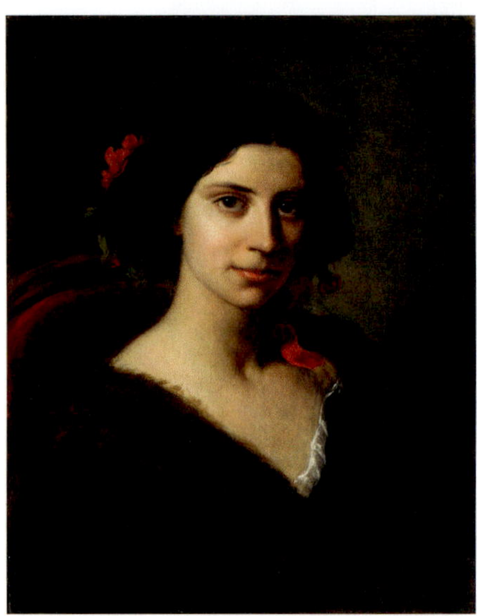 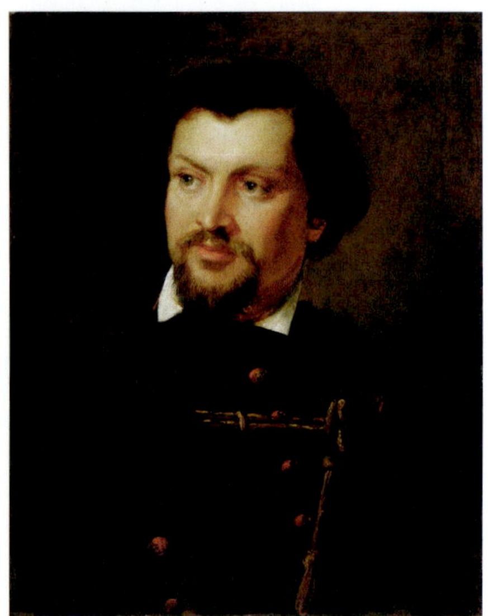

Carl Rahl was initially taught by his father, a painter and engraver, then continued his studies at the academies of art in Vienna, Munich, and Stuttgart. At first, he mainly painted portraits, although later he produced large historical scenes, influenced by Wilhelm von Kaulbach. He and August von Pettenkofen are seen as having made the Biedermeier style more relaxed; at the time, Rahl's work represented the progressive development of the style. Although Rahl was not particularly popular in Vienna, he was regarded by Hungarian painters as one of the most influential foreign masters. His eighty or so Hungarian students included such famous artists as Bertalan Székely and Mihály Munkácsy.

The portraits of Miklós Zichy and his wife, Franciska Festetich, were shown at the 1856 season-opening exhibition of the Pest Art Society. At the time, foreigners rarely featured in these exhibitions, but from 1855, Rahl received regular commissions from the upper echelons of Hungarian society. Typical of Rahl, although unusually for the period, the count and countess are shown in a natural pose, lending the portraits a sense of vitality. – BIB

Szvoboda Dománszky 2015, 63

Kaspar Clemens von ZUMBUSCH

(Herzebrock, 1830 – Rimsting, 1915)

Bust of Architect József Diescher, 1860s | Plaster, 88 × 54 × 34 cm
Donated by Hermina Diescher, 1904 | Inv. no. 56.16.U

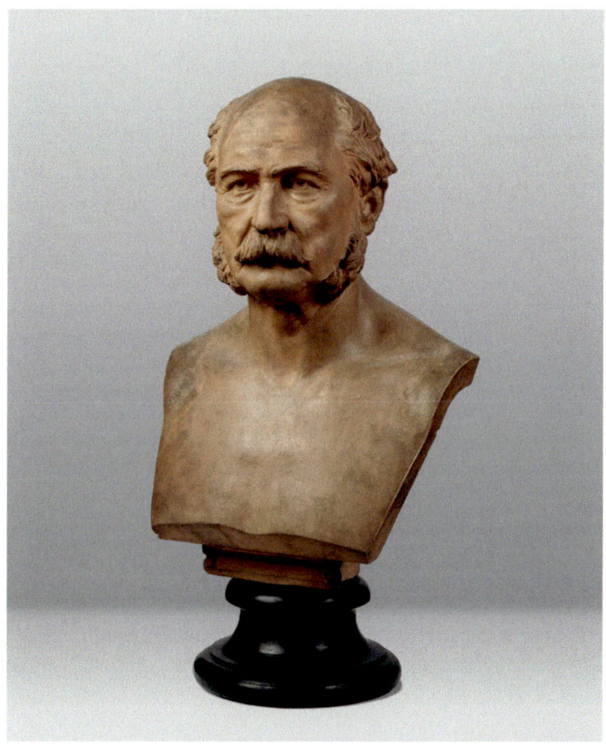

Zumbusch studied sculpture under Johann von Halbig at the Polytechnikum in Munich. On returning to Munich from a study tour in Rome, he mainly produced memorials, then, in 1873, he
was invited to teach memorial sculpture at the Vienna Academy. His numerous public sculptures, including the monumental memorial to Maria Theresa in front of the Kunsthistorisches
Museum, elevated him among the ranks of the most significant historicist sculptors. He also
produced several busts, which – unlike his heroic and idealised public sculptures – are more
realistic portraits. Among them is this painted plaster portrait of József Diescher, a Hungarian
architect of German descent.

Diescher designed many well-known buildings in Budapest, including the Mihály
Vörösmarty Grammar School and the Church of Saint Anna on Szervita Square. He knew
Zumbusch from the beginning of his career and requested him to produce a sculpture for the
family crypt in the Kerepesi Cemetery in Budapest, which he himself had designed and which
was built during his lifetime. The plaster model preserved in the collection of the Museum
of Fine Arts served as the basis for the carved marble bust that stands on the grave. – FT

Kőrösné Mikis 2016, 29

Franz von LENBACH

(Schrobenhausen, 1836 – Munich, 1904)

The Triumphal Arch of Titus in Rome, 1860 | Oil on canvas, 179 × 130 cm
Bequest of Count János Pálffy, 1912 | Inv. no. 245.B

The Triumphal Arch of Titus in Rome is one of the most important early works by Franz von Lenbach, who would go on to become the "Painter Prince" of Munich. In the autumn of 1858, Lenbach and his teacher, Karl von Piloty, a professor at the Munich academy, travelled to Rome, where Piloty produced studies for the composition *Nero Walking on the Embers of Rome* (see page 158) on which he was working at the time. The Triumphal Arch of Titus was a popular motif and was also painted by Piloty. Lenbach was captivated by the road leading to the Campo Vaccino, Rome's livestock market, the bustling atmosphere of the triumphal arch, the everyday scene of traders from the Campagna leaving the market, and the monumentality of the ancient building. While in Rome, the artist produced numerous drawings and an oil sketch for the painting, which he completed in Munich, although after returning home he produced further studies in the German countryside. Among them is a study of the little boy lying at the foot of the triumphal arch, which he later went on to paint as an independent composition. According to Lenbach's memoirs, he was an "admirer of nature" and had a "passion for sunlight". He referred to his painting of the triumphal arch, bathed in Italian light, as an "image of sunlight" (*Sonnenbild*). The intense illumination and powerful play of light and shadow highlight the painstakingly rendered details of the arch.

The painting was purchased by Count János Pálffy from the Kunstverein exhibition in Munich, presumably at the suggestion of Piloty, whose *Nero* painting had probably been commissioned by Pálffy. Eventually, both works were acquired from his collection by the Museum of Fine Arts. – DS

Munich 1986–1987, 218, cat. no. 55 | Rome 2003, 266, cat. no. XII.1

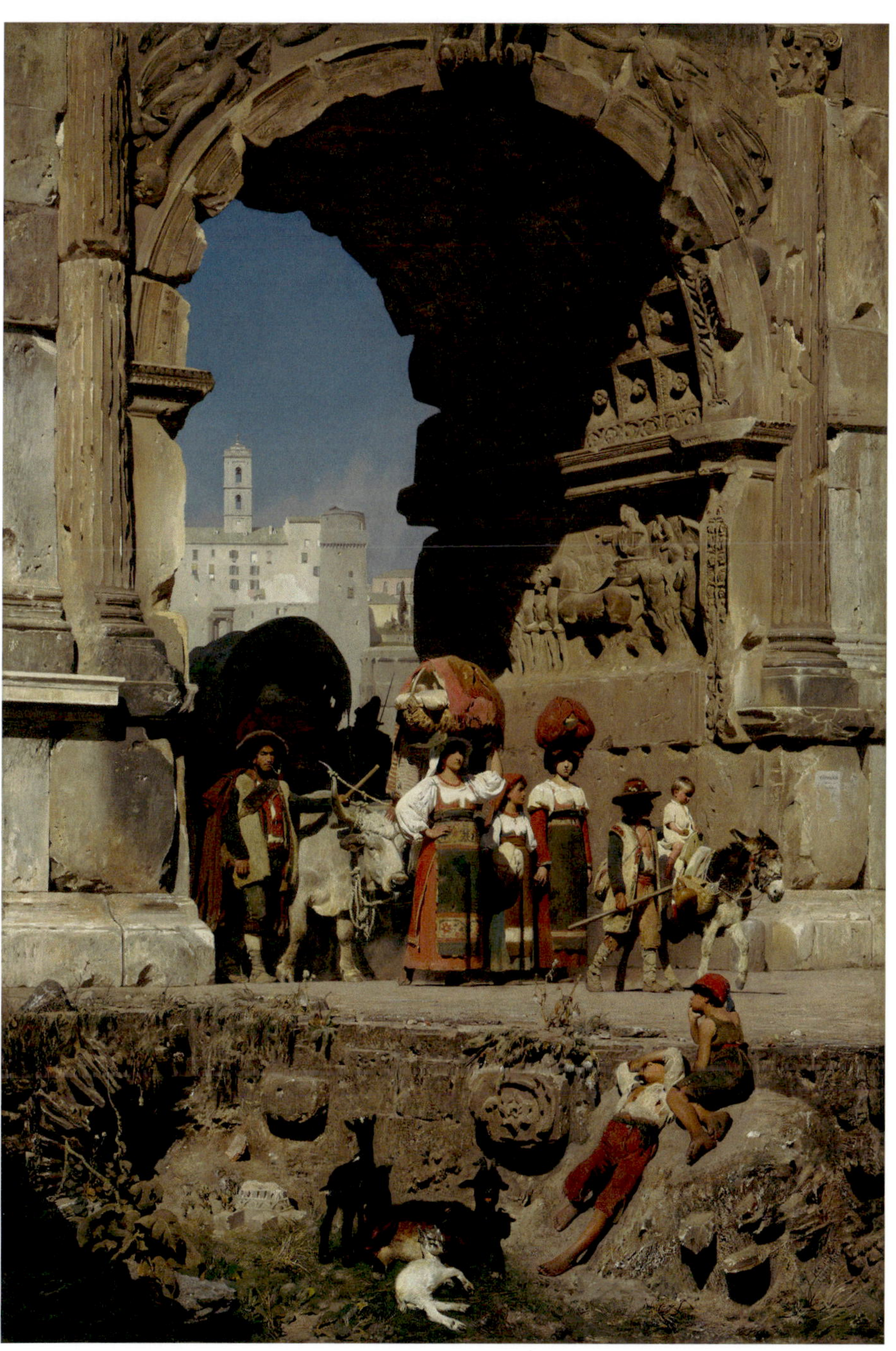

Eugène VERBOECKHOVEN

(Warneton, 1798 – Brussels, 1881)

Sheepfold, 1873 | Oil on canvas, 92 × 140 cm
Bequest of Count János Pálffy, 1912 | Inv. no. 262.B

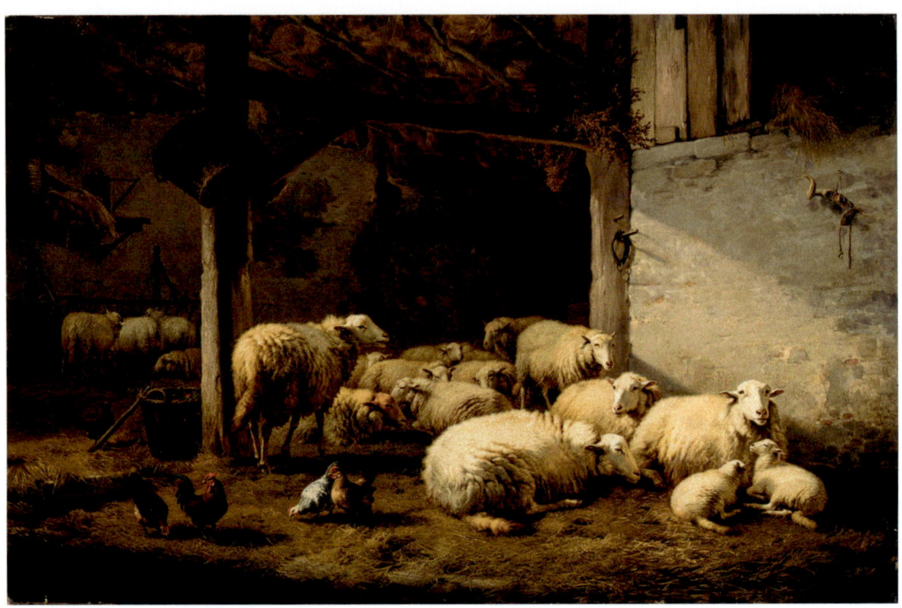

The Belgian painter Eugène Verboeckhoven specialised in animal painting, especially of sheep. As a youngster, influenced by his father, he first tried his hand at sculpture, and although he subsequently opted for painting, his initial experiences were put to good use. He was awarded a prize at the Brussels Salon at the age of just twenty-six. Highly successful throughout Europe, his work could be found in every important state and private collection. He painted mainly wild animals at first, later turning to grazing goats, cows, and sheep. Besides his meticulous execution, he borrowed his subtle colours and filtered light effects from the Dutch masters; the backgrounds of his paintings – the farms, stables, and village scenes – are also adapted from the old masters, translated into the nineteenth century and brought up to date.

His ability to paint multiple variations of the same species of animal lends vividness to his work. This is clearly apparent in the Budapest painting, acquired from the bequest of János Pálffy, in which the sheep, painted with anatomical accuracy, rest idyllically in the sheepfold. – BIB

Alvin 1885 | Dalemans 2001, 50–51

Théodule RIBOT

(Saint-Nicolas-d'Attez, 1823 – Colombes, 1891)

Plucked Fowl, ca. 1865 | Oil on canvas, 60 × 74.5 cm

Transfer, 1948 | Inv. no. 457.B

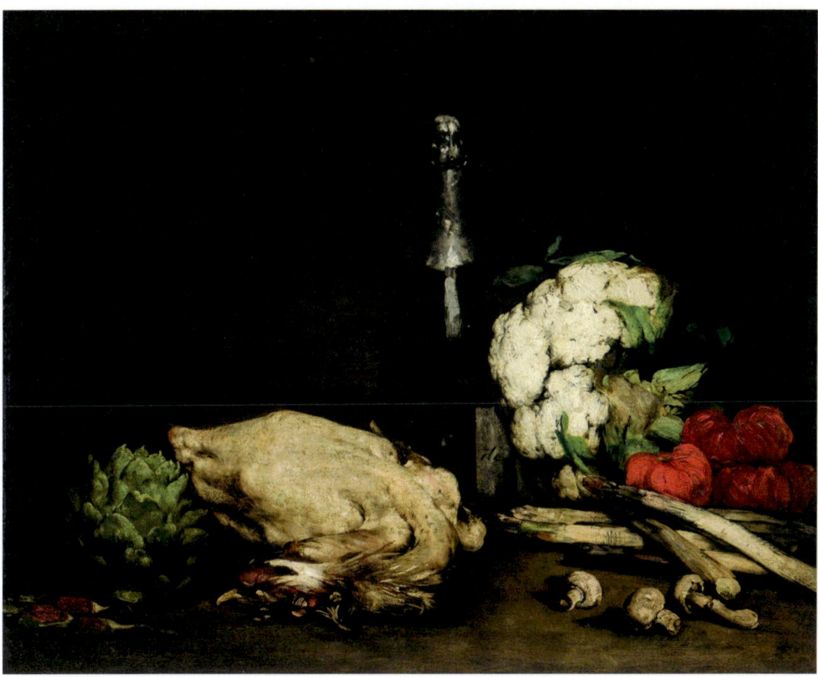

A self-taught painter, Théodule Ribot turned to the art of the past to develop his unique, realist style. He employed the powerful effects of light and shade of seventeenth-century Spanish and Dutch masters – especially Frans Hals and Rembrandt – in his dramatic, profoundly human, biblical scenes and his true-to-life contemporary genre pieces. Following in the footsteps of Jusepe de Ribera, Francisco de Zurbarán, and the eighteenth-century French painter Jean Baptiste Siméon Chardin, he also produced simple, spare still lifes depicting everyday objects.

The Budapest painting reveals Ribot's quintessential qualities as a painter. The ingredients on the kitchen table gleam against a deep black background: the artist has painted the radishes, artichoke, and the yellow skin and grey feathers of the plucked fowl using vigorous brushstrokes. The composition features a snow-white cauliflower and bright red tomatoes alongside a bottle of champagne that almost disappears into the background, complemented by spears of asparagus and a few mushrooms. Ribot selected the elements for his still life not primarily for their symbolic meaning but rather for their decorative, pictorial effect: his painting explores the contrasts between more or less vivid patches of colour and different textures, as well as the dynamic balance of the composition. – KAZS

Fukuoka–Matsuyama–Tokyo 1994, cat. no. 25 | Illyés 2001, 40–41

Rudolf von ALT

(Vienna, 1812 – Vienna, 1905)

Venice Scene, after 1864 | Oil on canvas, 52.6 × 79 cm
Bequest of Mihály Erny, 1871 | Inv. no. 160.B

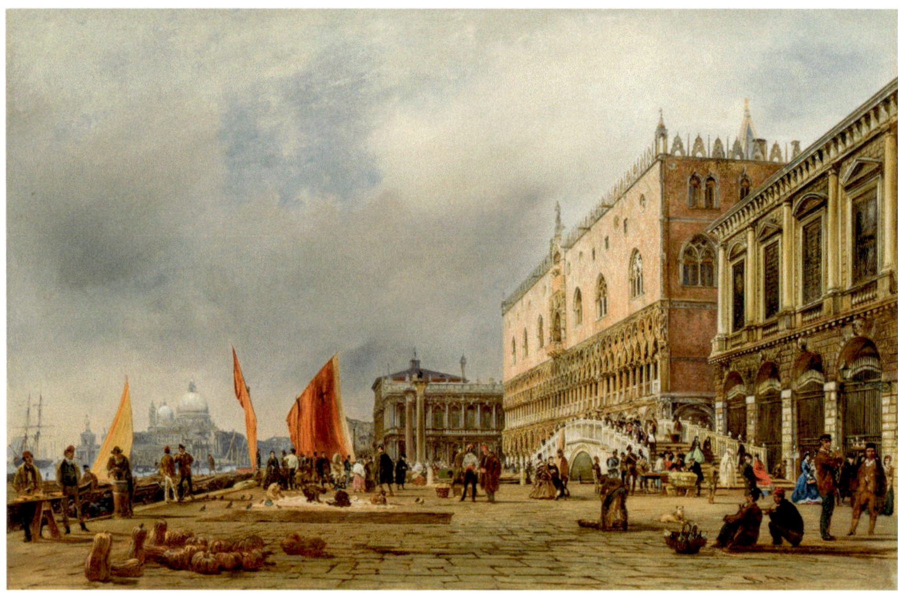

The most eminent of the Austrian vedutisti, Rudolf von Alt was trained by his father, Jacob. He then completed his formal studies at the Vienna Academy before making a tour of Europe. He enjoyed a long life, and his oeuvre spans the whole of the nineteenth century, from the golden age of the Biedermeier to the end of the century. His career brought him prizes, distinctions, and widespread recognition. In 1874, he was elected president of the Vienna Künstlerhaus, and in 1897 he became president of the pioneering Vienna Secession. He earned acclaim for drawings, prints, and watercolours that capture the sights, cities, and palaces of the Austro–Hungarian Monarchy. His flawless draughtsmanship was coupled with speed and accurate observation.

Venice had long been an important destination for art lovers. Alt visited the city on several occasions, returning home each time with numerous sketches, watercolours, and, more rarely, oil paintings. *Venice Scene* depicts the bustling waterfront of the Riva degli Schiavoni. The view is framed on the right by the magnificent Doge's Palace and the neighbouring building, in the centre by the Marciana Library, and in the background by the Basilica Santa Maria della Salute. Yellow and red sails form vivid patches of colour on the water. Alt showed four paintings of Venice at the Künstlerhaus in 1871, possibly including this Budapest work. – AS

Cifka 2000, 35 | Grabner et al. 2011, 145

Adolph MENZEL

(Wrocław [Breslau], 1815 – Berlin, 1905)

Sermon in the Beech Grove near Kösen, 1868 | Oil on canvas, 71 × 58 cm
Purchased from Bruno Cassirer (Berlin), 1926 | Inv. no. 386.B

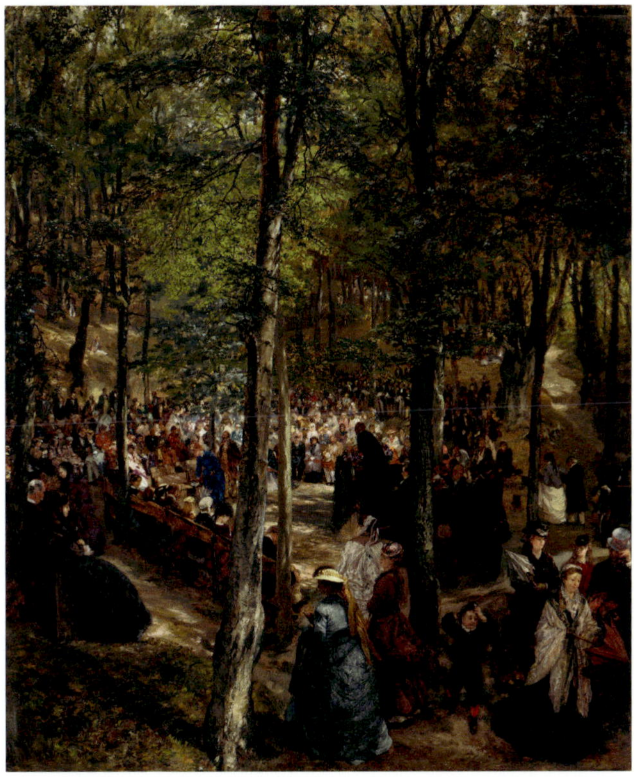

Adolph Menzel was one of the most revered German artists of the nineteenth century. His genre pieces and his history paintings are characterised by a dazzling wealth of details and intense realism. Beside his activities in Berlin, he travelled on several occasions to Paris from the 1850s, where he exhibited his works with great success.

The painting by Menzel in the Budapest collection shows people listening to a sermon held in a forest grove near Kösen (now Bad Kösen), a spa resort in Germany. The open-air scene is portrayed using dynamic brushstrokes: the sunlight filtering through the foliage makes the figures appear as vibrant patches amidst the dense green trees. Many among the well-to-do, elegant company are listening to the pastor's words in silence, while others are walking past the assembly inattentively: what we are witnessing is as much a social event as it is a religious ceremony. When creating the painting, the artists relied partly on sketches he had made on site, and partly on his memory, which explains the realistic, if somewhat hazy nature of his depiction. – AZSK

Nuremberg 1985–1986, cat. no. 36 | *Paris–Washington–Berlin* 1996–1997, cat. no. 125

Gustave COURBET

(Ornans, 1819 – La Tour-de-Peilz, 1877)

The Wrestlers, 1853 | Oil on canvas, 252 × 198 cm
Transfer, 1951 | Inv. no. 502.B

Gustave Courbet's embattled commitment to his artistic ideals and political opinions was central to his life. The great master of realist painting places this same struggle at the core of *The Wrestlers*. The setting is the racecourse behind the Arc de Triomphe in Paris. In the foreground, two athletes are wrestling, although the figures convey a sense of motionlessness and rigidity. Rather than movement, Courbet emphasises the anatomical details of the powerful yet contorted bodies, highlighting the strained muscles and bulging veins. The distinguished spectators occupy the stand behind them – strikingly, the contest is oriented towards the viewer of the painting rather than the distant, indistinct audience.

Thanks to restoration work in 2009, Courbet's intense colours have been revived, sharpening the contrast between the foreground figures and the background. The disparity apparent in terms of colours, proportions, and brushwork arise partly from Courbet's working method (he elaborated his figures in his studio, placing them before a more freely painted landscape), while also demonstrating how the painter's aim was to draw attention to the suffering, struggling masses rather than the bourgeois Parisian audience. This political overtone alludes to the social hardships of the period, and to the disenchantment of the years following the accession of Napoleon III. Rather than this, however, it was the full-blooded realism of its approach that led many critics to denounce the painting when it was shown at the 1853 Paris Salon. – AZSK

Herding 1991, 11–44 | Illyés 2001, 27–29

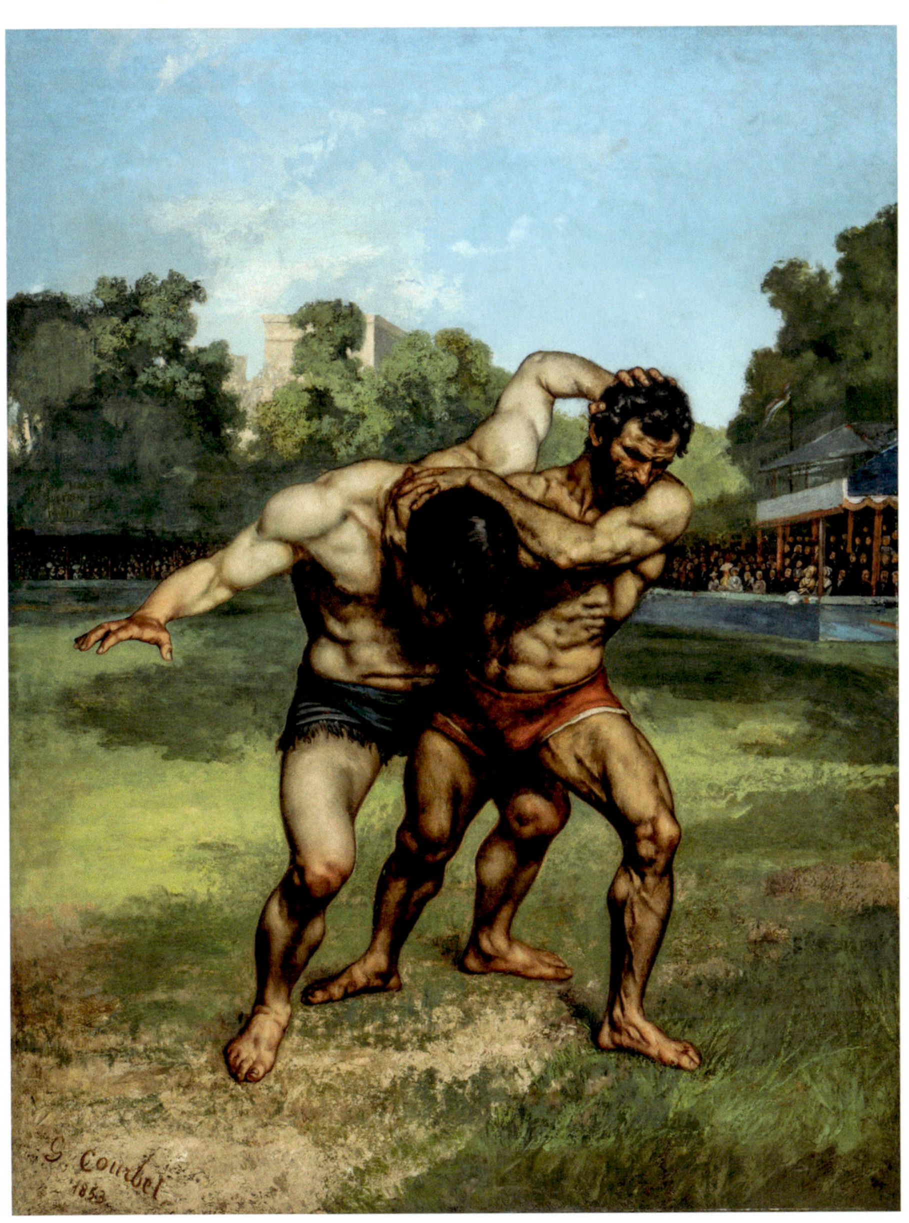

Thomas COUTURE

(Senlis, 1815 – Villiers-le-Bel, 1879)

The Bird-Catcher, 1857 | Oil on canvas, 42 × 61 cm
Bequest of Count János Pálffy, 1912 | Inv. no. 253.B

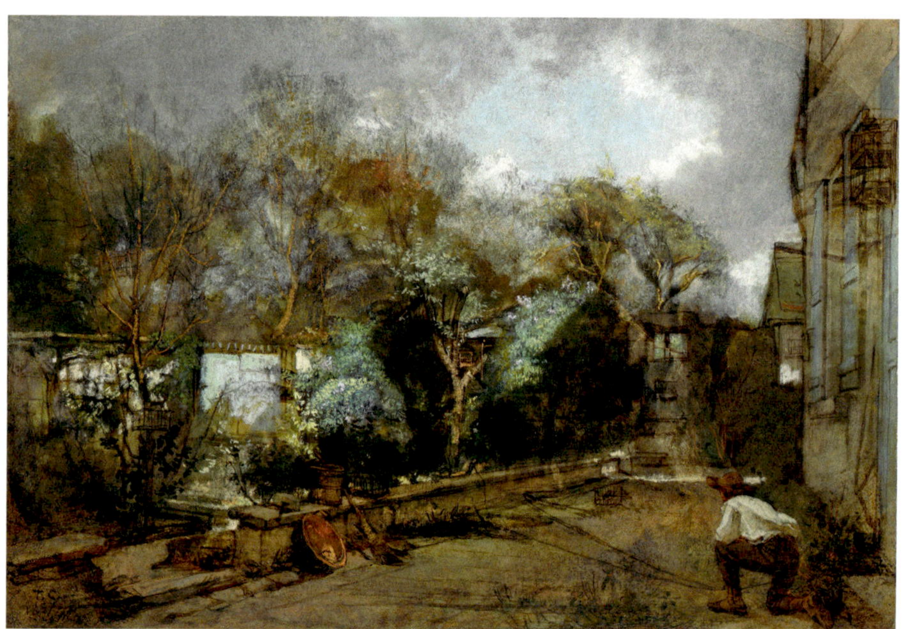

Thomas Couture was one of the most popular French painters of the mid-nineteenth century. He studied under such distinguished representatives of historical painting as Antoine-Jean Gros and Paul Delaroche. In terms of subject matter and technique, Couture is conspicuous for his versatility: besides paintings on historical themes, his repertoire includes landscapes, portraits, and allegorical compositions. In 1847, he opened his prestigious private school, where, as a painter and teacher he nurtured the talents of artists such as Anselm Feuerbach and Édouard Manet.

In the late 1840s, his hometown offered him the old bishop's chapel as his studio, and *The Bird-Catcher* is set in the courtyard of this chapel. The young hunter in the foreground, crouched on one knee, watches intently, waiting for the right moment to pull the string that will close the trap. The surrounding birdcages, which hang from the building and the trees, indicate his livelihood. Bird-catching, or fowling, is an ancient craft, the compelling embodiment of human ingenuity: in Couture's warm-toned genre painting, the birds are caught using traditional devices. – RM

Boime 1969, 48–56 | Illyés 2001, 30–31

Eugène FROMENTIN

(La Rochelle, 1820 – Saint-Maurice, 1876)

Reed Cutters by the Nile, 1871 | Oil on wood, 26.5 × 35 cm

Exchange, 1946 | Inv. no. 437.B

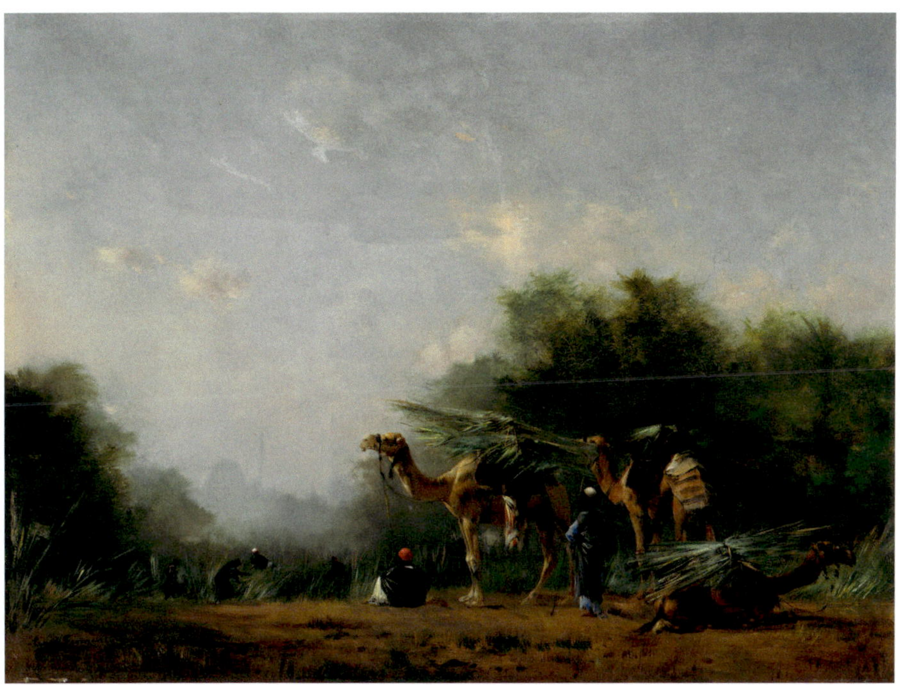

Eugène Fromentin was a prominent figure in French Orientalism. He also produced a substantial written oeuvre. Besides his psychological novel *Dominique*, published in 1863 and long extolled as a masterpiece, he also wrote travelogues and personal essays on art history. His paintings record his personal impressions of the East: he made several visits to Algeria, and in 1869 he travelled to Egypt, where he undertook a long boat trip on the Nile. The small panel painting was certainly inspired by this journey. It offers us a glimpse of everyday life in the contemporary, yet apparently timeless landscape: a group of Arab men are taking a rest on the riverbank beside their camels laden with freshly cut reeds. Interestingly, the legendary river itself – lifeline of the desert region and symbol of Egypt's great historical and commercial past – is barely visible: its presence is merely suggested by the distance between the two banks and the haze above its surface. The dome and minaret of a distant mosque are faintly discernible through the mist. The sky, vegetation, and clothing have been rendered in fresh, rich colours, while the entire composition is permeated with the atmospheric, golden sunlight of the East. – AZSK

Illyés 2001, 72–73 | Thompson and Wright 2008, 325

Édouard MANET

(Paris, 1832 – Paris, 1883)

Lady with a Fan (Jeanne Duval), 1862 | Oil on canvas, 90 × 113 cm
Purchased from art dealer Kurt Walter Bachstitz (Berlin), 1916 | Inv. no. 368.B

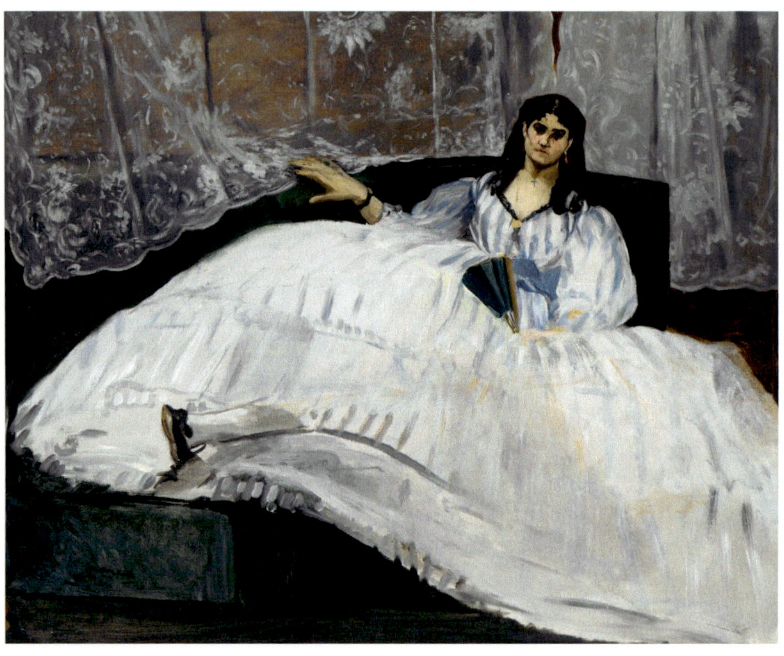

Charles Baudelaire, one of the foremost poets of the period spanning from romanticism to symbolism, made the acquaintance of Jeanne Duval in 1842. Of mixed race, the actress is the subject of Baudelaire's poem *Sed non satiata*: "Singular deity, brown as the nights, / Scented with the perfume of Havana and musk, / Work of some obeah, Faust of the savanna" (trans. William Aggeler). Even after the end of their almost ten-year affair, Baudelaire continued to support Duval, who was by then paralysed in one leg.

Manet painted the "black Venus" in 1862, at the height of his Spanish period. The unconventional composition is a stroke of genius: the canvas is dominated by the woman's enormous white crinoline. Through Manet's use of many different shades of white, the elaborate dress seems almost to take on a life of its own. The model's right hand rests on the back of the curved sofa, a counterpoint to her leg, which emerges from beneath her skirts. The discreet positioning of the leg, however, does nothing to conceal the model's tragic illness. Behind her, the lace curtain frames Jeanne Duval like a theatre box.

The painting was purchased during the First World War from a private collection in Berlin by the curator Simon Meller, whose expert recommendation drew attention to the colourist tradition of Spanish painting. The loose brushstrokes, that were to characterize the artist' style in his later years, were revealed by the restoration of the painting. – JG

Rouart and Wildenstein 1975, cat. no. 48 | *Paris – New York* 1983, cat. no. 27

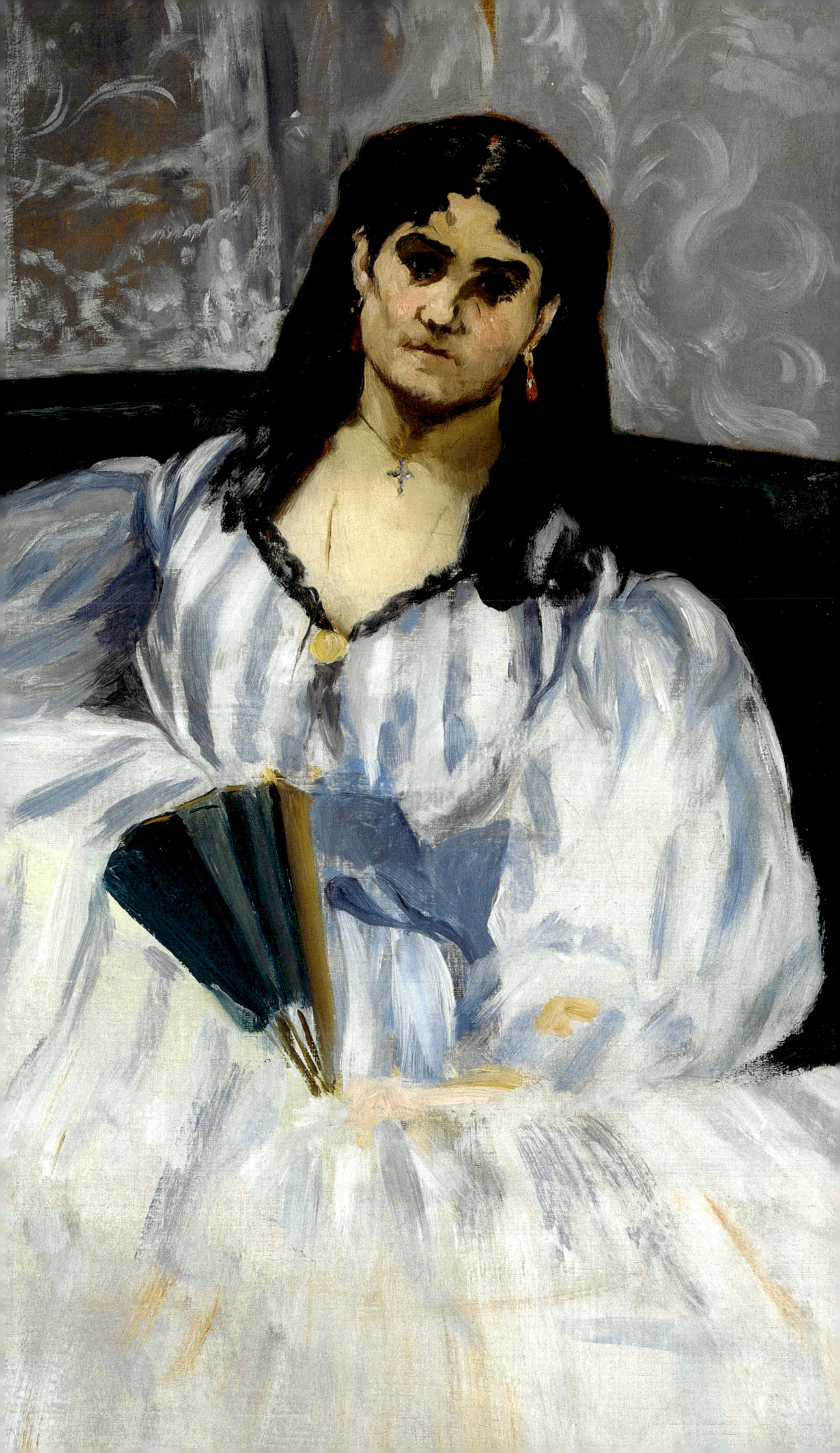

Jean-Baptiste Camille COROT

(Paris, 1796 – Ville-d'Avray, 1875)

Lady with Daisies, ca. 1870 | Oil on canvas, 78 × 58 cm

Transfer, 1946 | Inv. no. 501.B

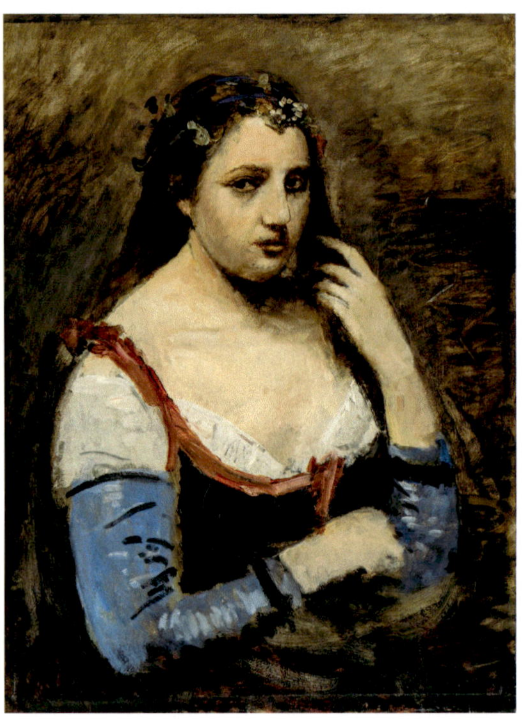

Although Camille Corot is known primarily for his harmonious and delicate landscapes, he also painted many figural works in the last two decades of his life. He often portrayed his female models dressed in Italian or Oriental clothing in life-size, half-length compositions. These paintings constitute a certain transition between portraits examining the sitter's individual features, personality, and state of mind, and head studies depicting a more idealised, general character.

His models are most often depicted in a natural or studio environment, but the brownish, dark background of the Budapest painting titled after the flowers decorating the woman's hair, remains indefinite. The hand movement of the round-faced model adjusting her hair, and her questioning look as she turns to the viewer provide the sensation of a captured moment. The unfinished, sketch-like painting gives insight into the artist's working method: Corot first sketched the dark background and then rendered the lighter tones. X-radiographs of the painting as well as visible alterations show that Corot was uncertain about the position of the arms and the tilt of the head, and that he repainted the composition in several places. – AZSK

Kovács 1957, 89–91 | Illyés 2001, 81-83

Wilhelm LEIBL

(Cologne, 1844 – Würzburg, 1900)

Portrait of Pál Szinyei Merse, 1869 | Oil on canvas, 139.5 × 102 cm
Donated by Pál Szinyei Merse in 1900 | Inv. no. 10.B

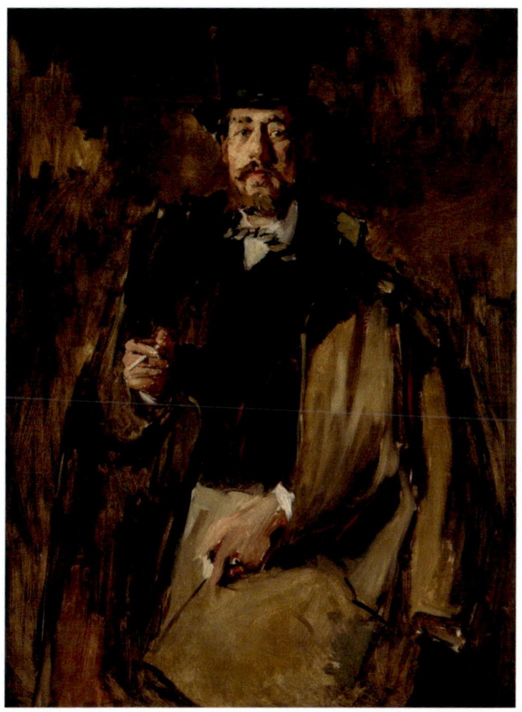

On account of his carefully observed rural genre scenes and precise rendition of human figures, Wilhelm Leibl is considered one of the most important figures of German Realism. His artistic approach was deeply influenced by Gustave Courbet, who had met with great success at the international exhibition in Munich in 1869. The German public – not least, Leibl, a student at the local academy – welcomed his works with admiration. The young painter met Courbet on several occasions during the Frenchman's stay in the Bavarian capital, and witnessed firsthand the dynamic, almost fevered tempo with which he painted.

Leibl made this portrait of Pál Szinyei Merse, his Hungarian friend and fellow student at the Munich Academy, in just a couple of hours, working under the spell of Courbet's example. He painted it directly onto the canvas, without making any preparatory studies. He executed this experiment with verve and boldness, breaking away from his methodical, meticulous realism. Leibl focused on the face and rendered the body in a sketchy manner, using tones of brown. His diffuse yet forceful brushwork shows that, besides Courbet, Leibl had also studied seventeenth-century Dutch painting, in particular the art of Frans Hals. – AZSK

Budapest 2021–2022a, cat. no. 113 | *Zurich–Vienna* 2019–2020, cat. no. 13

Albert-Ernest CARRIER-BELLEUSE

(Anizy-le-Château, 1824 – Sèvres, 1887)

Woman with Lilac, model: ca. 1880; cast: 1884 | Terracotta, 60 × 37 × 27 cm

Transfer, 1950 | Inv. no. 56.7.U

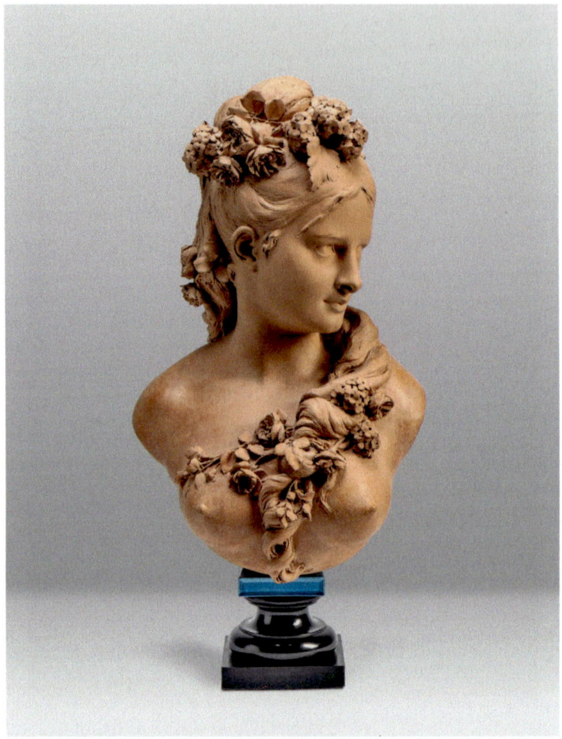

During his successful career, Albert-Ernest Carrier-Belleuse worked in many different fields of sculpture: besides regularly exhibiting portraits and statues inspired by mythological themes at the Paris Salon, he produced works of applied art and architectural ornamentation, and in 1875 he was appointed artistic director at the Sèvres porcelain factory. As one of the most sought-after sculptors of the Second Empire, he headed a busy workshop, even taking under his wing the young Auguste Rodin, who was his student and assistant between 1864 and 1871. The influence of the Italian Renaissance, along with the playfulness, grace, sensuality, and dynamism of the French Rococo are all perceptible in his work.

Carrier-Belleuse created numerous decorative busts of coquettish young women, in bronze, marble, and terracotta. These fantasy figures were individualised by their decorative elements – fruits, flowers, or drapery. The Budapest bust is one such figure: with her rounded shoulders, full breasts, and alluring gaze, she embodies the female ideal of the period, her charms enhanced by the clusters of lilac and roses threaded into her long hair. – AZSK

Illyés 2001, 116–117

Charles-Édouard BOUTIBONNE

(Pest, 1816 – Wilderswil / Interlaken, 1897)

Portrait of Baroness László Majthényi, 1862 | Oil on canvas, 121 × 85 cm

Purchased from László Protics, 1914 | Inv. no. 359.B

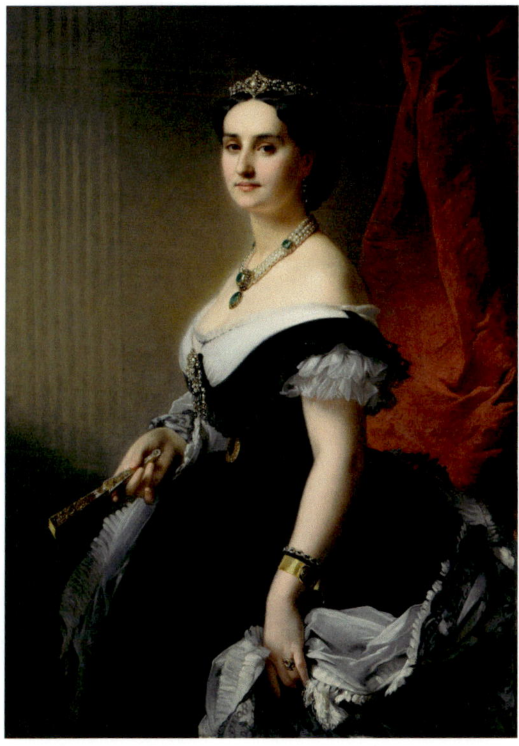

Charles-Édouard Boutibonne was born in Pest to French parents. He was trained by his father, Louis, a drawing master in Pest, later studying under Friedrich von Amerling in Vienna between 1832 and 1843. He then moved to Paris, where he was an assistant to the German painter Franz Xaver Winterhalter, who produced portraits of royalty and wealthy patrons in the then fashionable academic style. Boutibonne became successful under Winterhalter's patronage, painting genre scenes of elegant drawing rooms and portraits of the aristocracy, including Napoleon III and the Empress Eugénie. His work was regularly shown at the Paris Salon, as well as in Vienna and Budapest. He painted this portrait of Natália, wife of Baron László Majthényi, hereditary member of the Hungarian Upper House and lord lieutenant of Hont County, in Paris in 1862. The baroness poses before a plain background wearing a black velvet gown and lace shawl, with a tiara on her head, a large, matching brooch, and several strands of pearls set with emeralds. The tactile rendering of the different fabrics and finishes, and the use of subtle colour contrasts, are a testament to the painter's technical virtuosity. – AS

Fukuoka–Matsuyama–Tokyo 1994, 57, 152

Jozef ISRAËLS

(Groningen, 1824 – The Hague, 1911)

The Orphans of Katwijk, 1866 | Oil on canvas, 85 × 117.5 cm
Bequest of Count János Pálffy, 1912 | Inv. no. 255.B

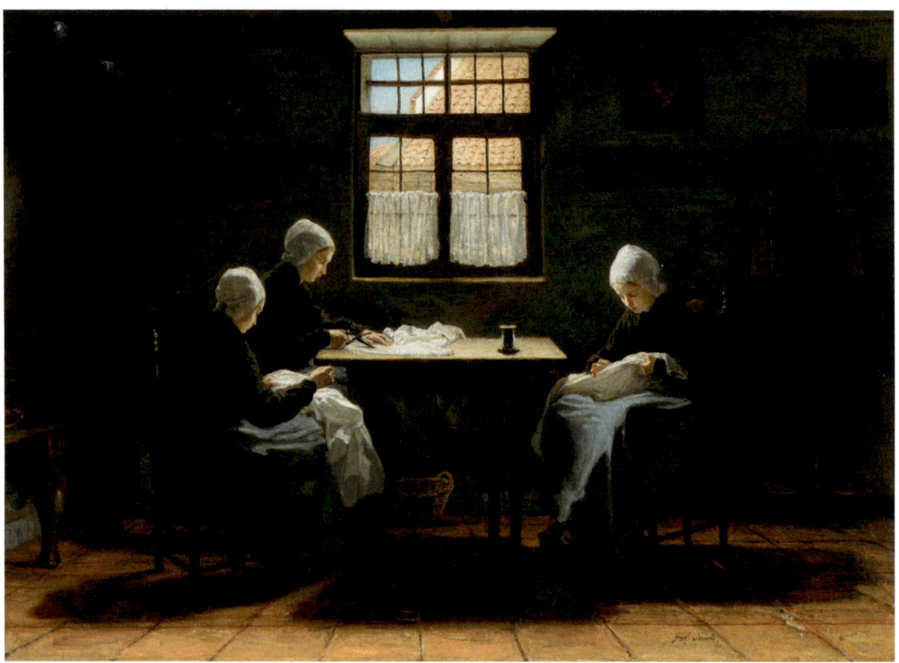

Jozef Israëls, one of the most significant artists of The Hague School, completed his studies in Amsterdam and at the École des Beaux-Arts in Paris. He then immersed himself in the study of the Barbizon school and the old Dutch artists, of whom Rembrandt exerted especially great influence on him. During his early period, he depicted romantic and historical scenes, but these early works did not bring him success. He returned to the Netherlands, and while staying in Zanvoort he discovered new themes through the observation of nature and rural life,thereby completely transforming his style and technique. His painting *The Orphans of Katwijk* received unanimous critical acclaim when it was shown at the 1866 Paris Salon. Sitting around a table in a humbly furnished room, we see three seamstresses in puritanical dress, wearing linen bonnets. The light filtering through the half-curtained window reflects off the snow-white fabrics, and the faces of the orphans. They do not speak, but instead concentrate on their monotonous work. Contemporary critics interpreted the work as a symbol of pure, Protestant lifestyle, with the three orphaned girls embodying simplicity, purity and honest toil.
– AS

Groningen–Amsterdam 1999–2000, 164, 165, 167 | *Tokyo* 2019, 169, 286, cat. no. 83

Eduard FRANKFORT

(Meppel, 1864 – Laren, 1920)

Studying the Talmud, ca. 1890 | Oil on canvas, 50 × 68 cm
Bequest of Count Dénes Andrássy, 1913 | Inv. no. 285.B

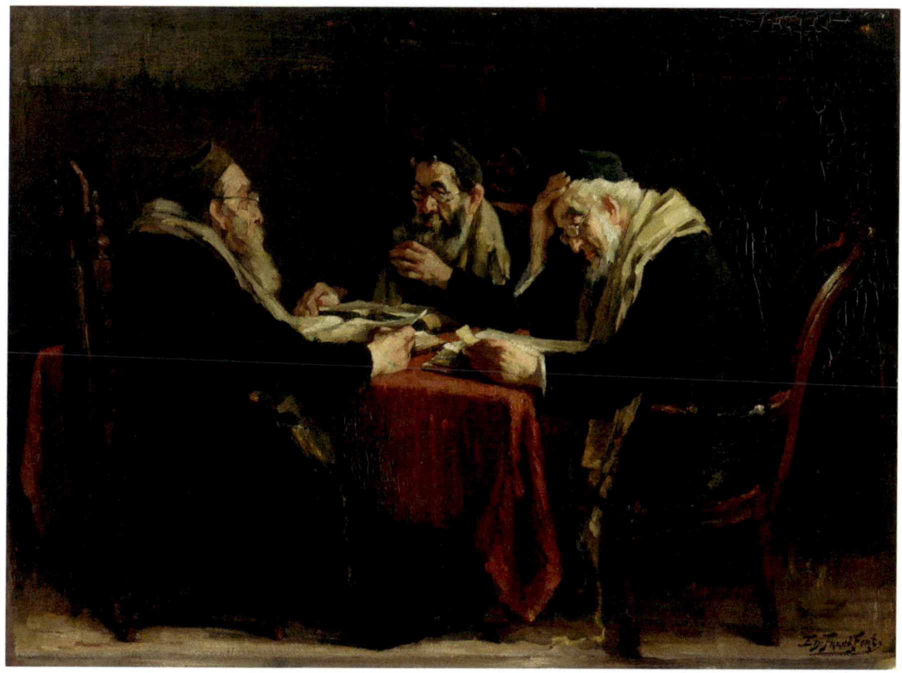

Born into a deeply religious Jewish family, Eduard Frankfort devoted himself to painting at a very early age. After formal training, first at the Royal Academy of Fine Arts in Amsterdam, then in Antwerp, he specialised in depictions of Jewish religious ceremonies and everyday life. In his paintings of religious ceremonies, he generally avoided the use of the slightly monotonous browns typical of the work of most students of Jozef Israëls, achieving chiaroscuro effects by using a wider palette of colours. In *Studying the Talmud*, however, the influence of Israëls is clearly apparent. The table, covered with a heavy burgundy tablecloth, and the three rabbis seated around it, dressed in traditional garments as they study the most important writings of Judaism, are all that stand out against the dark brown tones of the almost entirely homogeneous background. There are several known versions of this romanticised depiction of the scholars. The Budapest painting was probably purchased at the 1909 International Art Exhibition in Munich by Count Dénes Andrássy, who then left it in his will to the Hungarian state, together with his entire art collection. – AS

Budapest 1995–1996, 70 | Weiss-Blok 2017, 273–275

Alfred STEVENS

(Brussels, 1823 – Paris, 1906)

Woman with Harp, ca. 1870 | Oil on canvas, 80 × 57 cm | Purchased from Amélie Duez
at the 1908–1909 winter exhibition of the HNSFA | Inv. no. 218.B

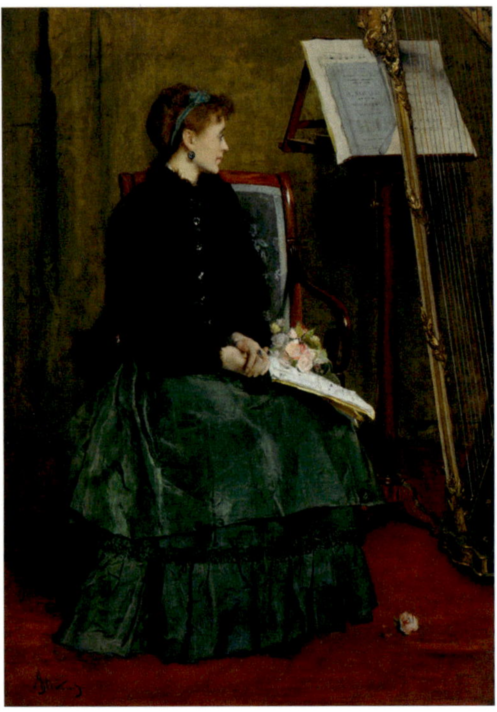

Belgian artist Alfred Stevens made a successful career in Paris, quickly rising to fame with his colourful, charming depictions of modern, fashionable women. His female figures are true epitomes of Parisian chic, often shown in sophisticated interiors, lost in lonely reverie.

Compared to some of his more exuberant *parisiennes*, the protagonist of the Budapest painting, whose model is unknown, is a rather modest, humble figure, sitting in an armchair with a few sheets of paper (maybe sheet music) and a lovely fresh bouquet resting in her lap. On the music stand, one can recognise the score of Mozart's opera *The Abduction from the Seraglio.* We witness a moment of waiting and contemplation, but her expression escapes us as she turns her face towards the instrument. The artist paid great attention to the rendering of her attire, with additional care for the deep green satin skirt, which gave the work one of its several titles, *Woman in Green.* Also called *The Harpist* or the *Rehearsal,* the painting once belonged to French artist Ernest Ange Duez, himself a renowned painter of the *parisienne.* The Museum of Fine Arts acquired the painting directly from his widow, the amateur singer Amélie Duez. – AZSK

Brussels–Amsterdam 2009, cat. no. 30 | *Tokyo* 2019, cat. no. 73

Albert NEUHUYS

(Utrecht, 1844 – Locarno, 1914)

Seamstress, ca. 1870–1876 | Oil on canvas, 60 × 50.3 cm
Purchased from the HNSFA's 1908–1909 winter exhibition | Inv. no. 215.B

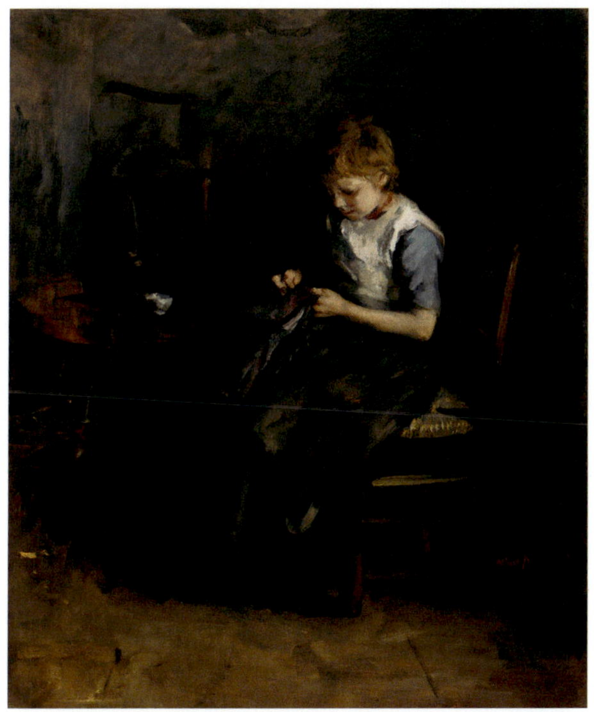

Albert Neuhuys initially worked in a lithographer's studio, and it was only when the studio went bankrupt that he turned to painting. Between 1868 and 1872, he studied at the Royal Academy of Fine Arts in Antwerp. Up until the late 1860s, he chiefly produced historical paintings, genre scenes and portraits. On returning to his native country, he lived first in Amsterdam, moving to the Hague in 1875. It was then that he made the acquaintance of Jozef Israëls, Anton Mauve, and Jacob and Matthijs Maris, the country's foremost artists. His return and his contact with artists of the Hague School, led to a change in Neuhuys's choice of subjects: he portrayed the everyday lives of agricultural labourers and weavers in their own homes, and favoured interiors.

The artists of the Hague School enjoyed huge international popularity in the late nineteenth century, including in Hungary. This painting won a state gold medal at the 1908–1909 winter exhibition at the Budapest Kunsthalle, after which it was purchased by the Museum of Fine Arts. In this intimate work, the figure of the little seamstress, absorbed in her work, is set against an extremely dark, almost homogeneous background of brown and blue tones. – RM

Heijbroek and Wouthuysen 1999, 54 | Matits 1995, 69–70

Franz von LENBACH

(Schrobenhausen, 1836 – Munich, 1904)

Katinka Kendeffy, Wife of Count Gyula Andrássy, 1875 | Oil on wood, 94 × 72.5 cm
Purchase, 1999 | Inv. no. 72.10.B

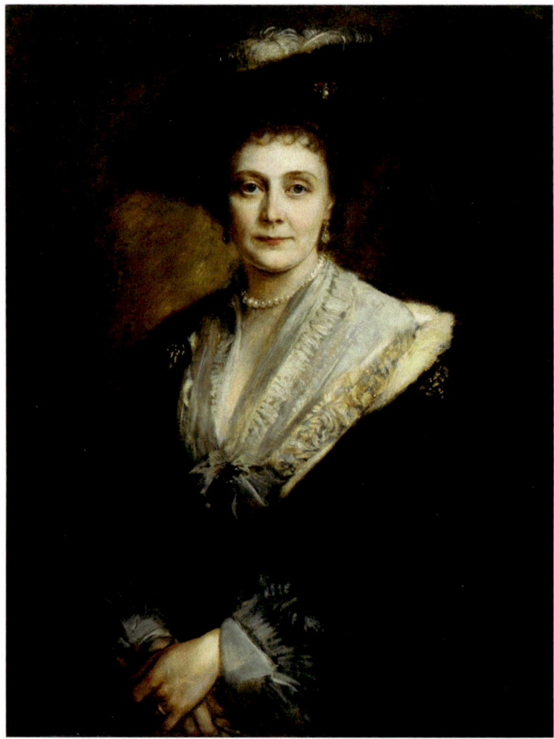

From the 1870s, Franz von Lenbach was one of the most popular portraitists in Europe. He was commissioned by aristocrats and politicians, and his clientele included the German emperors Wilhelm I and II, Otto von Bismarck, Franz Joseph I of Austria, Richard Wagner, and even Pope Leo XIII. Among the elite of Viennese society, he met the legendary patron of the arts Gyula Andrássy, foreign minister of the Austro-Hungarian Monarchy, and his wife, Katinka Kendeffy, who sat for this portrait.

    The countess's face, executed in delicate, diaphanous layers that radiate the intensity of her presence, is set in relief by the sketchy background and her baroque clothing. The white feather, pearl, and lace, gleaming against the brownish tones, has been painted in vigorous, visible brushstrokes. The popularity of costume portraits such as this was due in part to the masquerades enjoyed by the social elite and artistic circles. Hans Makart, the "Painter Prince" of Vienna, organised many such gatherings, at which his good friend Lenbach was a frequent guest. Besides Makart, the influence of Rembrandt is also striking in this painting, the allusion to the Dutch Master's portraiture reflecting the social standing of Lenbach's subject. – DS

Munich 1986–1987, 272, cat. no. 108

Cyprien GODEBSKI

(Méry-sur-Cher, 1835 – Paris, 1909)

Bust of Mihály Zichy, model: 1879; cast: 1879 | Bronze, 57 × 49.5 × 32 cm
Purchased from the artist, 1879 | Inv. no. 8367.U

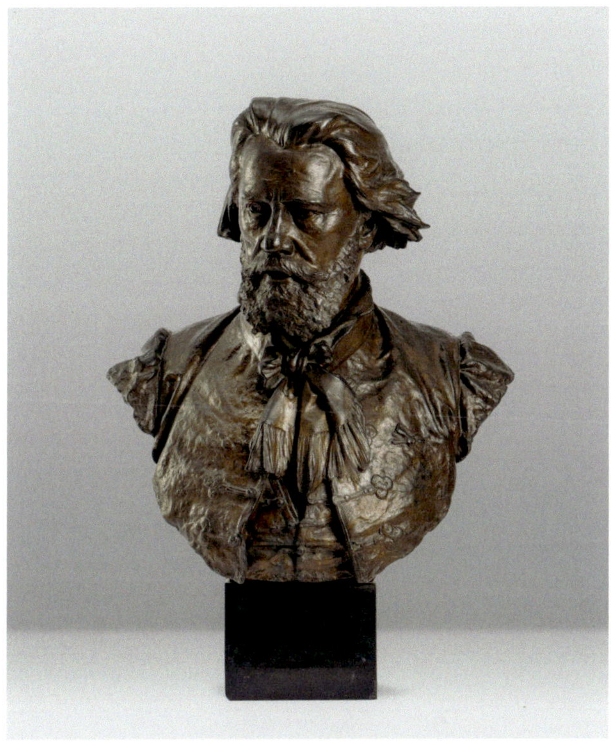

Cyprien Godebski, a French sculptor of Polish descent, achieved huge success with his portraits, allegorical compositions, and public monuments in France, Poland, and Russia alike. His circle of acquaintances included the Hungarian aristocrat, who, like him, enjoyed a successful and diverse international career: Zichy's romantic paintings and literary illustrations brought him popularity in his native country and Russia, while in Saint Petersburg he was employed in the court of the tsar. From 1874, Zichy lived in Paris, although he left the French capital in 1879, due partly to the controversy surrounding his daring allegorical composition *The Triumph of the Genius of Destruction*, a monumental painting addressing contemporary political issues that he submitted to the 1878 Paris Exposition. This may have been when Godebski produced this bust of the painter, shown at the 1880 Paris Salon. The sculpture depicts Zichy in a confident pose, capturing his expressive features and passionate character as well as the details of his Hungarian-style clothing, hair, and thick beard. Godebski dedicated the work to his friend, "an outstanding artist and true patriot". – AZSK

Berkovits 1964, 91 | Illyés 2001, 106–108

Louis-Ernest BARRIAS

(Paris, 1841 – Paris, 1905)

Bust of Mihály Munkácsy, 1879 | Bronze, 66 × 56 × 31 cm
Transfer, 1973 | Inv. no. 73.1.U

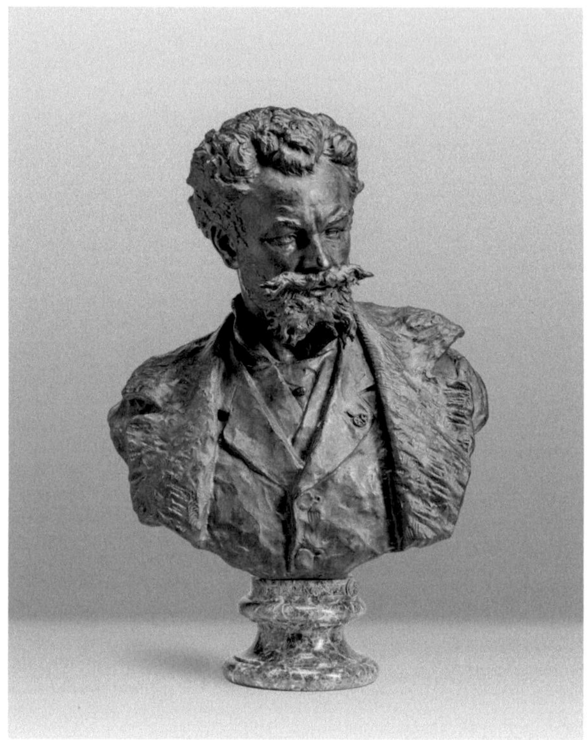

Mihály Munkácsy was one of the first Hungarian painters to gain widespread success in Paris, where he lived and exhibited regularly between 1870 and 1896. This bust was made at the time of the triumphant exhibition of *Milton dictating "Paradise Lost" to his Daughters* in the Austro-Hungarian section of the 1878 World's Fair in Paris, which earned him a gold medal and further increased his popularity.

The acclaimed, well-established sculptor Ernest Barrias was among Munkácsy's Parisian friends, and the Hungarian artist owned several of his works. Barrias exhibited this portrait of the painter at the Paris Salon in 1879. The critics lauded the dynamism of the likeness and its resemblance to the model. Barrias took special care to capture the painter's wavy hair and his thick moustache and beard, which the French public considered to be rather exotic. Munkácsy kept the bust for the rest of his life, presenting it in a prominent place in his elegant Parisian studio. After his death, it passed on to his widow, who then bequeathed it to the Hungarian state. Another version of the bust is displayed at the New York Public Library, together with Munkácsy's large painting of Milton. – AZSK

Lafenestre, 1908, 17, 96, 109 | *Budapest* 2005, 224, 225, cat. no. 119

Friedrich August von KAULBACH

(Munich, 1850 – Ohlstadt bei Murnau, 1920)

Portrait of Mrs Mihály Munkácsy, 1886 | Oil on canvas, 110 × 75 cm
Bequest of Mrs Mihály Munkácsy, 1917 | Inv. no. 373.B

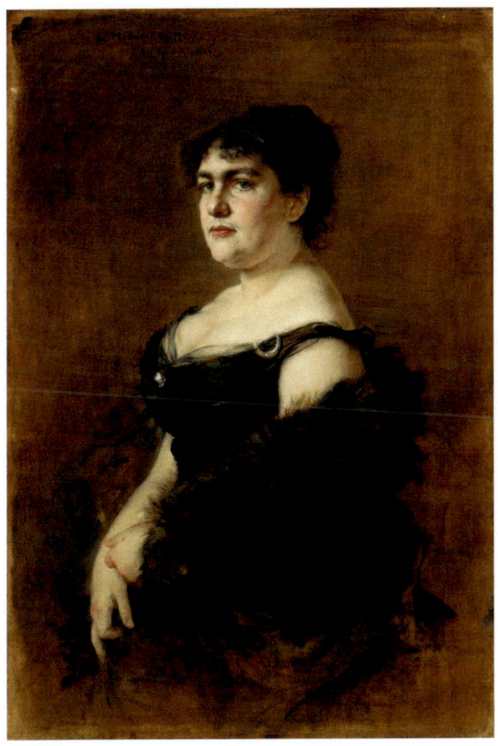

Friedrich August von Kaulbach's portrait of Mrs Mihály Munkácsy, née Cécile Papier, widow
of the Baron de Marches of Luxembourg, was painted in 1886. According to contemporary
sources, it hung in pride of place in the salon of the Munkácsys' mansion in Paris.

Besides offering emotional support, Cécile played an important role in her husband's career, contributing to his success through her efforts. Here, too, she is portrayed as
a confident and determined woman. The painting enjoyed international acclaim in its own day:
it featured prominently at the international portrait exhibition organised in Brussels in 1890.

Kaulbach has skilfully combined the realistic portrayal of his model with his virtuoso
depiction of her elegant, low-cut black dress and fur wrap. The model's pose, the wealth of
detail, and the delicate rendering of the skin are reminiscent of Titian's work *Girl in a Fur*. Portraits of this type generally give emphasis to the model's slenderness, thus Kaulbach, bearing
in mind Cécile's fuller figure, has deftly concealed her hips. The painting was acquired by the
Museum of Fine Arts in 1917 from the widow's bequest. – BIB

Bonn 2018, 164–165

Mathias SCHMID

(Tyrol, 1835 – Munich, 1923)

The Moralist, 1872 | Oil on canvas, 102.5 × 131 cm
Bequest of Count János Pálffy, 1912 | Inv. no. 257.B

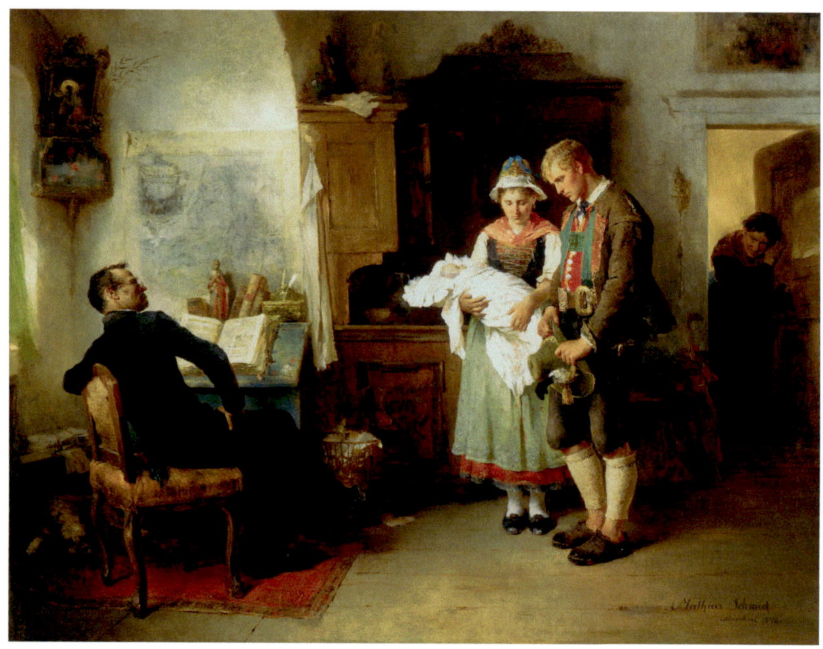

Mathias Schmid studied at the Academy of Fine Arts in Munich from 1855. He initially favoured religious subjects, although, despite having a patron, he went on to achieve greater acclaim with his humorous engravings depicting Tyrolean folk life, which were published in German periodicals. For many years he shared his time between Munich and Tyrol. On the advice of his friend, the painter Franz von Defregger, he joined the school of painting led by Karl Theodor von Piloty in 1869, and from then on his style and approach were defined by realism. Schmid portrayed the morality of his native country in critical, occasionally humorous paintings. He never dealt with the same theme more than once. His first real artistic breakthrough came at the 1873 World's Fair in Vienna, with the works *Handing in Confession Slips* and *The Moralist*. The latter painting centres on a couple dressed in distinctive Tyrolean costume. They have brought their illegitimate baby to the parsonage and are hanging their heads in shame. The modestly furnished room is decorated with a statue of the Virgin Mary and a map bearing the inscription "TERRA SANCTA PALAESTINA JUDAH ISRAEL". The village priest looks up from his book and stares sternly at the guilty couple with an air of moral superiority. An older woman peeps in at the open door, watching the scene with a smug smile. An engraving of the composition was also produced, attesting to its success. – AS

Luger 1999, 47–48 | Moser-Ernst and Marinelli 2023, 29–30, 153

Wilhelm LINDENSCHMIT

(Munich, 1829 – Munich, 1895)

After Work, Rest is Sweet, 1870s | Oil on wood, 60.5 × 47.5 cm
Purchase, 1875 | Inv. no. 105.B

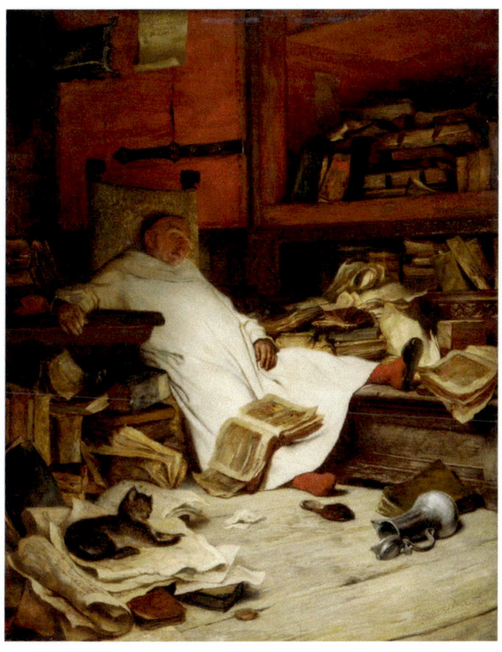

Wilhelm Lindenschmit was given his first painting lessons by his father and his uncle, a copperplate engraver. After studying in Munich, he pursued his training in Antwerp from 1849, and in Paris from 1851 to 1853. In 1875, he was appointed as a teacher of historical painting at the Academy of Art in Munich. He was greatly influenced by seventeenth-century Dutch genre painting, which he combined with the more pastose application of paint and more dynamic brushwork, inspired by the Barbizon School and Gustave Courbet. He undertook comprehensive teaching duties at the Munich academy alongside Karl von Piloty and Wilhelm von Diez, and his class was particularly popular among students interested in the latest French tendencies and the aspirations of the realists and the Barbizon School. Unlike Piloty, he avoided the more theatrical approaches of historicism and strove for historical fidelity. He regarded the art of Anthony van Dyck rather than Peter Rubens as his model. He also undertook work on mythological and religious themes and showed a particular interest in the events of the Thirty Years' War, the Reformation, and the Counterreformation.

The genre painting *After Work, Rest is Sweet* shows a Dominican monk slumbering peacefully among his books. Judging by the upended flagon, he may well have eased the day's burdens by imbibing alcohol of some kind. The warm-toned, homogeneous colouring and veiled humour suggest an inclination for amusing anecdote. – DL

Munich 1979 | Budapest 2009–2010, cat. no. 204

Victor Julien GIRAUD

(Paris, 1840 – Paris, 1871)

Lunch in the Studio, 1864 | Oil on canvas, 170 × 274 cm
Donated by Mrs Frigyes Killián, 1900 | Inv. no. 142.B

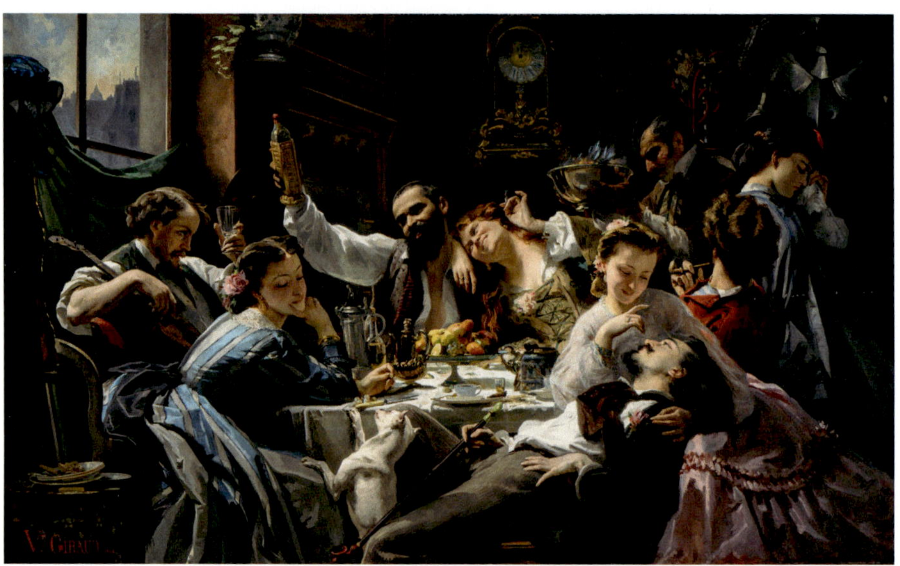

Born into a family of painters, the promising young artist Victor Giraud was killed during the siege of Paris in the Franco-Prussian War. Despite his tragically early death, his few remaining paintings leave no doubt as to his innate talent and artistic ambition.

In this life-sized work, known for many years as *The Bohemians*, he depicts a lively company of men and women at table, abandoning themselves to the pleasures of food and love. When Victor Giraud showed the composition in 1864, at just twenty-four years of age, it was only the second occasion on which his work had been exhibited in the Salon. The painting attracted attention, its libertinism even causing a minor scandal: according to contemporary critics, the permissive behaviour of the flirtatious young crowd – especially that of the coquettish, drinking, smoking woman – was an unworthy subject for such a large-scale, ambitious work of art. Several critics, however, praised the artist's confident, unfettered brushwork and vibrant colours, as well as the accurately observed details of the studio and of the subjects' poses and clothing. This is Giraud's most intimate and personal composition, a celebration of his own circle of friends and fellow artists, and a tribute to the pleasures of youth. – AZSK

Kovács 2017 | *Cologne* 2024, 132–133, cat. no. 8

Giacomo FAVRETTO

(Venice, 1849 – Venice, 1887)

Susanna and the Two Elders, 1887 | Oil on canvas, 91 × 143 cm
Purchased from the artist's heirs, 1899 | Inv. no. 141.B

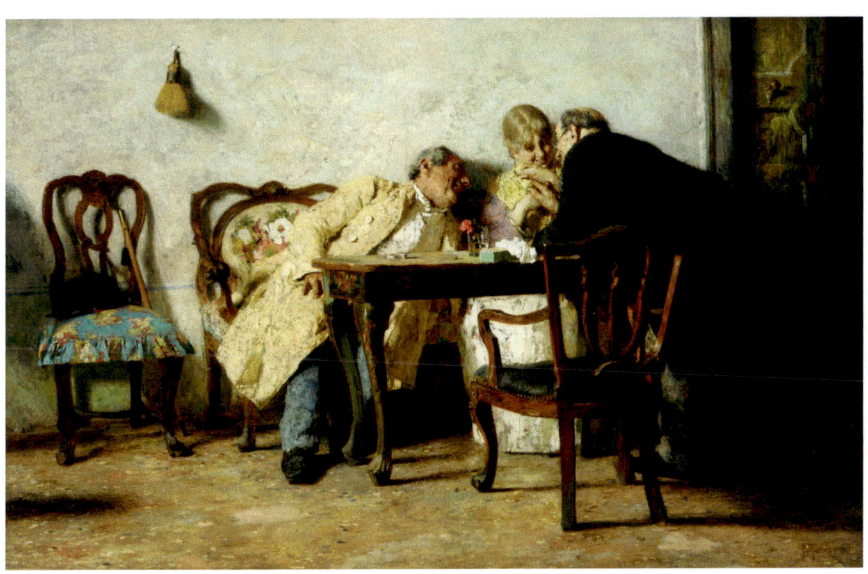

Favretto, who grew up in poverty in Venice, was a frail, sickly child, unable to help with the strenuous tasks in his father's carpentry workshop. Instead, he was employed in a stationery shop until the age of sixteen, sketching in his spare time: his drawings attracted attention, and his talents earned him the opportunity to train at the Academy of Art in Venice. Initially, he painted romantic historical scenes and genre pieces; his originally dry, academic drawing style blossomed into a relaxed and unfettered virtuosity that evoked the richly colourful palette of his great Venetian predecessors, making him the founder of a new kind of "Venetian realism". Widely known by his thirties, the artist was nicknamed "the Goldoni of the brush" by his contemporaries, due to his genre paintings that evoke cheerful scenes of everyday life and the streets and interiors of eighteenth-century Venice.

The fondness for anecdote that characterises Favretto's paintings is already apparent in his first masterpiece, painted in around 1878. In the present work, he reinterprets an Old Testament story from the Book of Daniel, giving it a contemporary setting. In this fresh, spontaneous scene, painted in bright blues and yellows and set in a middle-class interior, two older gentlemen are taking liberties with a young girl, who, while somewhat discomfited by their improper advances, does not reject them. – AL

Cifka 2000, 60–61 | *Rome–Venice* 2010, 50–51, 53, 93, 165, 186

V

Heroic Allegories, Evocative Costumes

René Théodore BERTHON   Wilhelm von KAULBACH

Vlaho BUKOVAĆ   Johann Peter KRAFFT

Hans CANON   Johann Baptist LAMPI the Younger

Josef DANHAUSER   Eugenio LUCAS VELÁZQUEZ

Alphonse Marie-Adolphe DE NEUVILLE   Hans MAKART

Jean-Baptiste Édouard DETAILLE   Jan MATEJKO

Wilhelm von DIEZ   Celestin MEDOVIĆ

Eduard ENGERTH   Raffaele MONTI

Jean Alexandre Joseph FALGUIÈRE   Karl Theodor von PILOTY

Édouard HAMMAN   Herman Frederik Karel TEN KATE

Jean-Baptiste ISABEY   Konstantinos VOLANAKIS (BOLANACHI)

Friedrich August von KAULBACH   Ernst ZIMMERMANN

The works in this section follow the main stylistic trends of the century; they are united by their thematic and intellectual correlations despite inevitable differences in approach. The depiction of scenes from mythology, religious history, or decisive historical events – the evocation of the past and the glorification of a vanished age – remained thematically important throughout the nineteenth century. The epitomisation of significant heroic events and historical figures of the period involved not only the paying of respect but even dressing up in historical masks and costumes.

In the curricula of the academies of Vienna, Munich, and Paris, scenes from cultural tradition ranked highest in the hierarchy of genres, and there were formal rules for their representation. The heroic events of the past and present not only provided the primary subject matter for official art training, and for works that followed the academic artistic style, but also frequently served as a starting point for freer experimentation. At the same time, representatives of "academic" or "official" art can be said to have aimed to achieve success for their historical depictions within the generally accepted imagery of the period, endeavouring to interpret cultic events in the context of their own era.

During the nineteenth century, the aspiration to historical fidelity and the demand for lived experience emerged as competition to the idealism of neoclassicism founded on allegories. Illustrious or tragic scenes in the nation's history took the place of edifying stories from mythology and religion. This sometimes took the form of propagandistic imperial patriotism (Peter Krafft), and at other times – by way of reaction – the expression of national identity. In the middle of the century, the focus turned to the lifelike depiction and accurate reconstruction of historical events, and heroic themes were brought to life by the inclusion of elements of genre painting. Personal, often tragic episodes in the lives of heroes, glorious, decisive battles, and important contemporary or recent events were depicted in such a way that viewers perceived them almost as their own, individual experience.

The demand for historical depictions did not decline in the successive new artistic waves of the last decades of the century. In contrast to the strict technique and didactic understanding of art typical of the masters of the Munich Academy such as Karl von Piloty and Wilhelm von Kaulbach, the great Viennese Painter Prince Hans Makart introduced an emotionally richer, more relaxed style, which became widely fashionable with the new approach to historical painting. Not only did this style influence many of the important representatives of the genre in Central Europe (Jan Matejko, Mihály Munkácsy, Vlaho Bukovać), but Makart's intense colours and powerful colour schemes even became the starting point for the Viennese symbolist reform movement – witness the emergence of Gustav Klimt.

Jean-Baptiste ISABEY

(Nancy, 1767 – Paris, 1855)

Portrait of Napoleon I, 1804–1814 | Oil on ivory, 7 × 5.8 cm
Donated by Mór Vitalis, 1876 | Inv. no. 96.B

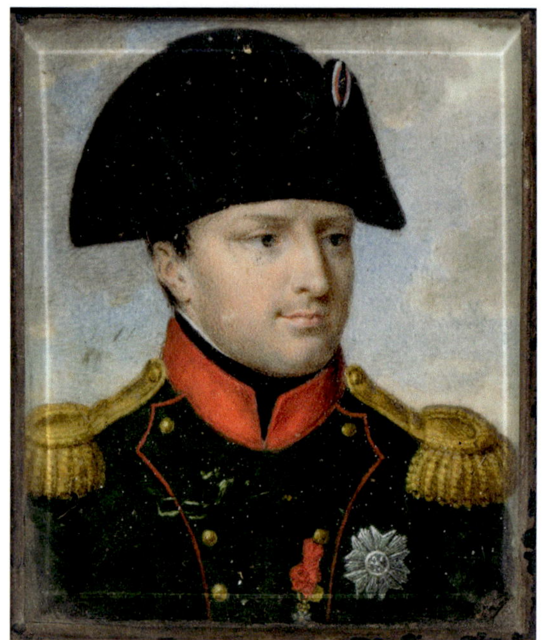

Although Jean-Baptiste Isabey was a pupil of the great historical painter Jacques-Louis David, he earned recognition not by painting monumental battle scenes or representative court portraits but as one of the most eminent miniaturists in France. Despite the country's constantly changing political situation, Isabey enjoyed unwavering popularity throughout his long career, painting portraits of the illustrious figures of the day – royal, imperial, and republican dignitaries, nobles, and revolutionaries. Even Napoleon commissioned many small, easily portable portraits from Isabey and his studio. These portraits were often mounted on the lids of decorative gilt boxes, which were presented to various European dignitaries. The Budapest miniature may perhaps have been one such portrait, depicting Napoleon after he's already crowned himself Emperor. The model's assertive features and the details of his dark-green uniform, complete with the red collar and gold epaulettes of the mounted guards, are rendered with a refined, meticulous technique. The emperor wears his trademark black hat, while pinned to his chest is a silver star, badge of the Grand Officer of the Legion of Honour that he founded. – AZSK

Malmaison-Nancy 2006

Johann Baptist LAMPI the Younger

(Trient [Trento], 1775 – Vienna, 1837)

Portrait of Emperor Francis I, 1804 | Oil on canvas, 281 × 216 cm
Transfer, 1951 | Inv. no. 497.B

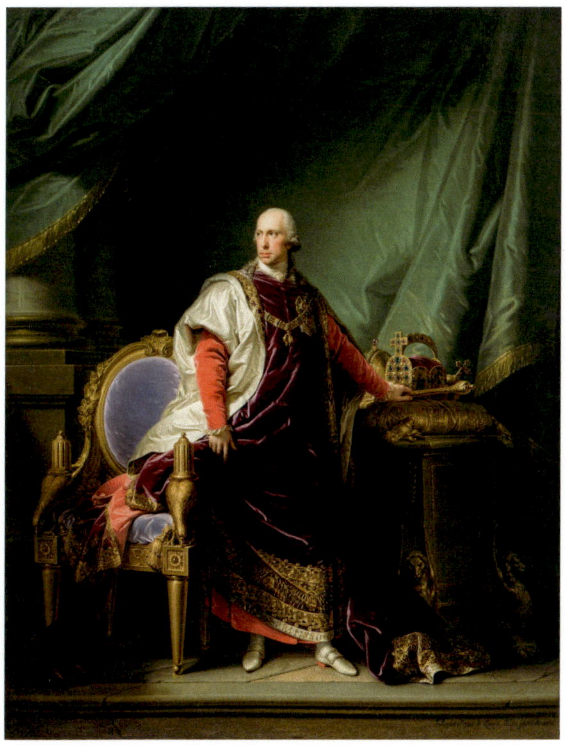

In 1804, after several years in the service of Empress Catherine the Great, Johann Baptist
Lampi the Younger returned to Vienna to take up a post in the court of Francis I, Emperor of
Austria. Lampi's royal portraits are rooted in the classical baroque tradition prescribed by rigid
court protocol and iconography. In this monumental, full-length portrait, produced for an unknown purpose, the emperor wears the full dress uniform of the Order of the Golden Fleece.
The medal of the order, which was founded in 1429 by Philip the Good, Duke of Burgundy,
was bestowed by the Holy Roman Emperor on members of the Catholic aristocracy and was
regarded as the highest state distinction. The emperor also wears the badge of the Order of
Saint Stephen, founded by Maria Theresa. On the table are the crowns of the Austrian Empire
and the Holy Roman Empire. As customary at the time of Louis XVI, the emperor is shown
standing next to his gilt throne, looking to the right, his hand resting on the sceptre: the pose
expresses the ideal of the sovereign active on his people's behalf. The globe and column in the
background are traditional symbols of monarchy, while the rich green velvet drapes enhance
the sense of grandeur. – DL

Trento 2001, 100 | Turin 2004–2005a, 101

Johann Peter KRAFFT

(Hanau, 1780 – Vienna, 1856)

Miklós Zrínyi's Sortie from Szigetvár, 1825 | Oil on canvas, 455 × 645 cm
Commissioned by public contributions, 1820 | Inv. no. 137.B

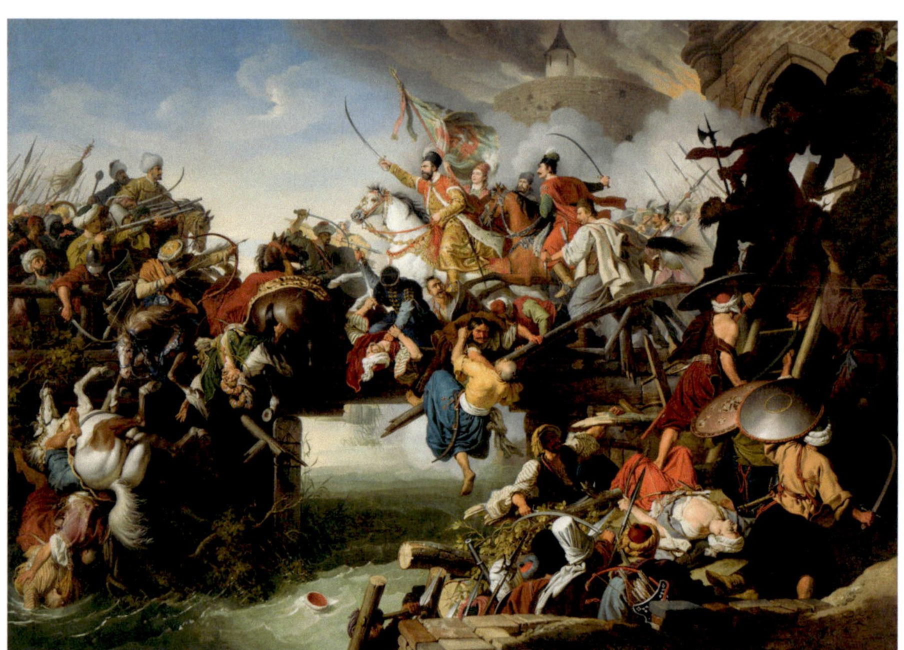

Johann Peter Krafft studied at the Vienna Academy between 1799 and 1802, and in Paris from
1802 to 1804 under Jacques-Louis David. Following a study tour of Italy in 1808, he settled in
Vienna. Besides being the prominent portraitist of the Habsburg Empire, he contributed to the
renewal of Austrian historical painting based on the French model. His large-scale commissions from the court were for dynamic historical paintings filled with life-size figures.

In 1820, Palatine Joseph ordered three large compositions from Krafft for the new
Hungarian National Museum, two of which were eventually produced: *The Coronation of Emperor Francis as King of Hungary*, and the Zrínyi painting. The works are expressions of imperial patriotism and the loyalty of the Hungarian nation to the Habsburg Empire. This image
recalls the final moments of the battle against the Ottomans at Szigetvár in 1566 – the sortie
by the defenders of the fortress. Although, according to reliable historical sources, in the face
of defeat the defenders blew up the castle gate and Zrínyi and his comrades charged out on
foot, Krafft shows the hero on horseback to enhance the dramatic effect. – DL

Cifka 1993b | *Vienna–Hanau 2016*, 112

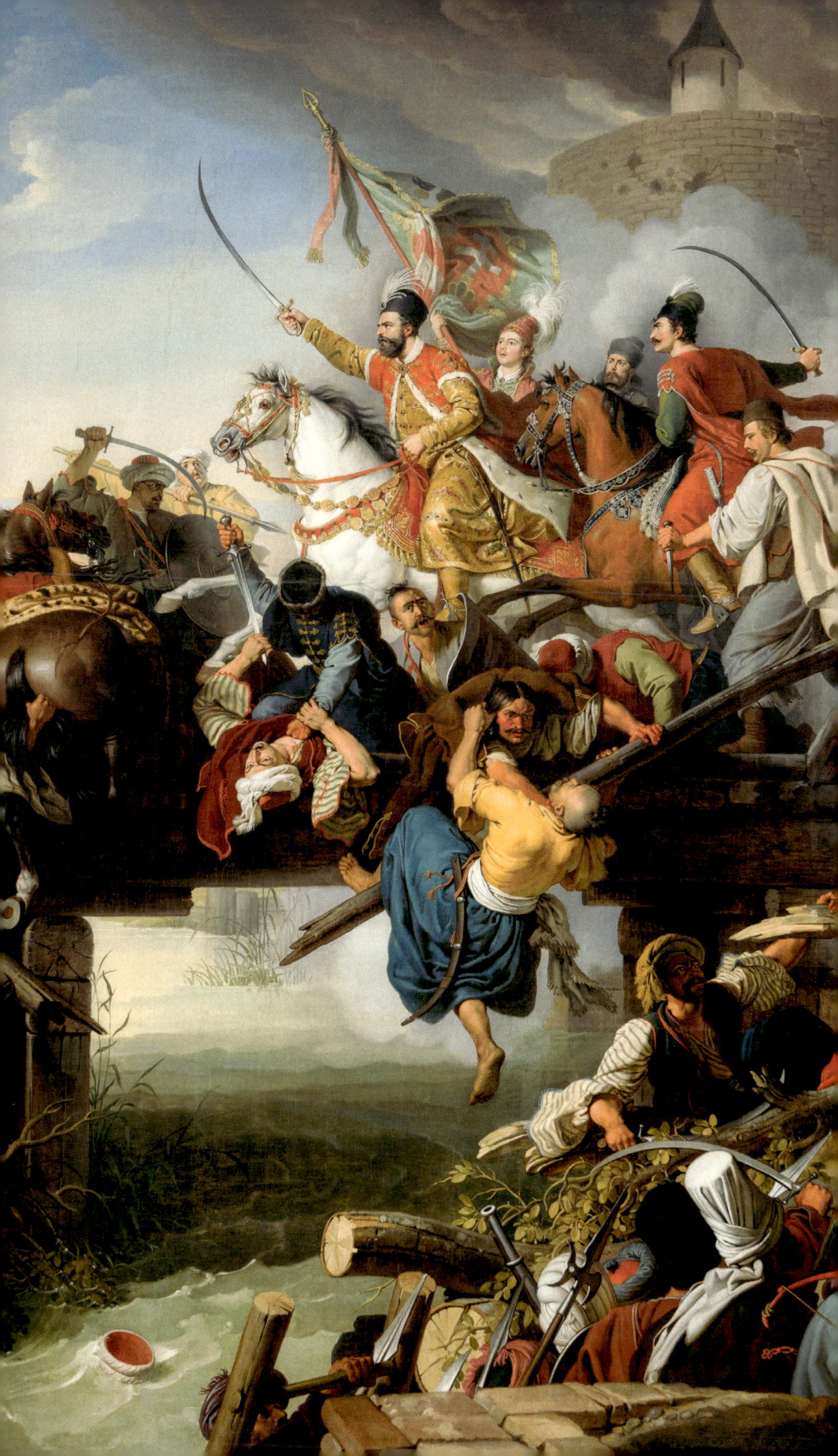

René Théodore BERTHON

(Tours, 1776 – Paris, 1859)

The Founding of the Abbey of Marmoutier by Saint Martin, 1822

Oil on canvas, 260 × 227.5 cm | Transfer, 1951 | Inv. no. 495.B

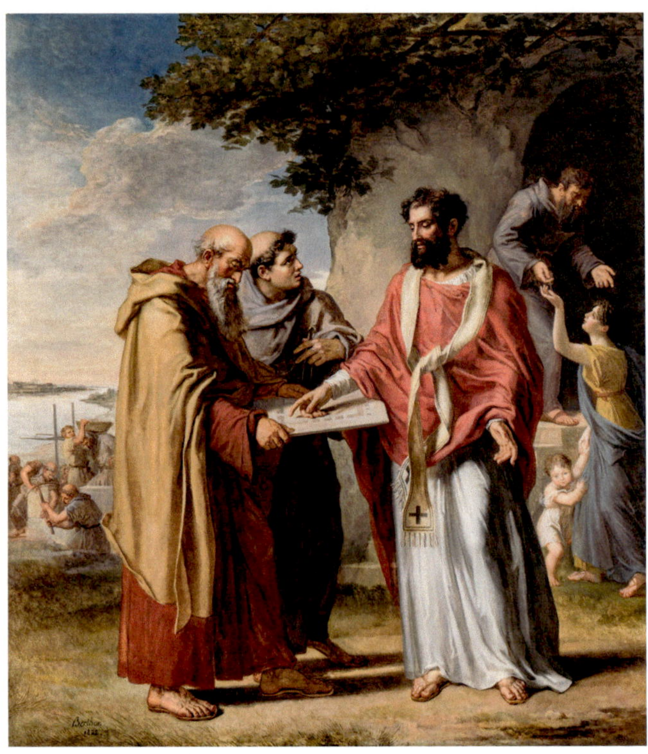

René Théodore Berthon studied the principles of neoclassical painting under Jacques-Louis David: his work is characterised by clear and elegant composition, powerful, elevated gestures, a muted palette, and precise execution. Besides being a successful portraitist, he also painted historical, mythological, and biblical themes and was much in demand during both the Napoleonic period and the Restoration.

It was no doubt due to his being a native of Tours that Berthon was commissioned to paint what was otherwise a rare artistic subject, taken from the life of Saint Martin. Born in 372 in Savaria – now Szombathely, Hungary – the saint founded the Abbey of Marmoutier, one of the earliest monasteries in France, near the city of Tours. In this large-scale painting, shown at the Paris Salon in 1822, Martin appears not in his episcopal robes but wearing a simple, classical garment: he is depicted examining the plans for the new building, while the construction work goes ahead in the background. A Benedictine monk standing at the entrance to the cave behind Saint Martin hands a rosary to a young mother, symbolising the evangelistic work of Martin and his companions. – AZSK

Illyés 2001, 8–10 | *Tours* 2016, cat. no. 13

Josef DANHAUSER

(Vienna, 1805 – Vienna, 1845)

Wallstein Is Buried Beneath an Oak Tree, 1832 | Oil on canvas, 103.5 × 84.5 cm
Donated by Archbishop János László Pyrker, 1836 | Inv. no. 174.B

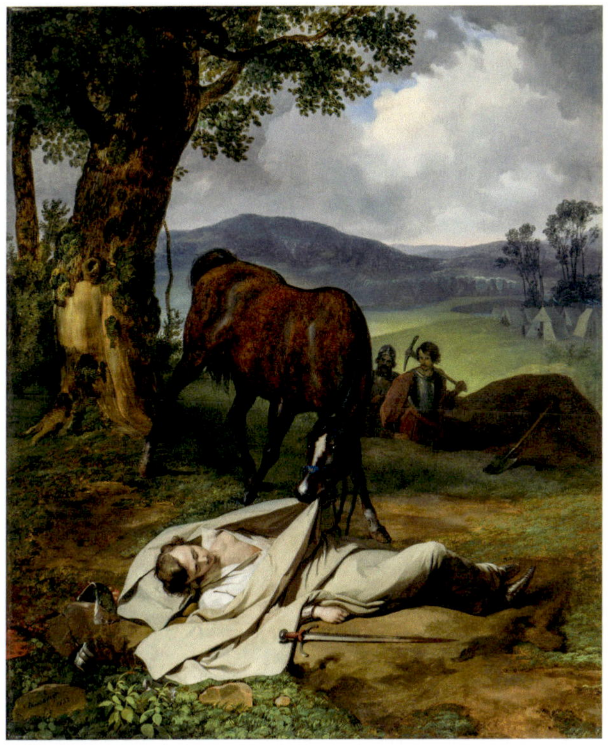

Josef Danhauser began his career as a historical painter. His first significant commission was for a series of paintings dedicated to the German king Rudolf I of Habsburg, legendary founder of the Habsburg dynasty. The basis for these works was the epic poem *Rudolph von Habsburg*, written by János László Pyrker, patriarch of Venice and archbishop of Eger, for which Danhauser produced illustrations for five scenes between 1825 and 1832.

Wallstein is Buried Beneath an Oak Tree is the final, closing work in the series: it shows Count Wallstein, one of the minor characters in the epic, whose moral crisis ended in suicide. Abandoned by his companions, only his horse takes pity on him. The theatrical composition and dramatic lighting lend sentimentality to the young knight's tragic death. Several versions of the painting are known, the Budapest work being the largest and most mature. The painting already clearly demonstrates the young painter's penchant for storytelling, anecdote, and moralising, which a few years later would make him one of the most sought-after genre painters in Vienna. – DL

Cifka 1990–1991, 23 | Grabner 2011, 32

Wilhelm von KAULBACH

(Arolsen, 1804 – Munich, 1874)

Baron István Prónay as Hamlet | Oil on canvas, 235 × 132.5 cm
Purchased from the artist's bequest, 1889 | Inv. no. 104.B

Wilhelm von Kaulbach was one of the most important painters in Munich in the nineteenth century. He became known primarily for his large-scale murals and ceiling paintings, many of which were destroyed in the Second World War. He produced the first version of *The Battle of the Huns* – the work that established his reputation – between 1834 and 1837. Commissioned by his later patron Count Atanazy Raczyński, the work was a source of inspiration for Franz Liszt, who wrote a symphonic poem by the same name in 1857. From 1849, Kaulbach worked for several years as a professor at the Academy of Fine Arts in Munich.

In this painting, Baron István Prónay, a member of an established Hungarian noble family, is depicted in an idealised setting, dressed as Hamlet. The Hungarian aristocrat, who was training to be an artist, was studying in Kaulbach's studio in Munich, where the students organised masquerades. Kaulbach was so taken by Prónay's strange, melancholy character that he produced this portrait of him as an actor in costume. The pensive young man, dressed in black hose, red jacket, and black velvet cape, fixes the viewer with a suggestive, somewhat defiant stare. However, rather than the attributes of an actor, the objects lying beside him on the grass – the portfolio of sketches and the folding stool – are the tools of a painter. The Hungarian National Museum purchased the painting in 1889, directly from Kaulbach's widow. – DL

Ostini 1906 | *Budapest* 2009–2010, cat. no. 160

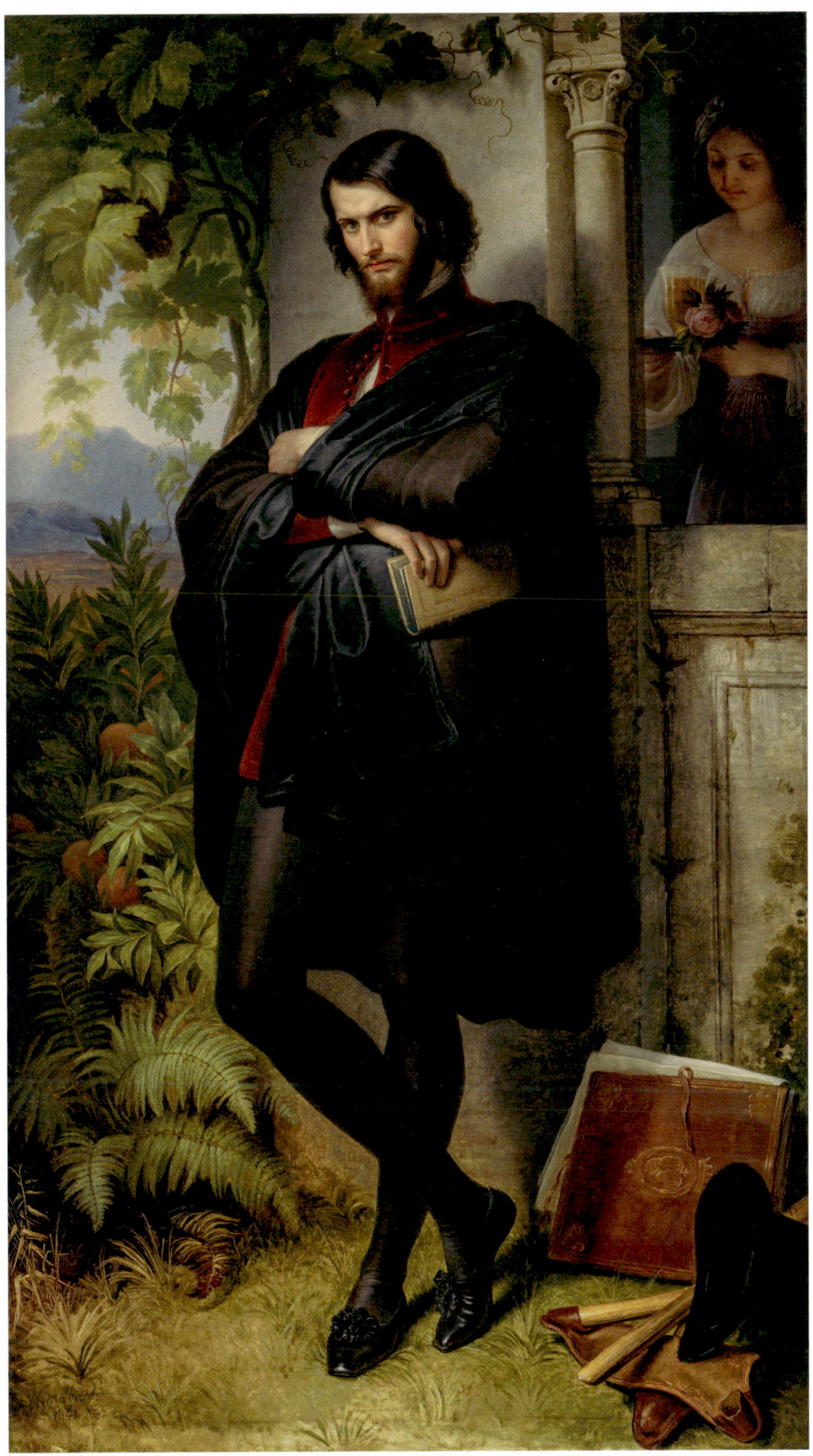

Hans CANON

(Vienna, 1829 – Vienna, 1885)

Portrait of a Man, second half of the 19th century | Oil on canvas, 65 × 52 cm

Donation, 1988 | Inv. no. 88.1.B

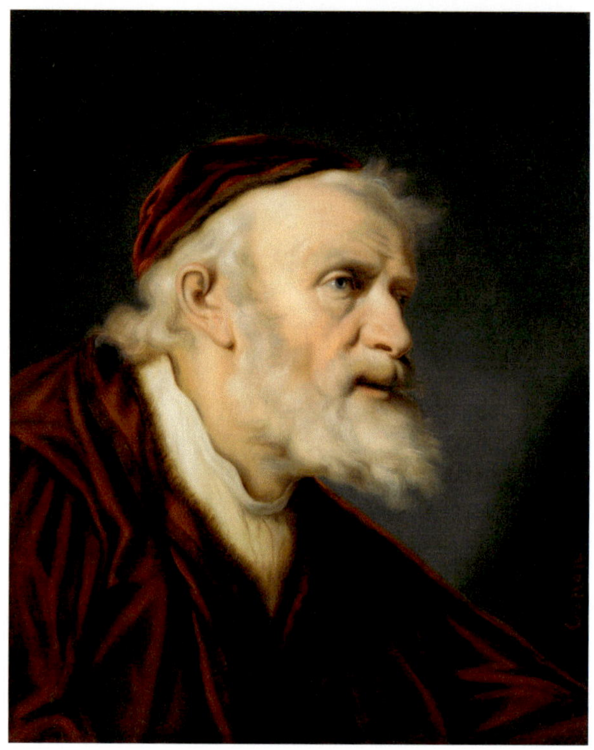

Alongside his contemporary, Hans Makart, Hans Canon was the most important master of Viennese historicism after Carl Rahl. He studied at the Academy of Fine Art in Vienna from 1845, and from 1847 in the studios of Ferdinand Georg Waldmüller and Rahl, while also serving as an officer in the imperial army until 1855. After travelling in the 1860s and 1870s in Western Europe, Italy, and the Ottoman Empire, and following a lengthy stay in Germany, he returned to Vienna in 1875, where initially he worked mainly on commissioned portraits. He was later asked to produce several monumental murals, the most important being the fresco *The Circle of Life* that adorns the cupola of the Natural History Museum in Vienna.

In terms of genre, the *Portrait of a Man* is a role portrait in costume or historicizing genre portrait. The masterfully executed three-quarter profile shows an elderly white-haired man dressed in a Renaissance-style velvet hat and robe. The dark background, white shirt and red gown create a subtle colour harmony with the tones of the man's complexion. The individualised features, furrowed brow, and penetrating gaze replicate the finest traditions of classical portraiture. – DL

Drewes 1994

Herman Frederik Karel TEN KATE

(The Hague, 1822 – The Hague, 1891)

Domestic Bliss, mid-19th century | Oil on canvas, 37 × 57.2 cm
Purchased from the HNSFA's 1875 exhibition | Inv. no. 115.B

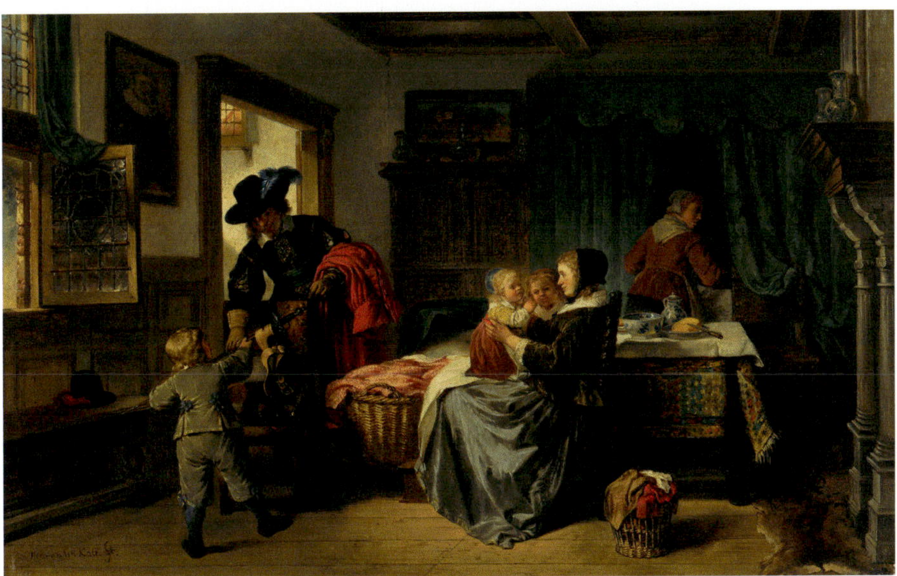

Herman Frederik Karel ten Kate began studying painting privately before enrolling at the Academy of Art in the Hague for one year. In 1841–1842, he visited Belgium, Germany, Italy, and France, and while in Paris, was the protégé of Jean-Louis Ernest Meissonier. In his early career he specialised in scenes from the Thirty Years' War and became popular for his depictions of soldiers. In the 1860s, he was elected director of the Academy of Art in The Hague. However, as the popularity of his work declined, he began to produce rococo scenes and genre paintings. This period saw a revival in the popularity of seventeenth-century Dutch genre painting, inn scenes, and simple depictions of everyday life. Taking seventeenth-century genre painting as his starting point, Ten Kate nevertheless significantly modernised the scenes and costumes. He painted several compositions with the title *Domestic Bliss.* The setting for the Budapest painting is a typically elegant Dutch room with wooden floor and beams, a stove, homely furnishings, and paintings on the wall. The woman of the house plays with her two young daughters, while the head of the family, who has just returned home, shows off his sword to his son. The contemporary popularity of both subject and painter are attested by the fact that this was the first nineteenth-century Dutch painting to be purchased for the public collection in Hungary. – AS

Matits and Sillevis 1992, 14–15 | *Budapest* 1995–1996, 68

Édouard HAMMAN

(Ostend, 1819 – Paris, 1888)

The Agony of Charles IX, 1851 | Oil on canvas, 81 × 68 cm
Bequest of Count János Pálffy, 1912 | Inv. no. 227.B

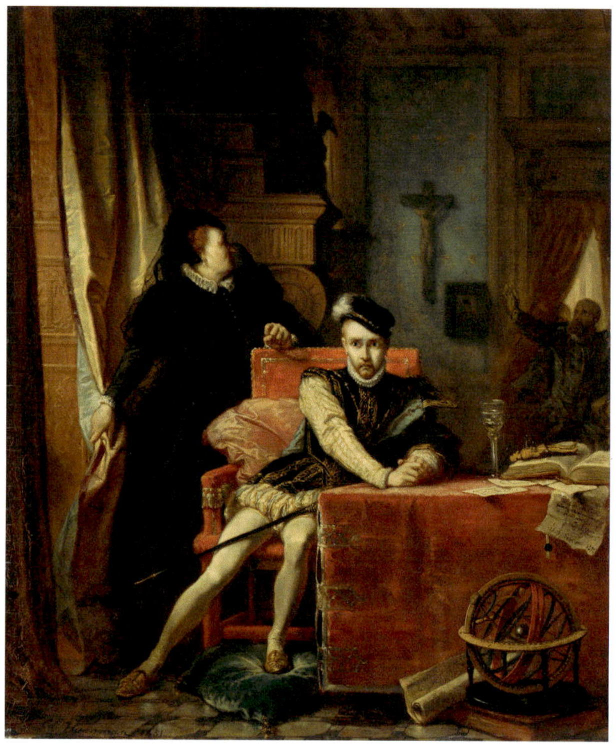

Dramatic episodes from sixteenth-century French history provided inspiration for many romantic historical painters and were a recurring theme in the work of the Belgian artist Édouard Hamman. This painting evokes the most notorious incident of the reign of the French king Charles IX. In 1572, a Catholic mob murdered thousands of Protestants in Paris on the night of Saint Bartholomew's Day. Hamman's scene is set the following morning, when the king, who had ordered the deaths of the Huguenot leaders only, and his mother, Catherine de' Medici, who had instigated the killings, are told of the escalating situation. On the table beside the decree, a wax figure lies on an open book, its body pierced with tiny daggers. This curious motif alludes to a story about Charles IX, according to which the king found a witchcraft poppet in the possession of one of his courtiers, whom he executed on a charge of attempted murder.

Hamman moved to Paris in 1846, where he mastered the colourism of the French Romantics and achieved great renown with works depicting the lives of famous artists, scientists, and monarchs. With their decorative settings and sentimental scenes, his historical genre paintings are reminiscent of contemporary theatrical performances. – CSJB

Térey 1913, 57–58 | Hostyn 1978

Hans CANON

(Vienna, 1829 – Vienna, 1885)

The Death of Philip II, after 1860 | Oil on canvas, 135 × 101 cm
Bequest of János Frohner, 1891 | Inv. no. 125.B

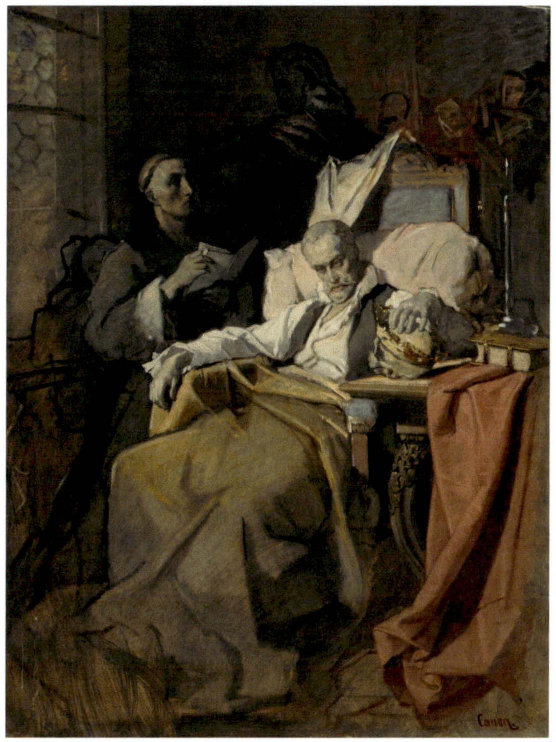

The controversial reign of the Spanish king Philip II of Habsburg, and his death in 1598, were popular subjects among nineteenth-century historical painters. The image of Philip as a religious bigot and proponent of the Inquisition became dominant in historiography, although his death can also be seen as symbolising the end of a glorious era. Severely ill, the king spent his last days in El Escorial, the palace he had had built. Canon's historical genre painting captures the human tragedy of the king's solitary death, as the priests keep their vigil around him. The crowned skull is an allusion to the transience of worldly power. Canon studied at the Academy of Fine Arts in Vienna. After travelling in Eastern and Western Europe, he taught at the Karlsruhe School of Art, founded by the Grand Duke of Baden, returning to Vienna in 1874. For reasons unknown, his painting of the death of Philip II remained unfinished, leaving the firm, vigorous sketch lines and thin layers of dilute paint clearly visible. Interestingly, the same subject was chosen by the artist's pupil, Ferdinand Keller, for the painting that earned him his first international success. – SD

Drewes 1994, 801 | Reyero 1999, 67–81

Karl Theodor von PILOTY

(Munich, 1826 – Ambach, 1886)

Nero Walking on the Embers of Rome, ca. 1861 | Oil on canvas, 446 × 582 cm
Donated by Count János Pálffy, 1872 | Inv. no. 106.B

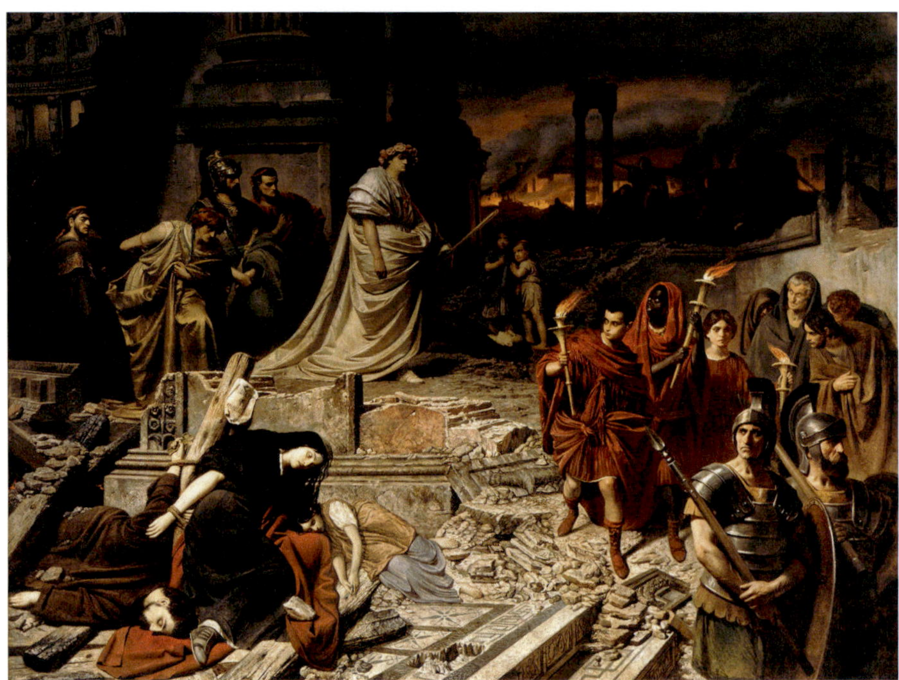

This important early work by Karl von Piloty, the foremost representative of historical painting at the Munich Academy, shows the emperor Nero making his way through the streets of Rome following the great fire in 64 CE. The dramatic composition combines two incidents that took place at different times: the raging fire, which continues to cause devastation in the background, and the execution of the Christian martyrs, who were later used as scapegoats for the catastrophe. Piloty visited Rome in 1858, where he produced many studies and sketches for this painting. The meticulously executed architectural details, the traces of mosaic flooring, and the fragments of the statue of the she-wolf that symbolised the ancient city are all allusions to past glory. Accused by certain ancient historians of deliberately setting fire to Rome, the emperor is shown glancing dispassionately, perhaps even arrogantly, at the remains of the city and at the victims. The tyrant's appearance reflects the image of Nero that emerged in the second half of the nineteenth century: that of a deranged and decadent despot.

The painting was commissioned by Count János Pálffy, however the subject was probably suggested by the artist himself. The collector intended the painting to hang in his palace in Bratislava, although he apparently changed his mind, donating the work to the Hungarian National Museum in 1872. – DS

Härtl-Kasulke 1991, 178–188, cat. no. II.5 | *Munich* 2003, 235–247, cat. no. 10

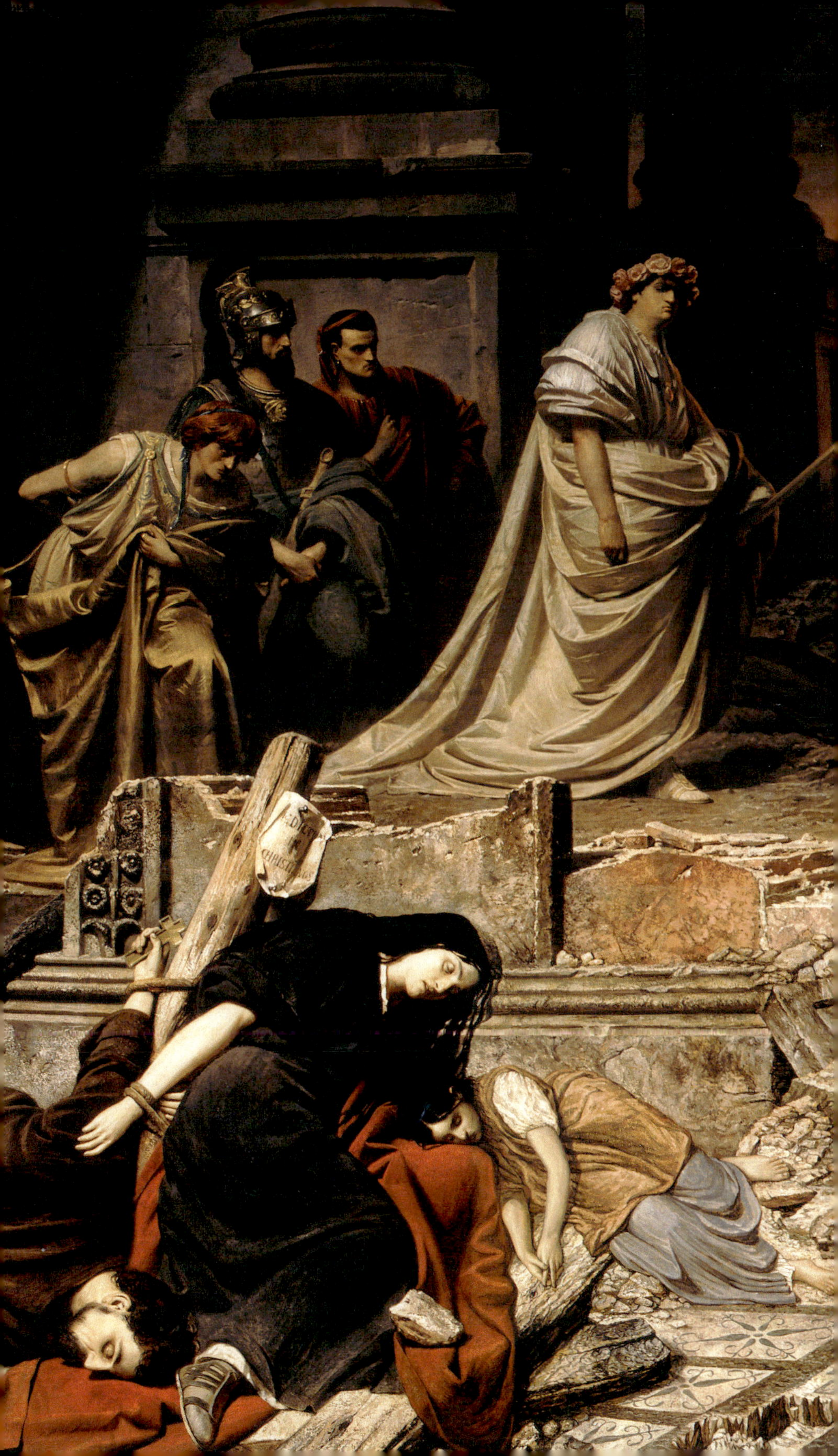
EDICT
CHRISTIANOS

Raffaele [Raffaello] MONTI

(Ticino, 1818 – London, 1881)

Bust of Emperor Ferdinand I of Austria, 1841 | Marble, 71 × 56 × 35 cm
Transfer from the National Museum of Hungarian History, 1943 | Inv. no. 8337.U

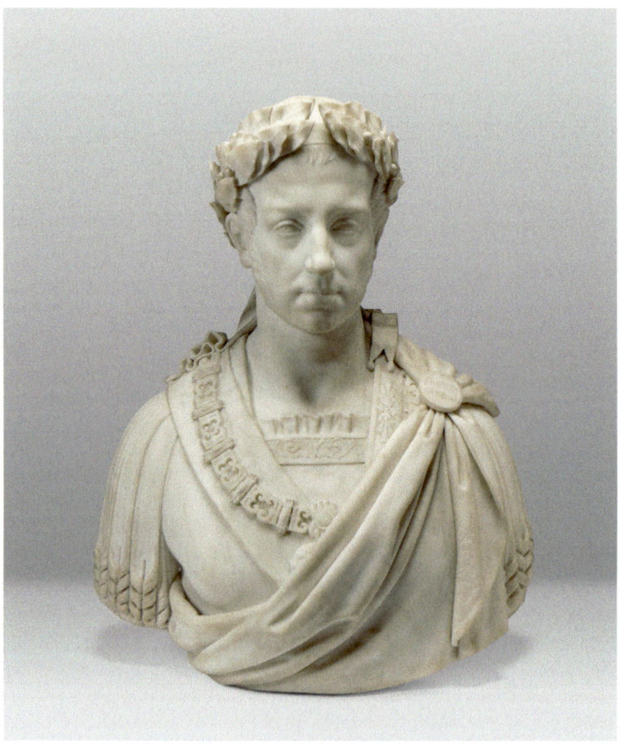

Despite his youth, Monti achieved acclaim in Milan and Vienna thanks to his sculptures. In 1841–1842 he was invited to spend time in Pest to work on the pediment of the Hungarian National Museum then under construction. The fact that he was asked to produce busts of the museum's architect, Mihály Pollack, as well as the president of the Hungarian Academy of Sciences, Count József Teleki, among others, indicates the esteem in which he was held. This archaising, idealised portrait of King Ferdinand V of Hungary and Emperor Ferdinand I of Austria was also produced at around this time. Based on a marble bust of the emperor by the Austrian sculptor Franz Anton Zauner (1796, Belvedere, Vienna), he is shown wearing a laurel wreath and the toga of a Roman emperor. The toga clasp features the royal motto (*Recta Tueri*, or "To defend the right"), while around his neck is the emblem of the Order of the Golden Fleece. The emperor, who was known as "the Benevolent", suffered from severe congenital disorders, including hydrocephalus and epilepsy; under political pressure, he was forced to abdicate shortly after the outbreak of the 1848 Hungarian Revolution in favour of his nephew, Franz Joseph. – AL

Dux 1857, 49 | Peregriny 1900, 543

Eduard ENGERTH

(Pszczyna, 1818 – Semmering, 1897)

The Coronation of Franz Joseph and Elisabeth, 1872 | Oil on canvas, 355 × 430 cm

Transfer, 1948 | Inv. no. 92.6.B

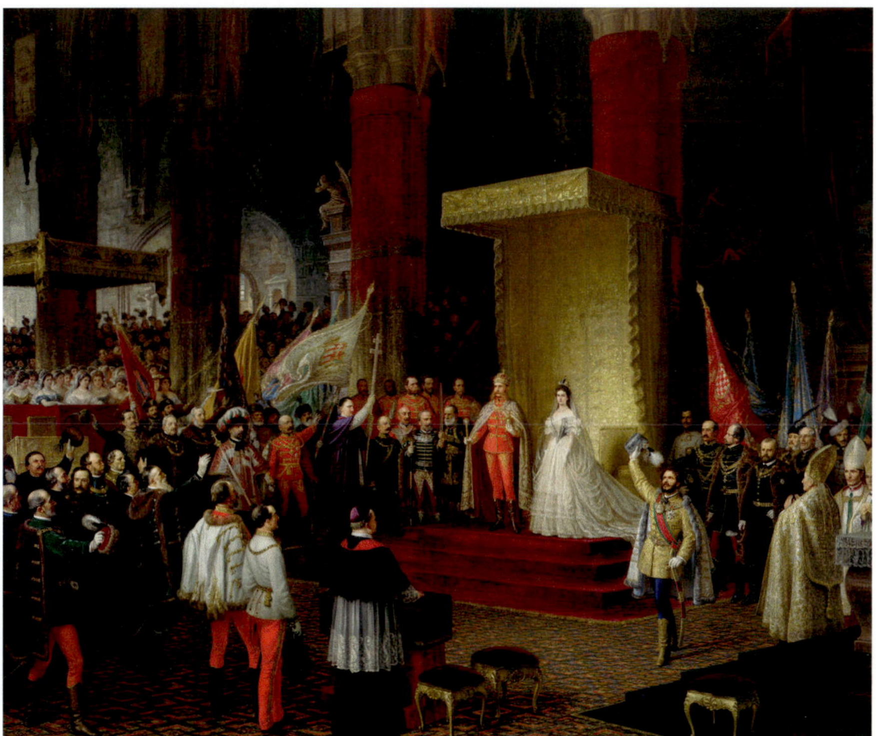

Engerth was probably commissioned by the Viennese court in the spring of 1867 to paint the coronation of Franz Joseph and Elisabeth. Following the restoration of the Buda Castle in the mid-nineteenth century, this large-scale work, which occupies an important place in cultural history, was displayed in one of the imperial rooms. The artist himself was present at the coronation, but there were many sources for the work: contemporary reports, drawings and engravings.

In the gorgeously decorated Church in Budapest, where the coronation took place, Engerth captures the decisive moment when the distinguished congregation – which included, among others, important figures in public office, church dignitaries, and members of the government – shouted a resounding "Long Live the King!" In addition to the royal couple, around thirty notable individuals can be identified in the painting, including Count Gyula Andrássy, Ferenc Deák, and József Eötvös; Engerth even smuggled his own portrait into the work. The combined effect of the composition, the angle of view, and the formality of the figures lends this painting a reserved theatricality. – RM

Vienna 1997, 88, cat. no. 7.3 | Papp 1997, 79–88

Eugenio LUCAS VELÁZQUEZ

(Madrid, 1817 – Madrid, 1870)

2 May 1808, mid-19th century | Oil on canvas, 59.5 × 79 cm

Transfer, 1952 | Inv. no. 480.B

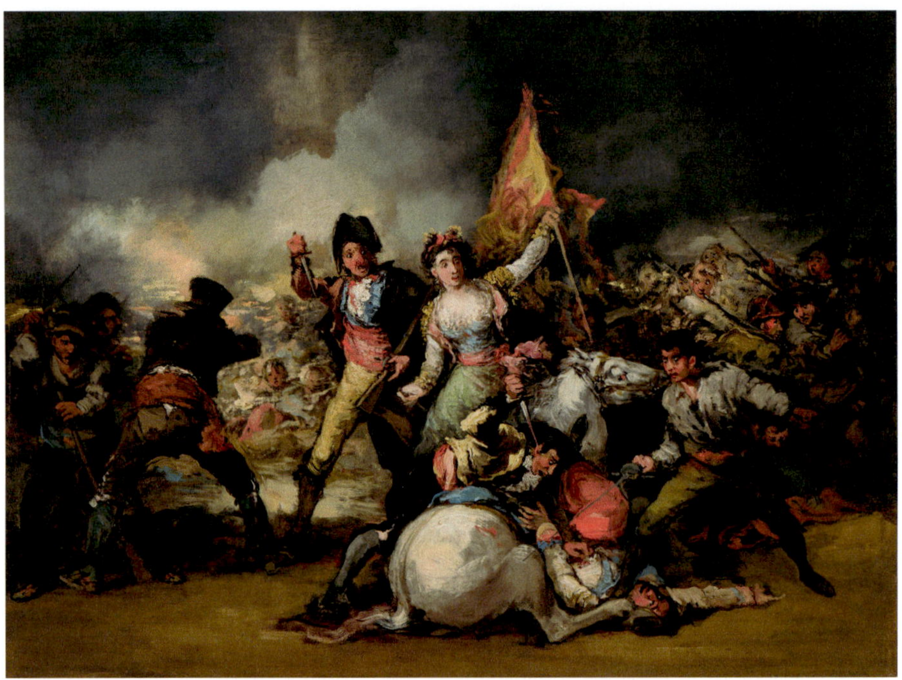

Francisco de Goya had numerous followers, among them Eugenio Lucas, many of whose paintings, including this one, were inspired by themes addressed by the great master. This dramatic, slightly theatrical work, conceived in the spirit of Romanticism, reveals Lucas's profound knowledge of his great predecessor's imagination. It records the moment when, on 2 May 1808, the population of Madrid revolted against the Napoleonic occupation, launching a bitter and furious attack on the French troops. Violence spread immediately through the streets, and although the rebels were shot by the French the following day, the flame of resistance remained unquenched: the uprising marked the beginning of the Spanish War of Independence, which lasted until 1814. In this composition, Lucas drew on his familiarity with Goya's work on the same theme: among other things, he borrowed the motif of the man stabbing the de-horsed Mameluke soldier (an Egyptian mercenary serving in Napoleon's army). The figure of the woman brandishing a flag in her raised left hand, however, is certainly inspired by Eugène Delacroix's 1830 work *Liberty Leading the People*, a painting that made a huge impression on Lucas when he saw it in Paris in 1852. – AL

Arnáiz 1981, 438 | *Madrid–Bilbao* 1996–1997, cat. no. 49

Jan MATEJKO

(Kraków, 1838 – Kraków, 1893)

The Battle of Varna, 1879 | Oil on wood, 58 × 91 cm
Purchased from the HNSFA's 1880 spring exhibition | Inv. no. 102.B

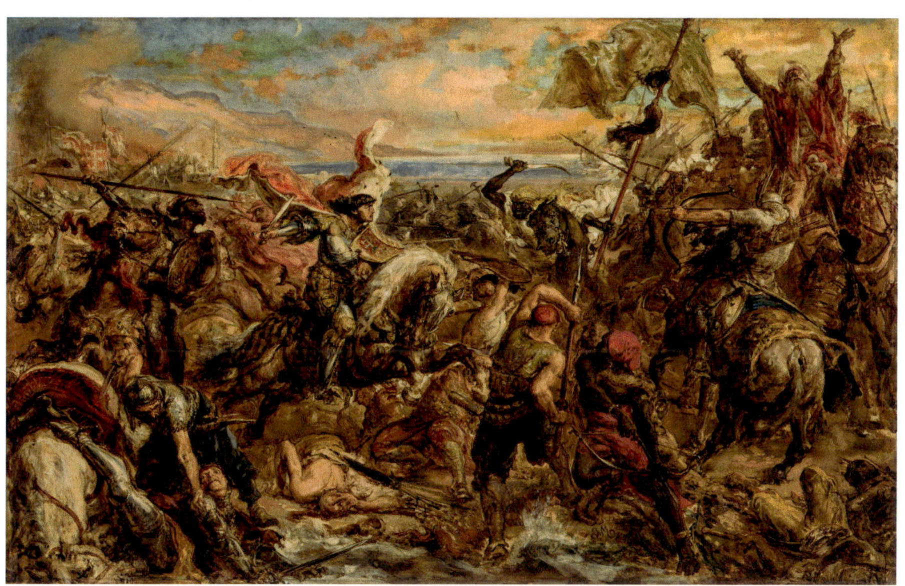

Jan Matejko was the most renowned Polish artist of the second half of the nineteenth century and an internationally important representative of historical painting. As early as the 1860s, however, he departed from the academic tradition in terms of composition and his use of colour. His depictions of historical events became an integral part of the national memory and a way of keeping it visually alive following Poland's loss of independence and the three-way partition of its territory.

Today, Matejko's colour palette often appears dark: like Mihály Munkácsy, he preferred painting with bitumen. Commemorating the battle of Varna that took place on 10th November 1444, this work was produced during Matejko's tenure as director of the Academy of Fine Arts in Kraków. It was presumably originally a colour sketch for a more monumental painting, although the final version was never realized. At the centre of the painting is the figure of Władysław III of Poland, riding courageously and heroically into battle against the army of Sultan Murad II. His troops suffered an ignominious defeat, and the king lost his life in the battle. In its passion and fervour, the scene echoes the earlier work of Eugène Delacroix. – BIB

Budapest 1995, 369–370 | Petneki 2018, 46

Konstantinos VOLANAKIS
[BOLANACHI]

(Heraklion, 1837 – Piraeus, 1907)

The Naval Battle of Lissa, 1869 | Oil on canvas, 169 × 283 cm
Purchased from the HNSFA's 1877–1878 winter exhibition | Inv. no. 84.B

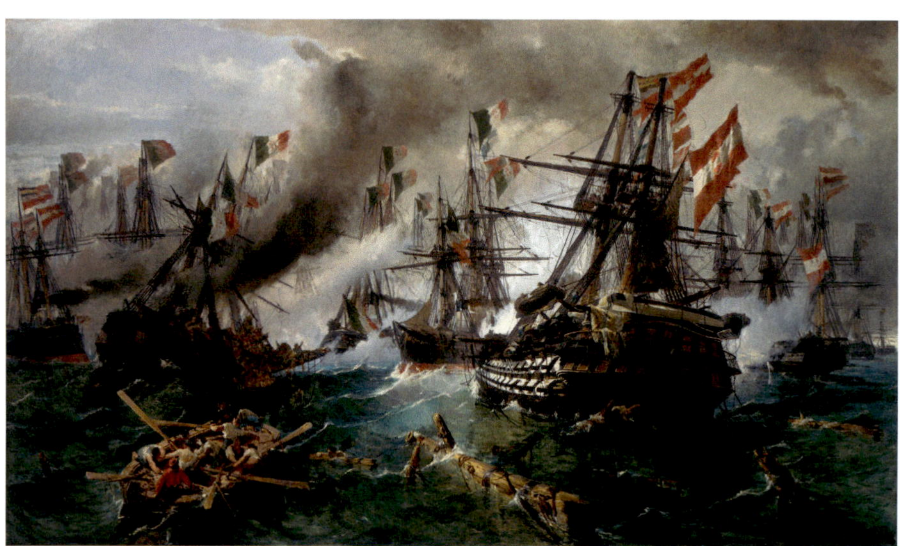

Konstantinos Volanakis studied historical painting in Munich, as a pupil of Karl von Piloty. It was then that he discovered seventeenth-century Dutch landscapes and naval battle scenes, becoming one of the foremost nineteenth-century masters in this field. In 1866, Volanakis won an international art competition announced by Emperor Franz Joseph on the theme "The Battle of Lissa". The winner was able to travel for two years on the battleships of the Austrian fleet, to study seascapes and types of ships. The 1866 war between Prussia, Italy, and Austria, which essentially ended in defeat for Austria, was begun by the Prussians, who, with Italian support, fought the Austrian Empire by land and sea. This painting records one of the dramatic moments during the naval engagement off the island of Lissa (today Vis, Croatia), which ended in victory for Austria. An excellent strategist, Admiral Wilhelm von Tegetthoff managed to prevail against a technically more advanced Italian fleet, which had twice the military force. The painting shows the *Kaiser*, the Austrian ship-of-the-line, sailing away from the viewer; in the foreground, a group of shipwrecked sailors fight for their lives, while in the centre, the *Re d'Italia* smoulders and sinks. – DL

Athens 2009 | Tóth 2012, 154

**Alphonse Marie-Adolphe
DE NEUVILLE**

(Saint-Omer, 1835 – Paris, 1885)

French Dragoon Captain, 1879
Oil on canvas, 46 × 38 cm
Donated by the artist, 1879
Inv. no. 65.B

**Jean-Baptiste Édouard
DETAILLE**

(Paris, 1848 – Paris, 1912)

Hungarian Hussar Major, 1879
Oil on canvas, 46 × 38 cm
Donated by the artist, 1879
Inv. no. 66.B

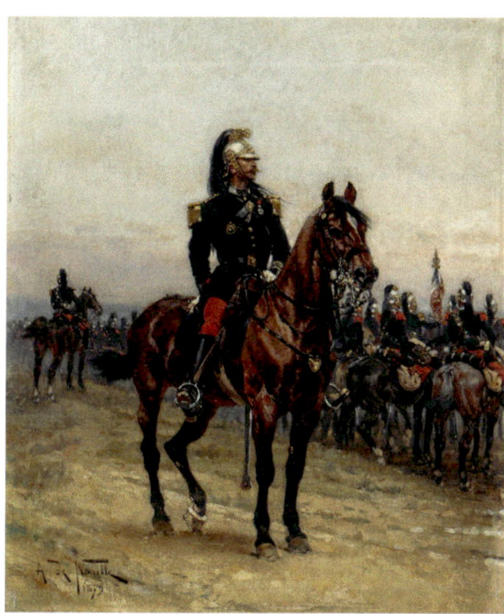 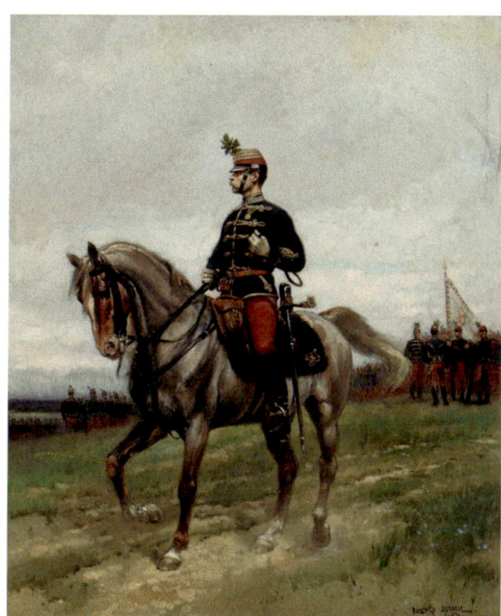

Édouard Detaille and Alphonse de Neuville were celebrated representatives of French military painting. The genre was particularly popular in the nineteenth century: the Paris Salon welcomed works by the two artists, which often depicted the heroic deeds and tragic events of the 1870–1871 Franco-Prussian War.

Curiously, these two paintings ended up in Hungary thanks to the extraordinary international interest evoked by the great flood in Szeged in 1879. The catastrophe in March that year claimed many lives; many of the city's buildings were damaged, and tens of thousands of people lost their homes. Details of the traumatic events were regularly reported in the French daily press and a fundraising event was organised at the Paris Opera House in aid of the victims on 7 June 1879: besides the money raised by the gala, Detaille and De Neuville each offered a work specially painted for the National Museum. The two paintings, similar in size and composition, form a pair: the French Dragoon captain and the Hungarian Hussar major seem almost to be in conversation, symbolising the friendship between the two nations. Both artists have emphasised the dignified appearance of the officers and the disciplined bearing of their horses, while the attention to detail and meticulous execution of the uniforms and weapons demonstrate the painters' expertise in military themes. – AZSK

Kaposy 1983, 133–134

Jean Alexandre Joseph FALGUIÈRE

(Toulouse, 1831 – Paris, 1900)

Diana, model: ca. 1882; cast: ca. 1890 | Bronze, 42.5 × 37 × 26 cm

Purchase, 1980 | Inv. no. 80.1.U

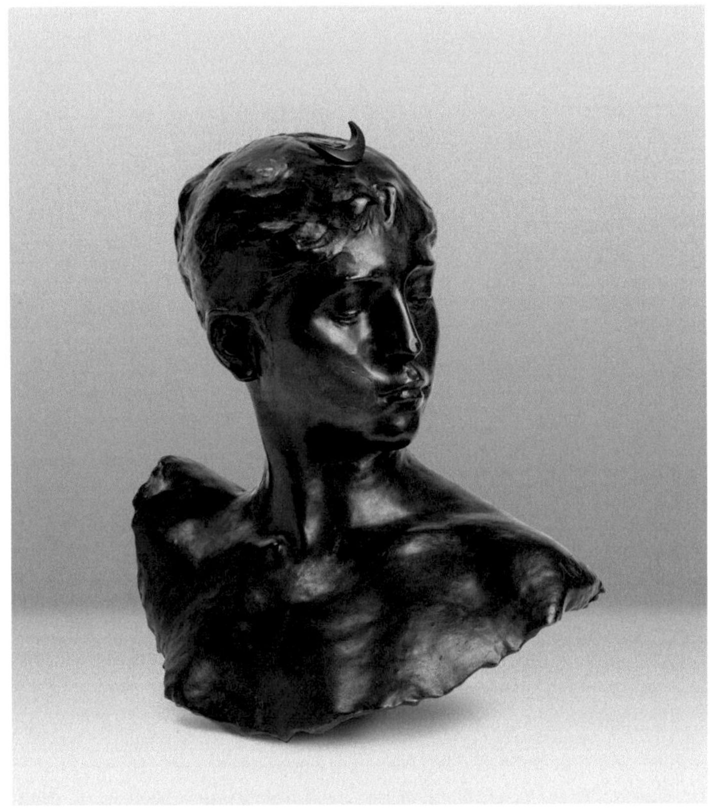

Alexandre Falguière was one of the most celebrated French sculptors in the second half of
the nineteenth century. The life-size statue of Diana, the roman goddess of the hunt, is one
of his best-known works. The statue, presented at the Paris Salon in 1882, was both a success
and a scandal at the same time, as many critics complained that the artist did not portray the
goddess in an idealised way. Instead of following classical tradition, Falguière opted for a realistic depiction of the female body, accentuating Diana's human character by emphasising her
natural proportions, her full figure, which was considered vulgar by many. Nevertheless, the
artist produced several variations on the same theme, including in one of his (relatively rare)
paintings, and his masterpiece also became popular as a bust. Only the crescent adorning the
forehead tells us that we are looking at Diana, but as the body is not present here to distract us
from the goddess's non-idealised facial features, the bust's defiant poise and striking profile
shines through to full effect. – AZSK

Illyés 2001, 134–135

Friedrich August von KAULBACH

(Munich, 1850 – Ohlstadt bei Murnau, 1920)

Pomona, 1878 | Oil on wood, 117.5 × 66 cm
Bequest of Count Dénes Andrássy, 1913 | Inv. no. 289.B

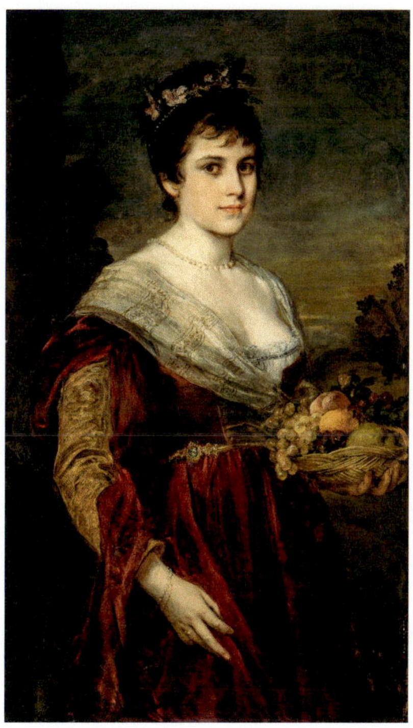

Friedrich von Kaulbach was one of the most sought-after German portraitists of his day; alongside Albert von Keller, he was regarded as one of the greatest masters of female portraiture. Together with Franz von Lenbach and Franz von Stuck, he ranks among the foremost nineteenth-century German painters. His charming, dignified models are dressed in the latest fashions. Early in his career, he was greatly influenced by the German renaissance, an impression subsequently complemented by that of late Flemish and Venetian art and the work of Karl von Piloty and his circle. In 1886, he succeeded Piloty as director of the Academy of Fine Arts in Munich.

This painting of Pomona, goddess of fruits and gardens who symbolises mature female beauty, is also known by the title *Ripe Fruits*. The artist has depicted his model with the archaic attire and attributes popular in his day, thus aligning the work with the costume paintings made fashionable by Makart. The colour palette evokes the portraiture of Anthony van Dyck, who made a great impression on Kaulbach. Count Dénes Andrássy purchased the painting in 1905 from the Galerie Heinemann in Munich, and it hung in the picture gallery of the Andrássy Castle in Krasznahorka (today Krásna Hôrka, Slovakia) until the count's death. – IBB

Peregriny 1914–1915/3, 227 | Ludwig 1981, 279–283

Wilhelm von DIEZ

(Bayreuth, 1839 – Munich, 1907)

A Fight at the Inn, 1904 | Oil on wood, 22.5 × 33 cm
Bequest of Count Dénes Andrássy, 1913 | Inv. no. 322.B

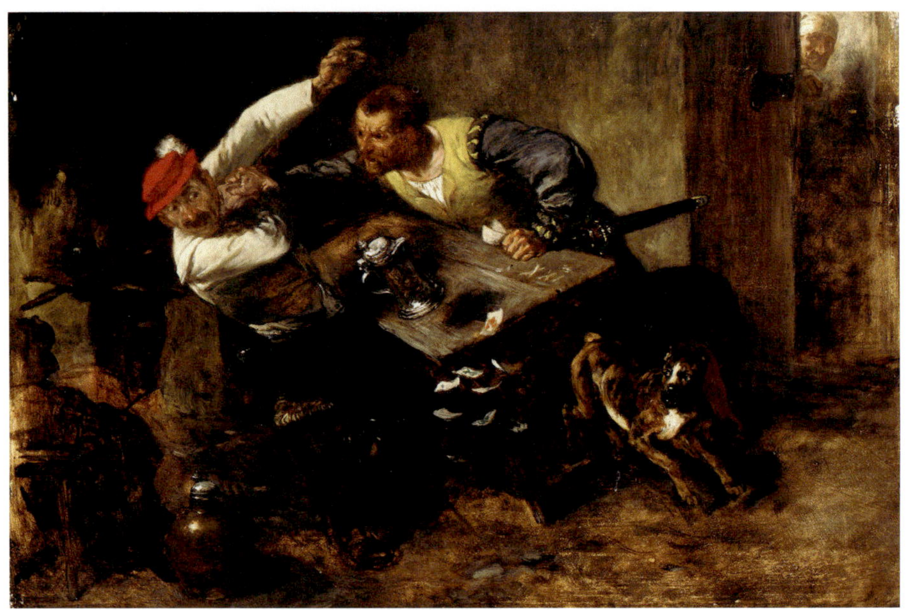

A teacher at the Munich Academy of Art from 1872, and a leading figure in the Munich School, Wilhelm von Diez contributed to the renewal of historical genre painting. Essentially self-taught, he perfected his technique primarily by copying the works of the seventeenth-century Dutch masters, especially Adriaen van Ostade, Adriaen Brouwer, and David Teniers, subsequently developing his own distinctive style. His dynamic, epigrammatic, realistic approach, with its emphasis on picturesqueness, imbued historical painting with unique colours and emotions: Diez was fond of anecdote and strove for picturesque effects, a way of seeing the world that he passed on to his students. His subjects were typically drawn from the Thirty Years' War, as well as the milieu of seedy inns. He tended to paint brawling figures, robbers, vagrants, and other distinctive characters, occasionally – as in this painting – seasoning his works with subtle humour. Dressed in seventeenth-century costume, the men have fallen out over a game of cards. Furious, the soldier has grabbed his drinking companion by the collar, knocking over the table in his temper, while in the background, a figure peeps into the room, observing the scene with disapproval. The glowing, pure yellow, white, and red colours against the bare, monochrome background emphasise the theatricality of the gestures. – AL

Kamm 1991 | *Budapest* 2009–2010, 26, 246

Ernst ZIMMERMANN

(Munich, 1852 – Munich, 1901)

Merry Story, 1880s | Oil on wood, 53.5 × 66.2 cm
Bequest of Count Dénes Andrássy, 1913 | Inv. no. 446.B

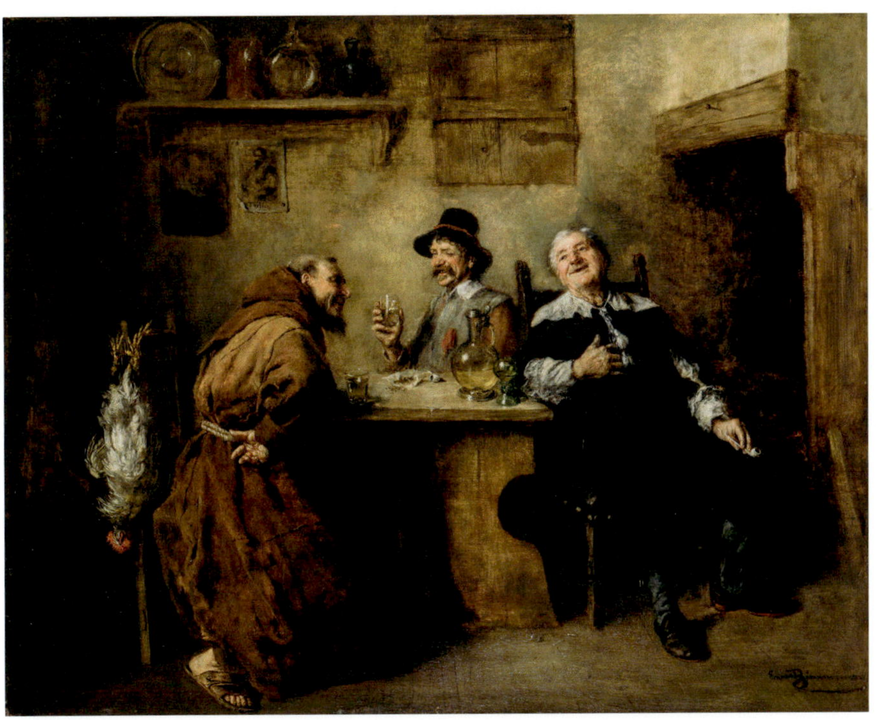

Less well known today, in the first half of the twentieth century Ernst Zimmermann was still considered the most highly skilled portraitist of the Munich school and the circle around Wilhelm von Diez. In his own day, however, he became famous for his religious paintings and still lifes with fish, although alongside these he worked in almost every genre of painting. Compared to the specialised representations of the period, his genre paintings include a variety of motifs. Besides the distinctive features of realism, they convey both humour and charm. He painted the family lives of the lower and middle classes and bustling inn scenes just as happily as scenes from the period of the Thirty Years War, which lasted from 1618 to 1648.

These latter paintings form a self-contained category of genre paintings, to which *Merry Story* also belongs. A man in a hat, who might well be an old soldier, sits at a wooden table in a seventeenth-century Dutch tavern along with a Franciscan monk, who is recounting the merry story, and an elegantly dressed, elderly burgher, who clutches his stomach as he laughs. The monk has probably been given the poultry that hang from the back of his chair by way of alms, a characteristic feature of the mendicant order. – BIB

Peregriny 1914–1915/3, 251 | Ostini 1902, 128

Hans MAKART

(Salzburg, 1840 – Vienna, 1884)

Masquerade, 1863–1865 | Oil on canvas, 100 × 232 cm
Bequest of János Frohner, 1891 | Inv. no. 126.B

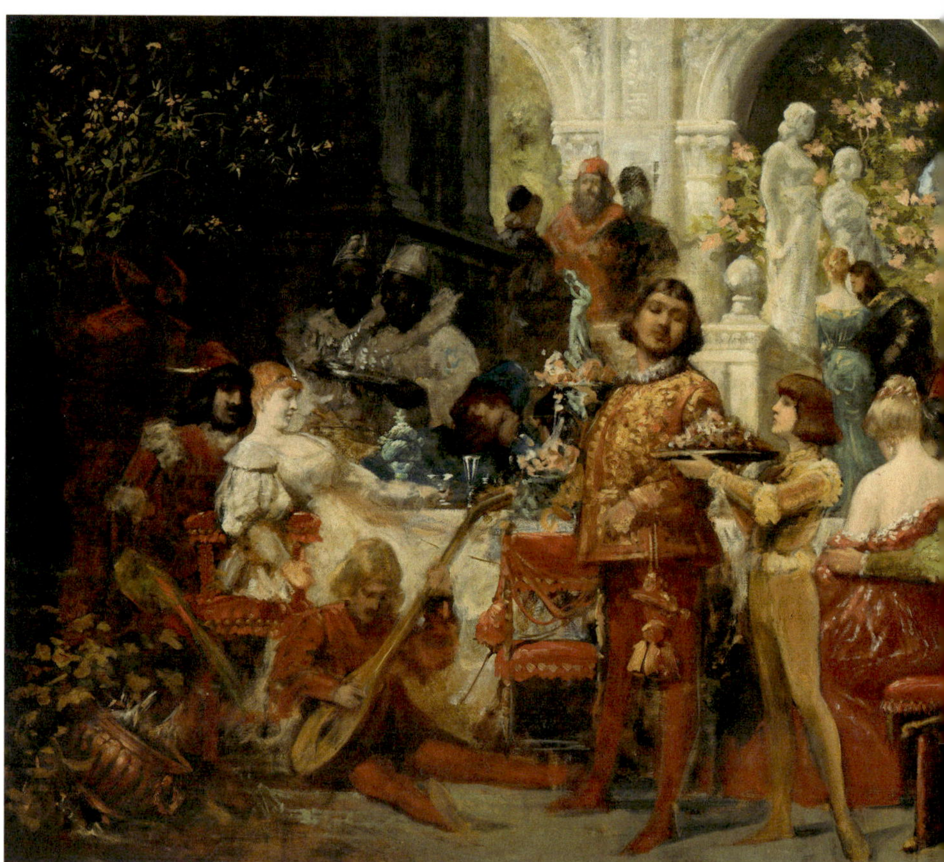

Hans Makart was a pupil of Karl von Piloty at the Munich Academy. He drew inspiration from historical and mythological sources for his large-scale, multi-figure, frieze-like paintings and decorative commissions. Complex compositional solutions and a virtuoso use of colour heighten the decadent sensuality of his works. His approach to history was somewhat eclectic: his paintings masterfully combine the colourism of the Venetian Cinquecento masters Titian and Veronese with the baroque excess of Rubens.

After Carl Rahl and Hans Canon, Makart was the most important artist during the period of urban development that took place in Vienna in the second half of the nineteenth century, the so-called Ringstrasse era, achieving acclaim as a decorative painter of the imposing buildings constructed in place of the old city walls. From the 1870s, in the spirit of *Gesamtkunstwerk*, he dominated the imperial capital for two decades with his taste, his lifestyle, and

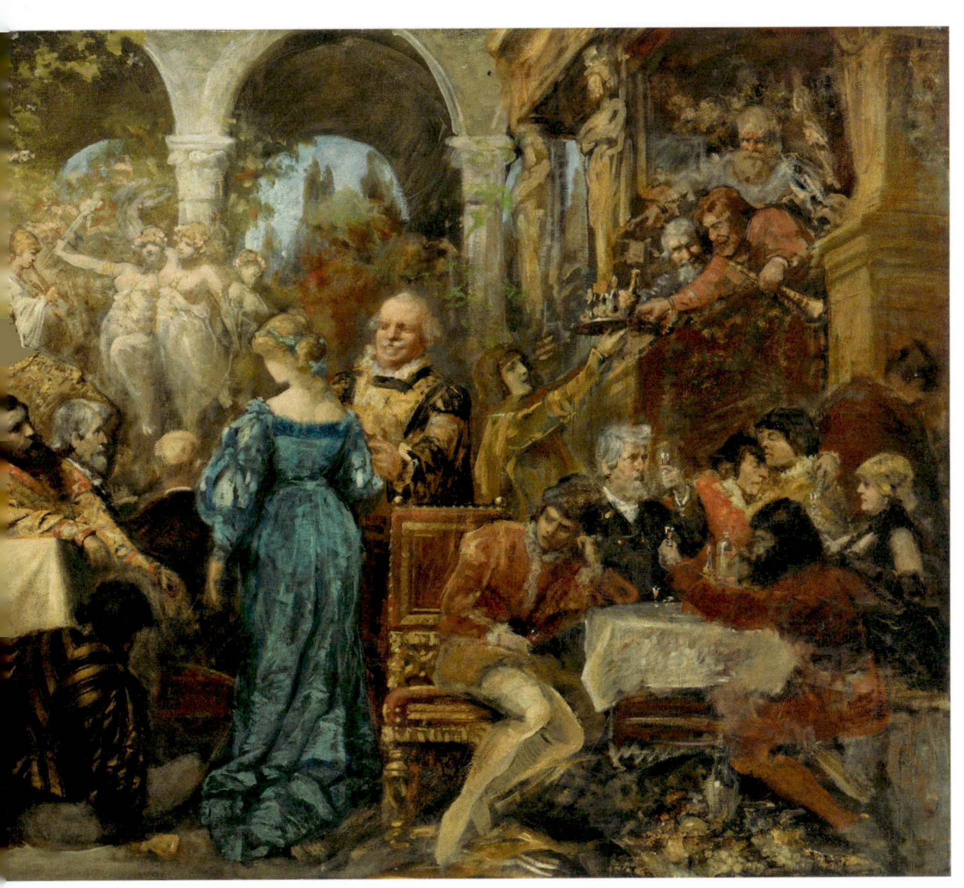

his painterly vision. His active period is even referred to as the Makart era, or *Makartstil*. In his legendary studio in Gusshausstrasse, Vienna, which served as a meeting place for the city's elite, he organised masquerades on historical themes. These parties culminated in the jubilee gala evening organised in 1879 for the silver wedding anniversary of the imperial couple, at which Makart appeared before the cheering Viennese public on horseback, dressed in a Rubens-era costume. His early death marked the end of an era: as the teacher of Gustav Klimt, he can be regarded as the forerunner of the Vienna Secession, and – due to his dynamic colourism – Viennese expressionism. – DL

Frodl 2013, 71 | Weitner 2017

Vlaho BUKOVAĆ

(Cavtat, 1855 – Prague, 1922)

Dubravka, 1894 | Oil on canvas, 300 × 215 cm | Purchased from the group of Croatian
exhibitors at Hungary's National Millennium Exhibition in 1896 | Inv. no. 7.B

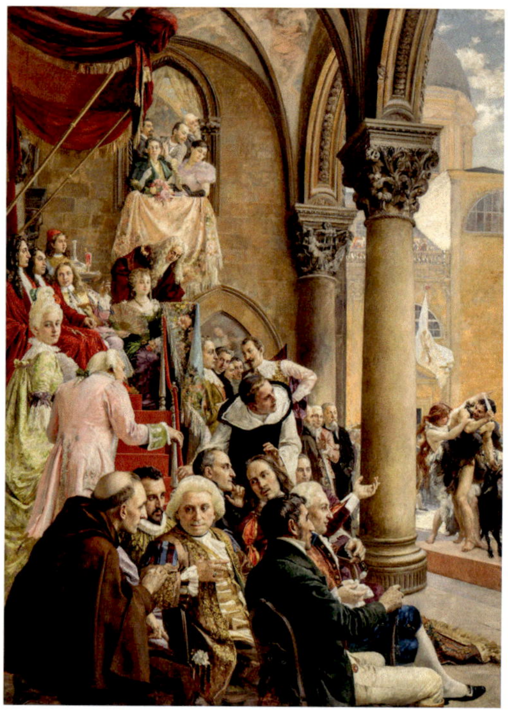

As chief curator of the Croatian art pavilion at the Millennium Exhibition held in Budapest in
1896, Croatia's most internationally acclaimed artist, Vlaho Bukovać, included several of his
own paintings among the exhibited works. During the exhibition, the Hungarian state purchased *Dubravka* for the newly established Museum of Fine Arts.

 The subject of the painting is the 1628 premiere of the pastoral drama *Dubravka*
by the Dalmatian poet Ivan Gundulić. Crucial to Croatian national consciousness, the drama
is the reworking of an ancient myth that would later become an allegory for the liberation of
Raguza (today Dubrovnik).

 The relationship between Hungary and Croatia was unstable during the Austro-
Hungarian Monarchy from 1867. Some of the works shown in the Croatian pavilion at the
Millennium Exhibition reflected these tensions. Through its depiction of illustrious personalities, *Dubravka* was intended as a demonstration of Croatian cultural development. The man
in the red cloak beneath the crimson baldachin is the dramatist Ivan Gundulić, while the
man applauding from the balcony is the painter himself. – BIB

Matits 1994 | *Zagreb–Budapest* 2020–2021, 309–310

Celestin MEDOVIĆ

(Kuna na Pelješcu, 1857 – Sarajevo, 1920)

The Sirmian Martyrs, 1895–1896 | Oil on canvas, 300 × 215 cm | Purchased from the group
of Croatian exhibitors at the National Millennium Exhibition in 1896 | Inv. no. 441.B

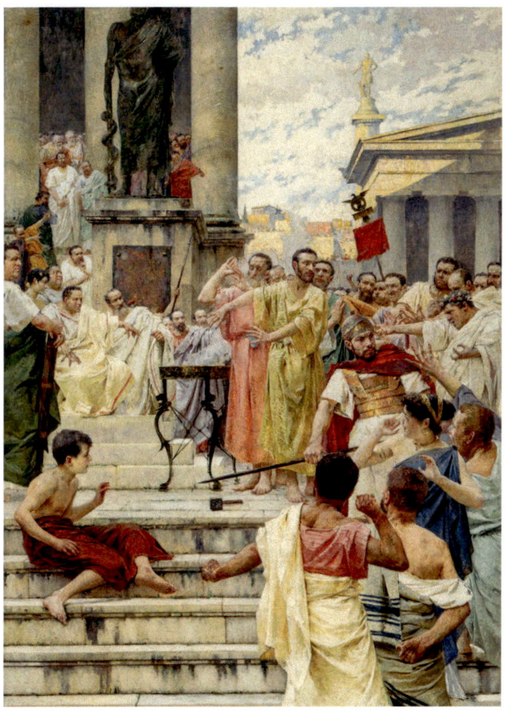

Celestin Medović was a Franciscan monk before studying at the Academy of Fine Arts in
Munich. His large-scale paintings depict key events in Croatian history. His earlier subjects
were typically ascetic, scholarly monks, while later he mostly painted still lifes and landscapes.

    The Sirmian Martyrs is a typical example of the influence of Munich historical paint-
ing and the Piloty school. The details are painted with meticulous realism, while the clothing
and setting are historically authentic. The work shows the death sentence passed on the
Christian Pannonian stonemasons, who, during the rule of Emperor Diocletian, having refused
to carve a statue of Aesculapius, the Roman god of healing, were locked into iron cages and
thrown into the river Sava. The incident took place in Sirmium, a city on the banks of the Sava
known today as Sremska Mitrovica. Medović depicts the sentencing of the four martyrs in the
square in front of an ancient temple. On the right of the painting stands the high priest, wearing a garland of flowers on his head; around him, the crowd calls for judgement on the stonemasons, while the judges tasked with deciding on the martyrs' fate are seated on the left. – BIB

Matits 1994 | *Zagreb* 2011–2012, 46

VI

Painting in the Open Air

Oswald ACHENBACH

Eugène BOUDIN

Anton BRAITH

Jean-Baptiste Camille COROT

Gustave COURBET

Charles-François DAUBIGNY

Narcisse Virgilio DIAZ DE LA PEÑA

Jules DUPRÉ

Paul Joseph Constantin GABRIËL

Paul GAUGUIN

Charles JACQUE

Albert LEBOURG

Adolf Heinrich LIER

Willem MARIS

Hendrik Willem MESDAG

Jean-François MILLET

Claude MONET

August von PETTENKOFEN

Camille PISSARRO

Johann Gualbert RAFFALT

Eduard SCHLEICH the Elder

Ivan Ivanovich SHISHKIN

Willem Bastiaan THOLEN

Constant TROYON

Jules Jacques VEYRASSAT

Friedrich VOLTZ

Individual elements of nature, or the grandeur of the landscape, have long been popular themes in painting, and working in situ has been part of the creative process for centuries. Before the nineteenth century, artists tended to produce sketches, or occasionally smaller studies, outdoors, typically in sketchbooks and using drawing utensils. What changed in the nineteenth century was that artists no longer looked to nature to provide ideological analogies or didactic allegories; instead, they set out in search of beautiful scenery, striving to capture directly the fleeting experiences enjoyed during their walks.

From the 1830s, a group of artists gathered in Barbizon, not far from Paris, to record their immediate impressions of the local woodlands. Various technical advances soon proved beneficial to their work: firstly, the invention of paint tubes (1841), and later, factory-primed canvases and portable easels. Such developments made it possible for artists to commit to canvas their observations of nature relatively quickly outdoors, even in adverse weather.

By the middle of the century, the method adopted in Barbizon had elicited a significant international response, attracting artists of other nationalities and further enhancing their popularity. The Barbizon group inspired several Dutch painters, who, in the early 1850s, likewise gathered to work in the countryside; having later settled in The Hague, they founded the style known as the Hague School. In contrast to the Barbizon artists, they deliberately chose warm, grey shades and subdued tones in an effort to capture the characteristically misty, hazy atmosphere of their surroundings.

Landscape painters based in Munich and Düsseldorf soon joined their French and Dutch peers, and via them, the method that came to be known as *plein air* painting also provided a model for aspiring artists in Central Europe. From the mid-1850s, Austrian artists who were drawn to the region around Szolnok adopted the *plein air* method to paint what was, to them, the exotic world of the Great Hungarian Plain.

In the 1860s, several young French painters visited the Barbizon region, attracted by the output of their older colleagues who were working there. By the following decade, these artists had developed their newly acquired techniques into the style that we know today as impressionism. The elements of impressionism – everyday themes, the depiction of objects using short, thick brushstrokes, the juxtaposition of unmixed colours, and the meticulous observation of shifting light effects – are all to be found in the various artistic practices of the day. However, the impressionists employed them systematically, on canvases that glowed with the luminous colours that became the exclusive hallmark of this group of artists in Europe in this period.

Large numbers of paintings by members of the Barbizon group were acquired by the museum with the bequest of Count János Pálffy. Dutch, German, and Austrian representatives of *plein air* painting were also popular guests at Hungarian exhibitions and their works were regularly purchased by the Hungarian state. The systematic collecting of impressionist paintings in the years following the opening of the Museum of Fine Arts brought to completion what is today one of the best-loved units within the collection.

Eduard SCHLEICH the Elder

(Haarbach, 1812 – Munich, 1874)

Landscape with Homecoming Cows, ca. 1870 | Oil on canvas, 85 × 123 cm

Purchased from the HNSFA's 1871 spring exhibition | Inv. no. 113.B

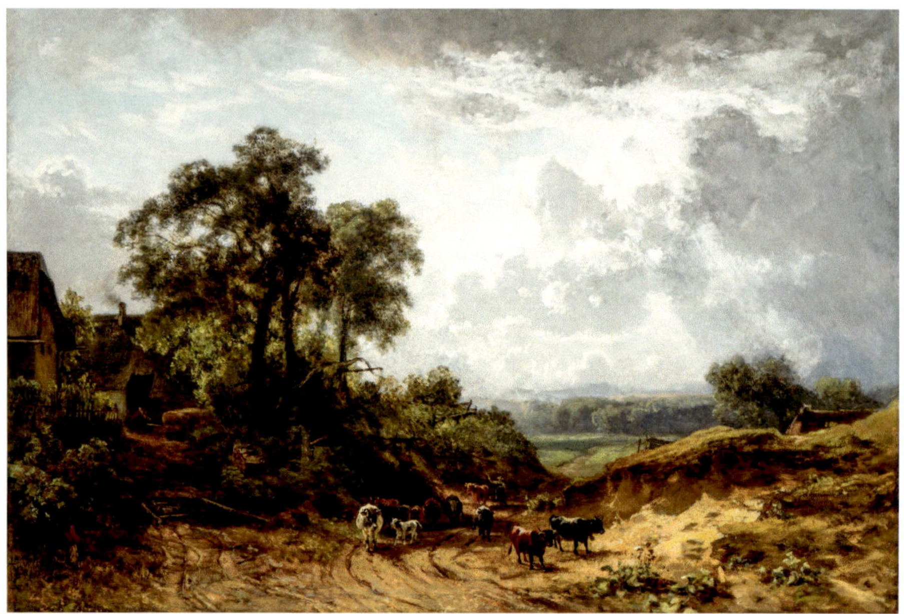

Eduard Schleich, the first realist *plein air* landscape painter of the Munich school, initially studied historical painting at the Academy of Fine Arts in Munich but was soon expelled for an alleged lack of talent. He earned success in around 1830 with his late romantic mountain landscapes, based on sketches made in Upper Bavaria and the Tyrol. He was greatly influenced by seventeenth-century Dutch landscape painting and the cosmic expanse of Rubens' landscapes; inspired by Rubens' work, he depicted the natural countryside of Upper Bavaria as a painterly vision of light, colours, and atmosphere.

  After extensive experimentation, his unique concept of landscape took shape in around 1850, when he suddenly rejected the intensive study of nature in favour of a more holistic view. He was able to lend a restrained grandeur to simple motifs, thus perpetuating the early nineteenth-century Munich traditions: in the painting *Landscape with Homecoming Cows*, he captures quite simple, mundane details, the less spectacular elements of the Bavarian countryside. This is the only one of the Museum of Fine Arts' five Schleich paintings that was not acquired from the bequest of Count János Pálffy. – BIB

Peregriny 1909/1, 283 | *Dijon* 1995, 284–285

Friedrich VOLTZ

(Nördlingen, 1817 – Munich, 1886)

Herd of Cattle, mid-19ᵗʰ century | Oil on wood, 24 × 53.2 cm
Bequest of Count Dénes Andrássy, 1913 | Inv. no. 351.B

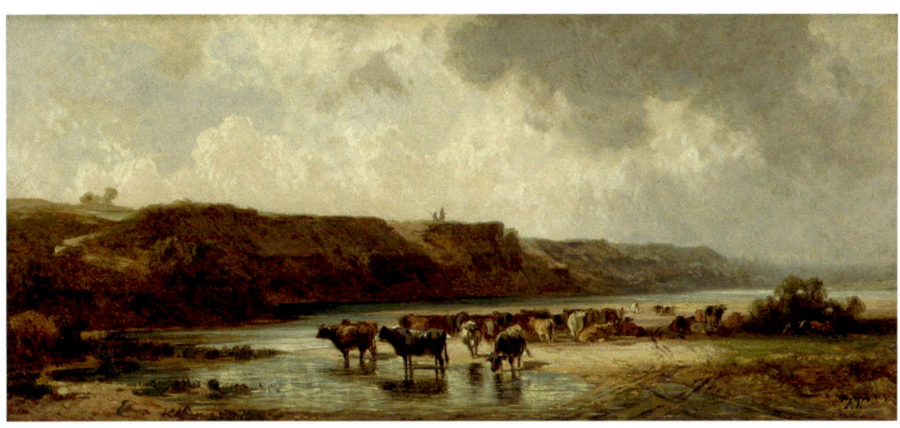

Friedrich Voltz, the second member of a family of three generations of artists, produced copperplate etchings and lithographs even as a teenager. He mastered the rudiments of art from his father, then for a brief time studied at the Academy of Fine Arts in Munich. However, the old masters, and especially the work of the seventeenth-century Dutch painters – Paulus Potter's *The Young Bull* (1647, Mauritshuis, the Hague), for example, came to be hugely significant in his oeuvre – as well as his direct experience of *plein air* painting during his summers in the Bavarian Alps, had a greater impact on him than his theoretical knowledge. Voltz initially painted horses, then, from the early 1840s onwards, bulls and cows, in each case producing portrait-style renderings that accentuated the characteristic features of the specific breeds raised at that time. He also produced idyllic landscapes similar to the present painting, in which tranquil, motionless animals are included as staffage. Here, the sky and the approaching storm clouds convey a sense of the changeability of nature; the light effects and shadows are muted, lending an underlying, pulsating tension to the work. His virtuoso paintings made Voltz one of the most famous German animal painters of his day. Towards the end of his life, he received the title of professor and was awarded the Order of Merit of the Bavarian state. – AL

Holland 1896, 276–280 | Peregriny 1914–1915/3, 267

Constant TROYON

(Sèvres, 1810 – Paris, 1865)

Cowherd, ca. 1860 | Oil on canvas, 77 × 103 cm
Bequest of Count János Pálffy, 1912 | Inv. no. 260.B

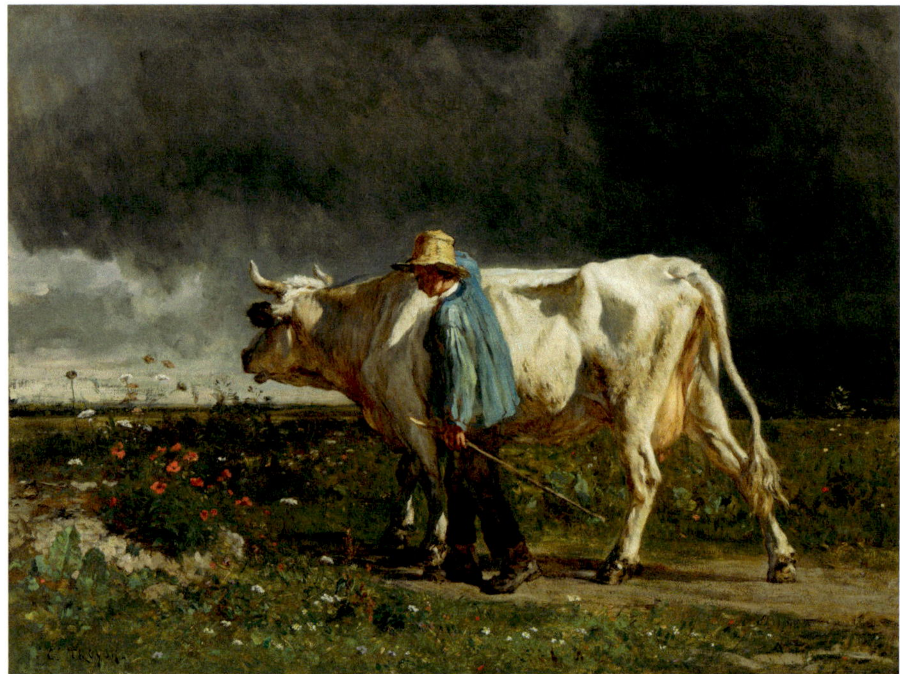

Constant Troyon was among those Barbizon School artists who were interested not only in the realistic depiction of the landscape but also in animal painting: cows resting or grazing, either in herds or alone, are a recurring subject in his works. Besides the direct observation of nature, Troyon, who started out as a porcelain painter, drew inspiration from the work of the seventeenth-century Dutch masters – especially Paulus Potter and Aelbert Cuyp, in whose paintings the cow is elevated into a noble motif.

The central figure in *Cowherd* is not the young peasant in his loose blue shirt and straw hat, but the massive, majestic white beast that almost dwarfs him. Cow and cowherd trudge side by side across the plain, in search of shelter from the approaching storm. The dramatic play of light before the rain, the golden rays of the sun, and the general effect of the dark grey, almost black clouds disrupt the uneventfulness of the everyday. Troyon conveys the contrast between the dark background and the light-coloured body of the animal with vigorous brushwork and a rich palette. The light falling from the side partly accentuates and partly obscures the subjects: the face of the resigned cowherd disappears into shadow, while the animal's huge, bony frame becomes almost sculptural. – AZSK

Shinjuku et al. 1992–1993, cat. no. 89 | Illyés 2001, 52–53

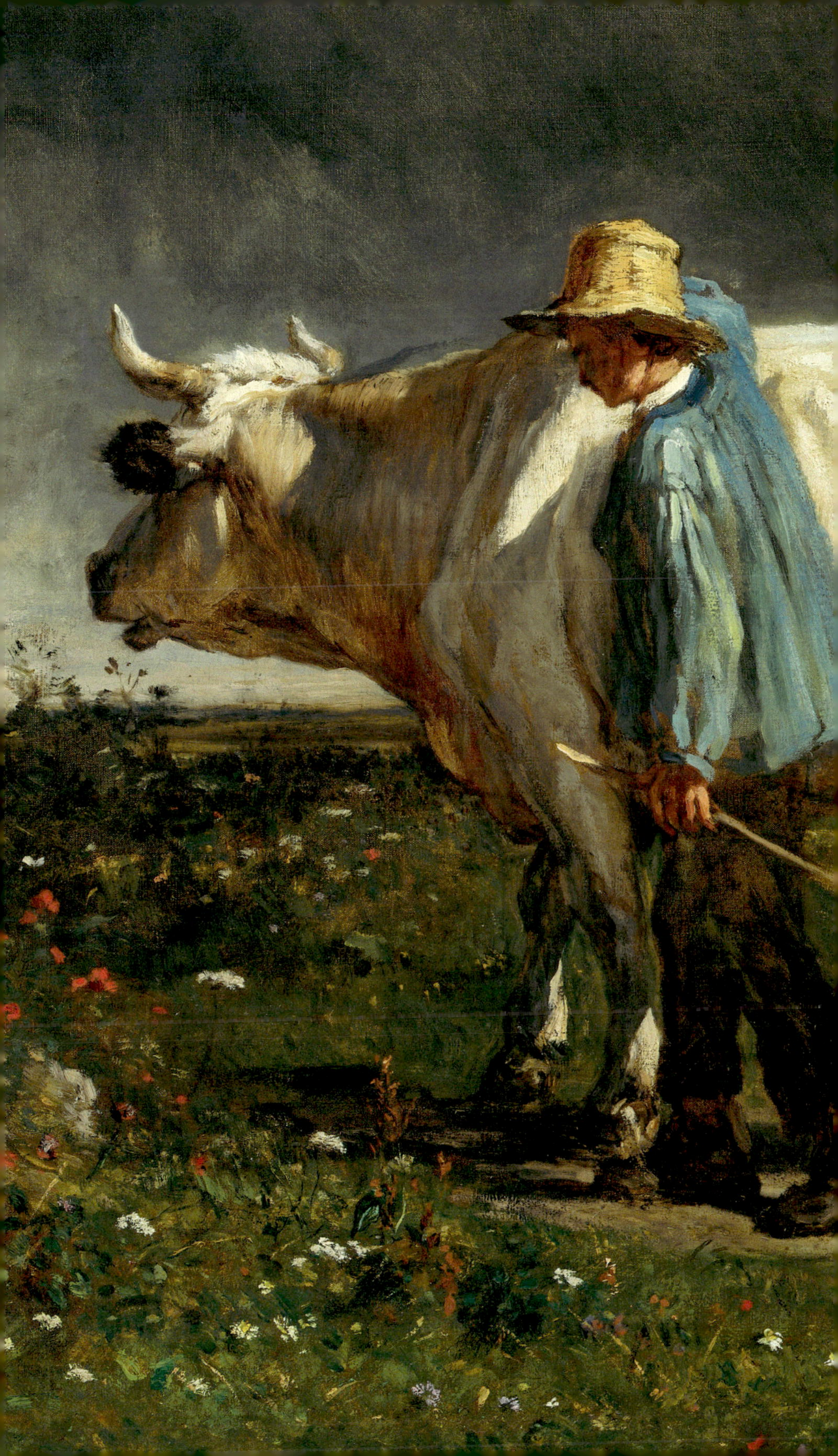

Narcisse Virgilio DIAZ DE LA PEÑA

(Bordeaux, 1807 – Menton, 1876)

Landscape, ca. 1860–1870 | Oil on wood, 32 × 44.5 cm
Purchased from the HNSFA's 1879–1880 winter exhibition | Inv. no. 67.B

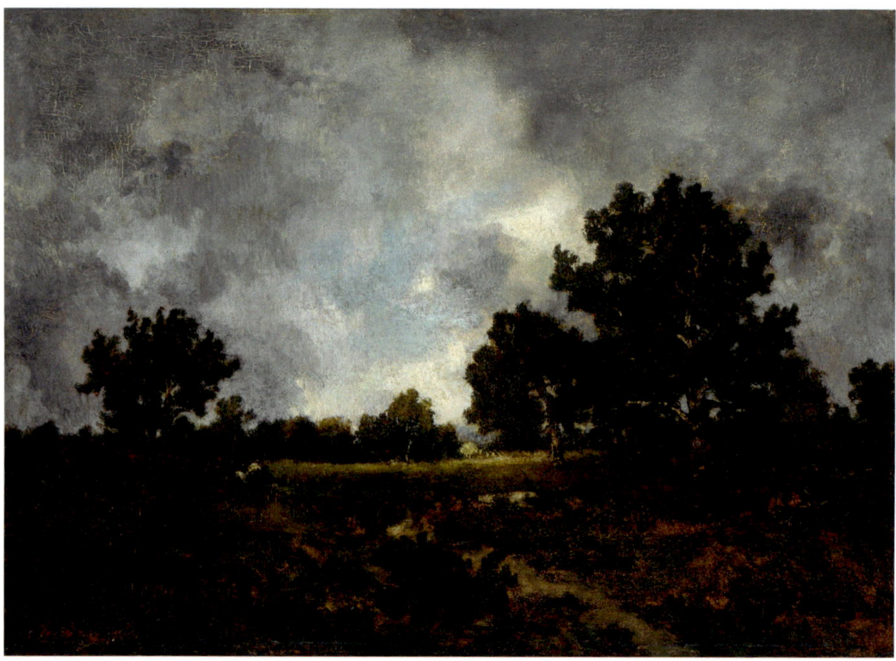

Narcisse Diaz, who was born in France to a family of Spanish descent, was a self-taught artist: he began his career as a porcelain painter before perfecting his technique by copying paintings in the Musée du Louvre. Although regarded as one of the defining figures of the Barbizon school, his rich and diverse oeuvre includes realistic landscapes, orientalist paintings, and romanticised mythological and historical scenes. From the 1830s – like his friends Théodore Rousseau and Jean-François Millet – he paid regular visits to the Forest of Fontainebleau and the surrounding area; these painters, who championed a new, realistic representation of landscape, drew inspiration not only from the direct observation of nature but also from the works of the seventeenth-century Dutch masters.

Diaz typically based his compositions on powerful colour effects and contrasts between light and shadow. In this small landscape, he employed the vigorous, pastose brushwork characteristic of the Barbizon school and a palette built on dark greens, browns, and greys. The foliage, outlined against the cloudy sky, the forest path, and the clearing are represented by patches of colour. Because of the use of bitumen pigment, Diaz's paintings have darkened over time, losing something of their original vibrancy. – AZSK

Illyés 2001, 42–43 | Miquel and Miquel 2006

Jules DUPRÉ

(Nantes, 1811 – L'Isle-Adam, 1889)

Farmstead, 1860–1865 | Oil on canvas, 36.5 × 57.5 cm
Purchased from Soma Rosenfeld, 1897 | Inv. no. 97.B

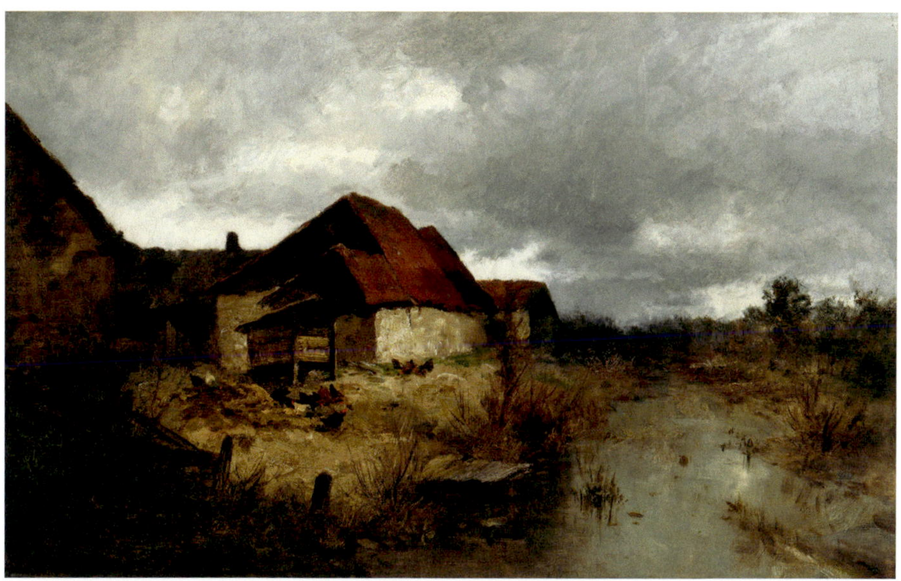

Jules Dupré began his career as a porcelain painter in his father's manufactory, although he soon switched to landscape painting. On a visit to England in 1831, he encountered the innovative, naturalistic landscapes being produced by British painters; the work of Richard Parkes Bonington and John Constable had a profound impact on his art. He cultivated a close relationship with members of the Barbizon school, especially Théodore Rousseau, with whom he regularly visited the Forest of Fontainebleau in search of new subjects.

Dupré typically painted landscapes without human figures: this depiction of a farmstead also features merely a group of derelict buildings, with a few hens scratching about in the yard. The sluggish stream and grey, cloudy sky intensify the gloomy atmosphere of the landscape: the scene is given life chiefly by the sensitive use of colour and the artist's distinctive technique. X-rays of the canvas have revealed an earlier still life of flowers beneath the landscape, painted upside down compared to the present composition. The fact that a subject of this kind is almost without precedent in Dupré's work makes it difficult to say whether he painted over one of his own compositions or reused a canvas belonging to a fellow painter. – AZSK

Aubrun 1974, cat. no. 747 | Illyés 2001, 44–45

Gustave COURBET

(Ornans, 1819 – La Tour-de-Peilz, 1877)

The Spring of Léri in Chassagne, 1863 | Oil on canvas, 65.5 × 81 cm

Transfer, 1945 | Inv. no. 458.B

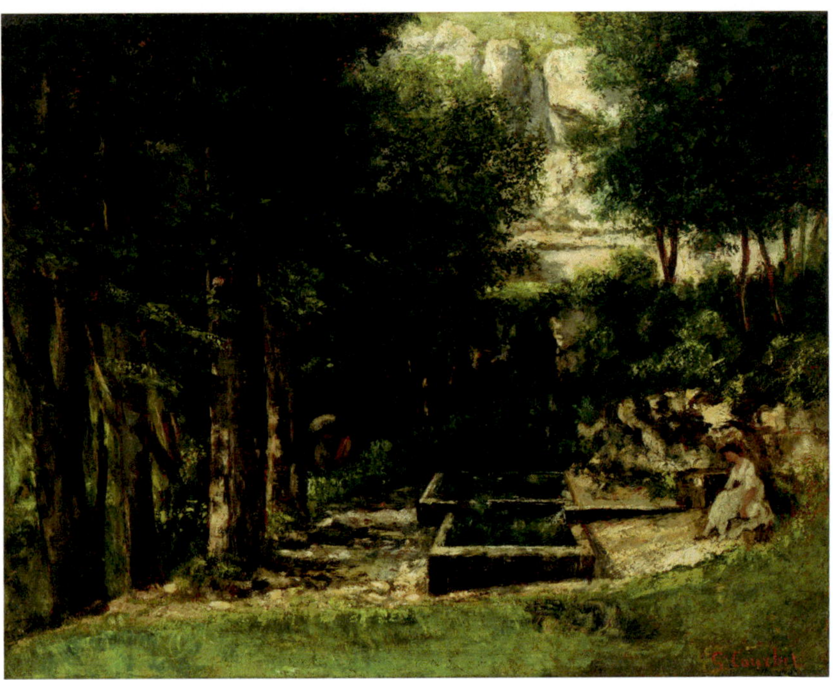

After his highly controversial, large-scale compositions painted in the 1850s, with their overtly political reflection on social issues, Gustave Courbet somewhat distanced himself from social commentary in the following decades, when landscape came to play an increasingly important role in his art.

For decades, this woodland scene was thought to have been painted near the town of Fouras, on the French Atlantic coast, and was known as *The Spring at Fouras*. With the help of the Musée Courbet, however, it has recently been established that the work in fact depicts the area around Ornans, the town in Eastern France where the artist was born. The spring of Léri in the tiny village of Chassagne-Saint-Denis has remained virtually untouched: the stone basins and the wall of rock in the background are still recognisable today. Comparing the painting with the original location, it becomes clear how Courbet has reduced the landscape to simple, distinctive shapes, and how he made bold use of the palette knife to render the summer vegetation and the effects of light and shadow. The artist has focused to such an extent on the depiction of the landscape that the viewer has to look closely to make out the figure of the young woman sitting next to the spring, and the painter seated at his easel in the background. – AZSK

Illyés 2001, 64–65 | Brunnarius 2023

Charles-François DAUBIGNY

(Paris, 1817 – Paris, 1878)

Moonrise, 1868–1873 | Oil on canvas, 172 × 305 cm
Bequest of Count János Pálffy, 1912 | Inv. no. 249.B

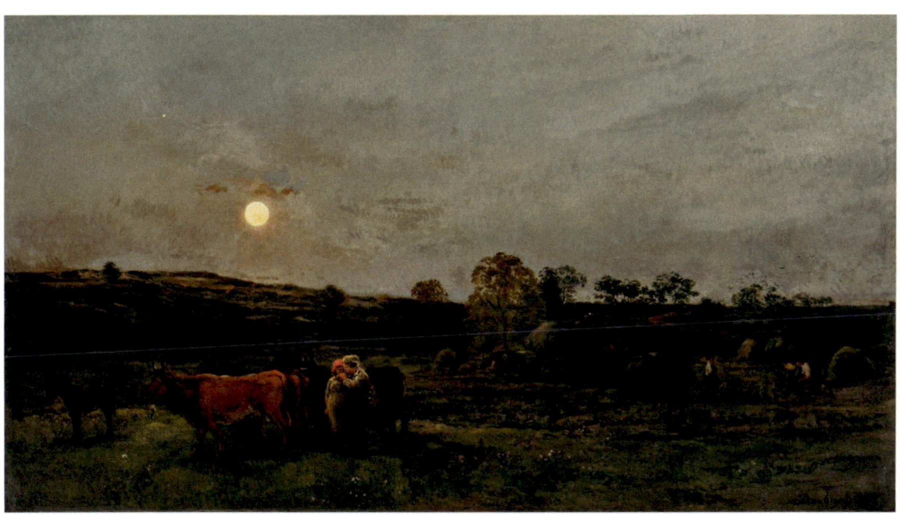

Charles-François Daubigny, one of the most prominent figures of the Barbizon school, owed his popularity to his brownish palette, reminiscent of the Dutch masters, and his sensitive, atmospheric depictions of nature. The subject of this imposing, large-scale painting is a young couple, flirting as they drive home the cows at dusk. The greyish half-light and the poetic approach turn the composition into a genuine peasant idyll. The painting was first shown at the 1868 Paris Salon, where it was given a somewhat mixed reception In the contemporary press. While many critics praised the subtle evocation of the sky and the landscape, others considered the artist's style to be overly sketchy. Most of the criticism, however, was directed at the artist's rendering of the moon: its bright glow was considered excessively yellow and intense. Daubigny subsequently modified the details that had attracted censure, probably for the 1873 Vienna World's Fair. The work was eventually shown at the 1878 Paris Exposition, where it now enjoyed complete success. Recent technical examinations of the painting have confirmed that the artist did indeed repaint the Moon. – AZSK

Kaposy 1979, 170–171 | Illyés 2001, 62–63

Charles JACQUE

(Paris, 1813 – Paris, 1894)

In the Pasture, 1875 | Oil on canvas, 81 × 65 cm
Purchased from the HNSFA's 1877–1878 winter exhibition | Inv. no. 76.B

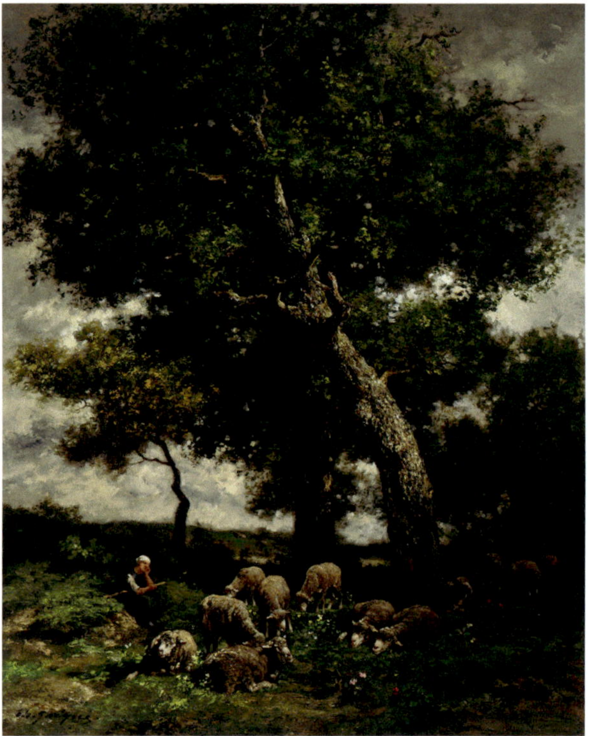

Charles Jacque began his career as an engraver and illustrator and taught himself the finer points of painting. Like his friend Jean-François Millet, he found both a home and his artistic subjects in Barbizon in the 1840s. The fact that he himself was involved in animal husbandry, and especially poultry farming and breeding, underlines his commitment to the peasant lifestyle.

In his bucolic paintings, based on subjects that he observed in nature, Jacque was fond of depicting the everyday events of village life: the shepherd, resting with his flock, was a recurrent motif in his work. *In the Pasture* is a realistic yet poetic depiction of a shepherdess daydreaming as she sits beneath a huge oak tree beside her resting, grazing sheep; the composition is permeated by a sense of harmony between people and animals, and by the simple tranquillity of peasant life. The rough surface of the bark, the dark green foliage, the rich texture of the wool, and the grey tones of the overcast sky are rendered in tiny specks of dynamically applied paint. This was one of the first contemporary French paintings to be acquired for a Hungarian public collection from the HNSFA's exhibitions. – AZSK

Bremen–Munich 1988–1989, cat. no. 5 | Illyés 2001, 48–49

Jules Jacques VEYRASSAT

(Paris, 1828 – Paris, 1893)

The Horse Fair, 1878 | Oil on canvas, 116 × 158 cm
Purchased from the HNSFA's 1880 autumn exhibition | Inv. no. 74.B

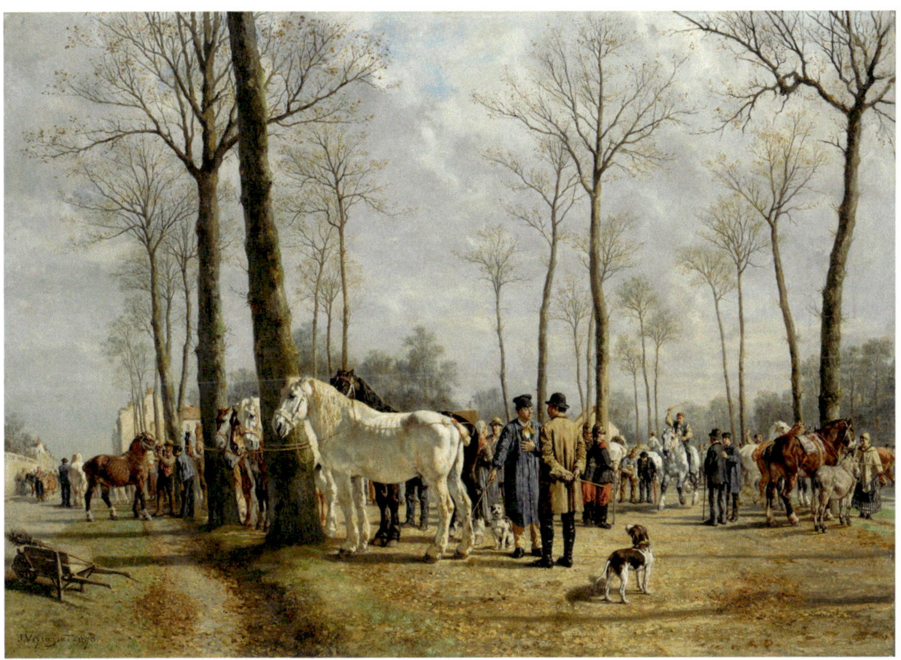

The French painter and engraver Jules Veyrassat worked in a style akin to the Barbizon School's realist approach to nature. His popular themes connect his art to the work of Constant Troyon and Charles Jacques, the animal painters of the Barbizon group. Horses regularly take centre stage in his genre scenes of everyday rural life; dubbed the "workhorse painter", the artist took particular pleasure in depicting the sturdy animals used for ploughing and driving.

This painting of the Fontainebleau horse fair, held on Saint Catherine's Day, was shown at the Paris Salon in 1878, then, in the following year, at the Salon in Antwerp. Most Belgian and French critics commended his sensitive rendering of light and the accurate depiction of the animals. Veyrassat has depicted in meticulous detail the prospective customers and horse traders haggling beneath the almost bare trees in the mild, late-autumn sunshine at the fair, which was held regularly near the forest at the end of November. Veyrassat renders the anatomical details of the different kinds of workhorses and their tranquil posture with characteristic expertise and artistic sensitivity. – AZSK

Montrosier 1882, 103 | Illyés 2001, 50–51

Jean-Baptiste Camille COROT

(Paris, 1796 – Ville-d'Avray, 1875)

Souvenir of Coubron, 1872 | Oil on canvas, 46 × 55.3 cm
Purchased from Galerie Bernheim-Jeune (Paris), 1915 | Inv. no. 362.B

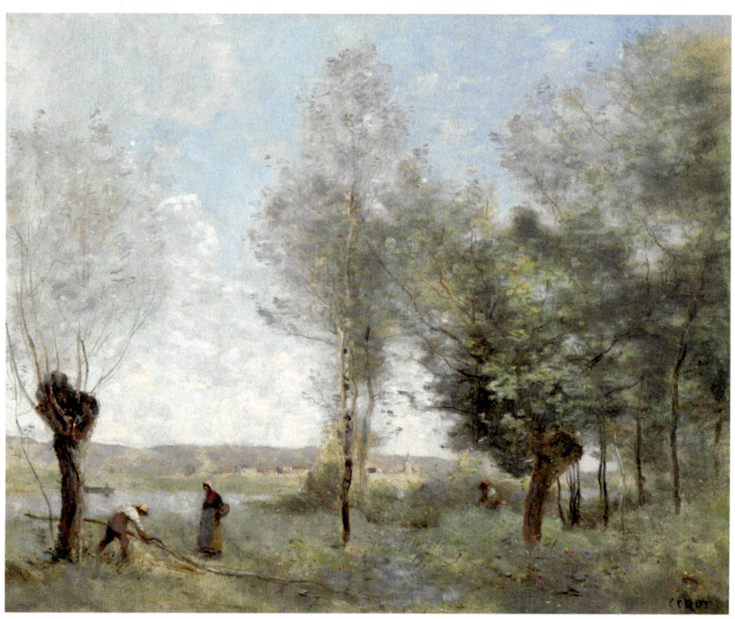

In the wake of the Paris Commune (1871), Corot visited a friend of his in Coubron, a doctor, with whom he stayed for some time. An admirer of the Italian landscape, Corot was fond of this hamlet near Paris; he found poetry in the woodlands by the village, and the small stream, and created a true Arcadia there for himself.

He painted five landscapes during excursions in 1872, including this master-piece, which Elek Petrovics, the newly appointed director of the Museum of Fine Arts, purchased for the museum's collection at the start of the First World War. Petrovics, and the curator Simon Meller, bought the painting in the knowledge that the museum was soon likely to acquire Camille Pissarro's early landscape *La Varenne-Saint-Hilaire* (page 187) from the collection of painter and art collector Ferenc Hatvany. These two works, along with a Boudin landscape (page 202), clearly illustrate how the depiction of light and atmosphere led to the mature impressionist style.

Corot's vaporous technique makes his Coubron paintings particularly attractive. Lightness of being floats above the landscape, while the village lies quietly hidden in the distance. The village was presumably left unscathed by internal political events in France, the Franco-Prussian War and its aftermath. However, the advances of civilisation gradually infiltrated into everyday rural life. Urban and village architecture was foregrounded in painting, while questions concerning the representation of nature were relegated to the background. – JG

Robaut 1905, cat. no. 2094 | Illyés 2001, 84–85

Camille **PISSARRO**

(Charlotte Amalie, 1830 – Paris, 1903)

La Varenne Saint-Hilaire, ca. 1863 | Oil on canvas, 49.6 × 74 cm
Donated by Ferenc Hatvany, 1918 | Inv. no. 377.B

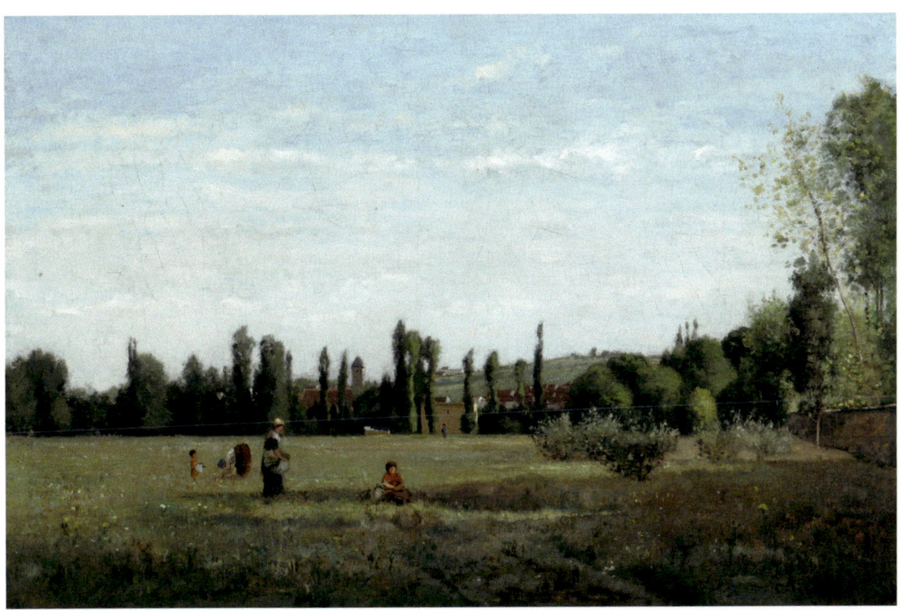

Camille Pissarro moved to the village of La Varenne Saint-Hilaire, not far from Paris, in summer 1863. Motifs found in the nearby settlements – Pontoise, Louveciennes, and Auvers-sur-Oise – prompted the painter to develop an objective, non-Arcadian approach to landscape painting. This unique perspective – along with Pissarro's talent for and interest in teaching – had a powerful impact on the younger generation of impressionists and post-impressionists.

The depiction of labourers in the meadow, the strong daubs of colour that structure the composition, the painting technique used for the meadow, and the soft brushstrokes that shape the trees connect this early Budapest painting with the work of Pissarro's great forerunners, Camille Corot and Jean-François Millet. However, already discernible in the background is the typical French village that would play such an important role in Pissarro's later landscapes. These features show the connection between the French landscape tradition and the vision of Paul Cezanne, Paul Gauguin, Paul Signac, Alfred Sisley and others. – JG

Pissarro and Durand-Ruel Snollaerts 2005, cat. no. 74 | *Verona 2013–2014*, cat. no. 77

Hendrik Willem MESDAG

(Groningen, 1831 – The Hague, 1915)

Winter's Day by the Seashore, ca. 1880 | Oil on canvas, 96 × 157 cm
Purchased from the HNSFA's 1881 spring exhibition | Inv. no. 136.B

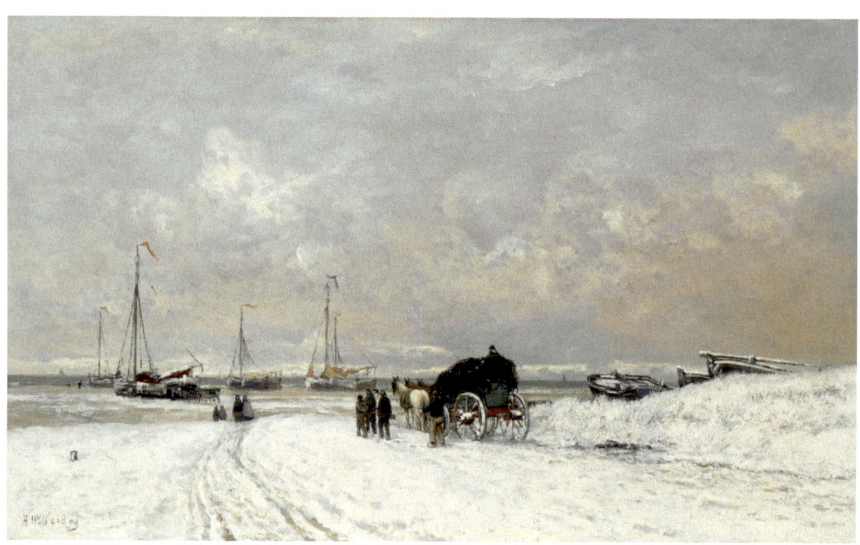

Mesdag's early career differed significantly from that of the other artists of the Hague School. Having decided to become a painter at the age of thirty-five, he trained in Brussels and made the acquaintance of the most talented Belgian painters. The sea soon became the focus of his interest: he painted countless views of the grey seas of his native country, filled with sailing boats and fishermen, from many different perspectives. Influenced by the seascapes painted by Gustave Courbet in the 1870s, his landscapes quickly became popular. His first real success came in 1870, when he won the gold medal at the Paris Salon. The painting *Winter's Day by the Seashore* was first exhibited in 1880, likewise at the Paris Salon; in the same year, it featured at the Salon in Ghent before going on display in Budapest. The painting offers a glimpse of the everyday hardships faced by the fishermen of Scheveningen during the winter months. Much of the painting is taken up by the sky, which is rendered in a muted palette; the loaded cart and staffage draw the eye towards the narrow stretch of coast and the sailing boats. The loose, easy brushwork suggests a familiarity with the impressionists. Besides paintings by representatives of the Hague School, his renowned art collection also contained works from the School of Barbizon. – AS

Poort 1989, 213 | *Turin* 2004–2005b, 351, cat. no. 63

Paul Joseph Constantin GABRIËL

(Amsterdam, 1828 – The Hague, 1903)

Morning Dew, ca. 1878 | Oil on canvas, 90 × 151 cm
Purchased from the HNSFA's 1879 December exhibition | Inv. no. 75.B

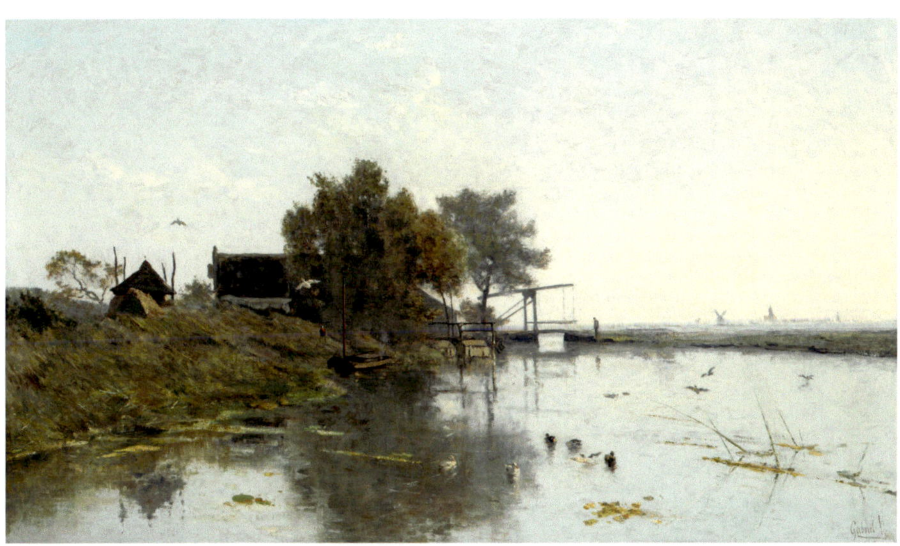

Gabriël belonged to the last generation of the Hague School, but rather than the warm, grey tones typical of the group's style, his landscapes are painted in bright colours that earned him the title "the colourist of the Hague School". *Morning Dew* is a characteristic example of Gabriël's landscapes: it depicts the polder of Kortenhoef, a settlement not far from Amsterdam. The artist visited the area frequently to paint what became known as "Gabriël's land". The work features the classic elements of Dutch landscape painting, including a glimpse of windmills on the hazy skyline.

A painting from the early 1880s by Willem Bastiaan Tholen, one of Gabriël's pupils – today in the Museum Boijmans Van Beuningen in Rotterdam – shows the artist at work beneath a sunshade, sitting in a rowing boat on the water, his paintbox in his lap. The invention of paint tubes in the mid-nineteenth century meant that artists were able to carry their paints with them without them drying out, making it possible to work outdoors. Gabriël presumably produced rough sketches of the polder, and a smaller version, today owned by a private collector, using the working method captured in Tholen's painting. The Budapest work, however – judging by its size – was probably completed in the studio, based on these sketches. – RM

Matits 1995, 68 | *Dordrecht* 1998, 13, cat. no. 35

Willem MARIS

(The Hague, 1844 – The Hague, 1910)

Grazing Cows, after 1880 | Oil on canvas, 56.5 × 85 cm
Purchased from Van Wisselingh & Co. (Haarlem), 1909 | Inv. no. 217.B

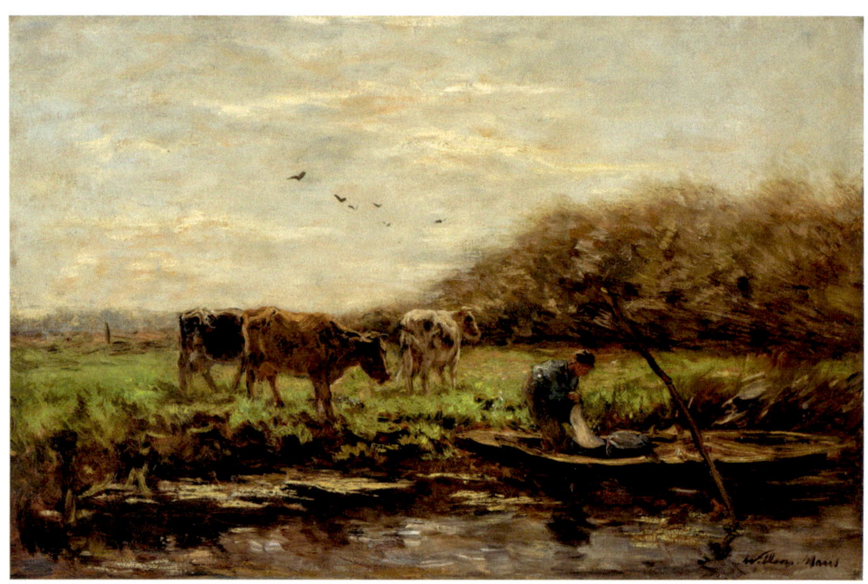

Willem Maris was a distinguished representative of the Hague School and the youngest of the famous Maris brothers. His works typically feature cows, ducks, pastures, and canals. He was greatly influenced by the seventeenth-century Dutch artist Paulus Potter. Although he is generally classified as an animal painter, Maris viewed animals merely as secondary elements in the natural world, therefore he can also justifiably be regarded as a landscape painter. Besides paintings, Maris also produced copperplate engravings and watercolours; he even participated in the founding of the Dutch Drawing Society, which was established in 1876. The goal of the society was to win recognition for watercolours as works of art in their own right: until then, audiences had associated the technique merely with sketches.

From 1880, Maris employed a loose style of brushwork that occasionally earned him the epithet "the impressionist of the Hague School". It was during this period that he painted *Grazing Cows*, which was purchased by the Museum of Fine Arts at the 1908–1909 Winter International Exhibition at the Budapest Kunsthalle. The Dutch material shown at the exhibition, introducing important Dutch artworks from the turn of the century, was brought to Budapest by the Dutch art dealer Elbert Jan van Wisselingh. – BIB

Boer 1900 | Heijbroek and Wouthuysen 1999, 52–54

Anton BRAITH

(Biberach an der Riß, 1836 – Biberach an der Riß, 1905)

Watering Cows, 1868 | Oil on canvas, 71.6 × 144 cm
Bequest of Count Dénes Andrássy, 1913 | Inv. no. 271.B

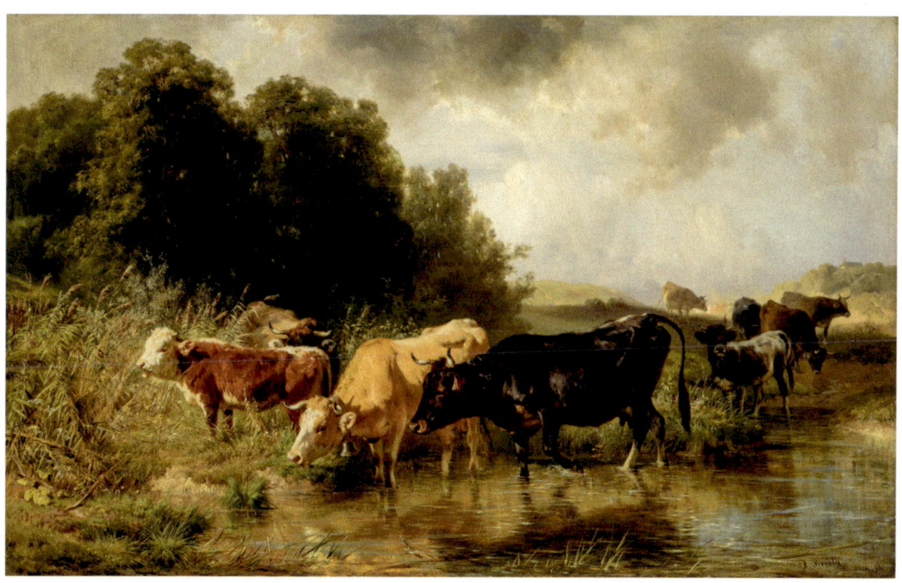

Anton Braith's talent was obvious even as a child, when he sketched the animals grazing in the Berghausen meadows. He was offered a place at the Stuttgart school of art at the age of fifteen. Early in his career he travelled frequently through Upper Bavaria to study nature. During these visits, he came into contact with painters from Munich, and under their influence he moved to the city in 1860. There, he mastered Karl von Piloty's draughtsmanship and use of vibrant colours, although he was never taught directly by the great master. He became a member of the Munich school and, following the death of Friedrich Voltz, was considered the greatest German animal painter. He was a lifelong friend of the painter Christian Mali: the two artists had a house built together in Munich, and both settled in Biberach at the end of their lives.

This painting by Braith dates from his early days in Munich, although from his second artistic period. Influenced by Constant Troyon, it was then that he began experimenting with placing groups of animals in the foreground, the first of the Munich painters to do so. Braith was also the first animal painter to produce large-scale works. – BIB

Bühler 1981a, 124–127 | Bühler 1981b, 59–62

Oswald ACHENBACH

(Düsseldorf, 1827 – Düsseldorf, 1905)

Italian Landscape, ca. 1852 | Oil on canvas, 56 × 81.7 cm
Purchased from the artist in 1875 | Inv. no. 108.B

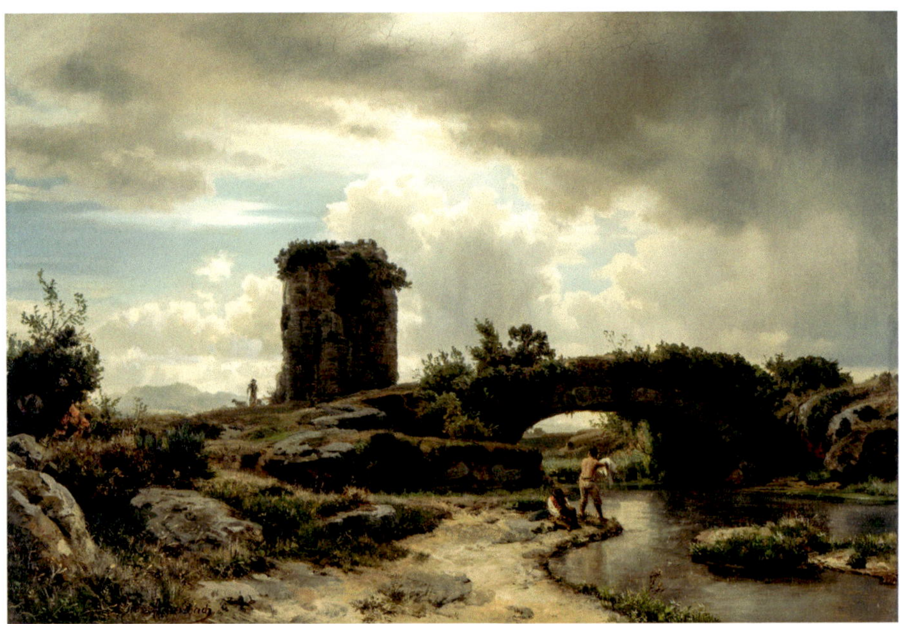

The Achenbach brothers, Oswald and Andreas, were among the most prominent and popular landscape painters in Düsseldorf, a city that had emerged as a centre of the arts by the mid-nineteenth century. Oswald's early work bears the influence not only of his brother, who was twelve years his senior, but also of the idealised landscapes of Johann Wilhelm Schirmer, his teacher at the Düsseldorf Academy. Following a visit to Rome and the surrounding countryside in 1850, the artist favoured Italy as the subject matter of his work. He finalised his compositions in his studio in Düsseldorf using sketches made during his travels. This early landscape shows the ruined tower of an ancient mausoleum in Campagna standing next to an atmospheric bridge overgrown with vegetation. The dramatic expanse of sky and the gently shimmering water were among Achenbach's favourite motifs in the 1850s. Although the elegance of this painting's structure, its meticulous detail, and its brown tones still point to the influence of Schirmer and the Düsseldorf tradition, Achenbach was here clearly already striving for the overall effect of the image, the rendering of atmosphere, and the visualisation of the silvery light that unifies the scene. His entire oeuvre was defined by the increasingly subtle synthesis of ideal and real, tradition and innovation. – DS

Potthoff 1995, 263, cat. no. 8 | *Düsseldorf* 1997, 50–51, 146, 217

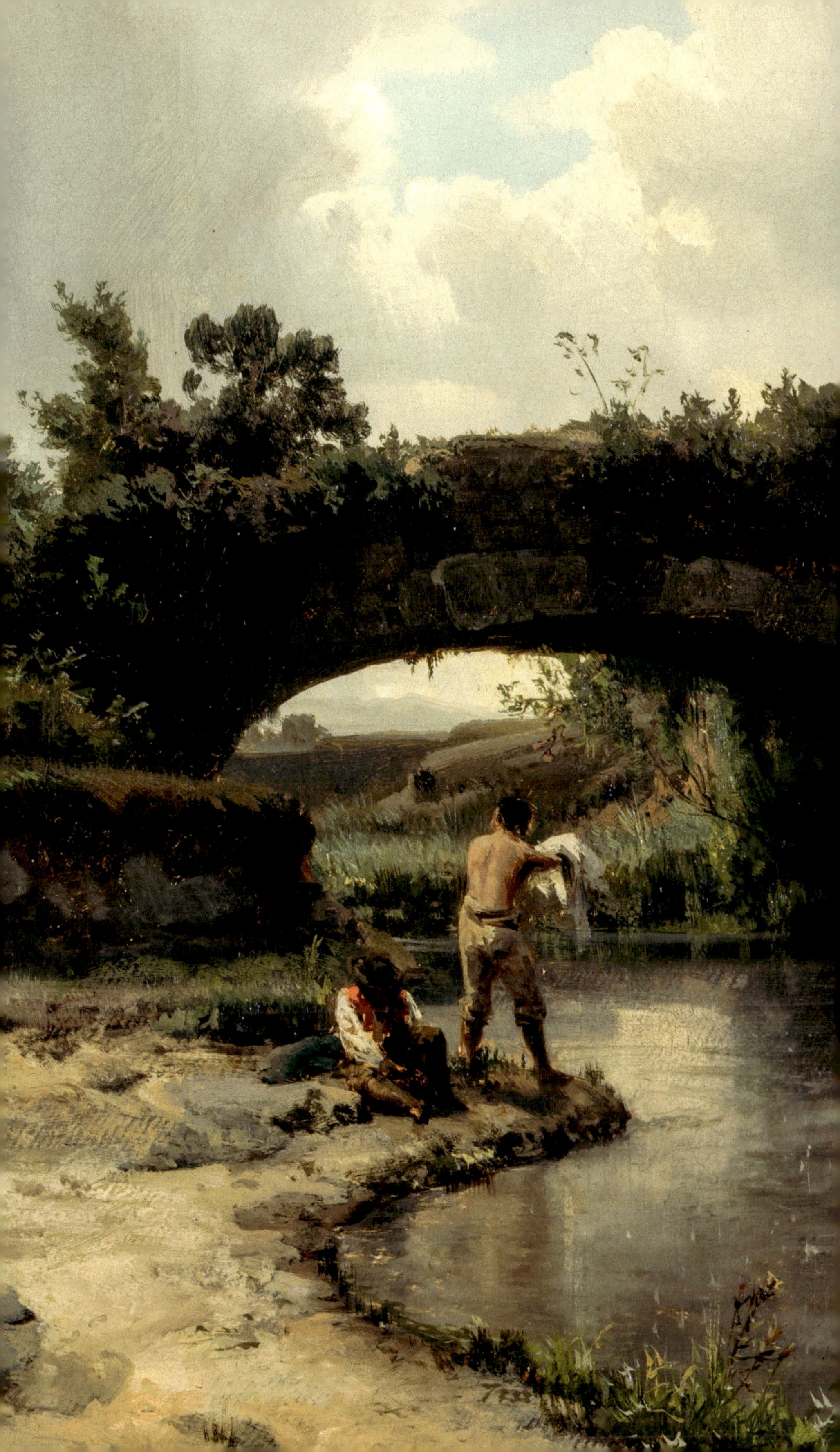

Adolf Heinrich LIER

(Herrnhut, 1826 – Varna, 1882)

The Mill, after 1867 | Oil on canvas, 44 × 48.5 cm
Bequest of Count Dénes Andrássy, 1913 | Inv. no. 340.B

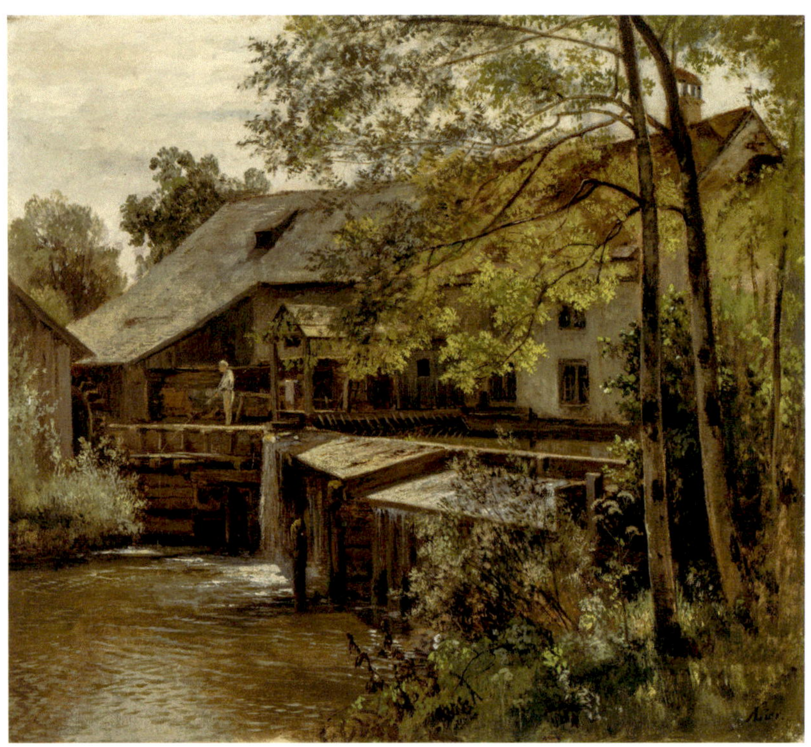

Due to the crisis in mid-nineteenth-century Munich landscape painting, artists turned away from the studio and began to work outdoors. This was the path chosen by Adolf Lier, who was then seen as the equal of his teacher, Eduard Schleich the Elder. It was through Schleich that Lier encountered the works of the Barbizon school and incorporated his experiences of traveling in France into his painting.

Lier restored to Munich landscape painting the prestige it had lost under Karl von Piloty and his followers, he embodied the transition between the Munich landscape painters under Schleich and the impressionists. In 1868, he opened a master's school at the Academy of Fine Arts in Munich, founding modern German landscape painting. The school attracted key landscape painters such as Hermann Baisch and the American Charles Miller.

Lier painted mainly spring and autumn scenes in the countryside around Munich. His landscapes are often bathed in moonlight or evening light, or shrouded in rain, and are dominated by warm brown or yellow tones. *The Mill* also features a landscape bathed in half-light, although the light piercing through the clouds sparkles on the surface of the water. – BIB

Peregriny 1914–1915/3, 260 | Eschenberg 1984, 267–268

Willem Bastiaan THOLEN

(Amsterdam, 1860 – The Hague, 1931)

Dawn, 1880s | Oil on canvas, 96 × 117 cm
Purchased from the HNSFA's 1887 autumn exhibition | Inv. no. 81.B

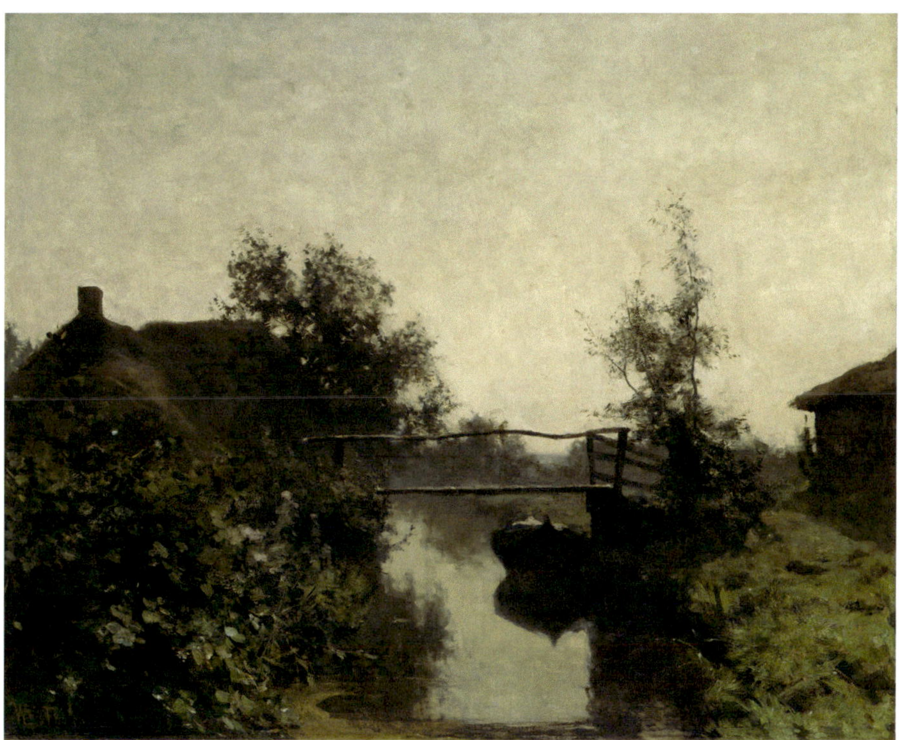

In 1876, Tholen studied the basics of art at the Academy of Fine Arts in Amsterdam and the Polytechnic School in Delft, although he only became a painter after his months working in the Brussels studio of Paul Joseph Constantin Gabriël. The two artists enjoyed a close professional relationship: they spent many summers painting outdoors together in the region of Kampen and Giethoorn. For both Gabriël and Tholen, it was important not simply to paint the landscape but also to convey its atmosphere. In 1887, Tholen settled in the Hague, where he played an active role in artistic life, joining the group of painters known as the Hague School, which at the time included Hendrik Willem Mesdag and Jacob and Willem Maris. Members of the group generally specialised in their own preferred field, while Tholen's choice of subject matter was wide ranging. In the case of the landscape held in Budapest, it was as important for him to convey the obscurity, utter stillness, and tranquillity of the dawn as it was to depict the broad canal, the wooden bridge, and the reflection of the leaves in the water. The success of the composition is evident from the fact that an engraving of it was later produced, and that it was the first of the artist's works to be acquired by a museum. – AS

Budapest 1995, 68 | *Paris–Dordrecht* 2019–2020, 70

August von PETTENKOFEN

(Vienna, 1822 – Vienna, 1889)

Fair in Szolnok, after 1851 | Oil on wood, 32.8 × 52.4 cm
Purchased from Eugen von Miller zu Aichholz (Vienna), 1908 | Inv. no. 209.B

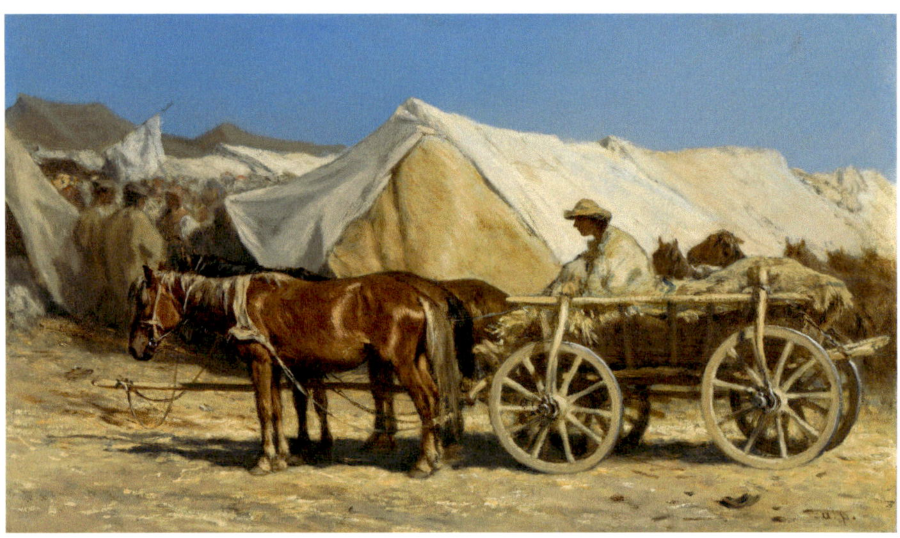

During his summers in Szolnok, Pettenkofen produced many small genre paintings, which he often repainted in a larger format and in greater detail on his return to Vienna. This may well have been the case with the Budapest painting *Fair in Szolnok* (occasionally also known as *Slovak Cart*), which bears the hallmarks of the placid realism typical of the Austrian painter. The painting is not dated, although we know for certain that from 1851, Pettenkofen visited Szolnok every summer to paint. This, for him, was a source of inspiration equivalent to the forest of Fontainebleau for the members of the Barbizon school: the quivering haze above the plain, colours glistening in the sunlight, models that appeared exotic to Western eyes, and the Tisza region's wilderness of wetlands.

In the Budapest painting, the Szolnok marketplace, bathed in brilliant sunlight beneath a dazzling blue sky, is veiled in a muted tone by the swirling dust of the Great Hungarian Plain. The hayrack of the two-horse cart in the foreground has already been lowered. The third horse has presumably been attached to the cart to be sold at the market by its owner, the man in the linen shirt and straw hat driving the cart. The painting hung on the wall of Emperor Franz Joseph's palace in the second half of the nineteenth century. – BIB

Weixlgärtner 1916, 502 | *Tokyo* 2019, 280–281

Johann Gualbert RAFFALT

(Murau, 1835 – Rome, 1865)

Pedlars on the Hungarian Plain, 1860s | Oil on wood, 24 × 32 cm
Purchase, 1993 | Inv. no. 93.2.B

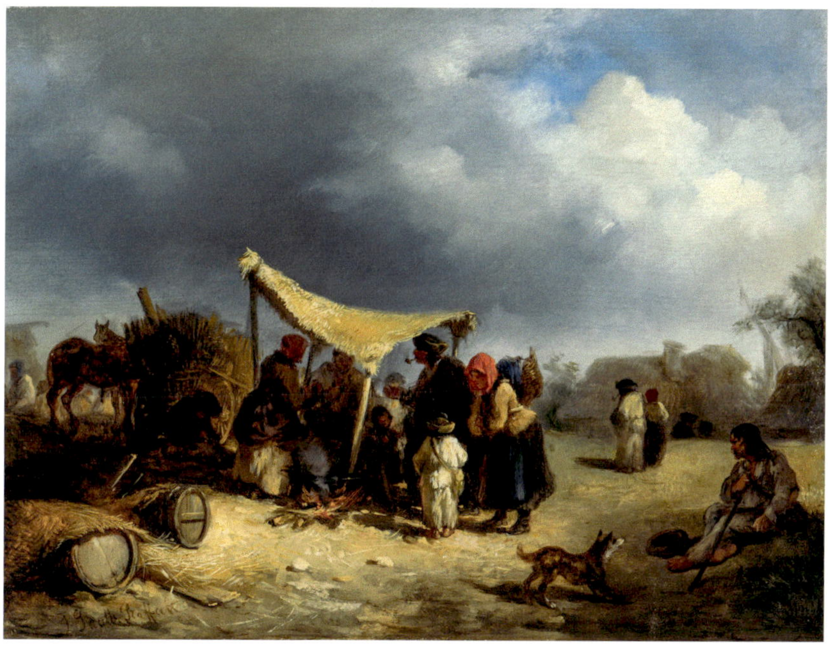

Johann Gualbert Raffalt was given his first lessons in painting by his father, the landscape artist Ignaz Raffalt. He attended the Academy of Fine Art in Vienna between 1850 and 1855, where he became a friend of August von Pettenkofen. Prompted by his older colleague, he turned his attention to the Hungarian Plain and the region around Szolnok. The isolated farms of the Great Hungarian Plain, the lives of the Hungarian Romani travellers, the sight of herds of horses galloping in the wild, and the stories of the robber bands and highwaymen of the Puszta had an exotic appeal for the young Vienna-educated painters who gathered around Pettenkofen. The young Raffalt's enthusiasm for Hungarian motifs earned him the nickname "Pusztamaler".

His approach to painting was determined by the growing fascination throughout Europe with distant, foreign cultures and exotic, eastern themes during the nineteenth century. Like many of his fellow painters, an interest in ethnography and anthropology also prompted him to paint more realistic landscapes and genre paintings during a career cut short by his early death. In this small painting on wood panel, the artist displays his skills in atmosphere and colourism. The apparent spontaneity of the composition, the brilliant blue of the sky, and the unaffectedness of the group gathered around the cooking pot beneath the awning all mark him out as a promising talent. – DL

Szvoboda Dománszky 2016, 63 | Kovács 2021, 82

Ivan Ivanovich SHISHKIN

(Yelabuga, 1832 – Saint Petersburg, 1898)

Forest Detail, second half of the 19th century | Oil on canvas, mounted on paperboard,
38 × 24 cm | Purchase, 1978 | Inv. no. 78.6.B

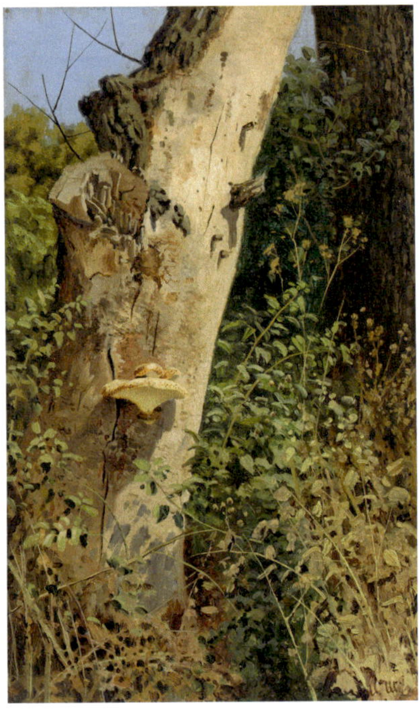

Ivan Ivanovich Shishkin, one of the most famous figures in nineteenth-century Russian landscape painting, studied in Saint Petersburg and several renowned Western European art schools. On his return home, he became a painter of Russian landscapes, then a professor of landscape painting in Saint Petersburg. He was a member of the group of Russian artists who, in 1863, rebelled against the rigidity of the academy and established the Society for Travelling Art Exhibitions, also known as the Peredvizhniki (The Wanderers). The Wanderers wanted Russian artists to be able to exhibit their works in as many places as possible, and to reach the widest possible audience, in the interests of creating a national art movement and making art accessible to the general public. Their travelling exhibitions also resulted in the first successes for Russian landscape painting, which had languished in the shadow of historical and portrait painting up until the middle of the nineteenth century.

Shishkin, whose meticulous observations of nature had provided him with a thorough knowledge of the depths of the forests and their vegetation, was a brilliant draughtsman, and his drawing skills are also apparent in his paintings. He was the first Russian artist to use colour shading in his paintings. He mostly painted majestically calm pictures of epic proportions, rarely depicting volatile human emotions in his works. – BIB

Niederhauser and Sargina 1979, 321 | Churak 2012

August von PETTENKOFEN

(Vienna, 1822 – Vienna, 1889)

By the Tisza, early 1850s | Oil on canvas, 18.5 × 28.3 cm
Donated by Móric Heim, 1920 | Inv. no. 381.B

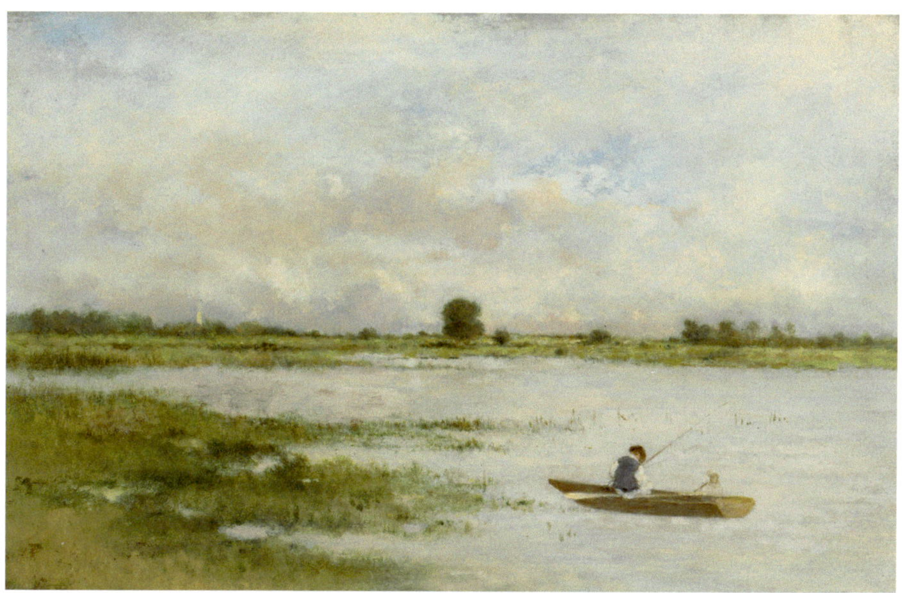

In the nineteenth century, Austrian artists discovered the Hungarian Great Plain as a subject for their paintings: for them, the distinctive Hungarian landscape represented the "exotic East". With the development of the railways, the town of Szolnok and the surrounding countryside became easily accessible to artists who were abandoning the constraints of academic painting and turning towards nature. The influence of French landscape painting and the Barbizon School made the light and atmosphere of the Great Plain even more appealing.

August von Pettenkofen, who visited Paris and Barbizon on several occasions, was one of the first artists to recognise the potential of the Hungarian Plain. The paintings he produced here might even be seen as ethnographic snapshots. The work, known as both *By the Tisza* and *Riverside Landscape*, plays on the contrast between the isolated figure of the fisherman and the Hungarian Plain stretching into infinity around him. The sweeping skyline above the river is broken by a single tree. What makes the area of wetland depicted in this painting so special is that this natural Tisza landscape, which was such a source of inspiration for contemporary artists, would disappear forever due to the river regulation that took place in the 1870s. – BIB

Cifka 1993a, 7

Jean-François MILLET

(Gruchy, 1814 – Barbizon, 1875)

View of the Puy-de-Dôme, 1866 | Pastel on paper, 55 × 68.2 cm
Purchased at the Henri Rouart auction (Paris), 1913 | Inv. no. 269.B

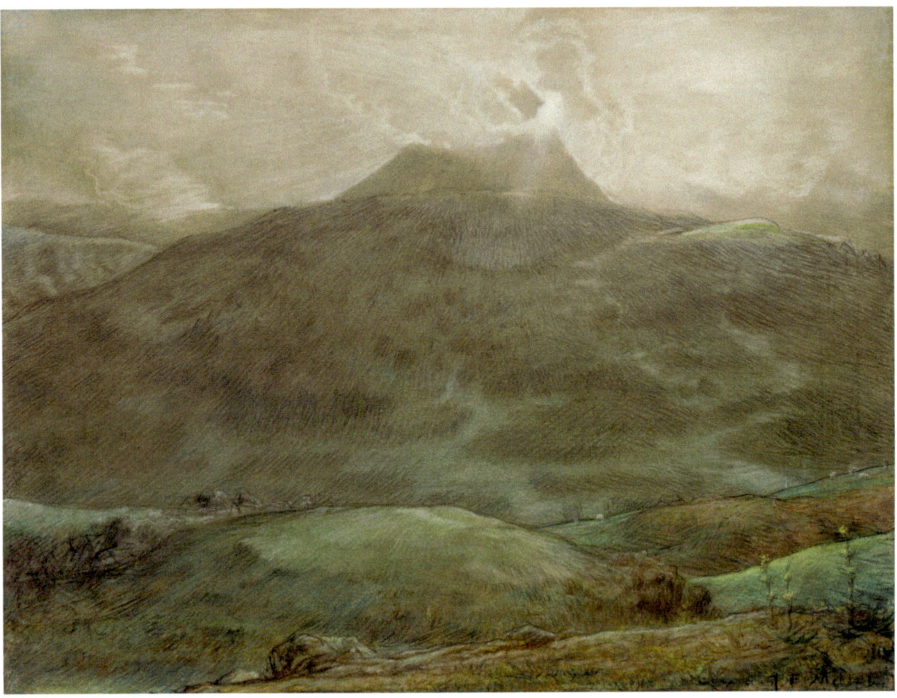

As one of the leading figures of the Barbizon School, Jean-François Millet became famous primarily for his genre scenes depicting everyday peasant life and the hardships of work in the field. However, the realist artist also painted numerous landscapes in the surroundings of Fontainebleau and in his native Normandy, occasionally exploiting the softness and subtle colour gradations of pastels besides working in oils. In 1866, a visit to the volcanic region of Auvergne in central France inspired several works.

The almost empty, monotonous landscape is dominated by the region's biggest volcano, the Puy-de-Dôme. The haze after a fall of rain brings to life an almost monochrome palette based on gradations of grey and green, while the sun's rays accentuate and sculpt the parallel lines of the hills. Light filters through the clouds visible behind the bare, majestic mountain, illuminating and almost transfiguring the countryside: the dramatic sky suggests the latent power of the dormant volcano. The work was owned by the famous French art collectors Émile Gavet and later Henri Rouart before being acquired by the Museum of Fine Arts in 1913. – AZSK

Illyés 2001, 46–47 | *Clermont-Ferrand 2002*, 44, 67, 119

Claude MONET

(Paris, 1840 – Giverny, 1926)

Breakwater at Trouville – Low Tide, 1870 | Oil on canvas, 54 × 65.7 cm
Purchased at the Julius Stern auction (Berlin), 1916 | Inv. no. 367.B

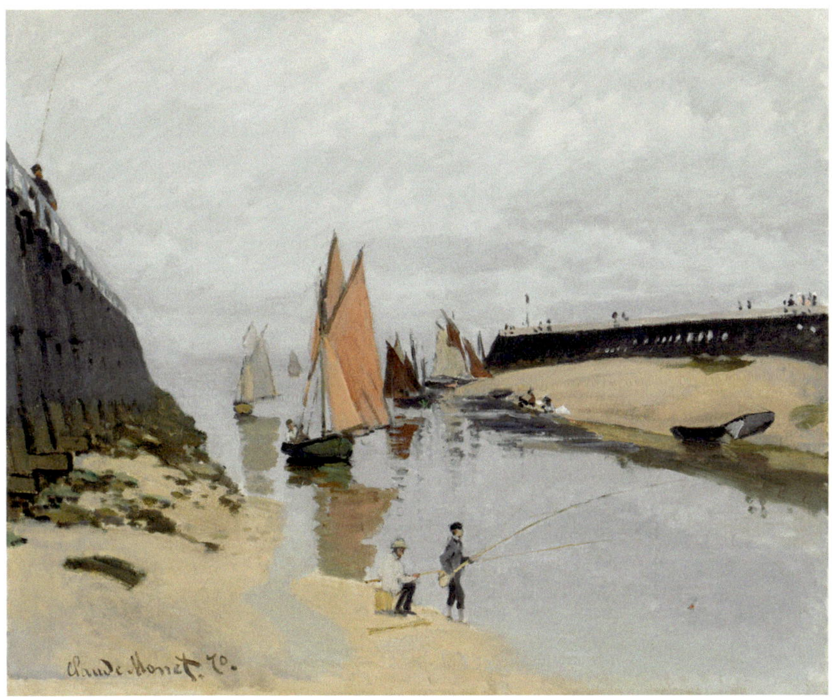

With three landscapes belonging to different periods of his career, Claude Monet is well represented within our collection. This painting shows the freshness of his early impressionist works. In June 1870, Monet spent his honeymoon in the fashionable seaside resort of Trouville in Normandy, where he often recorded the new phenomena of tourism. In this painting, though, there is not a single trace of the busy beaches, nor of the contemporary events of the Franco-Prussian War: as the river Touques flows into the sea, there is nothing to disturb the peace of the anglers. The restrained tones, the pictorial structure built up of strong diagonals and independent fields of colour, and the slightly overhead perspective, all recall the world of Japanese woodcuts. The apparently random composition is in fact designed with great care: the mass of the breakwater that seals the left-hand edge of the painting is countered on the right, where the dark band stretching along the line of the horizon marks the invisible boundary between the river and the sea. Monet's sensitive portrayal of the cloudy sky, which seems to merge with the water, reveals a direct observation of atmospheric effects. – AZSK

Illyés 2001, 90–91 | *Budapest 2003–2004*, cat. no. 19

Eugène BOUDIN

(Honfleur, 1824 – Deauville, 1898)

Portrieux, 1874 | Oil on canvas, 54.3 × 89.3 cm | Purchased at the spring exhibition
of the National Salon, Budapest from Galerie Le Pelletier (Paris), 1907
Inv. no. 202.B

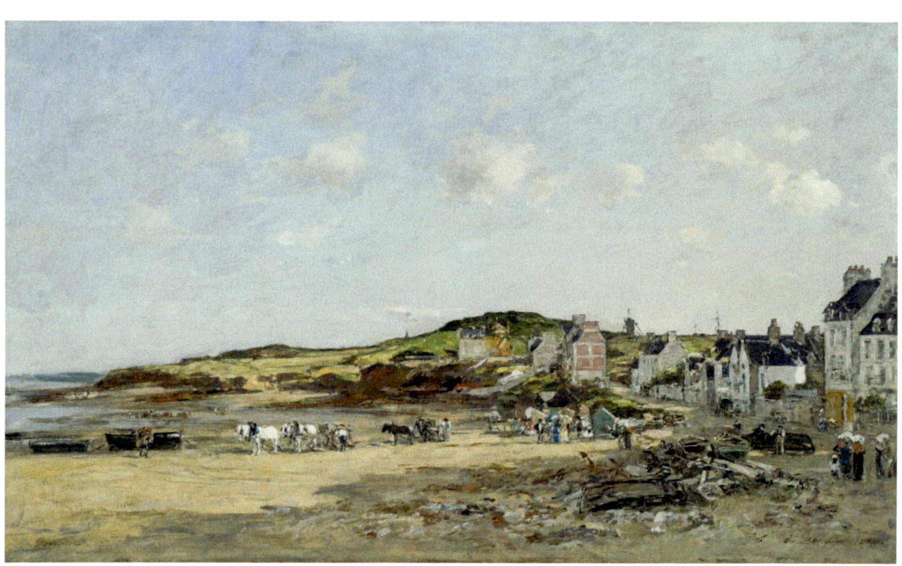

While Eugène Boudin, a native of Normandy, never took part in Impressionist exhibitions and
did not join the group, he played an important part in the birth of the movement on account of
his practice of painting outdoors and the brisk and lively brushwork with which he recorded
effects of light and air. Despite his success, he was often remembered chiefly as Claude Monet's master. After the two artists first met in 1856, the young Monet was quickly and profoundly impressed by Boudin's aesthetic ideas, technical advice and preferred motifs.

Although he often took as his subject matter the popular beaches of Normandy, in
particular Trouville, Boudin occasionally opted for the supposedly more 'primitive' coast of
Brittany. In the early 1870s he made a number of paintings around Portrieux, mainly depicting the rocky coastline and the ships stationed in the harbour. In this picture we are given
a glimpse of everyday life in the village. The whole canvas is executed with the painter's lively
brushwork, which gives a vivid clarity to the sunswept sandy beach. The sensitive rendering
of the slightly cloudy, pale-blue sky confirms Corot's claim that Boudin was the "king of the
skies". – AZSK

Schmit 1973, vol. 1, cat. no. 958 | Illyés 2001, 88–89

Albert LEBOURG

(Montfort-sur-Risle, 1849 – Rouen, 1928)

The Bridge at Charenton, 1887 | Oil on canvas, 34.5 × 64.5 cm

Transfer, 1953 | Inv. no. 504.B

203

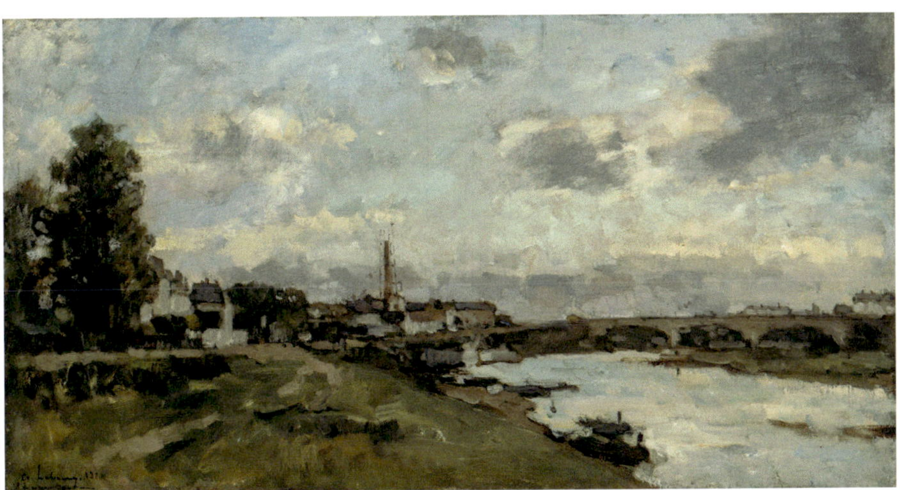

For several decades, this small, somewhat elongated riverside landscape was inventoried in the museum's collection under the name of the little-known French painter Edme Émile Laborne. Recent research has demonstrated, however, that it was actually the work of a much more acclaimed master, Albert Lebourg. Born in Normandy, Lebourg was known for his independent spirit; he was often associated with the impressionists, and he even exhibited with them twice, in 1879 and 1880.

The artist was extremely fond of painting riverbanks, and he would often set up his easel along the rivers flowing through the environs of Rouen and Paris, recording the gentle waves of the water, the sweeping progress of the clouds and the constant changes of the light. The motif of the bridge was among his favourites. The Budapest painting, which shows the freshness and painterly ease of his best artistic period, represents Charenton, a small town to the southeast of Paris, at the confluence of the Seine and the Marne, which inspired numerous paintings by Lebourg. The artist rendered the cloudy sky and the unique atmosphere of the increasingly industrialised area using bold, confident brushstrokes. – AZSK

Kovács and Lespinasse 2018

Paul GAUGUIN

(Paris, 1848 – Hiva Oa, Marquesas Islands, 1903)

Winter Landscape, 1879 | Oil on canvas, 60 × 81 cm
Purchased from the 1907 spring exhibition of the National Salon, Budapest | Inv. no. 204.B

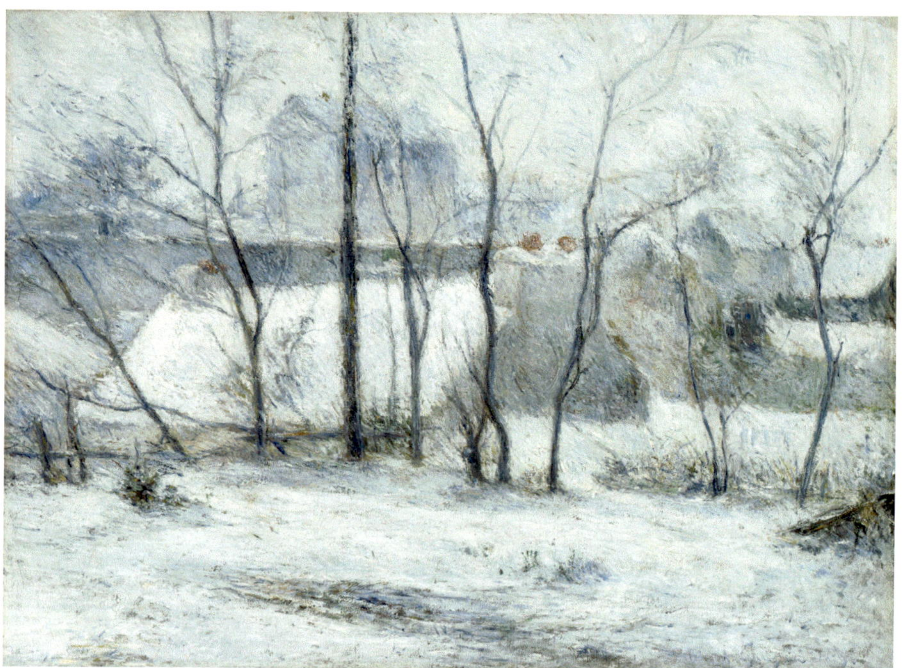

Nine years his junior, Gauguin was a huge admirer of Paul Cezanne, whose art he revered throughout his life. Having abandoned his job as a stockbroker to dedicate himself to painting – to the dismay of his practical, Danish-born wife Mette, with whom he had five children – he studied intensively not only the landscapes painted in around 1870 by the "father" of impressionism, Camille Pissarro, but also the compositions of Cezanne.

Gauguin made use of a winter and a summer landscape by Cezanne for his attractive fan designs but was also keen to imitate the older master's parallel brushstrokes in his early still lifes and landscapes. His own art collection included several works by Cezanne, as well as paintings by Pissarro. Completed in 1879, Gauguin's *Winter Landscape* was shown at the fifth impressionist exhibition organised the following year. The composition encapsulates the rich European landscape tradition.

Homage to seventeenth-century Dutch painting and the Italian mannerists was a new phenomenon in French art in the mid-nineteenth century. Gauguin too discovered and explored these pioneering approaches before choosing an entirely new path: inspired by his childhood memories of Peru, as well as by the islands' mythology and magical worlds of colour, he decided to move to Polynesia. – JG

Wildenstein and Crussard 2001, cat. no. 57 | Illyés 2001, 98–100

Claude MONET

(Paris, 1840 – Giverny, 1926)

Plum Trees in Blossom, 1879 | Oil on canvas, 64.3 × 81 cm
Purchased from the Galerie Arnot (Vienna), 1912 | Inv. no. 266.B

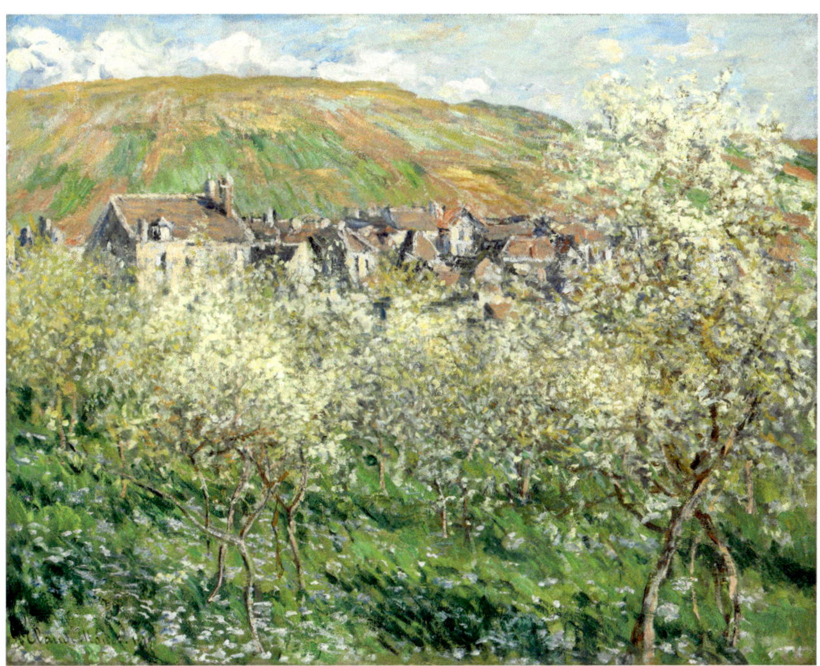

Between 1878 and 1881, Claude Monet rented a house in the village of Vétheuil on the bank of the Seine not far from Paris. The house and the pretty orchard surrounding it perhaps eased his pain: his paintings were not selling, his art dealer was of little help, and his wife and young son were ill. Bedridden since May 1879, his wife died in September that year.

Of the three Monet paintings in Budapest, it is *Plum Trees in Blossom* that illustrates every one of the stylistic features of impressionism. The onset of his beloved wife's illness coincided with the end of a long, cold winter, although when the spring blossoms appeared, Monet was still able to work with relative tranquillity.

There is still no consensus among experts as to whether this picture was painted outdoors in the garden at Vétheuil, or from a window of the house. The fresh, uncut grass and the flowering plum tree, clothed in brilliant white, form the first spatial layer of the painting, with the village behind them, and a hill rising beyond. The angle suggests that Monet was working from a window of the house, a vantage point favoured by several of his contemporaries, including Édouard Manet. – JG

Wildenstein 1974, cat. no. 520 | *Budapest* 2003–2004, cat. no. 81

Claude MONET

(Paris, 1840 – Giverny, 1926)

Three Fishing Boats, 1886 | Oil on canvas, 73 × 92.5 cm
Purchase, 1945 | Inv. no. 436.B

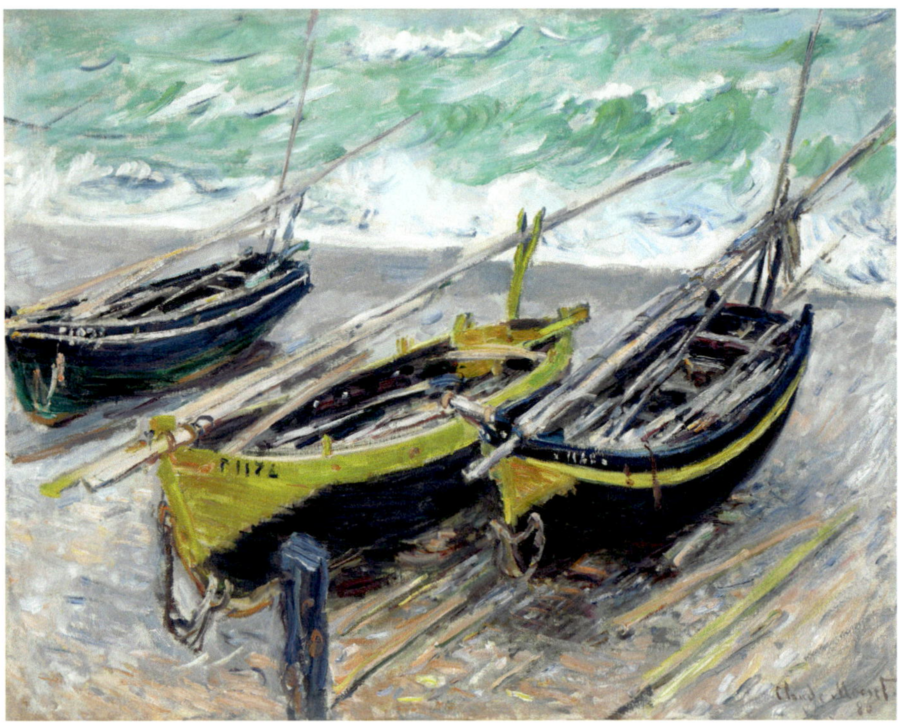

Throughout the life of Claude Monet, the movements of water, the ever-changing light and weather conditions of the sea remained a fundamental source of inspiration. *Three Fishing Boats* was painted in Étretat, a popular tourist destination in Normandy, probably in October or November of 1886. The harsh winter weather did not deter the painter from working in the open air, right in front of the motif. Among the works Monet devoted to this theme, this painting is one of the most radical. The seemingly random composition evokes the spontaneity of a photograph: the three boats are seen from above, the sky is not visible and the bow of the vessel on the left is cut off by the edge of the picture. With powerful and expressive brush-strokes, Monet depicted this scene in dim winter light, distinguishing between the materials of the different elements and following the forms with intense dynamism: the boats with their yellow, green and dark-blue colours are rendered with sweeping movements of the brush, following their curved structure, while the bright green and white waves striking the shore were formed with energetic upward slashes. The dynamic technique perfectly captures the motion of the wind and the water. – AZSK

Illyés 2001, 94–95 | *Budapest 2003–2004*, cat. no. 10

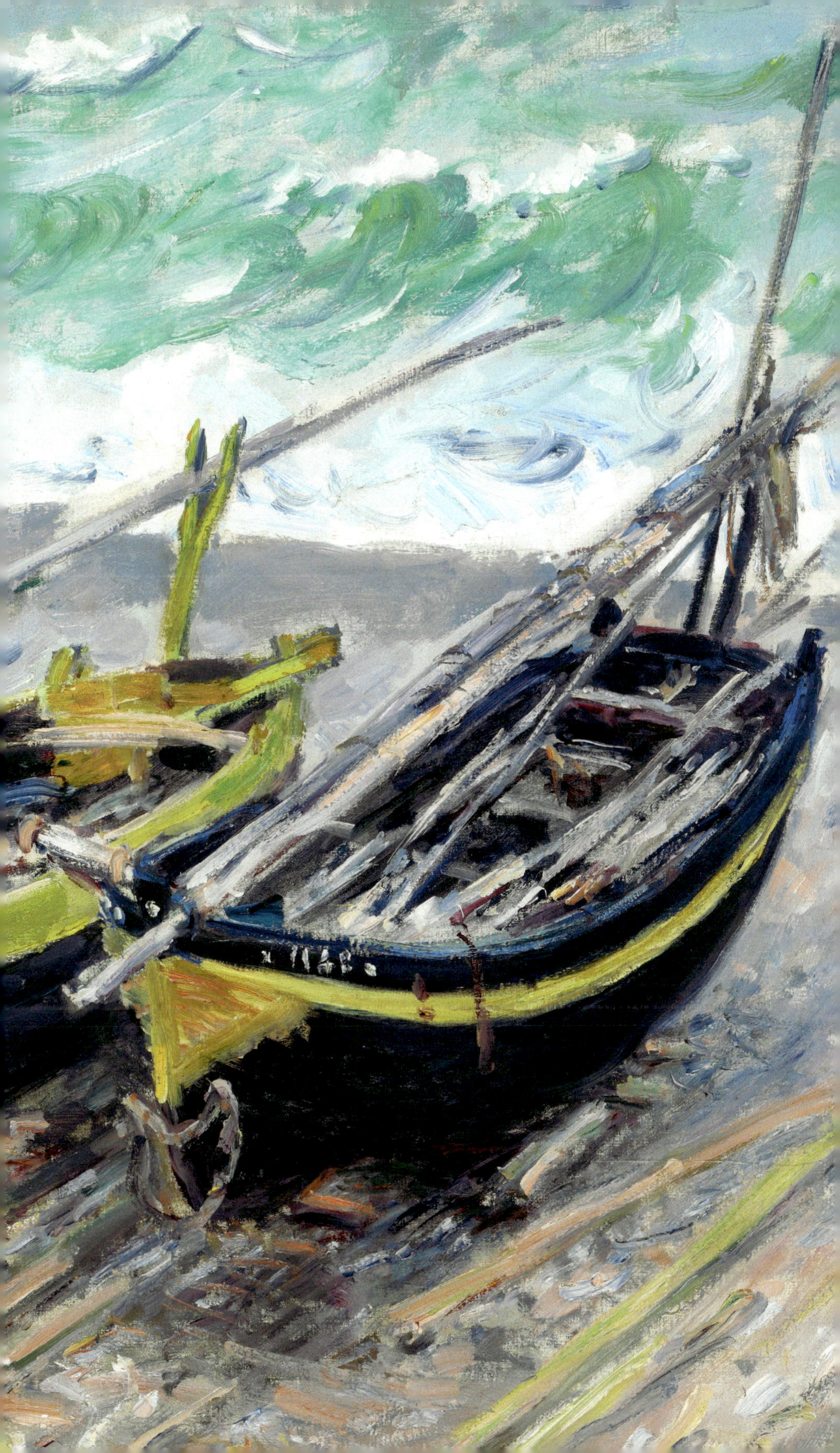

VII

The Observation of People and Their Surroundings

John Quincy ADAMS	Jules LAGAE
Jules ADLER	Constantin MEUNIER
Michael ANCHER	Paul MEYERHEIM
Hermann BAISCH	José MORENO CARBONERO
Jules BASTIEN-LEPAGE	Luigi NONO
Jean BÉRAUD	Auguste RODIN
Jacques-Émile BLANCHE	Anton ROMAKO
Józef CHEŁMOŃSKI	Lucien SIMON
Pierre Jacques DIERCKX	Stephan SINDING
Paul DU BOIS	Solomon Joseph SOLOMON
Auguste FEYEN-PERRIN	Gudmund STENERSEN
Walther FIRLE	Ettore TITO
Robert FRANGEŠ-MIHANOVIĆ	Laurits Regner TUXEN
José GALLEGOS Y ARNOSA	Fritz von UHDE
Edmond Georges GRANDJEAN	Frans VAN LEEMPUTTEN
Viggo JOHANSEN	Jan VERHAS
Pio JORIS	Théodore VERSTRAETE
Albert von KELLER	Ingebrigt VIK
Gotthardt KUEHL	Ignacio ZULOAGA

From the 1870s, visitors to the Paris Salon and to exhibitions held in the growing number of private galleries would have discerned a change in technique: a shift from realism to a more colourful, painterly world. Urban, everyday subjects were represented in lighter colours, taking a fresh, direct approach. The impressionists deliberately adopted a loose, sketchy style, experimenting with the properties of colour and boldly capturing the perceived colour effects of cast shadows. However, another, bigger group of painters, who reached larger audiences, were working with natural tones and accurately rendered forms. Rather than faithfulness to sensory experience, their work was dominated by the minute observation of reality, and in place of charming figures engaged in elegant urban life and carefree outdoor excursions, their protagonists were the destitute, poor peasants and day labourers.

An approach to painting characterised by the meticulous observation of people's everyday surroundings and behaviour had spread throughout the continent by the 1880s. Summarised under the label naturalism, this trend gradually gained ground at international exhibitions. A new generation of artists emerged alongside the respected representatives of realism. The international horizon also expanded, with artists from previously little-known countries and regions taking on a greater role. Belgian, Italian, Spanish, Scandinavian, and Central and Eastern European representatives of this shift in perspective were popular participants at exhibitions.

Munich was the most important centre of European art besides Paris. Art students from Scandinavia and Central Europe were attracted by the opportunity to train at the city's academy and growing number of private art schools, while an openness to contemporary foreign trends at exhibitions meant that success was within everyone's reach. Emerging and ambitious artists from Hungary also gathered in the Bavarian capital, acquainting themselves not only with the German masters but also with other leading representatives of the new wave of naturalism, including artists from France. Having travelled to Paris to study the works of these artists – primarily Jules Bastien-Lepage and Pascal Dagnan-Bouveret – in their place of origin, they forged their own unique style on their return to Munich.

In the 1880s and the first half of the following decade, paintings that later came to be recognized as belonging to the naturalist trend became increasingly prominent at exhibitions in the Budapest Kunsthalle – just as in Munich. These were the new favourites among exhibition audiences and art critics, and Belgian, Italian, and later Scandinavian and Spanish proponents of the style soon emerged alongside the eminent Austrian, German, and French masters. It was through their works that the Hungarian public first became acquainted with the new visuality that had already gained ground abroad. Representatives of naturalism were honoured with several gold medals by the Society of Fine Arts, while the state regularly purchased their works. As a result, the museum's collection includes a particularly rich selection of naturalist works from a broad geographical spectrum.

Auguste RODIN

(Paris, 1840 – Meudon, 1917)

The Age of Bronze, model: 1875–1876, cast: 1900 | Plaster, 181.5 × 66 × 51 cm
Purchased from the artist, 1900 | Inv. no. 1987.U

At the start of his career, Rodin worked as a decorative sculptor, first in Paris and later in Brussels. In 1877, while still virtually unknown, Rodin showed a life-size male plaster figure in Brussels under the title *The Vanquished One*. The figure later became known as *The Age of Bronze*. The initial title was an allusion to France's defeat in the Franco-Prussian War, while the later version – expanding the original political reference – is rather an allusion to humanity awakening to consciousness. The statue caused shock and scandal when it was first shown. In fact, on seeing the unprecedented subtlety and sensuousness of the modelling, some critics even accused the artist of having made the statue using a life cast of his model.

Gábor Térey, director of the National Picture Gallery, was drawn to the work of the now celebrated artist at the 1900 Paris Exposition. He subsequently commissioned a plaster cast for the brand new Museum of Fine Arts. By special request, the cast was given a bronze-coloured patina. Besides the masterful finish and brilliant nuances of colour, the special casting technique employed makes this life-size figure a rarity among Rodin's patinised plaster casts. – FT

Illyés 2001, 118–121 | *Budapest* 2012–2013, 37, 44, 51–54

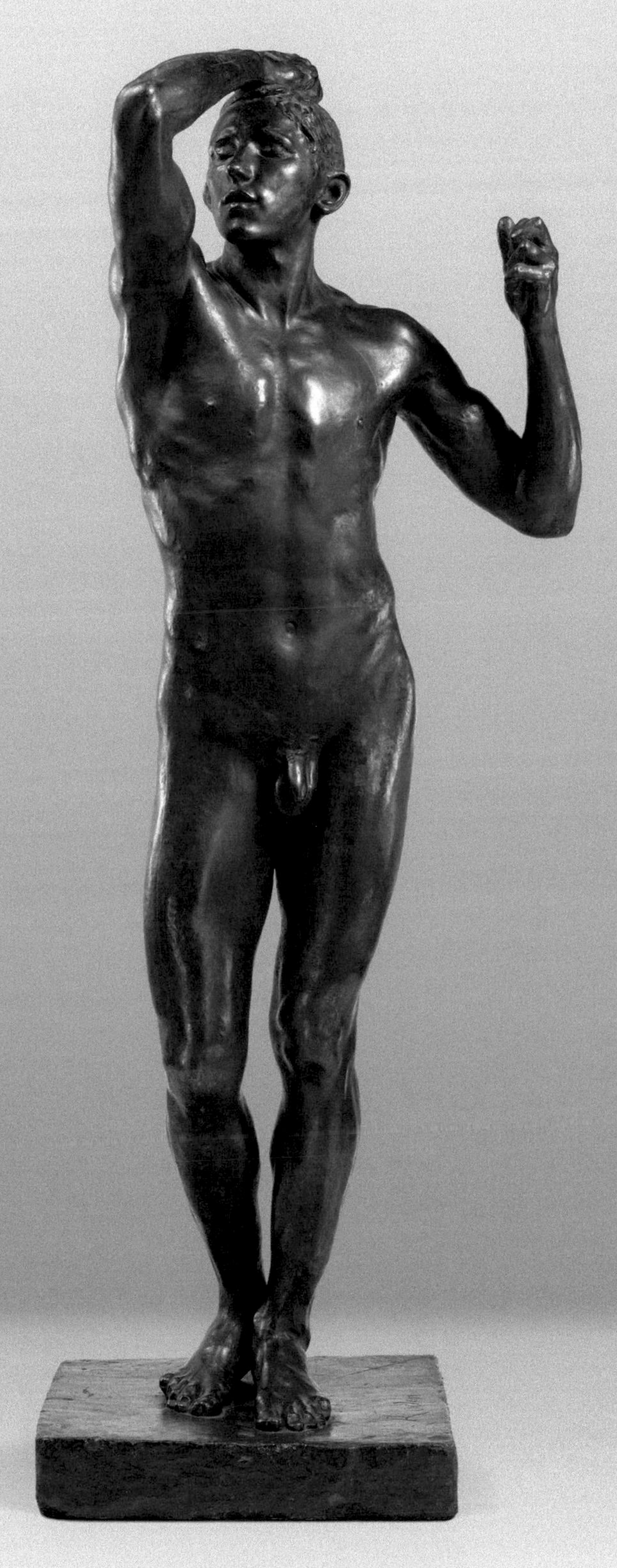

Auguste FEYEN-PERRIN

(Bey-sur-Seille, 1826 – Paris, 1888)

Fisherwomen of Cancale, 1881 | Oil on canvas, 118 × 158 cm
Purchased from the HNSFA's 1881 autumn exhibition | Inv. no. 80.B

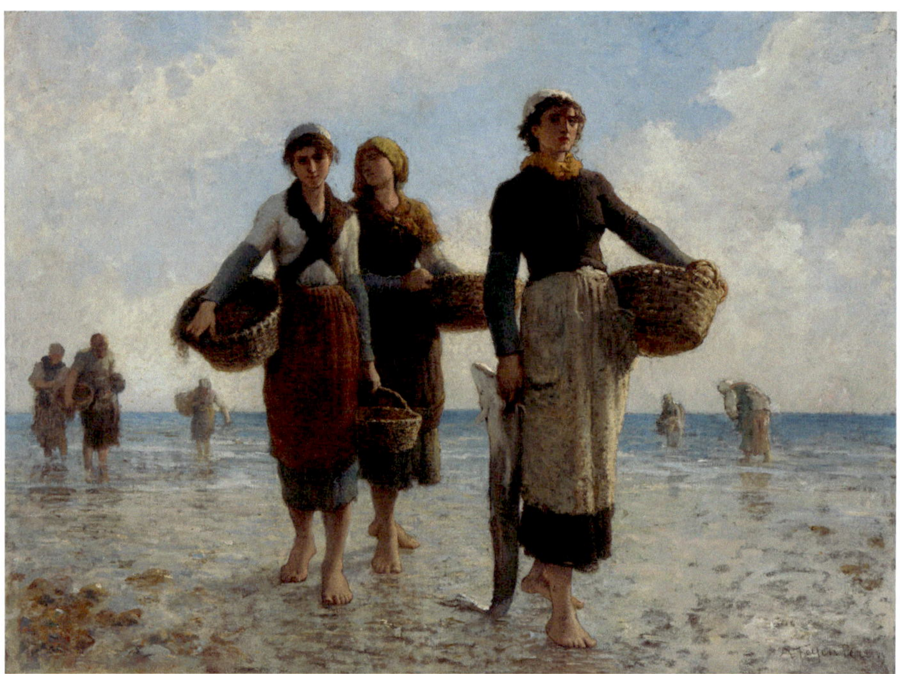

The now somewhat obscure Auguste Feyen-Perrin became popular in the last quarter of the nineteenth century as a painter of the women of Cancale. The small town on the Breton coast, known for oyster farming and fishing, inspired many of his compositions, which usually depict the everyday lives of local women.

His painting held by the Museum of Fine Arts, many variations of which are known, was quite successful in 1881 at the Paris Salon and at the autumn exhibition of the Hungarian National Society of Fine Arts. Its theme is the so-called "pêche à pied", the collecting of fish and mussels in shallow water at low tide. The composition focuses on three Cancale "graces" walking barefoot in the wet sand, wearing simple, unadorned attire, gracefully bearing their full baskets towards home. Their attractive, slender, yet noble and powerful figures emerge in front of a cloudy sky, seen slightly from below, which lends a kind of monumentality to their appearance. True to the poetic naturalism which made him popular, Feyen-Perrin did not depict the strain and fatigue of physical labour, but rather conjured up an idealised picture of traditional fishing life. – AZSK

Kovács 2021–2022

Jan VERHAS

(Dendermonde, 1834 – Brussels–Schaerbeek, 1896)

Alone, 1887 | Oil on canvas, 121 × 86 cm

Purchased from the HNSFA's 1887 autumn exhibition | Inv. no. 69.B

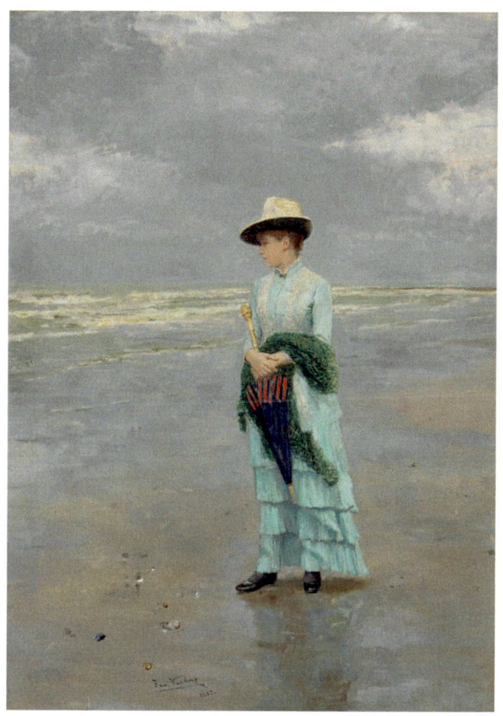

Known primarily for his charming paintings of children, the Belgian painter Jan Verhas spent most of his time on the coast at Heyst-sur-Mer from 1882. The main subjects of his later works are visitors at the resort, children in particular, strolling along the beach or riding donkeys, and local fishermen. Here, the painter set himself a new artistic goal: the sensitive rendering, using the *plein air* method, of the atmosphere of the Belgian coast, the reflection of light on the water, and the misty air. Contemporary critics commended Verhas's efforts to achieve the sensitive depiction of mood.

In this painting, the grey of the damp sand and the white churning waves emphasise the vibrant colours of the woman's dress. The boundary between sky and sea almost disappears; all that remains is an empty, monochrome background, enhancing the solitude of the figure, lost in her thoughts.

This melancholy painting won Verhas the gold medal reserved for foreign artists at the 1887 autumn exhibition held at the Budapest Kunsthalle. It was then that the Hungarian state purchased the work, which was generously being offered at half price. Because of its simple yet deeply emotional rendering, it was regarded by the public as a modern masterpiece. – CSJB

Fővárosi Lapok 1887, 2043 | Pasteiner 1888, 142–144

Jules BASTIEN-LEPAGE

(Damvillers, 1848 – Paris, 1884)

All Souls' Day, 1878 | Oil on canvas, 46 × 55 cm
Donated by the Friends of the Art Museums, Budapest, 1935 | Inv. no. 408.B

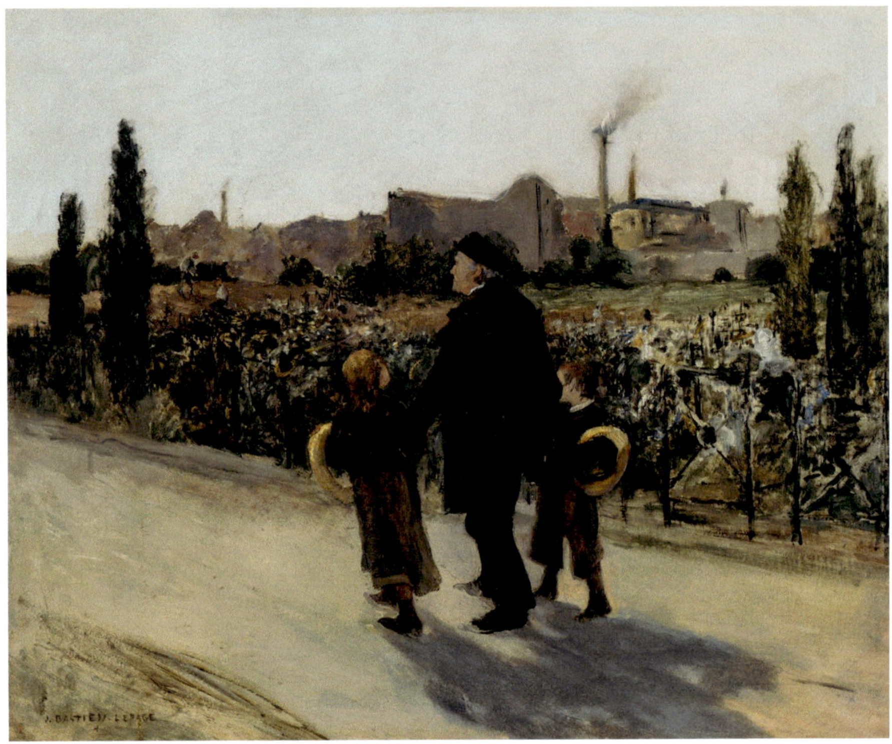

Jules Bastien-Lepage was one of the most successful French painters of the 1870s and 1880s. The Europe-wide popularity of the artist, who died at just thirty-six years of age, was largely due to his extraordinary ability to combine the precise, objective approach of naturalism with the light colours of *plein air* painting.

This small work was probably a sketch for a larger-scale composition that was never realised. Despite the delicate execution and limpid colours, the painting conveys a profound and sombre message about grief and the inevitability of death: the old man, with his stiff gait and slightly bowed posture, is on his way to the cemetery with the two children, to visit the graves of their loved ones and pay their respects. Although not explicit, the composition suggests that the children are taking their yellow wreaths to lay on their parents' grave. The factory chimneys rising in the distance are a reference to relentless modernisation, suggesting that time alters not only human beings but also their environment. The painting was acquired by the Museum of Fine Arts from the collection of Baron Adolf Kohner, one of the most important private collectors in Hungary in the early decades of the twentieth century. – AZSK

Aubrun 1985, 128, cat. no. 162 | Illyés 2001, 110–111

Jules BASTIEN-LEPAGE

(Damvillers, 1848 – Paris, 1884)

Shepherdess, model: ca. 1880; cast: ca. 1900 | Bronze, 32.5 × 21 × 19 cm
Purchase, 1952 | Inv. no. 52.601.U

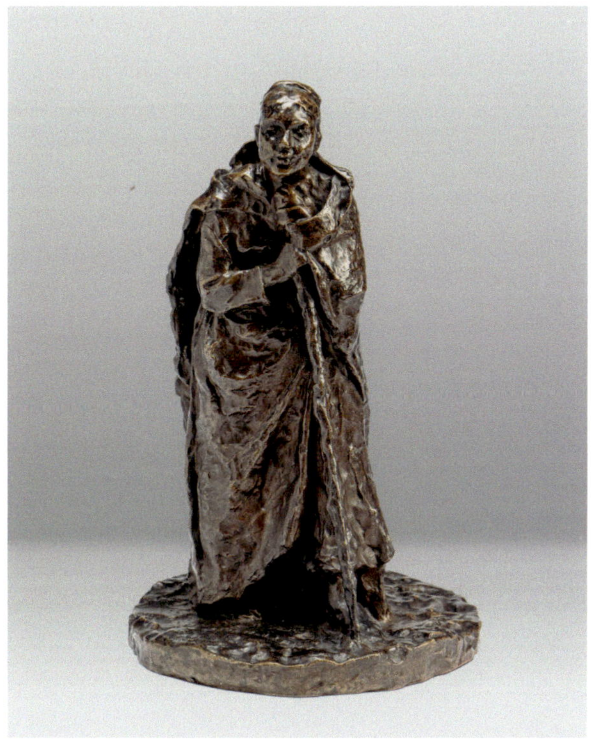

Besides his richly detailed, psychological portraits and highly acclaimed naturalist paintings of everyday peasant life, Jules Bastien-Lepage also produced a few sculptures during his short career. The *Shepherdess* is one of half a dozen known figurines: the small, loosely moulded figure, cast in bronze, leans on her long staff as she gazes into the distance. The rustic finish accentuates the simplicity of the girl's clothing and her pronounced facial features, which do not conform to the contemporary ideal of beauty. The various names given to copies of the sculpture reflect different interpretations of the work: some connect it with the artist's rural subjects, while others identify the shepherdess with Saint Joan.

Bastien-Lepage sparked considerable critical debate with a painting that he showed at the 1880 Paris Salon – a naturalistic portrayal of Joan of Arc together with the saints who appeared to her in her visions. Unusual psychic states, raptures and reveries are recurring elements in the painter's works, although the artist often left to the viewer to work out what lay behind the subject's meditations and enigmatic (vacant or ecstatic) gaze. – AZSK

Illyés 2001, 112–113

Théodore **VERSTRAETE**

(Ghent, 1850 – Antwerp, 1907)

Twilight in April, 1881 | Oil on canvas, 106 × 186 cm
Purchased from the HNSFA's 1882 autumn exhibition | Inv. no. 79.B

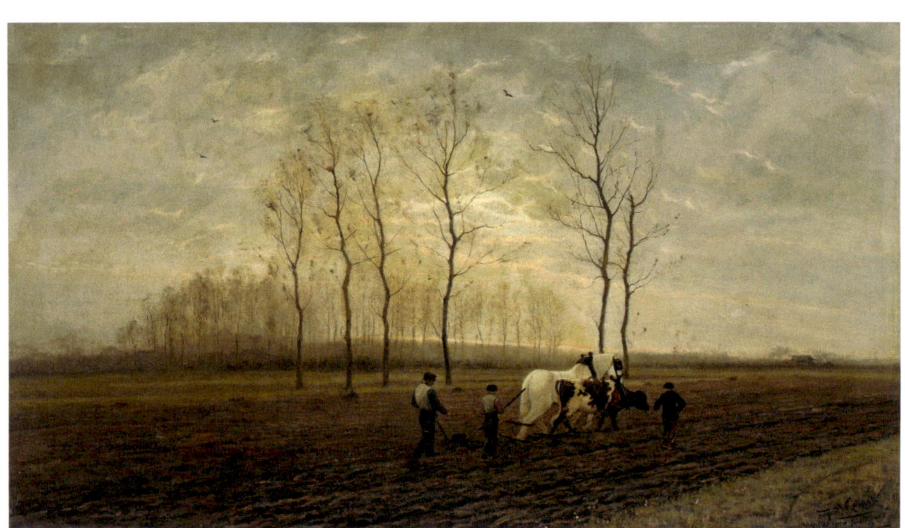

Théodore Verstraete studied at the Academy of Art in Antwerp between 1867 and 1878, and in 1883 became one of the founding members of Les XX, a group of artists in Brussels bringing together new artistic tendencies. As a representative of the naturalist *plein air* approach, he painted his landscapes on the coast of the Netherlands and in the countryside of Belgium; his peasant scenes depict everyday life with a sombre, poetic, and dignified tone.

Between 1879 and 1889, Verstraete lived and worked in the vicinity of Brasschaat in northern Belgium – it is this flat, uneventful Flemish landscape that is the setting for *Twilight in April*. Beneath the vast sky, work still goes on in the evening gloom: the peasant and his children pace intently beside the horse and cow that are pulling the plough. The almost bare trees and the golden sunlight filtering between the clouds evoke the reawakening of nature and the cycle of life and the seasons; the composition as a whole conveys the profound harmony and close connection between human beings and their environment. The painting was first shown at the 1881 Salon in Brussels, then in 1882 it featured in the autumn exhibition of the Hungarian National Society of Fine Arts. From there, it became part of the collection of the National Museum as one of its first contemporary Belgian acquisitions. – AZSK

Solvay 1906, 49, 105 | Weisberg 1992, 211–217

Frans VAN LEEMPUTTEN

(Werchter, 1850 – Antwerp, 1914)

Landscape with Cart and Flock of Sheep, 1889 | Oil on canvas, 50 × 88 cm
Purchased from the HNSFA's 1889–1890 winter exhibition | Inv. no. 86.B

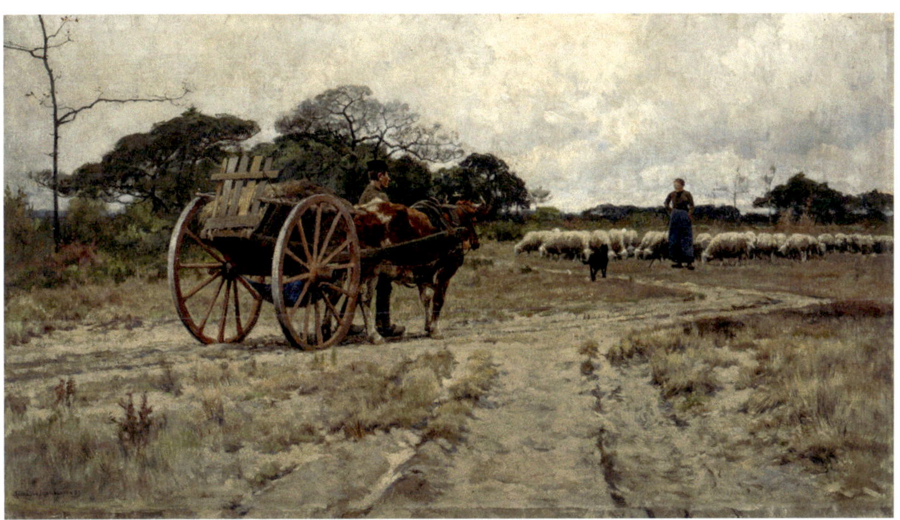

Frans Van Leemputten was born in a rural area, although his family soon moved to Brussels. His father, originally an agricultural worker, became a painting restorer at the Royal Academy of Fine Arts. As his father's assistant, Van Leemputten was introduced to the world of fine arts as a child and went on to study art in Antwerp. He earned wide recognition in the 1870s for his *plein air* paintings of Flemish village life. He was greatly influenced by, among others, his good friend Constantin Meunier and the Dutch landscape painter Paul Gabriël.

Van Leemputten's scenes, mainly depicting the countryside around Antwerp, the Campine, and the Brabant, avoid sentimentality and moralizing. He observed the peasants' clothing, everyday lives, and customs and committed them to canvas with meticulous attention to detail. In the late 1880s, agricultural workers pausing from their labours to converse beneath an overcast sky are a recurring subject in his paintings. This series includes *Landscape with Cart and Flock of Sheep*, in which the use of colour is in line with the artist's darker period. After the turn of the century, he employed lighter, brighter colours. – BIB

Weisberg 1992, 237 | Van Eldere 1995

Hermann BAISCH

(Dresden, 1846 – Karlsruhe, 1894)

Shrimp Fishermen, 1890 | Oil on canvas, 102 × 154 cm
Purchased at the 1890–1891 winter exhibition of the HNSFA | Inv. no. 117.B

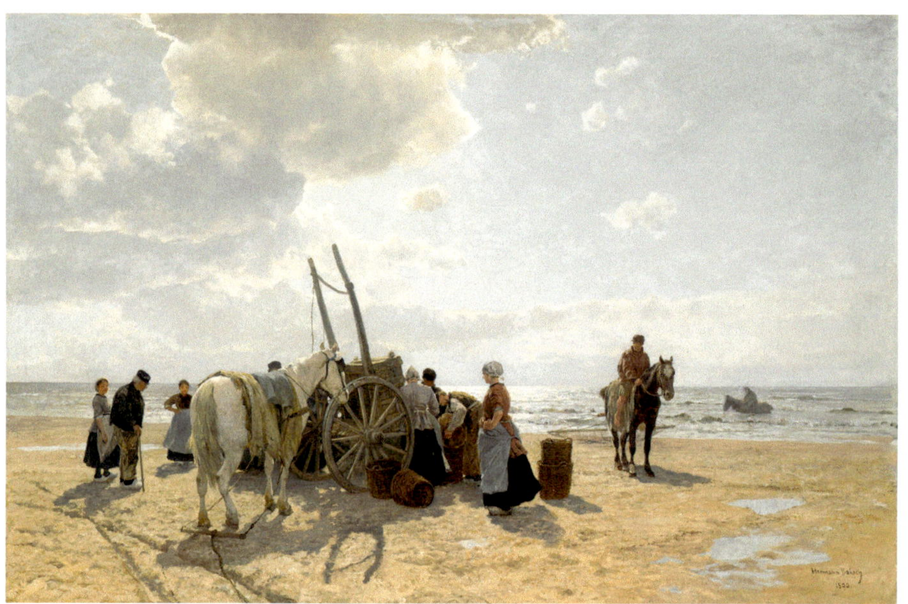

The German artist Hermann Baisch was best known for his village genre-paintings, rural landscapes, and animal depictions combining realistic and romantic elements, although he also produced a smaller quantity of more naturalistic works in Katwijk, on the coast of the Netherlands. The fishing village (which probably also inspired his painting in Budapest) attracted a large number of painters in the last quarter of the nineteenth century: the singular light, the simple fishing life, and the local clothing and customs provided them with new and attractive themes.

The fishermen on the beach are collecting shrimp using horse-drawn nets while the women are waiting for the fresh produce. What first captures the viewer's attention is the bright sunshine; Baisch depicted the light effects of the cloudy sky, the shadows on the shore, and the wet texture of the sand brilliantly. The tension in the composition derives from the fact that, while the artist depicted the scene with photo-realistic precision encompassing every detail, we still cannot see what the attention of all the characters is focused on: the fishermen turn away from the viewer, and the horse-drawn cart obscures the goods that are laid out. – AZSK

Ludwig 1981, 48–49

Józef CHEŁMOŃSKI

(Boczki, 1849 – Kuklówka, 1914)

In front of the Inn, 1872 | Oil on canvas, 58.5 × 116.5 cm
Bequest of Count János Pálffy, 1912 | Inv. no. 233.B

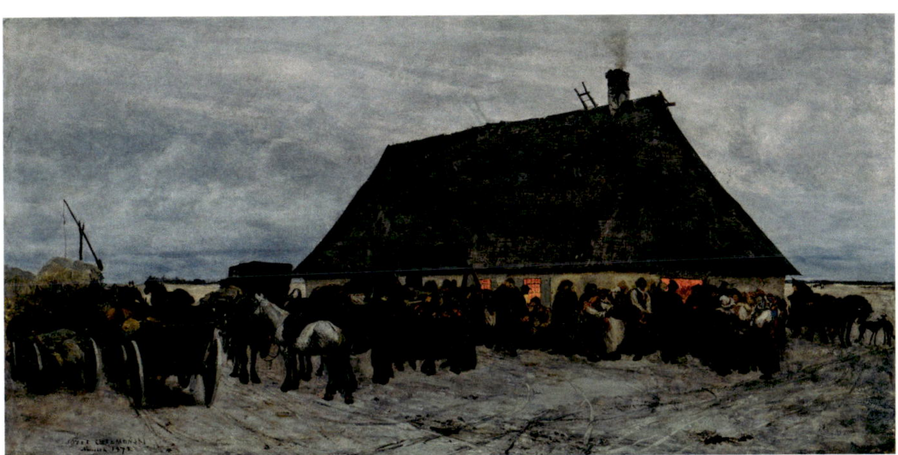

In contrast to the Kraków school, which shaped the foundations of the historical painting style associated with the name of Jan Matejko, which perpetuated the romantic tradition, the Warsaw school that influenced Józef Chełmoński introduced a realist turn to Polish painting. Chełmoński, who was also referred to as a folk painter, initially wavered between the influence of the academy and rural genre painting, but owing to the Polish artists he met while studying in Munich, he eventually opted for the latter path. His scenes, inspired by the lives of Polish peasants, were popular among British and American collectors.

He often set his scenes against a backdrop of snow-covered landscapes, achieving his intended dramatic effect by exploiting the contrast between the white and dark colours. The endless winter steppe likewise stretches into the distance in the painting *In front of the Inn*, while in the foreground, the Cossacks, escorting a group of men and women to their new homes, rest at an inn. The settling of Russian speakers in Polish-majority territories was a frequent occurrence in provinces under Russian rule in the nineteenth century. – BIB

Masłowski 1973 | Micke-Broniarek and Głowacki 2024, 40–41, cat. no. 21

Pio JORIS

(Rome, 1843 – Rome, 1921)

The Via Flaminia in Rome, after 1867 | Oil on canvas, 62.5 × 135 cm
Purchased from the HNSFA's 1893–1894 winter exhibition | Inv. no. 132.B

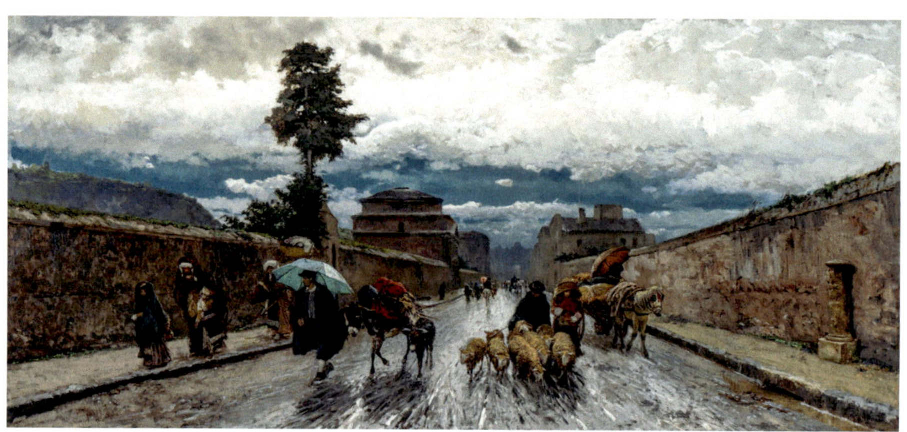

Having studied painting in Naples and Tuscany, in the late 1860s Pio Joris made the acquaintance of a circle of Spanish painters working in Rome. They were followers of Mariano Fortuny, whose work made a strong impression on Joris. These combined influences led him to
specialise in genre scenes, and his paintings attracted the attention of the Parisian art dealer
Alphonse Goupil, who also represented Mihály Munkácsy for a time. The two were probably
introduced to one another by Fortuny himself.

The Museum of Fine Arts owns two paintings by Joris. One is of the Via Flaminia,
which had been the most important road leading north out of the city in the days of the Roman
Empire. Along this road, shrouded in misty autumn colours and glistening in the rain, Joris
has depicted typical citizens of Rome, people leading donkeys and sheep, and market traders
sheltering beneath umbrellas. The Via Flaminia was home to many artists in Rome, including
Joris, who enjoyed a constant view of daily life on the street from the windows of his studio. The subject was so appealing that he painted it several times, and the different versions
– which include both oils and watercolours – were regularly shown at exhibitions. One of them
won a gold medal at the 1869 Munich International Art Exhibition. – BIB

Vinardi 2004, 571–573 | Piccioni 2011, 128–129

José MORENO CARBONERO

(Málaga, 1860 – Madrid, 1942)

Crossing the Guadalquivir, late 19th century | Oil on canvas, 44.5 × 34.4 cm
Purchased from the HNSFA's 1898 spring exhibition | Inv. no. 99.B

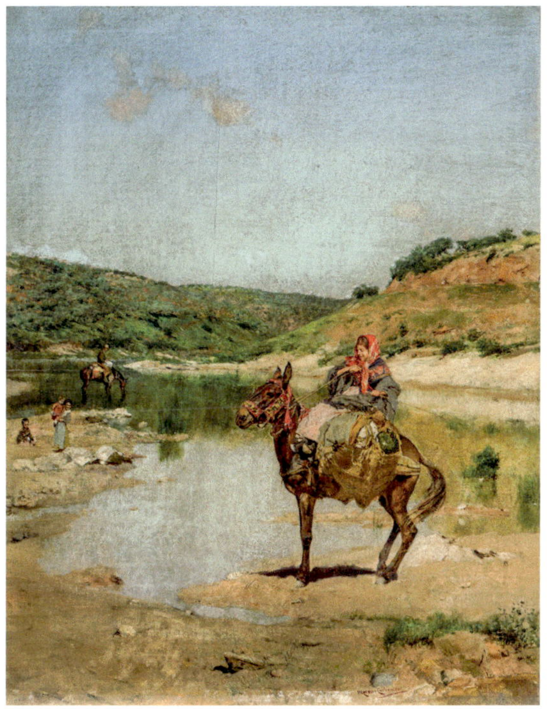

Crossing the Guadalquivir is one of several paintings by Moreno Carbonero in which he captures the people, the luminosity, and the atmospheric landscapes and towns of his native country. The clear waters of the river that cuts across Andalucia have played a central role in the lives of the region's inhabitants throughout history, while its banks have offered refreshment to weary travellers. The painter lyrically elevates the river, placing it at the centre of the composition; the radiant green of the vegetation, the azure of the sky, and the ochre of the barren soil, which tends in places towards brick red, converge in the reflective surface of the water. Dressed in traditional costume, the figures, whose movements seem almost frozen, convey a sense of timelessness.

Moreno Carbonero was outstandingly talented even as a teenager and became a highly successful artist, working in practically every genre. Although, following in the footsteps of his nineteenth-century predecessor and role model Mariano Fortuny, his most impressive works are his historical tableaux, his most popular paintings were the exquisite, small-format genre pieces that he executed with virtuoso brushwork. – AL

Peregriny 1909/2, 649, 744 | Tóth 2012, 165

Edmond Georges GRANDJEAN

(Paris, 1844 – Paris, 1908)

Equestrian Portrait of Mademoiselle Elise, 1883 | Oil on canvas, 53 × 43.9 cm
Bequest of Count János Pálffy, 1912 | Inv. no. 242.B

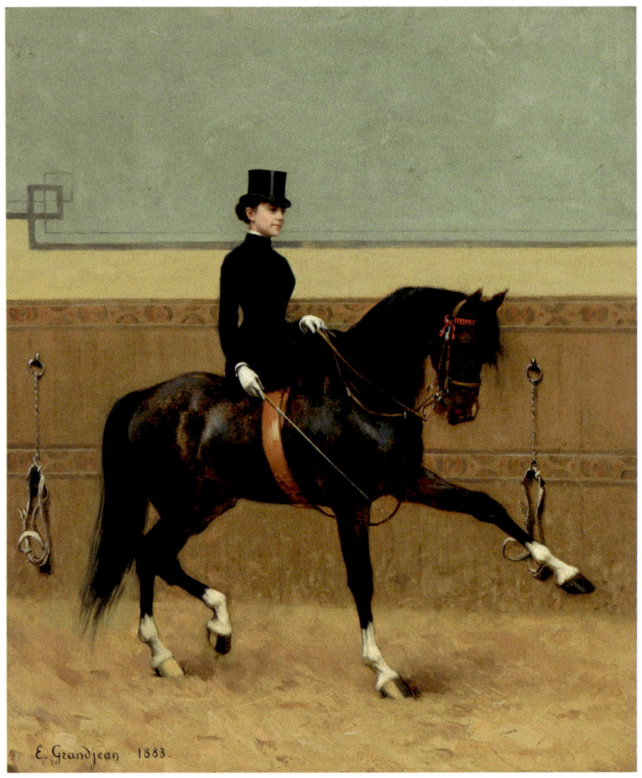

Edmond Georges Grandjean, who trained at the École des Beaux-Arts in Paris, was fond of painting the bustling streets of Paris, thus themes related to horses also occupy a prominent place in his work. From the spare composition of the Budapest painting, and the subject's elegant bearing, one would never suspect this to be a depiction of one of the most celebrated circus riders of her day. German-born Elise Petzold travelled throughout Europe, earning acclaim in Vienna, Dresden, and Berlin between 1875 and 1885, even instructing Empress Elisabeth of Austria in the finer points of dressage. Painted in 1883 in Paris, the portrait was shown at the Salon that same year. Although Elise was at the peak of her career at the time, she is depicted here practising, well away from the spotlight; seated in the saddle in simple clothes, she is absorbed in the complex sequence of steps. Her poise and figure are perfectly in harmony with the horse's body, as if she and her mount, Northern Star, were a single unit. The care that Grandjean took in committing the anatomy and silken coat of the stallion to canvas prove him to be a true specialist: this is as much a portrait of the horse as it is of its rider. – AZSK

Énault 1883, 65-66 | Kovács 2018

Jean BÉRAUD

(Saint Petersburg, 1849 – Paris, 1936)

At the Club, 1904 | Oil on canvas, 73.4 × 92.5 cm
Bequest of Count Dénes Andrássy, 1913 | Inv. no. 281.B

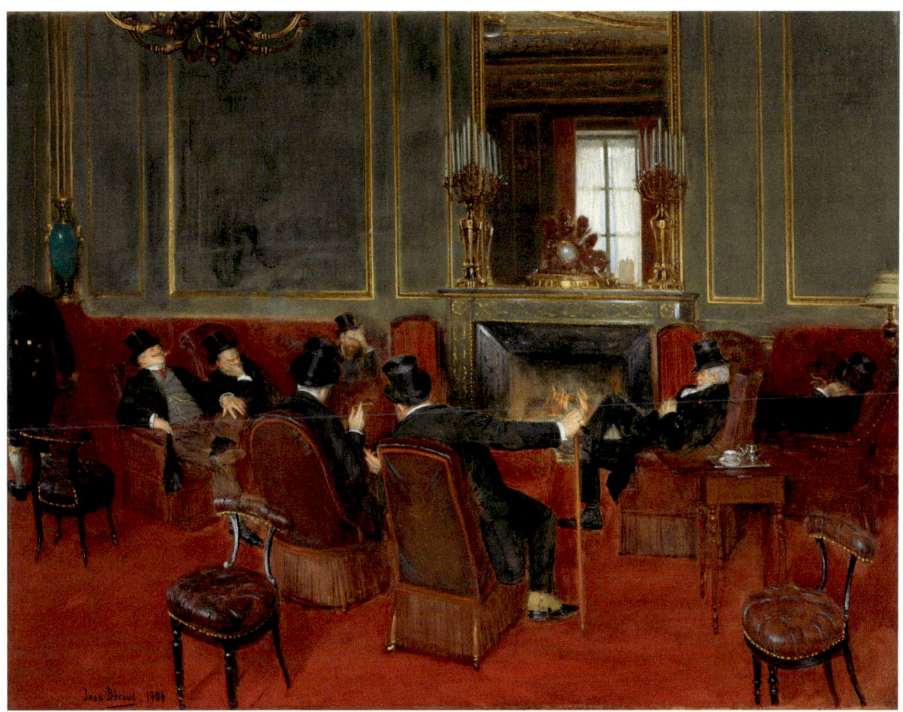

Jean Béraud made his name as a painter of modern urban life and attractive Parisian women. He also took an interest in the life of high society, thus private establishments reserved for the upper class, modelled on exclusive English gentlemen's clubs, provided the subject matter for several of his works, the present painting being perhaps the first on this theme. The men depicted in the painting, which was shown at the 1904 Salon of the Société nationale des Beaux-Arts in Paris, are undisguisedly bored: while two of them smoke and converse by the fire, some of the gentlemen sprawling in the armchairs have already dozed off.

While Béraud has depicted the scene with conspicuous irony, the painting is also remarkable for its compositional approach. The artist employed a reduced palette of just a few warm, deep colours. There is no central figure, and the gentlemen are positioned in such a way that their faces are either partly or entirely hidden. According to critics, the setting may have been the Cercle de l'Union artistique, also known as the Cercle de l'Épatant. This elite club, founded in 1860, supported cultural endeavours and regularly organised exhibitions. Although works by Béraud were featured in their shows, he may have intended this painting as a kind of mockery of the influential members of this artistic coterie. – AZSK

Fukuoka–Matsuyama–Tokyo 1994, cat. no. 31 | Offenstadt 1999, cat. no. 215

Luigi NONO

(Fusina, 1850 – Venice, 1918)

Walking Woman, 1891 | Oil on canvas, 126 × 72 cm
Donation, 1983 | Inv. no. 83.46.B

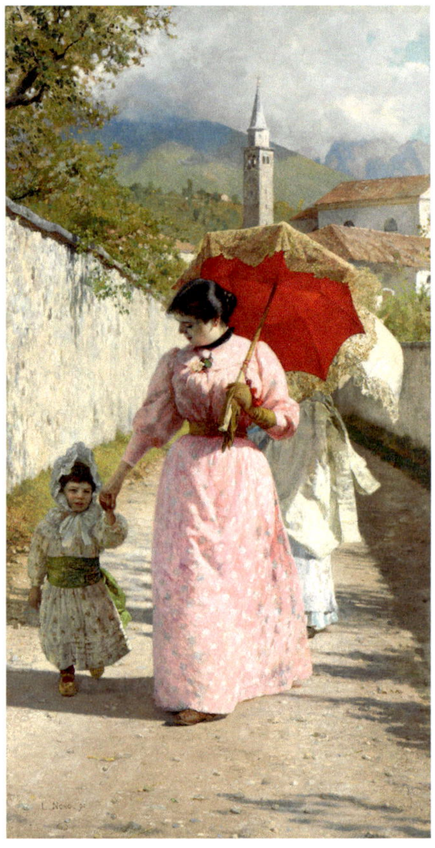

Luigi Nono studied painting at the Venice Academy between 1865 and 1871 and found his own unique style in landscape painting. His contemporaries saw him as a worthy successor to Giacomo Favretto, although while Favretto depicted the happy, humorous side of Venetian life, Nono became known primarily for paintings that captured the everyday lives of the poor and downtrodden.

    Walking Woman is one of his sunnier, more cheerful paintings. The subjects are the painter's wife, Rina Priuli Bon, and their daughter Maria. The tall white stone wall guides the eye up towards the church tower, the buildings, the sunlit countryside, and the cloudless blue sky. The setting for the walk is the village of Pedavena, in the Veneto region of Italy. Before painting this pleasant, idyllic scene, Nono took numerous photographs of the composition and of the individual subjects. – AS

Serafini 2006, cat. no. 455 | *Tokyo* 2019, cat. no. 99

Gudmund **STENERSEN**

(Ringsaker, 1863 – Oslo, 1934)

Midsummer Night, 1906 | Oil on canvas, 108 × 144.4 cm
Purchased from the HNSFA's 1906–1907 winter exhibition | Inv. no. 199.B

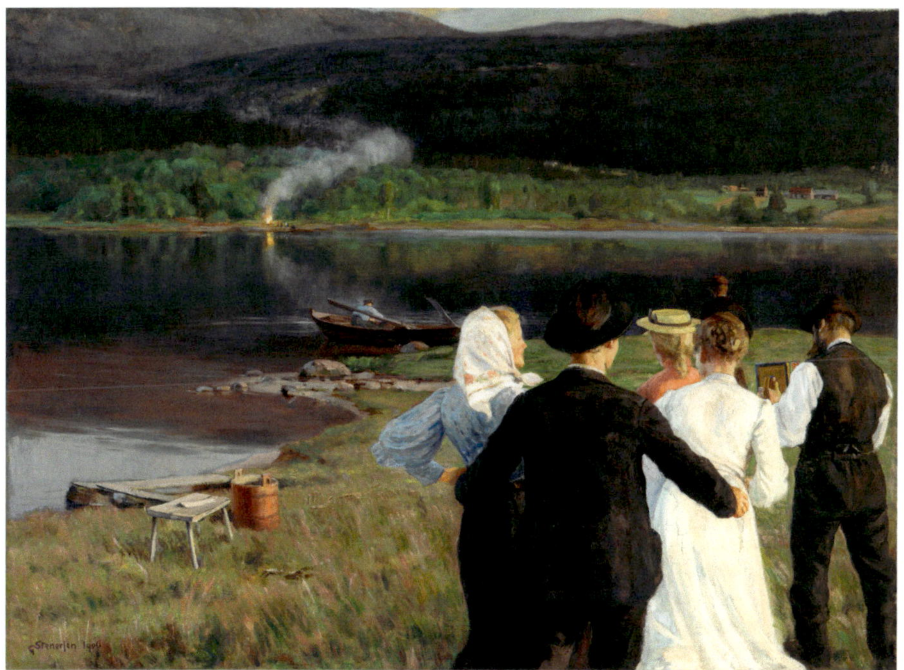

Having studied in Paris and Italy, Gudmund Stenersen joined the Jaeren artists' colony on his return home to Norway. He became known for his naturalist landscapes, although, like his contemporaries, he too produced several paintings of cheerful revellers gathering around the fire at the summer solstice. Saint John's Eve, or Midsummer Night, was a popular theme among Scandinavian painters in the late nineteenth and early twentieth centuries. It was still traditional at that time to light a fire on the shortest night of the year to ward off witches, illness, and misfortune.

In this work, Stenersen has confidently combined the elements of genre and landscape painting. In the foreground, five cheerful young people look towards the fire burning on the far side of the river, from which smoke spreads lazily across the beautiful, mountain-ringed landscape; on the water, a rowing boat prepares to set off. The artist has conjured up the appropriate mystical atmosphere through his use of bluish green shades. The painting was purchased by the Hungarian government from the 1906–1907 *Winter International Exhibition*, held in the Budapest Kunsthalle. – AS

Budapest 1995, 372 | *Tokyo* 2019, 195, 292–293, cat. no. 101

Fritz von UHDE

(Wolkenburg, 1848 – Munich, 1911)

The Sermon on the Mount, 1887 | Oil on canvas, 261 × 228 cm
Purchased from Rudolph Lepke's Kunst-Auktions-Haus (Berlin), 1899
Inv. no. 12.B

German painter Fritz von Uhde initially painted elegant genre scenes in the style of Mihály Munkácsy, although he later turned to religious painting and produced naturalist works. He was greatly influenced by Max Liebermann and by the colour and light effects of Dutch painting to which Liebermann introduced him. In 1883, Uhde moved to Munich, where he painted several series of religious paintings. His innovative approach to the subject matter influenced many Hungarian artists, including Tivadar Zemplényi and Hugó Poll.

His biblical scenes are populated with contemporary figures. His depictions of the life of Jesus do not include scenes that move the viewer to pity: the story of the Passion is entirely absent. Instead, he focused on episodes in which Christ demonstrates his compassion and love for people.

This is also the subject of *The Sermon on the Mount*, the most complete sermon of Jesus to have survived in the Bible, although it is probably a compilation of various teachings. The painting is Uhde's first biblical illustration to be set outdoors: the last rays of the setting sun illuminate the scene from the background. – BIB

Brand 1983, 70, 342 | Hessky 2018, 699

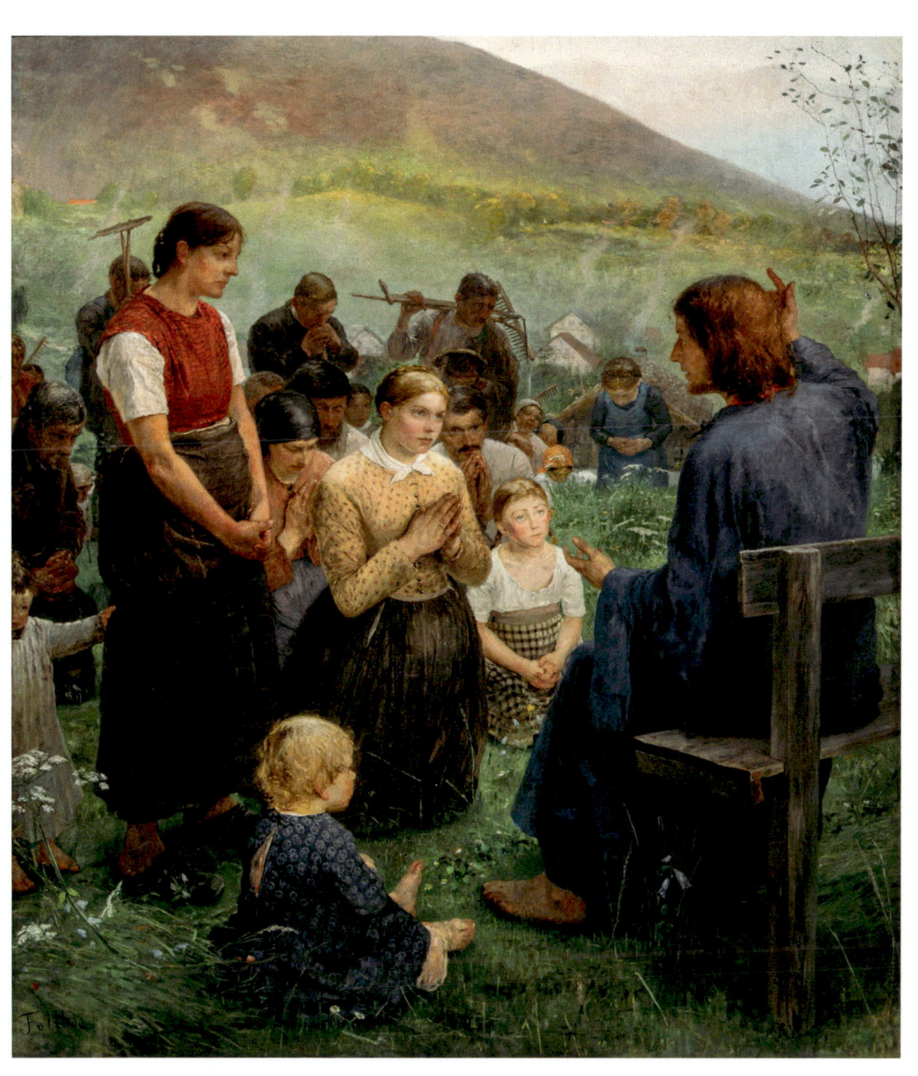

Walther FIRLE

(Wrocław, 1859 – Munich, 1929)

Sunday School, 1885 | Oil on canvas, 224 × 168.5 cm
Purchased from the HNSFA's 1887 autumn exhibition | Inv. no. 109.B

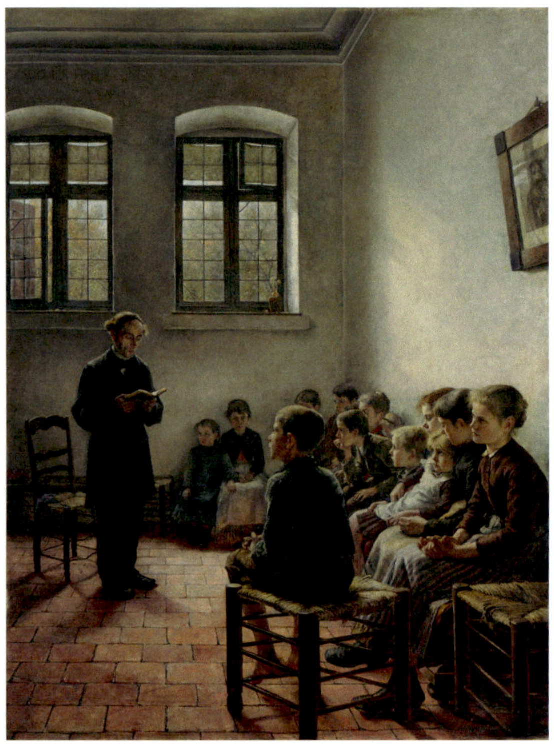

The profound humanity and empathy of the young Walther Firle's depictions of simple folk made him one of the most remarkable German painters of his day. Light plays an important role in his works: his aim was to demonstrate how light behaves in completely different environments. The acclaimed work *Sunday School*, the second large-scale painting of his career, is a prime example – a naturalistic, yet at the same time lyrical depiction of a plain, shabby room and an assortment of children. The spring light filtering through the windows, which modulates the colours with subtle transitions and pale tones, lends a melancholic atmosphere to the room, where the pupils – each with their own individual demeanour – listen in respectful silence to the teacher, who seems dwarfed beside them.

Having studied at the Munich Academy, Firle worked in Venice and the Netherlands; inspired by the interiors of the seventeenth-century Dutch painter Pieter de Hooch, as well as the approach to composition and the treatment of light of his contemporary, Jozef Israëls, Firle developed his own unique style, abandoning the artificiality of the Munich School and becoming a successful and sought-after painter of genre scenes in his day. – AL

Engels 1890, 128–131 | Firle-Rudolf 2013, 54–67

Gotthardt KUEHL

(Lübeck, 1850 – Dresden, 1915)

Courtyard of the Danzig Orphanage, ca. 1901 | Oil on wood, 75.7 × 59.3 cm
Purchased from the HNSFA's 1903 spring exhibition | Inv. no. 56.B

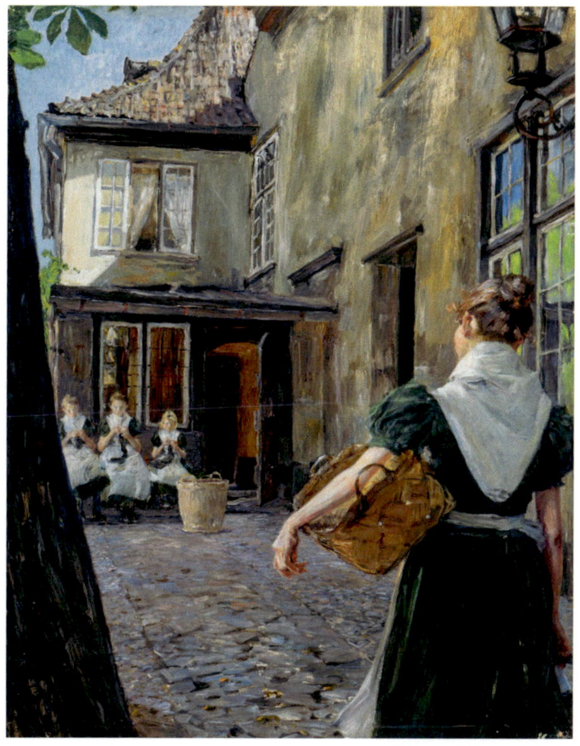

Gotthardt Kuehl was one of the first German artists, alongside Max Liebermann and Max Slevogt, to represent subjects taken from everyday urban life using impressionistic effects. His works frequently illustrate contemporary social issues: he painted numerous series from the mid-1880s depicting the orphanages of his native city of Lübeck, Danzig (Gdańsk), and others.

As a professor at the Dresden Academy of Art, Kuehl led study trips to Danzig with some of his students in the spring of 1900 and in the summer of 1901. There, Kuehl made sketches of the old town and several paintings of a characteristically naturalist subject – everyday life in the local orphanage. One of the works from this series is the Budapest oil painting. In the foreground, one of the orphan girls is shown from behind, walking into the courtyard with an empty basket under her arm – the viewer's eye is guided by the direction of her movement and the angle of her head. Three of her companions are sitting on a bench outside the building, absorbed in their knitting. The diligent girls wear the distinctive dark green uniform of the Danzig orphanage, along with white shawls and aprons. – RM

Dresden 1993, 207, cat. no. 446 | Warzecha 2022, 119

José GALLEGOS Y ARNOSA

(Jerez de la Frontera, 1859 – Anzio, 1917)

Christening, 1892 | Oil on wood, 56 × 40 cm

Transfer, 1950 | Inv. no. 452.B

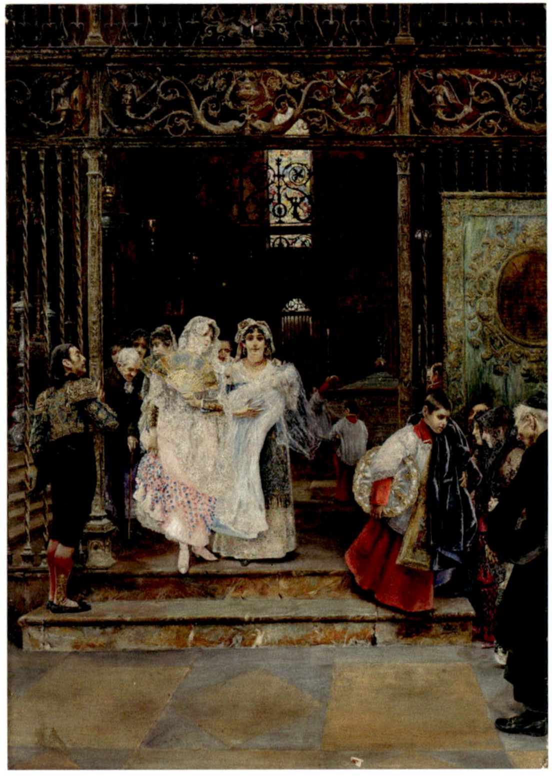

In the second half of the nineteenth century, small, highly detailed, meticulously executed paintings known as *tableautins*, depicting genre scenes inspired by the exotic, mythical world of the Orient, idyllic rural settings, or past ages, enjoyed huge popularity among the well-to-do Spanish bourgeoisie. Gallegos y Arnosa was an outstanding representative of this genre. He first achieved real recognition with paintings inspired by his travels in Morocco. He went on to paint typically Spanish church interiors, which became particularly fashionable after Mariano Fortuny's successful paintings on a similar theme. In his brilliantly executed paintings, he set his striking and dynamic scenes in the interiors of lavish baroque churches evoking the atmosphere of Southern Spain: rather than depicting one specific location, these are fictional interiors, composed out of a combination of individual decorative elements (wrought-iron latticework, carved and gilded embellishments) that he reused several times. In this painting, the artist portrays opulently dressed participants of various ages at a christening, with a typically Spanish figure – a toreador – on the left. – AL

Chofre García 2011, 197–226, 429–443

Pierre Jacques DIERCKX

(Antwerp, 1855 – Brussels, 1947)

Dining Room at the Orphanage, late 19th century | Oil on canvas, 98 × 132 cm
Purchased from the HNSFA's 1897 spring exhibition | Inv. no. 8.B

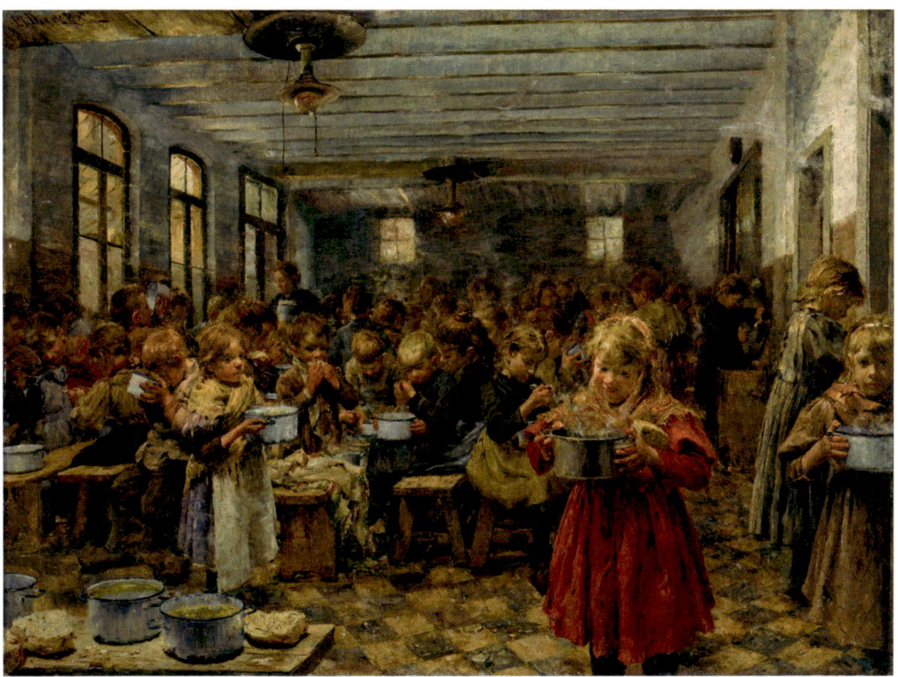

In the late nineteenth century, Pierre Jacques Dierckx and other renowned Belgian artists regularly showed their work in the bigger cities of Europe. In the 1890s, Hungarian audiences occasionally had the opportunity to see paintings by Dierckx in Budapest. Despite studying at the Royal Academy of Fine Arts in Antwerp, and later at the École des Beaux-Arts in Paris under Paul Baudry, it was his two Dutch colleagues Jozef Israëls and Albert Neuhuys who had the strongest influence on him in terms of style and choice of subjects. Dierckx's landscapes and genre scenes illustrate the simplicity and hardships of everyday life. His various compositions depict working peasant women, mothers caring for their children, and household tasks, while the orphanage in Antwerp was another frequent subject of his paintings. *Dining Room at the Orphanage* was purchased by the Hungarian state along with sculptures by Paul Du Bois and Charles Van der Stappen. Unusual in terms of subject and atmosphere, the composition shows a crowded room. The dominant grey, blue, and brown tones are interrupted only by the red dress of the little girl standing in the foreground holding a pot. The simple, everyday scene is both sad and homely at the same time. – AS

De Graef 1898, 173–178 | Tóth 2012, 102, 164

Constantin MEUNIER

(Etterbeek, 1831 – Ixelles, 1905)

Dock Worker, model: 1893; cast: after 1907 | Bronze, 220 × 119 × 92 cm
Purchased from the HNSFA's 1907 exhibition | Inv. no. 3859.U

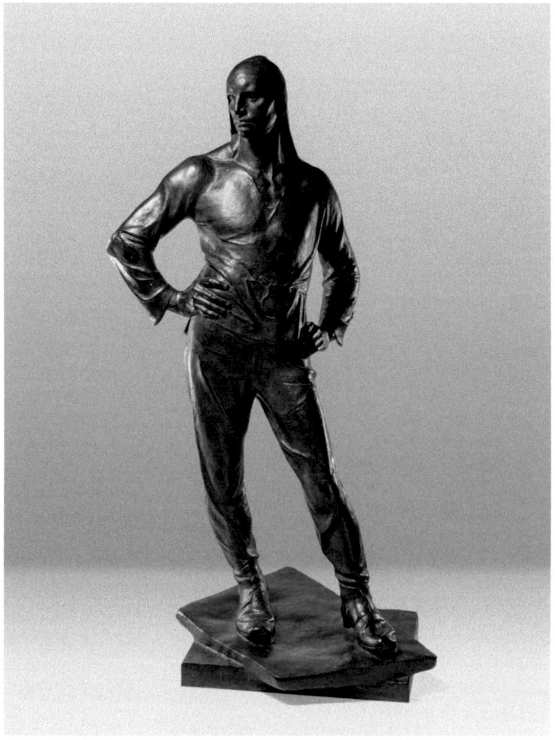

Although Constantin Meunier studied sculpture at the Brussels Academy, he produced paintings and drawings for almost thirty years. In 1878, he discovered the world of mines, furnaces, and factories, along with the labourers who worked in them, while travelling through Belgium with the writer Camille Lemonnier. This new-found subject matter gave impetus to his art in the early 1880s. His reputation took off after his work was shown at the Paris Salon. His art opened up a new perspective for modern sculpture. *Dock Worker* is one of his most famous sculptures, and copies of it can be found in numerous museums and cities. The sturdy male figure stands contrapposto, hands on hips, gazing confidently into the distance. His clothing hugs the contours of his body, revealing muscles built through hard labour. There is no trace of either physical or mental exhaustion; Meunier preserves the labourer's dignity, depicting him as a hero. The figure first appears among his sketches in around 1880, then in a painting (*The Harbour*, 1886, Musée Constantin Meunier, Brussels), while later he reworked the subject in several draft sculptures. This large bronze was commissioned by the museum, based on the small plaster cast shown in the Budapest exhibition. – AS

Meunier 1905, 76–77 | Soós 1964b, 24

Constantin MEUNIER

(Etterbeek, 1831 – Ixelles, 1905)

The Toilers of the Sea, model: 1898; cast: ca. 1900 | Bronze, 57 × 96 × 13 cm

Purchase, 1964 | Inv. no. 64.2.U

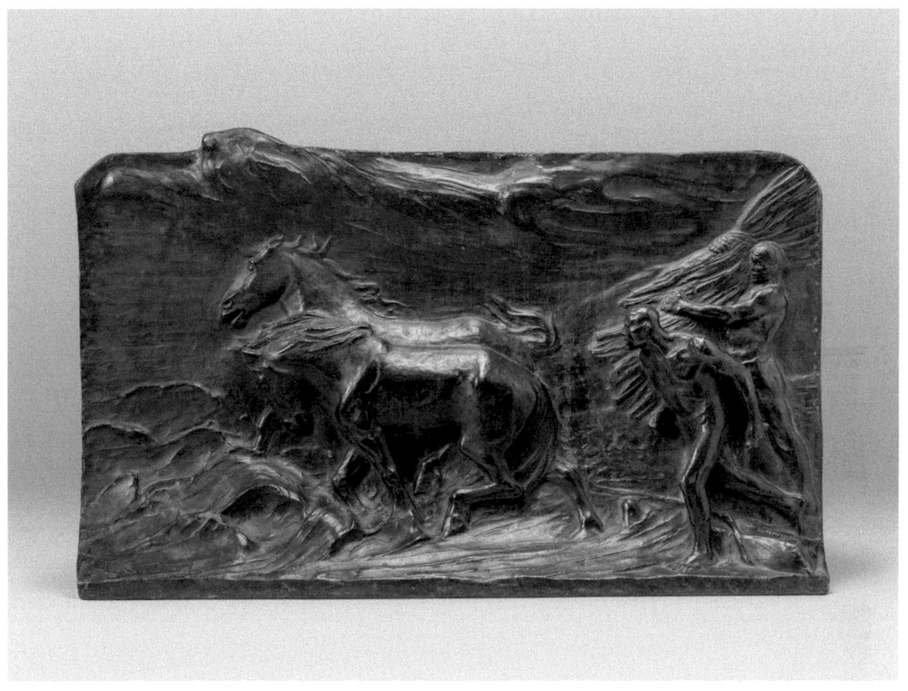

The construction of breakwaters is rarely depicted in relief works, although Meunier produced several copies on this theme. Built during the nineteenth century at the cost of enormous labour, these structures served to disperse the powerful waves, breaking them before they reached the shore. In the centre of the composition, two horses are shown between the shallow waves and the swirling clouds. Behind the horses, on the right of the relief, the figures of two half-naked men, muscled from work, appear almost as extras to the scene. One restrains the majestic horses, stick in hand, while the other carries a huge bundle of timber on his shoulder. The composition is harmonious, the curved, sinuous waves reflecting the influence of Art Nouveau, while the human figures have an extraordinary dignity and robustness. Besides everyday hard work, the relief evokes the heroic human struggle against nature, and humankind's ambition to tame the forces of nature. The title is a reference to Victor Hugo's 1866 novel about the ungovernable ocean, *Toilers of the Sea*, which is set on the island of Guernsey. After living in political exile from 1851, the writer moved to the island in 1855. The relief was shown at the 1907 Meunier exhibition in Budapest. – AS

Brussels 1993–1994, 496 | Cifka 1996c, 39–41

Paul MEYERHEIM

(Berlin, 1842 – Berlin, 1915)

Pair of Lions, ca. 1900 | Oil on wood, 52.6 × 68.2 cm
Bequest of Count Dénes Andrássy, 1913 | Inv. no. 282.B

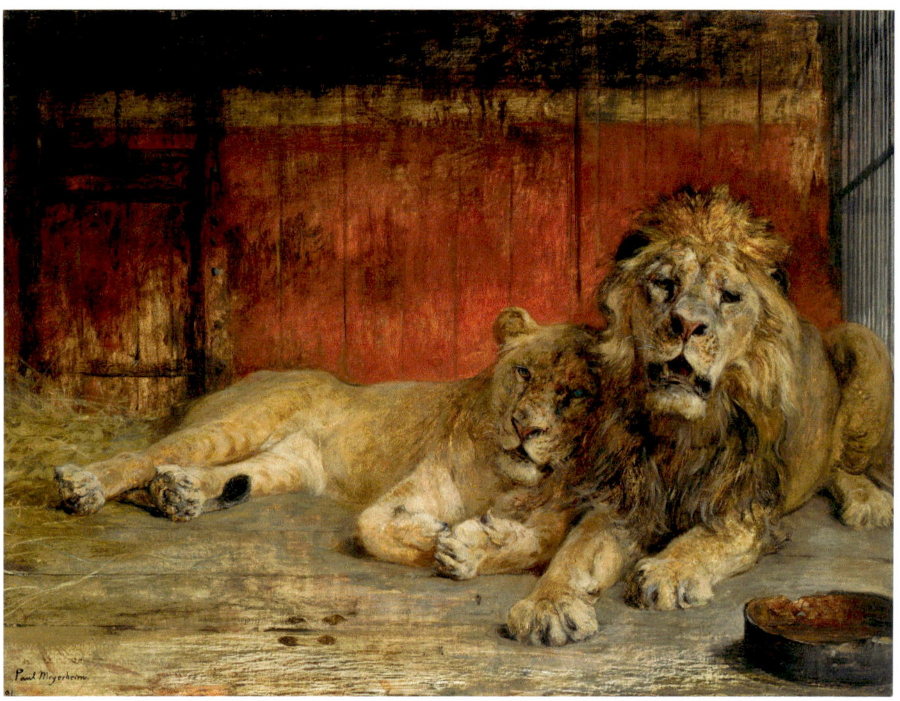

Born into a well-known German family of artists, Paul Meyerheim made his name as a painter of animals. He was a student of Adolph Menzel, an important contemporary representative of German realism and *plein air* painting, and the two became close friends. During their walks together, Meyerheim learned from his teacher the finer details of painting faithfully from life.

Meyerheim was particularly interested in painting exotic animals. He enjoyed spending time at the zoo observing the various species, and was equally fascinated by the world of travelling circuses. The painting *Pair of Lions* probably shows a circus cage, in which a majestic lion and lioness are resting. The painting is a richly detailed, lifelike representation of the captive animals, the red wooden panels providing a dramatic backdrop.

The work was purchased from the Galerie Heinemann in Munich by Count Dénes Andrássy, the last owner of Krásna Hôrka castle. The count was a regular visitor to Munich; he made the acquaintance of the artists who frequented the city and was keen to purchase their works for the picture gallery he had created in his castle. – BIB

Lippincott and Blühm 2006, 120–121 | Kunkel 2019, 66–71

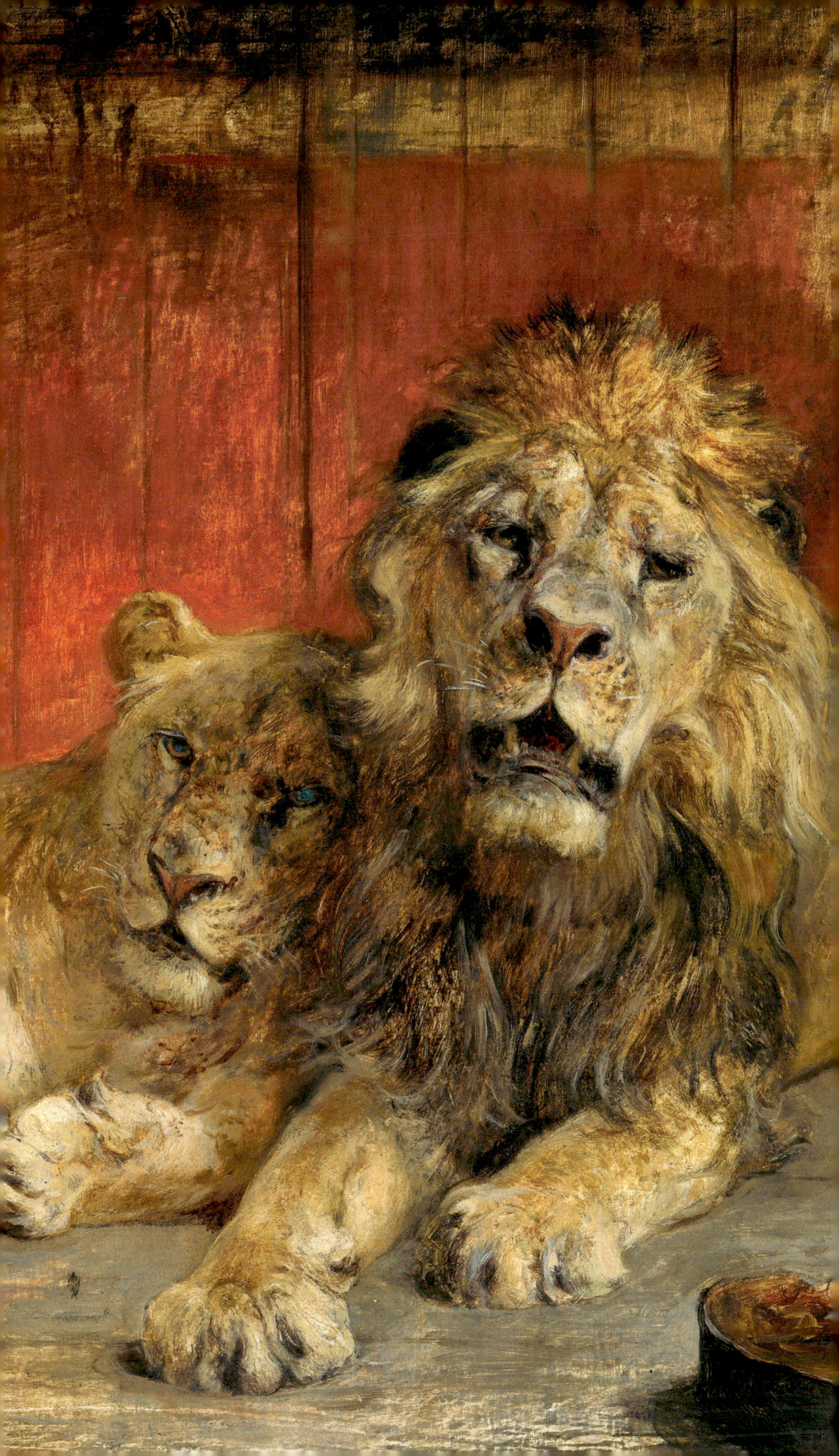

Albert von KELLER

(Gais, 1844 – Munich, 1920)

Woman in a Blue Dress, ca. 1900 | Oil on wood, 33.7 × 26.7 cm
Bequest of Count Dénes Andrássy, 1913 | Inv. no. 319.B

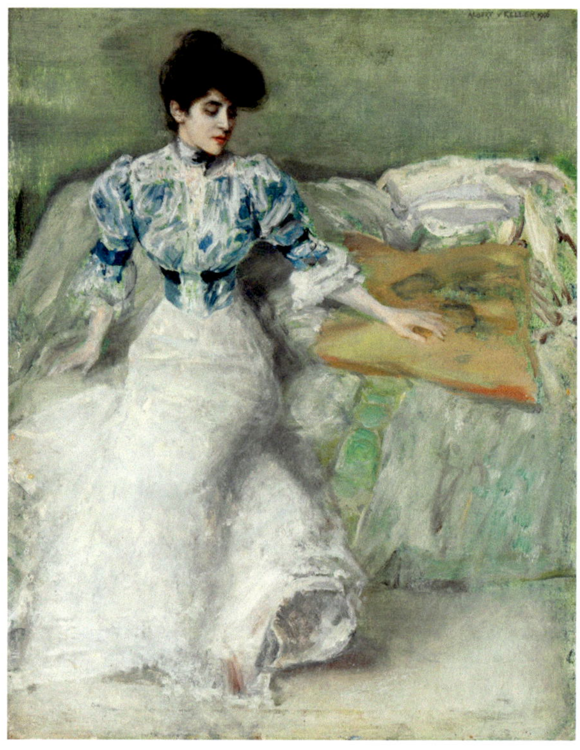

Albert von Keller originally trained as a lawyer but eventually decided to pursue a career as a painter, moving to Munich to study. In 1898, he was elevated to the rank of the nobility in recognition of his fame and reputation. As someone who moved in fashionable society, he devoted much of his oeuvre to salon paintings. He produced portraits of elegant women dressed in the latest fashions, posing in luxurious interiors. He was regarded as the most brilliant painter of female portraits in his day, with a gift for capturing the elegance of his subjects with his brush. Although he also developed an interest in paranormal phenomena and spiritism in the second part of his career, after the 1880s, influenced by the occultism espoused by Gabriel von Max, he never abandoned portraiture. Up until the 1890s, the intense use of colour typical of Hans Makart and Karl von Piloty continued to influence his work, but in the portraits he produced at around the turn of the century, there is already a greater use of impasto technique and a lighter colour palette. *Woman in a Blue Dress*, an illustration of the pretty yet melancholy turn-of-the-century female ideal, originates from this period. – BIB

Peregriny 1914–1915/3, 249 | Bott 2009

Ettore TITO

(Castellammare di Stabia, 1859 – Venice, 1941)

Head of a Woman, 1896 | Oil on canvas, 30.8 × 25.2 cm
Bequest of Tamás Szana, 1908 | Inv. no. 206.B

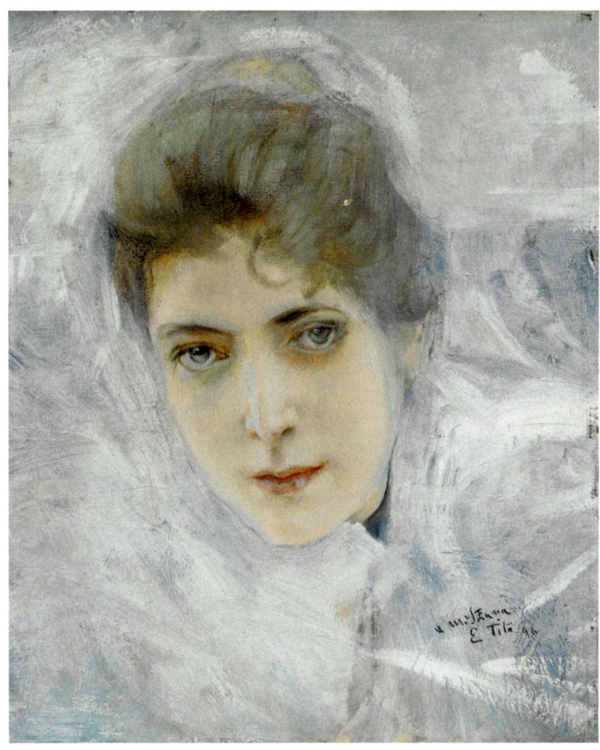

Known as a Venetian painter, Ettore Tito claimed Venetian descent through his mother, although he was in fact born in Castellammare, on the Bay of Naples. Based on early evidence of his excellent draughtsmanship, he was given a place at the Accademia di Belle Arti in Naples before reaching the required age. His painting is characterised by poetic realism, with an emphasis on the latter. He drew inspiration chiefly from the works of Giacomo Favretto – like him a Venetian painter – although among the old masters it was Giovanni Battista Tiepolo, and the colourful streets and harbours of Venice, that influenced his brilliant use of colour.

In this work, the face of a woman with porcelain-white skin emerges from a neutral, bluish grey background. While her identity is not known, what we do know is that she is an embodiment of Venetian beauty. The work bears the stylistic hallmarks of Art Nouveau, the suggestively painted, heavily made-up eyes and rouged lips at the centre suggesting the character of a "femme fatale". The painting was acquired by the museum from the bequest of writer, art critic, and art historian Tamás Szana, who was a great admirer and collector of Italian art. – BIB

Venice 1998, 205

Anton ROMAKO

(Atzgersdorf, 1832 – Vienna, 1889)

Portrait of August Wassermann, late 1870s | Oil on canvas, 106 × 76 cm
Bequest of Mrs. Izidor Strasser, née Mary Wassermann, 1947 | Inv. no. 433.B

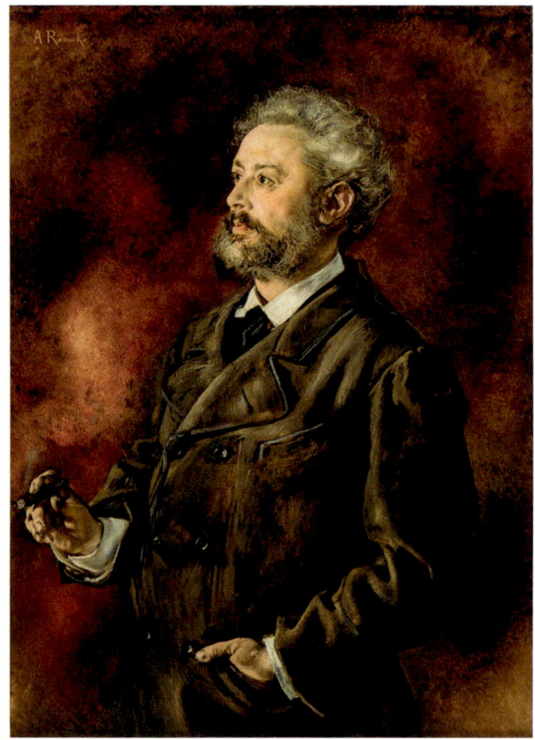

Although seen today as a great forerunner of the Vienna Secession and modernism, Anton Romako's work was hard to classify in terms of Austrian art in the nineteenth century and he remained a curious figure in the public mind. His personal life and artistic career were filled with peculiar twists and tragic turns. He was a pupil of Waldmüller at the Vienna Academy and attended Kaulbach's classes in Munich, although, restless by nature, he became embroiled in a series of conflicts even as a student. He spent most of his life outside Austria, living for around twenty years in Rome and visiting Paris, England, and even Hungary. His later work was given a rather negative reception in a Vienna dominated by Makart; in his own lifetime, his paintings were appreciated by only a few discerning collectors and intellectuals who were open to modernism – among them the Hungarian-born Lajos Hevesi. He achieved his greatest success as a portrait painter.

The subject of this extraordinarily fresh, richly textured, evocative portrait is the American diplomat and furrier August Wassermann, a man with German-Jewish roots who played an important role in the United States' purchase of Alaska from Russia. – LD

Reiter and Husslein-Arco eds. 2010 | *Vienna* 2018

Solomon Joseph SOLOMON

(London, 1860 – Birchington, 1927)

Portrait of Jeral Zangwill, 1894 | Oil on canvas, 91 × 71.2 cm
Purchased from the HNSFA's 1905 spring exhibition | Inv. no. 64.B

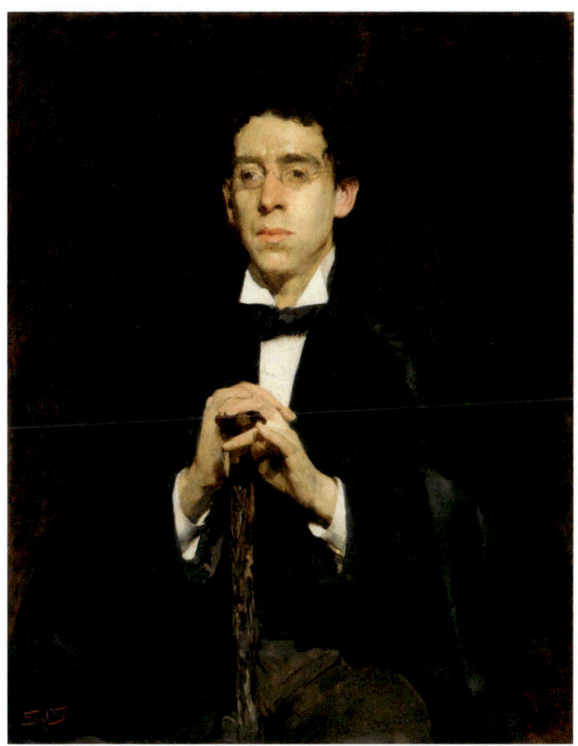

Solomon attended the Royal Academy of Art in London before pursuing his studies in the two most important centres of art, Paris and Munich. As a young man, he was influenced by one of his first teachers in Paris, Alexandre Cabanel, as well as by the painting of Frederic Leighton and George Frederic Watts. A figurative artist, he painted biblical and mythological scenes and colourful oriental bazaars, although it was in the field of portraiture that he produced some truly enduring works. He burst onto the scene with *The Portrait of Jeral Zangwill*. This English writer was a leading figure in the Zionist movement and became popular in America for his novels and writings exploring social aspects of Jewish life. Solomon depicts him not as a public figure but as a humanist scholar, writer, and close friend. The warm brown tones create a powerful contrast with the white of the shirt. Solomon painted this simple yet expressive portrait in barely six hours. The painting was reproduced in the same year it was completed; it featured a year later at an exhibition in Munich, and in 1903 at the International Art Exhibition in Venice. It won a gold medal at the spring exhibition in Budapest and was acquired for the national collection in 1905. – AS

Fülep 1988, 125 | *Turin 2004–2005a*, 66–67

Jules ADLER

(Luxeuil-les-Bains, 1865 – Nogent-sur-Marne, 1952)

Old Sailor, 1900 | Oil on canvas, 91.8 × 73 cm
Purchased from the International Exhibition of the National Salon, 1901
Inv. no. 22.B

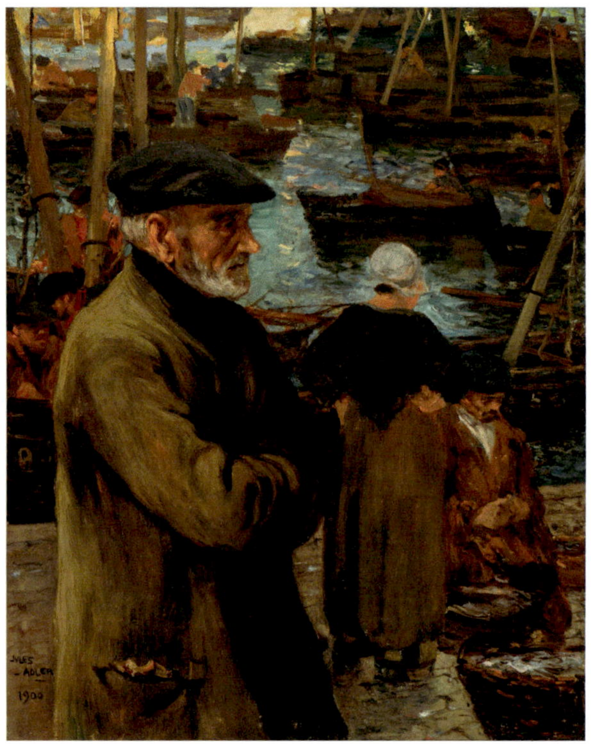

Jules Adler was a student of Pascal Dagnan-Bouveret, one of the leading proponents of French naturalism. Throughout his long life, he was committed to the portrayal of social conditions, and his political sensitivity is apparent in his depictions of the hardships of urban existence and the daily lives of the working class. He recorded the frequent strikes and workers' rallies of the turn of the century in monumental paintings that are heroic in feeling, emphasising the power of a crowd that moves as one. Besides painting city scenes, he occasionally visited the coast of Brittany: *Old Sailor* was painted in 1900, probably in Douarnenez. In the foreground stands an old man, his arms folded, gazing into the distance. Adler has painted the bearded face, simple brown coat, and black cap loosely yet accurately. In the background, we are given a glimpse of everyday life in a Breton port. The incoming boats, choppy sea, trading fishermen, and fish sellers form a lively, bustling scene. The painting was shown in the 1901 international exhibition of the National Salon in Budapest, which was largely dedicated to naturalist, symbolist works by the contemporary French school. – AZSK

Sinay and Sinay 2017, cat. no. JA 0107 S | *Balatonfüred* 2019, 9, 17, 53

John Quincy ADAMS

(Vienna, 1874 – Vienna, 1933)

Lilly, 1907 | Oil on canvas, 184.7 × 139.5 cm
Bequest of Count Dénes Andrássy, 1913 | Inv. no. 299.B

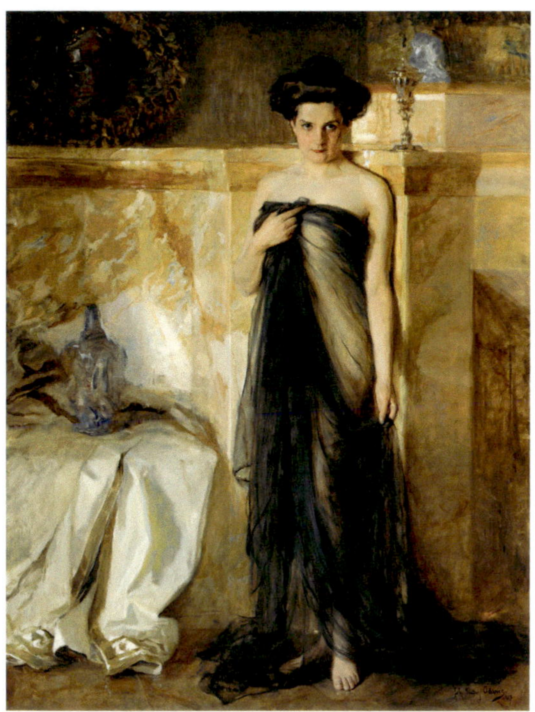

John Quincy Adams depicted his models with elegance and ease, and in the eyes of his contemporaries he assumed the place in Austro–Hungarian portraiture vacated by Hungarian-
born painter Philip de László on the latter's departure for London. His art closely resembles
that of de László.

Adams painted this portrait of Lydia Berger, a solo dancer with the Viennese court
opera who went by the stage name of Lilly, in his lavish studio at 5 Theresianumgasse in Vienna. The dancer's naked body is scarcely concealed by the transparent black veil. Ornaments
stand on the marble fireplace behind her and a white caftan is draped over the chair. In terms
of approach and atmosphere, the painting shows the influence of symbolism and Art Nouveau: painted here at the peak of her career, Lilly is depicted as a "femme fatale".

The painting was displayed at the 1907 autumn exhibition in the Vienna Künstlerhaus, where it even fetched the exorbitant price named by the artist. It was probably purchased by Count Dénes Andrássy, since not long afterwards – according to contemporary
press photographs – it could be seen in his castle in Krasznahorka (today Krásna Hôrka,
Slovakia). – BIB

Vienna 1986, 5–14 | Peyrer-Heimstätt 1995

Jacques-Émile BLANCHE

(Paris, 1861 – Offranville, 1942)

Reading Woman, ca. 1900 | Oil on canvas, 100 × 81.5 cm
Purchased at the International Exhibition of the National Salon, Budapest, 1901
Inv. no. 21.B

Although he was also a writer, music aficionado and art critic, Jacques-Émile Blanche is best known as a portrait painter. Over a period of several decades, the well-connected and highly sociable Blanche immortalised some of the most important figures of his time (Marcel Proust, Jean Cocteau, Igor Stravinsky) and wrote several volumes of memoirs.

His painting entitled *Reading Woman* features not one of his distinguished sitters, but the daughter of a locksmith living nearby, Lucie Esnault, who had been regular model for the painter since her childhood. Lucie is shown reading, bending over a book. Her figure is reflected in the mirror, which also reveals a tiny glimpse of Blanche himself working on the canvas: the artist's gaze stares back at us hauntingly. In this painting, executed around the turn of the century, Blanche sketched the background with verve, rendering Lucie's delicate skin, her chestnut hair, and the light ruffle of her muslin dress with loose brushwork. The palette, with its diverse shades of white, reveals the painter's admiration for Édouard Manet and James Abbott McNeill Whistler, whom he had known personally. – AZSK

Kovács 2023 | Roberts and Molines online, cat. no. RM 1506

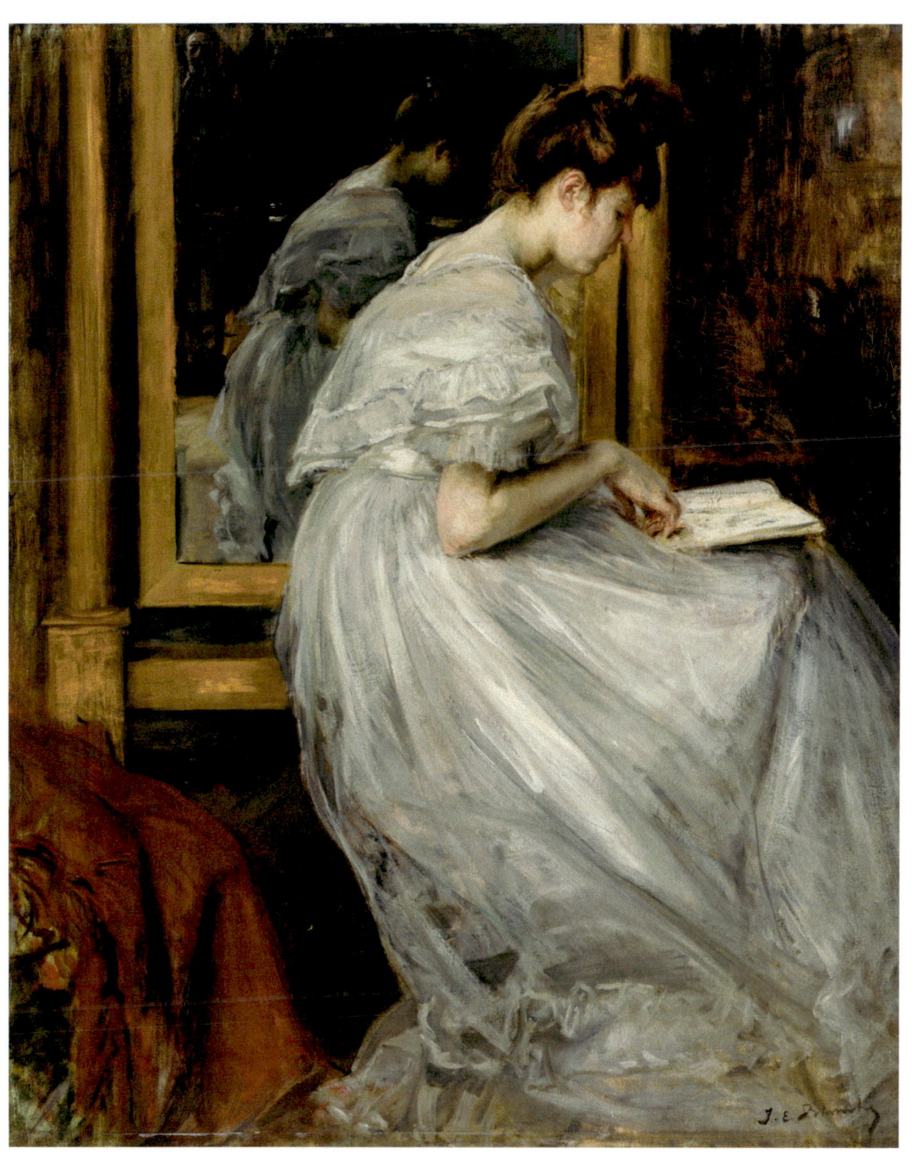

Jules LAGAE

(Roeselare, 1862 – Bruges, 1931)

Head of a Girl, ca. 1890 | Bronze, 26.5 × 22.5 × 15.5 cm
Purchase, 1980 | Inv. no. 80.2.U

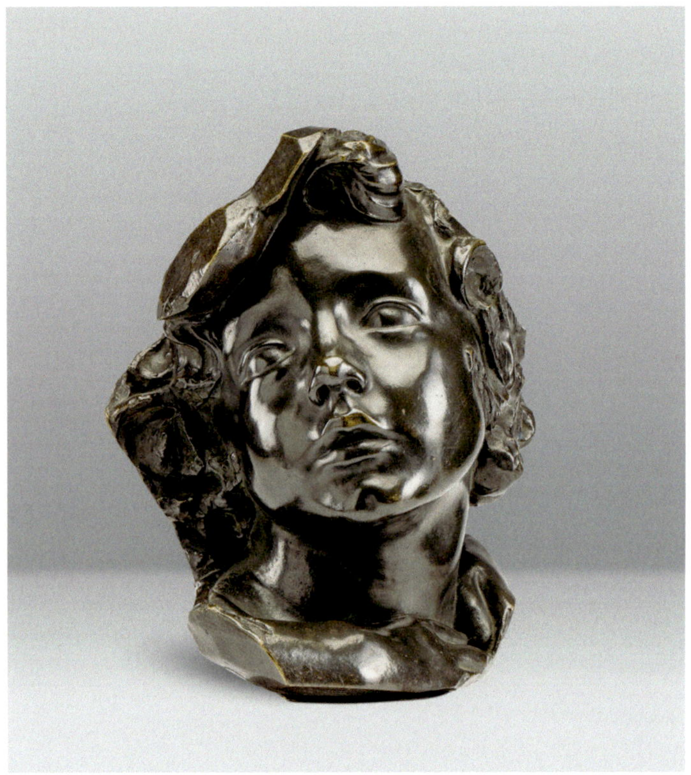

After studying sculpture at the Royal Academy of Fine Arts in Brussels, Jules Lagae continued his training at the Atelier Libre, the studio of Charles Van der Stappen, between 1882 and 1885. He lived in Italy from 1889 to 1892, where he was influenced by quattrocento sculpture, although he essentially remained a follower of Van der Stappen's naturalist style throughout his life. Besides public sculptures and monuments, he produced busts of the prominent artists and distinguished figures of his day. The collection of the Museum of Fine Arts includes bronze busts of the sculptor Julien Dillens, the art collector Léon Lequime, and the art historian Arnold Goffin, purchased by the Hungarian state in 1909, during the artist's lifetime.

Compact and precisely executed, Lagae's balanced sculptures attest to his painstaking study of his subjects. *Head of a Girl* was the last of Lagae's works to be acquired for the museum's collection. The model has never been identified, although at one time the figure was certainly part of a bust of two children, as borne out by the traces of two, sculpted hands at the neck. – AS

Vanzype 1935, 86–111 | *Brussels* 1990, 471–476

Paul DU BOIS

(Aywaille, 1859 – Uccle, 1938)

Madonna, late 19th century | Bronze, 41 × 36 × 28 cm
Purchased from the HNSFA's 1897 spring exhibition | Inv. no. 1524.U

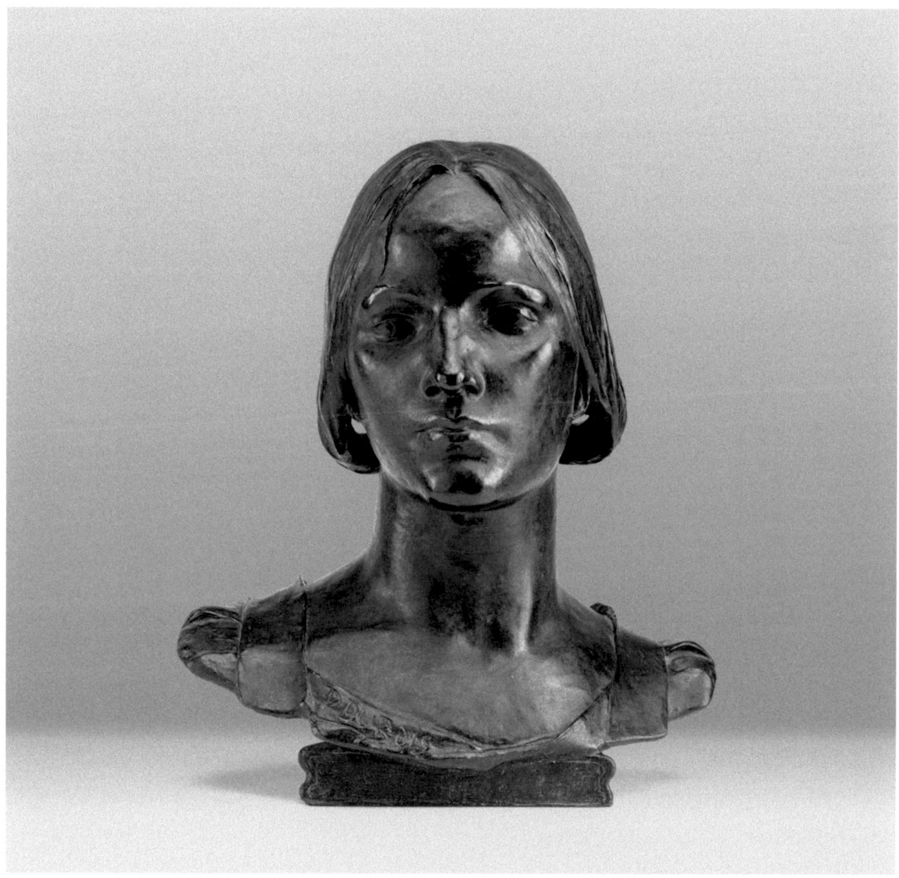

Besides public monuments, sculptural ornamentation, and tombs, Paul Du Bois's oeuvre included jewellery and items of applied art; examples of his work can be found in many European museums. Although Du Bois supported the artistic aspirations of the avant-garde, he himself remained a follower of the naturalist style, and his solidly executed sculptures were always marked by a sense of balance.

Although the Budapest bust is a portrait of the sculptor's wife, Alice Sèthe, the title of the work, *Madonna*, suggests that his wife is here the symbol of the idealised, selfless, pure woman, cast in bronze. Women were a favourite subject among turn-of-the-century artists, whether portrayed as the seductive, depraved *femme fatale* or as the embodiment of purity and innocence. – AS

Budapest 2001–2002, cat. no. 28 | *Budapest* 2022a, 17

Viggo JOHANSEN

(Copenhagen, 1851 – Copenhagen, 1935)

My Wife and Daughters, 1896 | Oil on canvas, 174 × 158 cm
Purchased from the HNSFA's 1906–1907 winter exhibition | Inv. no. 195.B

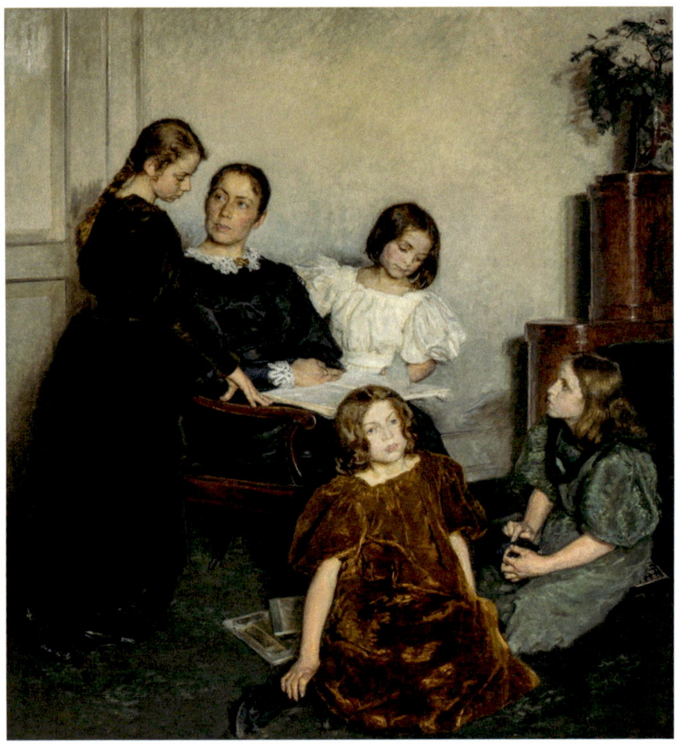

Viggo Johansen studied painting in Copenhagen from 1868 to 1875. After visiting Paris and the Netherlands in the 1880s, his palette became lighter, influenced by the Impressionists. He made his first visit to the small coastal resort of Skagen, which became an artists' colony at the end of the nineteenth century, at the invitation of the painter Michael Ancher. Although not smitten with the location, the place did have an impact on both his artistic development and his private life, and returned to paint the distinctive coastal landscape and the fishermen. Nevertheless, it was principally his genre scenes that brought him acclaim. In Skagen, he was introduced to his future wife, Martha Møller. The couple had six children. His family provided him with new subjects and inspired his art.

This painting is characterised by its balanced composition and the perfect equilibrium between light and dark colours. The influence of seventeenth-century Dutch painting can be felt in the intimacy of the everyday scene. The painting was shown at the third Venice International Art Exhibition before being purchased by the Hungarian state at the 1906–1907 winter exhibition in Budapest. – AS

Müller 1903 | *Tokyo* 2017, 155

Lucien SIMON

(Paris, 1861 – Combrit, 1945)

Madame Lucien Simon with Her Children, ca. 1902 | Oil on canvas, 171.5 × 193.5 cm
Purchased from the HNSFA's 1905 spring exhibition | Inv. no. 62.B

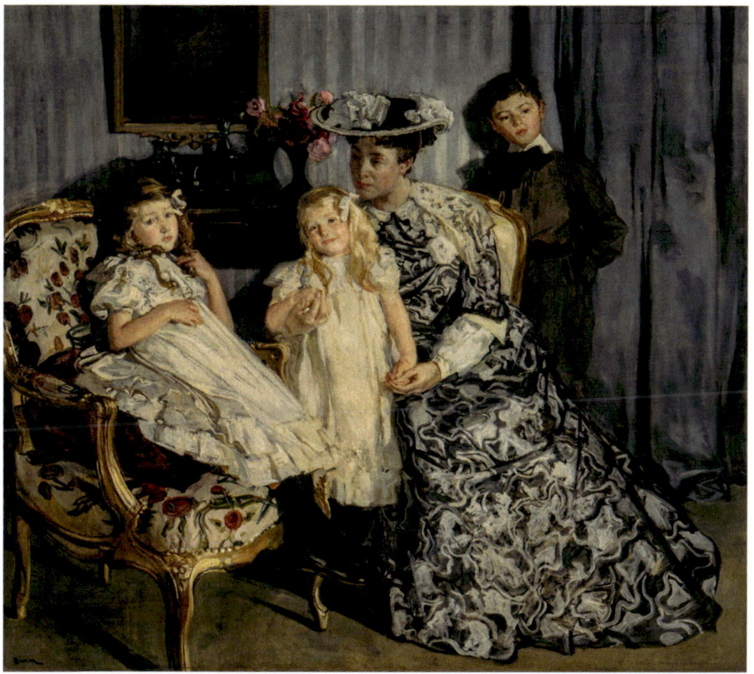

At around the turn of the century, Lucien Simon was a member of the *Bande noire* (Black Band), a group of painters who distanced themselves from the powerful colour and light effects of Impressionism. Alongside his Breton genre paintings, Simon achieved acclaim as a portraitist and as a painter of interiors. He produced numerous portraits of his family and children: the painting shown at the 1903 Salon of the Société nationale des Beaux-Arts in Paris also depicted his home and his loved ones.

 The subjects of this large-scale, representative, yet at the same time intimate portrait are depicted in an elegant, bourgeois setting, sitting in gilt armchairs. The whites, greys, and blacks of the background and clothing create a subtle harmony. In contrast to the rigidity of contemporary photographs, the painter has emphasised the informality of the poses and the play of glances: the painting conveys the complexity of family relationships, the vulnerability of childhood, and a sense of quiet melancholy. The only one smiling out from the painting is Charlotte, the blonde-haired child standing in the centre. The artist's wife, Jeanne, who was also a painter, has her arms around her youngest child, while keeping an anxious eye on Lucienne, who is beginning to fidget with boredom. Paul, who would go on to become a sculptor, lurks in the background, staring into the distance, aloof from the rest of the family. – AZSK

Illyés 2001, 158–159 | Cariou 2002, 50, 153

Auguste RODIN

(Paris, 1840 – Meudon, 1917)

The Kiss, model: 1884, cast: between 1898 and 1918 | Bronze, 71.5 × 43 × 44 cm
Purchase, 1968 | Inv. no. 68.1.U

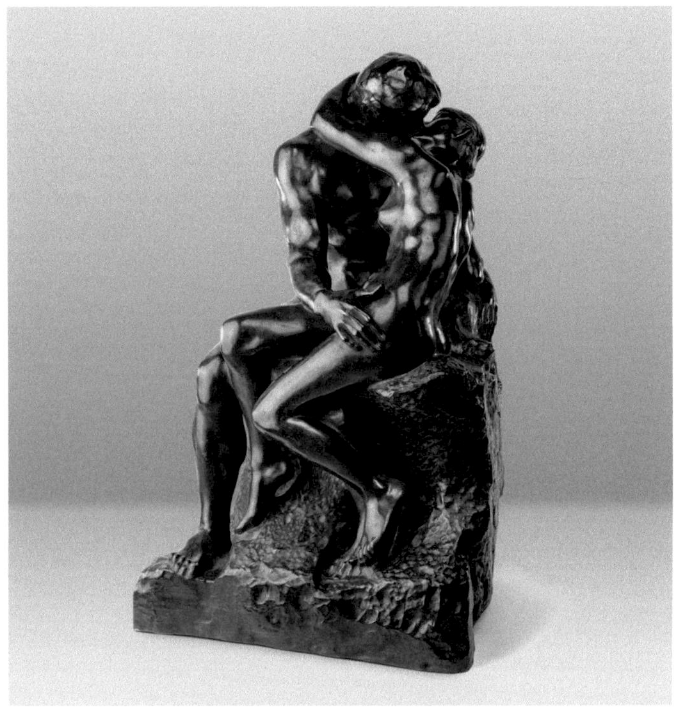

Auguste Rodin, the most influential master of modern sculpture, in 1880 was commissioned by the French state to produce a doorway for the main entrance to the planned new Musée des Arts Décoratifs. He selected passages from Dante's *Inferno* as the theme for the bronze reliefs on the doors. *The Gates of Hell* was a hugely labour-intensive piece, and the grandiose project was never completed. However, the designs provided countless ideas for other sculptures that later became famous.

The Kiss has an immediate connection with *The Gates of Hell*: in an early clay model of the latter work, the intertwined figures of Paolo and Francesca are depicted in exactly the same pose, although this was subsequently altered. By enlarging the original design and making it into an independent composition, he produced one of the most recognised pieces of modern sculpture. In addition to its sensual depiction of two human bodies intertwining, its popularity may partly be due to the fact that Rodin granted the Barbedienne casting company permission to create large numbers of bronze replicas of the model in various sizes – one such work was later sold to the museum by a private collector. – FT

Illyés 2001, 124–126

Stephan SINDING

(Trondheim, 1846 – Paris, 1922)

Couple, model: ca. 1887–1889; carving: ca. 1900 | Alabaster, 26 × 32 × 22 cm
Purchase, 1956 | Inv. no. 56.28.U

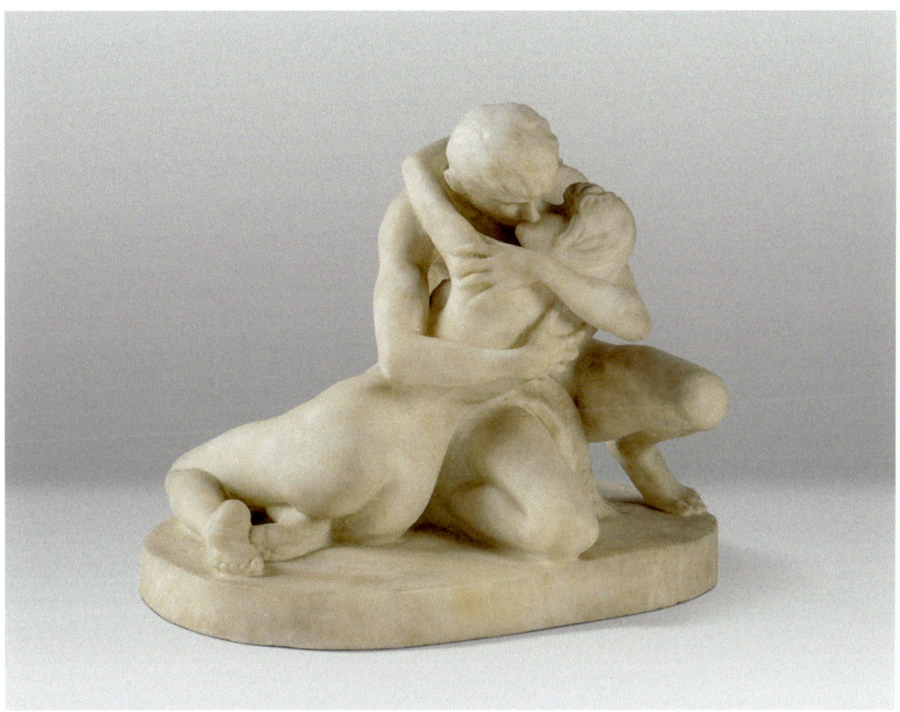

Stephan Sinding belonged to a well-known family of Danish artists of Norwegian origin: his younger brother, Otto, achieved acclaim as a painter, while his older brother, Christian, became a composer. Sinding studied art in Christiania (now Oslo) and Berlin and later lived in Rome, Paris, and Copenhagen. Although initially drawn to realism, he gradually aligned himself with the symbolists: the sensuality and expressivity of Auguste Rodin and the powerful physicality of the work of Michelangelo are both discernible in his sculptures.

The composition known variously as *Couple*, *Man and Woman*, and *Kiss* is one of Sinding's most popular works; like Rodin's famous sculpture *The Kiss* it is a celebration of infatuation and physicality. The couple's passionate embrace is the encapsulation of elemental yearnings and desires. The man wears a loincloth made from animal skin, indicating that the entwined figures are the primitive children of a golden age, free of the fetters of civilisation and morality. The life-sized sculpture was shown in 1891 at both the Paris Salon and the international exhibition in Munich, and numerous marble and bronze versions of it are known. This small-scale copy is made from alabaster, conveying the transparency and warm tones of human skin. – AZSK

Osborn 1904 | Coussange 1922, 239, 246–247

Ignacio ZULOAGA

(Eibar, 1870 – Madrid, 1945)

Portrait of Carlos Albarrán, "El Buñolero", 1901 | Oil on canvas, 180.3 × 100 cm
Purchased from the HNSFA's 1902 spring exhibition
Inv. no. 46.B

As an admirer of the old masters, Ignacio Zuloaga distanced himself from the artistic aspirations of his own day, and especially from the aesthetic approach of the Impressionists. He achieved fame as a portraitist, at the same time becoming one of the outstanding painters of so-called *regionalismo*, an artistic trend gaining ground at around the turn of the century, which foregrounded the values of the Spanish countryside: he was particularly fond of painting the various characters in the traditional folk culture of his native country. Prominent among such works are his lyrical paintings of toreadors and other bullfight participants. Executed in a muted palette, these paintings reflect his aspirations towards a realist approach.

As a young man, Zuloaga himself played an active part in several bullfights, thus he took great pains to convey in his portraits the unique atmosphere the of these contests, as well as the personality of his subjects. The man whose earlier job had earned him the nickname "El Buñolero", or the "doughnut seller", was a well-known figure in the Madrid bullring. It was he who let the bulls out of their holding pen into the bullring, a task he performed for sixty years, right up until the age of eighty-four. Zuloaga painted four portraits of Albarrán, all of them capturing his distinctive and eloquent features and the dignified bearing that he maintained even in his old age. – AL

Lafuente Ferrari 1949, 253 | *Budapest* 2023, cat. no. 10

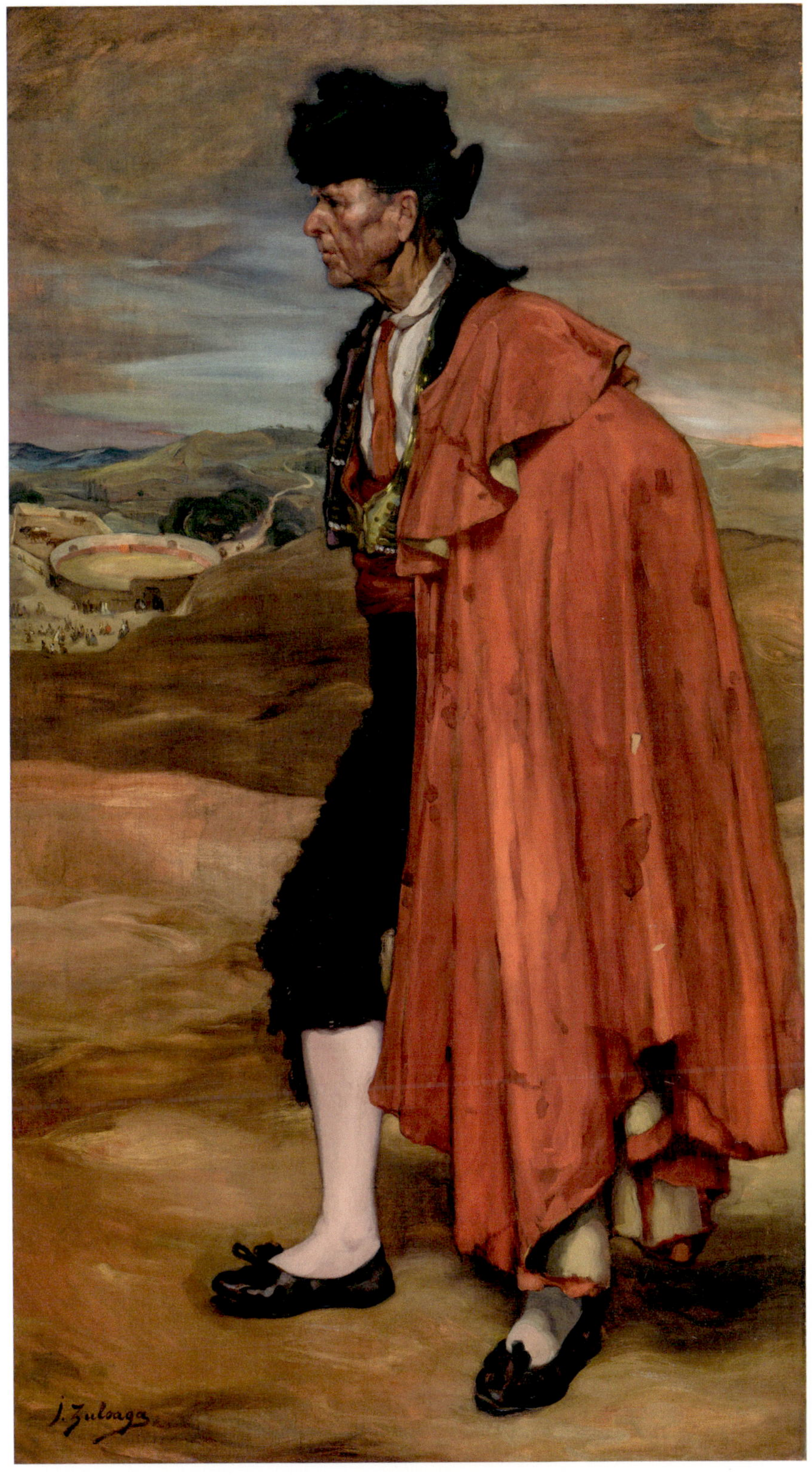

Ingebrigt VIK

(Øystese, 1867 – Øystese, 1927)

Old Age, 1907 | Marble, 94 × 44 × 68 cm
Purchased from the HNSFA's 1906–1907 winter exhibition | Inv. no. 3413.U

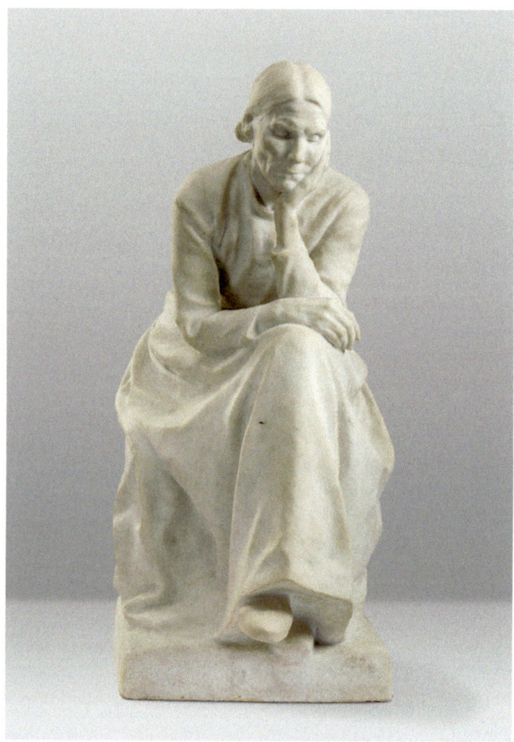

In the late nineteenth century, Norway was a poor country. Norwegian artists lived in difficult conditions and few besides the most prominent sculptor of the period, Gustav Vigeland, had an opportunity to succeed. One such artist was Ingebrigt Vik, who, like his contemporaries, studied at the Academy of Art in Copenhagen, and also lived there right up until 1892. He then returned to Norway, where, true to the national consciousness that had emerged at the turn of the century, he took inspiration from Norwegian peasant life to create his formally simple, naturalist sculptures that were influenced by the Belgian artist Constantin Meunier. Two of Vik's sculptures feature in the collection of the Museum of Fine Arts in Budapest: *Old Age*, and *Young Girl*, both of which are considered important pieces in his oeuvre.

Endowed with symbolic content, *Old Age* is a depiction of an elderly woman. The sculptor has fashioned her wrinkled face and unadorned clothing with no recourse to artistic beautification. The pose is inspired by a popular theme in the fine arts – the representation of an individual lost in contemplation, the most famous example being Auguste Rodin's *The Thinker*. – BIB

Storaas 1994, 47–50

Robert FRANGEŠ–MIHANOVIĆ

(Sremska Mitrovica, 1872 – Zagreb, 1940)

A Roman Citizen, 1893 | Marble, 65 × 35 × 30 cm | Purchased from the group of Croatian
exhibitors at the National Millennium Exhibition in 1896 | Inv. no. 1643.U

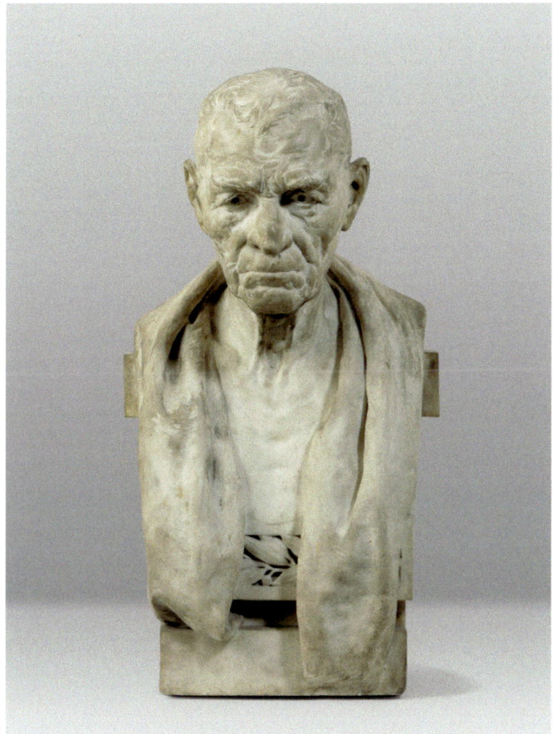

Sculptor and medallist Robert Frangeš-Mihanović was one of the exhibiting artists in the
Croatian arts pavilion at the 1896 Budapest Millennium Exhibition. Despite belonging to the
youngest generation of sculptors, Frangeš received the highest acclaim at the exhibition. Un
surprisingly, besides purchasing paintings by Vlaho Bukovać, Celestin Medović, and Bela Čikoš
Sesija, the Hungarian state also acquired works by Frangeš for the new Museum of Fine Arts.
According to contemporary sources, the sculpture *A Roman Citizen* achieved the greatest
success in the Croatian pavilion.

Its significance lies in the fact that it is the first non-idealised, psychological portrait
in the history of Croatian sculpture. The face of the elderly man, which Frangeš modelled on
the grandfather of the warden of the Vienna Kunstgewerbeschule has been rendered natural-
istically. Other variants of the work exist – besides the Budapest sculpture, there are several
versions to be found in Croatia. Some of these are similar in terms of their physiognomy yet
differ from the Budapest sculpture in various aspects – the absence of a plinth, the modelling
of the chest, or the rough, wrinkled material of the clothing. – BIB

Zec 2018, 368 | *Zagreb–Budapest 2020–2021*, 324

Michael ANCHER

(Rutsker, 1849 – Skagen, 1927)

Self-portrait, 1903 | Oil on canvas, 188.5 × 102 cm
Purchased from the HNSFA's 1906–1907 winter exhibition | Inv. no. 192.B

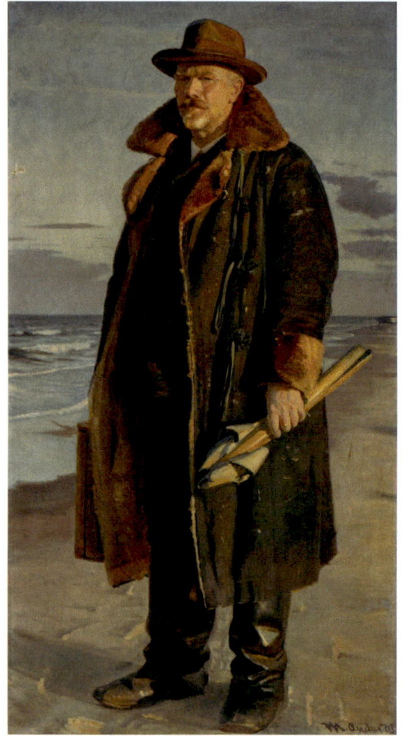

Like other members of the Skagen group, Ancher studied painting at the Royal Danish Academy of Fine Arts in Copenhagen. He visited Skagen in 1874 before moving there following his marriage to the painter Anna Brøndum. The couple welcomed many artists to their home, and by the end of the nineteenth century, the small northern resort had developed into an artists' colony. Scandinavian painters were attracted by the peninsula's unique natural milieu, special light conditions, and opportunities for *plein air* painting. The Skagen artists gradually broke away from the rigid traditions of the academy, preferring to emulate the realism of the Barbizon school, naturalism, and French impressionism. Besides the struggles of the local fishermen, Ancher's paintings capture the atmosphere of the coastal landscape. Most of his self-portraits were painted by the sea: he is typically depicted wearing his distinctive brown coat and hat, either working or, as in the Budapest portrait, carrying his painting utensils and folding stool. In 1906, this self-portrait was awarded the lesser national gold medal in Budapest. – AS

Peregriny 1914–1915/1, 457 | Svanholm 2004, 44–60

Laurits Regner TUXEN

(Copenhagen, 1853 – Copenhagen, 1927)

Portrait of the Painter Peder Severin Krøyer, 1904 | Oil on canvas, 184.3 × 116.8 cm
Purchased from the HNSFA's 1906–1907 winter exhibition | Inv. no. 191.B

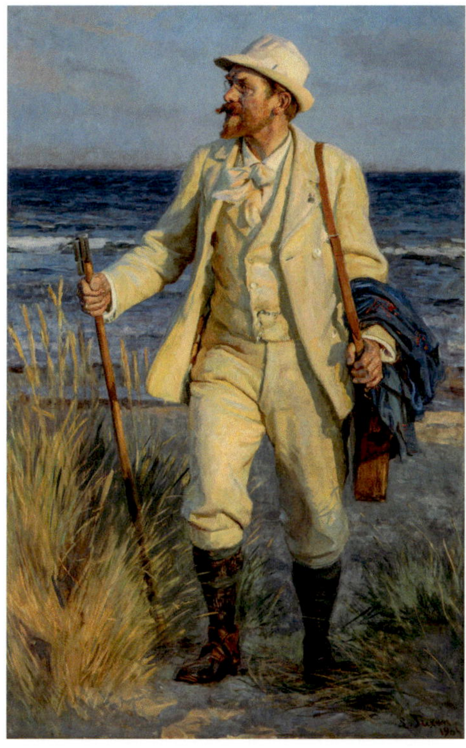

It is no coincidence that this full-length portrait of Krøyer should have been painted by Tuxen, since the lives of the two artists intersected at several points: both attended the Royal Danish Academy of Fine Arts at roughly the same time, where they were considered among the most talented students in their year. After graduating from the Academy, both pursued their studies at Léon Bonnat's school in Paris, and both belonged to the Skagen group of painters. They were among the founding members of the Kunstnernes Frie Studieskoler and both taught at the art school, which offered an alternative to academy-style teaching.

Tuxen painted the portrait of Krøyer on the beach in 1904. The setting is certainly Skagen, which lies at the northernmost point of Denmark. It was home to one of Europe's most important art colonies, in which Krøyer was a defining figure and a genuine driving force. Standing on the sand in his distinctive white suit, his paintbox slung from his shoulder and his painting smock draped over his arm, surrounded by gently rustling sedge and with the waves of the sea in the background, Krøyer might easily be setting off home after a day spent painting on the beach. – RM

Peregriny 1914–1915/1, 456 | *Paris 2021*, 207, cat. no. 52

VIII

Nature Imbued with the Spiritual

Oswald ACHENBACH
Olof Per Ulrik ARBORELIUS
Sir David Young CAMERON
Franz COURTENS
Pascal-Adolphe-Jean DAGNAN-BOUVERET
William Parsons Winchester DANA
Sir Alfred EAST
Pekka HALONEN
Eugen JETTEL
Fernand KHNOPFF
Émile-René MÉNARD
Carl MOLL
Adelsteen NORMANN
Edward Arthur WALTON
Alfred ZOFF
Heinrich von ZÜGEL

In the last quarter of the nineteenth century, audiences would certainly have been aware of an occasionally radical shift in tone and appearance in new works of art. However, it is only retrospectively that the nature of these changes has been articulated, since correlations among diverse trends are occasionally perceptible only with hindsight. One such characteristic change of direction was the revival of landscape painting and the imbuing of nature with "soul" or "spirit".

The increasingly successful *plein air* tendency attracted a group of Central European followers, whose depictions of nature were executed using similar methods but based on the effects of mood. In the 1950s, this group was widely referred to by the term *Stimmungsimpressionismus* or *Stimmungsnaturalismus* ("mood impressionism" or "mood naturalism"). This was the term applied to the circle of Austrian painters (Emil Jakob Schindler, Tina Blau, Eugen Jettel, Robert Russ, Rudolf Ribarz, Carl Moll) who had studied the *plein air* methods of the Barbizon and Hague Schools but who emphasised in their works the magic of the landscape's mood – which sometimes acquired a symbolist dimension. There is no apparent connection between their technique and the concept of optical analysis behind impressionism, with the possible exception of the use of lighter, vibrant, and pure colours – although this had by now become a general tendency, independent of what French artists were doing. In terms of technique, the approach might rather be classified as belonging under naturalism.

In the 1880s and the first half of the following century – together with *plein air* paintings – works that, in terms of their pictorial intensity, resembled, and frequently surpassed, those produced by Viennese painters, became increasingly prominent at exhibitions throughout Europe, eventually becoming the principal trend in landscape painting. Expanding the definition, we tend rather to encounter the label *Stimmungsmalerei* in the later art historical literature, chiefly in relation to German, Hungarian, British, and Scandinavian paintings. The recurrence of the prefix is telling: the epithet "mood" clearly points to the potential, contained within naturalist painting, that would become one of the starting points for the revival of painting in the 1890s and the emergence of symbolism. The popularity of naturalism throughout the continent played a huge role in predisposing the public towards a symbolist – or somewhat similar spiritualised – understanding of nature and the work of the Belgian artists Franz Courtens and Fernand Khnopff, the Glasgow Boys, and the Hungarian László Mednyánszky, while it also prepared the way for the Scandinavian cult of the mystical landscape. The new landscape painting, in which effects of mood were intensified by a renewal of the elements of painting, became part of the modernisation process, preparing the field for the radical artistic changes of the mid-1890s and remaining popular even in the twentieth century. Such works of art also enjoyed popularity at exhibitions in Hungary, and since a considerable selection were acquired for this collection, we have also classified them here as a distinct unit.

William Parsons Winchester DANA

(Boston, 1833 – London, 1927)

Solitude, 1877 | Oil on canvas, 107.5 × 215 cm
Bequest of Count János Pálffy, 1912 | Inv. no. 252.B

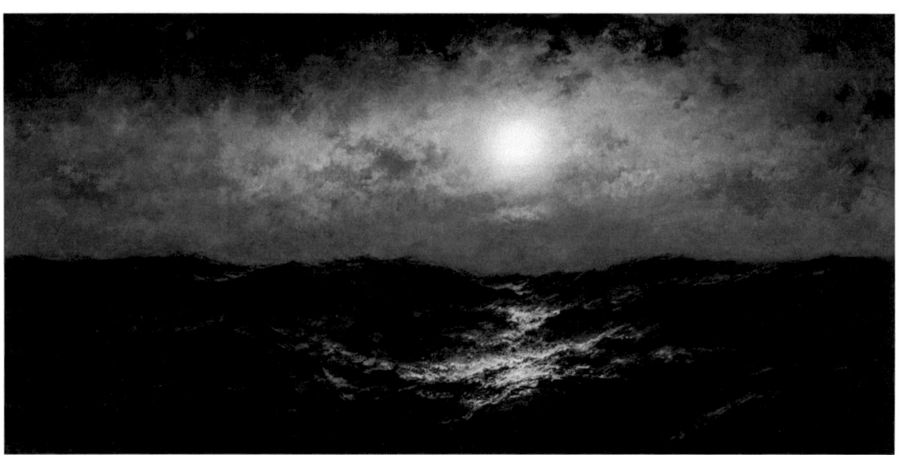

Born in Boston, William Parsons Winchester Dana enrolled at the École des Beaux-Arts in Paris in 1852. For many years, he split his time between France and America, before finally settling in London in 1878. Although his early paintings tended to be inspired by the sea, he later achieved acclaim as a painter of genre scenes. Dana regularly participated in exhibitions in America and at the Paris Salon. In 1878, his work was shown at the Paris Exposition, where he was awarded a third-class medal: enthusiastically received by French critics, it was the seascape held in Budapest that earned him the greatest recognition.

The wide, panoramic, simple composition is divided into two horizontal bands: the overcast sky and the stormy sea. Using subtle gradations of grey and blue, the painter has brilliantly captured the sea at night and the moonlight, veiled by clouds, illuminating the turbulent surface of the water. The infinite, almost empty space is majestic, spellbinding, and slightly haunting at the same time. Recent X-ray scans have revealed that originally, a large frigate has floated on the water, possibly the ship named Constitution, built at the end of the 18th century, which appeared on some of Dana's other pictures. By painting over it, the artist transformed his former historical landscape into an enigmatic modern composition. The new meaning of the work is highlighted by the title *Solitude*, which alludes both to human loneliness and the infinite desolation of the ocean. – AZSK

Dana 1927, 3, 6–7 | Spassky et al. 1985, 361–362

Sir Alfred EAST

(Kettering, 1844 – London, 1913)

A Haunt of Ancient Peace, 1896 | Oil on canvas, 126 × 183.5 cm
Purchased from the HNSFA's 1901 spring exhibition | Inv. no. 25.B

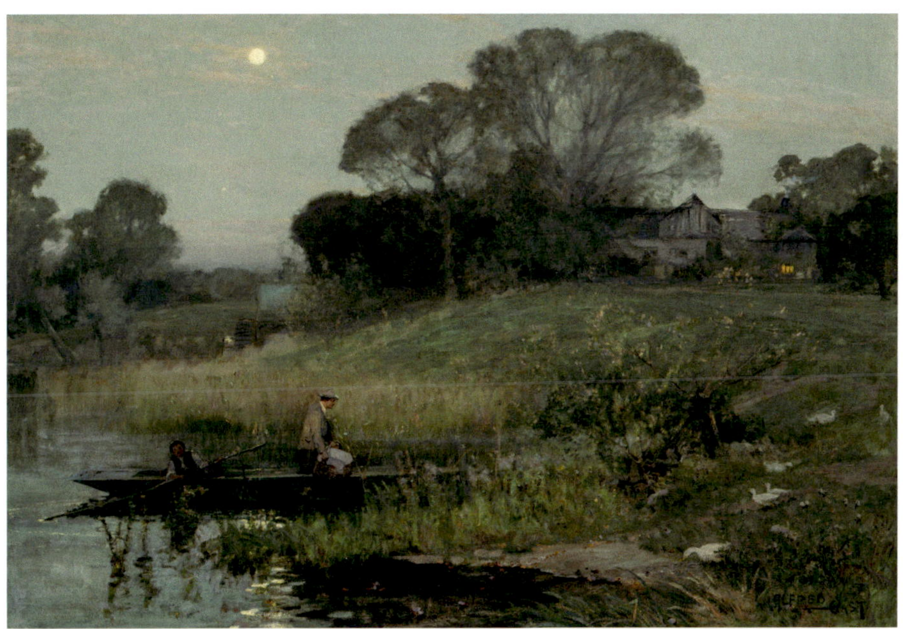

East took up painting in his mid-to-late thirties. He studied at the Glasgow School of Art, then travelled to Paris, where he was influenced by the naturalism of Jules Bastien-Lepage and the work of the Barbizon masters, Jean-François Millet and Camille Corot. After Paris and Barbizon, he visited Japan, Italy, Spain, Morocco, Egypt, and Sicily. In a relatively short time, he became the leading British landscape painter and from 1906 was president of the Royal Society of British Artists. Besides painting, he also wrote essays, and in 1906 he published the book *The Art of Landscape Painting in Oil Colour*.

He first showed *A Haunt of Ancient Peace* in Manchester, at the peak of his career in 1897, before it was exhibited in Budapest in 1901. In the foreground we see a figure – perhaps a fisherman or hunter – arriving by rowing boat, and ducks at the water's edge. Discernible in the background is the silhouette of an old building, with a light showing at one of its windows. The setting is presumably a millpond, although East may have produced the work in his Westminster studio. The restrained palette and composition reveal the influence of Corot. The viewer is captivated by the enigmatic tranquillity and unique, restrained colours of the large-scale painting. A smaller version of the work can be found in the collection of the Christchurch Art Gallery in New Zealand. – AS

Johnson and McConkey 2009, 49 | McConkey 2013, 24–32

Adelsteen NORMANN

(Bodø, 1848 – Christiania [Oslo], 1918)

The Nærøy-fjord in Norway, 1870–1887 | Oil on canvas, 215.5 × 322 cm

Exchange, 1887 | Inv. no. 70.B

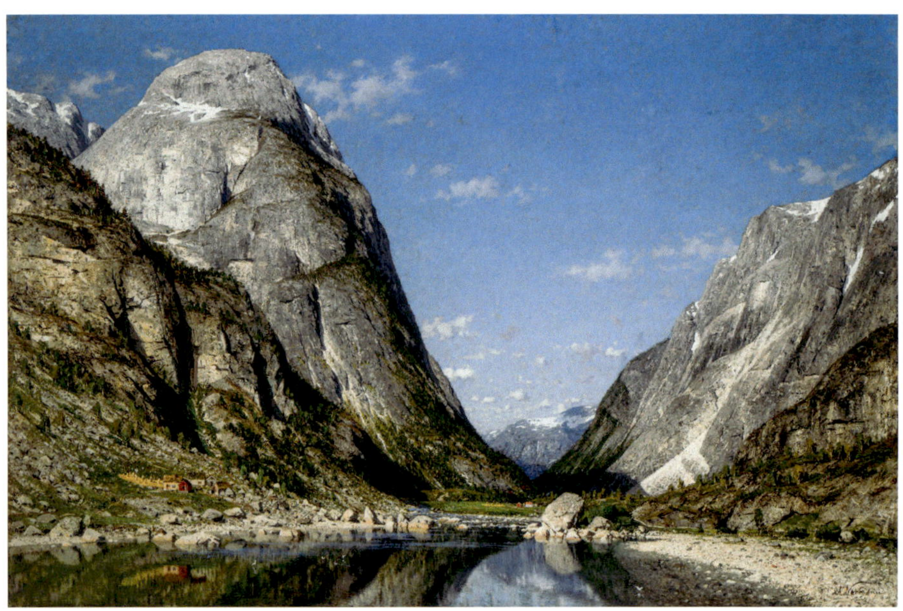

Adelsteen Normann was one of the most important Norwegian landscape painters of his day. He studied at the Academy of Art in Düsseldorf from 1869. The Düsseldorf landscape tradition left a profound mark on his art in terms of his use of colour, method of composition, and painting technique. From the outset of his career, Normann specialised in depictions of the Norwegian fjords, but having spent much of his life in Germany rather than Norway, he painted from sketches and photographs. His monumental landscapes soon brought him commercial success in Norway, Denmark, and Germany. He regularly exhibited at the World's Fairs and won medals at the Paris Salon in 1884 and 1889.

The Nærøy-fjord in Norway is one of the artist's most distinctive works, a brilliant depiction of the idyllic and at the same time majestic scenery: the few buildings, as traces of human civilisation, are scarcely perceptible below the towering peaks and vast expanse of blue sky. The reflection of the lofty mountains in the undisturbed stretch of water lends the composition a peculiarly dramatic, almost abstract character. Normann's influence extended beyond the fine arts: his work – which enjoyed extraordinary popularity among hotel owners – certainly contributed to the boom in Norwegian tourism. – DF

Aaserud 2013, 93

Olof Per Ulrik ARBORELIUS

(Orsa, 1842 – Stockholm, 1915)

Spring, ca. 1900 | Oil on canvas, 70 × 104.8 cm
Bequest of Count Dénes Andrássy, 1913 | Inv. no. 295.B

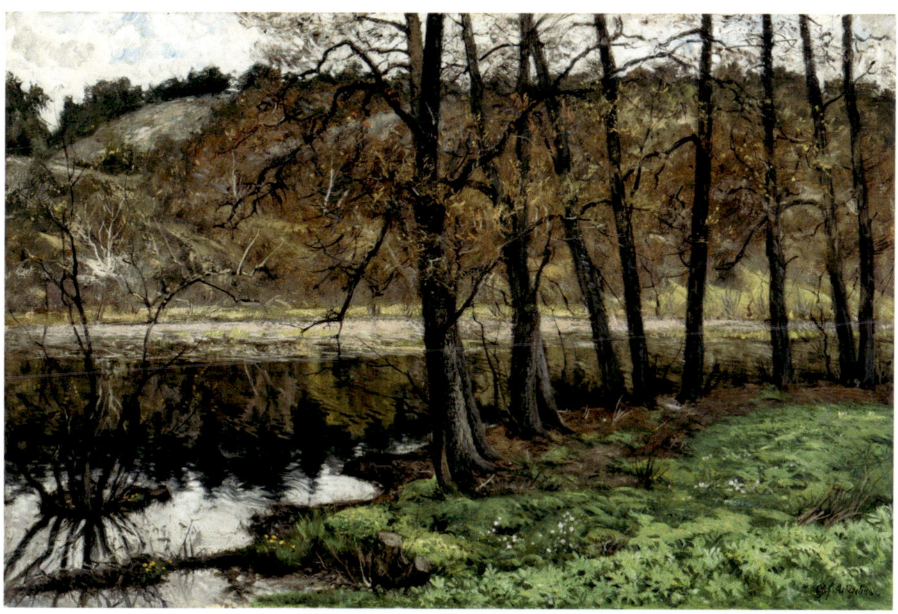

In the late nineteenth century, landscape painting in Sweden was influenced not only by the new artistic trends coming from other European countries but also by the unique atmosphere of Scandinavian nature, which lent the work of Swedish landscape artists a mystical quality. Olof Arborelius combined these influences with the skills he had acquired while studying in Düsseldorf. In this respect, another important influence on him was his teacher, Edvard Bergh, who, despite his Swedish origins, was associated with the Düsseldorf school of painting.

Arborelius was born in the town of Orsa, where his father served as a priest. On completing his studies he travelled, painting mainly Swiss and Italian landscapes, then, on his return home, he sought his subjects among the natural wonders of his native region, the province of Dalarna in central Sweden, as well as the mining district of Bergslagen. He was influenced by *plein air* painting, while a realist approach is also discernible in his attitude to nature. His work shows no traces of the symbolism of the 1890s. One of the hallmarks of his paintings is lush, vibrantly green forest vegetation, although he occasionally included members of the local population in his landscapes. In works such as this, he often painted forest lakes encircled by the tranquillity of native plants. – BIB

Peregriny 1914–1915/3, 230 | Arborelius n. d.

Oswald ACHENBACH

(Düsseldorf, 1827 – Düsseldorf, 1905)

Villa d'Este, 1892 | Oil on canvas, 119.5 × 150 cm
Bequest of Baron Albert Wodianer the Elder, 1892 | Inv. no. 17.B

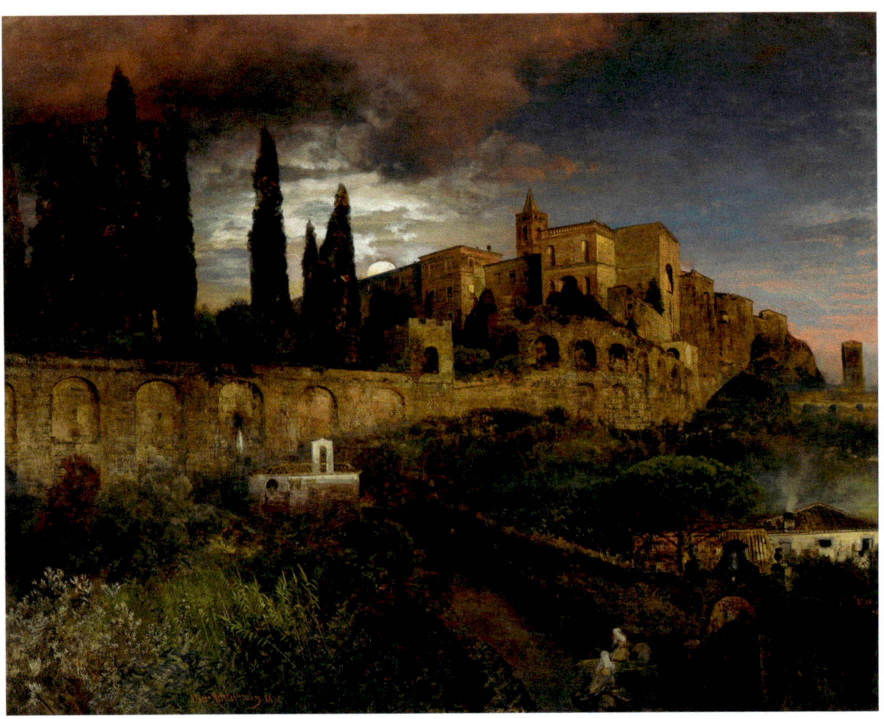

Oswald Achenbach was regarded as one of the leading landscape painters in Germany in his day. He and his elder brother Andreas, also a landscape painter, were the last prominent representatives of the Düsseldorf school of painting. Oswald's first visit to Italy in 1845 determined the subject matter of his paintings for almost the whole of his life. He combined elements of genre painting and landscape painting with remarkable sensitivity, conveying a variety of atmospheric effects. His meticulously executed paintings of the famed Italian countryside, cities, and everyday life enjoyed huge popularity among the bourgeoisie.

Surrounded by cypresses, the Villa d'Este in Tivoli appears in several of Achenbach's compositions from the 1850s onwards. The paint is applied in thick layers, typical of his later, mature style, with an emphasis on contrasting colours. In the foreground is an everyday scene: two peasants on donkeys and some monks. The southern wall of the gloomy Renaissance villa towers above the end of a pathway bordered with lush vegetation. The dramatic colour contrasts in the cloudy sky are achieved by the juxtaposition of the red glow of the setting sun and the silvery light of the rising moon. – AS

Potthoff 1995, 132, 289, 332 | Mai 1998

Émile-René MÉNARD

(Paris, 1862 – Paris, 1930)

Corsican Landscape in Autumn, ca. 1902 | Oil on canvas, 90.5 × 123.5 cm
Purchased from the HNSFA's 1903 spring exhibition | Inv. no. 57.B

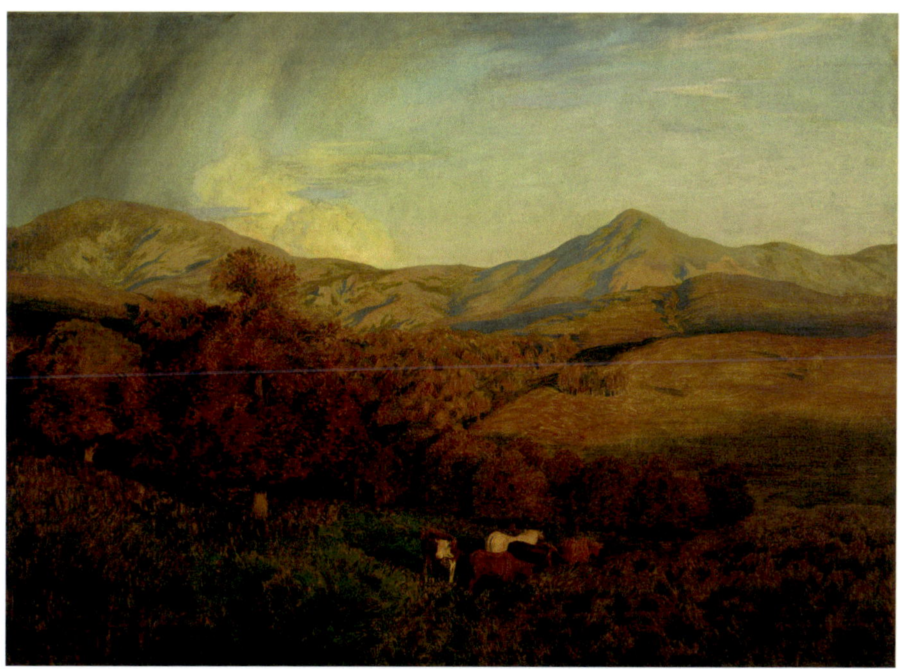

Born into an intellectual, art-loving family, René Ménard enjoyed a classical education and had a wide-ranging knowledge of the arts. In the 1890s, he joined the *Bande noire* (Black Band), a nowadays somewhat forgotten group of painters who rejected the light palette of Impressionism and its emphasis on capturing fleeting moments. Ménard also distinguished himself among his contemporaries with his sensitive perception of nature and his feel for the ancient world, and he became known as the painter of sunsets and autumn. His works evoked the idealised mythological landscape painting typified by Nicolas Poussin and Claude Lorrain, with the characteristically nostalgic, poetic tone of the fin de siècle. In his paintings, which often feature ruins and women reminiscent of nymphs, he aimed for harmony between human figures and nature, and for the unity of colours and composition. His painting of the island of Corsica was greeted with acclaim at the 1902 Salon of the Société nationale des Beaux-Arts in Paris. The landscape, bathed in the golden light of the setting sun, and the bare mountains in the background, are painted in Ménard's customary warm, harmonious palette. Nothing disturbs the tranquillity of the cattle grazing in the foreground: Ménard's rustic composition captures the grandeur and timelessness of the ancient landscape. – AZSK

Migeon 1902, 107, 112 | Illyés 2001, 162–163

Franz COURTENS

(Dandermonde, 1854 – Saint-Josse-ten-Noode, 1943)

Falling Leaves, 1888 | Oil on canvas, 219 × 183 cm
Purchased from the HNSFA's 1891–1892 winter exhibition
Inv. no. 87.B

Born in Belgium, Franz Courtens taught for twenty years at the Royal Academy of Fine Arts in Antwerp. He was made a baron by King Albert I in 1922 in recognition of his achievements. While his early style was defined by realism, he was later influenced by the Barbizon painters and impressionism. His large-scale, atmospheric landscapes, executed with flawless technique, brought him fame and popularity in the 1880s. Courtens produced several paintings of richly coloured autumn leaves. One of the most attractive is *Falling Leaves*, which he painted with vigorous brushstrokes and heavy impasto. The pictorial space is filled entirely with the arching, spreading trees of the Royal Park in Brussels, while the sunlight filtering through the branches glitters on the golden yellow foliage and falling leaves. A tiny figure carrying brushwood, scarcely perceptible on the wide, leaf-strewn path, directs the viewer's gaze to the end of the avenue, while at the same time indicating the height of the towering trees. The yellow, green, and brown tones radiate a sense of harmony. Prior to its acquisition by the Hungarian state in 1891, the painting won a gold medal at the 1889 Paris Exposition, and a year later was exhibited at the Paris Salon. – AS

Losonczi 1892, 123 | Muther 1907, 225–226

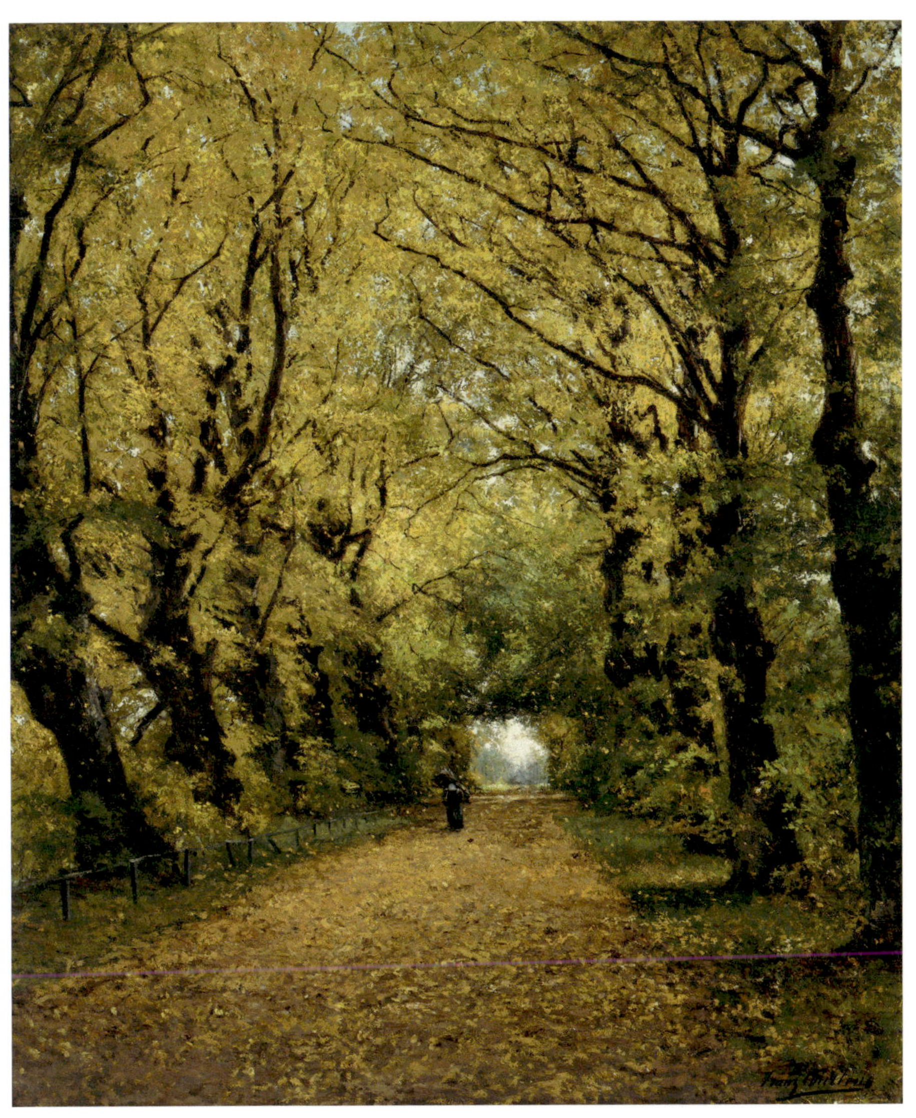

Eugen JETTEL

(Janovice, 1845 – Veli Lošinj, 1901)

Landscape near Staatz, 1898 | Oil on paperboard, 31.5 × 57 cm

Purchase, 1964 | Inv. no. 544.B

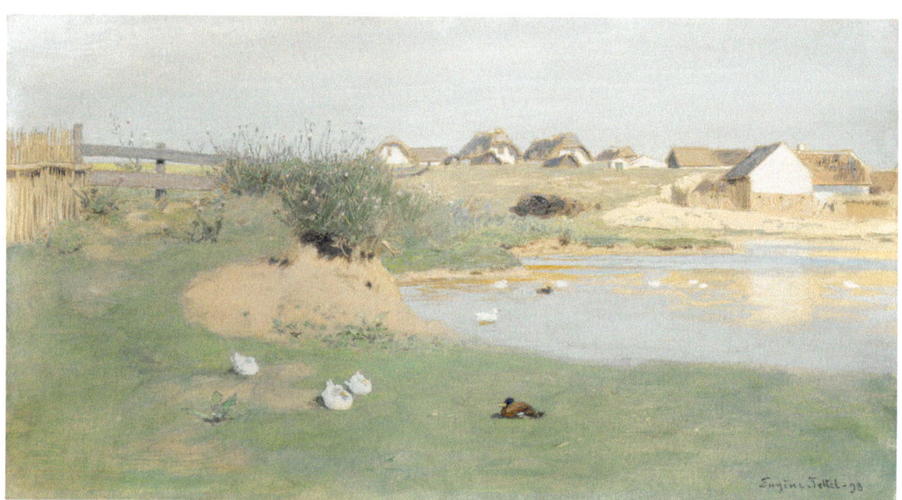

Czech-born Eugen Jettel was a student at the school of landscape painting founded by Zimmermann in Vienna. It was there that he became a good friend of August von Pettenkofen, who also had a great influence on his art. His breakthrough came when he was awarded gold medals for two of his paintings at the 1869 international exhibition in Munich. From 1873, he was employed by the art dealer Charles Sedelmeyer as his assistant in Paris. When their relationship deteriorated, he returned to Vienna in 1897, becoming one of the founders of the Secession movement.

His subjects and compositions were inspired by the Barbizon school and executed in a style of landscape painting popular in Austria in the second half of the nineteenth century – later known as *Stimmungsimpressionismus*, or "mood impressionism". From the 1880s, he typically used muted, glazed pastel colours, although his paintings nevertheless retained their melancholic quality. This depiction of the countryside near Staatz, in which the influence of French naturalism is already apparent, was painted in 1898, during the final period of his career. Here, the horizon is much closer than it was in the expansive views of the previous decade, as the painter focuses on a smaller, much more detailed sliver of the landscape. The ducks sitting in the foreground are recurring motifs in his work, as is the fence that marks the border of the neighbouring meadow. – BIB

Fuchs 1975, 251 | Kotoučová 2010, 64–65

Heinrich von ZÜGEL

(Murrhardt, 1850 – Munich, 1941)

The First Rays of Light, 1893 | Oil on canvas, 140 × 202 cm
Purchased from the HNSFA's 1894–1895 winter exhibition | Inv. no. 133.B

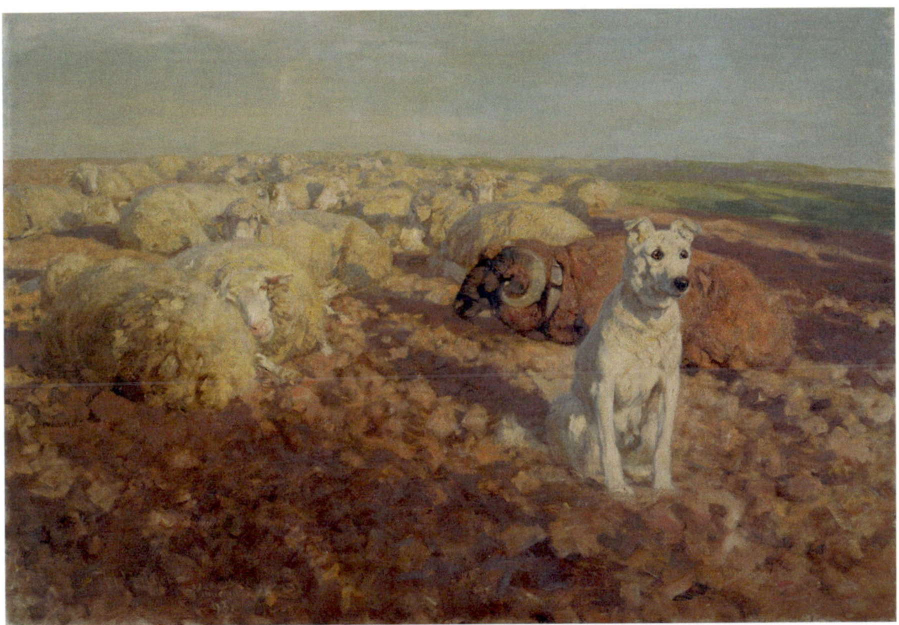

Heinrich von Zügel grew up in a sheep-breeding family, surrounded by animals, and became interested in animal painting at a young age. He studied art in Stuttgart and Munich. The co-existence of human beings and animals is a recurring theme in his work, and he was particularly fond of painting sheep and cattle. The pictorial space is often filled with monumental animals. Such was his interest in the animal world that in 1930, he was awarded an honorary degree in veterinary science by Giessen University. His son, Willy Zügel, achieved fame with his sculptures of animals.

In the first decades of his career, he employed loose brushwork and delicate tones, and his animals were meticulously executed. However, by the late nineteenth century, his colours had become more vivid and his brushstrokes broader, while his scenes were suffused with orange sunlight. It was at this time that he painted *The First Rays of Light*, depicting a dog guarding a flock of sleeping sheep, with the sunrise in the background. At this time, Zügel was spending his summers in Wörth, a village on the Upper Rhine, thus it is conceivable that the Budapest painting was inspired by the surrounding countryside. – BIB

Stransky 1916, 179 | *Budapest 2020*, 32

Edward Arthur WALTON

(Glanderston House, Renfrewshire, 1860 – Edinburgh, 1922)

The Stream, ca. 1900 | Oil on canvas, 91 × 121.5 cm
Purchased from the HNSFA's 1902 spring exhibition | Inv. no. 546.B

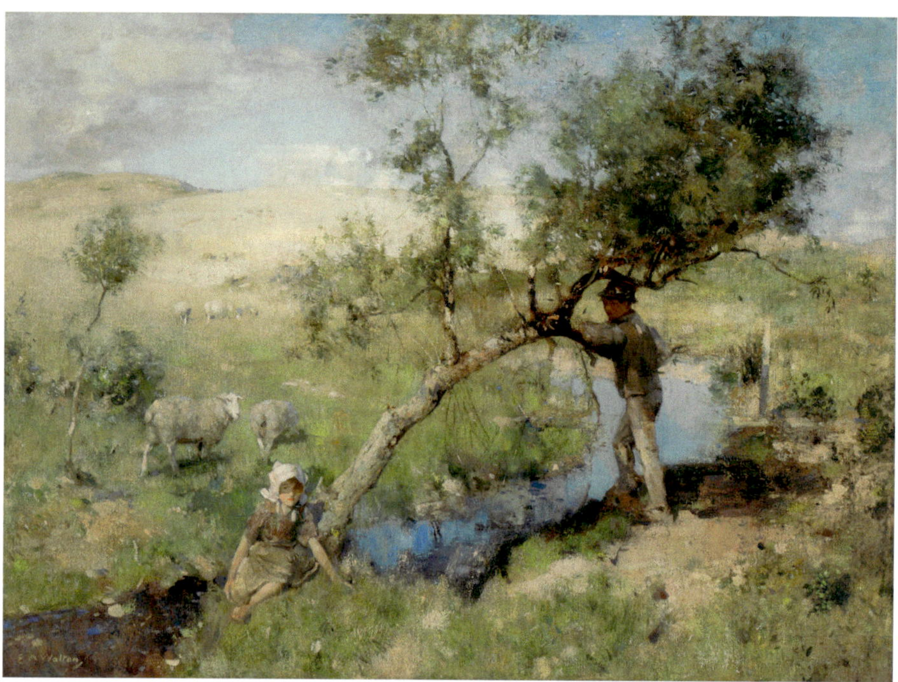

After studying at the Academy of Art in Düsseldorf, the Scottish painter returned to his native country and joined the circle of young painters that became known as the Glasgow School, or "Glasgow Boys". Having lost faith in the traditional precepts of academicism, they favoured the *plein air* methods of the Barbizon artists and the Hague School. The naturalism of Jules Bastien-Lepage made a particularly strong impression on them. Walton emerged as one of the leading figures among the Glasgow Boys, who, with their landscapes executed outdoors and their everyday subjects decoratively rendered in light colours, represent the beginnings of modernism in Scottish painting. Walton was a frequent visitor to Suffolk between 1894 and 1904, where he painted pastoral scenes. It was during this period that he produced *The Stream*, with its loose brushwork and fresh colours. At this time, he was living in London, where he was a neighbour of James McNeill Whistler: their close friendship led to the fulfilment of Walton's painting, as he turned from his earlier meticulous, realistic naturalism towards a more subjective approach. The subtle effect of his vivid landscapes, with their relaxed forms and lively colours, brought him widespread recognition throughout Europe. – FT

Budapest 1995, 371 | *Balatonfüred* 2019, 33

Sir David Young CAMERON

(Glasgow, 1865 – Perth, 1945)

The Square, Amboise, 1902 | Oil on canvas, 61.5 × 68.8 cm
Purchased from the HNSFA's 1903 spring exhibition | Inv. no. 52.B

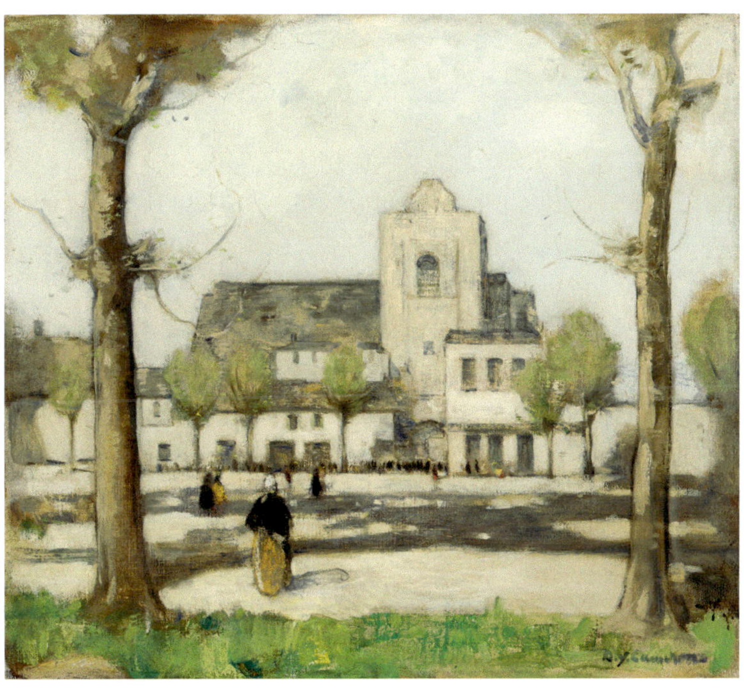

The Scottish painter and graphic artist studied at the prestigious schools of art in Glasgow and later Edinburgh. He grew up fascinated by J.M.W. Turner and Horatio McCulloch, the great masters of dramatic landscape painting, although in the vibrant artistic world of Glasgow he soon became acquainted with the atmospheric painting of the Hague School, James McNeill Whistler, and the Glasgow Boys. Their influence on Cameron was initially given expression in the form of etchings. He had already attained international acclaim with his print series when, in 1899, he moved to the Scottish Highlands: abandoning both portraiture and figurative studies – in both his etchings and, increasingly, his oil paintings – from then on, his subjects were exclusively architecture and landscapes.

In May 1902, while travelling in France, he visited the historic towns along the Loire. In the copperplate etchings that record the stops on his journey, it was the architecture of the narrow medieval streets that interested him above all, while he adopted a broader perspective in his watercolours and oil paintings. Among the latter is this painting of the square in front of the Church of Saint Florentin in Amboise. The work is striking for the closed composition typical of his other cityscapes, although here the more muted tones cast an elegiac veil over the surroundings. – FT

Peregriny 1914–1915/1, 344 | Smith 1992, 43

Pascal-Adolphe-Jean DAGNAN-BOUVERET

(Paris, 1852 – Quincey, 1929)

Landscape with Trees, ca. 1900 | Oil on canvas, 62 × 48 cm

Purchase, 1986 | Inv. no. 86.22.B

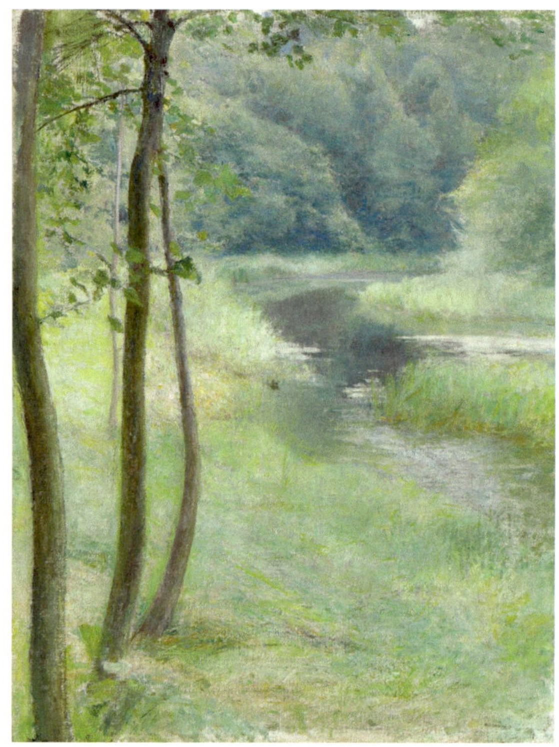

Along with Jules Bastien-Lepage, Pascal Dagnan-Bouveret was a leading representative of the French naturalist school and gained international recognition. Although, in the 1870s and 1880s, he made his name through genre paintings of everyday rural life and of religious processions in Brittany, he gradually became less committed to realism: around the turn of the century, he started to produce monumental compositions infused with deep religiosity and symbolist overtones.

As one of the chief proponents of naturalist *plein air* painting, he produced most of his works outdoors, yet landscapes tend to appear merely as backdrops to his genre scenes. His landscape paintings are less well-known and make up only a small proportion of his oeuvre. This painting is characterised by its vivid green tones and lively brushwork. The scene is framed on the left by the darker accent of the three tree trunks, while the small stream meanders freely on the right. Trees obscure the horizon, and there is no glimpse of the sky in the hazy background. The contained composition and almost monochrome palette help to immerse the viewer in this simple, uneventful, yet atmospheric landscape. – AZSK

Fukuoka–Matsuyama–Tokyo 1994, cat. no. 24

Pekka HALONEN

(Lapinlahti, 1865 – Tuusula, 1933)

Spring Frost, 1906 | Oil on canvas, 35.3 × 26 cm
Donated by Izor Halmos, 1924 | Inv. no. 383.B

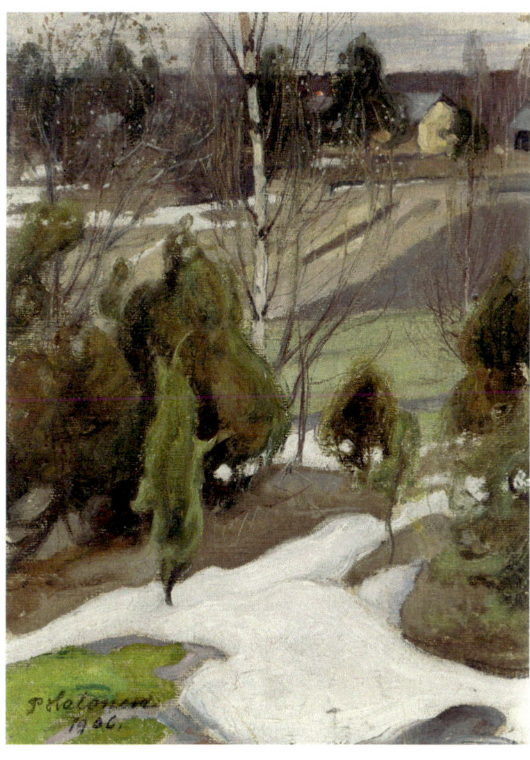

The winter views painted by Pekka Halonen after 1895, largely in Eastern Finland, stand out
from among the artist's other landscapes. The paintings are evocations of the season that
defined the face of Finland for almost six months each year. Halonen always worked outdoors,
even when temperatures fell below freezing. He conveys the bright, sunny, albeit frozen aspect of this predominant season, as well as its gloomy, grey, forbidding side. The small-scale,
portrait-format landscape preserved in Budapest is a sensitive depiction of the transition to
spring following the long, northern winter. Patches of snow of various sizes are still visible
on slopes that are gradually turning green. A few houses are discernible at the top of the hill,
while the sky is no more than a narrow strip at the top of the painting. Halonen's patches of
restrained colour can be traced back to the synthetism of Paul Gauguin, which he combines
with Art Nouveau–inspired curves. Alongside Western European artistic trends, Halonen was
influenced by Japanese art: he began collecting Japanese woodcut prints following his third
visit to Paris. – AS

Let me See! 2015, 44–45

Fernand KHNOPFF

(Grembergen, 1858 – Brussels, 1921)

The Stream near Fosset, 1897 | Oil on canvas, 40 × 32 cm
Purchased from the HNSFA's 1902 spring exhibition
Inv. no. 42.B

Fernand Khnopff was a permanent member of Les XX and exhibited his work with the group, which was founded in Brussels in 1883. His mystical, allegorical paintings were highly esteemed by his contemporaries, and the critics of his day regarded him as the greatest of the Belgian symbolists. He submitted seven works to the spring exhibition at the Budapest Kunsthalle in 1902, which he imagined being shown in three thematic groups. The themes, which formed tightly arranged units both conceptually and in terms of their actual positioning, were: "Dreams", "Solitude", and "Paintings after Nature". The small oil painting purchased by the Hungarian state belonged to the last of these groups.

Landscapes play a somewhat subordinate role in Khnopff's oeuvre, although they can be considered part of a comprehensive, idealistic concept of life and nature. He often painted natural motifs from the area around Fosset, his estate in the Belgian Ardennes. Rather than capturing fleeting impressions, this forest scene, too, emphasises the enigmatic, immaterial aspect of the landscape. It is chiefly the vibrancy and translucency of the dominant green tones in this almost monochromatic painting that evoke an atmosphere of transcendence. – FT

Paris–Brussels–Hamburg 1979–1980, cat. no. 96
Budapest 1995, cat. no. III.5.3

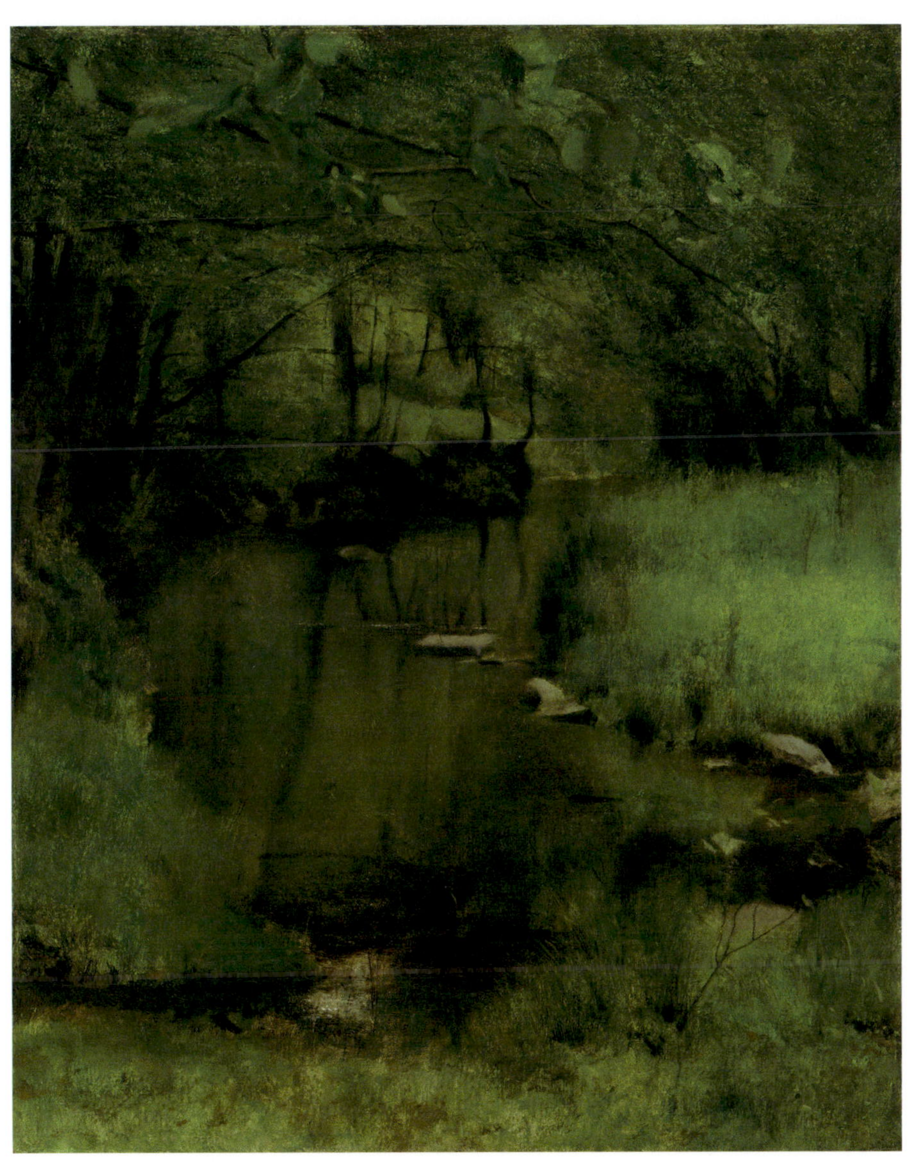

Alfred ZOFF

(Graz, 1852 – Graz, 1927)

Evening Sunshine in Chioggia, ca. 1900 | Oil on canvas, 37 × 49.9 cm
Bequest of Count Dénes Andrássy, 1913 | Inv. no. 333.B

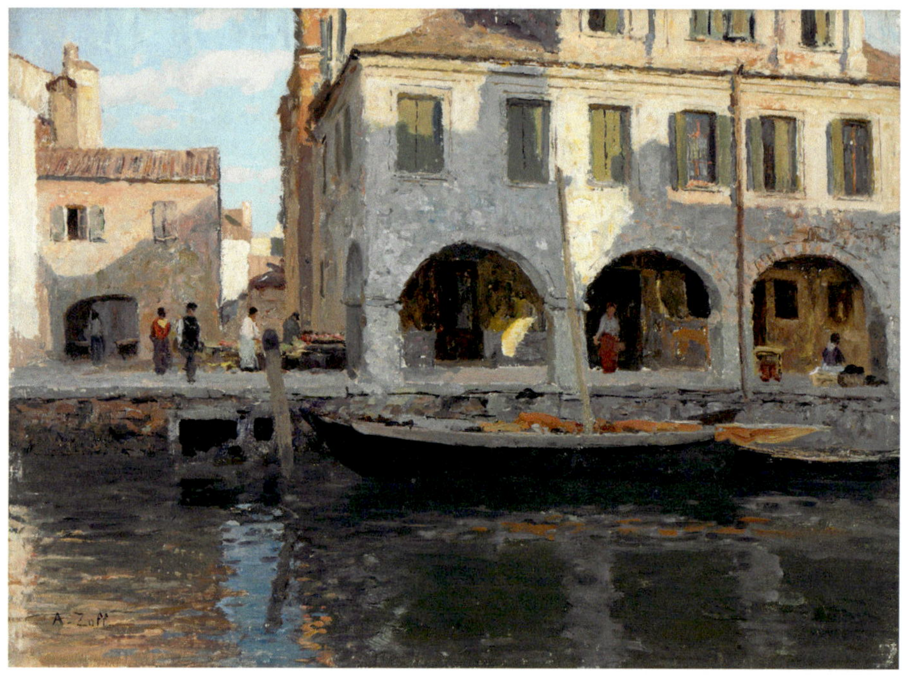

Alfred Zoff was initially a medical student before studying painting in Vienna and at the Karlsruhe Academy of Fine Arts. In Karlsruhe, he became acquainted with the art of the Barbizon school, prompting him to move beyond the realism represented by his teachers and associated with the Biedermeier tradition; in the second half of the nineteenth century, he began working in the style then popular in Austria, which later became known as "mood impressionism". His brushstrokes become broader and more pastose. He spent a great deal of his time travelling, preferably by ship, being particularly fascinated by the sea, waves, and atmospheric phenomena. He had a special fondness for the Italian Riviera, which he visited regularly. He produced numerous oil sketches during his travels, which he subsequently worked into larger-scale paintings in his studio. Clients who commissioned seascapes from him included the cream of contemporary Austrian society – entrepreneurs, aristocrats, art collectors, and even Franz Joseph himself, who was a great admirer of his work and who owned a total of eight of his paintings. The setting chosen for the Budapest painting was the small Italian town of Chioggia, known as "little Venice", where Zoff captured the harbour in the light of the setting sun. – BIB

Wigger ed. 2015, 4 | Peer 2021

Carl MOLL

(Vienna, 1861 – Vienna, 1945)

Winter Courtyard, 1905 | Oil on canvas, 100 × 100 cm
Purchase, 1982 | Inv. no. 83.69.B

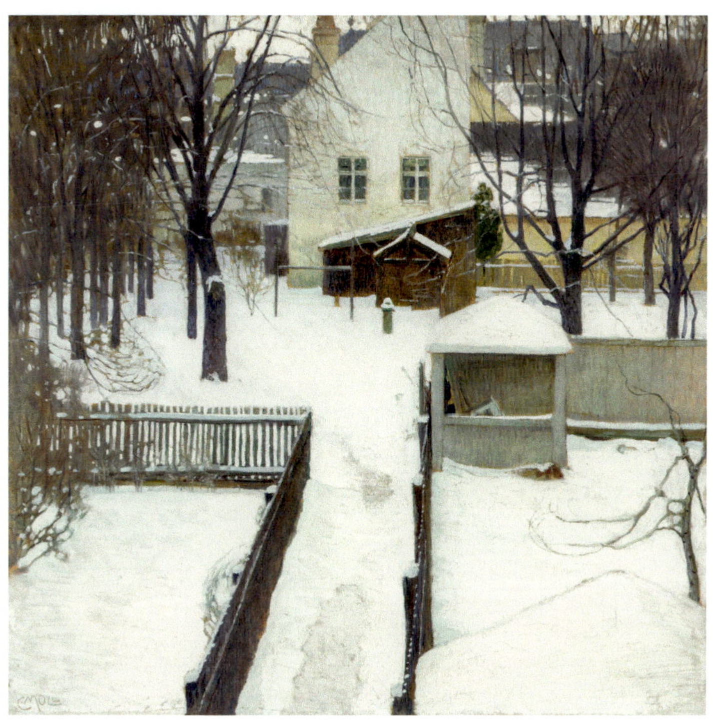

Having abandoned his studies at the Academy of Fine Arts in Vienna, Carl Moll became a student of Emil Jakob Schindler, who taught him to paint atmospheric landscapes and free himself from the constraints of *plein air* naturalism. In 1897, he was one of the founders of the Vienna Secession and was even its president in 1900–1901. As a member of the radical, experimental group of friends that gathered around Gustav Klimt, he played an active role in the creation of an independent institutional system for the fine arts and in the renewal of artistic forms.

In 1901, Moll commissioned the celebrated Secessionist architect Josef Hoffmann to design a villa for him in the Hohe Warte district of Vienna, which became a central location frequented by progressive artists. This work shows its snow-covered garden, with part of the building in the background. The balanced harmony and lyrical mood of the painting can be attributed to the influence of Schindler. Yet the tightly balanced composition adheres to the aesthetic principles of revolutionary Viennese architecture, which, with its clean lines and strict internal arrangement, also had a powerful impact on contemporary painting. – FT

Dijon 1995, cat. no. 189 | *Madrid* 2017, cat. no. 87

IX

Hidden Correlations

———

Arnold BÖCKLIN
Rupert BUNNY
Eugène CARRIÈRE
Jules-Clément CHAPLAIN
Alexandre-Louis-Marie CHARPENTIER
Maurice DENIS
Jules DESBOIS
Akseli GALLEN-KALLELA
August GAUL
Pekka HALONEN
Ludwig von HERTERICH
Adolf von HILDEBRAND
Jules Joseph LEFEBVRE
Maximilian LENZ
Yrjö LIIPOLA
Hans MAKART
Gabriel von MAX

Ivan MEŠTROVIĆ
Constantin MEUNIER
George MINNE
Carl O'LYNCH OF TOWN
Leo PUTZ
Pierre PUVIS DE CHAVANNES
Auguste RODIN
Anton ROMAKO
Égide ROMBAUX
Oscar ROTY
Giovanni SEGANTINI
Jean Paul SINIBALDI
Hans STOLTENBERG-LERCHE
Franz von STUCK
Fritz von UHDE
Charles VAN DER STAPPEN
Anders ZORN

By the time the European public had become familiar with the work of the impressionists, artists were already setting off in new directions. Naturalism, like impressionism, which, in terms of its basic principles, was regarded as a branch of naturalism – the final phase of painting tied to visual perception – were on the wane. In the final decades of the century, aesthetic doctrines calling not for the subjugation of the world by reason, but for the perception and sensualisation of the forces concealed behind the appearance of reality achieved widespread popularity. This movement in literature and painting was given the overall name "symbolism". Its representatives argued for an art that conveyed thought and internal states of mind through the unique idiom of the given branch of the arts. They demanded freedom of imagination and creativity and sought independent opportunities for art that could not be substituted by any other means.

In Paris, a city that was regarded as the crucible of European art, the distinguished forum of publicity, the Salon, was flooded with works evoking enigmatic scenes from ancient mythology or based on the sensuousness of the exotic world of fantasy. The innovative paintings of Pierre Puvis de Chavannes attracted particular attention and great respect. By the end of the century, they had earned the unanimous acclaim of reformers keen to break away from the principle of visual perception. Through the simplification of forms and monolithic figures, even his small-scale paintings convey an impression of monumentality. Paul Gauguin was the first to respond to these possibilities, aiming for a similar monumentality in his own works. These were the starting point from which Maurice Denis went on to formulate the principles of modern art and to develop his own unique style.

The cultural vibrancy of the *fin de siècle* led to far-reaching changes not only in France but in most of the countries of Europe. Alongside Paris, Brussels emerged as a focal point of cultural life and the most important centre of international symbolism. The innovative works of sculpture shown in exhibitions there elicited enormous interest and signalled the renascence of Belgian culture. In German-speaking areas, the younger generation of artists were influenced primarily by the paintings of Arnold Böcklin – in which the idyllic world of mythology was encompassed within an atmosphere of mystery. Through the revival of traditional themes, Böcklin's followers, primarily Franz von Stuck, founded the distinctive Munich tendency in symbolism, which provided the aesthetic starting point for the German Jugendstil movement. The emphasis on emotionality in Böcklin's technique, the effects of mood achieved by the intensification of colour, and, in certain works, the sense of threat, led to a liberation of the means of expression in the works of the next generation. As a distinguished professor at the Academy of Fine Arts, Stuck helped to launch the artistic careers of some of the outstanding figures of twentieth-century modern art, including Vasily Kandinsky, Paul Klee, and Josef Albers.

An alliance of reform-minded artists and architects in Austria founded the Vienna Secession in 1897, with Gustav Klimt as its president. Two of the valuable works in the collection are by Carl Moll and Maximilian Lenz, both founding members of the Secession, an association that brought together progressive artists while representing a variety of stylistic tendencies. The Northern Italian artist Giovanni Segantini was a regular participant in the Secession's large-scale international exhibitions.

Arnold BÖCKLIN

(Basel, 1827 – San Domenico di Fiesole, 1901)

Spring Evening, 1879 | Oil on wood, 67.4 × 129.5 cm
Bequest of Count Dénes Andrássy, 1913
Inv. no. 294.B

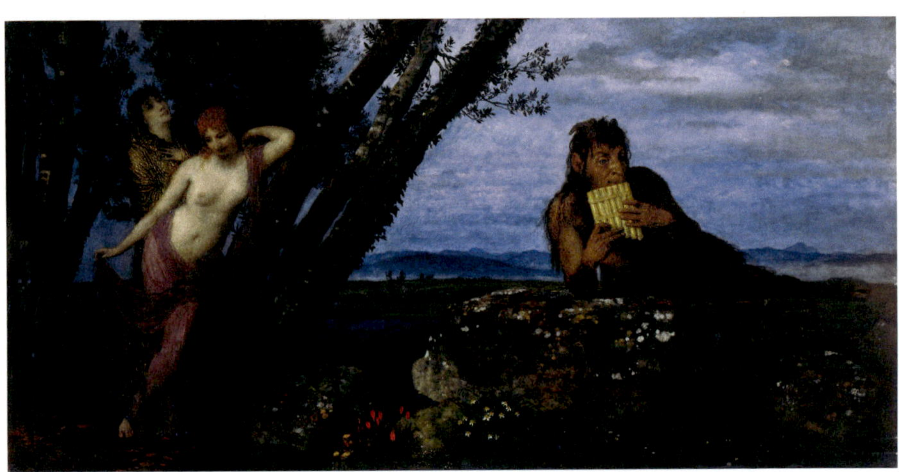

Born in Switzerland, Arnold Böcklin travelled to Rome for the first time in 1850 at the sugges-tion of the renowned art historian Jacob Burckhardt. Böcklin later returned to Italy on several occasions, and the countryside around Rome and the relics of the past had a profound impact on his art. In 1874, he moved to Florence for a number of years, and it was here that his elegiac composition *Spring Evening* was painted.

Pan playing on his pipes, and the hidden nymphs of the forest (dryads) who listen to his music, emerge from the charmingly painted landscape as elements of the reassuring natural world. We know of several versions of the scene. Böcklin had a nostalgic love for the ancient traditions of the Mediterranean and for the harmonious golden age of unity with na-ture. From the 1870s, his romantic landscapes and idyllic scenes were imbued with a power-ful atmosphere that became the trademark of his most important works. His paintings were filled with mythological figures – sirens, naiads, centaurs, and mermen. Intense colours and at-mospheric effects lend Böcklin's work a peculiar appeal, while the expressive force and unique pictorial world of his paintings made him one of the most important figures in the symbolist generation. – FT

Andree 1998, cat. no. 332 | *Basel–Paris–Munich 2001–2002, cat. no. 55*

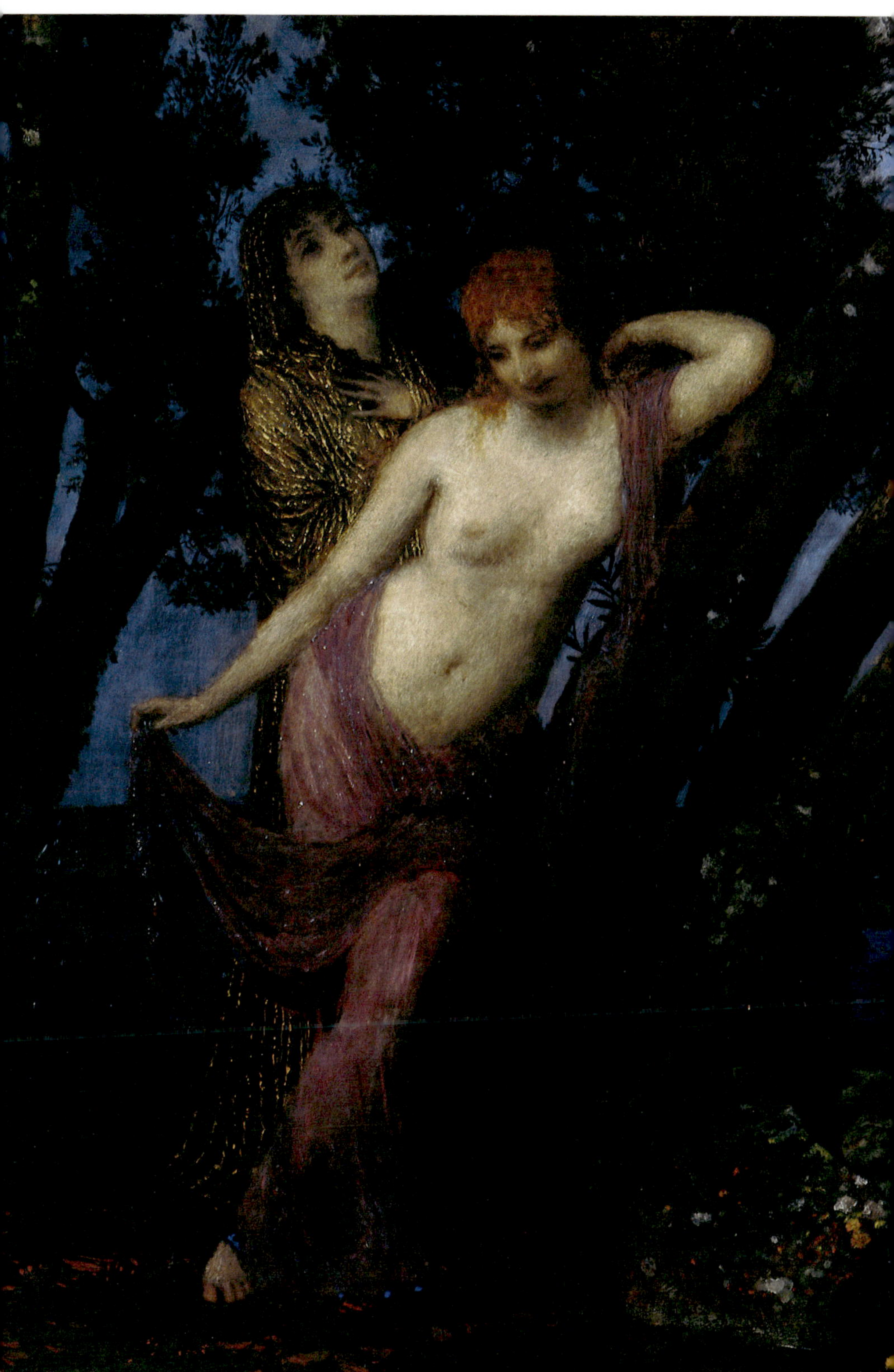

Arnold BÖCKLIN

(Basel, 1827 – San Domenico di Fiesole, 1901)

Centaur at the Village Blacksmith, 1888 | Oil on wood, 78.5 × 100 cm
Purchased from Kunsthandlung J. P. Schneider jr. (Frankfurt am Main), 1901
Inv. no. 26.B

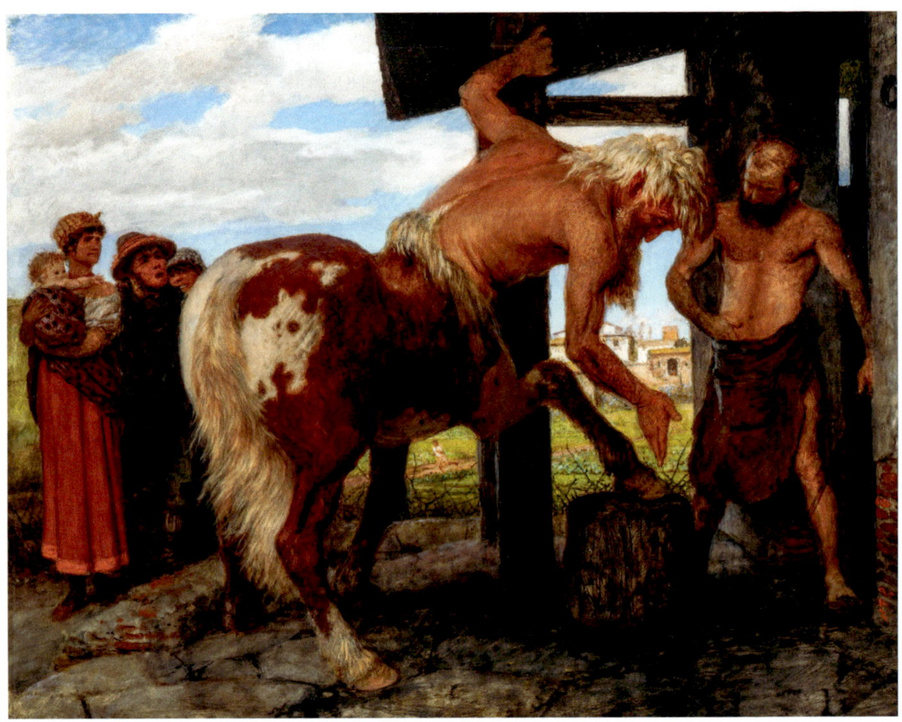

After living for a time in Florence, Böcklin settled in Zurich in 1885, and in the same year began work on his painting *Centaur at the Village Blacksmith*. He recalled coming up with the idea for the painting while out for a walk, when he started imagining what would happen if a mythical creature were to appear in the fields and terrify the local population. The work took three years to complete, and he painted the figures from his imagination rather than after models. Originally, the painting featured two centaurs, who were frightening the villagers. Later, however, the mood of the composition changed: the earlier terror has disappeared from the onlookers' faces, and they observe the unusual situation with interest. The blacksmith, too, merely seems perplexed by this unaccustomed task. The earthly and mythological figures, placed in a natural setting and painted with naturalistic precision, interact with one another quite naturally. Unlike traditional depictions of centaurs, this imaginary creature seems almost human, and the whole situation is humorous rather than disturbing. According to Böcklin, in order to convey the centaur's mannerisms, he had to imagine himself in its place. – FT

Andree 1998, cat. no. 408 | *Tokyo* 2019, cat. no. 106

Hans MAKART

(Salzburg, 1840 – Vienna, 1884)

Nessus Carrying off Deianeira, ca. 1882 | Oil on wood, 142 × 93 cm
Purchased from Gyula Szlávik, 1887 | Inv. no. 100.B

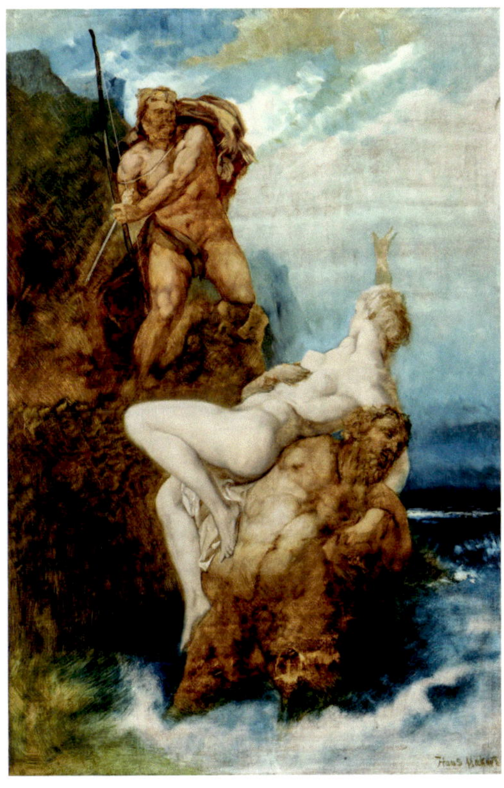

Both celebrated and censured by his contemporaries, from the 1870s until his death in 1884 Hans Makart was acclaimed in Viennese cultural and public life as the Painter Prince. This painting is a detail from one of his major works, *Bacchus and Ariadne*, held in the Belvedere in Vienna, although it has its own independent iconography. Rendered with baroque dynamism, the monumental figure of Heracles draws his bow as he looms above the centaur who is carrying off his wife, Deianeira. According to the myth, as Heracles hastens to Deianeira's aid he fatally wounds the centaur, although his victory also seals his defeat. Convinced by the dying centaur, Deianeira makes a lethal potion, believing it will ensure Heracles' faithfulness. Deianeira gives her husband a shirt steeped in poison, and having put it on, he dies a painful death. In all of the variants of the myth, Heracles' death is caused by Nessus exacting revenge from beyond the grave. It is in this context that we should interpret the triad formed by the two colossal male figures, rendered in ochre and umber tones, and the graceful, marble-white figure of the woman, as the tragic culmination of a dramatic tale of jealousy. – DL

Bodnár ed. 2002, 268 | Frodl 2013, 270

Anton ROMAKO

(Atzgersdorf, 1832 – Vienna, 1889)

Young Girl at the Mirror (The Allegory of Vanity), ca. 1880 | Oil on canvas,
mounted on wood, 104 × 82 cm | Purchase, 2024 | Inv. no. 2024.6.1.B

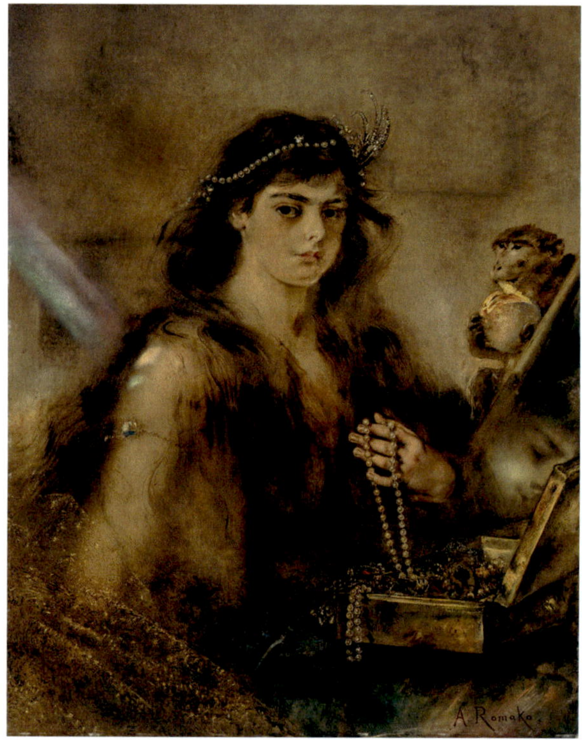

Anton Romako is an idiosyncratic, hard to classify figure in nineteenth-century Austrian painting. He was taught by Ferdinand Georg Waldmüller at the Vienna Academy and Wilhelm Kaulbach in Munich, although his difficult temperament got him embroiled in numerous conflicts while a student. He spent much of his life outside Austria: he lived in Rome for around twenty years and visited Paris, England, and even Hungary several times.

This work reflects Romako's lofty style and eccentricity. In iconographical terms, its precursors can be found among baroque allegories of vanity, which typically feature a young woman standing before a mirror, lost in the contemplation of her own beauty. Here, the highly realistic monkey eating a piece of fruit, the overflowing jewellery box, and the glimmer of a (ghostly) face in the mirror all refer to the allegory of vanity and anticipate the decadent aesthetic of the Vienna Secession, associated with Gustav Klimt. Romako's female figures are not ideal types of beauty: his models were real individuals, whose unconventional charms he captured with great sensitivity. Romako's bold, expressive brushwork and use of colour are discernible in this painting. – DL

Novotny 1954, 184 | Reiter and Husslein-Arco eds. 2010

Gabriel von MAX

(Prague, 1840 – Munich, 1915)

Hearing, ca. 1900 | Oil on canvas, 59.5 × 43.5 cm

Transfer, 1951 | Inv. no. 498.B

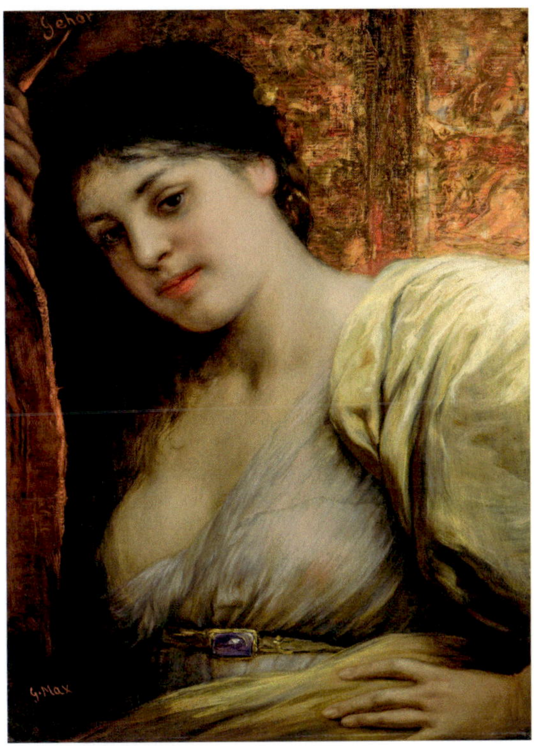

Born into a family of Czech artists, Gabriel Max's talents were recognised early and he became a student at the Prague Academy at just fifteen years of age. After a brief stay in Vienna,
he continued his training at the Munich Academy between 1863 and 1867 as a student of Karl
von Piloty, and later his assistant. In Munich, he became friends with two Hungarian painters:
Pál Szinyei-Merse and Gyula Benczúr. Max later married Benczúr's sister. Max's romantic genre paintings and religious works were conspicuous for their unusual, rarely depicted scenes.
He painted the mystical revelations of Christian visionaries and martyrs, as well as extraordinary spiritual states. He had a longstanding interest in science, but was also fascinated by the
occult and spiritism, which became fashionable at the turn of the century, and by the hidden
depths of the human soul.

Allegories of the five senses had been popular in the arts for centuries, inspiring
works by Jan Brueghel, Pieter Paul Rubens, Rembrandt, and Hans Makart. As the allegory of
hearing, Gabriel Max depicted an ethereal, radiant young woman, her head slightly inclined as
she listens. The predominantly gold background intensifies the sense of mystery. – AS

Gunma–Sapporo–Tokyo 1981, cat. no. 47 | *Fukuoka–Matsuyama–Tokyo* 1994, 46, 149, cat. no. 8

Franz von STUCK

(Tettenweis, 1863 – Munich, 1928)

The Kiss of the Sphinx, 1895 | Oil on canvas, 162.5 × 145.5 cm
Purchased from the HNSFA's 1895–1896 winter exhibition | Inv. no. 124.B

After graduating from the Academy of Fine Arts, Franz von Stuck quickly emerged as the leading artist in Munich. In 1892, he was one of the founders of the Secession, a group of artists working independently of academic institutions. In 1895, he became a leading teacher at the Academy of Fine Arts in Munich but was also highly respected for his support to young, progressive artists. He helped launch the careers of several painters who would go on to become prominent figures in twentieth-century modern art. Stuck's works embody the mysterious realm of the symbolist imagination. They combine the masterful handling of form and sculptural qualities with powerful pictoriality. *The Kiss of the Sphinx* was painted in the same year he was appointed professor at the Academy. The motif of the traveller who kisses a statue with a human head and the body of a lion, bringing it to life while condemning himself to destruction, was introduced by Heinrich Heine in the poem that forms the preface to the third edition of *The Book of Songs* (1839). Stuck's painting is a metaphor for the seductive, destructive *femme fatale*. The demonic woman's sensual curves emerge from the depths of shadow. Each stylistic device he employs – the tension of the confined composition, the raw colours and bulky proportions – intensifies the sense of brutal eroticism. – FT

Amsterdam 1995–1996, 19–22 | Munich 2008–2009, 80

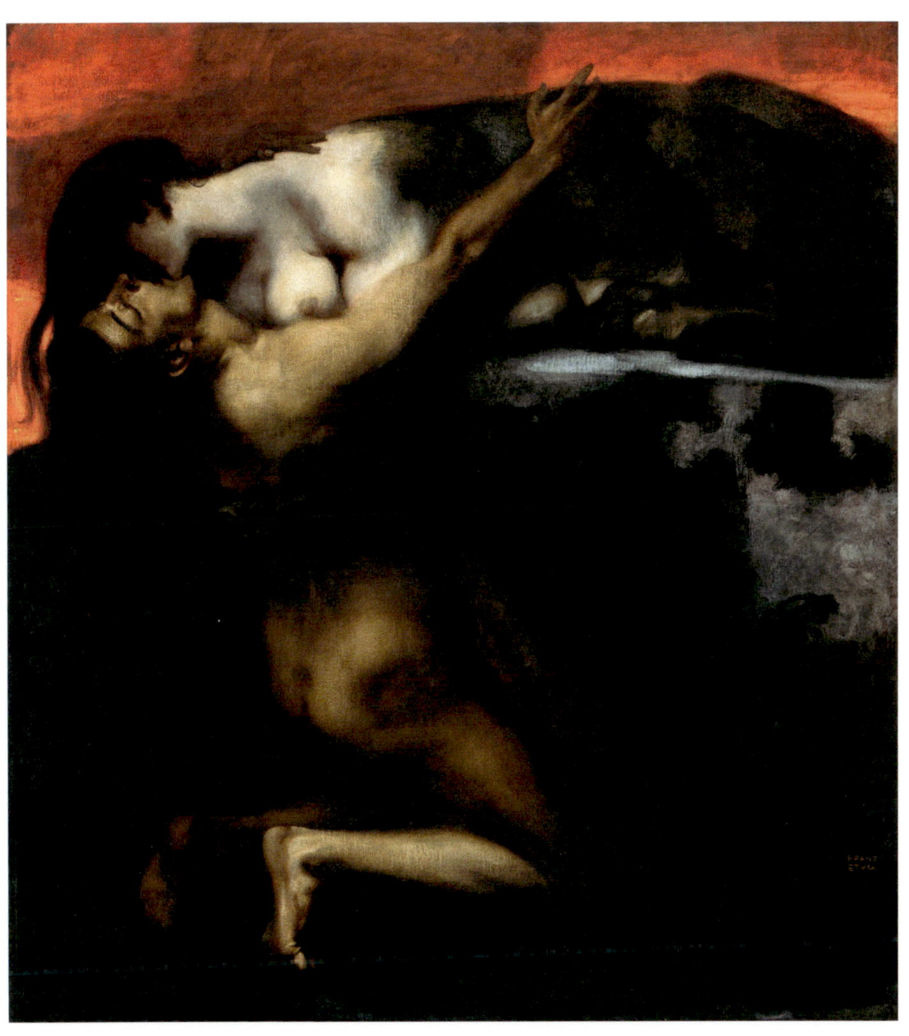

Franz von STUCK

(Tettenweis, 1863 – Munich, 1928)

Spring, 1902 | Oil on wood, 70.4 × 68.5 cm
Donated by Count Dénes Andrássy, 1911 | Inv. no. 224.B

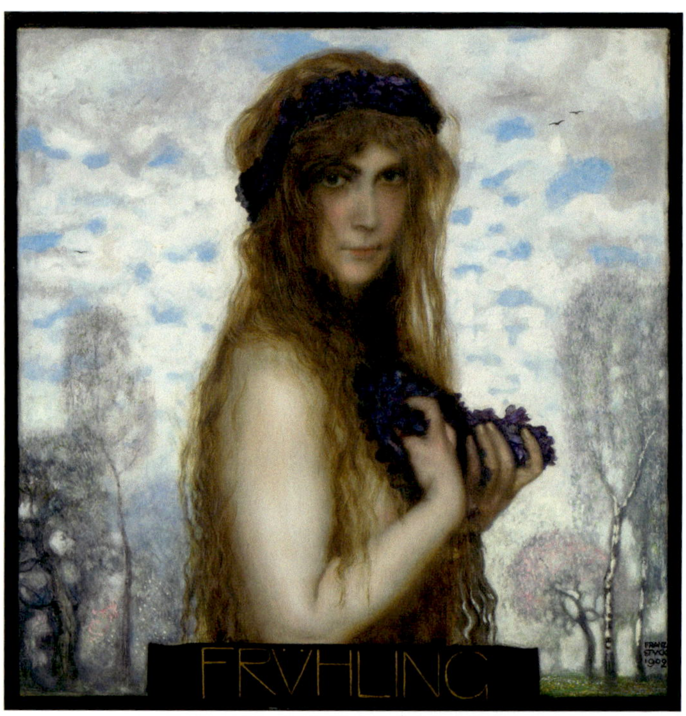

The unattainability of women and the battle of the sexes were one of the most popular themes in the symbolist period. The representation of the sensuous, seductive *femme fatale* and her destructive desires is a recurring motif in Stuck's work. He produced several versions of the allegorical composition *Spring*, the Budapest painting being the first. The woman fixes the viewer with her dark, bewitching eyes. Each of the stylistic devices employed by the artist – the pale blues and pinks, and the soft, enigmatic outlines – intensifies the sense of eroticism. In symbolist imagery, spring meant a break with the past, the dawn of a new era. In the final years of the century, the various branches of fine and applied art became far more closely connected than ever before, and the boundaries between genres began to blur. The painterly aspect of symbolism was coupled with the decorativeness of the Jugendstil. Besides the enigmatic mood and emotional force conveyed by the painter's technique, another striking feature of this allegory of spring is the decorativeness of Stuck's almost square composition, especially the carpet-like pattern of clouds in the background and the wavy lines of the branches. – FT

Voss 1973, cat. no. 249 | *Frankfurt–Birmingham–Stockholm 2000*, cat. no. 91

Jules Joseph LEFEBVRE

(Tournan, 1834 – Paris, 1912)

Ondine, 1881 | Oil on canvas, 151 × 92.5 cm

Purchased from the artist at the 1885 summer exhibition of the HNSFA | Inv. no. 71.B

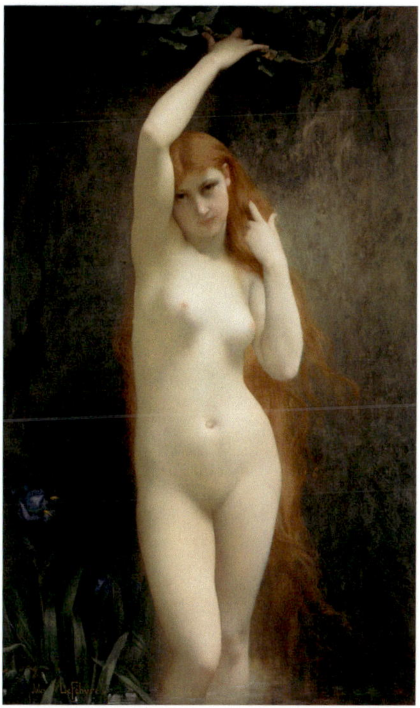

Jules Joseph Lefebvre was a renowned representative of the grand tradition of French painting: in 1861 he was awarded the Prix de Rome, and as a member of the jury of the Salon and a professor at the École des Beaux-Arts and the Académie Julian, he played a leading role in the Parisian art scene.

Lefebvre earned his fame mostly as a painter of nudes depicting allegorical, literary or mythological figures. In his delicately painted works, he masterfully combined the perfection of the classical female ideal with the observation of the model, virginal purity with sensuality. The life-size *Ondine*, executed in 1881, focuses on a single red-haired figure shown frontally, her elegant contrapposto emphasising the suppleness of the body. Her immaculate whiteness recalls the smoothness of classical marble sculptures, while also paying homage to *The Spring* (Musée d'Orsay, Párizs) by Jean-Auguste-Dominique Ingres. The success of the work at the 1881 Salon is partly due to the fact that his portrayal of the female body was justified by a lofty theme from Germanic mythology, the story of a water nymph who gains a soul by marrying a man. *Ondine* also caused a sensation at the summer exhibition of the Hungarian National Society of Fine Arts in 1885, where it was acquired by the Hungarian state. – AZSK

Illyés 2001, 108–109 | Kovács 2015–2016

Charles VAN DER STAPPEN

(Saint-Josse-ten-Noode, 1843 – Brussels, 1910)

Imperious Chimera, before 1895 | Marble, 78.5 × 58 × 43 cm
Purchased from the HNSFA's 1897 spring exhibition
Inv. no. 1546.U

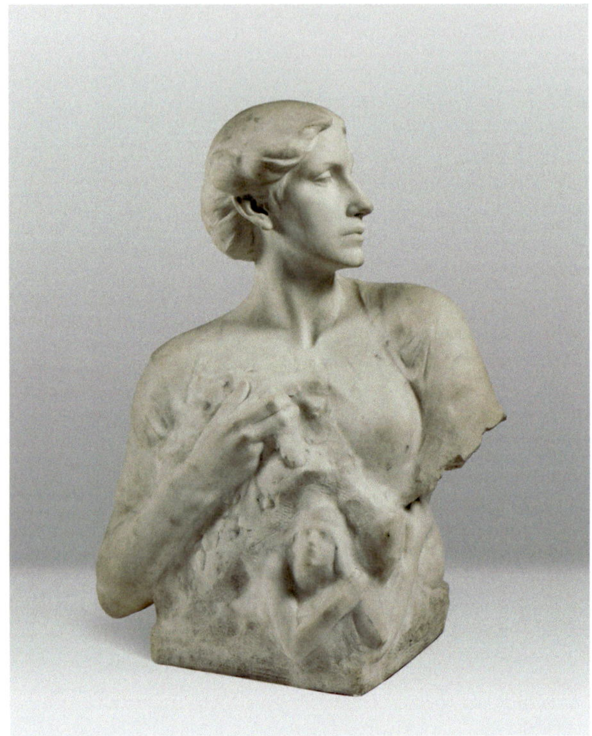

A pioneering artist, Charles Van der Stappen sought to free Belgian sculpture from its academic shackles and guide it on a progressive path. His art is based on a love of nature, and he drew inspiration from clear and simple forms. His figures, depicted in a state of repose, are rendered with suggestive power. His subjects are characterised by a kind of austere charm. Besides sculptures, he produced works of applied art and decorative objects in gold and ivory, and was even involved in costume and jewellery design.

With its heroic effect, *Imperious Chimera* is a perfect example of his expressive vision. The three symbolic figures appearing on the pedestal convey the emotional state of the depicted subject and the thoughts that torment her. The sculpture was purchased for the Museum of Fine Arts by the Hungarian state in 1897 from the spring international exhibition of the Society of Fine Arts. It was subsequently shown with various titles, including *Hubris* and *Pride*. The original French title – *Impérieuse chimère* – has an abstract ambiguity befitting symbolist art. – BIB

Van Lennep 1990, 578 | *Brussels* 2010, 97–98

Égide ROMBAUX

(Schaerbeek, 1865 – Uccle, 1942)

The Daughters of Satan, model: 1903; carving: 1909
White limestone, 205 × 156 × 114.5 cm | Purchased from the HNSFA's
1908–1909 winter exhibition | Inv. no. 3910.U

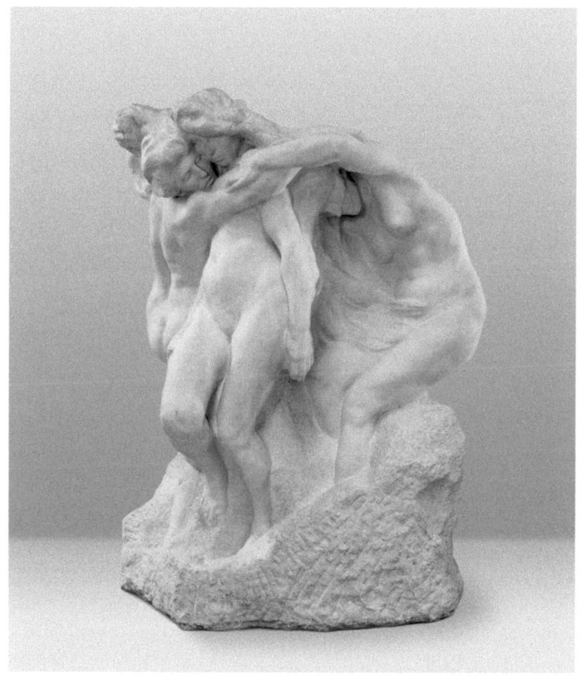

The talents of sculptor Égide Rombaux were nurtured at the Académie Royale des Beaux-Arts in Brussels, which he attended as a student and where, from the 1890s, he also taught. His stay in Florence between 1889 and 1892 had a huge influence on his style, as did contemporary French sculpture, especially Rodin's oeuvre. The more mystical Symbolist trend, typically associated with Belgium, is apparent primarily in his choice of themes.

The *Daughters of Satan* was first executed by Rombaux himself as a marble sculpture in 1903 (now held in the Musées Royaux des Beaux-Arts de Belgique, Brussels). In his grandiose, dramatic masterpiece, Rombaux turned to a popular theme among the decadent circles of the *fin de siècle*: only sickness, ruin, and damnation await those who fall victim to the seductive, diabolic beauty of these women. Based on this first work, the sculptor produced further copies in marble, plaster, and limestone. Following its exhibition in Brussels, it appeared in many of the main international art shows in Europe after 1900 (Paris, Amsterdam, Milan, Berlin, Barcelona). In Budapest, the *Daughters of Satan* was awarded a gold medal at the 1908–1909 winter exhibition of the HNSFA, and was then acquired by the Museum of Fine Arts. – LK – AZSK

Grandmoulin 1951, 269, 283 | *Budapest 2022a*, 29

Oscar ROTY

(Paris, 1846 – Paris, 1911)

Paris-Lyon-Méditerranée, 1901 | Silver, 45 × 59 mm

Purchase, 1966 | Inv. no. 66.21.P

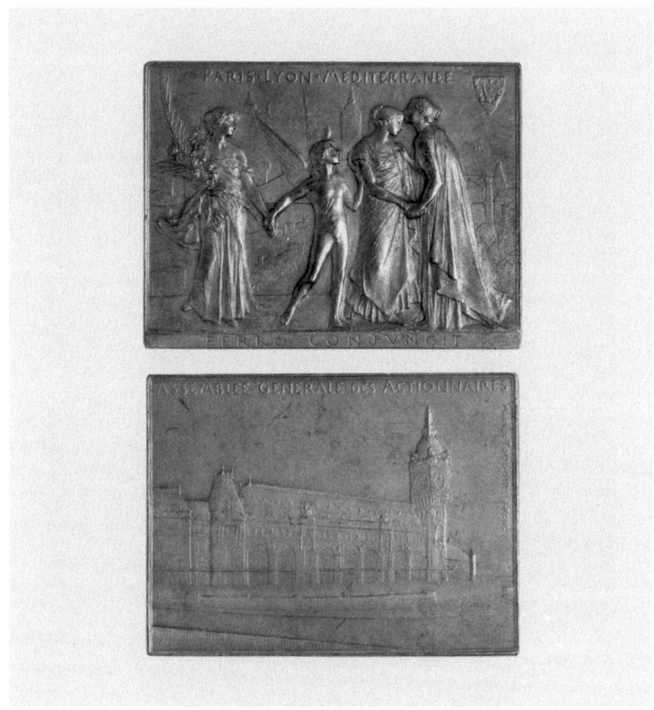

Oscar Roty enjoyed a successful career as a designer of plaquettes and medals. Besides requests for portraits, he received numerous state commissions in the context of the French Third Republic, and his work contributed to shaping the new symbolism of republicanism. It was Roty who designed the famous figure of the woman sowing seeds, which, from 1897 onwards, appeared on French francs and later French stamps, and which survives to this day, in a slightly reworked form, on euro coins.

This silver plaquette by Roty was commissioned by the Paris–Lyon–Méditerranée railway company, which was founded in 1857. The line linking the capital with the city of Lyon, as well as with Marseille and the increasingly popular Mediterranean Coast, was personified in the form of three allegorical female figures dressed in classical attire. The women's graceful movements and the subtle details of their robes are rendered with meticulous care. The figures are linked by a nude, winged genius, just as trains bring people and provinces closer together in space and time. The other side of the plaquette features the eclectic building and distinctive clock tower of the Gare de Lyon in Paris: the station was rebuilt for the Paris Exposition in 1900. – AZSK

Kunz 1913, 118 | *Paris* 2012, 102–103

Adolf von HILDEBRAND

(Marburg, 1847 – Munich, 1921)

Autumn, 1888 | Terracotta, 121 × 83 × 15 cm
Purchased from the artist's heirs, 1922 | Inv. no. 5897.U

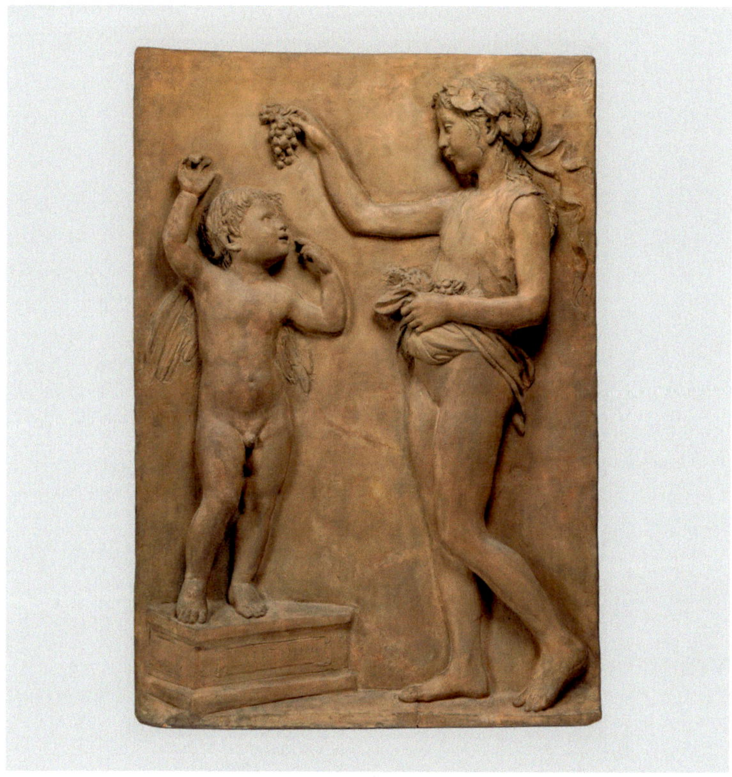

After studying briefly in Nuremberg and Munich, Hildebrand travelled to Italy. In 1873, he purchased the abandoned building of the Convent of San Francesco di Paola, near Florence, which for many years served as his home, studio and as a meeting place for artists, composers, and intellectuals. The relief work *Autumn* may have been part of a "Four Seasons" series to decorate the convent. Besides the traditions of Antiquity and the Renaissance, Hildebrand's art was heavily influenced by the painter Hans von Marées, with whom he worked for a while in Italy. This is apparent in the arrangement and gestures of the figures in *Autumn*. The composition rests on the balance between the background and the figures, between simplified shapes and subtle details. The idealised figures, modelled on Hildebrand's own children, are arranged with a delicate rhythm within their narrow confines. Hildebrand wrote of his faith in the autonomy of sculptural expression and in the timeless laws of art that can be discerned from a study of nature and the Old Masters. His most famous treatise, *The Problem of Form in Painting and Sculpture* (1893), determined European attitudes towards sculpture for decades. – DS

Heilmeyer 1902, 54 | Esche-Braunfels 1993, 154–155

Giovanni SEGANTINI

(Arco, 1858 – Schafberg, 1899)

The Last Effort of the Day, 1884 | Oil on canvas, 117 × 82 cm
Purchased from the International Exhibition of the Glaspalast, Munich, 1901
Inv. no. 143.B

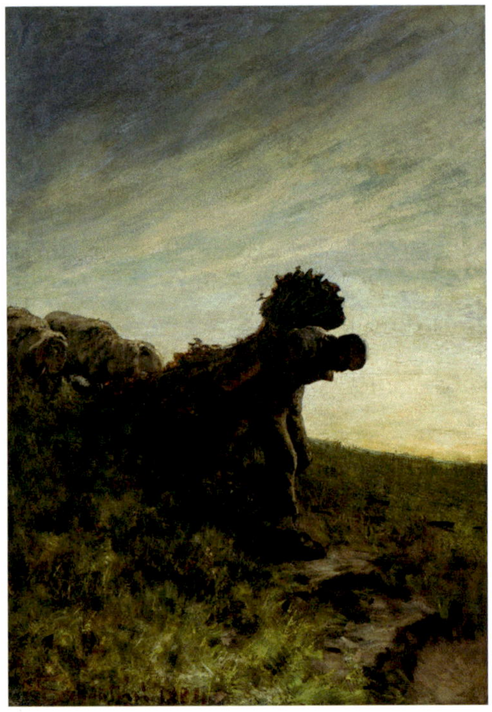

Born in Tyrol, Segantini lost both parents at the age of eight and was raised by his half-siblings in extreme poverty. He studied at the Accademia di Belle Arti di Brera in Milan, but after three years began to teach himself. In 1881, he moved to a village near Lake Como. There he produced *plein air* paintings of peasants and shepherds. Over the next decade, his approach evolved: uniform tonality was replaced by the colourist technique that he had developed by the 1890s.

Segantini was influenced by the work of Anton Mauve and Jean-François Millet, a striking example of this being *The Last Effort of the Day*. His early paintings, produced in nature, are not taken directly from life: his works are characterised by a certain naturalist symbolism. His paintings reflect moods and express compassion for the subjects. In this almost monochrome painting, the figure stooping beneath his heavy load of brushwood becomes one with his surroundings. Segantini's oil paintings did not constitute the final composition: he continued to strive for the most eloquent expression of his ideas in further drawings executed in his studio. There are four extant sketches of this painting, too, in which the artist increasingly distanced himself from the original subject. – FT

Quinsac 1982, cat. no. 389 | *Milan* 2014, 164, cat. no. 44

Fritz von UHDE

(Wolkenburg, 1848 – Munich, 1911)

The Entombment of Christ, ca. 1894 | Oil on canvas, 43.4 × 61 cm
Bequest of Count Dénes Andrássy, 1913 | Inv. no. 291.B

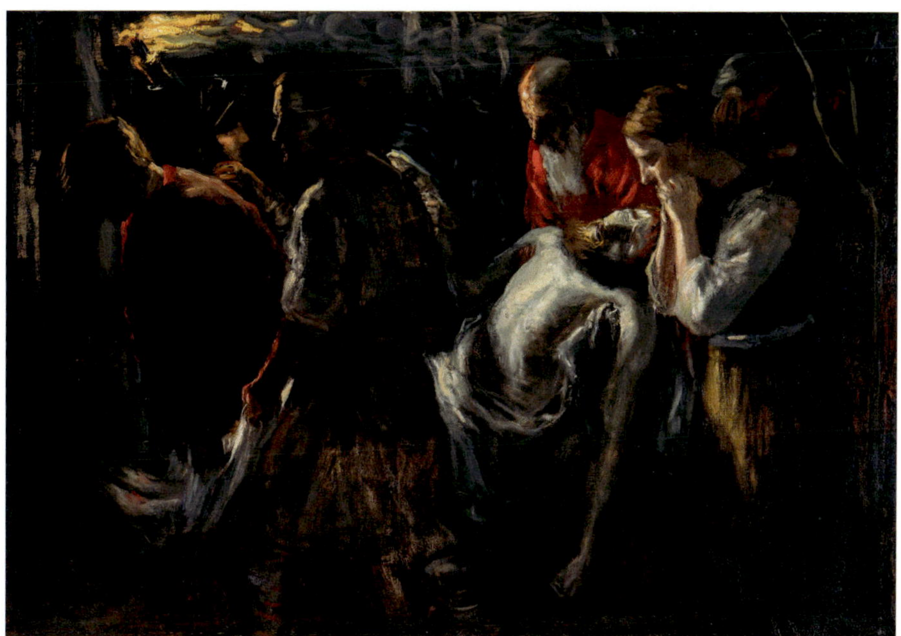

Fritz von Uhde was one of the pioneers of German *plein air* painting and realism, although he made his name as a painter of religious subjects. As a young man, he was taught by the Hungarian painter Mihály Munkácsy, who became a close friend and continued to have a huge influence on Uhde's later work, especially when it came to painting models, and the techniques of colour mixing and application. Uhde's paintings are characterised by a profound social awareness: he portrayed his biblical figures as simple people of their own day, in a poor, peasant setting, creating considerable controversy in church circles as a result.

Uhde probably painted *The Entombment of Christ* as a sketch for the larger, final version that hangs in the Bautzen museum. Unlike traditional representations of the subject, which depict the moment the body is laid in the stone tomb or sarcophagus, Uhde focuses instead on the group of mourners making their way to the grave. The dramatic effect of the scene is heightened by the grieving Galilean women who accompany the funeral procession, as well as the light of the torches that illuminate the body of the Redeemer. In the background can be seen the weeping figure of Mary, dressed in her traditional blue robe. – BIB

Peregriny 1914–1915/3, 228 | *Zwickau – Limbach-Oberfrohna – Barth 2011–2012*, 166–167

Pierre PUVIS DE CHAVANNES

(Lyon, 1824 - Paris, 1898)

Mary Magdalene, 1897 | Oil on canvas, 116.5 × 89.5 cm

Purchased from Adolf Kohner, 1930 | Inv. no. 389.B

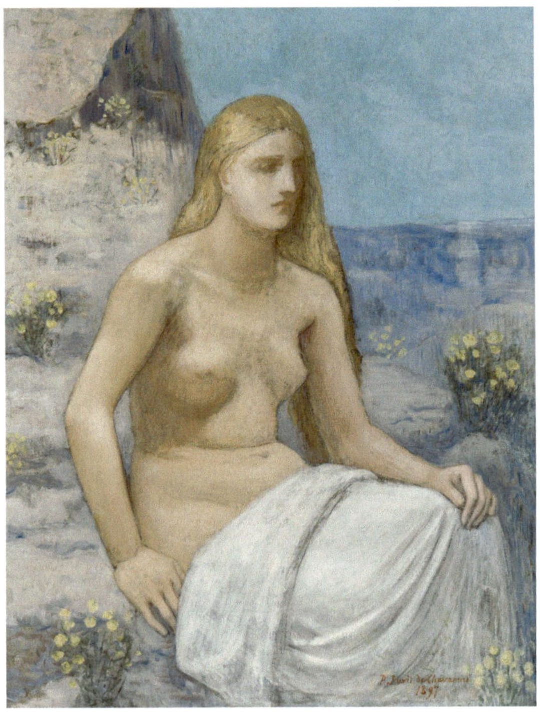

Pierre Puvis de Chavannes was one of the most influential French painters of the second half of the nineteenth century. His oeuvre furthered the classical tradition of painting, while at the same time, his simplification of forms, his technique reminiscent of frescoes, and his poetic approach made him one of the precursors of symbolism. Although he made his name primarily with his large-scale mythological and allegorical murals, he also played an important role in the renewal of religious painting.

In this image of Mary Magdalene, the saint appears in what was, according to legend, her final refuge – the cave of Sainte-Baume in Provence. The half-naked female figure is shown in contemplation, absorbed in her thoughts. The austere landscape, bathed in brilliant southern sunlight, is evoked by means of a few rocks and a brilliant blue sky. In what would be one of his last works, Puvis de Chavannes returned to a theme that inspired him thirty years earlier (1869, Städel Museum, Frankfurt). This time he avoided any superfluous detail and chose not to show the saint's traditional attributes. In its absolute purity, the composition is as much a study of a nude figure as a melancholic representation of the saint's meditations.
– AZSK

Illyés 2001, 145–148 | Brown Price 2010, cat. no. 431

Constantin MEUNIER

(Etterbeek, 1831 – Ixelles, 1905)

The Prodigal Son, model: 1895; carving: ca. 1900 | Marble, 93 × 40 × 84 cm
Purchased from C. Jacques-Meunier (Brussels), 1908 | Inv. no. 3856.U

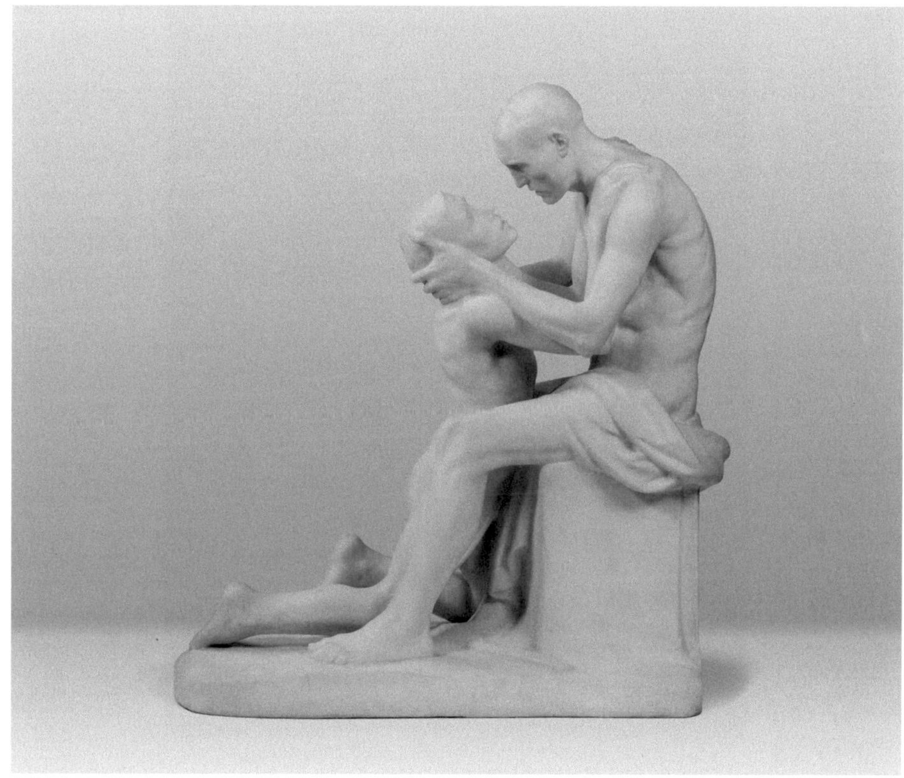

Meunier studied sculpture at the Brussels Academy, although he switched to painting after
a few years. He was drawn to religious subjects in his early career. Even after returning to
sculpture, he chose biblical themes, among them the parable of the Prodigal Son. According
to the story in the Gospel of Luke, the younger son claimed his inheritance and left his father's
house to see the world. Having squandered all his possessions, he returned home. Meunier
shows the son kneeling before his father, filled with remorse. The old man looks at his son with
love and forgiveness, gently taking the young man's head in his hands. Both are naked, their
sinewy muscles perfectly proportioned, their loins covered by a cloth. Meunier produced two
versions of the touching story. In the first, smaller version, the father has a beard, making him
seem older; the artist exhibited this version in 1892 at the Salon de la Société Nationale des
Beaux-Arts. This sculpture, a plaster version of which was shown at the 1907 Meunier exhibition in Budapest, was created three years later. The marble version of the exhibited work was
offered for sale to the museum by the artist's brother-in-law. – AS

Soós 1964b, 21 | *Brussels* 1993–1994, 474

Maurice DENIS

Granville, 1870 – Saint-Germain-en-Laye, 1943

Maternal Bliss, 1895 | Oil on canvas, 81 × 65 cm
Donated by Mrs Adolf Kohner, 1934 | Inv. no. 401.B

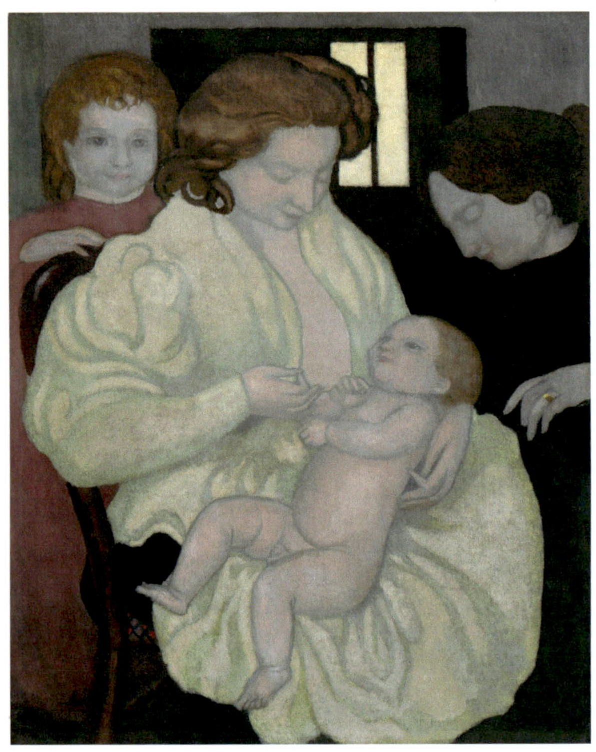

Maurice Denis was a founding member of *Les Nabis* in 1888, and he was also their principal theorist. The word *nabi* means "prophet" in Hebrew; the members of this group saw themselves as prophets of a new kind of mystical and ornamental art, which rejected the teachings of Impressionism.

In this work Denis immortalised his young wife, Marthe, breastfeeding their first-born son – an image which resembles a secular Madonna. The closely cropped image and the lack of pictorial depth intensify the sense of intimacy, creating a unified and harmonious group consisting of the family and the neighbour girl visiting the baby. This picture bears the uniform, flat planes of colour and the strong contours which characterised the aestheticism of Les Nabis. The palette is soft and subdued – out of the dark background emerges the bright patch of Marthe's dress, with its arabesque pleats echoing the stylised, reddish-brown curls of her hair. Tragically, this painting became a heart-wrenching memorial to a brief period of maternal bliss: not long after it was painted, the baby Jean-Paul died, at only a few months' age. – AZSK

Illyés 2001, 152–153 | *Tokyo* 2019, cat. no. 117

Eugène CARRIÈRE

(Gournay-sur-Marne, 1849 – Paris, 1906)

Maternity, ca. 1890-1900 | Oil on canvas, 49 × 64.5 cm
Purchased at the sale of the G. Bing Collection (Hôtel Drouot, Paris) in 1927
Inv. no. 388.B

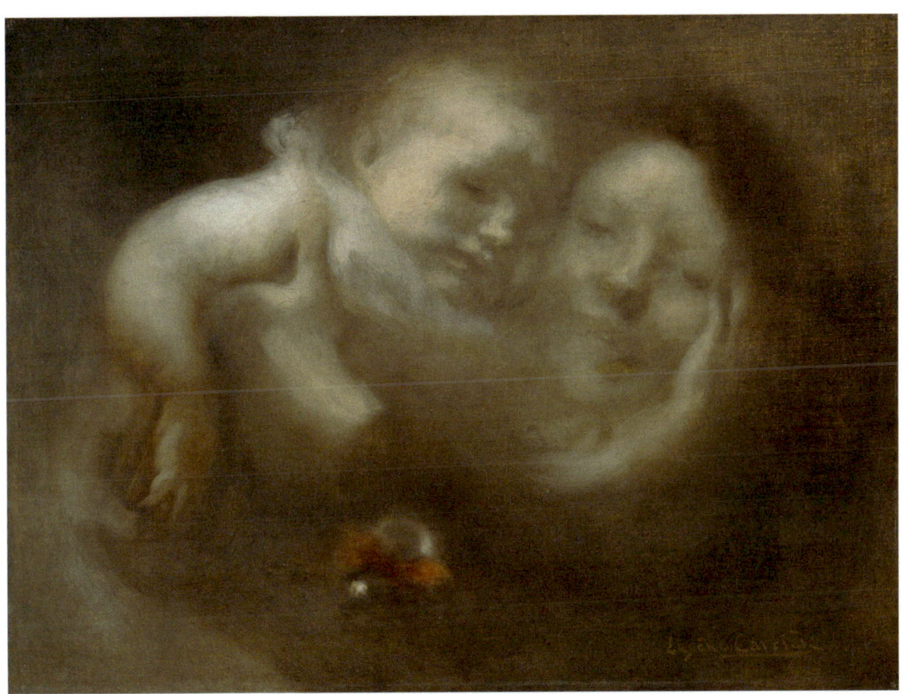

Eugène Carrière was an unusual figure of late-nineteenth-century French art. Developing a unique style, he never joined any artistic group or movement. Although his later work can be linked in some aspects to Symbolism, his blurry, monochromatic style, his emotional approach remained entirely personal.

This painting, focusing on family, maternity, and intimacy, is a fine example of the painter's characteristic technique and themes. The composition centres around two figures, a young woman and a baby, who are shown very close to the picture plane, and occupy almost all the pictorial space. The painter concentrated on their faces and the affection evident in their expressions and gestures. They are locked together in a tight and warm embrace; the interplay of arms and hands forms an arabesque that unites the whole composition. The only patch of colour is provided by the reddish ribbon in the foreground. The overall blurry tonal effect, the delicate play of light and shadow also contribute to this unity: all forms dissolve in the brown mist surrounding them. Depicting an instant of maternal bliss, this painting has the evanescent, hazy quality of distant, happy memories. – AZSK

Illyés 2001, 154–155 | Nora-Milin, Lamarre, and Rapetti 2008, cat. no. 419

Anders ZORN

(Mora, 1860 – Mora, 1920)

Mother and Child, 1900 | Oil on canvas, 100 × 81 cm
Purchased from the artist, 1904 | Inv. no. 61.B

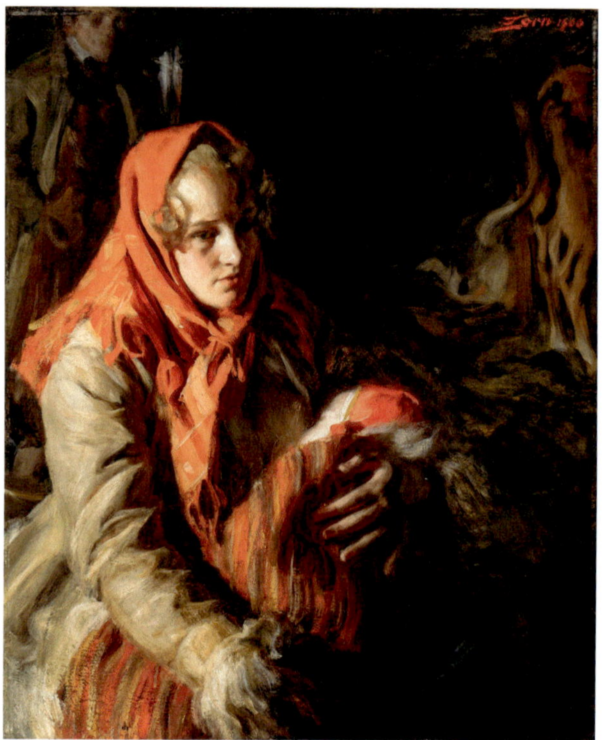

Anders Zorn was the most renowned Swedish painter of his day and achieved international acclaim at the turn of the century. After studying in Stockholm and spending some time in London, he lived in Paris for almost a decade before eventually making his home in Mora in his native Sweden. Among international artistic trends, he was mostly influenced by naturalism and impressionism. His oeuvre includes genre paintings of rural Sweden, landscape paintings, as well as paintings of modern urban life and portraits of the urban population.

His painting *Mother and Child*, also known as *Madonna*, is unique in his oeuvre and allows for several possible interpretations. What is, at first glance, a mundane scene is in fact filled with religious symbolism. The Virgin Mary is depicted in contemporary clothing, while the male figure of the Holy Family can be discerned against the dark background, along with the outline of an animal. In his autobiographical notes, Zorn identified the child as himself: he was born out of wedlock and grew up without a father. He produced three versions of the painting, the Budapest version being the last. A copperplate engraving was also made of the composition. – AS

Zorn 2004, 200, 164, 166 | Boston 2013, 116

Ivan MEŠTROVIĆ

(Vrpolje, 1883 – South Bend, 1962)

Motherly Care, 1904 | Granite, 70 × 60 × 60 cm
Donated by Ernő Fränkel, 1918 | Inv. no. 5240.U

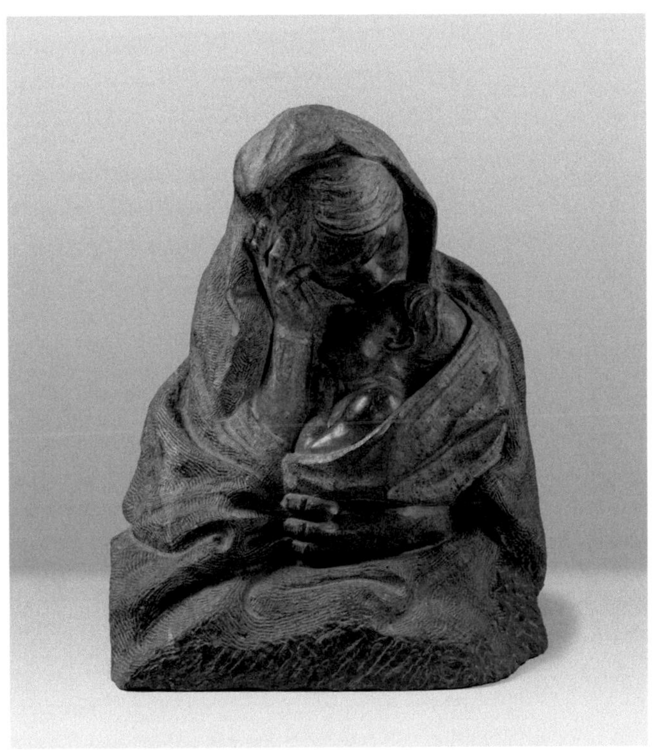

Croatian artist Ivan Meštrović was born into a poor peasant family. During his studies in Vienna he befriended Auguste Rodin, who would later refer to Meštrović as a greater artist than himself. A religious man, Meštrović often depicted biblical subjects. From 1903, he regularly took part in exhibitions of the Vienna Secession, showing works that were symbolist in content but naturalist in character, much like those of Gustav Klimt. Like Klimt, Meštrović frequently depicted turning points in human life.

His early work *Motherly Care* is a significant piece in his oeuvre. The intimacy of the portrayal of the mother, holding her child to her breast, contrasts with the austerity of the grey Belgian granite. The work incorporates the most typical components of Meštrović's art: the restless contours, the decorative grooves, and the execution of the surface follow the stylistic features of the Vienna Secession, while the tensely clenched fingers of the left hand are suggestive of expressionism. The sculpture was purchased by Emperor Franz Joseph from the 1905 exhibition of the Zagreb Art Pavilion.– BIB

Kečkemet 1969, 8 | Kraševac 2017, 113

Giovanni SEGANTINI

(Arco, 1858 – Schafberg, 1899)

The Angel of Life, 1894 | Mixed techniques on paperboard, 59.5 × 47.9 cm
Purchased from a private owner in Vienna through the mediation of the Vereinigung
bildender Künstler Österreichs, 1901 | Inv. no. 24.B

After years of vicissitude and deprivation in his youth, Segantini moved to the Swiss Alps in 1886. He and his partner lived a life of true poetic asceticism, far from the public eye, while the crystal-clear light of the alpine landscape led him to adopt a new artistic idiom. The gleam of the snow-covered peaks and the translucent mountain air had an immediate impact on his technique, resulting in works whose philosophical content was infused by symbolism. With paintings composed from pure colours and tiny adjacent lines, he became a pioneer of Italian divisionism.

His *Maternità* paintings, produced in the 1890s, occupy a special place among his monumental landscapes and transcendental mountain scenes. Permeated with the sublimity of turn-of-the-century Art Nouveau and symbolist art, the series illustrates two extremes – steadfast, tender motherly love and demonic evil. The Budapest painting, a mature example of his new style, is perhaps the most sensitively executed of all the compositions belonging to the first category.

The branches of the dry tree in which they are seated weave protectively around the mother and child, who are elevated above the realm of reality. Designed by the artist, the exquisitely carved frame forms an integral part of the work. – FT

Quinsac 1982, cat. no. 567 | *Milan 2014*, 235, cat. no. 104

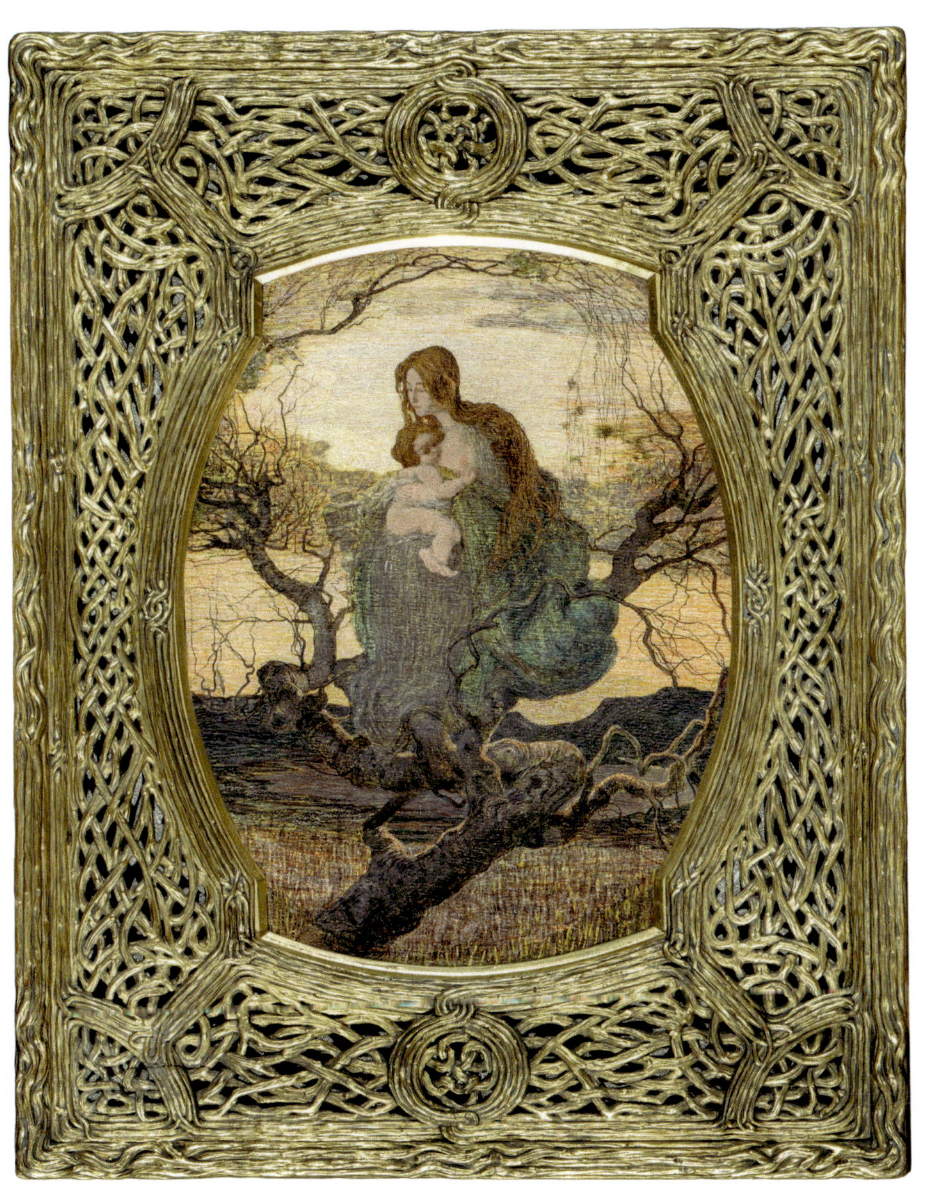

Auguste RODIN

(Paris, 1840 – Meudon, 1917)

Eternal Springtime, model: 1884; carving: 1901 | Carrara marble, 75 × 81 × 44 cm
Purchased from the artist, 1900 | Inv. no. 3394.U

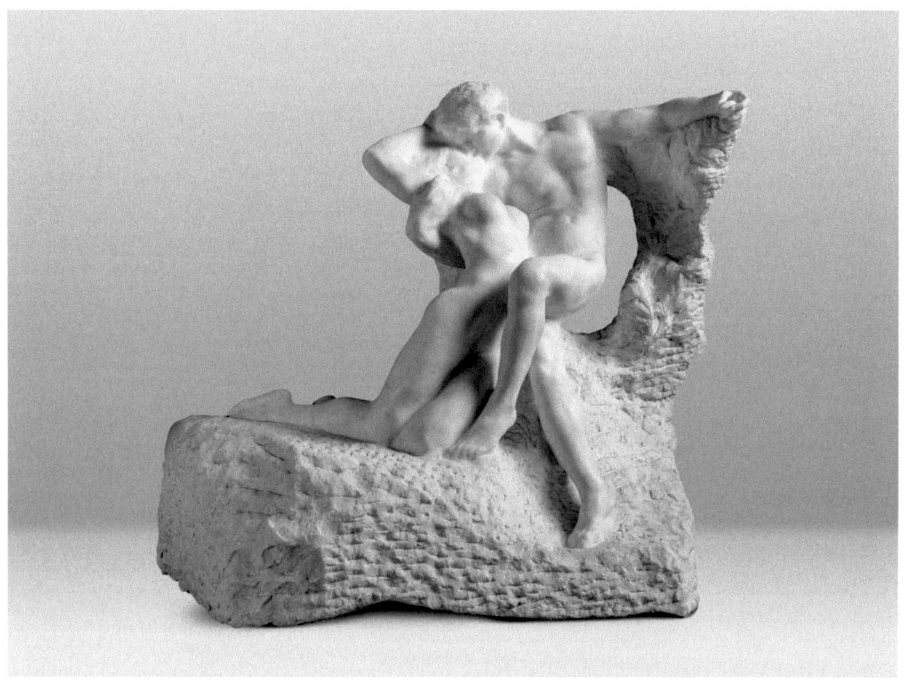

Rodin modelled the *Eternal Springtime* in 1884, the same year as *The Kiss*, and there is an undeniable similarity between the two. While ardent desire and unbridled sexuality are often among the sculptor's subjects, he was fascinated first and foremost by the beauty of the human body. However, he opted for different approaches when modelling the two works: in *The Kiss*, the viewer's gaze is held by the closed circle of the couple's embrace, while what is spellbinding here is the sensual bodies' liberation from the solid block that encases them.

In 1882, Rodin sculpted a small nude torso with an arched back, which he then incorporated into the upper left-hand corner of his grandiose project, *The Gates of Hell*. Later he reworked the pose of the female figure to some extent and complemented it with a male figure, thereby creating the work *Eternal Springtime*. The sculptor was fascinated by the tragic fate of Dante's two characters, Paolo and Francesca, whose romance inspired this sensual expression of the universal theme of physical love. The sculpture was modelled in 1884, and several versions of it were subsequently made. A personal meeting with Rodin during the Paris Exposition in 1900 led to the Hungarian state commissioning a new marble copy. What is striking about the Budapest composition is the way in which the smoothly polished figures emerge from the rough block of marble. – FT

Illyés 2001, 127–128 | *Budapest* 2012–2013, 46, 57

Jules DESBOIS

(Parçay-les-Pins, 1851 – Paris, 1935)

Leda, model: 1891; carving: 1900 | Marble, 36.5 × 54 × 40.5 cm | Purchased from
the International Exhibition of the National Salon, Budapest, 1901 | Inv. no. 1984.U

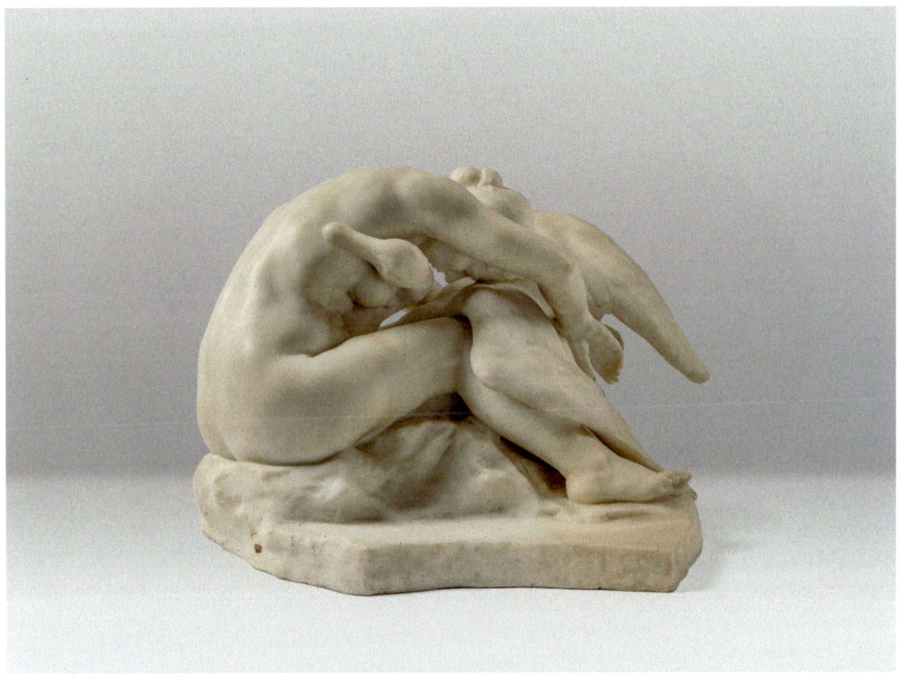

In addition to his mythological, allegorical compositions, the French sculptor Jules Desbois
became widely known for his exquisite Art Nouveau–style objects of applied art. His career
was defined by his artistic dialogue with Auguste Rodin: in 1884, he became the renowned,
older sculptor's assistant. Desbois, however, was more than a student: he soon inspired his
master, and the two artists enjoyed a mutual influence. Unlike Rodin, Desbois was proficient
in many different techniques, working in wood, stone, and metal

His sculpture *Leda* is a modern, symbolist interpretation of an ancient myth – Zeus's
union with Leda, whom he seduces in the guise of a swan. The embrace of the human and
animal bodies creates a strange yet sensual and harmonic unity: the work is reminiscent of
Michelangelo in the boldness of its composition and the passion of its approach. A plaster
model of the sculpture was shown at the 1891 exhibition of the Salon de la Société nationale
des Beaux-Arts, and owing to its success, a version carved out of marble was exhibited in
1896. Contemporary critics emphasised the pagan eroticism of the sculpture, and the raw,
unvarnished depiction of the subject. – AZSK

Huard and Maillot 2000, 9–22 | Illyés 2001, 138–139

Jules-Clément CHAPLAIN

(Mortagne-au-Perche, 1839 – Paris, 1909)

Medal of the Paris Exposition, 1900 | Bronze, diameter: 64 mm
Transfer, 1956 | Inv. no. 56.745.P

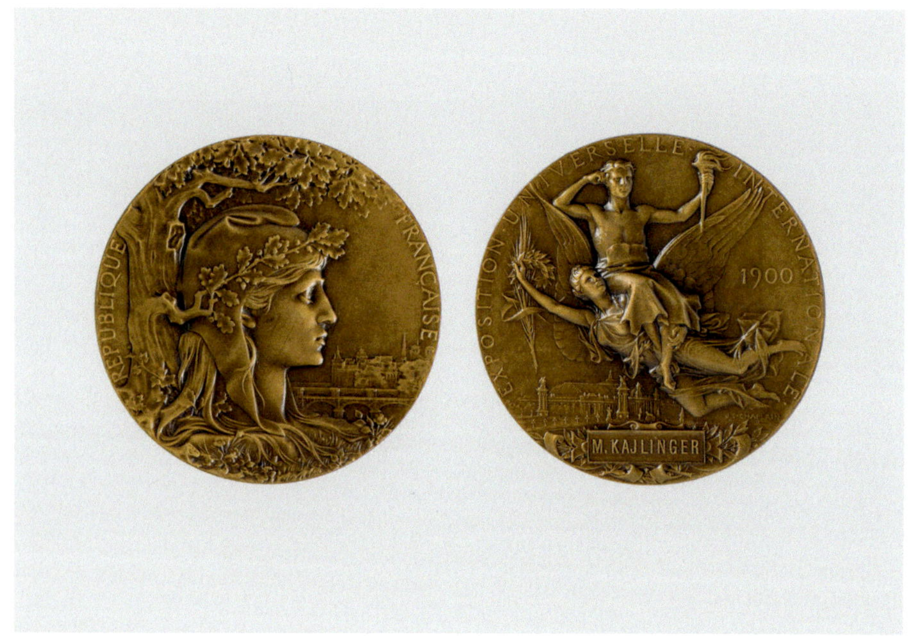

Jules Chaplain was one of the most celebrated medallists in France in the nineteenth century: during his successful career, he won the Prix de Rome scholarship in 1863, became a member of the Academy of Arts in 1881, and was appointed art director of the Sèvres porcelain manufactory in 1896. He designed countless medals and plaquettes for both private clients and the state, and in around 1900 was commissioned to design the medal awarded to prize winners at the Paris Exposition. The medal features Marianne, the personification of the French Republic: her stern profile is accentuated by her Phrygian cap and the oak branches that frame her face, while a view of Paris is discernible behind her. On the reverse, a male figure holding a torch is borne on the wings of Fame, with the Grand Palais, built for the Paris Exposition, in the background. The inscription "M. Kajlinger" indicates that the medal was awarded to engineer Mihály Kajlinger, director general of the Budapest Municipal Waterworks. The medal was acquired for the Municipal Picture Gallery's collection as part of the Pompéry bequest in 1940 and was later transferred to the Museum of Fine Arts. Two other copies are preserved in the Collection of International Art after 1800, including the bronze medal awarded to architect Alajos Hauszmann, who designed the building that houses the Supreme Court in Budapest and who was also responsible for the reconstruction of the Palace in Buda. – AZSK

Paris 2012, cat. nos. 111, 112

Alexandre-Louis-Marie CHARPENTIER

(Paris, 1856 – Neuilly-sur-Seine, 1909)

Chess, ca. 1896 | Bronze, 76 × 146 mm
Purchase, 1966 | Inv. no. 66.9.P

Dominoes, ca. 1896 | Bronze, 77 × 146 mm
Purchase, 1966 | Inv. no. 66.8.P

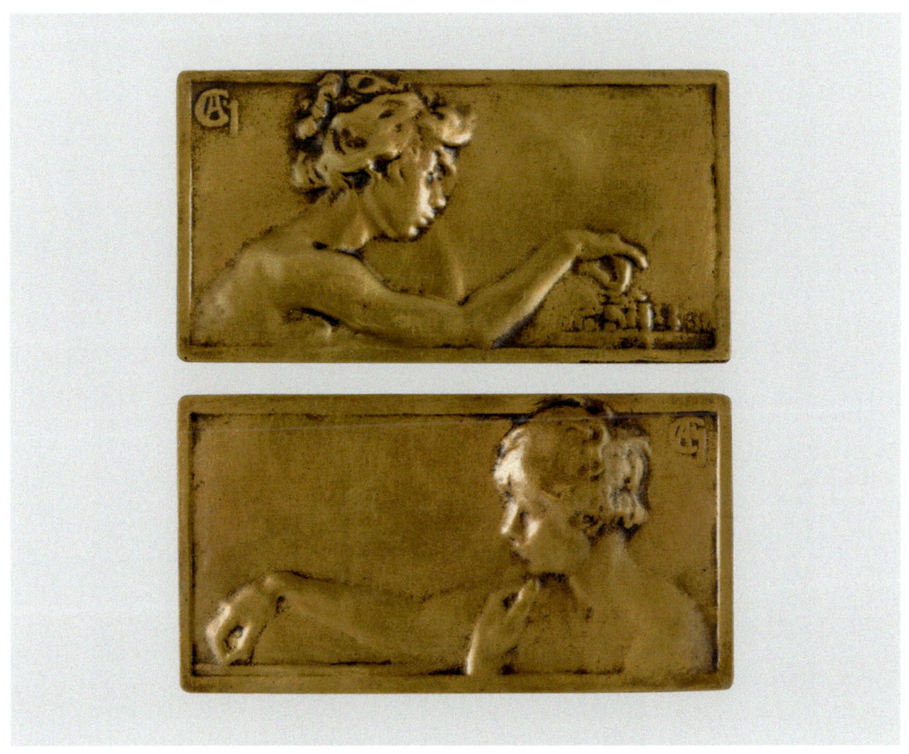

Alexandre Charpentier, one of the founders of French art nouveau, was a truly versatile artist. He promoted the equality and unity of different artistic forms, experimenting with almost every technique, material, and genre in the course of his career: he was simultaneously a sculptor, painter, illustrator, medallist, and furniture designer. His art was informed by the realistic approach of naturalism and the decorativeness of art nouveau alike. He produced hundreds of medals and plaquettes: his portraits of artists and writers, like his allegorical figures, enjoyed huge popularity, and his work can also be found in the Museum of Applied Arts in Budapest. Nine of his plaquettes are preserved in the Collection of International Art after 1800, including *Painting* and *Sculpture*, as well as the simultaneously mundane and lyrical representations *Singing* and *The Violin*, symbolising the spirit of music. The personifications of chess and dominoes are also related to this group of works: the complementary, exquisitely executed youthful figures evoke the playful yet serious world of games. Originally intended as door lock plates, then independently produced on decorative boxes and as plaquettes, they reflect the Gesamtkunstwerk sensibility that characterised Charpentier's work. – AZSK

Pandur 1997, 111–142 | *Paris* 2008, 146–147, 159

Ludwig von HERTERICH

(Ansbach, 1856 – Etzenhausen, 1932)

Nocturne, ca. 1900 | Oil on canvas, 207 × 114 cm
Purchase, 1984 | Inv. no. 84.6.B

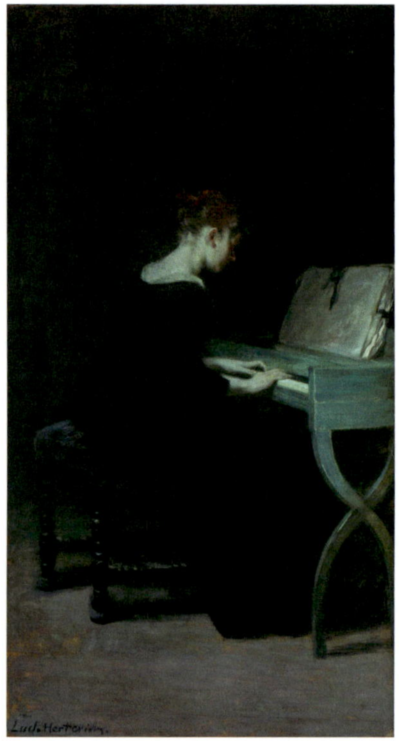

Herterich was initially taught by his sculptor father before joining the circle around Wilhelm von Diez at the Munich Academy of Arts. During his tour of Italy, he was influenced primarily by the monumental paintings of Raphael and Mantegna, but was also enthralled by the broad, dynamic brushstrokes of Diego Velázquez. He received several prestigious awards for his decade-long teaching work at the Munich Academy, including a noble title. He was one of the founders of the Munich Secession in 1892. With age, he turned from monumental, historicising depictions of knights and saints towards more intimate subjects inspired by romanticism and symbolism. He was one of the pioneers of German *plein air* painting.

Herterich was deeply fascinated by interactions among colours; he favoured white, which he referred to as "the most colourful of all colours". The Budapest painting is a wonderful example of his discerning colourism. He conveys the beauty of the young pianist, represented in an undefined space and time, through the graceful curve of her neck and the delicate movements of her hands. The enigmatic quality of the work might also be interpreted as an allegory of the soul immersed in music. – DL

Herterich 1909, 239–249

Franz von STUCK

(Tettenweis, 1863 – Munich, 1928)

The Dancer, 1897 | Bronze, 63 × 30 × 35 cm
Purchase, 1964 | Inv. no. 65. 1.U

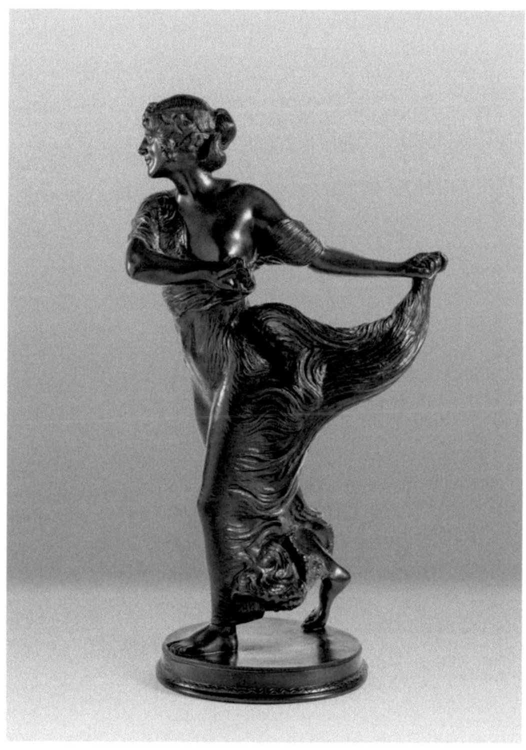

Compared to his painted oeuvre, Stuck's sculptural legacy is quite small, consisting of only fourteen statues and as many reliefs. His debut sculpture was the 1891 work *The Athlete*, a cast of which was purchased as early as 1893 by the Hungarian state. Its companion piece, *The Dancer*, was produced several years later, in 1897. While Stuck's own features are supposedly discernible in *The Athlete*, his *Dancer* was modelled on the American Mary Lindpainter, whom the artist married in the same year the sculpture was executed. Standing on a circular base, her body is shown in a twisting pose. Although her movements and the folds of her dress reflect the graceful, flowing lines of Art Nouveau, frozen mid-spin rather than effortlessly dancing. The woman's features and hair are reminiscent of the stylised sculpture of classical Greece. These two small statues occupy an extremely important place in Stuck's oeuvre. He had a cast of each made for the studio of his new villa in Munich, which were later placed in separate niches as part of his famous "Altar of Sin". The decorative statues, modelled on husband and wife, can also be interpreted as symbolising feminine grace and masculine strength. – AS

Passau–Munich, 1993–1994 | *Amsterdam* 1995–1996, 51

George MINNE

(Ghent, 1866 – Laethem-Saint-Martin, 1941)

Bust of a Woman, model: 1899; carving: ca. 1906–1907
Carrara marble, 72 × 61 × 36 cm | Purchase, 1956 | Inv. no. 56.30.U

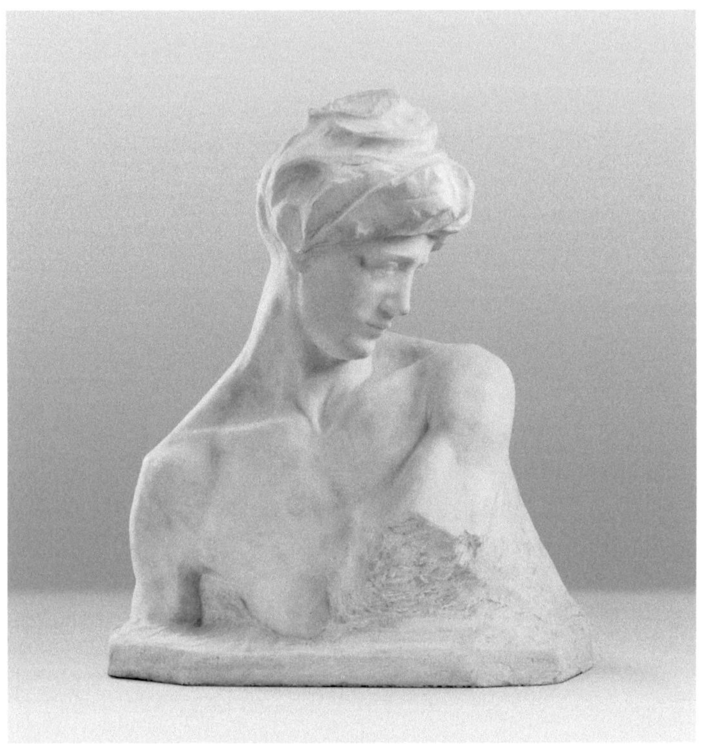

George Minne, a key Belgian Symbolist sculptor at the turn of the century, studied at the academies of art in Ghent and Brussels before continuing his training independently in Paris. His early sculptures already reflect his unique vision: his contemporaries saw him as a natural genius, who discovered his own style right away. He drew inspiration not from the classic renaissance and baroque traditions, but from the gothic art of the Netherlands and the work of his fellow sculptor Rodin. In 1890, his work was shown for the first time at an exhibition of the most progressive group of artists in Brussels, Les XX (the Twenty), a group that he himself joined the following year. He strove to capture complex emotions and states of mind.

The first version of this bust was produced in 1899 and was titled *Melancholy*. In the same year, he produced similar compositions (such as the bust in the Folkwang Museum, Essen), which may be associated with the memorial to the Belgian symbolist poet and novelist Georges Rodenbach in Ghent. This bust featured in the 1908–1909 winter international exhibition in the Budapest Kunsthalle, where it was acquired for the famous collection of Baron Adolf Kohner. – AS

Molnos 2018, 132–133 | *Budapest 2022a, 23*

George MINNE

(Ghent, 1866 – Laethem-Saint-Martin, 1941)

Nun, after 1894 | Bronze, 44.5 × 48.5 × 37 cm
Donated by Adolf Wertheimer, 1927 | Inv. no. 6213.U

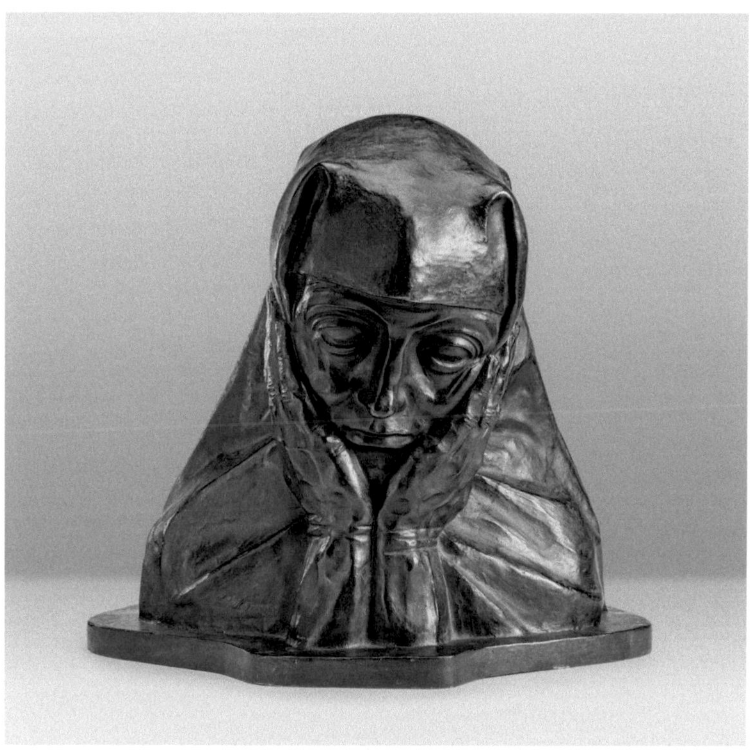

Early in his career, Minne won acclaim as a graphic artist. His sensitivity and his interest in mysticism brought him into contact with the symbolist poets and writers of his day, many of whom commissioned him to produce illustrations for their poetry.

Minne's sculpture *Nun* can be associated with the poem *Oraison* (Prayer), from Maurice Maeterlinck's 1889 volume *Serres chaudes* (Greenhouses). The first version of the sculpture, which was carved from wood, was likewise given the title *Prayer*. Numerous versions of the work exist, the variations in the title – *Mourning Woman*, *Prayer*, and *Devotion* – indicating the artist's ambition to illustrate a specific mental state. The rigorously self-contained, expressive triangular composition conveys a contemplative state of utter dejection, anguish, sorrow, and despair, in which the only refuge is prayer.

This is one of the most famous of Minne's early works, produced before the turn of the century. The originality of his approach influenced the subsequent generation of artists, in particular some of the followers of German Expressionism. – AS

Pudles 1985, 122 | *Budapest* 2022a, 21

August GAUL

(Grossauheim, 1869 – Berlin, 1921)

Tomcat, 1901 | Bronze, 14.3 × 19 × 7 cm
Purchased from the HNSFA's 1902 spring exhibition | Inv. no. 2198.U

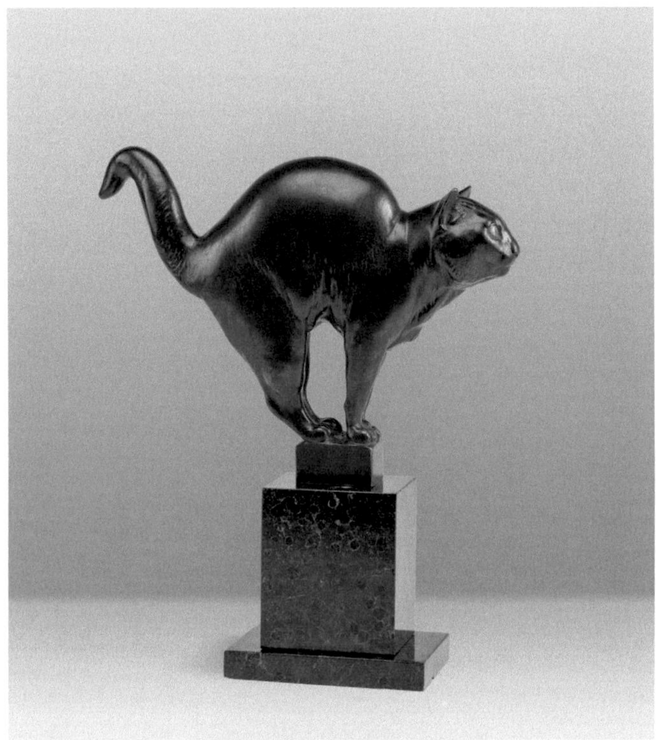

August Gaul is regarded as one of the foremost animal sculptors of the nineteenth century. He studied at the State Drawing Academy in Hanau before attending the Academy of Art in Berlin, in the meantime gaining practical experience in a goldsmith's workshop. He discovered his favourite theme during visits to the Berlin Zoological Garden. Fascinated by the behaviour of the animals, he strove to capture their characteristic movements in sketches. This led to an opportunity to work on the lions adorning the *Kaiser Wilhelm Monument* designed by Reinhold Begas. After returning from a study trip to Rome, he became a founding member of the Berlin Secession and a defining figure in the city's artistic life. His work was sold by the famous Berlin art dealer, Paul Cassirer.

Early in his career, he was influenced by naturalism, although his mature style is typically more stylised. Fifteen copies of the small-scale work *Tomcat* were cast. The animal's dynamism and temperament are perfectly conveyed by its arched back, raised tail, and stance. The sculpture was first shown in 1901 at the Secession exhibition, and every copy of it had sold within a few years. It was recast with slight alterations after Gaul's death. – AS

Rosenhagen 1905, 14 | *Berlin–Hamburg–Hanau* 1999, 189, cat. no. 17

Hans STOLTENBERG-LERCHE

(Düsseldorf, 1867 – Rome, 1920)

Henrik Ibsen, ca. 1900
Bronze, diameter: 8.7 cm
Donated by Dr Pál Hámos, 1925
Inv. no. 56.1659.P

Anti-Darwinist Allegory, ca. 1900
Brown glass, diameter: 10.2 cm
Donated by Dr Pál Hámos, 1925
Inv. no. 56.1689.P

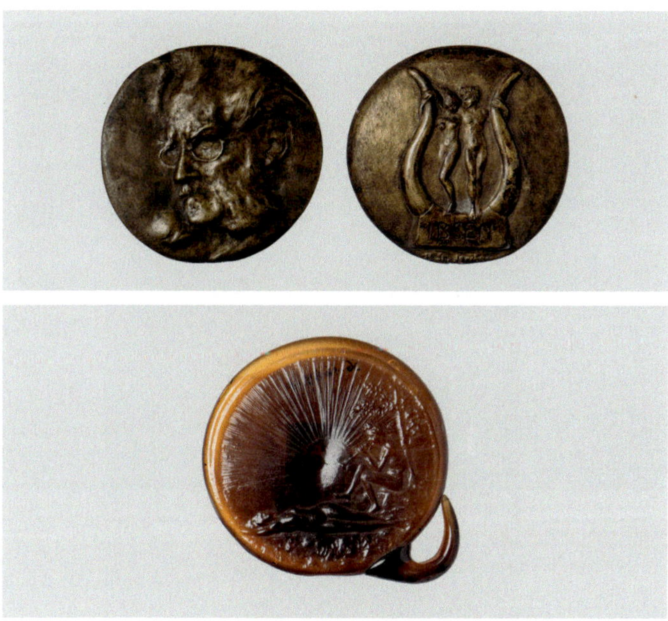

Of Norwegian origin, Hans Stoltenberg-Lerche worked initially as a ceramicist and as an illustrator for German periodicals before turning to the applied arts and sculpture. Between 1891 and 1900, he studied painting in Paris, as a student of Eugène Carrière, mastering the figurative language of Art Nouveau. He regularly exhibited his work at the Paris Salon over a period of twenty years before eventually settling in Rome. Although he never resided in Norway, he was greatly influenced by Norwegian applied arts. He represented the country at numerous International exhibitions and cultivated a strong relationship with Norwegians in Paris and Rome.

He applied his exquisite, richly imaginative motifs on majolica, glass, enamel, and jewellery. His principal inspiration was marine flora and fauna, which he studied during his regular visits to the aquarium in Naples. Although his sculptures represent a more realistic tendency, his glass and ceramic works are distinctively Art Nouveau in style.

The Museum of Fine Arts has a collection of forty-three medals and plaquettes by Lerche, including a portrait of the playwright Henrik Ibsen, illustrating Lerche's close connections with Norwegian culture. The distinctively shaped *Anti-Darwinist Allegory*, made from brown glass and inspired by the arts and crafts movement, depicts an idyllic scene with an Art Nouveau feel. – BIB

Petrovics ed. 1927, 208 | Fahr-Becker 2004, 290–291, 410–411

Maximilian LENZ

(Vienna, 1860 – Vienna, 1948)

A World, 1899 | Oil on canvas, 121.5 × 186 cm
Purchased from Julius Leitner (Vienna), 1900 | Inv. no. 20.B

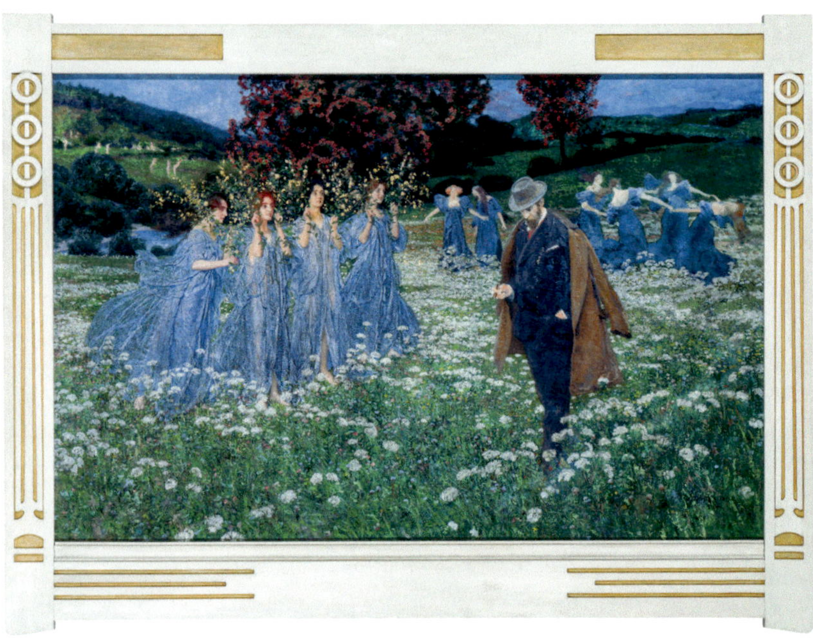

Maximilian Lenz was a typical turn-of-the-century Viennese artist, who, besides painting, also worked as a sculptor, graphic designer, and wood engraver. He was a friend of Gustav Klimt, a member of the Vienna Künstlerhaus in the early 1890s, and one of the founders of the Secession in 1897. This work was reproduced in *Ver Sacrum*, a journal with a reputation for its progressive aesthetics.

Known as both *A Life* and *A World*, this is one of Lenz's most important paintings and was first shown in 1899, at the fourth Vienna Secession exhibition. It features a man, deep in thought, apparently oblivious to the beauties of his surroundings and the circle of women dancing towards him as he walks through the meadow. A peculiar tension arises between the man's modern, civilised, urban appearance and the enigmatic, bewitching female figures, drifting and dancing with abandon. The painting is dominated by the impressionistically rendered cold pastel colours typical of Lenz, which he liberally counterbalances with the vivid yellow, red, pink, and white smudges of the flowers. The flowing, graceful movements of the dancing figures may have been inspired by the pioneering ideas of the American dancer and choreographer Isadora Duncan, who popularised the free and natural motion of the body. The painting might also be interpreted as a lyrical expression of the essential ambiguity that characterised symbolist art: the contrast between bleak reality and the idealised dream world. – DL

Budapest 2010–2011, 116 | *Museum Guide 2018*, 249

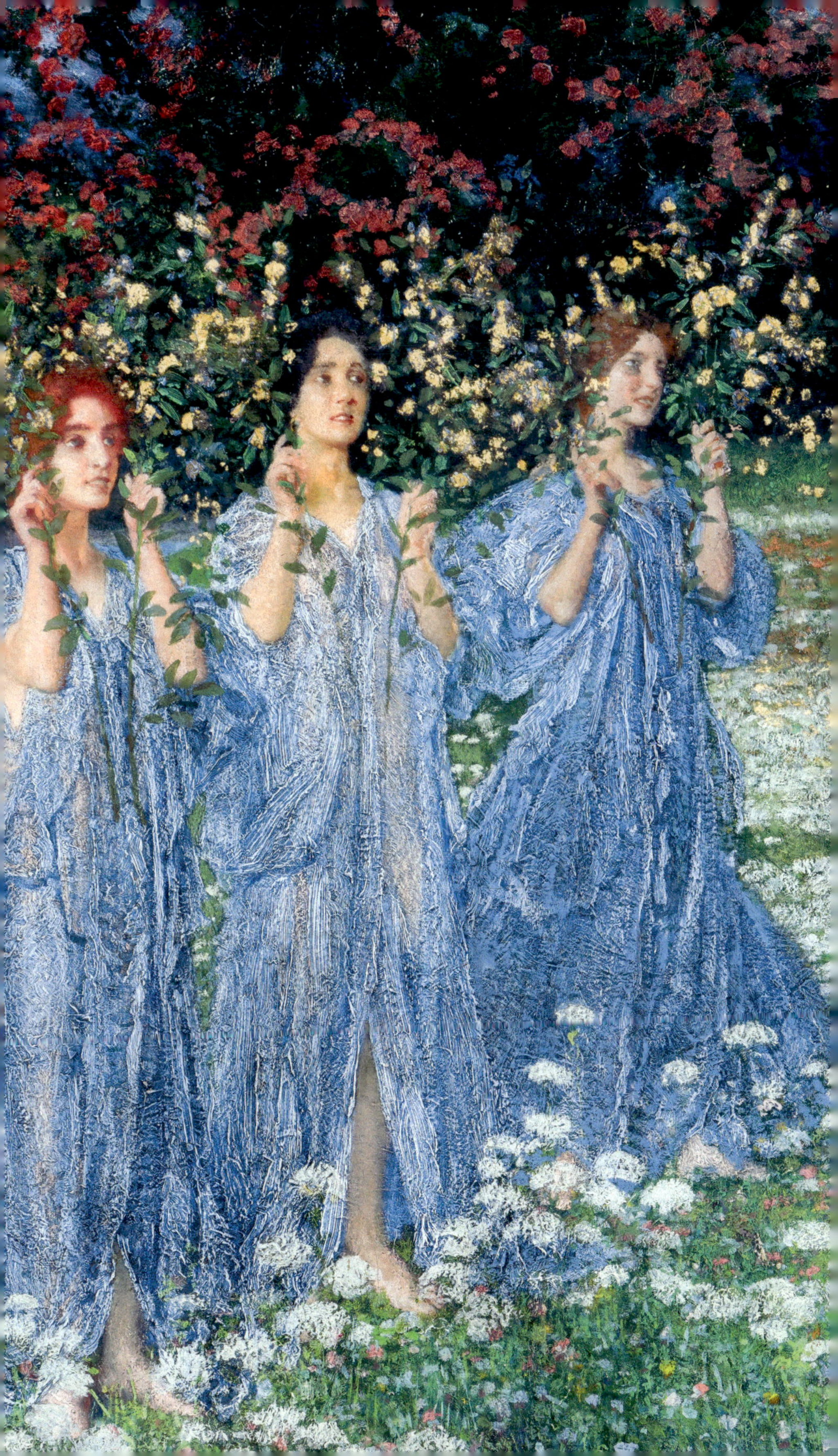

Jean-Paul SINIBALDI

(Paris, 1857 – Bourg-en-Bresse, 1909)

Break of Day, 1893 | Oil on canvas, 181 × 271 cm
Purchased from the HNSFA's 1893–1894 winter exhibition | Inv. no. 129.B

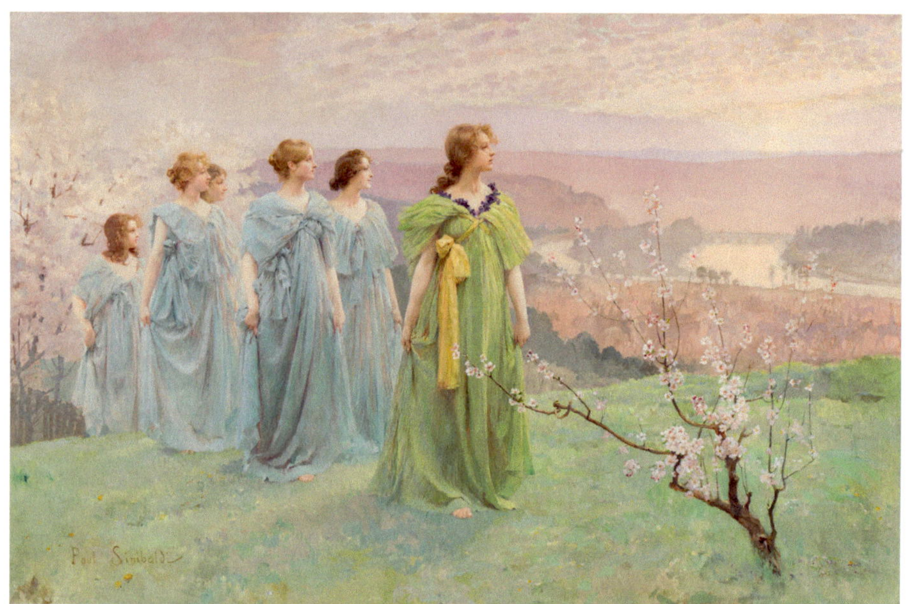

Trained at the École des Beaux-Arts in Paris, Paul Sinibaldi enjoyed a successful career, winning prizes at the Salon as well as the 1900 Paris Exposition. He was also a recipient of the Legion of Honour and became famous for his impressive, large-scale paintings, although as an eclectic artist it is difficult to associate him with any concrete trend: his art shows traces of academicism, naturalism, and symbolism.

Due to its enigmatic subject and controversial critical reception, *Break of Day*, which was shown at the 1893 exhibition of the *Salon des artistes français*, deserves particular attention. The allegorical scene is set in a slightly Japanese-style landscape, dominated by pastel colours: a group of young women stand on a plateau that rises above a valley, gazing into the distance. Below them, the mounted soldiers riding along the riverbank are almost obscured in mist. The unusual composition was greeted with incomprehension by Parisian critics, although not long afterwards, when the work was shown in Budapest, it was interpreted by the Hungarian press as an allegory of revanchism: the mounted soldiers were understood as the French army marching towards the German Empire, and the female figures as the hope that France would one day take revenge for its defeat at the hands of the Prussians in 1870. – AZSK

Kovács 2019 | Lespinasse 2023

Leo PUTZ

(Merano, 1869 – Merano, 1940)

Idyll, ca. 1890 | Oil on canvas, 112.3 × 96.5 cm
Purchased from the HNSFA's 1902 spring exhibition | Inv. no. 45.B

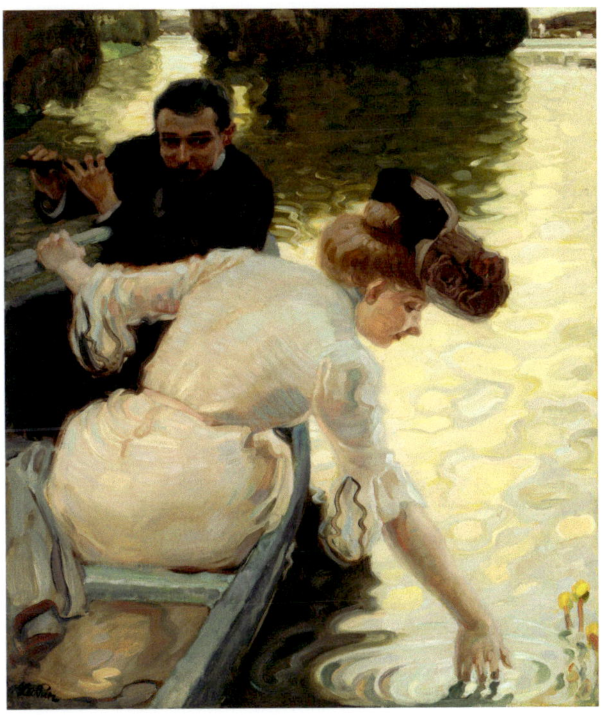

Leo Putz studied painting first in Munich, and then at the Académie Julian in Paris. Although his teacher in France, William-Adolphe Bouguereau, followed the official, academic style of painting, the early works of Édouard Manet and Pierre-Auguste Renoir made a huge impression on the young Putz. On his return to Munich, he joined the artistic movement that emerged around the journal *Jugend*. Many of his paintings were later reproduced in its pages. In 1901, he became a member of Die Scholle, a Munich-based group spiritually akin to the Vienna Secession. The painting *Idyll* can be associated with his early period, the most important in his oeuvre.

The couple in the rowing boat are probably artist friends of Putz. The picture space is taken up almost entirely by the figures, and by the gently rippling water. The effect of the painting is extraordinarily decorative, thanks to the sinuous brushstrokes, the intense colours, and the harmony between them. In 1901, the work was shown at the eighth International Art Exhibition at the Glaspalast in Munich, and the following year was introduced to the public in Budapest. – AS

Budapest 1995, 152, 371 | *Tokyo* 2019, cat. no. 107

Pekka HALONEN

(Lapinlahti, 1865 – Tuusula, 1933)

In the Stone-Quarry, 1903 | Oil on canvas, 175.5 × 123 cm
Purchased from the HNSFA's 1906–1907 winter exhibition | Inv. no. 197.B

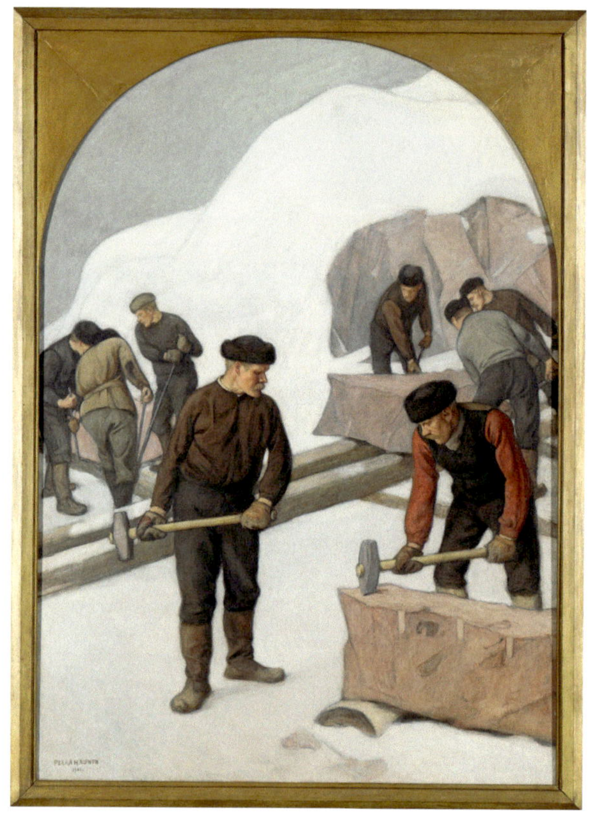

Together with Akseli Gallen-Kallela, Pekka Halonen played a leading role in the creation of a
Finnish national style that was based on international art trends. After completing his studies
in Helsinki, from 1890 he regularly visited Paris, where he became acquainted with the art
trends then in vogue. The influence of Jules Bastien-Lepage can be felt in his early works. In
the summer of 1894, he became a student of Paul Gauguin, who had returned from his first
trip to Tahiti. He incorporated Gauguin's synthetism into his painting, and stylized, decorative
lines can be observed in his later works. After his return to Finland, the focus of Halonen's
interest shifted to the characteristic Finnish landscape and Finnish people. The figure of the
Finnish peasant became for him a key symbol of the country. Around the turn of the century,
Halonen's figural compositions became increasingly monumental and decorative. In his painting *In the Stone-Quarry*, men in traditional fur hats work in a snowy landscape, the figures
forming a vivid contrast with the pale background. – AS

Helsinki 2008, 218, 395 | Kokkinen 2019, 134

Yrjö LIIPOLA

(Koski, 1881 – Koski, 1971)

Despair, 1907 | Wood, 26 × 13.4 × 19.2 cm
Purchase, 2023 | Inv. no. 2023.1.1.U

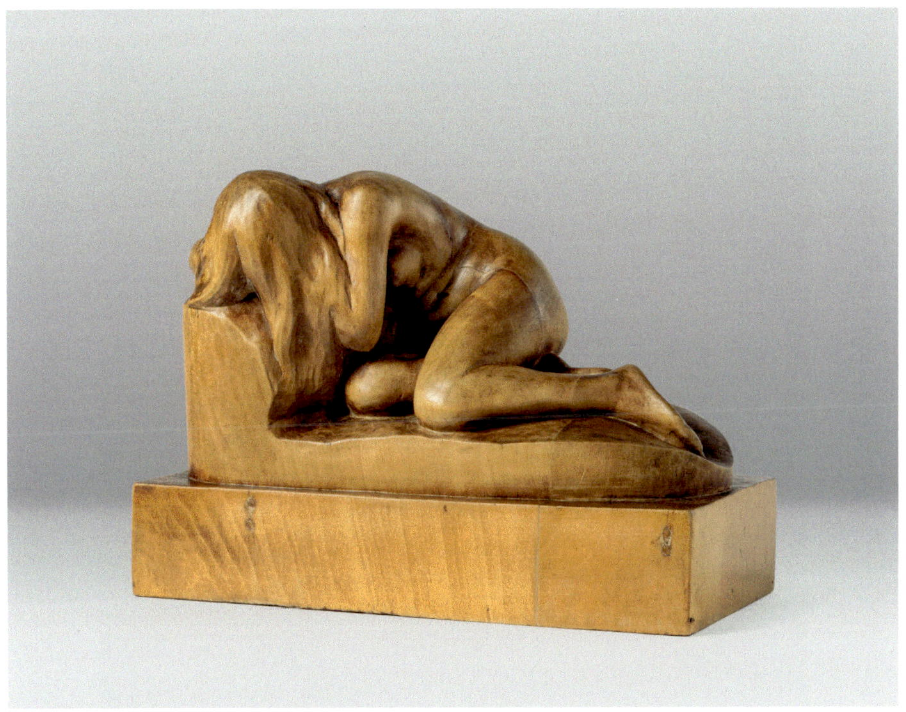

Yrjö Liipola came from Finland to Hungary in 1904 as a political refugee, fleeing a tsarist Russian conscription order. He did not lose contact with his homeland, however, and in Finland he is still considered a great national sculptor. In Hungary, meanwhile, Alajos Stróbl and Ede Kallós became his teachers, and he cultivated close friendships with the key figures of the Gödöllő Art Colony, thanks to whose influence certain features of the Hungarian Art Nouveau style can be found on his works. He later became the Finnish ambassador to Budapest, and when he moved back to Finland in 1934, he was made Hungarian consul there.

Liipola predominantly made small sculptures and portraits from marble, terracotta and bronze, of which the Museum of Fine Arts of Budapest possesses a number of important examples. Few of his wooden sculptures have survived, which is why the work entitled *Despair* is considered so unique, as it displays symbolist features typical of the period. The success of the composition depicting a naked woman with unbound hair lying on the ground is shown by the fact that the Hungarian Applied Arts Association bought it for reproduction, and the Zsolnay Porcelain Manufactory in Pécs has been producing a porcelain version of the statue since the 1930s. – BIB

Rolla 1971 | Tuomisto 2011, 54–55

Akseli GALLEN-KALLELA

(Pori, 1865 – Stockholm, 1931)

Young Faun, 1904 | Oil on canvas, 67 × 65 cm
Purchased from the HNSFA's 1906–1907 winter exhibition | Inv. no. 196.B

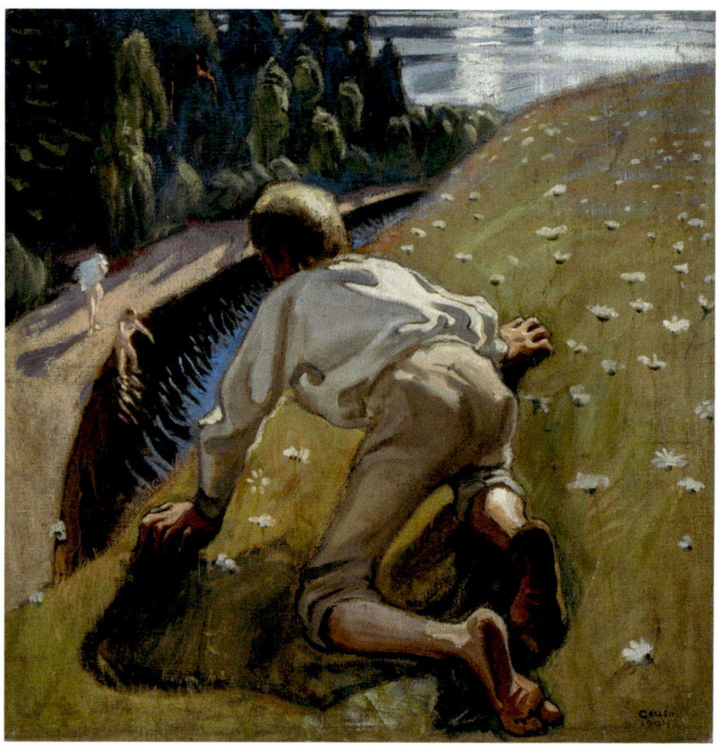

Akseli Gallen-Kallela is one of the defining figures in Finnish art. At the end of the nineteenth century, his initially realist approach gave way to a highly stylised, mystical, and decorative symbolism. The patriotic artist favoured subjects taken from the Finnish national epic, the *Kalevala*. His landscapes celebrate the peculiar beauty of nature in Finland: in the small Budapest painting, too, he focused on rendering the powerful light of the hot summer sun and capturing the atmosphere of the waterside scenery. Gallen-Kallela opts for an unusual angle, painting the young boy from above as he spies from the top of the hill: the unsuspecting girls bathe without any idea that they are being watched. By means of the slightly ironic title, the artist compares this modern-day peeping Tom with the mythological figure of a faun pursuing the nymphs, thereby highlighting the timelessness of his subject – human curiosity and carnal desire.

Gallen-Kallela cultivated close ties with Hungary and his work was regularly shown in Budapest. *Young Faun* was acquired by the Museum of Fine Arts from the 1906–1907 international exhibition of the Society of Fine Arts. – AZSK

London 2010, cat. no. 211 | *Vienna* 2024, 97

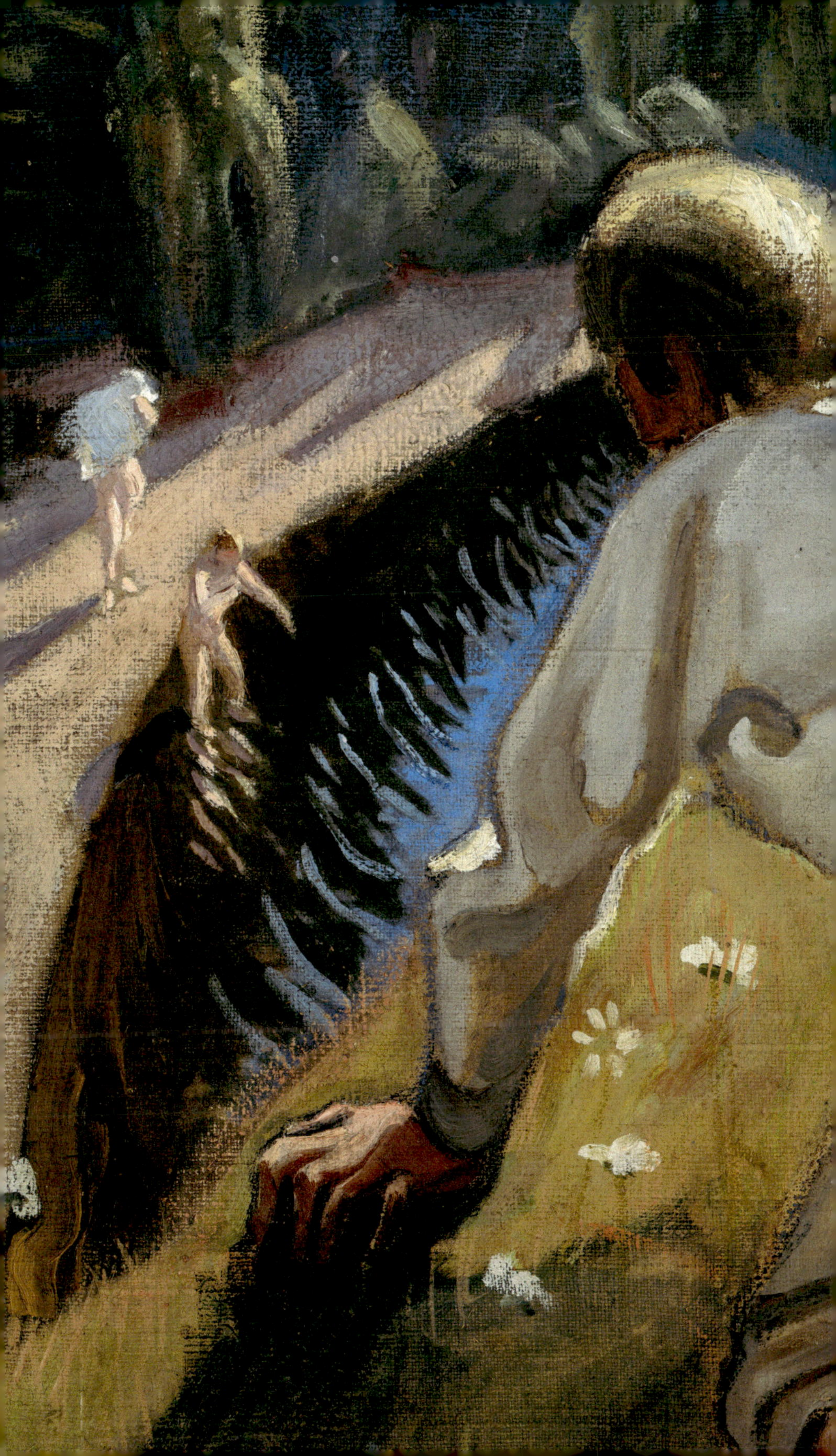

Rupert BUNNY

(Melbourne, 1864 – Melbourne, 1947)

Women on the Shore, ca. 1894 | Oil on canvas, 49 × 65 cm

Purchase, 1964 | Inv. no. 545.B

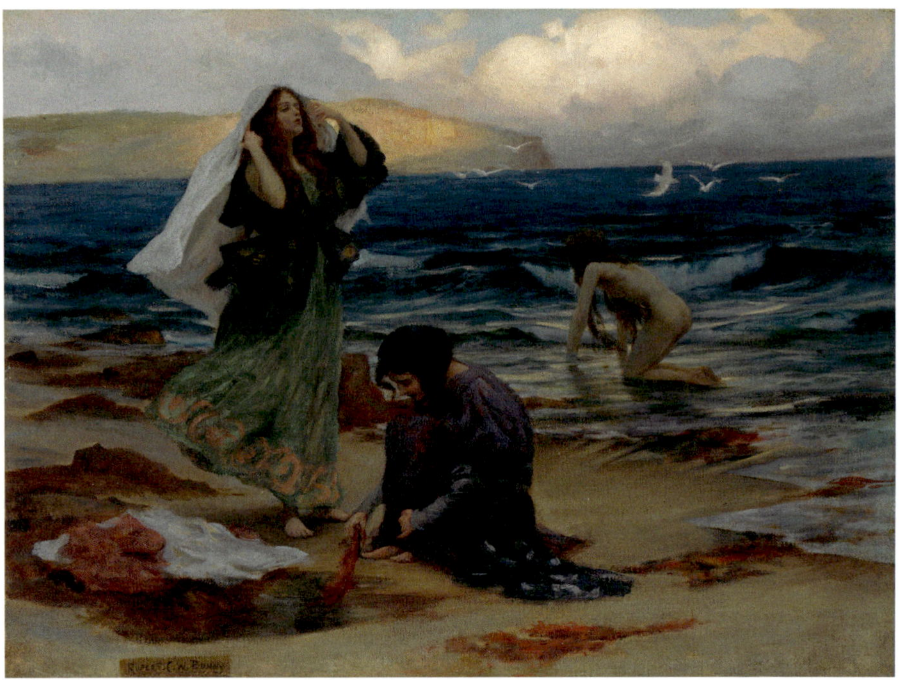

After spending a year and a half in London, the Australian painter moved to Paris in 1885. The first works he submitted to the Salon were large-scale mythological and biblical compositions. His paintings were characterised by a meticulousness of technique acquired from his teacher, Jean-Paul Laurens, although the imaginative powers of the French symbolists also left a vivid impression. Bunny quickly became one of the most recognised foreign artists in cosmopolitan Parisian society, among both audiences and critics. He was a frequent visitor to Étaples in Normandy, which was home to a sizeable English-speaking art colony. The coastal scenes painted there at the turn of the century combine the real and the imaginary, while the Pre-Raphaelite ideal of femininity is foregrounded in his figures. In 1888, he made the acquaintance of the Hungarian writer Zsigmond Justh, and the two became close friends. Bunny visited Justh in Hungary several times and regularly took part in international exhibitions at the Budapest Kunsthalle. – FT

Mánfai 2017 | Thomas 2017, 86, cat. no. 069

Carl O'LYNCH OF TOWN

(Ljubljana, 1869 – Genoa, 1942)

The Blue Lake, 1908 | Oil on card, 47 × 62.3 cm
Bequest of Count Dénes Andrássy, 1913 | Inv. no. 304.B

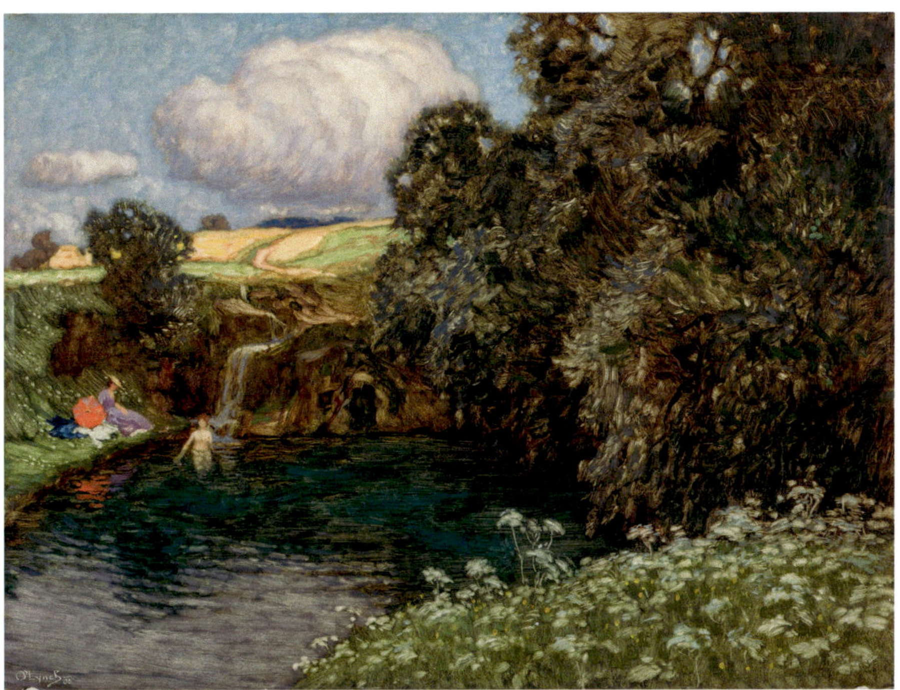

The painter's Irish ancestors had emigrated after taking part in the Jacobite Risings in the late seventeenth century. Carl O'Lynch of Town began studying drawing in Graz before attending the academies of fine art in Vienna and Munich. He founded a painting studio in Munich, where he kept in contact with the circle around Emil Jakob Schindler, at the same time regularly exhibiting his work in Graz and Vienna. Between 1904 and 1906, he was a member of the Hagenbund group, which brought together local progressive artists in the years following the internal conflicts within the Vienna Secession. O'Lynch regularly travelled in Europe, and wherever he went – be it southern beaches or Alpine crags – he indulged in his favourite pastime of landscape painting. From the outset, his paintings bore the hallmark of symbolism, an influence that is striking in the idyllic scene depicted in *The Blue Lake*. His approach to landscape involves the accentuation of atmospheric elements by means of pure, intense colours; besides the synthesising of forms, attention is drawn to the decorative proliferation of lines. The landscapes painted by O'Lynch at the turn of the century won him recognition as one of the foremost Styrian painters of his day. – FT

Peregriny 1914–1915/3, 238 | *Graz 2014–2015*, 281

X

Artistic and Individual Autonomy

Pierre BONNARD

Paul CEZANNE

Paul GAUGUIN

Henry LEROLLE

Alexandre LUNOIS

Aristide MAILLOL

Camille PISSARRO

Pierre-Auguste RENOIR

Medardo ROSSO

Henri de TOULOUSE-LAUTREC

Paul TROUBETZKOY

The most striking aspect of the new artistic phenomena that shook fin-de-siècle Paris was the attempt to move beyond the passive recording of sensory impressions. The demand for a more distinct separation of painting from visual perception was discernible even among impressionists from the second half of the 1880s, by which time the group had already broken apart. Its members were experimenting with new trends: Claude Monet was fascinated by the complete disintegration of forms, Pierre-Auguste Renoir by neoclassicist form, and Camille Pissarro by the scientific aspects of pointillism. Paul Gauguin, who had likewise become a master of impressionist technique during his association with the group, later strove for a mode of expression that he referred to as synthetism, specifically rejecting the idea of capturing surface impressions perceptible to the eye.

In the artistic kaleidoscope of Paris, countless tendencies emerged in parallel, the shared features of which – beyond the questioning of traditional values – long remained difficult to distinguish. The various artistic groupings all made their appearance under independent names – neo-impressionism, the Pont-Aven School, synthetism, the Nabis, etc. – some of them subsumed under the broad concept of "symbolism". The term "post-impressionism", coined in 1910 by the English art critic Roger Fry, refers to the French artists of the generation that followed (and responded to) impressionism. Distinguishing themselves from painting based on visual perception, which had culminated in impressionism, they sought opportunities for autonomous artistic expression. Two outstanding individuals from this period, Paul Cezanne and Paul Gauguin, became highly influential figures for later generations of modern artists through their use of colours and shapes as independent means of expression that endowed their images with a unified structure and harmony. These two painters represent most strikingly the connection between the fin de siècle and the tendencies that subsequently emerged.

The changes that took place at the end of the century occurred on several planes simultaneously, and artistic reform emerged from the clash between divergent attitudes. The liberation of forms, the adoption of dynamic pictorial expression, and above all the toppling of the bastions of academic art ultimately took place in every artistic centre. The art of the period is extremely heterogeneous, differing hugely from country to country. Liberation from centuries-long constraints allowed free rein to countless variations on individual experimentation. The most influential works were not those that followed and recreated generally typical, widely accepted stylistic and thematic features, but those characterised by individual ingenuity. This period saw the emergence of artistic personalities in the modern sense of the term – artists who established trends not only through their creative output but also by means of their sheer existence. It was a period when personal life became inseparable from artistic practice.

Paul CEZANNE

(Aix-en-Provence, 1839 – Aix-en-Provence, 1906)

Le Buffet, ca. 1877–1879 | Oil on canvas, 65.5 × 81 cm
Donated by Ferenc Hatvany, 1917 | Inv. no. 371.B

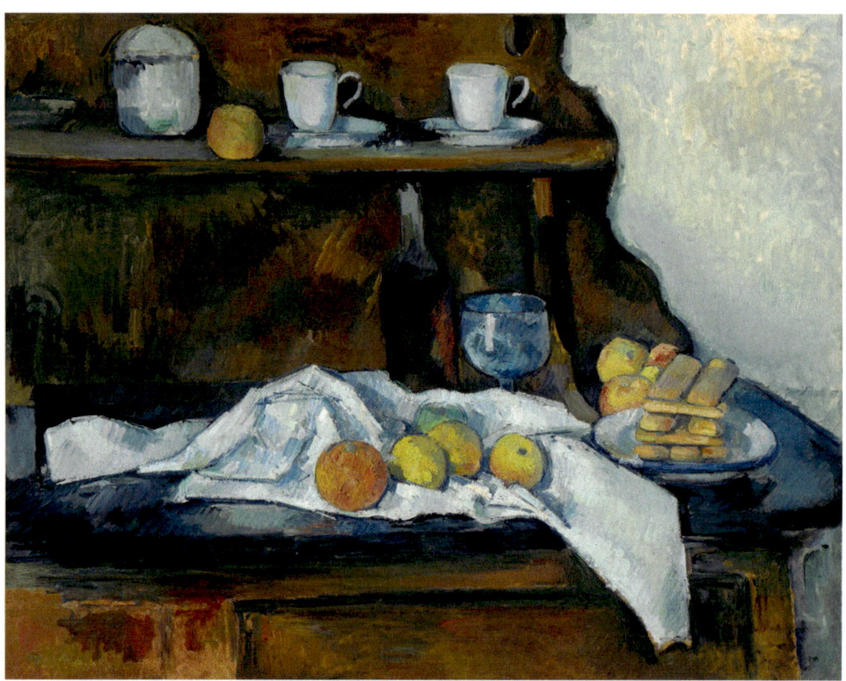

This painting by Paul Cezanne perfectly illustrates an observation made by the distinguished art critic Ernő Kállai, editor of the journal *Bauhaus*: "Cézanne took as his ideal the solid, sculptural forms of the old masters. His ambition was to create a solid, painterly construct from the ethereal colours of the impressionists... in his still lifes, he applied paint to canvas in small dabs, from which the forms and mass of the depicted objects gradually emerged. A balance of tone was sought between two adjacent dabs of colour."

Besides the use of colour, the composition here is extraordinary. The carved side panels of the dresser, the geometric patterns of carefully arranged tableware, fruits, and ladyfingers, the interplay of shapes, and the structural brushwork make this a key work. Cezanne's early "baroque" period and the "builderly painting" that he perfected from the 1880s, are both discernible here. In places, his brushwork reflects a movement forward from impressionism. Restoration of the painting in 2012 brought into relief the strong contrast between the loosely brushed ash blue of the wall in the background and the thickly applied paint that shapes the white tablecloth in the foreground, with its powerful structure and angular lines. These solutions, which Cezanne himself called his small "sensations", were later adopted by other artists, including Paul Gauguin in his early paintings. – JG

Cezanne catalogue, cat. no. FWN 746 | *Budapest 2021–2022b*, cat. no. 97

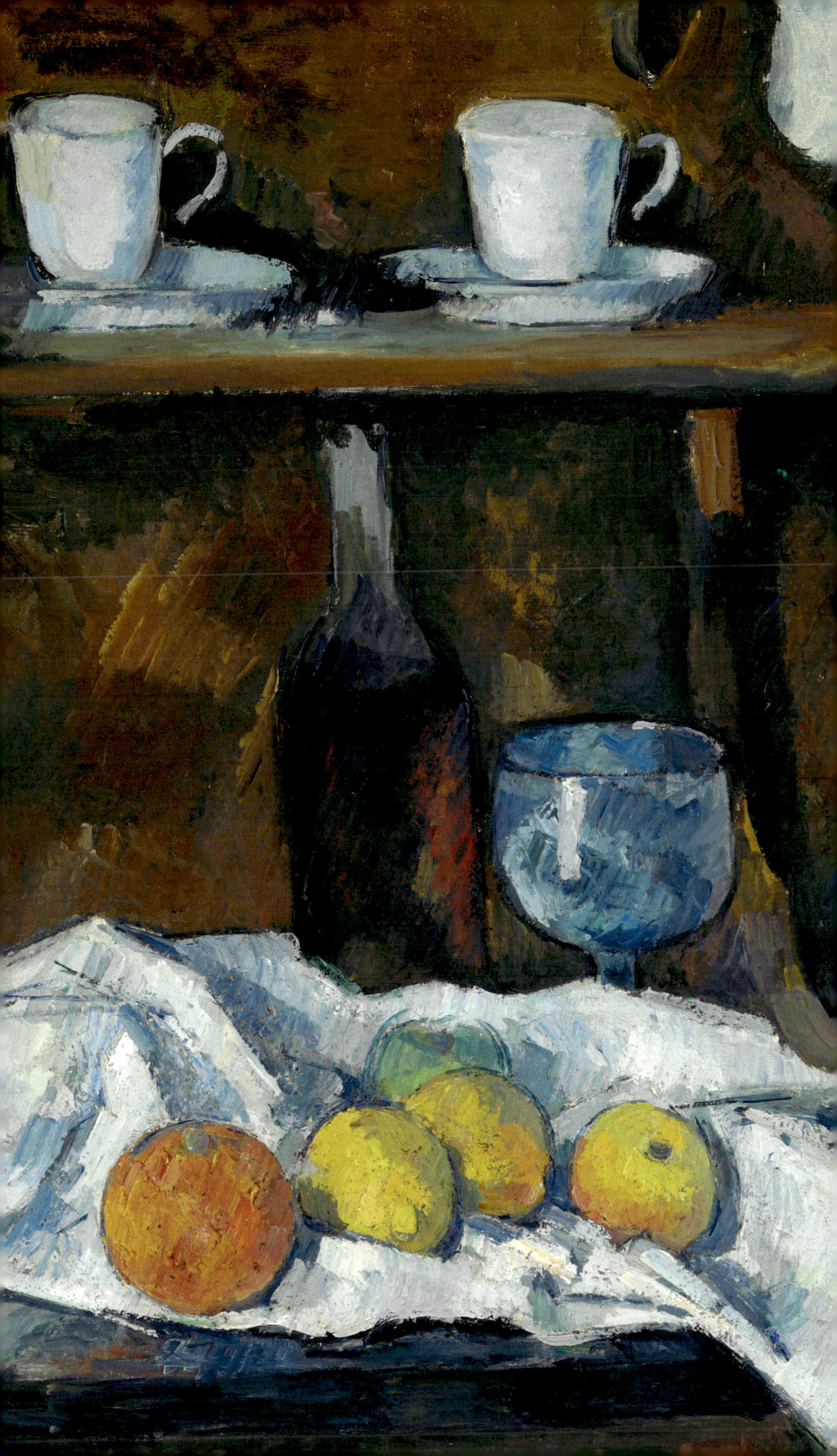

Pierre-Auguste RENOIR

(Limoges, 1841 – Cagnes-sur-Mer, 1919)

Reclining Nude (Gabrielle), 1903 | Oil on canvas, 65.3 × 155.3 cm

Purchase, 2019 | Inv. no. 2019.1.B

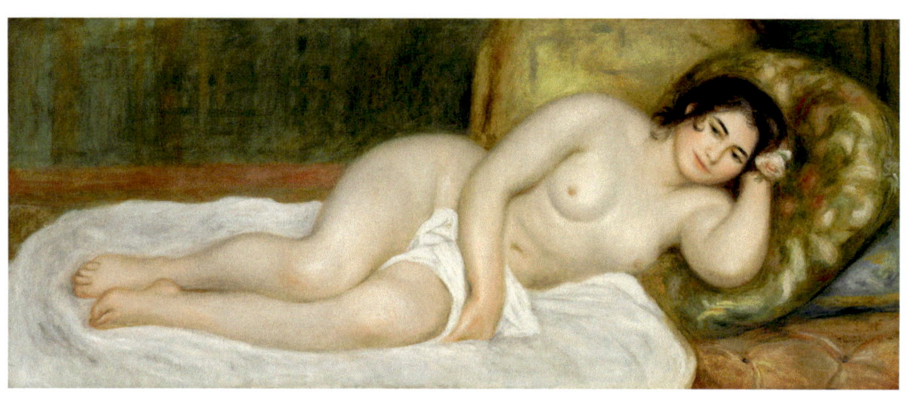

Renowned as a painter of *joie de vivre*, Pierre-Auguste Renoir always kept the human figure at the centre of his oeuvre. Besides his light-hearted scenes of everyday life and his delightful portraits, the nude remained a major focus throughout his career. With the outstanding, almost life-size reclining nude he created in 1903, Renoir pays homage to great masters such as Giorgione, Titian and Ingres, while maintaining his own sensual touch. Restrained brushwork and a harmonious use of colour characterize the picture, made in his classicizing manner of the turn of the century. The central figure, Gabrielle Renard, was one of his favourite models, and the inspiration for many of his later works. Renoir repeated the composition three times, with some modifications. Later variations of this first version are kept in the Musée d'Orsay and the Musée de l'Orangerie in Paris. The nude was first exhibited at the Salon d'Automne in Paris in 1905, where, next to the younger representatives of the avant-garde, Renoir was celebrated as an established exponent of the modern tradition. Although it was included in the December 1907 exhibition of the National Salon in Budapest, the painting was acquired by the Museum of Fine Arts only in 2019, becoming one of the major acquisitions in the history of the institution. – AZSK

Dauberville and Dauberville 2010, cat. no. 3502 | *Budapest* 2023–2024, cat. no. 68

Pierre-Auguste RENOIR

(Limoges, 1841 – Cagnes-sur-Mer, 1919)

Bust of a Young Girl, ca. 1895 | Oil on canvas, 56.5 × 47 cm

Purchase, 1945 | Inv. no. 435.B

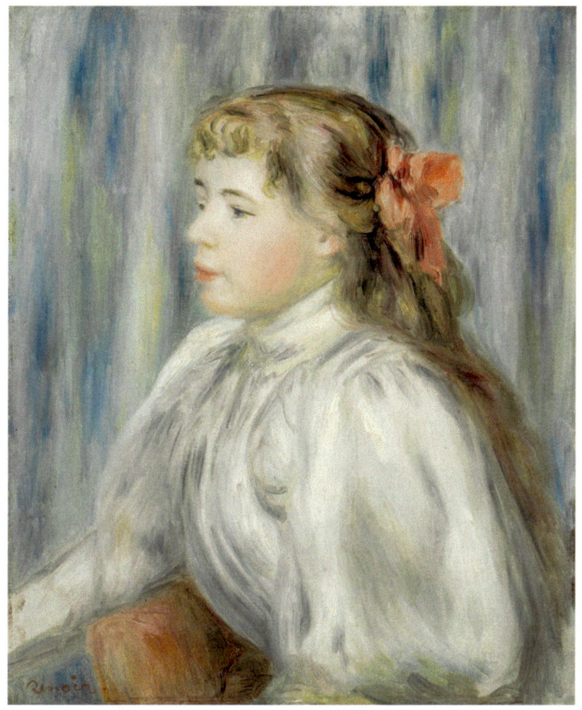

Although Pierre-Auguste Renoir was one of the most revered impressionist masters, the artist turned away from the impressionist approach during the 1880s, deemphasising the rendering of the fleeting moment to devote himself to a more traditional way of painting inspired by Raphael and Jean-Auguste-Dominique Ingres, primarily emphasising line and drawing.

This charming depiction of a young girl was made by Renoir in a later period when he returned to a looser, freer way of painting, and can be dated around 1895 based on stylistic grounds. The details of the model's garment, a white blouse with a high, tight collar and large, puffed sleeves fashionable at the time also confirm this datation. The young girl occupies most of the picture plane; she is sitting on a reddish armchair that echoes the hue of her lips and the ribbon in her hair. Renoir depicted her blue eyes, rosy cheeks, and light brown hair with subtle, delicate brushstrokes. Her figure also harmonises beautifully with the blurred, blue, white and green stripes in the background. The lack of expression and psychological characterisation suggest that the work was not intended as a portrait, but rather as a study of form and colour. – AZSK

Illyés 2001, 104–105 | *Budapest 2023–2024*, cat. no. 52

Aristide MAILLOL

(Banyuls-sur-Mer, 1861 – Banyuls-sur-Mer, 1944)

Kneeling Girl, model: ca. 1900; cast: 1902–1917 | Bronze, 18 × 12 × 11 cm
Donated by Marcell Nemes, 1917 | Inv. no. 5038.U

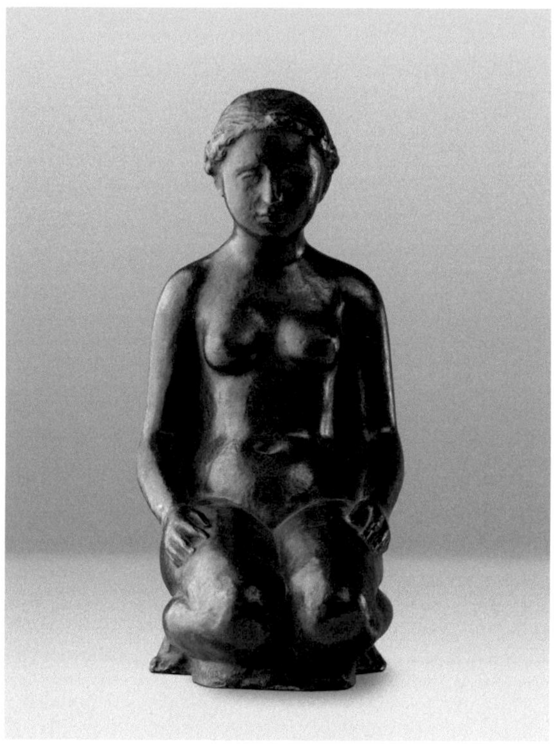

Having started out as a painter, Maillol then began producing tapestry designs until forced to abandon this work due to eye disease. In the 1890s, he developed a close friendship with József Rippl-Rónai, which would prove important to the careers of both artists. In the middle of the decade, Maillol began creating small figures from clay, and from then on, he focused exclusively on sculpture. In contrast to the dynamism and sensuality of Rodin, his work is characterised by restraint, simplicity, and balance. By his own admission, he was more interested in beauty than idiosyncrasy.

Maillol fired the clay figure of the kneeling girl himself. The modelled figure was among the small-scale compositions purchased by art dealer Ambroise Vollard and shown in his gallery in 1902. This was the first occasion on which Maillol's newly produced series of sculptures were shown alongside his paintings and tapestry designs. The exhibition proved hugely successful artistically, although in the interests of financial profit, Maillol transferred full rights over the bronze casts to Vollard. One of these casts was purchased by Marcell Nemes and donated to the Museum of Fine Arts. – FT

Illyés 2001, 164–166 | Berger-Lebon 2021, cat. no. 5

Aristide MAILLOL

(Banyuls-sur-Mer, 1861 – Banyuls-sur-Mer, 1944)

Leda, model: ca. 1900; cast: 1902–1904 | Bronze, 28.5 × 14.5 × 13.5 cm
Purchased at the auction of the Julius Stern Collection, Galerie Paul Cassirer (Berlin), 1916
Inv. no. 4990.U

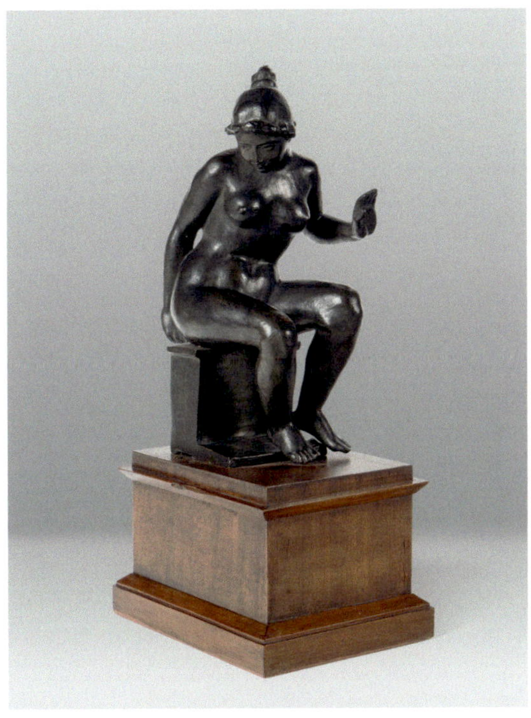

All of Maillol's sculptures take the female body as their subject, with no hidden literary or allegorical meaning. Although he gave some compositions mythological names, these were merely allusions to classical sculptural tradition. The renowned art critic Octave Mirbeau wrote enthusiastically about the small composition *Leda*, a cast of which he had purchased from the exhibition held in 1902 in the gallery of Ambroise Vollard. Mirbeau quotes the artist's explanation that although the composition originally included a swan (the guise adopted by Zeus to approach Leda, in Greek mythology), he was unhappy with the result and left it out. Thus, it is merely Leda's eloquent gesture that suggests the other character in the story. Mirbeau showed the sculpture to Auguste Rodin, who also expressed his admiration: "What is so wonderful – and I might even say timeless – about Maillol's work is its craftsmanship, its intellectual purity, clarity, and harmony."

Leda brought Maillol his first real success and became one of his most famous sculptures. This cast was purchased from Vollard in 1904 by the financier and art collector Julius Stern and was subsequently acquired by the Museum of Fine Arts. – FT

Illyés 2001, 164–166 | Berger-Lebon 2021, cat. no. 6

Paul **GAUGUIN**

(Paris, 1848 – Hiva Oa, Marquesas Islands, 1903)

Black Pigs, 1891 | Oil on canvas, 91 × 72 cm
Purchased from the exhibition *Great French Masters of the 19th Century*,
Ernst Museum, Budapest, 1913 | Inv. no. 355.B

Gauguin's childhood in Peru had a lifelong influence on his artistic outlook. The first works that he painted after he left France for Tahiti already show enigmatic correlations between dream and reality, fiction and objectivity, myth and everyday life. These paintings convey both physical and spiritual truths. The titles, whether in French or the language of the native people, are extremely telling. In his memoir, *Noa Noa*, which he illustrated with sketches and water-colours, Gauguin gave an account of his life on the island, and his Tahiti sketchbook is filled with images of the local people, their surroundings, and exotic plants and animals, including the indigenous black pigs.

Painted on rough jute canvas, figures familiar from Gauguin's other paintings are arranged here in a picturesque composition. The totem pole towering above the hut may be one of the artist's own marvellous carvings, since there were very few original, ancient examples left in Tahiti in around 1891. – JG

Wildenstein 1964, cat. no. 446 | *Verona* 2013–2014, 320–321, cat. no. 75

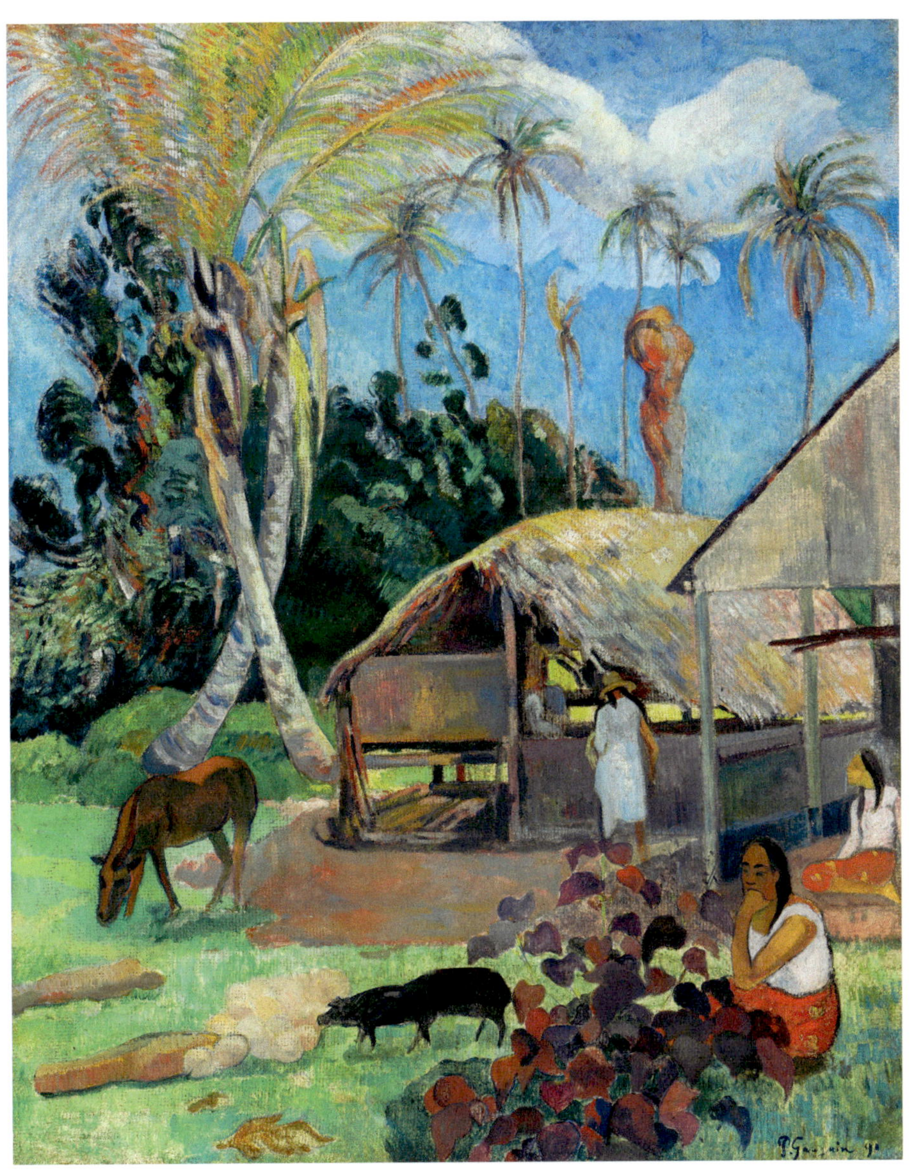

Camille **PISSARRO**

(Charlotte Amalie, 1830 – Paris, 1903)

The Pont Neuf, 1902 | Oil on canvas, 55.3 × 46.5 cm
Purchased at the spring exhibition of the Budapest National Salon
from the Galerie Durand-Ruel, Paris, 1907 | Inv. no. 205.B

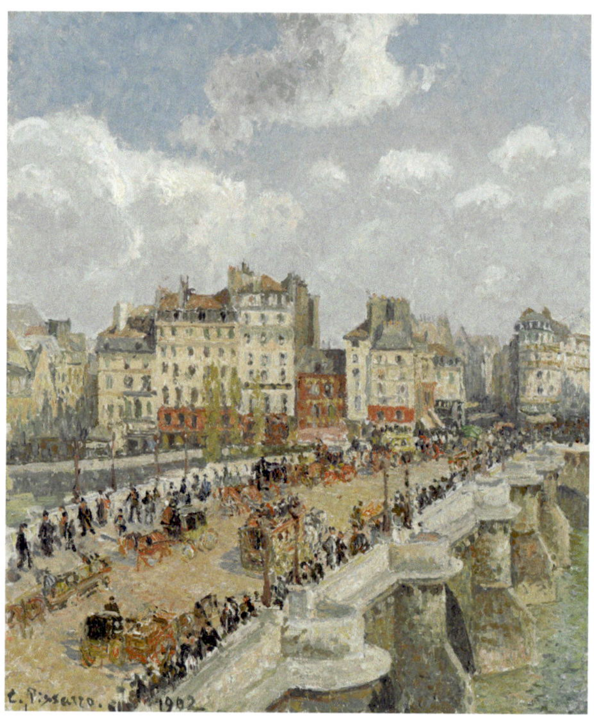

Pissarro produced a dozen of paintings of the Pont Neuf, the oldest stone bridge in Paris, capturing the elegant limestone structure spanning the Seine in both morning and afternoon light, in snow, rain, and sunshine. The aging painter, who suffered from eye disease, always viewed the scene from the same spot, observing the busy traffic and houses on the opposite bank from the window of his apartment on the Île de la Cité. The painting's structure is defined by the powerful diagonal of the bridge: the crowds that line the road and the central flow of carriages follows the same dynamic line. The Budapest painting captures the play of bright sunlight and vibrant colours. Although by this time Pissarro had long abandoned the strict, time-consuming methods of neo-impressionism, he cleverly adapted the technique he had mastered alongside Georges Seurat and Paul Signac: his use of pointilliste brushwork is most apparent in the slightly rippled surface of the water and the depiction of the bustling crowds. In this painting, however, the tiny dots of pure colour are used not primarily as a means of optical colour blending but rather to convey dynamic movement. – AZSK

Illyés 2001, 101–103 | Pissarro and Durand-Ruel Snollaerts 2005, cat. no. 74

Henry LEROLLE

(Paris, 1848 – Paris, 1929)

Bathing Women, ca. 1902 | Oil on canvas, 219 × 150 cm
Purchased from the HNSFA's 1903 spring exhibition | Inv. no. 49.B

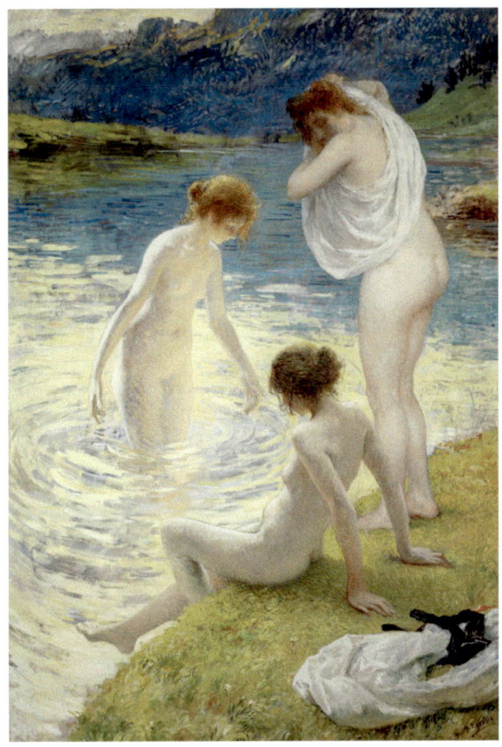

Henry Lerolle, painter, musician, art patron and collector, was a major figure on the Parisian art scene at the turn of the century, who enthusiastically embraced the formal innovations of his impressionist and symbolist contemporaries. He collected works by Edgar Degas, Maurice Denis, Pierre-Auguste Renoir and Pierre Puvis de Chavannes, among others. The combined influence of these artists can be discerned in this painting *Bathing Women*, but Lerolle found his own unique fusion of the impressionists' sensual grace and symbolist decorativeness.

Lerolle's painting lacks mythological or historical allusions, and the figures are so similar in appearance that they could be sisters: one is standing on the grassy bank, while her companion is about to enter the river; the third young woman is already knee-deep in water. It is as if we were following a sequence of movements. The three figures form a self-contained oval that echoes the concentric waves. Lerolle paid particular attention to the ripples on the surface, which almost become one with the reflection of the sun, highlighting the white bodies of the women. The work appeared at the Salons of La Libre Esthétique in Brussels and the Société Nationale des Beaux-Arts in Paris in 1902. – AZSK

Kovács 2020 | Lerolle 2022, 204–205, 245, 265

Alexandre LUNOIS

(Paris, 1863 – Le Pecq, 1916)

The Bullfight, ca. 1897 | Pastel on paper, 62.3 × 83.2 cm
Purchased from the National Salon International Exhibition, 1901 | Inv. no. 23.B

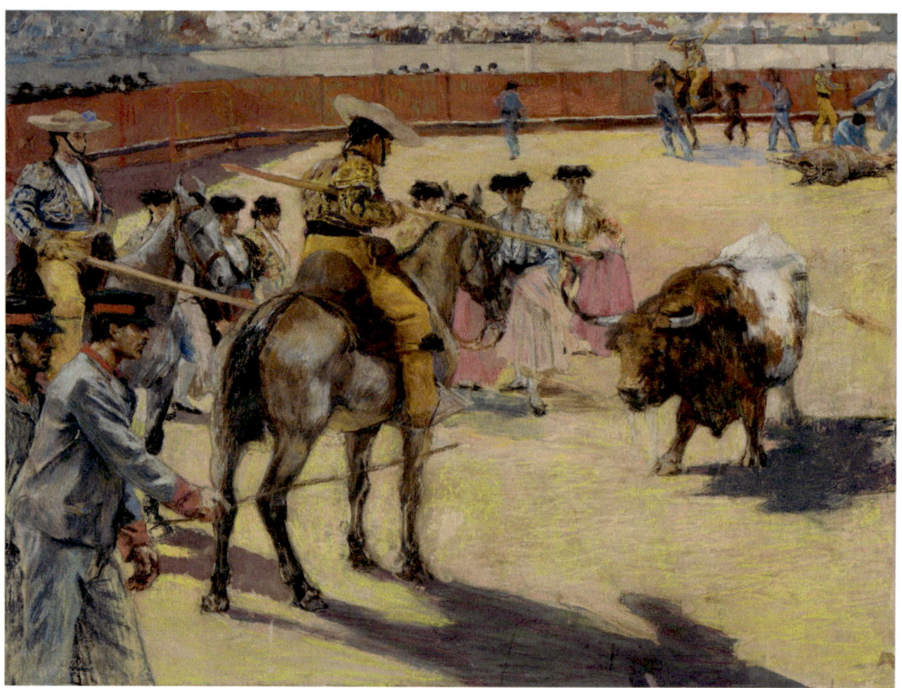

Alexandre Lunois is one of several nineteenth-century French painters who obtained their most telling artistic inspiration during their travels abroad: besides the exotic landscapes of West Africa, he was inspired by the folk characters and traditions of Spain, including bullfights. His compositions draw not only on his personal experiences: he also used details from paintings by Édouard Manet, as well as photographs taken at bullfights by Jean Laurent. Lunois generally painted in pastels – as he did in the case of this work from his bullfighting series – later reproducing the images as colour lithographs.

 This painting captures a moment of tension integral to the first third of a bullfight – the so-called *tercio de varas*: preparing to attack, the bull stares down the picador (the horseback bullfighter), who provokes the animal with his lance until it displays its real strength and true temperament. Lined up and ready behind the picador are his assistants, the *monosabios*. Nothing can save the solitary animal watching in the foreground: it can no more escape its fate than the dead horse that lies on the ground behind it. – AL

André 1914, 78, 202 | *Budapest* 2023, cat. no. 11

Henri TOULOUSE-LAUTREC

(Albi, 1864 – Malromé, 1901)

These Ladies in the Dining Room, 1893–1895 | Oil on cardboard, 61 × 81 cm
Purchased from the exhibition *Great French Masters of the 19th Century*,
Ernst Museum, Budapest, 1913 | Inv. no. 356.B

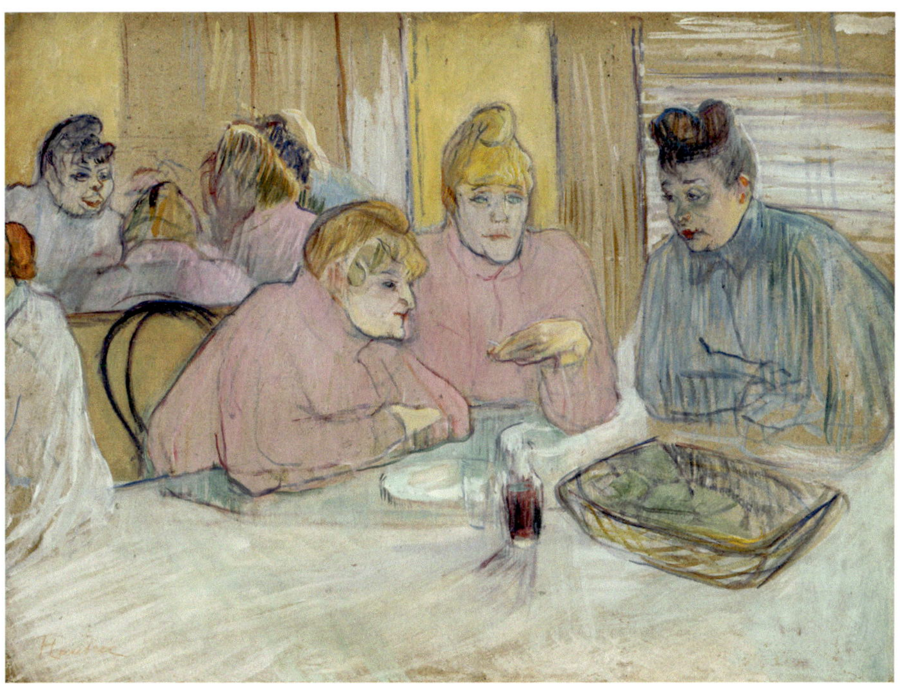

This painting by Toulouse-Lautrec shows the dining room of a popular brothel that operated at 6 Rue des Moulins in Paris. From 1884, Lautrec lived in Montmartre, where he keenly observed the various characters in his surroundings. He had an affinity for the world of Parisian courtesans. Because of his own physical disabilities, he sympathised with the women who were forced to make a living in this way, depicting their onerous existence not with the realist devices of Émile Zola but in a style akin to symbolism. He recorded the prostitutes' lives for around three years, between 1893 and 1895. His sympathy was given expression through his symbolist approach, while his subject was very similar to the kind of human pain described in the novels of Guy de Maupassant.

There is no moralising, only compassion. At the same time, both painter and writer had a profound insight into the lives of the desperate people they observed in the brothels and coffeehouses. The Budapest composition captures this psychological awareness. The mirror, in which the face of the fourth woman appears, reflects the complex duality of the lives of the socially marginalised. – JG

Dortu 1971, cat. no. 499 | *Budapest* 2014, cat. no. 1

Medardo ROSSO

(Turin, 1858 – Milan, 1928)

Impression of a Concierge, 1887 | Bronze, 45 × 37 × 21 cm
Transfer, 1951 | Inv. no. 52.139.U

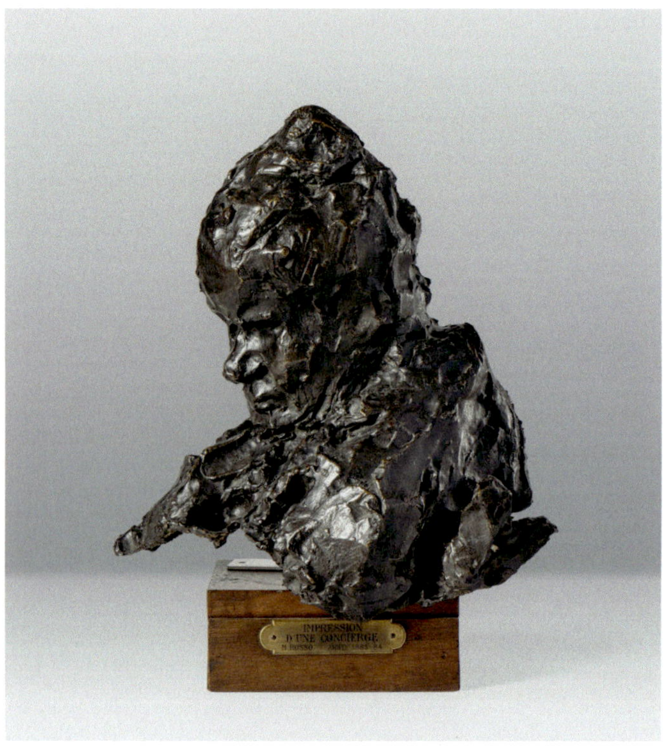

Rosso is regarded as one of the precursors of modern sculpture. After studying briefly at the academy, and following his first, realist sculptures, he gradually discovered his own unique style in around 1882. He would rework a particular theme several times, producing sculptures from plaster, bronze, and even wax. Like the impressionists, he too looked for his subjects in modern urban life and was interested in light and shadow, the capturing of first impressions, and three-dimensional representation. The first version of *Impression of a Concierge* dates from 1883–1884. The caretaker or concierge became a popular figure in literary works following the publication in 1882 of Émile Zola's novel *Pot-Bouille*, set in a Parisian apartment building. Rosso may have been familiar with the novel and drawn inspiration from it, as it was translated into Italian by one of his friends, Felice Cameroni. The Budapest bronze depicts the elderly caretaker of an apartment building on Via Montebello in Milan. Depicted in semi-profile, the head is extraordinarily expressive, as if the old woman has been caught dozing. According to Rosso's memoirs, he worked very quickly on this piece, constantly mindful of the fleeting impression made on him by the woman as he passed her. – AS

New York 1963, 24–25 | Frankfurt 2020, 134–135, 137, cat. no. 53

Paul TROUBETZKOY

(Verbania, 1866 – Verbania, 1938)

Seated Woman, 1908 | Bronze, 38 × 37 × 37 cm

Transfer, 1951 | Inv. no. 52.147.U

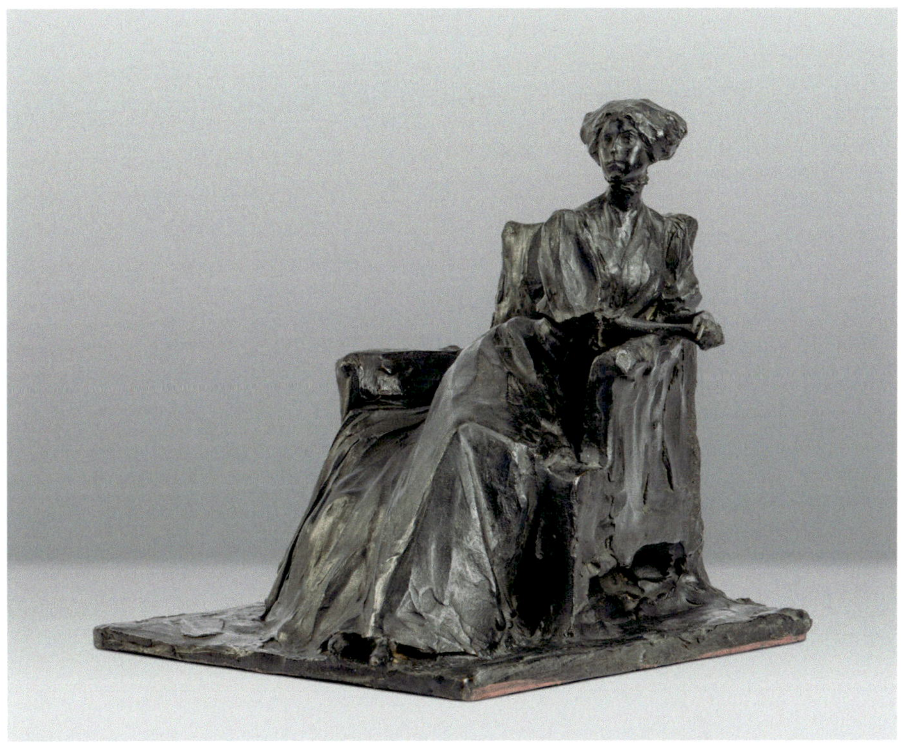

Paul Troubetzkoy was an important representative of turn-of-the-century sculpture and one of the most popular artists of his day. His father was a Russian prince from an old aristocratic family, and his mother was an American opera singer. His parents settled in Italy, where Paul was born. As a young adult, he was involved in managing his family's estates, although his interest soon turned towards sculpture. He studied in Milan, in the studio of Ernesto Bazzaro.

Through Bazzaro, the origins of Troubetzkoy's distinctive style can be found in the work of the Italian sculptor Giuseppe Grandi and the Milanese avant-garde movement Scapigliatura, which was known for its expressive, indistinct forms. In addition, he was greatly influenced by Auguste Rodin and Medardo Rosso. Troubetzkoy broke with the traditions of the academy and experimented with new approaches to light and form. His bronzes, which convey a sense of both virtuosity and sketchiness of execution, capture fleeting impressions.
– BIB

Bacher 1959, 11 | *Verbania* 1990, 176–177

Pierre **BONNARD**

(Fontenay-aux-Roses, 1867 – Le Cannet, 1947)

Grandmother and Child, 1894 | Oil on wood, 33 × 42 cm
Purchased at the auction of the collection of Adolf Kohner, 1934
Inv. no. 406.B

Dining Room at Grand-Lemps, 1899 | Oil on canvas, 53.5 × 61 cm
Purchased at the auction of the collection of Adolf Kohner, 1934
Inv. no. 400.B

A member of the Nabis, Pierre Bonnard initially favoured stylised, heavily contoured shapes and the flat, decorative approach of Japanese art. His outlines gradually acquired greater fluidity, as he rendered forms in vibrant spots of intense colour. The indistinct figures in *Grandmother and Child* have been depicted using this loose technique: the narrowly cropped composition focuses on an elderly woman and a little child – probably the artist's mother and one of his nephews – the warm colours reinforcing the intimacy of the scene. The figures appear against an almost abstract, geometrically articulated background, juxtaposing different patterns.

Bonnard's other work, likewise based on the motif of the family table, was executed using an even looser technique. In around 1900, Bonnard produced several paintings of gatherings at his family's estate in Grand-Lemps. Here, however, the focus is not on members of the family: the old woman drinking her coffee and the slightly hesitant figure of the girl standing next to her are almost squeezed out of the composition by the dramatic curve of the table. Set against an indistinct background, the central motif, the still life, is presented from an unusual angle: the tabletop, spread with a white cloth, seems almost to tip towards the viewer, highlighting the empty plates and the fruit bowls' rich dabs of colour.

Both works come from the renowned collection of Adolf Kohner, whose Budapest home was decorated with works by Pierre-Auguste Renoir, Paul Gauguin, and Vincent van Gogh. – AZSK

Dauberville and Dauberville 1968, cat. no. 69 and cat. no. 387
Illyés 2001, 148–149, 150–151

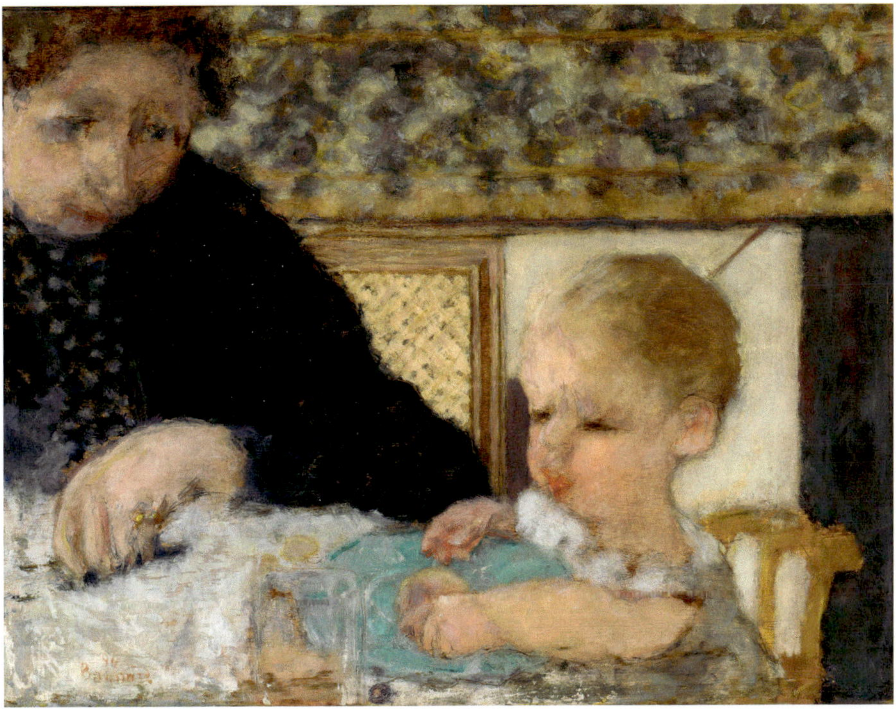

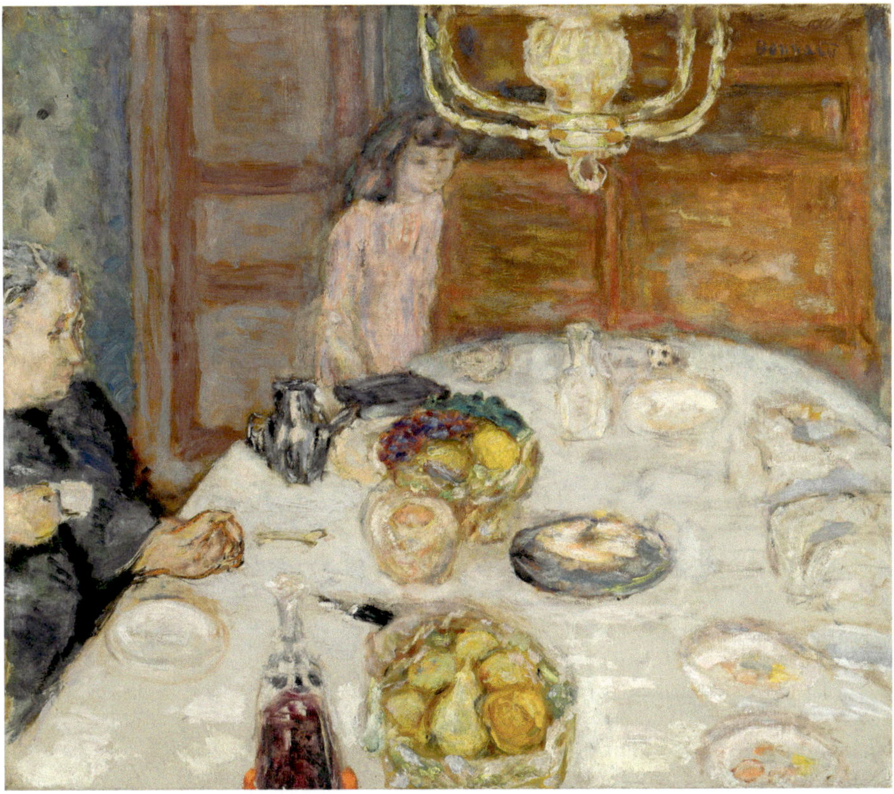

Appendix

Bibliography
Index of Artists

Bibliography

Aaserud 2013
Aaserud, Anne. *Adelsteen Normann. Fra Bodø til Berlin.* Stamsund: Okrana Akademisk, 2013.

Aix-en-Provence 2008
Coutagne, Denis. *François Marius Granet (1775–1849). Une vie pour la peinture.* Exh. cat. Musée Granet, Aix-en-Provence, 2008. Paris: Somogy éditions d'art, 2008.

AKL 1997
Allgemeines Künstlerlexikon. Die Bildenden Künstler aller Zeiten und Völker. Vol. 16. Munich/ Leipzig: Saur Verlag, 1997.

Allgemeines Lexikon 1915
Allgemeines Lexikon der bilden-den Künstler von der Antike bis zur Gegenwart. Vol. 11. Edited by Hans Vollmer, Ulrich Thieme, Felix Becker, and Frederick Charles Willis. Leipzig, 1915.

Allgemeines Lexikon 1921
Allgemeines Lexikon der bilden-den Künstler von der Antike bis zur Gegenwart. Vol. 14. Edited by Hans Vollmer, Ulrich Thieme, Felix Becker, and Frederick Charles Willis. Leipzig, 1921.

Alvin 1885
Alvin, Louis. *Eugène-Joseph Verboeckhoven.* Brussels, 1885.

Amsterdam 1995–1996
Becker, Edwin. *Franz von Stuck 1863–1928. Eros & Pathos.* Exh. cat. Van Gogh Museum, Amsterdam, 1995–1996. Amsterdam: Van Gogh Museum, 1996.

Amsterdam–Helsinki 2010–2011
Illusions of Reality. Naturalist Painting, Photography, Theatre and Cinema, 1875–1918. Edited by Gabriel P. Weisberg. Exh. cat. Van Gogh Museum, Amsterdam; Ateneumin Taidemuseo, Helsinki, 2010–2011. Brussels: Mercatorfonds, 2010.

André 1914
André, Édouard. *Alexandre Lunois, peintre, graveur et lithographe.* Paris: H. Floury, 1914.

Andree 1998
Andree, Rolf. *Arnold Böcklin. Die Gemälde.* Basel: Friedrich Reinhardt Verlag / Munich: Prestel Verlag, 1998.

Arborelius n. d.
Arborelius, Olof. https:// www.lexikonettamanda. se/show.php?aid=18860, Konstnärlexikonett Amanda (last accessed: 6 June 2024).

Arnáiz 1981
Arnáiz, José Manuel. *Eugenio Lucas. Su vida y su obra.* Madrid: Montal, 1981.

Athens 2009
The Poet of the Sea, Contantinos Volanakis 1837–1907. Edited by Marilena Z. Cassimatis. Exh. cat. Theocharakis Foundation, Athens, 2009. Athens: Aikaterini Laskaridis Foundation, 2009.

Atlanta–Seattle–Denver 1999
Impressionism: Paintings Collected by European Museums. Edited by Ann Dumas and Michael E. Shapiro. Exh. cat. High Museum of Art, Atlanta; Seattle Art Museum, Seattle; Denver Art Museum, Denver, 1999. New York: Abrams, 1999.

Aubrun 1974
Aubrun, Marie-Madeleine. *Jules Dupré 1811–1889. Catalogue raisonné de l'œuvre peint, dessiné et gravé.* Paris: Léonce Laget éditeur, 1974.

Aubrun 1985
Aubrun, Marie-Madeleine. *Jules Bastien-Lepage 1848–1884. Catalogue raisonné de l'œuvre.* Paris: M. M. Aubrun, 1985.

Bacher 1959
Bacher, Béla. *Modern külföldi szoborgyűjtemény.* A Szépművé-szeti Múzeum állandó kiállításai-nak ismeretterjesztő katalógusa 2. Exh. cat. Budapest: Museum of Fine Arts, 1959.

Balatonfüred 2019
Rivers, Lakes, Seas. Vitalizing Water. Water Motifs in 19th Century European and Hungarian Paintings. Exh. cat. Vaszary Gallery, Balatonfüred, 2019. Balatonfüred: Vaszary Gallery / Museum of Fine Arts – Hungarian National Gallery, 2019.

Basics 2018
Basics, Beatrix. "Kortárs esemé-nyek ábrázolásai." In *A magyar művészet a 19. században. Képzőművészet,* 335–40. Edited by József Sisa, Júlia Papp, and Erzsébet Király. Budapest: MTA Bölcsészettudományi Kutatóközpont / Osiris, 2018.

Bätschmann 1997
Bätschmann, Oskar. *Ausstellungs-künstler. Kult und Karriere im modernen Kunstsystem.* Cologne: DuMont, 1997.

Basel–Paris–Munich 2001–2002
Arnold Böcklin. Eine Retrospek-tive. Edited by Bernd Wolfgang Lindemann. Exh. cat. Kunst-museum, Basel; Musée d'Orsay, Paris; Neue Pinakothek, Munich, 2001–2002. Heidelberg: Edition Braus im Wachter Verlag, 2001.

Benezit 2006
Benezit Dictionary of Artists. Vol. 1. Paris: Gründ, 2006.

Béraldi 1885
Béraldi, Henri. *Les Graveurs du XIXe siècle.* Vol. 1. Paris: L. Conquet, 1885.

Berger–Lebon 2021
Berger, Ursel and Élisabeth Lebon. *Maillol (re)découvert.* Montreuil: Gourcuff Gradenigo, 2021.

Berkovits 1964
Berkovits, Ilona. *Zichy Mihály élete és munkássága (1827–1906).* Budapest: Akadémiai Kiadó, 1964.

Berlin–Hamburg–Hanau 1999
Der Tierbildhauer August Gaul. Edited by Ursel Berger. Exh. cat. Georg Kolbe Museum, Berlin; Ernst Barlach Haus, Hamburg; Hanau, Museen der Stadt Hanau, 1999–2000. Berlin: Nicolai, 2000.

Bodnár ed. 2002
A Szépművészeti Múzeum – vezető. Edited by Szilvia Bodnár. Budapest: Szépművészeti Múzeum, 2002.

Boer 1900
Boer, H. de. *Willem Maris.* The Hague: P. G. Zürcher, 1900.

Boime 1969
Boime, Albert. "Thomas Couture and the Evolution of Painting in Nineteenth Century France." *The Art Bulletin* 51, no. 1 (1969): 48–56.

Bonn 2018
Malerfürsten. Edited by Doris H. Lehmann and Katharina Chrubasik. Exh. cat. Bundeskunsthalle, Bonn, 2018. Munich: Hirmer, 2018.

Boston 2013
Anders Zorn. A European Artist Seduces America. Edited by Oliver Tostmann. Exh. cat. Isabella Stewart Gardner Museum, Boston, 2013. London: Paul Holberton Publishing, 2013.

Bott 2009
Bott, Gian Casper. *Albert von Keller. Salons, Séancen, Secession.* Zurich: Hirmer, 2009.

Brand 1983
Brand, Bettina. *Fritz von Uhde. Das religiose Werk zwischen künstlerischer Intention und Öffentlichkeit.* Mainz: Privately published, 1983.

Bremen–Munich 1988–1989
Französische Kunst des 19. Jahrhunderts aus dem Museum der Bildende Künste Budapest. Gemälde, Aquarelle, Zeichnungen. Exh. cat. Kunsthalle Bremen, Bremen; Neue Pinakothek, Munich, 1988–1989. Bremen: Kunsthalle Bremen, 1989.

Brescia 1994
Giuseppe Canella 1788–1847. Paesaggi e vedute nei Civici Musei di Brescia. La memoria figurativa 2. Edited by Maurizio Mondini. Exh. cat. Brescia: AAB Edizioni, 1994.

Brescia 2008
La natura come paesaggio. Dipinti e disegni "dal vero" del primo Ottocento nelle raccolte dei Civici Musei di Brescia. La memoria figurativa 23. Edited by Maurizio Mondini. Exh. cat. Brescia: AAB Edizioni, 2008.

Brown Price 2010
Brown Price, Aimée. *Pierre Puvis de Chavannes. A Catalogue Raisonné of the Painted Work.* Vol. 2. New Haven / London: Yale University Press, 2010.

Brunnarius 2023
Brunnarius, Isabelle. "Restaurer la Fontaine de Léri peinte par Gustave Courbet, des passionnés se mobilisent." *France 3 Régions,* 15 January 2023. https://france3-regions.francetvinfo.fr/bourgogne-franche-comte/doubs/restaurer-la-fontaine-de-leri-peinte-par-gustave-courbet-des-passionnes-se-mobilisent-2693458.html (last accessed: 14 January 2023).

Brussels 1990
La Sculpture Belge au 19ème siècle. Edited by Jacques van Lennep. Exh. cat. Musées Royaux des Beaux-Arts de Belgique, Brussels, 1990. Brussels: La Générale de Banque, 1990.

Brussels 1993–1994
Ollinger-Zinque, Gisèle et al. *Les XX et La Libre Esthétique: honerd jaar later = cent ans après.* Exh. cat. Musées Royaux des Beaux-Arts de Belgique, Brussels, 1993–1994. Brussels: Musées Royaux des Beaux-Arts de Belgique, 1993.

Brussels 2010
Charles van der Stappen 1843–1910. Edited by Michel Draguet, Francisca Vandepitte, and Angélique Demur. Exh. cat. Musée Royaux des Beaux-Arts de Belgique, Brussels, 2010. Gent: Snoeck, 2010.

Brussels–Amsterdam 2009
Alfred Stevens, Bruxelles – Paris (1823–1906). Exh. cat. Musées Royaux des Beaux-Arts de Belgique, Brussels; Van Gogh Museum, Amsterdam, 2009. Brussels: Mercatorfonds / Musées Royaux des Beaux-Arts de Belgique, 2009.

Budapest 1995
Aranyérmek, ezüstkoszorúk. Művészkultusz és műpártolás Magyarországon a 19. században / Goldmedaillen, Silberkränze. Künstlerkult und Mäzonatur im 19. Jahrhundert in Ungarn. Edited by Katalin Sinkó. Exh. cat. Magyar Nemzeti Galéria / Ungarische Nationalgalerie, Budapest, 1995. Budapest: Hungarian National Gallery, 1995.

Budapest 1995–1996
A hágai iskola. A 19. századi holland festészet mesterművei a Haags Gemeentemuseum gyűjteményéből. Edited by Mariann Gergely and Anna Szinyei Merse. Exh. cat. Hungarian National Gallery, Budapest, 1995–1996. Budapest: Hungarian National Gallery, 1995.

Budapest 2001–2002
A lélek mélységei. Belga szimbolisták / Les Passions de l'Âme. Les symbolistes belges. Edited by De Croes, Catherine, Jean-David Jumeau-Lafond, and Michel de Reymacker. Exh. cat. Musée des Beaux-Arts de Budapest, 2001–2002. Hungarofest Kht., Budapest: Museum of Fine Arts, 2001.

Budapest 2003–2004
Monet et ses amis. Edited by Judit Geskó. Exh. cat. Museum of Fine Arts, Budapest, 2003–2004. Budapest: Museum of Fine Arts / Vince Kiadó, 2003.

Budapest 2005
Munkácsy a nagyvilágban. Munkácsy Mihály művei külföldi és magyar magán- és közgyűjteményekben / Munkácsy in the World. Mihály Munkácsy's Works in Private and Public Collections at Home and Abroad. Edited by Ferenc Gosztonyi. Exh. cat. Hungarian National Gallery, Budapest, 2005. Budapest: Szemimpex, 2005.

Budapest 2009
Borsos József festő és fotográfus (1821–1883) / József Borsos Painter and Photographer (1821–1883). Edited by Petra Kárai and Nóra Veszprémi. Exh. cat. Hungarian National Gallery, Budapest, 2009. Budapest: Hungarian National Gallery, 2009.

Budapest 2009–2010
München magyarul. Magyar művészek Münchenben 1850–1914. Edited by Petra Kárai and Nóra Veszprémi. Exh. cat. Hungarian National Gallery, Budapest, 2009–2010. Budapest: Hungarian National Gallery, 2009.

Budapest 2010–2011
Nuda Veritas. Gustav Klimt and the Origins of the Vienna Secession 1895–1905. Edited by Marian Exh. cat. Museum of Fine Arts, Budapest, 2010–2011. Budapest: Museum of Fine Arts, 2010.

Budapest 2011
Markó Károly és köre. Mítosztól a képig / Károly Markó and his Circle. From Myth to Vision. Edited by Gábor Bellák, Zoltán Dragon, and Orsolya Hessky. Exh. cat. Hungarian National Gallery, Budapest, 2011. Budapest: Hungarian National Gallery, 2011.

Budapest 2012–2013
Rodin és a Szépművészeti Múzeum / Rodin and the Museum of Fine Arts, Budapest. Cabinet Exhibitions of the Department of Art after 1800 VIII. Edited by Ferenc Tóth. Exh. cat. Museum of Fine Arts Budapest, 2012–2013. Budapest: Museum of Fine Arts, 2012.

Budapest 2014
The World of Toulouse-Lautrec. Edited by Zsuzsa Gonda and Kata Bodor. Exh. cat. Museum of Fine Arts Budapest, 2014. Budapest: Museum of Fine Arts, 2014.

Budapest 2020
Állatok. Állatábrázolás a 19. századi festészetben. Edited by Zsófia Medzihradszky. Exh. cat. Magyar Mezőgazdasági Múzeum, Budapest, 2020. Budapest, 2020.

Budapest 2021–2022a
Canvas and Cult. Pál Szinyei Merse (1845–1920) and His Art. Edited by Orsolya Hessky, Réka Krasznai, and Adrienn Prágai. Exh. cat. Hungarian National Gallery, Budapest, 2021–2022. Budapest: Museum of Fine Arts – Hungarian National Gallery, 2021.

Budapest 2021–2022b
Cezanne to Malevich. Arcadia to Abstraction. Edited by Judit Geskó. Exh. cat. Museum of Fine Arts, Budapest, 2021–2022. Budapest: Museum of Fine Arts, 2021.

Budapest 2022a
Az eszmény felé. Belga szimbolista szobrászat a Szépművészeti Múzeum gyűjteményéből / Towards the Ideal. Belgian Symbolist Sculpture from the Collection of the Museum of Fine Arts / Vers l'Idéal. Sculptures symbolistes belges de la collection du musée des Beaux-Arts. Cabinet Exhibitions of the Department of Art after 1800 12. Edited by Anna Zsófia Kovács and Ferenc Tóth. Exh. cat. Hungarian National Gallery, Budapest, 2021–2022. Budapest: Museum of Fine Arts – Hungarian National Gallery, 2022.

Budapest 2022b
Divine Seduction. Erotica and Passion in Five Centuries of Mythological Depictions. Edited by Júlia Tátrai, Vilmos Tátrai, Exh. cat. Museum of Fine Arts, Budapest, 2022. Budapest: Museum of Fine Arts, 2023.

Budapest 2023
Harc a fenevaddal. A bika a spanyol és a mediterrán kultúrában / Battling the Beast. The Bull in Spanish and Mediterranean Culture / En lucha con la bestia. El toro en la cultura española y mediterránea. Cabinet Exhibitions of the Department of Art after 1800, 13. Edited by Adriána Lantos. Exh. cat. Hungarian National Gallery, Budapest, 2023. Budapest: Museum of Fine Arts – Hungarian National Gallery, 2023.

Budapest 2023–2024
Renoir. The Painter and His Models. Edited by Cécile Girardeau, Anna Zsófia Kovács, and Paul Perrin. Exh. cat. Museum of Fine Arts, Budapest, 2023–2024. Budapest: Museum of Fine Arts, 2023.

Bühler 1981a
Bühler, Hans-Peter. "Braith, Anton." In *Münchner Maler im 19. Jahrhundert,* 124–27. Bruckmann Lexikon der Münchner Kunst 1. Edited by Ludwig Horster. Munich: Bruckmann, 1981.

Bühler 1981b
Bühler, Hans-Peter. "Braiths Aufstieg – Das Nahbild." In *Anton Braith, Christian Mali. Tiermalerei der Münchner Schule,* 59–62. Mainz am Rhein: Philipp von Zabern Verlag, 1981.

Cariou 2002
Cariou, André. *Lucien Simon.* Quimper: Éditions Palantines, 2002.

Castelnuovo ed. 1990
La pittura in Italia. L'Ottocento. Vol. 2. Edited by Enrico Castelnuovo. Milan: Electa, 1990.

Cezanne catalogue
The Paintings, Watercolors and Drawings of Paul Cezanne. Online catalogue. https://www.cezannecatalogue.com/catalogue/entry.php?id=334 (last accessed: 16 February 2025).

Chofre García 2011
Chofre García, María del Carmen. *Tras los pasos de Fortuny: El universo pictórico de José Gallegos Arnosa y Salvador*

Sánchez Barbudo. PhD. diss. Universidad de Sevilla, Sevilla, 2011.

Churak 2012
Churak, Galina. "Russian Painters in Düsseldorf. Rapprochements and Parallels." In *The Düsseldorf School of Painting and its International Influence 1819–1918*, 318–19. Edited by Bettina Baumgärtel. Exh. cat. Museum Kunstpalast, Düsseldorf, 2011–2012. Petersberg: Michael Imhof Verlag, 2012.

Cifka 1980
Cifka, Brigitta. "Tableaux de Ferdinand Georg Waldmüller en Hongrie." *Bulletin du Musée Hongrois des Beaux-Arts* 55 (1980): 83–94.

Cifka 1990–1991
Cifka, Brigitta. "Josef Danhauser in Ungarn." *Mitteilungen der Österreichischen Galerie* nos. 78–79 (1990/1991): 16–46.

Cifka 1993a
Cifka, Brigitta. *XIX. századi Gyűjtemény*. Museum guide. Budapest: Museum of Fine Arts, 1993.

Cifka 1993b
Cifka, Brigitta. "'L'empereur François couronné roi de Hongrie' par J. P. Krafft." *Bulletin du Musée Hongrois des Beaux-Arts* 79 (1993): 49–61.

Cifka 1996a
Cifka, Brigitta. "Gemälde von Friedrich von Amerling in Museum der Bildenden Künste." *Bulletin du Musée Hongrois des Beaux-Arts* 84 (1996): 61–68.

Cifka 1996b
Cifka, Brigitta. "Il dipinto di Gaspare Landi nel Museo delle Belle Arti di Budapest." *Strenna Piacentina* (1996): 111–14.

Cifka 1996c
Cifka, Brigitta. "Egyedi példány? Ajánlás XIX. századi bronzszobrok gyűjtőinek." *Új Művészet* 7, no. 7 (1996): 39–41.

Cifka 2000
The 19ᵗʰ Century Exhibition. Edited by Brigitta Cifka. Budapest: Museum of Fine Arts, 2000.

Cifka 2003
Cifka, Brigitta. "Sir Joseph Noel Paton's Madonna with the sleeping Christ and the infant Saint John the Baptist." *Bulletin du Musée Hongrois des Beaux-Arts* 99 (2003): 93–99.

Clermont-Ferrand 2002
Roux, Nathalie and François Gibert. *Jean-François Millet: Voyages en Auvergne et Bourbonnais 1866–1868*. Exh. cat. Musée Roger-Quilliot, Clermont-Ferrand, 2002. Paris: Seuil, 2002.

Cologne 2024
Paris 1863–1874. Revolution in der Kunst. Vom Salon zum Impressionismus. Edited by Barbara Schaefer. Exh. cat. Wallraf-Richartz-Museum & Fondation Corboud, Cologne, 2024. Cologne: Wienand, 2024.

Coussange 1922
Coussange, Jacques de. "Stephan Sinding (1946–1922)." *Gazette des Beaux-Arts*, April 1922, 237–48.

Craske 1997
Craske, Matthew. *Art in Europe 1700–1830. A History of the Visual Art in an Era of Unprecedented Urban Economic Growth*. Oxford: Oxford University Press, 1997.

Crielesi 2019
Crielesi, Alberto. "Il pittore Filippo Agricola: alcuni inediti per un doveroso riscatto." *Strenna dei Romanisti*, 21 April 2019, 119–40.

Czére ed. 2006
Museum of Fine Arts. Highlights from the Collection. Edited by Andrea Czére. Budapest: Museum of Fine Arts, 2006.

Dalemans 2001
Dalemans, René. "Eugène Verboeckhoven." In Id., *Ombre et lumière. La Peinture en Belgique aux XVIIIe et XIXe siècles*, 50–51. Brussels: Éditions Artis-Historia, 2001.

Dana 1927
Dana, Robert W. *William Parsons Winchester Dana (1833–1927). Biographical note*. Unwin London: Brothers, 1927.

Dauberville and Dauberville 1968
Dauberville, Jean and Henry Dauberville. *Bonnard. Catalogue raisonné de l'œuvre peint (1906–1919)*. Éditions Bernheim-Jeune, Paris, 1968.

Dauberville and Dauberville 2010
Dauberville, Guy-Patrice and Michel Dauberville. *Renoir. Catalogue raisonné des tableaux, pastels, dessins et aquarelles (1895–1902)*. Vol. 3. Paris: Bernheim-Jeune, 2010.

De Graef 1898
De Graef, Gustave. *Nos artistes anversois*. Anvers: J. Theunis, 1898.

Dijon 1995
Budapest 1869–1914. Modernité hongroise et peinture européenne. Edited by László Beke and Emmanuel Starcky. Exh. cat. Musée des Beaux-Arts de Dijon, Dijon, 1995. Paris: Adam Biro, 1995.

Dordrecht 1998
Paul Joseph Constantin Gabriël, 1828–1903. Colorist van de Haagse School. Edited by Moniek Peters. Exh. cat. Dordrecht Museum, Dordrecht, 1998. Dordrecht: Dordrecht Museum / Kleef: Stichting B.C. Koekkoek-Huis / Zwolle: Waanders Uitgevers, 1998.

Dortu 1971
Dortu, Madeleine Grillaert. *Toulouse-Lautrec et son œuvre*. New York: Collectors Editions, 1971.

Dresden 1993
Gotthardt Kuehl, 1850–1915. Edited by Gerhard Gerkens – Horst Zimmermann. Exh. cat. Dresden, Staatliche Kunstsammlungen, 1993. Seeman, Leipzig, 1993.

Drewes 1994
Drewes, Franz Josef. *Hans Canon (1829–1885). Werkverzeichnis und Monographie*. Vols. I–II. Hildesheim: Olms, 1994.

Dux 1857
Dux, Adolf. *A Magyar Nemzeti Múzeum. Útmutató ennek Műkincsgyűjteményeiben*. Pest: Lampel Róbert, 1857.

Düsseldorf 1997
Andreas und Oswald Achenbach. "Das A und O der Landschaft." Edited by Martina Sitt. Exh. cat. Kunstmuseum Düsseldorf, Düsseldorf, 1997. Cologne: Wienand, 1997.

Eckhart 1986
Eckhardt, Mária. *Liszt Ferenc Emlékmúzeum.* Budapest: Liszt Ferenc Zeneművészeti Egyetem, 1986.

Eisenstadt 1995
Die Fürsten Esterházy. Magnaten, Diplomaten und Mäzene. Exh. cat. Esterházy Castle, Eisenstadt, 1995. Eisenstadt: Burgenländischen Landesregierung, 1995.

Énault 1883
Louis Énault, *Paris-Salon 1883,* Paris, E. Bernard et Cie, 1883.

Engels 1890
Engels, Eduard. "Walther Firle." *Kunst unserer Zeit. Eine Chronik des modernen Kunstlebens,* 1:113–42. Vol. 12. Munich: Franz Hanfstaengl, 1890.

Esche-Braunfels, 1993
Esche-Braunfels, Sigrid. *Adolf von Hildebrand.* Berlin: Deutscher Verlag für Kunstwissenschaft, 1993.

Eschenberg 1984
Eschenberg, Barbara. *Spätromantik und Realizmus. Vollständiger Katalog.* Munich: Hirmer Verlag, 1984.

Fahr-Becker 2004
Fahr-Becker, Gabriele. *Art Nouveau.* Hamburg, 2004.

Feuchtmüller 1983
Feuchtmüller, Rupert. "Johann Matthias Ranftl." In Österreichisches Biographisches Lexikon 1815–1950, 413–14. Vol. 8. Vienna: Verlag der Österreichischen Akademie der Wissenschaften, 1983.

Feuchtmüller 1987
Feuchtmüller, Rupert. *Friedrich Gauermann (1807–1862).* Rosenheim: Rosenheimer Verlagshaus, 1987.

Feuchtmüller 1996
Feuchtmüller, Rupert. *Ferdinand Georg Waldmüller.* Vienna/Munich: Verlag Christian Brandstätter, 1996.

Fierens 1931
Fierens, Paul. *Joseph Stevens 1816–1892.* Brussels: Édition des cahiers de Belgique, 1931.

Firle-Rudolf 2013
Firle-Rudolf, Angelika. "Walther Firle. Einst berühmt – heute vergessen." In *Das Künstlerdorf. Von Spitzweg bis Campendonk,* 54–67. Edited by Peter Amann and Bero von Fraunberg. Munich: Apex, 2013.

Fővárosi Lapok 1878
Fővárosi Lapok, 20 December 1878, 1421.

Fővárosi Lapok 1887
"Az őszi műtárlat II. Külföldi képek." *Fővárosi Lapok,* 9 October 1887, 2041–43.

Frankfurt 2020
En Passant. Impressionism in Sculpture. Edited by Alexander Eiling and Eva-Mongi Vollmer. Exh. cat. Städel Museum, Frankfurt am Main, 2020. Frankfurt am Main: Prestel, 2020.

Frankfurt–Birmingham–Stockholm 2000
SeelenReich. Die Entwicklung des deutschen Symbolismus 1870–1920. Exh. cat. Schirn Kunsthalle, Frankfurt; Birmingham Museum and Art Gallery, Birmingham; Prins Eugens Waldemarsudde, Stockholm, 2000. Munich/London: Prestel, 2000.

Frodl 2013
Frodl, Gerbert. *Hans Makart. Werkverzeichnis der Gemälde.* Weitra: Bibliothek der Provinz, 2013.

Fuchs 1975
Fuchs, Heinrich, *Eugen Jettel.* Vienna: privately published, 1975.

Fukuoka–Matsuyama–Tokyo 1994
The 19th Century European and Hungarian Paintings from the Budapest Museum of Fine Arts and the Hungarian National Gallery. Edited by Nobuyuki Senzoku. Exh. cat. Art Museum, Fukuoka; Ehime Prefectural Museum of Art, Matsuyama; The Bunkamura Museum of Art, Tokyo, 1994. Sendai: NHK Promotions, 1994.

Fülep 1988
Fülep, Lajos. *Egybegyűjtött írások I. Cikkek, tanulmányok 1902–1908.* Budapest: MTA Művészettörténeti Kutató Intézet, 1988.

Gaunt 1964
Gaunt, William. *Concise History of English Painting.* London: Thames and Hudson, 1964.

Genthon 1956
Genthon, István. "A Modern Külföldi Képtár." In *A Szépművészeti Múzeum (1906–1956),* 210–17. Edited by Ö. Gábor Pogány and Béla Bacher. Budapest: Képzőművészeti Alap Kiadóvállalata, 1956.

Geskó and Molnos 2003
Geskó, Judit and Péter Molnos. "Histoire des collections d'œuvres impressionnistes françaises en Hongrie." In *Budapest* 2003, 15–32.

Gonda 2001
Gonda, Zsuzsa. "A bécsi dioszkuroszok. Johann Nepomuk Ender és Thomas Ender művészi pályája." Johann Nepomuk Ender (1793–1854) Thomas Ender (1793–1875) emlékkiállítás Magyar Tudományos Akadémia Művészeti Gyűjtemény 2001. február–május, 11–84. Edited by Gábor György Papp. Exh. cat. Budapest: Magyar Tudományos Akadémia Művészettörténeti Kutató Intézete, 2001.

Grabner 2011
Grabner, Sabine. *Der Maler Josef Danhauser. Biedermeierzeit im Bild. Monografie und Werkverzeichnis.* Vienna: Böhlau Verlag, 2011.

Grabner et al. 2011
Grabner, Sabine, Marianne Hussl-Hörmann, Herbert Giese, Michael Kovacek, and Marie Luise Sternath. *Rudolf von Alt 1812–1905. Die Ölgemälde.* Vienna: Christian Brandstätter Verlag, 2011.

Grandesso 2003
Grandesso, Stefano. *Pietro Tenerani 1789–1869*. Milan: Silvana, 2003.

Grandesso 2008
Grandesso, Stefano. "Gaspare Landi e la riforma del gusto nella pittura storica." In *La pittura di storia in Italia. 1785–1870. Ricerche, quesiti, proposte*, 12–27. Edited by Giovanna Capitelli and Carla Mazzarelli. Cinisello Balsamo: Silvana Editoriale, 2008.

Grandmoulin 1951
Grandmoulin, Léandre. *Notice sur Égide Rombaux, membre de l'Académie*. Brussels: Académie Royale, 1951.

Graz 2014–2015
Grazer Kunst – Aufbruch in die Moderne? Paul Schad-Rossa und die Kunst in Graz. Edited by Gudrun Danzer and Peter Pakesch. Exh. cat. Neue Galerie Graz Universalmuseum Joanneum, Graz, 2014–2015. Graz: Neue Galerie Graz, 2014.

Graz 2023
Die Alpen im Blick. Der Landschaftsmaler Franz Steinfeld. Edited by Gudrun Danzer and Günther Holler-Schuster. Exh. cat. Neue Galerie Graz Universalmuseum Joanneum, Graz. Graz: Leykam, 2023.

Groningen–Amsterdam 1999–2000
Dekkers, Dieuwertje and Martha Kloosterboer. *Jozef Israëls 1824–1911*. Exh. cat. Groninger Museum, Groningen; Joods Historisch Museum, Amsterdam, 1999–2000. Zwolle: Waanders, 1999.

Gunma–Sapporo–Tokyo 1981
Exhibition of the Collection of the Budapest Museum of Fine Arts and the Hungarian National Gallery. Edited by Anna Szinyei Merse. Exh. cat. Prefectural Museum of Modern Art, Gunma; Tokyu Department Store, Sapporo; Tokyu Department Store, Nihonbasi, 1981. Tokyo: Tokyo Shimbun, 1981.

Hamburg 2015
Franz Ludwig Catel. Italienbilder der Romantik. Edited by Andreas Stolzenburg and Hubertus Gassner. Exh. cat. Hamburger Kunsthalle, Hamburg, 2015. Michael Imhof Verlag, Hamburg, 2015.

Hanfstaengl 1895
Die Kunst unserer Zeit. Eine Chronik. Modernen Kunstlebens XVIII. Munich: Franz Hanfstaengl Kunstverlag, 1895.

Härtl-Kasulke 1991
Härtl-Kasulke, Claudia. *Karl Theodor Piloty (1826–1886). Karl Theodor Pilotys Weg zur Historienmalerei 1826–1855*. Munich: Kommissionsverlag UNI-Druck, 1991.

Heijbroek and Wouthuysen 1999
Heijbroek, Jan Frederik and Ester L. Wouthuysen. *Portret van een kunsthandel. De firma Van Wisselingh en zijn compagnons, 1838-heden*. Zwolle: Waanders, 1999.

Heilmeyer 1902
Heilmeyer, Alexander. *Adolf von Hildebrand*. Leipzig: Hesse und Becker, 1902.

Helsinki 2008
Pekka Halonen. Edited by Anna-Maria von Bonsdorff. Exh. cat. Helsinki: Ateneumin taidemuseo, 2008.

Herding 1991
Herding, Klaus. *Courbet. To Venture Independence*. New Haven / London: Yale University Press, 1991.

Herterich 1909
Herterich, Ludwig von. "Aus meinem Leben." *Kunst und Künstler. Illustrierte Monatsschrift für bildende Kunst und Kunstgewerbe* 7 (1909): 239–49.

Hessky 2018
Hessky, Orsolya. "A zsánerfestészet és változatai." In *A magyar művészet a 19. században. Képzőművészet*, 692–703. Edited by József Sisa, Júlia Papp, and Erzsébet Király. Budapest: MTA Bölcsészettudományi Kutatóközpont / Osiris, 2018.

Hofmann 1987
Hofmann, Werner. *Das irdische Paradies: Motive und Ideen des 19. Jahrhunderts*. Munich, 1974.

Holland 1896
Holland, Hyacinth. "Voltz, Friedrich." In *Allgemeine Deutsche Biographie*, 276–80. Vol. 40. Leipzig: Duncker & Humblot, 1896.

Horváth 1924
Horváth, Henrik. "Magyar műpártolók a klasszicizmus és romanticizmus Rómájában." *Napkelet* 2, no. 8 (September–October 1924): 284–88.

Hostyn 1978
Hostyn, Norbert. "Kunstschilder Edouard Hamman. Bondige chronologie van zijn leven en werk." In *Ostendiana III*, 135–45. Oostende: Oostendse Heem- en Geschiedkundige Kring "De Plate", 1978.

Huard and Maillot 2000
Huard, Raymond and Pierre Maillot. *Jules Desbois (1851–1935). Une célébration tragique de la vie*. Paris: Le Cherche midi éditeur, 2000.

Illyés 2001
Illyés, Mária. *Œuvres françaises du XIXe siècle*. Les Collections du Musée des Beaux-Arts, Budapest 4. Translated by László Csejdy. Budapest: Musée des Beaux-Arts, 2001.

Jensen 1994
Jensen, Robert. *Marketing Modernism in Fin-de-Siècle Europe*. New Jersey: Princeton University Press, 1994.

Jensen 2007
Jensen, Robert. "Measuring Canons. Reflections on Innovation and the Nineteenth-Century Canon of European Art." In *Partisan Canons*, 27–54. Edited by Anna Brzyski. Durham: Duke University Press, 2007.

Jeszenszky 1952
Jeszenszky, Sándor. *Az Országos Szépművészeti Múzeum háborús veszteségeinek jegyzéke. Háborús műtárgyveszteség jegyzékek I. füzet.* Budapest: Múzeumok és Műemlékek Országos Központja, 1952.

Johnson 1986
Johnson, Lee. *The Paintings of Eugène Delacroix. A Critical Catalogue.* Vol. 3. Oxford: Clarendon Press, 1986.

Johnson and McConkey 2009
Johnson, Paul and Kenneth McConkey. *Alfred East. Lyrical Landscape Painter.* Bristol: Sansom & Company Ltd., 2009.

Kamm 1991
Kamm, Stefanie. *Wilhelm von Diez 1839–1907. Ein Künstler zwischen Historismus und Jugendstil.* Munich: Utzverlag, 1991.

Kaposy 1979
Kaposy, Veronika. "Madeleine Fidell-Beaufort – Janine Bailly-Herzberg: Daubigny." *Acta Historiae Artium* 25 (1979): 169–73.

Kaposy 1983
Kaposy, Veronika. "Dessins de Forain au musée des Beaux-Arts." *Bulletin du Musée Hongrois des Beaux-Arts* 60–61 (1983): 133–34.

Kapp 1911
Kapp, Julius. "Franz Liszt-Bildnisse." *Blätter der Gemäldekunde* 7, no. 3 (September–October 1911): 37–43.

Kastel 1983
Kastel, Ingrid. *Franz Eybl 1806–1880.* Diss. Universität Wien, Vienna, 1983.

Kečkemet 1969
Kečkemet, Duško. *Ivan Meštrović. Der einzige Weg Künstler zu werden ist arbeiten.* Zagreb: Spektar, 1969.

Keil 2009
Keil, Robert. *Heinrich Friedrich Füger 1751–1818. Nur wenigen ist es vergönnt das Licht der Wahrheit zu sehen.* Vienna: Amartis, 2009.

Kokkinen 2019
Kokkinen, Nina. *Totuudenetsijät. Vuosisadanvaihteen okkulttuuri ja moderni henkisyys Akseli Gallen-Kallelan, Pekka Halosen ja Hugo Simbergin taiteessa.* Turku: Turun Yliopisto, 2019.

Kotoučová 2010
Kotoučová, Veronika. *Eugen Jettel (1845–1901).* MA diss. Palacký University, Olmütz, 2010.

Kovács 1957
Kovács, Éva. "Les tableaux de Corot en Hongrie." *Bulletin du Musée National Hongrois des Beaux-Arts* 11 (1957): 85–91.

Kovács 1988
Kovács, Mária. "Des manuscrits de Liszt à Morlanwelz." *Studia Musicologica Academiae Scientiarum Hungaricae* 30, nos. 1–4 (1988): 321–32.

Kovács 2015–2016
Kovács, Anna Zsófia. "L'*Ondine* de Jules Lefebvre: un nu académique français dans les collections du Musée des Beaux-Arts." *Bulletin du Musée Hongrois des Beaux-Arts* 120–121 (2015–2016): 147–64.

Kovács 2017
Kovács, Anna Zsófia. "*Le déjeuner dans l'atelier* de Victor Giraud." *Bulletin du Musée Hongrois des Beaux-Arts* 122 (2017): 187–205.

Kovács 2018
Kovács, Anne Sophie. "*Haute école, par Mlle Élisa de Vienne* : Une amazone moderne d'Edmond Georges Grandjean." *Bulletin du Musée Hongrois des Beaux-Arts* 123 (2018): 147–68.

Kovács 2019
Kovács, Anna Zsófia. "*Aurore* de Paul Sinibaldi: allégorie insondable ou métaphore politique?" *Bulletin du Musée Hongrois des Beaux-Arts* 124 (2019): 119–35.

Kovács 2020
Kovács, Anna Zsófia. "*Les Baigneuses* d'Henry Lerolle." *Bulletin du Musée Hongrois des Beaux-Arts* 125 (2020): 207–28.

Kovács 2021
Kovács, Éva. "Black Bodies, White Bodies – 'Gypsy' Images in Central Europe at the Turn of the Twentieth Century (1880–1920)." *Critical Romani Studies* (June 2021): 72–93.

Kovács 2021–2022
Kovács, Anna Zsófia. "Auguste Feyen-Perrin, *La pêche à pied. Souvenir de Cancale.*" *Bulletin du Musée Hongrois des Beaux-Arts* 126 (2021–2022): 133–50.

Kovács 2023
Kovács, Anna Zsófia. "*La Liseuse.* Redécouverte d'une peinture de Jacques-Émile Blanche." *Bulletin du Musée Hongrois des Beaux-Arts* 128 (2023): 233–46.

Kovács and Lespinasse 2018
Kovács, Anna Zsófia and François Lespinasse. "De Laborne à Lebourg: un paysage d'Albert Lebourg redécouvert au Musée des Beaux-Arts de Budapest." *Bulletin du Musée Hongrois des Beaux-Arts* 123 (2018): 223–30.

Körner 2013
Körner, Stefan. *Nikolaus II. Esterházy und die Kunst. Biografie eines manischen Sammlers.* Vienna/Cologne/Weimar: Böhlau Verlag, 2013.

Kőrösné Mikis 2016
Kőrösné Mikis, Márta. "Család-történet és életpálya." In *Diescher József. Építészet és mesterség,* 11–31. Edited by Violetta Hidvégi and Katalin Marótzy. Budapest: Budapest Főváros Levéltára, 2016.

Kraševac 2017
Kraševac, Irena. "'To Art Its Freedom.' Gustav Klimt and Ivan Mestrović." In *The Challenge of Modernism. Vienna and Zagreb around 1900,* 112–29. Edited by Stella Rollig, Irena Kraševac, and Petra Vugrinec. Exh. cat. Belvedere, Vienna, 2017. Vienna: Belvedere Publications, 2017.

Kruse 1901
Kruse, John. *Petter Gabriel Wickenberg 1812–1846.* Stockholm: Ivar Haeggström, 1901.

Kunkel 2019
Kunkel, Alexander. "Der König der Löwen. Die exotische Tierwelt des Paul Meyerheim." *RIZE Magazine* 15 (2019): 66–71.

Kunz 1913
Kunz, George Frederick. "The Late Louis Oscar Roty: His Life Work and His Influence on the Past and Future of Medallic Art." *American Journal of Numismatics (1897–1924)* 47 (1913): 93–119.

Lafenestre 1908
Lafenestre, Georges. *L'Œuvre de Ernest Barrias.* Paris: Renouard, 1908.

Lafuente Ferrari 1949
Lafuente Ferrari, Enrique. *Obras de juventud de Zuloaga.* Arte Español. Vol. 18. Madrid: Sociedad Española de Amigos del Arte, 1949.

Lauzac 1859–1861
Lauzac, Henry, Lépaulle. In *Galerie historique et critique du dix-neuvième siècle.* Vol. 2. 515–17. Paris: La galerie historique, 1859–1861.

Lerolle 2022
Lerolle, Aggy: *Henry Lerolle. Paris 1848–1929.* Paris: Société des amis d'Henry Lerolle, 2022.

***Les Lucs-sur-Boulogne – Paris* 2013**
Félicie de Fauveau, l'amazone de la sculpture. Edited by Jacques de Caso and Sylvain Bellenger. Exh. cat. Historial de la Vendée, Les Lucs-sur-Boulogne – Musée d'Orsay, Paris, 2013. Paris: Gallimard, 2013.

Lespinasse 2023
Lespinasse, François. "Poses, mon beau village de Paul Sinibaldi à Eugène Tirvert." *Les Amis de l'École de Rouen*, November 2023. https://peintresecolerouen.blogspot.com/2023/11/poses-mon-beau-village-de-paul.html (last accessed: 10 November 2024).

***Let me See!* 2015**
Let me See! Guide on Guided Tours. Edited by Edina Deme. Budapest: Museum of Fine Arts, 2015.

***Linz* 2013**
Schultes, Lothar. *Johann Baptist Reiter.* Exh. cat. Nordico Stadtmuseum, Linz; Schlossmuseum Linz, Linz, 2013. Salzburg: Pustet, 2013.

***Linz–Grafenegg* 1990**
Bilder des Lebens. Johann Baptist Reiter und der Realismus des 19. Jahrhunderts. Edited by Lothar Schultes. Exh. cat. Museum Francisco Carolium, Linz; Schloss Grafenegg, Grafenegg, 1990. Linz: Oberösterreichisches Landesmuseum, 1990.

Lippincott and Blühm 2006
Lippincott, Louise, and Andreas Blühm. *Fierce Friends. Artists and Animals, 1750–1900.* Amsterdam: Merill, 2006.

***London* 2010**
Treasures from Budapest. European Masterpieces from Leonardo to Schiele. Ed. David Ekserdjian. Exh. cat. Royal Academy of Arts, London, 2010. London: Royal Academy of Arts, 2010.

***London – New York* 2000**
1900. Art at the Crossroads. Edited by Robert Rosenblum, MaryAnne Stevens, and Ann Dumas. Exh. cat. Royal Academy of Arts, London; Solomon R. Guggenheim Museum, New York, 2000. New York: Abrams, 2000.

***London–Leicester–Liverpool* 1974–1975**
British Sporting Painting 1650–1850. Introduction by Oliver Millar. Exh. cat. Hayward Gallery, London; Leicestershire Museum and Art Gallery, Leicester; Walker Art Gallery, Liverpool, 1974–1975. London: The Art Council of Great Britain, 1974.

Losonczi 1892
Losonczi Lipót. "A Műcsarnok Téli tárlata." *Budapesti Szemle* 69, no. 181 (1892): 119–28.

Ludwig 1981
Ludwig, Horst. *Münchner Maler im 19. Jahrhundert.* Vol. 1. Munich: Bruckmann, 1981.

Luger 1999
Luger, Petra R. *Mathias Schmid. Ein tiroler Maler in München 1835–1923.* Innsbruck: Verlagsanstalt Tyrolia, 1999.

***Madrid* 2017**
Obras maestras de Budapest. Del Renacimiento a las Vanguardias. Edited by Guillermo Solana and Mar Borobia. Exh. cat. Museo Thyssen-Bornemisza, Madrid, 2017. Madrid: Museo Thyssen-Bornemisza, 2017.

***Madrid–Bilbao* 1996–1997**
Obras maestras del arte español: Museo de Bellas Artes de Budapest. Exh. cat. Banco Bilbao Vizcaya, Madrid; Museo de Bellas Artes, Bilbao, 1996–1997. Madrid: Banco Bilbao Vizcaya, 1996.

Mai 1998
Mai, Ekkehard. "Der Sehnsucht Traum und Wirklichkeit – Oswald Achenbach Zwischen Romantik, Realismus und Salon." In *Düsseldorf* 1997, 43–56.

***Mainz* 2012**
Shur, Norbert, et al. *Die Nazarener – vom Tiber an den Rhein: Drei Malerschulen des 19. Jahrhundwerts.* Exh. cat. Landesmuseum, Mainz, 2012. Regensburg: Schnell und Steiner, 2012.

Makela 1990
Makela, Maria. *The Munich Secession. Art and Artists in Turn-of-the-Century Munich.* Princeton: Princeton University Press, 1990.

***Malmaison–Nancy* 2006**
Jean-Baptiste Isabey, Portraitiste de l'Europe. Exh. cat. Musée national des châteaux de Malmaison et de Bois-Préau, Malmaison; Musée des Beaux-Arts de Nancy, Nancy, 2006. Paris: Réunion des musées nationaux, 2006.

Mánfai 2017
Mánfai, Melinda. "Egy angol festőről, aki ausztrál – Rupert C. W. Bunny (1864–1947) magyar kapcsolatai." *MúzeumCafé* 61, no. 5 (October–November 2017): 200–209.

Mascalchi 2012
Mascalchi, Silvia. *Félicie de Fauveau. Una scultrice romantica da Parigi a Firenze*. Florence: Leo S. Olschki, 2012.

Masłowski 1973
Masłowski, Maciej. *Józef Chełmoński*. Warsaw: Wydawnictwa Aertystyczne i Filmowe, 1973.

Matits 1994
Matits, Ferenc. "A Szépművészeti Múzeum 19. századi horvát festményeinek kapcsolata egy zágrábi képciklussal." *Pavilon. Építészet–Művészet–Történet*, no. 9 (1994): 39–41.

Matits 1995
Matits, Ferenc. "19. századi festmények a Szépművészeti Múzeumban." In Budapest 1995–1996, 65–71.

Matits and Sillevis 1992
Matits, Ferenc, and John Sillevis. "Haagse School in Hongaars bezit." *Pulchri* 20, no. 1 (1992): 14–15.

Mátray 1846
Mátray, Gábor. *Pyrker János László egri patriarcha-érsek képtára a' Magyar Nemzeti Muzeum képcsarnokában*. Pest: Trattner és Károlyi Nyomda, 1846.

McConkey 2013
McConkey, Kenneth. "Every Picture was a Design. The poesie of Alfred East (1844–1913)." *The British Art Journal* 14, no. 1 (2013): 24–32.

Meier-Graefe 1904
Meier-Graefe, Julius. *Entwicklungsgeschichte der modernen Kunst*. Stuttgart: Kessinger, 1904.

Meller 1915
Meller, Simon. *Az Esterházy Képtár története*. Budapest: Országos Magyar Szépművészeti Múzeum, 1915.

Meunier **1905**
Constantin Meunier et son œuvre. Paris: Éditions de la Plume, 1905.

Micke-Broniarek and Głowacki 2024
Micke-Broniarek, Ewa, and Wojciech Głowacki. *Józef Chełmoński, 1849–1914*. Vols. 1–2. Warsaw: Muzeum Narodowe w Warszawie, 2024.

Migeon 1902
Migeon, Gaston. "René Ménard." *Art et décoration* 11 (January-February 1902): 101–12.

Milan **2014**
Segantini. Il ritorno a Milano. Edited by Annie-Paule Quinsac. Exh. cat. Palazzo Reale, Milan, 2014. Milan: Skira, 2014.

Miquel and Miquel 2006
Miquel, Pierre and Rolande. *Narcisse Diaz de la Peña*. Vol. 1. Paris: ACR Édition, 2006.

Molnos 2018
Molnos, Péter. *Lost Heritage. Hungarian Art Collectors in the Twentieth Century*. Budapest: Kieselbach Gallery and Auction House, 2018.

Montargis **2010**
Lemeux-Fraitot, Sidonie, and Stephen Bann. À l'épreuve du noir. *Girodet et la lithographie*. Exh. cat. Musée Girodet, Montargis, 2010–2011. Montargis: Musée Girodet, 2010.

Montrosier 1882
Montrosier, Eugène. *Les Artistes modernes*. Vol. 3. Paris: Hachette, 1882.

Moser-Ernst and Marinelli 2023
Moser-Ernst, Sybille, and Ursula Marinelli. *Mathias Schmid. Gegen den Strich gemalt*. Innsbruck: Tyrolia Verlag, 2023.

Munich **1979**
Die Münchner Schule 1850–1914. Edited by Eberhard Ruhmer. Exh. cat. Neue Pinakothek, Munich, 1979. Munich: Bayerische Staatsgemäldesammlungen, 1979.

Munich **1986–1987**
Franz von Lenbach 1836–1904. Edited by Winfried Ranke and Ingeborg Geith. Exh. cat. Städtische Galerie im Lenbachhaus, Munich, 1986–1987. Munich: Prestel, 1987.

Munich **2003**
Großer Auftritt. Piloty und die Historienmalerei. Edited by Reinhold Baumstark and Frank Büttner. Exh. cat. Neue Pinakothek, Munich, 2003. Cologne: DuMont, 2003.

Munich **2008–2009**
Franz von Stuck. Meisterwerke der Malerei. Edited by Margot T. Brandlhuber and Michael Buhrs. Exh. cat. Museum Villa Stuck, Munich, 2008–2009. Munich: Hirmer, 2008.

Museum Guide **2018**
Museum Guide – Hungarian National Gallery. Museum of Fine Arts – Hungarian National Gallery, Budapest, 2018.

Muther 1907
Muther, Richard. *The History of Modern Painting*. Vol. 3. London: J. M. Dent & Co. / New York: E. P. Dutton & Co., 1907.

Müller 1903
Müller, Sigurd. "Viggo Johansen." In *Kunst. Organ for dansk kunst og kunsthaandvaerk*. Copenhagen: A. Jacobsen, 1903.

New York **1963**
Scolari Barr, Margaret. *Medardo Rosso*. Exh. cat. The Museum of Modern Art, New York, 1963. New York: The Museum of Modern Art, 1963.

Niederhauser and Sargina 1979
Niederhauser, Emil, and Ludmilla Sargina. *Az orosz kultúra a XIX. században. Európa nagy korszakai*. Budapest: Gondolat, 1979.

Nora-Milin, Lamarre, and Rapetti 2008
Nora-Milin, Véronique, Alice Lamarre, and Rodolphe Rapetti. *Eugène Carrière 1849–1906. Catalogue raisonné de l'œuvre peint*. Paris: Gallimard, 2008.

Novotny 1954
Novotny, Fritz. *Der Maler Anton Romako*. Vienna/Munich: Anton Schroll, 1954.

Nuova Enciclopedia Popolare Italiana 1857–1864
Supplemento Perenne alla Nuova Enciclopedia Popolare Italiana. Vol. 1. Turin: Unione Tipografico-Editrice, 1857–1864.

Nuremberg 1985–1986
Meisterwerke europäischer Malerei aus ungarischen Museen. Edited by Carlo Pirovano and Gabriella Borsano. Exh. cat. Germanisches Nationalmuseum, Nuremberg, 1985–1986. Milan: Electa International, 1985.

Nyerges 2008
Nyerges, Éva. *Spanish Paintings. The Collections of the Museum of Fine Arts, Budapest.* Budapest: Museum of Fine Arts, 2008.

Offenstadt 1999
Offenstadt, Patrick. *Jean Béraud 1849–1935. The Belle Époque. A Dream of Times Gone By. Catalogue raisonné.* Cologne: Taschen / Wildenstein Institute, 1999.

Ornans 2011
Thomas-Maurin, Frédérique, Julie Delmas, and Élise Boudon. *Courbet, Clésinger. Œuvres croisées.* Exh. cat. Musée Gustave Courbet, Ornans, 2011. Besançon: Éditions du Sekoya, 2011.

Osborn 1904
Osborn, Max. "Stephan Sinding, Sculptor." *Brush and Pencil* 14, no. 1 (April 1904): 1–9.

Osten-Sacken 2023
Osten-Sacken, Caroline von der. *Die Malerfamilie Tischbein. Geschichte eines Aufstiegs.* Petersberg: Michael Imhof Verlag, 2023.

Ostini 1902
Ostini, Fritz von. "Ernst Zimmermann." In *Die Kunst unserer Zeit. Eine Chronik des modernen Kunstlebens* 13, no. 2 (1902): 113–32.

Ostini 1906
Ostini, Fritz von. *Wilhelm von Kaulbach: mit 143 Abbildungen nach Gemälden und Zeichnungen.* Künstler Monographien. Leipzig: Velhagen und Klasing, 1906.

Ottino della Chiesa 1968
Ottino della Chiesa, Angela. "Luigi Bisi." In *Dizionario Biografico degli Italiani.* Vol. 10. Rome: Istituto della Enciclopedia Italiana, 1968. https://www. treccani.it/enciclopedia/luigi-bisi_(Dizionario-Biografico) (last accessed: 1 November 2024).

Pálinkás 1942
Pálinkás, László. "Marco Casagrande nella storia delle relazioni artistiche italo-ungheresi del secolo XIX." *Olasz Szemle / Studi Italiani in Ungheria* 1, no. 5 (September–October 1942): 733–52.

Pandur 1997
Pandur, Ildikó. "Les œuvres d'Alexandre Charpentier et le musée des Arts décoratifs de Budapest." *Ars Decorativa* 16 (1997): 111–42.

Papp 1997
Papp, Katalin. "Edouard von Engerth: Le Couronnement de François-Joseph Ier à Buda en 1867." *Bulletin du Musée Hongrois des Beaux-Arts* 87 (1997): 79–88.

Paris 1994–1995
Delacroix. Le Voyage au Maroc. Edited by Brahim Alaoui. Exh. cat. Institut du Monde Arabe, Paris, 1994–1995. Paris: Flammarion, 1995.

Paris 1997
Alfred De Dreux. Le Cheval, passion d'un dandy parisien. Edited by Marie-Christine Renauld. Exh. cat. Fondation Mona Bismarck, Paris, 1997. Paris: Action artistique de la ville de Paris, 1997.

Paris 2005
Girodet 1767–1824. Edited by Sylvain Bellenger. Exh. cat. Musée du Louvre, Paris, 2005. Paris: Gallimard, 2005.

Paris 2008
Charpentier-Darcy, Madeleine, Emmanuelle Héran, Marie-Madeleine Massé, and Dominique Morel. *Alexandre Charpentier (1856–1909). Naturalisme et Art nouveau.* Exh. cat. Musée d'Orsay, Paris, 2008. Paris: Musée d'Orsay, 2008.

Paris 2012
Chevillot, Catherine, and Édouard Papet. *Au creux de la main. La médaille en France aux XIXe et XXe siècles.* Exh. cat. Musée d'Orsay, Paris, 2012. Paris: Skira / Flammarion, 2012.

Paris 2021
Harbo Lehmann, Mette, and Dominique Lobstein. *L'Heure bleue de Peder Severin Krøyer.* Exh. cat. Musée Marmottan Monet, Paris, 2021. Paris: Hazan, 2021.

Paris–Dordrecht 2019–2020
Willem Bastiaan Tholen (1860–1931). Een gelukkige natuur. Edited by Marieke Jooren. Exh. cat. Fondation Custodia, Paris; Dordrechts Museum, Dordrecht, 2019–2020. Bussum: Uitgeverij Thoth, 2019.

Paris – New York 1983
Cachin, Françoise, Charles S. Moffett, Michel Melot, and Juliet Wilson-Bareau. *Manet 1832–1883.* Exh. cat. Grand Palais, Paris; Metropolitan Museum of Art, New York, 1983. New York: Metropolitan Museum of Art, 1983.

Paris – New York 2018–2019
Delacroix, 1798–1863. Edited by Sébastien Allard and Côme Fabre. Exh. cat. Musée du Louvre, Paris; The Metropolitan Museum, New York, 2018–2019. Paris: Éditions du Louvre / Hazan, 2018.

Paris–Brussels–Hamburg 1979–1980
Fernand Khnopff 1858–1921. Edited by Frans Boenders, Hubert Juin, Günter Metken et al. Exh. cat. Musée des Arts décoratifs, Paris; Musée Royaux des Beaux-Arts de Belgique, Brussels; Kunsthalle, Hamburg, 1979–1980. Brussels: Ministère de la Communauté française de Belgique, 1979.

Paris–Washington–Berlin
1996–1997
*Adolph Menzel 1815–1905.
Between Romanticism and
Impressionism.* Edited by Claude
Keisch and Marie Ursula Riemann-
Reyher. Exh. cat. Musée d'Orsay,
Paris; National Gallery of Art,
Washington; Alte Nationalgalerie,
Berlin, 1996–1997. New Haven/
London: Yale University Press,
1996.

***Passau–Munich** 1993–1994*
*Franz von Stuck. Gemälde, Zeich-
nung, Plastik aus Privatbesitz.
Ausstellung zum 130. Geburtstag.*
Edited by Gerwald Sonnberger.
Exh. cat. Museum Moderner
Kunst, Passau; Villa Stuck,
Munich, 1993–1994. Passau:
Museum Moderner Kunst, 1993.

Pasteiner 1888
Pasteiner, Gyula. "A
képzőművészeti társulat őszi
tárlata." *Budapesti Szemle* 53,
no. 133 (1888): 138–51.

Peer 2021
Peer, Peter. "A Master
of Austrian Landscape Painting
on International Paths." In *Alfred
Zoff. Die Faszination des Meeres,*
12–24. Exh. cat. Galerie & Edition
Martin Suppan, Vienna, 2022.
Vienna: Edition Suppan, 2021.

Peregriny 1900
Peregriny, János. *A Magyar
Nemzeti Múzeum Képtárának
leíró katalógusa.* Budapest:
Athenaeum, 1900.

Peregriny 1909
Peregriny, János. *A Magyar
Nemzeti Múzeum képtárának
festményei és grafikai állaga,
2. rész. 1–2.* füzet. Budapest:
Athenaeum, 1909.

Peregriny 1914–1915
Peregriny, János. *Az Országos
Magyar Szépművészeti Múzeum
állagai. 3. rész. Új szerzemények.*
1–3. füzet. Budapest: Országos
Magyar Szépművészeti Múzeum,
1914–1915.

Petneki 2018
Petneki, Áron. „*Oh az ecset
nagy szónok!" Jan Matejko és
a magyarok.* Budapest: Rézbong
Kiadó, 2018.

Petrovics 1918
Petrovics, Elek. "A Szépművészeti
Múzeum újabb szerzeményei."
*Az Országos Magyar Szépművé-
szeti Múzeum Évkönyvei,* no. 1
(1918): 191–92.

Petrovics 1921
Petrovics, Elek. "Múzeumok
és gyűjtők." *A Műbarát,*
15 February 1921, 2–4.

Petrovics 1926
A modern szoborgyűjtemény.
Foreword by Elek Petrovics.
Budapest: Országos Magyar
Szépművészeti Múzeum, 1926.

Petrovics 1927
"A Szépművészeti Múzeum
1924–1926-ban." In *Az Országos
Magyar Szépművészeti Múzeum
Évkönyvei,* 197–217. Vol. IV. 1924–
1926. Edited by Elek Petrovics.
Budapest: Országos Magyar
Szépművészeti Múzeum, 1927.

Peyrer-Heimstätt 1995
Peyrer-Heimstätt, Alexandra.
"Der Wiener Maler John Quincy
Adams." Thesis, Universität Wien,
Vienna, 1995.

Piccioni 2011
Piccioni, Matteo. "Pio Joris
(1843–1921) e la pittura a Roma
nel secondo Ottocento." *Storia
dell'arte* 28, no. 128 (2011):
122–48.

**Pissarro and Durand-Ruel
Snollaerts 2005**
Pissarro, Joachim, and Claire
Durand-Ruel Snollaerts. *Pissarro.
Catalogue critique des peintures –
Pissarro. Critical Catalogue
of Paintings.* 3 vols. Paris:
Wildenstein Institute / Milan:
Skira, 2005.

Poletti and Richarme 2000
Poletti, Michel, and Alain
Richarme. *Barye. Catalogue
raisonné des sculptures.* Paris:
Gallimard, 2000.

Poort 1989
Poort, Johan. *Hendrik
Willem Mesdag (1831–1915).
Oeuvrecatalogus.* Wassenaar:
Stichting Mesdag Documentatie,
1989.

Potthoff 1995
Potthoff, Mechthild. *Oswald
Achenbach. Sein künstlerisches
Wirken zur Hochzeit des
Bürgertums. Studien zu Leben
und Werk.* Cologne/Berlin:
P. Hanstein, 1995.

Probszt 1927
Probszt, Günther. *Friedrich von
Amerling. Der Altmeister der
Wiener Porträtmalerei.* Zurich/
Leipzig/Vienna: Amalthea-Verlag,
1927.

Pudles 1985
Pudles, Lynne. "The Symbolist
Work of George Minne."
Art Journal 45, no. 2 (1985):
120–29.

Pulszky 1875
Pulszky, Ferenc. "A muzeumokról."
Budapesti Szemle, no. 8 (1875):
242–57. Republished in *Pulszky
Ferencz kisebb dolgozatai,* edited
by Antal Dr. Lábán, 218–40.
Budapest: Magyar Tudományos
Akadémia, 1914.

Quinsac 1982
Quinsac, Annie-Paule. *Segantini.
Catalogo generale 2.* Milan:
Electa, 1982.

**Reiter and Husslein-Arco eds.
2010**
*Anton Romako, Pionier und
Aussenseiter der Malerei des
19. Jahrhunderts. Monografie
mit Werkverzeichnis.* Edited
by Cornelia Reiter and Agnes
Husslein-Arco. Weitra:
Bibliothek der Provinz, 2010.

Renauld 2008
Renauld, Marie-Christine.
*L'Univers d'Alfred de Dreux 1810–
1860, suivi du catalogue raisonné.*
Arles: Actes Sud, 2008.

Reyero 1999
Reyero, Carlos. "El siglo más
grande de todos los siglos.
La época de Carlos V y Felipe II
en la pintura de historia." In *La
época de Carlos V y Felipe II en
la pintura de historia del siglo XIX,*
25–86. Exh. cat. Museo Nacional
de Escultura Valladolid, Valladolid,
1999. Toledo: Sociedad Estatal
Centenario Felipe II y Carlos V,
1999.

Ricordi autobiografici 1900
*Ricordi autobiografici di Adamo
Tadolini scultore (vissuto dal
1788 al 1868).* Edited by Giulio
Tadolini. Rome: Tipografia di Balbi
Giovanni, 1900.

Robaut 1905
Robaut, Alfred. *L'Œuvre de Corot.
Catalogue raisonné et illustré.*
Vol. 3. Paris: H. Floury, 1905.

Roberts and Molines online
Roberts, Jane, and Muriel
Molines. *Jacques-Émile Blanche
1861–1942. Catalogue raisonné.*
https://www.jeblanche-
catalogue.com/fr/jacques-
emile-blanche-1512-lucie-
esnault-lisant (last accessed:
14 November 2023).

Rolla 1971
Rolla, Margit. "A 'Liipola-Múzeum'
Finnországban." *Művészet* 12,
no. 7 (1971): 10–11.

Rome 1989–1990
*Bertel Thorvaldsen 1770–1844
scultore danese a Roma.*
Edited by Elena Di Majo et al.
Exh. cat. Galleria Nazionale d'Arte
Moderna, Rome, 1989–1990.
Rome: De Luca, 1989.

Rome 2003
Rome–Venice 2010
*Giacomo Favretto. Venezia,
fascino e seduzione.* Edited by
Paolo Serafini. Exh. cat. Chiostro
del Bramante, Rome; Museo
Correr, Venice, 2010. Milan:
Silvana Editoriale, 2010.

Rosenblum and Janson 1984
Rosenblum, Robert, and Horst
Woldemar Janson. *Art of the
Nineteenth Century. Painting
and Sculpture.* London:
Thames and Hudson, 1984.

Rosenhagen 1905
Rosenhagen, Hans. *Bildwerke
von August Gaul.* Berlin:
Paul Cassirer, 1905.

Rouart and Wildenstein 1975
Rouart, Denis, and Daniel
Wildenstein. Édouard Manet.
Catalogue raisonné. Vol. 1.
Peintures. Lausanne/Paris:
La Bibliothèque des Arts, 1975.

Sandoz 1974
Sandoz, Marc. *Théodore Chassériau 1819–1856. Catalogue raisonné des peintures et estampes.*
Paris: Arts et métiers graphiques,
1974.

Schmit 1973
Schmit, Robert. *Eugène Boudin
1824–1898. Catalogue raisonné
de l'œuvre.* Paris: Galerie Schmit,
1973.

Schorske 1979
Schorske, Carl E. *Fin-de-siècle
Vienna. Politics and Culture.*
New York: Alfred A. Knopf, 1979.

Serafini 2006
Serafini, Paolo. *Il Pittore Luigi
Nono (1850–1918). Catalogo
Ragionato dei dipinti e disegni.*
Vol. 2. Turin: Umberto Alemandi,
2006.

Sernagiotto 1881
Sernagiotto, Luigi. *Natale e Felice
Schiavoni. Vita, opere, tempi.*
Venice: Longo, 1881.

Sinay and Sinay 2017
Sinay, Jacques and Thibault Sinay:
*Catalogue raisonné des oeuvres
de Jules Adler.* Paris, 2017.

Shinjuku et al. 1992–1993
*European Landscapes from
Raphael to Pissarro. Museum of
Fine Arts Budapest, Hungarian
National Gallery.* Edited by Ildikó
Ember. Exh. cat. Mitsukoshi
Museum of Art, Shinjuku; Ishi-
bashi Museum of Art, Kurume;
Kintetsu Nara Hall, Nara; Yamaga-
ta Museum of Art, Yamagata;
Sogo Museum of Art, Yokohama,
1992–1993. Tokyo: Nihon Keizai
Shimbun, 1992.

Smith 1992
Smith, Bill. *D. Y. Cameron.
The Visions of the Hills.* Edinburgh:
Atelier Books, 1992.

Solvay 1906
Solvay, Lucien. *Le Paysage et les
paysagistes. Théodore Verstraete.*
Brussels: G. Van Oest & Cie, 1906.

Soós 1963
Soós, Gyula. "Sept bas-reliefs
en plâtre de Thorvaldsen." *Bulletin
du Musée Hongrois des Beaux-
Arts* 23 (1963): 97–100.

Soós 1964a
Soós, Jules. "Les nouvelles
acquisitions de la Collection
des Sculptures Modernes."
*Bulletin du Musée Hongrois des
Beaux-Arts* 25 (1964): 107–12.

Soós 1964b
Soós, Gyula. *A XIX–XX. századi
szoborkiállítás. A Szépművészeti
Múzeum állandó kiállításainak
ismeretterjesztő katalógusai.*
Budapest: Szépművészeti
Múzeum, 1964.

Spassky et al. 1985
Spassky, Natalie, et al. *American
Paintings in The Metropolitan
Museum of Art.* Vol. 2. New York:
Metropolitan Museum of Art,
1985.

Stockholm 1976
Lindwall, Bo, Georg Nordensvan,
and Carl August Adlersparre.
Pehr Wickenberg. Exh. cat.
Prins Eugens Waldemarsudde,
Stockholm, 1976. Stockholm,
1976.

Stoll 1923
Stoll, Adolf. *Der Maler Joh.
Friedrich August Tischbein und
seine Familie. Ein Lebensbild nach
den Aufzeichungen seiner Tochter
Caroline.* Stuttgart: Strecker
und Schröder, 1923.

Storaas 1994
Storaas, Reidar. *Poesi i stein og
bronse. Bilethoggaren Ingebrigt
Vik.* Bergen: Nord 4 bokverksted,
1994.

Story 1895
Story, Alfred Thomas. *The Life
and Work of Sir Joseph Paton
Her Majesty's Limner for Scotland.*
London: Art Journal Office, 1895.

Stransky 1916
Stransky, Josef. *Modern Paintings
by German and Austrian Masters.*
New York: [The De Vinne Press],
1916.

Svanholm 2004
Svanholm, Lise. *Northern
Light. The Skagen Painters.*
Copenhagen: Gyldendal, 2004.

Szmrecsányi 1911
Szmrecsányi, Miklós.
"Visszapillantás az Országos
Magyar Képzőművészeti Társulat
50 éves múltjára." *Művészet* 10,
no. 3 (1911): 144–48.

Szombathely 2001
*Antique Background. Ancient
Themes and Motifs in the
European and Hungarian Fine
Arts in the 16th–19th century.*
Edited by Mónika Zsámbéky.
Exh. cat. Szombathelyi Képtár,
Szombathely, 2001. Szombathely:
Szombathelyi Képtár, 2001.

Szombathely et al. 2005–2006
Rejtett szépségek. A nő ábrá-
zolása a 19. század kezdetétől
a századfordulóig. Festmények,
szobrok, grafikák a 100 éves
Szépművészeti Múzeum gyűjteményéből. Ed. Varga Ágota.
Exh. cat. Szombathely, Szombathely Gallery – Kaposvár, Vaszary
Gallery – Debrecen, Kölcsey
Congressional Centre – Kecske-
mét, Cifrapalota – Szeged, Móra
Ferenc Museum, 2005–2006.
Museum of Fine Arts, Budapest,
2005

Szvoboda Dománszky 2007
Szvoboda Dománszky, Gabriella.
*A Pesti Műegylet története.
A képzőművészeti nyilvánosság
kezdetei a XIX. században
Pest-Budán.* Miskolc: Miskolci
Egyetem, 2007.

Szvoboda Dománszky 2015
Szvoboda Dománszky, Gabriella.
"Külföldi kiállítók megjelenése
Pesten, 1840–1866." *Tanulmá-
nyok Budapest múltjából* 40
(2015): 19–78.

Szvoboda Dománszky 2016
Szvoboda Dománszky, Gabriella.
*Nézők és képek Pest-Budán.
A Pesti Műegylet története és
a képzőművészeti nyilvánosság
kezdetei a 19. században.*
Budapest: Kovács Gábor
Művészeti Alapítvány, 2016.

Térey 1913
Térey, Gábor. *Katalog der
Gemäldegalerie des Grafen
Johann Pálffy.* Budapest:
Hornyánszky, 1913.

Térey 1916
Térey, Gábor. *Országos
Szépművészeti Múzeum. A Régi
Képtár teljes leíró lajstroma az
összes képek hasonmásával.
Byzánci, olasz, spanyol, portugál
és francia mesterek.* Budapest/
Berlin: Bard Gyula Kiadása, 1916.

Thomas 2017
Thomas, David. *The Life and Art
of Rupert Bunny. A Catalogue
Raisonné in Two Volumes.*
Vol. 1. Melbourne: Thames &
Hudson Australia, 2017.

Thompson and Wright 2008
Thompson, James, and Barbara
Wright. *Eugène Fromentin
1820–1876. Visions d'Algérie
et d'Égypte.* Paris: ACR Édition,
2008.

Tokyo 2017
*Skagen: An Artists' Colony
in Denmark.* Edited by Hiroya
Murakami. Exh. cat. The National
Museum of Western Art, Tokyo
2017. Tokyo: National Museum
of Western Art / Western Art
Foundation, 2017.

Tokyo 2019
*Treasures from Budapest.
European and Hungarian
Masterpieces from the Museum
of Fine Arts, Budapest and the
Hungarian National Gallery.* Edited
by Iwata Takaaki and Ágnes
Pablényi. Exh. cat. The National
Art Center, Tokyo, 2019. Tokyo:
The National Art Center, 2019.

Tóth 2007
Tóth, Ferenc. "Pulszky Károly
tragédiája új dokumentumok
tükrében." *Művészettörténeti
Értesítő* 56 (2007): 233–58.

Tóth 2010
Tóth, Ferenc. "Collecting
'Contemporary Art' at the
Museum of Fine Arts." *Bulletin
du Musée Hongrois des Beaux-
Arts* 112–113 (2010): 137–52.

Tóth 2012
Tóth, Ferenc. *Donátorok és
képtárépítők. A Szépművészeti
Múzeum modern külföldi
gyűjteményének kialakulása.*
Budapest: Szépművészeti
Múzeum, 2012.

Tóth 2017
Tóth, Ferenc. *Mű–Kincs–Tár.
Művészeti közgyűjtemények
Magyarországon, 1802–1906.*
MúzeumCafé könyvek 3.
Budapest: Szépművészeti
Múzeum, 2017.

Tournai 1987
*Louis Gallait (1810–1887).
La Gloire d'un romantique.* Edited
by Serge le Bailly de Tilleghem.
Exh. cat. Musée des Beaux-
Arts de Tournai, Tournai, 1987.
Brussels: Crédit communal, 1987.

Tours 2016
*Martin de Tours. Le rayonnement
de la cité.* Edited by Sophie Join-
Lambert. Exh. cat. Tours: Musée
des Beaux-Arts de Tours, Milano :
Silvana editoriale, 2016.

Trento 2001
*Un ritrattista nell'Europa delle
corti. Giovanni Battista Lampi
1751–1830.* Edited by Fernando
Mazzocca, Roberto Pancheri,
and Alessandro Casagrande.
Exh. cat. Castello del
Buonconsiglio, Trento, 2001.
Trento: Provincia Autonoma
di Trento, 2001.

Turin 2004–2005a
*Da Raffaello a Goya. Ritratti dal
Museo di Belle Arti di Budapest.*
Edited by Vittorio Sgarbi, Daniela
Magnetti, and Vilmos Tátrai.
Exh. cat. Palazzo Bricherasio,
Turin, 2004–2005. Milan: Electa,
2004.

Turin 2004–2005b
*Gli impressionisti e la neve.
La Francia e l'Europa.* Edited by
Marco Goldin. Exh. cat. Palazzo
della Promotrice delle Belle Arti,
Turin, 2004–2005. Treviso:
Linea d'ombra, 2004.

Tuomisto 2011
Tuomisto, Aira. *Keihästyttö ja
Metsänpoika. Kuvanveistäjä Yrjö
Liipolan Taide Unkarin Kaudella
1904–1934.* Saarijärvi: Fenix-
Kustannus, 2011.

T. V. 1993
T. V. [Tátrai, Vilmos]. "Le Musée
des Beaux-Arts en 1992." *Bulletin
du Musée Hongrois des Beaux-
Arts* 79 (1993): 89–97.

Valence 1993
Callerun, Ferdinand, and Philippe Grunchec. *Joseph-Fortuné Layraud. Itinéraire d'un peintre drômois au XIXe siècle.* Exh. cat. Musée de Valence, Valence, 1993. Valence: Musée des Beaux-Arts et d'archéologie de Valence, 1993.

Van Eldere 1995
Van Eldere, Dirk. *Frans Van Leemputten (1850–1914).* Ghent: Pandora – Snoeck-Ducaju & Zoon, 1995.

Van Lennep 1990
Van Lennep, Jacques. *La Sculpture belge au 19ème siècle.* Brussels: La Générale de Banque, 1990.

Vanzype 1935
Vanzype, Gustave. "Notice sur Jules Lagae." *Annuaire de l'Académie, Bruxelles, Académie royale des sciences, des lettres et des beaux-arts de Belgique* (1935): 86–111.

Venice 1998
Archivi della pittura veneziana. Ettore Tito (1859–1941). Edited by Alessandro Bettagno. Exh. cat. Fondazione Cini, Venice, 1998. Milan: Electa, 1998.

Verbania 1990
Paolo Troubetzkoy 1866–1938. Edited by Gianna Piantoni and Paolo Venturoli. Exh. cat. Museo del Paesaggio, Verbania, 1990. Turin: Il Quadrante, 1990.

Verona 2013–2014
Verso Monet. Storia del paesaggio dal Seicento al Novecento. Edited by Marco Goldin. Exh. cat. Palazzo della Gran Guardia, Verona, 2013–2014. Milan: Silvana, 2013.

Vienna 1962
Biedermeieraustellung. Friedrich Gauermann und seine Zeit. Exh. cat. Servitenkloster, Gutenstein-Mariahilfberg; Gauermannhof und Postl-Mühle, Miesenbach, 1962. Vienna: Niederösterreichisches Landesmuseum, 1962.

Vienna 1985
Traum und Wirklichkeit Wien 1870–1930. Edited by Tino Erben. Exh. cat. Künstlerhaus Wien, Vienna, 1985. Vienna: Museen der Stadt Wien, 1985.

Vienna 1986
Wiener Gesellschaft im Portrait. Der Maler John Quincy Adams. Edited by Sylvia Eisenburger. Exh. cat. Akademie der bildenden Künste, Vienna, 1986. Vienna: Gesellschaft der Freunde der bildenden Künste, 1986.

Vienna 1993
Wiener Biedermeier. Malerei zwischen Wiener Kongress und Revolution. Edited by Gerbert Frodl and Klaus Albrecht Schröder. Exh. cat. Kunstforum der Bank Austria, Vienna, 1993. Munich: Prestel Verlag, 1992.

Vienna 1997
Engerth, Ruediger. *Eduard von Engerth: 1818–1897.* Exh. cat. Historisches Museum der Stadt Wien, Vienna, 1997. Vienna: Eigenverlag des Historischen Museums der Stadt Wien, 1997.

Vienna 2003
Friedrich von Amerling 1803–1887. Edited by Sabine Grabner. Exh. cat. Österreichische Galerie Belvedere, Vienna, 2003. Vienna: Österreichische Galerie Belvedere / Leipzig: Seemann, 2003.

Vienna 2016
Ist das Biedermeier? Amerling, Waldmüller und mehr. Edited by Husslein-Arco. Exh. cat. Österreichische Galerie Belvedere, Vienna, 2016. Vienna: Österreichische Galerie Belvedere / Munich: Hirmer Verlag, 2016.

Vienna 2018
Anton Romako. Beginn der Moderne / Anton Romako. The Beginning of Modernism. Edited by Marianne Hussl-Hörmann and Hans-Peter Wipplinger. Exh. cat. Leopold Museum, Vienna, 2018. Cologne: Verlag der Buchhandlung Walther König, 2018.

Vienna 2024
Akseli Gallen-Kallela, Finnland erfinden / Picturing Finland. Edited by Stella Rollig, Arnika Groenwald-Schmidt. Exh. cat. Österreichische Galerie Belvedere, Vienna, 2024. Verlag der Buchhandlung Walther und Franz König, Köln. 2024.

Vienna–Hanau 2016
Johann Peter Krafft. Maler eines neuen Österreich. Edited by Agnes Husslein-Arco, Katharina Bechler, Rolf H. Johanssen et al. Exh. cat. Österreichische Galerie Belvedere, Vienna; Historisches Museum Hanau Schloss Philippsruhe, Hanau, 2016. Vienna: Museen der Stadt Wien, 2016.

Vinardi 2004
Vinardi, Monica. "Pio Joris." *Dizionario Biografico degli Italiani.* Vol. 62. 2004. https://www.treccani.it/enciclopedia/pio-joris_(Dizionario-Biografico)/ (last accessed: 5 November 2024).

Voss 1973
Voss, Heinrich. *Franz von Stuck 1863–1926.* Munich: Prestel, 1973.

Wappenschmidt 1998
Wappenschmidt, Toni. "Meer und Land des Andreas Achenbach." In *Düsseldorf* 1997, 57–63.

Warzecha 2022
Warzecha, Jasper. *Gotthardt Kuehl und der "Figürliche Impressionismus".* Berlin: Logos, 2022.

Washington – New York – Minnesota 1982–1983
Northern Light. Realism and Symbolism in Scandinavian Painting, 1880–1910. Edited by Kirk Exh. cat. Corcoran Gallery of Art, Washington; The Brooklyn Museum, New York; The Minneapolis Institute of Arts, Minnesota, 1982–1983. New York: Brooklyn Museum, 1982.

Weisberg 1992
Weisberg, Gabriel P. *Beyond Impressionism. The Naturalist Impulse in European Art, 1860–1905.* New York: H. N. Abrams, 1992.

Weiss-Blok 2017
Weiss-Blok, Rivka. "'Religiosity' in Dutch Jewish Art in Nineteenth and the Early Twentieth Century." In *The Religious Cultures of Dutch Jewry,* 270–95. Edited by Yosef Kaplan and Dan Michman. Brill's Series in Jewish Studies 58. Leiden/Boston: Brill, 2017.

Weitner 2017
Weitner, Bettina. *Das Kostüm bei Hans Makart. Seine Auseinandersetzung mit Historie in Malerei, Theater, Festzug und Künstlerfest.* Munich: Herbert Utz Verlag, 2017.

Weixlgärtner 1916
Weixlgärtner, Arpad. *August Pettenkofen 1822–1889.* Vienna: Gerlach & Wiedling, 1916.

Wigger ed. 2015
Kunsthandel Widder. Gelegenheiten. Edited by Roland Wigger. Vienna: Bibliothek der Provinz, 2015.

Wildenstein 1964
Wildenstein, Georges. *Gauguin.* Paris: Les Beaux-Arts Éditions d'études et de documents, 1964.

Wildenstein 1974
Wildenstein, Daniel. *Claude Monet. Biographie et catalogue raisonné.* Vol. 1. 1840–1881. Peintures. Lausanne/Paris: La Bibliothèque des Arts, 1974.

Wildenstein and Crussard 2001
Wildenstein, Daniel, and Sylvie Crussard. *Premier Itinéraire d'un sauvage: Catalogue de l'œuvre peint (1873–1888).* Milan: Skira / Paris: Seuil, 2001.

Wurzbach 1879
Wurzbach, Constant von. *Ein Madonnen-Maler unserer Zeit. Eduard Steinle.* Vienna: Verlag der Manz'schen k. k. Hofverlags- und Universitäts-Buchhandlung, 1879.

***Zagreb* 2011–2012**
Mato Celestin Medović – retrospektiva. Edited by Vesna Kusin and Igor Zidić. Exh. cat. Galerija Klovićevi dvori, Zagreb, 2011–2012. Zagreb: Galerija Klovićevi dvori, 2011.

***Zagreb–Budapest* 2020–2021**
Ars et Virtus: 800 Years of Shared Cultural Heritage. Edited by Marina Bagarić et al. Exh. cat. Galerija Klovićevi dvori, Zagreb; Magyar Nemzeti Múzeum, Budapest, 2020–2021. Zagreb: Galerija Klovićevi dvori, 2020.

Zec 2018
Zec, Daniel. "Opaske uz pojedina djela Roberta Frangeša Mihanovića: primjer zbirke kiparstva Muzeja likovnih umjetnosti u Osijeku." In *Imago, imaginatio, imaginabile. Zbornik u čast Zvonka Makovića,* 365–82. Zagreb: Filozofski fakultet Sveučilišta u Zagrebu, 2018.

Ziegler 2001
Ziegler, Hendrik. "Neue Forschungen zu den Brüdern Andreas und Oswald Achenbach." *Kunstchronik* 54, no. 4 (2001): 179–84.

***Zorn* 2004**
Anders Zorn. Självbiografiska anteckningar. Edited by Brigitta Sandström. Mora: Zornsamlingarna, 2004.

***Zurich–Vienna* 2019–2020**
Wilhelm Leibl. The Art of Seeing. Edited by Bernhard von Waldkirch and Marianne von Manstein. Exh. cat. Kunsthaus Zürich, Zurich; Albertina, Vienna, 2019–2020. Munich: Hirmer Verlag, 2020.

***Zwickau – Limbach-Oberfrohna – Barth* 2011–2012**
Vogel, Gerd-Helge. *Die Göttlichkeit des Lichts. Fritz von Uhde (1848–1911).* Exh. cat. Kunstsammlungen Zwickau, Zwickau; Schloss Wolkenburg, Limbach-Oberfrohna; Vineta-Museum, Barth, 2011–2012. Zwickau: Städtische Museen, 2011.

Index of Artists

Editor:
Ferenc TÓTH

Project coordination:
Anna Zsófia KOVÁCS

Copy-editor:
Dóra DEKOVICS, Ilona KAPPANYOS, Mónika ZOMBORI

Translation:
Rachel HIDEG, Steve KANE

Layout:
Lídia TAKÁCS

Image processing:
Roland SZÁNTÓ

Reproduction rights:
Sylvia CSEH

Our special thanks go to Kornél FARKAS, Henriett GALAMBOS, János MAROSI and László NAGY
for their advice and help in the preparation of this publication.

For their help in the realisation of this collection guide, we owe thanks to all colleagues
of the Museum of Fine Arts – Hungarian National Gallery who contributed their assistance.

ISBN 978-615-6595-90-4

Printed by EPC

Published by László BAÁN General Director
© Museum of Fine Arts – Hungarian National Gallery, Budapest, 2025

Fonts: Approach, Roboto Mono and Roc Grotesk; dimensions: 147 × 235 mm.
Paper types: ClaroBulk 1.1 vol 135 g/m² (text block); coated paper 300 g/m², matte foil (cover).

On the cover:
Paul Gauguin, *The Black Pigs*, 1891, detail; Akseli Gallen-Kallela, *Young Faun*, 1904, detail

Inside cover:
Anne-Louis Girodet de Roucy-Trioson: *The Odalisque*, ca. 1820, detail
Égide Rombaux: *The Daughters of Satan*, 1909, detail